Greasing the Pan: The "Best" of Paul T. Riddell

Cover by Madelyn Z

Fantastic Books
PO Box 243
Blacksburg VA 24060
www.wilderpublications.com

ISBN 10: 1-60459-721-6
ISBN 13: 978-1-60459-721-9

First Edition

Greasing the Pan: The "Best" of Paul T. Riddell

Volume 1 of the Proverbs 26:11 Papers

By Paul T. Riddell

Table of Contents

Acknowledgments

A generally accepted attitude in the music industry is that any act that releases a "Best Of..." album is generally trying to cash in on past glories before its members finally accept that a life of tours and snorting coke out of the butt-cracks of 15-year-old groupies is all over. (It's particularly sad when the group wasn't around long enough to justify such a collection: in 1996, when the Portland-based proto-whiner rock act Quarterflash announced that it was releasing a "Best Of..." album, any number of wags noted that the only hit the group ever had was 1982's "I'm Gonna Harden My Heart" and asked "So...is it going to be a CD single?" I'm pretty sure that I lost a job in Portland because I echoed that sentiment, not knowing that the owner of the company was a friend of the band's lead singer.) In television, running a "Greatest Hits" episode is a sign that the budget for the season was all burned up, so putting out an episode full of "flashbacks," usually with the flimsiest of plot devices as adhesive, is an accepted way of saving a few dollars and keeping the schedule at the same time. As far as articles and columns are concerned, though, it's a long-established tradition to collect the brightest and best of an author's work, especially when said author is reaching a milestone (50 years of writing, the 100th novel, being with the same publisher for 10 years without going on a blood-soaked rampage through the editorial offices that leaves 72 dead and gooses the author's backlist). This attitude gains particular heft when many of the periodicals that contained the original columns/articles stopped publishing in the late Ordovician and many of the only existing copies are in the author's files. Since I had an incredible aptitude during my writing days for finding venues most likely to fold in the space of a year and pumping out an incredible amount of work before the publisher locked the doors and moved to a country without extradition treaties, this means that many of the pieces contained herein have an audience that simply had no way in Hell of reading them in their original formats.

This collection exists due to the determination of friends, fans, and other masochists who kept harping "Riddell, you really need to go back to writing." Since I'll get a hot Clorox enema before I do so except on my terms, this will have to do. Firstly, I'd like to thank Warren Lapine for picking up the volume (after it had been sitting with another publisher for two years while he preened for World Fantasy Convention photo shoots and composed "Hot Editors I'd Like To Pork" featurettes), but equal credit goes to Joey Shea and Cheryl LeBeau, Ernest Hogan and Emily Devenport, Paul Mears, Scott Roser, Harlan Ellison, Pat Cadigan,

Cyndy Milam, and the assembled loons over at the Texas Triffid Ranch blog (http://www.txtriffidranch.com). I'd especially like to thank my wife Caroline, for support, advice, and the occasional cricket bat to the side of my skull. If I've forgotten anyone, it's not due to malice but to impending senility: considering that my first publication was twenty years ago next month as I write this, that's a lot of people met, connected with, and misplaced over the intervening years.

However, it's also necessary to thank those who *really* inspired the resurrection of this volume. There's no need to bring up the names of the innumerable editors and publishers who convinced me that quitting writing was the best option. Their dying in obscurity is thanks enough.

However, if there's anyone to whom I'd like to dedicate this book, it's to my youngest brother Martin. He thought that he was following in the spirit of his big brother when he quit studying engineering and decided to pursue a career as an actor. Instead, he ended up convincing his big brother that struggling toward fame and fortune only count if you stand a chance of getting it...or having it in a venue that's worth a fart in a high wind. If not for his example, I probably never would have quit writing, and I'd probably be dead by now if I hadn't. And might I mention to the ladies out there that he's single and a ringer for Bill Hicks?

Introduction: On Pan Greasings and Essay Writings

Long before he became famous for starring opposite Keanu "Whoa" Reeves, Alex Winter was a film director as well as an actor. Best known today for the gonzo comedy *Freaked*, Winter directed a series of short films while in college and shortly afterwards, and one of the best of those short films went by the title *Entering Texas*. *Entering Texas*, starring the members of the Texas rock band the Butthole Surfers, followed the misadventures of a tourist family as they were exposed to the dubious joys of "family style barbecue": in one scene, a resident redneck (played by Butthole Surfers lead singer Gibby Haynes) asks our tourists "Would y'all like some scorpion tea?," and when they assent, he lights up a Coleman camp stove, puts a skillet atop the flame, drops his pants, and starts masturbating into the skillet. Naturally, the film doesn't actually *show* anything other than Gibby's grinning mug, and when our tourists look over the Coleman backplate to see what's going on, one says "Oh, he's just, um, greasing the pan, dear. It's, uh, *special* grease."

When I first saw this short with my best friend Paul Mears, that phrase became a well-used in-joke. Mears has had a bullshit meter with a hair trigger for the nearly thirty years I've known him, and when exposed to a line of utter stupidity or arrogance that set off that meter, he'd just look back, grin, and intone "It's *special* grease." Naturally, "greasing the pan" became our code word for "jacking off in public": in Dallas, where far too many people would lie, and do a bad job of it, solely because admitting the truth was some strange admission of failure, it was a necessary code word that wouldn't start a scene. "Greasing the pan" became the perfect way to express the *status quo*, whether it be narcissistic bands, arrogant businessmen, or completely clueless science fiction fans trying to convince the world that someone was going to give them million-dollar advances to direct blatant *Star Wars* ripoffs and bad *Dungeons & Dragons* adventures.

It also became the perfect analogy for writing, or at least for writing for science fiction magazines.

Hi. I'm Paul Riddell, and I'm a former skiffy writer. (Hi, Paul.) Between the end of 1988 and the middle of 2002, I spent an inordinate amount of time writing for a variety of publications, starting with film reviews for science fiction and horror zines best relegated to obscurity and ending with columns and articles for any number of professional venues. In that time, I ended up getting a bit of a reputation for smartaleck asides and (occasional) thoughtful commentary. In the end, though, I finally shut things down, told the venues for whom I was still writing that I'd sooner get a hot Clorox enema than return to writing, shut down the Web site that collected all of those articles and essays, put up a note reading "It's all over: go home," and quit cold turkey. In the nearly three years since I quit, I've had a few people for whom I wrote in the past ask if I wanted to come back; to the ones for whom I still cared, I'd gently but firmly decline. For the rest, the phrase "Not only 'no' but 'FUCK NO'" was used quite often. For a while, I was yelling it so loudly that it shook the windows out of their frames.

In that time, quite a few old friends, former editors or former compatriots at various publications, and other souls who knew me when I was consumed with the need to write would ask me why I quit. "After all, you never came close to making a living off your writing income. You dealt with editors who paid their writers when it was convenient to do so, you dealt with publishers who shouldn't have been trusted with pet rocks. You dealt with a community of readers who threaten violence against anyone who dares suggest that *Battlestar Galactica* (either version) isn't the culmination of human cultural development, and who spent their time alternating between bitching about your urge to push for something better and then who bitched when you decided that the battle wasn't worth the energy. With all of that, why would you want to quit?"

Why would I want to leave, when faced with all of that? Gee, ya got me.

Truthfully, you'd never figure it by listening to its proponents, but science fiction is nearly as dead as the Western. For all of the noise made by its fans about how science fiction was the literature of the future, its fans are some of the most reactionary, backwards-looking people anyone would care to meet, where trying to resurrect lousy TV shows and sequels to movies that nobody else wanted is of more importance than actually trying to *make* that future. Fifteen years ago, I coined the term "Church of Saint Spock the Pointyeared" to describe the mindset: science fiction fans act like religious fanatics, told that they're the anointed solely because of their ability to memorize otherwise worthless trivia, and certain that they'll be the ones that benefit when someone else creates the future that they keep reading about. Participating in politics to make sure that this future happens? Not a chance: *Enterprise* is on. There's no time to work toward resolving real-world issues because we're too busy learning conversational Klingon or living in *Star Wars* shantytowns or writing *Buffy the Vampire Slayer* fanfiction. Even if you look at science fiction fandom as a hobby, it's still combined with that level of fanaticism: "I can't get a job and move out! I can pay for my anime DVD bills or rent, but not both!"

And yet these same people can't understand why science fiction fans get such derogatory treatment in popular portrayals of fandom. *Obviously,* the "mundanes" are jealous of furries and Trekkies and Cat Piss Men, and since they aren't chosen, they'll never understand why so many of us are perfectly willing to live in squalor so long as we have enough money to purchase that life-sized Boba Fett figure with the fully functional orifices. Sure, they're jealous: and if you buy that, I have some great land at the bottom of Hudson Bay that I'll sell you real cheap.

The fact that most people in the science fiction community, both literary and media, simply don't want to understand is that science fiction is just as disposable as any other fad movement. The magazines that started the movement were usually loss-leaders created because a publisher noted the economics of scale in publishing and realized that publishing four magazines costs exactly the same as publishing three, and the editors were perfectly willing to work for insulting pay in order to Live the Dream. The big publishers of science fiction books? Half are similar loss-leaders for huge media conglomerates who notice the skiffy imprints about as much as you notice individual Islets of Langerhaans, and the other half are ego projects run on a shoestring by people who Believe. Same with the magazines today: if the message science fiction was supposed to impart was as important as fans would have us believe, don't you think that Conde Nast or Time Warner would be publishing whole lines of science fiction magazines to compete with *Cosmopolitan* or *Maxim?* If the books were that important, don't you think that mainstream authors would be falling over themselves to write science fiction instead of trying to distance themselves from the label "science fiction writer"? If the field was a noble one, worthy of the name, don't you think that the current editors at Tor and Baen and Del Rey would have been flushed out years ago by a wave of English majors from Columbia University backstabbing their way to the top? If science fiction fans weren't perpetuating the worst stereotypes of themselves, then wouldn't the most accessible figure representing fandom in popular culture be someone other than the Comic Shop Guy in *The Simpsons?*

About twenty years ago, being the good Catholic boy I was raised to be, I came incredibly close to following a calling to the priesthood, and the only reason why I'm not Father Paul right now is because I had a major crisis of faith. Well, not a crisis of faith, *per se,* but a crisis in wondering if the effort was going to the right cause. In the middle of 2002, I had the same sort of crisis, and realized that playing heretic for the Church of Saint Spock was still being involved. And so I left the punsters and the fanfic addicts and the failed engineers and the bad libertarians to their delusions, and stopped expending the energy. In that time, I haven't regretted the decision. If I'm going to grease any pans, I'm going to do it in private.

And that's where this collection comes in. For the last seven years, I've had readers call or write and ask "So, why don't you make up a book full of those articles and get it out to where I can buy a copy?" Well, aside from the fact that collections of columns only sell in this business if your name is Harlan Ellison (most agents won't even touch collections of newspaper columns because they're generally so unprofitable, which explains why one local "humor" columnist in my home town had to publish his via a vanity press financed by a local strip club), it's a matter of whether or not the people clamoring for such a collection can be bothered to buy it. However, poor Warren Lapine, whose brain is still permanently damaged from the one article he bought from me in 2001, thought that this might be a profitable compilation thanks to the wonders of modern technology, so this volume (along with its sister *The Savage Pen of Onan*, a compilation of the *Hell's Half-Acre Herald* columns I wrote between 1998 and 2002) puts the articles worth reprinting into a dead-tree format. And now it's time to put up or shut up.

If the experience of going through these lumps of chronal detritus has taught me anything, it's that I don't much like the person I used to be. Even more than I want to grab a time machine, go back to 1985, and beat the shit out of the fanboy I used to be, I want to go back to 1997, impress upon my previous self the time, energy, and money I spent on the assembled material herein, impress further the path that life would take if I hadn't fought to promote magazines and newspapers unworthy of that effort, and then break my previous self's legs to set the perception. It's not just that I had a real problem with repeating myself (in order to prevent spending months on reediting essays that don't otherwise need the revision, I've left most of these articles and essays intact other than spelling and syntax errors in the original manuscripts): it's that I was certain that people were reading and paying attention. Once I got past that delusion, I became a much happier person.

Anyway. Enjoy the collection and its sister, wonder about the references to cultural icons long dead and forgotten, and wince at how passionate I was for these at the time. "Paul T. Riddell" is dead and forgotten, too, and it's time to move on.

—Paul Riddell
January 29, 2009

A Disclaimer About People, Places, and Events

You know how every movie that isn't a documentary has that little disclaimer reading "This is a work of fiction. All characters, locations, and events are fictitious and any similarity to individuals living or dead is purely coincidental"? Well, this collection is composed of columns written in the distant past, so some of the people mentioned may be dead, many of the venues may be defunct, and all of the events are now a part of someone's dysfunctional history. When I make mention of "my wife," I was referring to my now-ex-wife. Likewise, feel free to try to hunt down any of the venues, magazines, TV programs, or any other cultural artifact mentioned in these pages, but when you find out that they've been dead for the last decade, try not to look too surprised, okay? (And while we're at it, just because I endorsed a particular subject, venue, publication, or individual back then, don't take this as an automatic assumption that I still have an interest. In other words, I really don't give a damn about Warren Ellis' latest project, so don't bother telling me about it, 'kay?)

On Science Fiction and Science Fiction Fandom

Because one of the most accessible venues for the beginning writer is the science fiction magazine, I ended up writing quite a lot for them. They pop up like mutant mushrooms after a good deluge of acid rain: a few disability checks or inheritances, a copy of Adobe InDesign swiped from the last job before security arrived for the escort of shame, and a complete lack of anything approximating a business plan, and suddenly Chuck C++ Programmer or Sadie Bored Housewife becomes an editor/publisher. Since these venues are always looking for writers willing to offer content for free or on the vague promise of pay "one of these days," I bought into the popular fiction that "paying your dues" meant "working for free for magazines that drop dead after four issues." Considering the subject, that meant writing about it, and as can be told by the output, I was very enthusiastic about it. Sadly deluded that I or anyone else could make a difference and bypass the people perfectly happy to keep the genre from doing anything different, but awfully enthusiastic.

"The Sound of One Genre Beating Off" or "If Charles Brown's Head Exploded, Would There Be A Sound?"

Few things in life are more reviled than the "authority" who rules by intimidation. Nearly everyone in the movie industry loathes Rex Reed and Michael Medved, but they still kiss the hineys of two insufferable hacks whose opinions are already bought (Medved, by the religious right; Reed, by whomever can pay the most for publicity perks). Nobody in music trusts anything that *Rolling Stone* or *Spin* have to say, yet both magazines clear small fortunes in advertising revenue for the privilege of a positive review of a label's latest Pearl Jam ripoff.

And then there's *Locus*.

For the last twenty years, *Locus* has ruled the SF field: not for merit, but because it was about the only source of information available to writers about the business aspects of the genre. Every month, the news out of Oakland, California has influenced the SF community in ways the fiction magazines never could: the fates and fortunes of writers and editors as they related to their peers rested in the little pink mitts of a gnome named Charles N. Brown.

Now, if *Locus* were one of many critical magazines, and if it were a readable product, then I wouldn't be ranting and raving and carrying on, but the magazine has reached the point where not only is the emperor naked, but somebody swiped his best tattoos, too, and he's trying to pry out most of his own dental work with a grapefruit spoon. Ever since Fritz Leiber died, *Locus* has been (at its worst) nothing but a wankfest for the more publicity-minded writers and editors in SF, and at its best the genre's equivalent of *People* magazine. Step right up, folks: give the Phleabitten One a good rim job, and win a free career in science fiction! *Locus* used to provide a valuable service to the SF community, and most of the awards it garnered were deserved, but not any more.

Admittedly, *Locus* is not the only critical magazine on the market, but it is the only one with decent distribution. *Science Fiction Chronicle*, while being much better at carrying information one can use (witness the market listings), still has problems with getting decent spots in magazine racks, and the others don't do too much better. When was the last time you saw *Science-Fiction Studies* outside of a major university library, or *The New York Review of Science Fiction* outside of a literary science fiction convention? By default, *Locus* gets the recognition some of the others now deserve.

This may sound like sour grapes. However, this is a hypothesis that can be tested: remember the 1993 Hugo Awards? Remember when *SF Chronicle* won the "Best Semi-Pro Magazine" Hugo by a margin of one vote? Well, could Borders and Barnes & Noble have had anything to do with that? I don't know about everywhere else, but the *Chronicle* only became available in Dallas when these two superstores started placing it in the SF section of the magazine rack. Otherwise, and it's still true with *NYRSF*, asking about it in the local SF and comics shops gets the response of "Uh, never heard of it. We've got *Locus*..."

Okay, enough with the preamble. Now it's time for the howitzers. Let's base further commentary on personal experience, shall we?

About a year ago, I was asked by Chris DeVito, the editor of *Fuck Science Fiction* and *Proud Flesh*, to compose an essay on the horrors of the small press field. Nothing grand: just a hatchet job on the booger-eating morons who made writers' lives miserable. You know the kind: the prima donnas who beg writers for stories and essays, take a year or more to pubish (if at all), hack up said stories and articles without asking for a rewrite, and then scream and moan about the solidarity of SF when the bullshit meter goes off the scale and the writers bail out. I've been burned by a plethora of the little vermin, and the only payback I was ever going to get was going to be kharmic. The piece was entitled "So You Want To Be A Writer, You Poor Bastard?," and it appeared in the second issue of *Fuck SF*.

To keep from reprinting the whole essay, our pertinent point is this: when debating the merits of writer's magazines, I slammed *Locus* in the same breath as *The Writer* and *Writer's Digest*. Specifically, I wrote "*Locus* is...read only by wannabes who think that their stories will get million-dollar advances, authors hoping to read whatever brain-damaged review of their work is due out (I suspect that the reviewers there are paid in raw meat and/or sunlight to allow them to photosynthesize), and the staff at *Pulphouse* checking to see what picture of Kristine Kathryn Rusch gets run *this* issue." Not very nice at all, but then being threatened with excommunication from *Locus* was akin to telling me that I can't eat green peppers ever again or that I won't get that cameo in *Jurassic Park II* or that Kim Basinger won't go to bed with me. Yeah, yeah, Jesus wept, but I didn't.

Anyway, the article went to the usual places, and I wasn't surprised when Chuck Brown printed his "1994: The Year In Review" issue and failed to make a mention of either *Fuck SF* or *Proud Flesh* in the overview of magazines. He spent his time slamming the publications whose editors didn't pay obesiance (*NYRSF*, *SF Eye*, and our own *Tangent*) and making kissy faces to the ones who did (*F&SF*, *Asimov's*), but not a word about *Fuck*. Gosh, I was so surprised and disappointed that I wanted to slice my wrists with a cheese grater and give myself a John Bobbitt with a Salad Shooter. The utter shame of not being treated as part of the SF community...the horror! The horror!

Gosh, could it have been anything we said? I mean, if we said anything to offend Chuck, we'd be glad to apologize...about the time the Texas Rangers win the Superbowl.

The thesis is at hand. While I received no official comment, either pro or con, about the essay, I had quite a number of pros come up to me at conventions and other gatherings and tell me how much they agreed with the assessment of *Locus*. Mind you, they wouldn't say these things themselves, but they sure were glad somebody said them. Unlike Yours Truly, they cared enough about their careers to tread softly when the big bad Brown came stalking by. They acted like early mammals at the feet of a dinosaur, only Chuck has a lot more in common with *Barney nonsapiens imbecilis* than Tyrannosaurus rex.

This seems to be the thrust of the matter. Most of the field cannot stand *Locus* or what it's done to the genre, but these poor saps love the field too much to be excommunicated from it. Too many of them have found themselves screwed by Chuck on one thing or another, but they see Barney and think Godzilla. They won't send their press releases and review copies, as I have, to *SF Chronicle* instead, and they won't confront Chuck with the fact that he's masturbating for a captive audience and they'd all love to leave if he didn't have the keys to the doors.

With all of the fear and loathing toward Chuck held by the field, why the hell is he still publishing? Take a look through the ads and the "Writers and Editors" section for a few clues. Although recent issues have finally dropped the constant photos of Kristine Kathryn Rusch (and mind you, I don't think she influenced anything–I suspect that the brilliant *Pulphaus* parody by Gordon Van Gelder, Robert K.J. Killheffer and a cast of dozens had more to do with this than anything), we have lots more of Poppy Z. Brite. Admittedly, Ms. Brite's two talents make the hopelessly hetero males among us bark at the moon (why do I get the feeling that she's the only writer in the field who will be introduced at conventions with a choir of frat boys singing "Shut Up And Show Us Your Tits"?), but do we really need yet another photo every month? Christ, Chuck, if you're going to be such a dirty old man, why don't you just ritually onanize an X-rated boxed set of 8x10 glossies of her and get it over with in private?

Sycophancy, while a social vice comparable to licking one's genitalia in public, isn't a capital offense...yet. (If it were, Richard Corliss at *Time* would have sung "Mr. Bojangles" on the electric chair for nearly twenty years of rim jobs for George Lucas and Steven Spielberg alone.) The real indictment lies with the advertising versus the review section. *Spin*, for example, is a master at giving great reviews to advertisers, thus explaining the rise of such scum as Stone Temple Pilots and Smashing Pumpkins, but *Spin* doesn't pitch itself as a social necessity on a par with toenail clippers and metal forks. The vast majority of positive reviews in any issue of *Locus* come from books published by either Tor or Baen Books, and guess who supplies the vast majority of the ads? (A hint: it ain't Arkham House or Ziesing, that's for damn sure.) Better yet, how many of you want to bet that Newt Gingrich's new SF books through Baen will get great reviews?

(A little aside to really piss off Jim Baen and Tom Doherty: the 1994 election proved three things. Firstly, Oliver North proved that a known felon could run for office and stand a chance of winning. Secondly, Marion Barry proved that a convicted criminal could run for office and not only win by a decisive majority, but be forgiven of his crimes by the electorate. Thirdly, Newt proved that a sociopathic science fiction fanboy could attain one of the highest offices in the land. With this in mind, ladies and gentlemen, may I present the next president of the United States, Mr. Charles Manson. Hey, we have to have someone more rational than Phil Gramm in the '96 campaign.)

Now we talk about change. After losing two years in a row to Andy Porter and *SF Chronicle*, the crew at Locus Publications has made a few changes, comparable to putting aluminum siding on a crack house. In response to *SFC*'s market listings, *Locus* tried its own listings for a while, but apparently abandoned them due to negative comments (well, can you imagine why? Could it have anything to do with having to be honest about the chronic lateness of *Pulphouse*? Or the ongoing screw jobs quite a few editors do to their writers concerning pay and editorial freedom?) Blessedly, we have no more photos of K.K. Rusch posing in a softball uniform, and Tom Maddox's "The Electronic Frontier" column, while no replacement for Fritz Leiber's "Moons and Stars and Stuff" (a quick note to somebody: why doesn't someone gather all of these columns into a collection?), at least considers the power of the World Wide Web as a serious competitor to the zine, both in timeliness and distribution. All the changes, though, still make *Locus* resemble a Romero zombie: it walks, it (tries to) talk, but it's still dead, and the only saving grace we can give it is a bullet to the brain. If we don't, then we deal with it limping around the house, chewing on the cat, pissing itself in the middle of the living room, and filling the area with the enticing aroma of rotting flesh.

Here's the resolution: what are we going to do about this? Well, we could boycott all of the advertisers with *Locus*, but that wouldn't do much good: the *Star Trek* geeks would get their fill of minddribble fantasy and war-porn all too easily anyway, and Chuck would take out his tantrums on the writers and editors who don't have massive rightwing backing. We could boycott *Locus* itself, but we're not the ones who read the magazine: the yearly polls Chuck runs every year show that a goodly number of his readers are first-timers or fanatics who have subscribed for years, so don't expect too much response from them.

This leads us to our third option: Do It Yourself. Rather than bitch about the situation, et's push for the improved circulation of other critical magazines. Grab your friends and drop copies of NYRSF, SF Eye, and Tangent in their laps; buy subscriptions for out-of-town friends for their birthdays. If you have connections to distributors or retailers, nag the hell out of them until they carry the magazines, and make damn sure you pick up your copies when they come in (stores won't order new magazines if you nag and then refuse to buy). Send copies to small book and magazine publishers: they might not know about them, and knowledge is power. Send copies of your magazine to Factsheet Five: you'll get better response for your alternative magazine there than with Locus, as F5 will at least acknowledge the receipt of your publication. Attend cons where Chuck is scheduled to speak, and pelt him with garbage the moment he starts with his mumblings about how nobody reads reviews and how it isn't worth his time to review anything that isn't published by Tor or Baen. When receiving junk mail from Locus advertisers, write "PISS OFF" in black marker on the return forms, and make sure you don't put a return address on the envelope when you return it minus the stamp. Support writers and editors who have had problems with Chuck and let them know you'll help. And whatever you do, remain above the law. It doesn't help your cause if you get busted for doing it.

Just remember: the next time you see a huge writeup on the latest convention in Locus with Gardner Dozois appearing in more than four photos, you could have stopped this. Friends don't let friends buy Locus.

—Tangent, Spring 1995

Postscript: Considering the source, nothing made me happier than reading the "Year In Review" section of The Year's Best Science Fiction 13 anthology and reading how Gardner Dozois referred to me as "a Hunter Thompson wannabe of sorts." I've said it before and I'll say it again: better a Hunter Thompson wannabe than a Tina Brown wannabe, fat boy.

On the other hand, I have more regrets that Frank Sinatra and Sid Vicious combined, and one of my biggest regrets, other than my first marriage, is that I slammed Poppy Brite like this for no reason. We became friends a while back, and I still cry "Mea culpa" in my sleep from time to time.

"Convention Carousing" or "Why Science Fiction Needs A Respite From Costume Competitions"

Peter David asked it about comics, but I'm going to ask it about genre writing in general: why don't we have a convention that's a convention?

Yeah, you're thinking, there goes that asshole Riddell, beating on fanboys again. Well, I have to admit they're easy targets, but I have a madness to my method.

Without exception, science fiction, fantasy, and horror conventions aren't really for the pro writers. They aren't for anyone but fans, really. Ever since the earliest days of fandom, cons were entertainment for fans; the pros either attended because they wanted to rub noses with fellow fans, or they were paid to attend and make nice. This isn't a bad thing in itself, but the genre needs a little more.

Several years ago in his "But I Digress" column in *Comic Buyer's Guide*, Peter David noted this as well. In fact, he suggested a critter later known as "Pro/Con," where pros in the comics business sat down and compared notes. Writers took tips from other writers, artists took notes on others' techniques, and writers and artists tried to work out some of the gulf between writing a script and drawing it. According to quite a few people involved, it was a tremendous success. All I suggest is that we move the concept into literary science fiction/fantasy/horror and fine-tune it. Lord knows, we need it..

Here's the logic behind the call to arms. Certain members of the genre community are sources of information for the others, and nearly everyone has a question that could be answered by anyone else. Have a question about screenplays? Ask the writers who have managed to break into Hollywood. Want to know more about certain magazines? Ask the folks who write for small-press publications on a regular basis. What about editing, religious themes, or the difference between llamas and ostriches as pack animals? Well, there's someone out there who has those answers: I get calls from folks on such diverse topics as the Viking lander soil analyses, Australian palaeontology, and road maps to Dallas' Grassy Knoll, so I know I'm not alone in this.

Also, consider how much work gets done by pros at conventions anyway. Since most of *Tangent*'s readership consists of fairly established writers and editors, we all have stories of how we attended one con or another, met some people in the throes of heavy drinking/heavy petting/throwing Trekkies out of a 30th-story window, and made friends for life. Some of these friends have information you needed right then; others have it when you need it the most.

We also have precedent for a convention of this type. Readercon, one of the best literary conventions on the East Coast, makes it a point to stick to the literary aspects of the genre. It has no masquerade and no dance, and anyone seen in a costume is gently escorted to the door, so pros tend to outnumber fans by nearly three to one. Although it isn't quite what we're looking for, it comes close: it's one of the few conventions around in which the odds of being assaulted (physically, verbally, or olfactorially) by an obnoxious fan are right up there with the odds for the Texas Lottery.

Now, I'm not slamming cons out of hand: I've been to many well-run cons, where the staff had its act together and the programming was to make happy. Sad to say, these are the worst cons to attend to meet fellow writers, because everyone wanders around in a daze, trying to see everything at once.

Let me give two examples. One con I attended in '94 was one of these wunnerful cons, where the pros nearly outnumbered the fans, and the place was full of neat folks like Scott Edelman, Paul Di Filippo, Stephen Brown (editor of *SF Eye*, for those three readers not familiar with the man), Judith Merril, Mark Rich, Hal Clement, and Joey Shea. Well, I think the people were there, because so much was going on that nobody could get together with anyone else. All I remember was a blur of faces as folks came up, shook hands, mumbled "HeyPaulnicetomeetyouIhaveapanelseeya," and shot off to prior commitments so fast they left shock waves. It could have been my breath, but I'm not sure.

Compare this to a con I attended a year earlier. I was one of about seven pros who attended, mostly because the con committee didn't start contacting pros until the Tuesday before the con, and most of them had real lives. (I only attended because my girlfriend at the time had never been to a convention, and I think she regretted her curiosity.) Panels were canceled, registration had no idea where pro badges were, and I had a crazed gamer throw a chair at me because he didn't like my informed opinion that most role-filling games are a waste of time better utilized for more productive things like smoking crack. I managed to have a wonderful time talking to the other pros, though: we were all in the bar, grumbling in our Dr. Peppers about stringing up the con chairman by his one testicle and using him as a Viking piñata. We all felt like old Army buddies after that one.

Here's what I propose: I don't know about the particulars, but I have the generalities for a convention solely for the pros in the business. Let's call it

Working Con, because that's what we're going to be doing.

Firstly, let's start with the attendance. As much as I hate to be a snob about this, Working Con is not a convention for those fans who want to become writers. We have a lot of cons which give them advice from old pros: we're trying to help the old pros get new viewpoints and ideas. Although I don't know how a committee would run this, I suggest requiring each and every attendee to show samples of their work. We all know the people who claim to be writers and artists, but amazingly never have any proof that they're really writing scripts for Babylon 5 or whatever. Let's nip that right in the bud by requiring each conventioneer to file a copy of a magazine or a book with the attendee's work inside. We open it to fanzines as well as prozines (some of the best work I've seen in years came from magazines with circulations of less than one thousand), and we put no time limit on the age of the submission (maybe we'll have examples of pros who wrote something forty years ago and stopped, and just needed a new idea to get going again).

(We have a little precedent for this: the American Bookseller's Association convention in Chicago only allows people in the book business, and they're rather tight about keeping others out. If they opened up to everyone, they'd be too busy dealing with spectators and people wanting freebies to be able to work with bookstore managers and distributors.)

Secondly, we want *everyone* out here. We want artists, if only so they can offer their viewpoint on how stories get published. We want editors so they can talk with writers and artists and address some grievances, such as poor communications and slow response time. We want publishers so we all get an idea of what they're looking for in books, so we don't have to depend upon telepathy. We want distributors so we can work on getting publications out to the general readership. We want the radicals and the reactionaries so we can compare viewpoints, and we want the tiny with the giants so we can see the difference between those who make their living from million-print runs and those who publish because their consciences force them to choose between postage and food.

Thirdly, we'll need a change in the standard dealer's room. The traditional science fiction convention differs from a "real" convention in that very few dealers give things away. Because we exclude fans, Working Con guarantees a much better response to freebies than at most cons: I know far too many fans who grab sample books and magazines at cons with the expressed purpose of taking them home and selling them to the local used bookstore (if you're going to do that, what's the point of taking them in the first place?). I advocate offering dealer's booths just the same as usual, only we push for getting magazine and book publishers to attend and solicit commentary from writers and artists in an active role. Artists could do the same thing: since any art show wouldn't be crowded with full-head profiles of Brent Spiner and Sculpey figurines of dragons, this would give the artist a chance to show off work without the urge to sell it right then and there. Even if only one artist manages to sell a painting or a sketch to an editor during the course of the convention, that's still a damn sight better than the results at most cons.

Fourthly, this has to be non-political. If this turns into, say, a SFWA-only event, we might as well throw it all away. I hate to be the one to express commonly-held attitudes in public again, but the Science Fiction Writers of America has become a geek club on a par with Mensa. Instead of being a real union or guild, such as the Screen Writer's Guild (and we could use a real guild; imagine striking the larger magazines until they paid writers something approximating the pay offered by non-genre magazines; when the SFWA standard is a whole three cents per word when most "real" magazines offer sixty or more, one can see the reason why writers and artists need to organize), SFWA seems to accept damn near anyone for the purpose of forming a club. Neophyte writers want to join SFWA, but they don't know why, and I'm willing to bet that other editors feel the same way I do: with very few exceptions, seeing the letterhead that lists SFWA and HWA is a screaming neon sign saying "crappy story enclosed; please flush at first opportunity."

Let's put it another way (and I'm certain I'll hear lots of calls for my scalp for this one; telling me that I'll never become a member of SFWA is akin to telling me I can never eat green peppers again, so save it for later): thanks to a subscription to *Science News*, half of my junk mail is now addressed "Dr. Paul T. Riddell." While my ego goes into overdrive, the "Dr." before my name has about as much significance and heft in the real world as the letters "SFWA" would after it. Titles only mean something if they're earned.

Anyway, as I was saying, this needs to remain non-political, in all senses of the term. Working Con cannot become a house organ for the Scientologists, nor can it become a SFWA-only event, nor should it exclude participants because the committee doesn't like their work. (Sorry, but I'm a very non-political animal, and petty politicking drives me up the wall.) Next issue, I'm going to go a bit further into this subject, but let's just say that everyone at an event like this should have at least one interesting point to add to a discussion, no matter how opinionated or obnoxious. Everyone might be amazed at the difference between meeting someone in person and just reading their words.

Okay, now we move to financing. Because we aren't going to need security or a Green Room or any of the other things most cons need when dealing with both pros and fans, we chop out a good chunk of the cost right there. Since everyone should pay their own way (yes, it's a tax writeoff, but one even the most anal-retentive IRS agent won't question), we don't need to charge a huge admission such as that charged by WorldCon each year (since Working Con won't have awards voting, that's one headache that won't require huge staffs). I'm probably wrong, but I'm thinking about an admission fee of $50, payable in advance. This fee would cover administration, the usual badges and schedules, and the costs of suites for panels. If Working Con swings, say, a thousand pros, it's on its way toward profitability, and the rental of tables in the dealer's room to publishers and interested individuals should help a bit more.

Numero Five-o, let's look at programming. Right off the top of my head, I can think of a good hundred subjects that should be covered at Working Con; most of them are answers to questions we all had as fledgling writers but couldn't find anyone to give those answers to us. For instance, I'd like to form a panel of agents and writers who proudly refuse to use agents and hear all of the reasons why one should and should not get a literary agent. We could also use a panel run and moderated by agents on what writers and artists should look for in choosing an agent. After all, one bad experience with a bad agent can sour a pro on them forever, so better to be forewarned as to spotting the fakes, eh?

(That's an idea: invite agents, too. This way, the agents can chat with writers and artists and decide as to whom they want to represent. This way, the agents don't have to deal with the wannabe-writers who believe that old cock-and-bull routine about how writers make $37.50 an hour, and they'll have the time to talk to their clients firsthand.)

(Y'know, I want to hunt down the idiot who came up with that "$37.50" story and let Whitley Strieber's aliens make him/her squeal like a pig. Working with that logic, I allegedly worked 12 hours this year, and I'm pretty certain most of the wonderful people reading *Tangent* didn't work that much if the story were true. I mean, don't you hate explaining to your grandmother that you saw a huge amount of work get published over the space of the year, but you still work 60 hours a week to pay for food and rent?)

Okay, here's a few more: how about a panel hosted by editors for various small-press magazines on tips they picked up to increase circulation or improve publicity? A seminar on using computer art programs such as Photoshop for covers and interior illustrations? The possibilities and pitfalls of Web publications? The best sources for hard science data, when the story is due the next morning? Which works better on deadline: coffee or ginseng soda? What writer's resources, such as *Tangent*, *Factsheet Five*, and *Scavenger's Newsletter*, exist for pros wanting to break out into new markets, and which ones do the pros recommend? How does one get a new magazine into chain bookstores, and what deals with the distributor devils should one avoid? What sort of news coverage would we like to see in *Locus* and *Science Fiction Chronicle*? And what about those pesky screenplays and comic scripts anyway?

The floor is now open; all I've done is present the bare concepts. Whether we want to admit it or not, we all need a convention like this, and we can thank Peter David for suggesting it in the first place. Now it's up to us.

—*Tangent, Fall 1996*

Postscript: Oh, this one produced a lot of passive-aggressive whimpering from SFWA regulars, an incredibly defensive "rebuttal" from James Van Pelt on how "editors don't really flush your manuscript if you put 'Member, SFWA' on the letterhead," and an equally ridiculous complaint from then-HWA president Brian Lumley over how "neither [Riddell's] cup nor his loo will be filled on my account": none of which actually addressed the issue. Not that this is surprising, considering the number of losers whose memberships to SFWA and the HWA are as relished as their memberships to the L-5 Society or the Joss Whedon Fan Club.

"The San Antonio WorldCon" or "If Life Gives You Lemons, Grab Some Salt and Tequila and Make A Margarita"

So you're planning to attend the WorldCon in San Antonio this year, are ya? Well, congratulations: if you've never been to Texas before, you're in for a blast.

Speaking as someone who spent more than half of his life in the Lone Star State, I can say that Texas grows on you: get caught in a dust storm, and those little Texas seeds stick right to you and you spend the rest of your life at the dermatologist's getting rocks and the occasional lump of river mud excised. However, most folks get the impression that Texas is an uncivilized place, where they'll turn a corner and run into James Franciscus lassoing tyrannosaurs or something similar. Rest assured, this no longer happens: the last tyrannosaur in Texas died during the State Fair in 1958, so now all we have are ankylosaurs and troodontids. You don't even see the ankylosaurs at the rodeos any more, as their armored backs tore up cowboys' jeans something fierce.

About the only place that comes close to paralleling Texas is Australia, and the similarities are stunning, with flat, brushy plains everywhere (only Texas has mesquite instead of eucalypts); weird critters (armadillos, longhorns, and horned toads instead of koalas, kangaroos, and Moloch lizards), lousy top-40 music (ZZ Top and Deep Blue Something instead of INXS and Men At Work), and gonzo movie material (Bill Paxton, *Texas Chainsaw Massacre*, and Joe Bob Briggs instead of Judy Davis, *The Road Warrior*, and Robin Pen). The climate is comparable, the people are cloned from each other, and both have a long-held tradition of independence and self-sufficiency. All Texas needed was Captain Cook instead of La Salle exploring the Galveston coast, and the analogy would be complete.

Most of the negative vibes about Texas come from popular media, and with good reason: a good chunk of that impression is based on Dallas, and Dallas is a scary place. If Hunter Thompson was right in saying that Las Vegas is what the whole world would be doing every Saturday night had the Nazis won the war, Dallas is what the whole world would be doing the subsequent Sunday morning. (This is in comparison to Portland, Oregon, which resembles a horrible cloning experiment involving the characters in the British TV series *The Young Ones*, with far too many Ricks and Mikes and nowhere near enough Vyvians. All of the Neils are down in Eugene, by the way.) Television and film don't help matters; thanks to Dallas, everyone the world over thinks that Texas is full of sociopathic greedheads who assassinate presidents out of boredom. Well, that's true for Dallas, but not for the rest of the state. One well-placed thermonuclear device in the Southern Methodist University campus would not only cut the national population of dittohead business majors in half, but it would make the rest of the state a lot nicer.

Another perception is that Texas is full of ignorant shit-kickers who chew tobacco and fornicate with pigs and chickens. This is also true, but only in certain areas. As a general rule, the closer the area comes to Arkansas and Oklahoma, the scarier the area. San Antonio and Austin are smack dead in the middle of the state, so they're safe, but watch out for places like Texarkana, Waxahatchie, Grapevine, and Lewisville. (Lewisville's really scary: what else can be said about a town whose high school football team bears the name "The Fighting Farmers"? I could reveal also that the team's fight song is "You Said You Was A Virgin, But Your Baby Ain't Named Jesus," but that would be cruel...)

San Antonio, on the other hand, is the most beautiful city in Texas, if not in the whole Southwest (with Fort Worth as a very close second). Not only does it contain an infinitude of possibilities, but it's also a hop away from Austin, the state capital and well-known center of Texas music. (Mind you, to a Texan, or anyone else raised in a western state, a "hop" is any drive of less than eight hours.) Oh, you're going to looooove WorldCon in San Antonio...if you don't melt in 103-degree heat and 97-percent humidity during the end of summer.

Anyway, I'm not going this year, but I can't let you go without a few suggestions as to things to see and do, as well as a few things to avoid.

Firstly, there's that lingo of yours. Texian is a separate language than the syntax of the South, although it has the same effect upon anyone born north of the Mason-Dixon Line (Molly Ivins once pointed out that a Southern accent automatically subtracts a good thirty IQ points from the speaker in the eyes of non-Southerners, and a lot of people, an ex-girlfriend of mine included, spend an obscene amount of time and money to erase all traces of the Texas twang). Texian is a combination of Southern patois, with touches of Spanish, Irish, and German, and a lot of mutation of its own. Ergo, don't depend upon phonetic pronunciation: "mesquite" is pronounced "muh-SKEET," "tire" is "tar," "barbed wire" is "bob war," and "H. Ross Perot" is "that gohdamn midget sumbitch." "Waco" is likewise pronounced "WAY-co" instead of "Wacko," but the Branch Davidians and Baylor University made that point moot a long time ago.

If'n you want to talk Texan, you have to get the right resources. Plant your butt down in that chair in front of the TV and start with the absolutely dead-on Fox series *King of the Hill*, and go from there to the movie *The Whole Wide World* (which not only does a damn good job at dramatizing the life and career of Robert E. Howard, but shows off the town of Bastrop, Michael Moorcock's new home turf; Cross Plains, Howard's home town, was never so hilly, but the film managed to catch the dryness and the incessant cicada buzzing) and the Alex Winter short *Entering Texas* (for the "greasing the pan" sequence, if nothing else). After that, go to the CD rack and plug in Cricket Taylor's album *Let Me Lead You To Sin*; not only is she one of the best blues musicians in Texas, but she's one of the few decent people in Dallas. While you're listening to Cricket, alternate between the complete run of Garth Ennis' comic *Preacher* from Vertigo (gad, it's scary how a Belfast boy managed to capture the soul of Texas) and anything Joe Lansdale has ever written. Suddenly have a hankering for a can of Ranch Style Beans? If so, the treatment worked. (To simulate the experience of a Texas WorldCon, just add a few doses of Evan Dorkin's *The Eltingville Comic Book, Science Fiction, Fantasy, Horror, and Role-Playing Club* comic series to the mix; a lot of the people involved this year haven't forgotten nor forgiven the book *Squashed Armadillocon*.)

Food is another consideration, seeing as how the Riverwalk area next to the Convention Center in San Antonio is full of the stuff. Texas barbecue isn't quite as good as Memphis barbecue, if only because Texans use beef instead of pork, but it has its moments. However, be warned about the jalapeño peppers they serve at most establishments: these aren't the wimpy pickled ones you get in Boston or Vancouver, but peppers from Satan's own backside, and they'll leave third-degree burns up and down your GI tract. The same warnings apply to chili: Texans have a long tradition of throwing chunks of any available carcass into a pot of chili (the real traditionalists use armadillo), but beware any chili that contains macaroni. Kidney beans instead of pinto beans are barely tolerable, but no reputable cook in Texas would ever serve chili with elbow macaroni unless they were trying to cover the distinctive flavor of dog or water moccasin. (And take my word for it: while rattlesnake is pretty good, water moccasin tastes like the fat on a pot roast, while copperhead tastes like kerosene. Better stay away from the snakes for a while, anyway.)

Beer is another sore subject. I don't drink, thanks to my reaching drinking age in Wisconsin (a winter in Wisconsin would have turned Jim Morrison into a teetotaler and Sid Vicious into a DARE parent), but I have an appreciation of a good glass of well-chilled local beer. Most turistas make the assumption that to attain the Texas experience, they must drink at least one bottle of Lone Star. Folks, Lone Star is a foulness used in this state to rip off tourists and strip paint, so shun it at all costs. (From what I understand, Australians do the same thing with Foster's: only tourists and other idiots would drink that swill.) If you feel the urge to partake of rotten hops juice, go for either Shiner Bock (the official drink of the University of Texas at Austin) or the Celis Raspberry Bock. Just don't expect any microbrew garbage; Texans have better things to do than bore everyone else silly with prattling about brewing and bottling when the end result tastes like strained coyote urine.

Now, longtime conventioneers will laugh at me for saying this, but San Antonio offers a lot to do besides wander around the WorldCon. The obvious attraction is the Alamo, right across the street from the convention center, if you don't mind busting your ass on the smooth-as-glass flagstones everywhere and landing in the cactus gardens. Catty-corner from the convention center is the Ripley's Believe It Or Not Wax Museum, and then we have the whole Riverwalk to play with. However, the best expenditure of entertainment dollars comes from cramming 1500 fellow conventioneers into your rented Saturn and high-tailing it to The Snake Farm, about 45 minutes north of San Antonio on I-35. Forget Seaworld: instead of watching a bored killer whale do backflips, watch albino boa constrictors eat things larger than their heads. (Back about a decade ago, a buck got you a fresh white mouse in a little paper bag, which you could then drop into a pit full of angry rattlesnakes. The Snake Farm still has the pit full of rattlers, but the Austin branch of the Animal Liberation Front whined about it, so now they have to feed the rattlers in the off-hours when the patrons can't watch. Besides, nothing's quite as barbaric as the chihuahua races in Laredo; as ol' Joe Bob likes to point out, most of the jockeys in this sport weigh over 250 pounds, and the dogs usually take all day to travel a whole seven feet.)

Within the convention itself, we have many joys: the most important one lies with the Friday and Saturday night dances, which shall expose the world to the talents of the DJ troupe Radio Free Oz. This team of dozens, led by mutants Mike Battle and Jim Reader, were the DJs at my wedding, so I can attest to their inability to play boring music; the song played for the groom's dance was the Ramones' "I Wanna Be Sedated," and things went downhill from there. (Mike and Jim are old friends, so remember one thing: anything they say about me is a goddamn lie, understand? The woman was dead when I got there, and I swear I don't know what she was doing with that LP of Jackson Browne's *Lawyers In Love...*)

Finally, we have the entertainment value of Texas politicians. Like most states in this wonderful Union of ours, Texas makes a point of assigning the village idiots to high political office, on the idea that they cause less trouble in Austin or Washington than they would at home. However, something in the water produces some mighty idiotic village idiots, especially in its two US Senators, but Kay Bailey

Hutchison and Phil Gramm also have connections to the science fiction community. Hutchison resembles one of the most famous maternal images in SF cinema: every time she grins, half of her audience (including her staff) asks "Where the hell is Sigourney Weaver and a forklift when you need 'em?" Gramm and his advocates, however, embrace the philosophy of another set of famed SF characters: whenever faced with mention of Gramm's ongoing ethics violations or of his horrendous Presidential election campaign, they all raise their plumber's helpers and start shrieking "EX-TER-MI-NATE!!!" Keep an eye open for the two at WorldCon; Gramm in particular loves to take credit for events with which he had no connection (out there, we call it "Grammstanding"), so make sure never to get between him and a TV camera, or he'll stomp you like a redheaded stepchild.

Finally, you might come to like Texas so much that you won't leave, which is okay with most natives so long as you aren't from Colorado or Michigan. Becoming a Texas resident is insanely easy: just declare that you plan to become a permanent resident one of these days, and you'll be as free of state income taxes as a native. All George Bush had to do was rent a suite in a Houston hotel to become a resident, so take a closer look at those mobile homes on the way from the airport. Best thing, in Texas, if you don't like the state, sit in that trailer for a week and at least one twister will deposit you in North Dakota, West Virginia, or Oregon, thus making you wish the twister would bring you back. Me, I'm just clicking my bootheels together and wishing "In brightest day, in darkest night..."

—*Tangent, Summer 1997*

Postscript: Intended to appear at the 1997 WorldCon, it might have been quite popular...if the magazine hadn't actually seen print the following Halloween. As it was, I had quite a few friends in Texas who heard about the various incompetencies of the convention committee before the event, and I faithfully relayed those to editor Dave Truesdale. He kept poo-poohing me "It can't be that bad" until after the convention, where he allegedly wandered the hotel, grabbing people by the lapels, and crying "Riddell said it was bad, but I didn't believe him! God help me, I didn't believe him!"

"Distribution Paradigms, Part 1" or "What Do You Mean, 'Borders Doesn't Carry Proud Flesh?'"

Hands up: how many readers have seen a copy of *File 770* or *Lan's Lantern* on the stands somewhere? Howzabout *The New York Review of Science Fiction?* Or *Nova Express, Speculations,* or *Eidolon?*

A few issues ago, I ranted and railed about how writers needed a union, not quite realizing the bind all of us ~ editors, writers, publishers, and artists, as well as readers ~ face by remaining in our business. Simply put, the best way to guarantee that we can revitalize the genre is by fixing the weak link in the publishing process: distribution.

In a better world, magazine readers would hear about a magazine, buy a subscription, and everyone would be happy. Problem is, no matter how noble any of us are, our first instinct when informed of a new magazine is to look for it on the magazine stand at the local bookstore. We usually don't buy a subscription until we get the chance to pick up at least one copy and poke, prod, sniff, taste, and incidentally read it. It's a holdover of our primate heritage: for all of our levels of sophistication, a certain monkey holdover tells us that whatever we see isn't real until we get confirmation from at least one other sense. (And if that isn't how we think, just explain to me why you see a "Wet Paint" sign and feel compelled to touch the paint "just to make sure," hm?) Oh, we'll get a subscription, one of these days, but only after we've seen a few issues on that stand, and we've taken them home and poked and prodded them into the recycling bin or the magazine collection. This works for everything else: if we didn't have the primal urge to see and touch something before we buy it, mail-order catalogues would have wiped out traditional retail a century ago.

(My wife Liz, Isabella Rossellini to my Dennis Hopper, points out that women are much more likely to buy magazine subscriptions than men. I'd like to see a serious breakdown of circulation based on sex, seeing as how I keep getting conflicting reports on the percentage of women who buy SF magazines, and which magazines they buy. Obviously, the subject matter dictates the sale: the more nearly-nude women on the cover, the less likely that its main readership is female.)

Books and magazines are a tougher sell than most products, because of the effort required to make that fateful decision to buy. Before becoming comfortable enough to buy a book, don't you read a few pages first? Sure, the author's name or the cover illustration might pique your fancy, but you need a little taste before you take the time to consume it all. Magazines are even tougher: the first issue you taste might be sweet and satisfying, but what guarantee do you have that the next one tastes the same? A new editor or publisher might take over between one issue and the next, or the cover illustration on the next might scare you off, or that great taste from the first issue may have been transitory and the rest of the magazine's run bears the gentle tang of emery cloth. In many ways, buying issue-to-issue is a safer proposition than buying a subscription: the new issue may sell out before you get to the bookstore, but that's a better sensation than feeling ripped off by buying a two-year subscription to a pile of compost. Also, spending $5 for each issue isn't quite as big a chunk of disposable income: the average magazine subscription is $20, which is enough for a first-run movie for two plus popcorn, which really seems like a lot of money when it goes to buy a sub for a magazine that dies after its first issue or enters into a six-year hiatus between issues.

Another point about subscriptions is the incentive to buy one in the first place. Compare the ease of walking into a local bookstore with a wad of bills and buying the newest issue of *SF Age* as compared to buying a subscription. Consider the ordering fiasco inherent with most subscription deals: the reader has to fill out the enclosed ordering card (if the magazine has one; otherwise, the reader either cuts out the order form or has to make a photocopy of it to keep from mutilating the magazine), write out a check (or go through the rigamarole of getting a money order), hunt down an envelope and stamp, enclose and sign everything, and hope and pray that the Post Office doesn't lose everything. Now consider the additional factors of foreign subscriptions, with more than a few requiring payment in local currency, and the inability of many publishers to take advantage of the ease of credit or debit cards, and making the road trip to the bookstore isn't quite so horrendous.

Now, when most people hear about a magazine, the first thing they do is ask for a copy from the bookstore. Human nature. If it isn't on the shelves, about half of them ask a clerk, and if the store doesn't carry it, they assume the clerk will order a few copies. The other half just assume "Oh, they don't have it" and carry on, and this doesn't consider the number of people who catch a cover out of the corner of the eye, pick up the rest of the magazine, and decide to take it home. (To quote John Lydon a little out of context, "I don't know what I want, but I know how to get it.") And here's where the fun begins.

When we give a magazine name to a clerk, we're assuming (a) the clerk can get the magazine, (b) the clerk wants to get the magazine, and (c) the magazine will arrive in the bookstore before Hell freezes over or we see another *Star Wars* movie, whichever comes first. In a perfect world, we wouldn't have to worry about the first two (sadly, I've had bad experiences with stores whose employees would rather lie to customers than take the time and the effort to find out if indeed they carried a particular magazine, much less order them), but the third is the clincher. We'd assume that the clerk takes the name, calls up the publisher, and picks up a huge stack of new issues. Unfortunately, what really happens is that the clerk pores through a catalogue supplied by his/her magazine distributor, and if said magazine isn't one the distributor carries, no amount of begging in the world will change that situation.

We always have exceptions. Some bookstores cultivate relationships with editors and publishers, who drag in stacks of magazines on a consignment basis or other financial arrangement, but most simply don't have the time to hunt down each and every little magazine customers ask for. Sorry, but that's the way of the world: the bookstore can't afford to expend phone and employee hours for a $3 magazine if only one or two people plan to buy it.

Even if the magazine gets a distributor, the odds are against it. The big boys, such as Eastern News Distribution and Ingram Periodicals, usually have no interest in carrying magazines with a print run of 10,000 or less (and remember, that's the magic number for a magazine being considered for a "Best Prozine" Hugo), so any enterprising publisher has to work with the small boys. While not to malign the smaller distributors, they carry just about everything, which means literary science fiction magazines have to compete for catalog space with aliens-killed-Elvis zines and nude yoga newsletters. Magazine buyers for bookstores (often enough, the clerk we talked about earlier) peruse through the distributor's catalogue and buy based on the information in the catalogue; if they don't know customers want it, they might take a chance, but not often.

The magazine buyer is another killer, because we cannot expect the buyer to know or care anything about science fiction. More often than not, said buyer might have an interest in any number of magazine categories except SF: from the catalogue, s/he couldn't tell the difference between *The New York Review of Science Fiction* and *Star Wars Insider*, but orders based on a need to fill shelf space. Ergo, we get magazine sections where *Absolute Magnitude* finds itself crammed in with *Fate* and *Locus* with Cracked.

If anything, the big chain stores aggravate the problem. Go look for the "sci-fi" section in any Borders, and look at the racks. In almost every store I saw while researching this column, the SF magazines were bunched up on the bottom shelves: either among the movie magazines (not helped by the SF connections afforded by *Cinefantastique* and *Starlog*), the comics (*Mad, Cracked,* and *Funny*

Times), or the flakozoid UFO magazines. They're usually on the bottom: the area that's eye-level for the kids. In other words, someone's decided that science fiction can't attract anyone but kids, no matter how well they build up the SF book section.

(Interestingly, while Barnes and Noble may be a bit lacking in SF magazines, the buyer at B&N certainly enjoys horror magazines, because I keep seeing plenty of them in alongside the literary journals. This is merely an observation: while I might question the emphasis on horror from time to time, the chain stores have a different clientele than the average independent store carrying genre magazines. While many department heads tell me that the standard-sized magazines sell rather well, they point out that they can't move *Asimov's* or *F&SF*; while the digest size made perfect sense for standard newsstand sales because it guaranteed that the magazines appeared in the front of the rack, now they end up piled at the bottom of the rack, where few if any readers notice them.)

Okay, so we've taken on the customers, the buyers, and the distributors. Now we look at the ultimate insult to all of the small-press publishers out there. Most distributors sell on a returnable basis: they ship the magazines, and if they sell, the distributor sends along the money to the publisher after taking its cut. However, the distributor or the bookstore usually pitches any unsold magazines, so a publisher gleefully awaiting a check necessary for continued publication of a magazine that can't move at the bookstores very often gets a notice saying "we only sold x copies" and doesn't get so much as the unsold copies for his/her trouble. In effect, if Magazine X gets shoved behind *Femme Fatales* or *World of Fandom* and then pulled by the magazine buyer to make room for new product, the publisher's screwed. For all intents and purposes, the publisher could take the money necessary to print up that many copies, run it through a tree mulcher, and get more enjoyment than by sending off a few hundred-odd copies to the distributor.

(I had a very interesting talk with the head of the science fiction section at Powell's City of Books, the country's largest independent bookstore, about SF magazine distribution. He told me that he'd love to carry a bevy of SF magazines, but he can't convince the distributor to send more. He said "I'd order 15 copies of *Locus*, and they'd send me 10. Then when I'd call up and say, 'You know, I could move another 15 copies without any problems', they'd send me four.")

We also can't forget the foreign magazines: in the past few years, we've seen a boom in publishing from Canada, Australia, and Ireland, and that's just in the English-speaking world. (Ernest Hogan has been having a great time telling everyone within earshot about the number of SF writers in Latin and South America, and what sort of interest may be available in America for Russian,

German, and Japanese fiction magazines?) Very few even figure into distribution in the US (five points to the folks who point out *Aurealis*, a very nice Australian digest that seems to appear in the most interesting places in the States), but they could build up a very good readership in the country that, like heavy industry, didn't necessarily invent the genre but brought it to its current level of popularity. As of now, though, the odds that any foreign publisher can afford to throw copies and/or money away by sending copies to American distributors is pretty damn slim: Australia, for instance, has a booming SF magazine field because of a series of government grants to help finance local product, and these magazines have a hard enough time finding an audience in their native land.

Comic shops used to be another possibility for alternate distribution: when I first started researching this essay, I started asking "Hey, a lot of the folks who frequent comic shops also read SF; why not push for improved relations with comic distributors?" Well, that fell through after realizing that the only comics distributor of any importance any more, Diamond Distribution, cut back on its orders of noncomics material sometime last year. (The whole sordid tale of how the comics field lost its distributors is a nasty one, involving the greedheads at Marvel Comics, and beyond the scope of this article.) Even considering that most (but certainly not all) comic shops won't order anything from a noncomic distributor if held at gunpoint and that more and more comic shops close each day because the market in comics speculation (which kept many shops alive as speculators bought fifteen copies of the last lump of crap by Rob Liefeld) has bottomed out, the dwindling numbers of comic shops around have to watch their bottom line, so we can't blame them for trying anything that could bounce them into bankruptcy.

(Last summer, *Locus* editor Charles Brown ran an editorial commenting on distribution problems, noting that while he used to depend upon a certain number of sales to comic shops, that revenue stream has disappeared. While readers of this column know that I'm not necessary fond of Mr. Brown and his magazine, this illustrates the dilemma for the entire supergenre: for all of the many complaints, *Locus* is an exceptionally popular magazine with a ready-made audience...and it has problems with getting onto stands. If *Locus*, with nearly 30 years of history behind it, can't get into stores, what chance do the rest of us have?)

Now lest anyone think I'm being overly nice this issue, I have reason: nobody wins. Next issue, I'll look at the demise of Fine Print distribution, its effect on many of the magazines reviewed in *Tangent*, and the possibility of starting a separate distributor solely for genre magazines. (A hint: considering the cost of starting up a legitimate distribution company in the face of the changing bookstore scene, we might have to look for alternatives to standard distribution, and promotion on the Internet isn't one of 'em.)

—Tangent, Spring 1998

Postscript: Sadly, this column appeared in the last print edition of Tangent, *and the magazine went online-only shortly afterwards. Hail and farewell. The rest of the small-press magazine market promptly followed*

"Distribution Paradigms, Part 2a: Promotion and Advertising" or "Pimping Your Magazine For Fun And Profit"

The Story Thus Far: In the last issue of Tangent, *this column discussed the beginnings of the problems with genre magazine distribution, particularly concerning smaller magazines. Future installments will cover some of the more worrisome trends in magazine distribution, especially the recent purchase of Ingram Distribution by Barnes & Noble and the death of Fine Print, as well as some possible solutions that are affordable to the average publisher.*

In the "1997: The Year In Review" issue of *Locus*, editor Charles Brown noted the declining circulation of the larger SF/fantasy/horror magazines, and noted that a subscription promotion on the part of *The Magazine of Fantasy and Science Fiction* would probably help boost its total numbers this year. Those who read these columns on a regular basis know that Mr. Brown and I see eye-to-eye about as often as would Garth Brooks and Marilyn Manson, but this time Mr. Brown was spot-on. If anything, he hit one of the major problems with all of the genre magazines: promotion.

Coming from a background in zines, I keep hearing the same lament from small publishers everywhere; "Oh, if I could just get a decent distributor, my zine would be a huge hit." If the publisher then promotes it so people will know to look for it when it's distributed, that's true, but that part's never considered. To far too many in the publishing business, once the hatchling magazine comes away from the bindery, it's supposed to fly on its own, and if it falls and splats on the sidewalk, that's the fault of the readership that didn't catch it.

Science fiction magazines are in a unique situation: out of all of the fiction genres once available in magazine format fifty years ago, science fiction is the only one remaining that's still available in any real quantity on a typical newsstand. With the exception of porn magazines, SF magazines are about the only place left in American publishing where one can sell short fiction of any type (a few wags might comment on the similar audiences for both SF and porn, but I'm not going to go there), and for all of the whining by Thomas Disch and Jonathan Lethem about the rampant immaturity of SF, that immaturity of SF compared to other forms of fiction may be the reason why it still survives.

Even so, the ongoing song among publishers of genre magazines is that their readership keeps getting older and older. With the exception of *SF Age*, whose circulation and acceptance among readers since 1992 has been impressive, the circulation of the Big Three (*Analog*, *Asimov's*, and *F&SF*) keeps dropping year after year, and the demographics keep leaning toward the Geritol set.

Seeing as how most of my friends are now either having kids for the first time or seeing their children through the horrors of high school, I've had the opportunity to talk with a few who enjoy science fiction. One in particular, David Nance, gave me an interesting insight into the mind of the typical 14-year-old SF reader, an insight that I'd forgotten. We're still seeing new SF readers popping up all of the time; it's just that they aren't bothering to get their fiction from magazines.

Here's part of David's logic. Back when the genre first started out, the magazines were the only regular outlet for SF or fantasy available. Ask someone who remembers when the films *Destination Moon* or *The Seventh Voyage of Sinbad* came out: they'll probably remember these films being all the talk among fans of the fantastic at the time. Nowadays, any monthly or bimonthly magazine has to compete with nearly daily reruns of three *Star Trek* franchises, two *Hercules* franchises, *Babylon 5*, and the Sci-Fi Channel. Considering that the average genre magazine costs close to the price of a new book, David and his friends would rather buy a new or used book that they know is going to be worth the money than take a chance with a magazine. If they buy magazines, it's generally going to be something media-related, like *Starlog* or *Sci-Fi Universe*, where they can get the skinny on the next big movie or TV show: short fiction magazines doesn't interest them at all.

(A possible side-effect of the changing of the SF crowd is illustrated, literally, by the number of movie or TV-related covers for *SF Age* within the last two years. While purists may complain, I've seen new readers pick up copies of *SF Age* and buy them, instead of putting them back on the rack, time and again solely because their interest was hooked by a *Babylon 5* cover. As a matter of full disclosure, I write for both *SF Age* and its sister publication *Sci-Fi Universe*, but I can't help but wonder how many subscribers to *SF Age* start with the media stories and then find themselves enthralled by the fiction inside.)

One also has to remember the fact that the average teenager generally has no money, so any money spent on entertainment has to last. When genre magazines were common and books, even paperbacks, were rare, buying a subscription made sense, but with a typical subscription running at the same price as four paperbacks, the paperbacks make more sense, especially when the magazine might put out four issues a year. To a 14-year-old, a year is a hell of a long time, and four paperbacks in the hand are worth more than four to twelve promised all year long.

It's not enough to understand the problem, though: the reason promotion is so necessary is that these teenagers eventually get money, and their buying patterns as adults are going to be based on their experiences as kids. A little name recognition goes a long way, and these future subscribers aren't getting any reason to look at the name of the Big Three magazines, not to mention any others.

Let's look at it another way. The three big methods used in our genre to promote a magazine, either new or existing, is to pass out subscription cards, promote it at conventions, or get reviews or endorsements from other magazines. None of these methods work for these new readers.

Firstly, as mentioned in the last column, trying to get someone to subscribe sight unseen to a magazine is getting harder all the time. The cost of a subscription to *Tangent*, for instance, could buy tickets for two to a first-run movie plus popcorn, so anyone plunking that $20 for a subscription is gambling that the magazine will live long enough to give a reader the requisite 4, 6, or 12 issues. Look at the people who subscribed to *Thrust* back in 1993: when it closed shop, all of the subscriptions were assumed by *SF Eye*, and the *Eye* has put out a whole three issues in that five years.

(In the past three years, I've heard several people, including one contributor, refer to *SF Eye* as "The Last Dangerous Magazine," although not in print. Personally, I find this nickname to be offensive and possibly libelous: the contributors to *The Last Dangerous Visions* were *paid* for their troubles.)

Promotion at conventions doesn't work for similar reasons. Remember what I said about teenagers having no money? Well, expecting the average 14-year-old to pay $25 for a three day pass to a local convention and then give a publisher $20 for a subscription, or even $5 for a sample issue, is folly. Worse, most magazines assume that setting up a table at a con and expecting people to storm the table is the key to success: generally, especially at media-related SF conventions, the people who show up with money aren't going to spend it on magazines, and everyone else will want a free copy. Free copies are a great way to get name recognition, but most small magazines can't afford to give ten copies away, much less the 100 copies or more necessary to make a real impression. Besides, any attendees of a convention are already True Believers in the power of SF: real promotion goes after those who may not know anything about science fiction but might be intrigued enough to pick up a magazine if it contained content they wanted.

Endorsements and ad trading might work, except that this implies that someone is buying those other magazines. For the record, I first heard of *Tangent* not through contacts, or because I saw a copy in a bookstore somewhere, but because I noticed an ad on the inside front cover of *Mindsparks* nearly five years ago. Some may notice that (a) *Mindsparks* is no longer in publication, and (b) the chain store where I was able to pick up a copy no longer exists. As related in the previous column in this series, the room allocated SF magazines at the local Borders and Barnes & Noble keeps getting smaller all the time. Trading ads with another magazine implies that the other magazine is available to readers and will be bought by them: trading a full page of space that theoretically could be sold to a paying advertiser for a space that may not run for another three years is just a little counterproductive.

Now that this is said and done, the next consideration is trying to convince editors and publishers to promote their magazine. While researching this series of columns, I kept hearing the same mantra: "It's a great idea, but it's been tried before, and it didn't work." This is, of course, the response I receive when I ask why the Big Three Digests don't move to a standard magazine format so that the chain stores will display it better. In that case, the response I hear is "Well, *Analog* tried that back in the Sixties, and it didn't work, so it won't work now." As anyone looking at the date on a paycheck will note, it ain't the Sixties any more, and publishing rules that worked then are counterproductive at best and potentially fatal when used this close to the lee of 2000.

Firstly, the stigma of promotion has to end. Lawrence Person of the exemplary *Nova Express* gives out free copies of his magazine to any registered attendee of an upcoming WorldCon, and has for the last two years, and he gets nothing but abuse for it because of some unspoken code that SF people should not campaign for Hugos and that magazines really shouldn't promote themselves at all. Not only is this a fallacy (an ungodly number of Hugo nominees and winners campaign to get their name and picture in *Locus* and *Science Fiction Chronicle*, which has the same effect), but it's counterproductive. Those who happen to like wasting money should start a cocaine habit: anyone who starts and maintains a magazine has at least the hope of turning it into a success, and refusing to succumb to crass promotion guarantees that nobody will buy a particular magazine because they've never heard of it. Even if the people who receive copies of *Nova Express* never buy a subscription or vote for it come Hugo time, they'll still have a better idea of what *Nova Express* prints in its pages than any of the other Hugo nominees in any given year.

Secondly, let's take out another fallacy. Contrary to popular opinion, promoting a magazine does not mean sending out the editor to a convention to talk about his/her genitalia, nor does it mean buying space in a convention dealer's room and acting like the proprietor of the local newsstand ("If ya want it, buy it; this ain't a library."). I'm not saying that editors and writers should ignore conventions (if anything, a properly planned con schedule can do wonders for letting fans know that a magazine exists, as well as give new readers a chance to meet writers and editors), but the usual strategy of manning a table at a con is a waste. To attract new readers and subscribers, editors have to consider that they have to press the flesh with the public in order to get them to consider spending their cash for an editor's product. To all of you editors reading this: if you have any money whatsoever, spend at least some on promotion, even if it's a slew of photocopies of a subscription notice. Passing out free copies to those who really want to read your magazine (as opposed to dumping a stack of old issues on a table at a convention for those seeking freebies) is much better, but anything that gets the magazine exposure is Nothing But A Good Thing. By putting a human face on a magazine, those with long memories will keep coming back, and not just to ask "So, do you take unsolicited submissions?"

Thirdly, more magazines should consider hiring or borrowing someone who knows something about publicity. Editors shouldn't be expected to be whizzes in all aspects of magazine publishing, but you'd be amazed at how many people will volunteer to pitch a product that they like, and for nothing up front. I'm one of them: with each issue of the print *Tangent*, I usually buy 100 copies or so and pass them out to friends, family, and anyone else willing to read my diseased meanderings. By doing this, I drop a large amount of money in my editor's lap when he needs it the most. I also make sure that when I'm told "I've looked all over for a copy of *Tangent* and I can't find it anywhere," instead of kvetching "Yeah, things are tough all over, so why don't you subscribe," I can reach into my satchel and say "Well, here's a copy, and God bless us, every one!" I seriously doubt that my freebies might lead to *Tangent* getting a mention in *The New York Times*, but I treat everyone who gets a copy with that level of respect, and it's generally paid off.

A pamphlet I picked up a decade ago on the subject of self-publishing started with the comment "If you aren't planning to make money from your publication at some time in the future, get out of the business now." If talent were more important than advertising strategy, then *bOING bOING* and *Mondo 2000* would have stomped *Wired* and *Nightmare Before Christmas* would have beaten *Jurassic Park* like a redheaded stepchild. However, we don't live in that sort of world, and the only way to let new readers know about the joys of the genre's magazines is to make a good sales pitch. A spot of advertising might not help a whole lot, but, as the joke goes about the woman who suggested an enema for the guest of honor at a funeral and was rebuffed with the fact that it was a little too late for that, it can't hurt.

—*TangentOnline, January 1999*

Postscript: Considering that Realms of Fantasy *was just shut down a couple of days ago as I read this, following* Science Fiction Age *and a plethora of smaller magazines into eBay oblivion, we can see exactly how well anybody paid attention to this advice. Right now,* The Magazine of Fantasy & Science Fiction *is going bimonthly to save money,* Analog *and* Asimov's *regularly get an annual readership that would have relegated them to fanzine status 25 years ago, and online magazines such as* SCI Fiction *are casualties along with the print magazines, but the genre is doing great!*

"Web Publishing" or "Internet: The Fandom Menace"

At first view, the Internet seemed to be the savior of the science fiction magazine. When the World Wide Web first started as a buzzword back around 1994, the possibilities seemed endless for the disenfranchised writers and editors of the world. Instead of requiring the money and resources necessary to print a magazine, not to mention the inefficiency of current magazine distribution (which guaranteed that the only people who made money were the ones who could afford to ship hundreds of thousands of copies), anybody could put up a Web site full of material. Hell, it was a license for making money, wasn't it?

Yeah, if only it were that easy. Up front, setting up an Internet presence made perfect sense for small-press and niche magazines: instead of paying the money necessary for printing, collating, binding, mailing, and distributing, which could run thousands of dollars per issue, a Web site could be built for nearly nothing, and could draw a potentially larger audience than any print magazine ever could. In reality, the demographics were off: yes, the Web has the potential to reach millions of people, but maybe only hundreds may have an interest in a particular magazine. Setting up a Web site required a basic understanding of Web design, and even a well-designed site that was poorly promoted could and would flop. Many online magazines were (and will continue to be) hobbies, with the same potential as standard zines in that their editors and contributors went on to other things or became overwhelmed by the amount of work necessary for basic maintenance. The only real difference is that print zines rarely remain as members of the living dead for years after their last publication (although the number of old copies of *SF Eye* still rotting in Borders stores across the country seems to belie this), while ghost sites still haunt their little corners of cyberspace years after their editors lost interest, diverted their attentions, or died.

Speaking as a relative veteran of the Web (I was building and maintaining sites back in 1994, when nobody knew a URL from an SUV), I've seen 'em all. I've been burned by online magazines that published maybe two issues before the publisher skipped town, shafted by publishers who planned to make millions from putting their magazine online but weren't willing to pay for advertising, and drowned with queries of "This guy contacted me; is he trustworthy?" Just like the print end of the genre. The difference is that while I still don't know what Shawna McCarthy is looking for at *Realms of Fantasy* (and since I don't write fantasy, I haven't gotten around to asking), I have a tiny bit of wisdom about the Web. To begin:

Anyone publishing on the Web may not necessarily increase the available audience. Back in 1994, when the Web was relatively new, it was relatively easy to set up a Web site that rapidly built up a serious following. Back then, with an estimated 10 to 18 million Web pages, anyone trying to get online didn't have that many options available, and good sites were passed on via word of mouth or E-mail. Today, not only is a new site competing with an estimated 5 billion pages of material, much of which may be better than that site, but the volume is so high that nobody can keep up with it anymore. (Witness the problems with the online directory Yahoo!: the site's biggest problem to date is trying to keep up with all of the changed and flat-out obsolete listings cluttering its archives, and the situation is unlikely to get better.) A new editor may try to start a new magazine or adapt an existing print magazine to the Web and find that readers are drowning in information as it is.

Contrary to popular opinion, science fiction isn't necessarily seeing a renaissance: the people interested in it are making more money than ever before thanks to the Internet and the corresponding boom in technology companies, but we really aren't seeing a huge boom in the number of folks who tire of *Cosmopolitan* and decide to read *Absolute Magnitude* instead. However, due to the history of the Web and the demographics of those likely to get a computer in the first place (not every computer owner is an SF fan, but SF fans are more likely than most to buy a computer), the Web seems to be full of SF fans and their Web sites. They may be interested, but they may not be interested in reading online fiction: just as in fandom in the real world, the fascination seems to lie in televised and cinematic SF, and getting readers away from the multitude of *X-Files*, *Babylon 5*, and *Squashed Armadillocon: The Movie* Web sites may be folly.

I suspect that this is part of the reason why *Tomorrow SF*'s Web experiment failed, besides the fact that it was a little too early and it charged for subscriptions (see below). If a magazine had decent distribution but failed to sell at the newsstand, it probably wouldn't do too much better online. While a Web site may help a magazine with a very distinct niche market (*Carpe Noctem* and *Tangent*, for instance) or one unable to get a distribution deal (or unable to afford to publish a few thousand more copies solely for sale at superstores), it may not.

This may change in the near future, as the cost of Web access and the tools necessary to hook up go down. Right now, most estimates of Web penetration suggest that maybe 40 percent of the United States population has easy access to the Internet (and that's including schools and libraries), which compares to the early days of television: TV didn't really take off until television set prices dropped to the point where the average Joe could afford to buy one. As with television, the Internet was the province of hobbyists; when a significant proportion of the industrialized world population has easy and affordable Internet access, we'll probably see many more neophyte SF fans checking out magazine offerings. (Right now, Australia is working its hardest to become the most wired country on the planet, especially in establishing satellite links to outlying towns, and the Internet won't be a true world medium until North America, Europe, and the rest of the Pacific Rim catch up.)

Print magazines have one and only one reason to set up a Web site: to sell magazines. The first column in this series mentioned the problems with getting potential readers to shell out cash for a single issue or a subscription to a magazine, and those problems amplify with a Web site. If someone visits your site, rest assured that they're interested in buying your product, but only if you make it easy for them to do so. Putting up compelling content in a Web site is a great way to get people to come back to your site, but if you make it hard for them to buy the print version, they'll keep visiting the site rather than buy a subscription. This means having to work out some kind of commerce situation: putting up a notice saying "Send checks payable to (fill in the blank)" is pointless. A good portion of Web users have or have access to a credit card, and they don't want to wait any longer than they have to in order to get their magazines. Setting up some sort of E-commerce solution is essential: Web shoppers tend to be impulse shoppers, and if you make the purchase of a subscription easy, they'll buy and then tell their friends to buy. If you require them to go through the rigmarole of writing out a check and sending it through Snail Mail, they'll probably take a walk unless they can't live without your product.

The situation gets worse with the Web because of foreign purchasers. Visa, MasterCard, and American Express are nicely universal, and credit card orders from Australia, Japan and Lithuania are still good. This works equally well in reverse: look at the number of Australian magazines, for instance, that could benefit from selling subscriptions to American readers who want to read these magazines but can't get them in their local bookstores. The last thing a magazine needs is the delay caused by potential subscribers who have to go through a currency exchange to pay for the new issue.

My advice? Start looking for a company that can process credit card or CyberCash orders. That's a direct order: at a time when everyone whines about how subscription orders to genre magazines keep going down, passing up on sales is more than ridiculous. It's flat-out suicidal.

Web sites had better have incredible content if they expect to charge for

subscriptions. The justification of buying a subscription to a print magazine lies with its physical mass: the magazine is wonderfully low-tech, allowing reading in the bathroom, on the beach, in a car, or anywhere with enough light for reading. For the expense, it can be stored, traded, resold, cut up for clip art, or otherwise utilized long past its effective shelf life. Best of all, for the casual reader, missing an issue or two at the newsstand won't cost anything.

The reason why subscriber-only Web sites, with very few exceptions, fail is because of basic viewer laziness. Getting a magazine in the mail is relatively passive: it pops in the mailbox, and the reader has the option of reading it then, reading it while eating lunch, being dumped in the bedroom and read before going to sleep, or ignored and left in the paper recycling bin. No matter what happens to that magazine, the subsequent issues keep coming so long as the subscription is valid. The reader's only participation in the distribution of a magazine via subscription is the choice to open and clean out the mailbox.

Compare that to reading a magazine on a Web site. The reader has to start up a computer, make an Internet connection, type in the site's URL or use a bookmark, wait for it to download, and then read it off a screen. Reading an online magazine is prohibitively expensive for those in a plane or at the beach, and the thought of using thousands of dollars of equipment to read a story is pretty absurd anyway. Even with a laptop, reading an online magazine is exasperating for those trying to read in bed or on the loo, and considering that most internet service providers disconnect accounts that are open but inactive for more than ten minutes or so, someone finishing the latest Ramsey Campbell novella and then trying to read the next story usually finds himself/herself disconnected.

(Yes, one may print out individual stories or articles, but consider that this forces the reader to use his/her own paper, ink, and printer. They'd be better off getting a print copy in the first place.)

In the book *Web Pages That Suck*, authors Vincent Flanders and Michael Willis point out that Web users will wait for only two sorts of images: those of naked or dead bodies. The same principle works for Web sites: the only sites that can get away with charging a subscription fee are those supplying images of naked and/or dead bodies. *Upside* magazine recently ran an article on how the porn industry managed to accelerate developments in Web technology by requiring improvements in video transmission and credit card transactions, and all of that tied to the fact that porn sites offer immediate gratification to their visitors. Considering the amount of free content available on the Web as is, fiction and news sites had better have some incredible material if they expect to get paying visitors. *The Wall Street Journal* can justify charging for access to its Web site, but seeing as how a general news and literature site like *Slate* lasted a year as a subscriber-only Web site (and that's with the nearly unlimited funds of Microsoft subsidizing it) before going back to offering everything for free, what chance does a subscriber-only science fiction site have of remaining solvent?

Remember the dictum of "Internet Years." For those unfamiliar with the term, time on the Internet goes roughly the same as dog years: one year of real time is the equivalent of seven years on the Web. This means that while readers of a print magazine may tolerate an issue a year (especially if it's a niche publication, or so damn good that they're willing to wait), they'll stop showing up to a Web site that hasn't had any new content in over three months. Visitors generally visit a site looking for new material, and nothing turns off a visitor faster than the little notice on the bottom of a page that reads "Last revised April 21, 1995." (Imagine buying a subscription to a magazine whose next issue is due out in 2031, and you'll understand the situation.) Trust me: individuals visiting a site that contains old, dead material will do one thing, and that's head to the nearest similar site with more recent information or entertainment.

Not to flog the deceased equine, but take a peek at the site for *SF Eye*. Considering that *SF Eye* at one time had greater cachet than *Mondo 2000* and *Wired* combined, one would think that this would be a perfect site for new, constantly updated material (and yes, I know all about editor Steve Brown's situation right now). Instead, the entire site, while aesthetically pleasing, is painfully out of date. The last addition to the site was at the end of 1997, about the same time the last issue saw print (and about the time it started receiving the nickname "The Last Dangerous Magazine"), and nothing has been added since. Besides a thumbnail of each issue, intended to snag potential subscribers, the site contains a link to the two John Shirley books published by Eyeball Books (both sold out, so advertising them is pretty much counterproductive for anyone not willing to search for them in used bookstores) and nothing else. Aside from the material on the last print issue, the site is identical in appearance to when it came online in 1996.

Now, compare this to *Event Horizon*, Ellen Datlow's baby. *Event Horizon* is a model for what online magazines should be: alongside the usual exemplary stories expected of Ms. Datlow are essays, reviews, and a regular contest. The staff updates the content on a regular basis (usually about every two weeks), guaranteeing that visitors have a reason to keep coming back. I wouldn't be so presumptuous as to predict the future success of *Event Horizon*, but if it fails, it won't be due to its site maintenance or its content.

This doesn't mean that the poor editor has to produce a whole new issue every week (although Craig Engler at *SF Weekly* (http://www.scifi.com/sfw) has managed to do just that, give or take a week, for the past four years). Even one new article, story, or review per week is enough content to demonstrate that the site isn't dead. When one considers that a bimonthly magazine such as *SF Age* could put out a story and two departments a week and still have material lying around by the time the next issue came out, the idea of having to publish a whole new issue every week is a bit ridiculous.

Be prepared to spend as much on a good site as you would on a print publication. I'm currently writing a book on effective Intranet design entitled *Chimps With Shotguns*, because giving a Web editor to someone without understanding of basic Web design is like giving shotguns to chimpanzees: it guarantees a mess, and someone's probably going to get hurt. The person hurt is going to be the publisher of that site: nothing turns off visitors to a potentially great site faster than multi-colored fonts, tacky animated graphics, and bad navigation, and visitors who don't come back never buy products.

Fact is, any idiot can set up a site claiming to be a magazine, and many do. However, setting up an effective site...well, that's a different situation. This requires being willing to pay for stories from established talent, paying for illustrations (cheap clip art stolen off the Web won't cut it), paying for site maintenance and upkeep, and setting aside the time to do it right. Very rapidly, that "cheap" Web site gets to be a bit expensive, eh?

This happens with magazines as well; the difference is that the editor/publisher of a print magazine can sell off copies. Web sites generally depend upon sponsorship and advertising, so work on that content: good stories will pull in advertisers, which helps pay for more good stories. Priming this pump may take a while, so be prepared to wait a while: as in print, the wannabe Web editors usually give up after a couple of months when they find that they can't make millions from publishing in a fortnight, leaving the playing field open for the determined and competent.

The proof that it's worth it comes from comparing various sites. A good site doesn't have to be expensive: witness *The Orphic Chronicle*, edited by S. Kay Elmore. Kay can't afford to pay print rates for stories, but she manages to find plenty of real gems, and it's all in a rather intuitive interface that allows first-timers to find everything they need when they need it. If and when the Hugo Awards allow nominations for online publication, sites like *The Orphic Chronicle* will most likely offer the greatest competition to the print magazines.

This is in contrast to any number of cheesy sites set up by wannabe editors that offer to publish stories so they can get general recognition. I won't name names, but these generally work on the same assumption as Faces International and other head-shot "modeling agencies": "Submit to us and we'll get your stories out so they can be recognized," as if Gardner Dozois and Gordon Van Gelder have nothing better to do with their time than visit personal home pages looking for misplaced talent. Because any dingbat can claim to be an editor on the Web, the only people taken seriously are those with professional credentials behind them and/or those who pay for submissions. It's the same difference as between talking to some Cretin Tarantino wannabe who plans on making his first film once someone discovers him and gives him a $1 million director's fee, and someone who's already putting out demo reels. The science fiction industry and Hollywood are both full of nutcases on either side of professionalism, but the work usually speaks for itself.

Because of that ease in publishing on the Web, the stigma will remain on Web publications the way television news was downplayed by newspapers in the Forties. While Web publishing is a great idea, the culture as a whole has a bit more respect for magazines that put out at least one dead-tree version every few months or so. In another ten years, this may change: an increase in the price of paper and a continuation of the decrease in the price of computers may combine with an acceptance of Web-only magazines, but that's going to be a while.

Giving away content makes money. Yes, one might figure that putting stories, articles, and essays on the Web negates any chance of making money from reprints, but the opposite is true. A magazine that specializes in genre-related news (*Locus*, f'r instance) could hide all of its information, giving only highlights on its Web site, but that won't encourage readers to subscribe. Instead, by giving out everything, a magazine increases its reputation and its reach, thus encouraging visitors to subscribe. Never underestimate the appeal of a dead-tree version of a magazine: once visitors see that your magazine has regular, consistent value, they'll want to subscribe or buy single issues, just to save on the printer bill.

A good corollary is Suck.com, a Web-based commentary and satire site. Established in August 1995, the site rapidly built up a rather fanatical following based on its daily content, gaining enough of a reputation to justify publishing a book of the best essays last year. While I don't have any statistics on sales of the book, the fact that a Web site's content inspired a book should come as an object lesson: those same essays are still up on the Suck.com Web site, but visitors are willing to pay for a low-tech version, and that book also draws in readers who may not have had any interest in the Web before, but want more after they've finished the book.

(As yet another aside, writers should consider this as well. I know, I know:

giving out stories is anathema. In the case of the Web, though, writers allowing ongoing publication of their stories online not only increase their readership [I had no idea how many Australians liked my work until I set up my own Web site], but that also encourages new sales to standard magazines. "If you liked his/her story in *Event Horizon*, check out the new novella in *SF Age* and *Asimov's!*")

Which brings up additional content. Since Web sites don't suffer the limitations of print (layout, page count, word count, etc.), a Web site is a great place to test out new columns and features. The Web site for the *Dallas Observer* demonstrates this well: as well as the standard Web reprints of its paper version, the *Observer* regularly runs features and columns intended for online purposes only. If a regular feature gains enough popularity, an editor can justify moving it to the print version, and a few notes in the print version along the lines of "Take a look at all the extra crap we have online!" help draw new visitors to the Web site. Offer enough unique content in both, and everybody wins.

As usual, this column only touches on the basics of Web publication: a comprehensive look would require a book, and it would be out of date the moment it saw print. However, this is a nexus for the genre: while nobody seems to be making a profit from online magazines yet, that may change in as little as a year, and legitimate print SF magazines may be the minority by 2005. Those who investigate the technology and the limitations now have the best chance of getting established by the time a majority of of the world population has access to the Web, and it'll be too late for those who lollygag.

—*Tangent Online, July 1999*

Postscript: It shouldn't be any surprise that most of the online venues mentioned in the preceding column are now long-dead, particularly the ones that I thought would be around for years. It also shouldn't be surprising that most of those venues died before the dotcom crunch, not after.

"Distribution Paradigms Continued: Building A Distributor Out Of Common Household Items"

Okay, so the genre magazine business is in serious trouble. Science fiction magazines have always been a marginal portion of the periodical landscape, and the inability of many editors and publishers to look at them as anything but a hobby threatens to flood that particular hill just as interest in the genre was starting to peak. Most are unknown to anyone outside the business, the Web hasn't exactly turned them into media powerhouses, and writers, editors, and publishers are too busy parading around conventions to do anything about letting the general public know they exist. Bookstores don't have any reason to put them in plain sight, they're getting crowded out by movie and UFO rags, and the number of bookstores keeps plummeting as Borders and Barnes & Noble keep advancing on indie booksellers like glaciers advancing on a herd of mammoths. If this were a movie, we'd be expecting Superman or Mighty Mouse to save the day; if this was an art film, everyone would die in despair, but with classy clothes. (In actuality, I figure the death of the genre magazine will resemble the end of Sam Peckinpah's *The Wild Bunch*, but that's just me.)

The death of Fine Print Distribution on Pearl Harbor Day 1997 cut off many small press magazines from their places at the newsstand, and the business still hasn't quite recovered. Ingram Distribution, one of the big magazine distributors in the United States, started to carry some of the more successful zines after Fine Print bought the farm, but it had problems of its own. Upon hearing word that Barnes & Noble was planning to purchase Ingram last year, many independent booksellers boycotted Ingram and refused to order books or magazines from the company; the deal fell through, especially under the threat of a Department of Justice investigation, but the lull in orders still hurt many smaller magazines that don't have advertising as a significant portion of their revenue. A few small press distributors, such as Desert Moon, have tried to fill the ecological niche left by Fine Print, only their problem lies with finding outlets willing to carry magazines with a circulation of less than 10,000 copies per issue.

Because of this, the natural question asked by many in the genre is "Well, why can't the science fiction industry start its own distribution system?" It's a very valid question, and had someone started one back around, say, 1965, we might be standing pretty right about now. As of 1999, though, the logistics are immense, and the entire face of the distribution scene has changed so much since then that if the expense didn't leave the project stillborn, the market would finish it off.

Before we go into the details of why a new distributor probably wouldn't work, let's recap the basic situation with selling magazines through stores. Most magazines make their money from advertising: they promise a certain number of copies to be delivered to stores and homes, and they base their advertising rates on that circulation. For all intents and purposes, most major magazines are already paid for before they go to the printer: ad revenue covers all of the expenses. (Since magazines are more durable than newspapers, many make the assumption that each copy is read by three people before it's archived or thrown away, so those hypothetical three people are included in the breakdowns of ad cost. A variation on this is how weekly newspapers and ad sheets can afford to be free: most weekly newspapers have a little disclaimer stating "The first copy is free, and all others are $1.95." The paper's staff knows full well nobody who picks up three or five or ten copies is going to send in a check for those copies, so the assumption is that each copy went to one distinct individual, minus the random check for ten copies that they may receive from time to time.) At this point, sales in stores are gravy: the real money is in subscriptions and advertising. If *Time* expected to recoup its expenses solely off newsstand sales, each issue would probably run about $10 a copy, if not more.

With a large-circulation magazine, the current distribution system works very well, as the main intent is to get copies in front of as many eyeballs as possible. A bookstore or newsstand that sells a copy of *Time* or *Popular Science* makes its share of the cover price, usually fifty percent, and the publisher can afford to send out as many as the store can sell. This doesn't work for small press magazines, where that same fifty percent is the general cost of publication. The main purpose of newsstand sales for a science fiction magazine (and let's face it: compared to *Time* or *Wired*, every magazine in this business qualifies as "small press") isn't to make money from the sale, but to gain exposure and possibly sell subscriptions. In a perfect world, a publisher could make money from every sale of a magazine, but quite a few factors conspire to keep that from happening.

Since bookstores can't afford to waste the time necessary to contact the publisher of each and every magazine and submit an order for the new issue, and the publishers can't afford to waste the time and effort necessary to submit invoices, pack up and ship copies, and send dunning notices to the occasional deadbeat, the magazine industry depends upon distributors. In their perfect form, distributors collect orders for magazines (and books, toys, and anything else a store may want to sell, but I'm getting ahead of myself) from book and magazine stores, submit orders from the individual publishers, receive the shipments of copies, send them to the stores, collect the money owed for each sold copy as well as any unsold copies, dispose of the unsold copies, and present the publisher with a final check. In exchange for those services, distributors take a percentage of the revenue from each magazine to cover their expenses.

As explained before, larger magazines either have sufficient advertising revenue that each issue makes a profit before it hits the presses, or they have sugar daddies that keep them solvent while they try to find their audiences. Because of this, the ten to fifteen percent of the cover price charged by a distributor is minor: any money finally received from the sale of an issue is welcome, but not absolutely necessary. A small press magazine, on the other hand, offers its own unique challenges. Since very few zines have their own ad department, and certainly aren't taking care of all of their expenses from ads, money is a bit tight. If a $5 copy of *Tangent* costs $2.50 to print, the bookstores expect to keep 40 to 50% of the cover price themselves, and the distributor wants another 15%, publishing *Tangent* solely for the magazine stand is a money-losing proposition. Factor in that most existing distributors won't waste their time with any magazine with a circulation of less than 10,000 copies per issue, and trying to get a distribution deal is financial suicide.

We have alternatives to this. Since publishing costs go down relative to the number of copies printed, most publishers can get out four magazines for the price of three. Sovereign Media (the folks who bring you *SF Age*, *Realms of Fantasy*, and *Sci-Fi Entertainment*, as well as the late *Sci-Fi Universe*) realized this back in 1997, but the leader in SF publishing right now has to be DNA Publications, owned by Warren Lapine. Putting such diverse magazines as *Dreams of Decadence*, *Absolute Magnitude*, *Weird Tales*, and *Pirate Writings* under one banner was absolute brilliance: not only is DNA able to take advantages of the economics of scale by consolidating print runs, but DNA also consolidates the support staff necessary to handle the financial side of each magazine. Orders for the magazines come to one address, which means that one person can fill orders, deposit checks, and enter subscribers into a database instead of one per magazine. Similarly, DNA's promotional literature takes advantage of the inherent procrastination of most subscribers. Why fill out four subscription forms and send four separate envelopes with four separate checks when one will do?

This attitude isn't new. Anyone familiar with the early history of the science fiction community may remember that most early SF magazines were intended to take advantage of these same factors: a publisher may not have made much money from a new SF magazine, but considering that by publishing four magazines they were getting one for free, even a small profit was an improvement. However, DNA and its crew should take credit for trying something drastically different: instead of buying up defunct magazines or creating new ones, DNA helps shelter existing magazines and allows them to survive and thrive in the current publishing climate.

This consolidation also helps other magazines, if only because copies of *Absolute Magnitude* on the stands helps draw interest from people who may be interested in science fiction but need that little extra push to read it on a regular basis. In previous columns on the subject, I mentioned that the main problem facing the genre is the decline in younger readers. By making sure that genre magazines remain on the shelves, and that they drop to a price where the average teenage reader can justify blowing $3 on a magazine instead of a matinee, we start to hook a whole new generation of SF readers.

Which leads us right back to our current situation: distribution. Editors and publishers can put out as much product as they want, but if nobody knows that the product exists, it's a waste of money. For any time in the foreseeable future, newsstand distribution is going to be one major path to getting the audience we all crave, although not the only one.

The first thought is to start a homegrown distribution system. On first thought, this sounds easy: run a distribution outlet through your home, and get these magazines out on the stands somewhere, even if it starts with St. Louis and then goes elsewhere. At least, that's what I thought, until I crossed paths with one David Davisson, a reviewer at *Nova Express*. Not only was David an old high school classmate (the guy who in fact introduced me to the works of Harlan Ellison, among others, so he's the one to blame for the way I turned out), but he worked for Fine Print Distribution in Austin, Texas until its closing, and he disabused me of the notion of a DIY network.

David noted first off that running a real distribution outlet is expensive. Since zines have a much lower profit margin than big magazines, Fine Print collected a huge number of zines to offset that margin. Storage of those zines is going to be expensive, so put down a good pile of cash for the warehouse necessary to protect those magazines from the elements. That large a body of zines requires sophisticated database software to keep track of accounts payable and accounts receivable, as well as how many orders for a zine versus the actual number of copies available, and this software isn't available off-the-shelf at CompUSA. Plan to throw a hefty chunk of change at a programmer to design this software, as well as to upgrade and maintain it as necessary. Still with me? Good, because you're going to need a workforce to fill orders, field queries from bookstores that might want to carry your magazines, send off catalogues to those bookstores, nag others who haven't made an order in a while, threaten to break the legs of those who haven't paid their bills, pay the utility bills, and make coffee. Naturally, with a workforce, ethical business owners are going to pay through the nose for health insurance, worker's compensation insurance, liability insurance, and overtime pay, as well as all of the free coffee necessary to help motivate the workforce in the morning. (Unethical ones can skip out on these, if they don't mind losing an inordinate amount of inventory to disgruntled employees who figure that they have nothing to lose.) Have anywhere between $100,000 and $1 million to spend to start up a magazine distributor? If not, you're not going anywhere.

Back when I first started working on the problems with magazine distribution, Jeff VanderMeer made what at first seemed to be a reasonable suggestion: why didn't the Science Fiction Writers of America start up its own distribution center? Well, aside from the question of who was going to manage this, the finances get in the way. I bounced this idea off Paula Guran, and she backslapped me until I saw the light: SFWA simply doesn't have the money or the resources to support something like this. Oh, it might happen...if we could convince every member of SFWA and the Horror Writers of America to chip in $5000 toward a new distribution center. Considering how little on average a SFWA or HWA member makes from writing each year, we're better off waiting for Bill Gates to finance the whole gig.

This isn't to say that SFWA and HWA couldn't do more to convince its members to support magazines other than submitting stories. Since buying subscriptions gives more direct cash to magazines, which allows them to publish more or larger issues, which means that said magazines have more room for stories, an effort by SFWA and HWA to make public service announcements to its members about how subscribing to magazines after sending submissions is The Right Thing To Do (comparable to the "Read A Child A Newspaper Every Day" campaign by the Newspaper Association of America) might help current magazines and sprout new ones. SFWA and HWA also need to consider ways to let those outside the SF community know about existing magazines, as school lectures and press releases are a good start toward building name recognition for everyone involved. However, they simply don't have the money or the manpower necessary to run a distribution center on their own.

Let's assume for the moment that we were somehow able to get the cash necessary to start a real distribution center: let's say that, for just one moment, that everyone between me and the British Throne died and I hocked the Crown Jewels shortly after the coronation to finance a real international distribution center for genre magazines. (Hey, it could happen. If *Tangent* can get three Hugo nominations in a row, anything's possible.) Better yet, let's say that I run this as a charity, so the distribution center takes out nothing for the cost of distributing

Asimov's and *Cemetery Dance* and *Plot!* Now we deal with the joys of getting those magazines into stores and getting paid for our efforts.

In an editorial in *Locus* nearly two years ago, editor Charles Brown pointed out that one of the main outlets for his magazine, comic shops, dried up when the distributors died. Back in 1993, Marvel Comics started a distributor's war by declaring that Hero's World would be the only distributor authorized to carry Marvel titles, which caused every other comic company to try to set up similar exclusive agreements with other distributors. When the smoke finally blew away three years later, only one real distributor, Diamond, was left alive, as all the others had either been assimilated by Diamond or had gone bankrupt. (One side-effect of all of this was that Marvel declared bankruptcy itself at the end of 1996, and is still trying to work its way toward solvency, which prompts the understandable response of "Good riddance to bad rubbish.") After Diamond took over, it gradually trimmed away all non-comic-related items from its catalogue, which meant that any number of genre-related magazines suddenly lost that many outlets.

As a child of the Eighties, I remember the early days of the comics direct market, and my local comic shop carried many genre magazines that were otherwise unavailable to me or to anyone else in the area. (My home town was good for cross-burnings, book-burnings, and brother-sister marriages, and not much else.) The readers frequent the shops, and all we have to do is get past the retailers.

Before I write the following, I would like to emphasize that in the course of researching this series of columns, I have met a multitude of retailers who honestly care about genre magazines, and who would bend over backwards and snatch dimes off the ground with their teeth if they thought it would help sales. For every retailer I met whom cared about the genre, though, I met at least two lazy, insufferable bastards who couldn't be trusted to sit the correct way on a toilet seat (to steal from Rowan Atkinson). The good folks aren't the subject of this attack, and in fact deserve declarations of sainthood all around: the bastards, on the other hand...

Considering the fact that most bookstores and comic shops have their own problems right now, many understandably go the easy route when purchasing magazines. They pull out the catalogues they already have, and make orders through them. Any new genre distributor would have to allocate even more money to contacting the magazine buyer of every large, medium, and small bookstore in the United States (and elsewhere, if we wanted to go international) and drop catalogues in their laps and hope that they put in orders. The superstores make things even more interesting: all of Barnes & Noble's magazine buying is coordinated through the New York headquarters, and more of the buying at Borders goes through Ann Arbor, Michigan instead of the individual store. If they have no interest in our catalogue, we're missing out on at least half of the outlets in the country, and the figures get more aggravating when one considers the expansion both superchains plan for Europe and Australia.

Even if we get the catalogues to buyers, we have no guarantee that they'll use them. I faced this personally about five years ago, when the manager of my favorite comic shop in Dallas asked me about the availability of zines in his shop. Since my wife managed a bookstore at the time, she gave me a Fine Print catalogue, and I gave it to the manager, highlighting the neat SF magazines carried by Fine Print. (Okay, I admit it: I was stoked on seeing some of the magazines I wrote for up on the shelves, and I had dreams of autographing each and every copy of *Science Fiction Eye* that came in.) He oohed and aahed for about an hour, and he told me that he'd put in an order in a week. About two months later, I asked him how the order went, and he told me "Well, I haven't gotten around to it yet," implying that putting in an order with Diamond was easier than getting off his butt and contacting a new distributor.

This behavior isn't surprising: compared to the dolts who lie to customers about how a particular magazine "should be in next week" rather than admit that they won't carry it, it's actually quite refreshing. Unfortunately, it doesn't help the shop, it doesn't help the distributor, and it sure as hell doesn't help the publisher. Customers are willing to bounce around a bit from store to store if they stand a chance of getting a magazine, but pull a bait-and-switch too many times, and they'll give up.

And then there's the matter of payment. Most bookstores and newsstands are good about payment for sold copies of magazines, but some are notorious for paying when they damn well feel like it. Borders and Barnes & Noble are well-known in the magazine business for paying their invoices if and when it seems like a good idea, and Fine Print had regular problems with getting money from them. This of course impacts the magazine: since most zines can't afford to print the next issue until they receive the money from the last issue, many go months or even years without a new issue while Borders deliberates whether it should pay its bills. (Many big bookstores work this way, on the logic of "You need us more than we need you," but it's not isolated to the big stores. Shortly before I left Oregon at the end of 1997, I dropped off copies of *Wetbones*, *Cyber-Psychos AOD*, and *Tangent* on consignment with two stores, and the managers in charge swore that they would get checks to me as each magazine sold. To this day, I have yet to receive a check for any of the magazines, and repeated phone calls and E-mail messages get ignored.)

To make things even more creative, we have to consider the creative bookkeeping used by stores to keep for paying for magazines. We're not talking about "pulping," the practice of destroying unsold copies of magazines, although nothing is quite so aggravating as a magazine telling paying customers that it can't send sample copies because all of the copies went to the distributor, and then hearing that the stores sent them all back to the distributor to be pulped. (Again, in this hypothetical distribution center, we'd return all unsold copies to the publisher for possible resale, although with the cost of UPS shipping, I'm obviously building dream castles and measuring for drapes.) The June 1999 issue of *Locus* made mention of a curious practice of Barnes & Noble making the publisher responsible for all damaged or stolen magazines as a condition of sale. Since most Barnes & Noble patrons seem to consider the magazine rack to be a free reading room next to the café, I can understand the damage inflicted by ignorant patrons on the magazines. (I once watched one character spill coffee all over the interior of a magazine he was reading, close it, carry it between forefinger and thumb while coffee spurted out both ends, and put it back on the rack and grab a new copy. He then went back to his seat and started reading where he left off, while the crappucino-dripping copy he left behind oozed over the rest of the shelf, ruining the copies behind it. I almost gave the man an enema with the espresso machine, but my wife stopped me from committing capital murder: in Texas, ripping out a man's throat with your teeth is considered cannibalism.)

It's still a curious practice, though. If a customer at a car dealership takes a Saturn out for a test drive and wraps it around a telephone pole, General Motors isn't expected to eat the cost of the car. If someone breaks into a pet shop and steals all of the bearded dragons and leopard geckos, the pet store still has to pay the breeder for the stock. If a parent lets his/her child into a glass shop and the anklesnapper proceeds to destroy $10,000 of crystal after trying to play "Bombardment" with the understandably reluctant clerk, Waterford hasn't signed a contract saying that the store doesn't have to pay for all damaged or destroyed merchandise. But Barnes & Noble can require just that of publishers who wish to sell their magazines in Barnes & Noble SuperStores. Hmmm.

The final insult comes with the tracking of magazine sales. On the surface, the idea of bookstores tracking the number of magazines sold per store is a valuable one, especially for demographic purposes or for future orders. Barnes & Noble is currently in the process of testing a new tracking system, that keeps tabs on the exact number of magazines sold. Previously, all magazines were logged in as "magazines (generic)," but the new system, if implemented, will track every copy of every carried magazine in every store.

In many ways, this system offers hope for understanding the buying habits of the general public. Better tracking could allow better display procedures: if the SF magazines sell much better when at eye level instead of the bottom-shelf-up-in-the-alcove section that most stores keep them in (right between *Cracked* and *Fate*), then maybe we'll get better-designed magazine sections. Then again, seeing as how magazines are generally a loss-leader designed to get the browser to buy books, maybe not. This system might also finally nail down how many copies are shoplifted, how many are damaged, and how many are "liberated" to the employee break room or in an employee's backpack. I'm measuring for drapes again, though, so let's bring up the danger.

The danger of this system lies in the sporadic publishing of most genre magazines. By keeping tabs on exactly how many copies sell per issue and when, the buyers at Barnes & Noble can micromanage their orders, buying only enough copies and no more. Well, that does nothing for new readers (after all, if B&N ascertains that only three copies of *Pirate Writings* sell per issue, and five people specifically hunt for that magazine, two are going to go home unhappy, and Arioch help the magazine that gets enough press that dozens of people go to the store to snag a copy), and it's not all that bad for weekly or monthly magazines. After all, with this database, the magazine buyer can keep tabs on an average sale, and orders accordingly: *Rolling Stone* can have a particularly poorly selling issue, such as the Sex Pistols issue back in 1977, but orders will be based on averages. The same holds true for the SF digests, since they generally keep a monthly or bimonthly schedule. It's the small magazines that are going to get slammed.

Because of their hobby status, most small genre magazines come out whenever the publisher gets enough money to send in an order to the print shop. They may advertise themselves as a triannual or quarterly, but any "quarterly" in this business that gets three issues out per year is doing pretty well, all things considered. The laws of statistics start to kick in with the B&N system: let's say the first issue of a new magazine gets carried by B&N, and the company orders fifteen copies per store. Five copies sell, but B&N orders fifteen copies of the next issue. Five copies of this one go out the door, only enough word of mouth gets around that fifteen customers at each store check back each day for the third issue. Well, it's been a year since the magazine premiered, so B&N follows through and orders five. If this zine came out more often, the system might have seen this sort of demand coming, but with three issues a year, one poorly selling issue could throw off the numbers and guarantee that another year would go by before orders picked up. As we all know, the magazine could be dead by then, especially if the publisher has been mailing off fifteen copies per store to the distributor and getting paid for five.

Considering the changes in the bookselling business in the last ten years, standard distribution is out for most genre magazines. The ones that already have distribution deals are good for now, but ongoing problems with distributors could affect them as well, and the smaller magazines simply cannot afford to take the kind of losses that they've been receiving since about 1992. In the next installment, I'll look at one possible solution: it may not work, and it may be impractical, but it just may beat the current system and keep the genre's magazines alive.

—TangentOnline, October 1999

Postscript: This was the last article I ever wrote for Tangent, *online or print, but it was a good place to stop. It's always good to know when to leave the party, even though I still miss working for the magazine from time to time. It joined most of the other magazines mentioned here, and even now it acts, as Sean Lindsay of "101 Reasons to Stop Writing" put it about my work, as an exercise in digital archaeology.*

"Would You Like Fries With That Franchise?"

As *Star Trek* reaches toward the one-third-century mark this year, its progeny are in trouble. Ticket sales and reviews of *Star Trek: Insurrection* hovered somewhere between anaemic and bathetic, the ratings on *Voyager* are so uninspiring that UPN would have cancelled the show four years ago had it not been a *Star Trek* franchise, and *Deep Space Nine* finally put itself out of our misery. Some fans talk about how, without some serious revision, the whole *Star Trek* conglomerate could go under in the next few years.

Well, to quote a childhood role model on the death of Elvis, good riddance to bad rubbish. If *Star Trek* in its multiple forms continues in its current surge toward self-destruction, the only people who'd complain about its demise are the fanboys who cannot conceive of life without a view of Two of 39D, er, I mean, Seven of Nine every Wednesday night. For the rest of the world, it'll have about as much impact as the cancellation of *The Brady Bunch*. Let's face it: *Star Trek* has been around, in one form or another, for 33 years, and it desperately needs an overhaul.

That's not to say that the beast is dead: if the crew at Paramount that currently micromanages its cash cow was to let up a bit, its popularity could and would surge again. The details may vary, but here are a few suggestions.

Bring In Some Fresh Blood. Even diehard fans admit that the first improvement necessary to save the franchises is to get producer Rick Berman to step down. I advocate stripping down the entire production team and replacing them with folks who (a) love *Star Trek* and (b) know something about the rest of science fiction. Some of the best episodes of the original series were written by big-name SF writers (Theodore Sturgeon, Norman Spinrad, Harlan Ellison, and Robert Bloch, among others), and a few big SF names brought on as consultants and scripters could help goose the series and movies into shape. As is, too many episodes over the last few years have been gimmicks (the "Trials and Tribble-ations" episode of *DS9* was thoroughly pointless) or near plagiarisms (the notorious "Lost World" episode of *Voyager* just begged for a lawsuit from Robert Sawyer), and hiring writers who actually know something about science fiction just might improve both films and shows.

Along that line, the franchises desperately need a new head makeup artist, and fast. Michael Westmore's work was always mediocre at best, and both the series and movies could use an artist that could make alien aliens. In a perfect world, Paramount would hire someone like Rob Bottin or John Vulich, as the current work is a step down from that in the original series, and that's saying something.

Remember the Credo "Anyone Can Die At Any Time." Part of the boredom factor with the current franchises is that characters leave only because the actor wants to quit the show. If viewers knew that all of the characters could die in a space battle, for instance, and know the battle wasn't in a parallel universe or a dream, the tension would be much greater (c'mon, admit it; nobody *really* worried when Kirk or Picard was in a "life-threatening" situation). Some fans may not like it, but change is good for everybody else.

As an idea, instead of full-blown series, why not a regular set of miniseries on UPN? Considering the number of potential storylines involving the Starfleet Corps of Engineers, the Federation Secret Service, or the equivalent of the Navy SEALs, a miniseries of, say, three two-hour segments offers enough time for a self-sufficient story, plenty of action, and more character development than what's available in a standard film. Because the audience may never see these characters again, the writers and actors can take chances on motivations and situations. A miniseries format also allows a linear storyline without getting too bogged down in detail; seeing as how the staff writers on *DS9* spent the last season copying everything else on *Babylon 5*, why not copy that instead?

What about the rest of us? Here's the underlying reason for the poor ratings and box office receipts: sure, the fans are exceedingly happy, but the only way the *Star Trek* franchises are going to grow is by attracting new audiences. This means making the show friendlier to casual viewers and not the dweebs who memorize the numbers stenciled on bulkheads. Coordinating the series and films so that someone unfamiliar with the *Star Trek* universe can at least follow the action, without dumbing it down, is the way to go.

Yeah, these may be extreme measures, and not too many fans will appreciate the comments. But considering the source, would the folks at Paramount trust this advice if it came from anyone else?

—Previously unpublished

Postscript: This was intended to be my 11th column for Sci-Fi Universe. *Unfortunately, the magazine was shut down due to various situations in the summer of 1999. On the bright side, two things happened. Firstly, every magazine that could even come close to caring about Paramount's woes with its cash cow, from* Cinescape *to* Salon, *put out similar articles, so I certainly wouldn't have been the first. (I would have been the only one calling for the show's extinction, instead of submitting soppy fanboyish screeds as if the franchise was worth saving, but I always try to make as many enemies as possible.) Secondly, the "Rant" column was moved over to the new SCI FI magazine, with a whole new subject. Due to various issues, this became the Column That Time Forgot, so it appears here in print form for the first time.*

"The Steve Irwin of Science Fiction?"

A couple of years ago, I took the time to catch the short-lived *Sci-Fi Entertainment* news show on our esteemed channel, and I caught probably the best missed opportunity this side of the Sex Pistols passing over *Saturday Night Live*. One of the show's reporters had snagged Jerry Pournelle and Gregory Benford at a convention and was interviewing them on general genre questions. Naturally, the reporter was trying to tie the interview to the Sci-Fi Channel, and he switched from literary questions to other media. When asked if either happened to recommend any genre TV shows or films, they admitted that they didn't like much of anything on television or film at the time. Actually, the proper adjective to describe their response was "mealy-mouthed," but that's their business.

Working in the literary side of science fiction, I understand the attitude most writers have toward the movie and TV side of the business. It gets frustrating to see the latest Spider Robinson or Jeff VanderMeer or Ernest Hogan get crowded off the bookshelves to make room for the latest *Star Wars* novel, and most writers and editors have a dismissive attitude toward either screen. However, neither group seems to be doing much to attract new readers to the genre: thanks to television and film, SF concepts flood the general public, and the public keeps going back to lousy TV shows solely because nobody gives them any alternatives. Even worse, the genre attitude toward "mundanes" tends to aggravate things. (We fans tend to have a bit of an attitude problem about the genre, where we kvetch about being outcasts but badmouth anyone from the outside who wants to get in, but that's material for another column.)

The situation is that science fiction needs an evangelist. We need someone who can not only help consolidate the people in the business, but attract new readers and viewers curious about the genre but with no idea where to start. A good example is in the computer industry, where Linus Torvalds and Guy Kawasaki used two completely different styles to garner interest in the Linux and Macintosh operating systems, respectively. Admittedly, Torvalds is about as quiet as Kawasaki is fervent, but they presented a human face to the industry, with none of the cliché of the arrogant technoweenie that infests most news coverage of the business. Compare that to Microsoft's attitude, and no wonder those Bill Gates-as-Borg, "We are Microsoft. Resistance is futile." T-shirts are so bloody popular.

Now, science fiction has some evangelists already: look at what J. Michael Straczynski has managed to do with *Babylon 5*. Not only did he keep pushing an intriguing and accessible TV show that brought in a lot of new faces, but he constantly incorporated little aspects that made *B5* fans run to the library. To this day, I wonder how many fans rushed to pick up a copy of Alfred Bester's *The Demolished Man* or the works of H.P. Lovecraft just because of little hints in the show. However, Mr. Straczynski and others working with television are just the start: we need someone who can turn the promotion of the genre into a full-time job, without being toadying or patronizing. We need a Steve Irwin.

For the unfamiliar, Steve Irwin is the host of the Australian TV program *The Crocodile Hunter*, currently running in the States on the Animal Planet cable channel. Since Australia is loaded with exotic reptiles, each episode of *The Crocodile Hunter* features Steve in distant locales, wrangling with some of the world's most venomous snakes or other unsuspecting herps. Some of his stunts come off as thoroughly insane (in particular, his work with saltwater crocodiles, which have no compunctions about eating humans), but he honestly and truly loves reptiles, and a lot of that love rubs off on his audience. Even viewers who loathe reptiles get caught up, especially when he grabs a tiger snake (one of the deadliest snakes in the world) and asks "Ooh, isn't he a beauty?"

Admittedly, too much Steve Irwin could be hard to take, but just picture him running amok at a WorldCon. ("Now, this is a fully grown Klingon, and I've got him by the toe so he can't bite me. By crikey, he's a beauty!") Better yet, imagine someone with Irwin's intensity and charisma promoting our genre, mentioning the wastes of time but pushing the material that deserves the attention. The last thing we need is a typical blow-dried TV anchor or fannish toad: we need an evangelist who can recommend novels to TV viewers and movies to diehard literary snobs, and who looks as if s/he is having the time of his or her life doing so. Anyone up for the job?

—SCI FI, June 2000

Postscript: Um, yeah. Yet another case of Riddell's reverse oracle powers, especially since just about everyone in Australia looks at Steve Irwin as an example of how Americans will go nuts over just about anything. On the other hand, I had a grand time out by the Pachyrhinosaurus statues in front of the Royal Tyrrell Museum in Drumheller, Alberta a few years back, grinning wildly and telling the crowd "This one's about three meters long, that's about ten or eleven feet, and now I'm going to sneak up behind and jam my thumb up his butthole. This'll really piss him orf!" I'm amazed I wasn't deported.

"To Rick Berman: A Modest Proposal"

A few months ago, the online magazine *Salon* ran a very entertaining article about the escapades of the denizens of the Usenet newsgroup alt.simpsons and how they've achieved immortality of sorts. After years of fannish kvetching about continuity gaffes and "Well, if I ran the show..." tirades, the writers and producers decided to pay tribute to those who have nothing better to do than whine on Usenet about how Homer keeps getting dumber every season...through the persona of the unnamed fanboy running "Android Al's Comics Emporium." Thanks to a regular posting headline, "Worst Episode Ever" is now a show catchline up there with "Whassamatta, Homah?"

Even though science fiction fandom is one of the most diverse groups in pop culture today, we still keep coming back to the popular stereotype of the science fiction fan: the humorless fat oaf whose obsessive behavior garners all of the popularity of a cigarette dealer in a dynamite factory. While it's unfair to judge the rest of fandom by that standard, it's also hard to deny that popular perceptions of science fiction fans as singleminded geeks doesn't have a basis in fact. Sure, we can laugh at the guy in "Android Al's," but most of us are also laughing nervously "There but for the Grace of God go I..."

On one point, use of the Web and Usenet has improved communication between television creators and their fans in a way scarcely believable, and nobody could have predicted ten years ago that this sort of communication might improve ongoing shows as the years went on. Thanks to e-mail, producers now get immediate feedback on story arcs and new characters, and fans understandably get the impression that someone in Hollywood is paying attention to their concerns and interests. The danger comes from those who feel that a show's cast and crew "owe them" for their patronage, as if McDonald's owes extra Big Macs or a private audience with Ronald McDonald to a regular customer.

If it isn't about *The Simpsons*, it's about the *Star Trek* franchises. Just look at the number of self-proclaimed "Treksperts" now stamping their widdle feet and throwing tantrums because Paramount won't acknowledge their ability to memorize useless facts about *Star Trek* and let them have a say in how *Voyager* turns out. They whine "Well, I give up," as if they had any influence in the first place, and threaten to pick up their toys and play elsewhere, as if they were invited in the beginning. *Voyager* is one extremely messed-up show, but last I heard, the producers weren't soliciting the edicts of science fiction magazine columnists, editors, and readers. (The whimperings of these spurned lovers are almost as pathetic as the gleeful butt-kissers who hope to get quoted in promotional material by sucking up to everyone involved in a production, but why beat on *Entertainment Weekly* more than usual?)

Sure, I have ideas about some of my favorite shows. I'd love to see some creative pruning of the cast rolls on *Buffy the Vampire Slayer*, and I'd like to see even more character development on *Farscape* (just why *is* Pilot so friendly to our escapees, instead of turning the ship around and turning them in at the first opportunity?). I'd love to see Sid Vicious take on Kurt Cobain on *Celebrity Deathmatch*, and I even have some ideas about improving *Star Trek: Voyager* that don't involve blowing up the ship and pretending that the show never existed. The difference here is that while I may express my likes and dislikes, and I'm lucky enough to have approximately 800 words every issue in which to do it, I'm not a writer for these shows, nor a producer, so my opinion means squat. And guess what? Neither does anybody else's.

If we fans have ideas about how a television program should go, and the cast and crew have other ideas, then we can either hang on and be surprised (delightfully or otherwise), or we can change the channel and watch reruns of *Frasier* instead. If the cast and crew take a show in a direction other than what fans want, that's the responsibility of those whose jobs are on the line if the show flops, not the couch potatoes who invest nothing more than an hour or so out of every week. To quote from the film *The Producers*, "I am ze writer. You are ze audience. I outrank you!"

Better yet, if anyone reading this has a better idea for an ongoing TV series than what they're already seeing, pitch it and produce it. Just don't be surprised to discover yourself up to your armpits with letters from armchair screenwriters who "know" they could do better.

—SCI FI, August 2000

"Making the Future"

The year isn't halfway over, and we're already seeing the opinion columns in the daily newspapers: "Whatever happened to the future? Whatever happened to the flying cars and personal jetpacks we were promised? Where are the manned Mars bases and the solar sail spaceships? WHERE!?"

Even discounting the number of columnists who really crave a return to the Good Old Days when one could remain warm by burning Wiccans and heretics, this is a question that really doesn't deserve an answer, mostly because those people asking about it aren't about to do a thing to make the future they're complaining about. Let me explain.

Right today, in 2000, we have technological and social marvels that weren't even science fiction back in 1975, when 2001 was just a movie. I can walk into a store right now and buy a self-encapsulated iMac that has more computing power than whole rooms of datacrunchers back in '75, and connect to a worldwide network that allows me to talk to friends in New Zealand. 25 years ago, planets other than the ones in our solar system were purely theoretical, as were black holes, mag/lev bullet trains, test tube babies, and remote presence submersibles exploring the *Titanic*. So we aren't sending manned missions to Jupiter right now, and we don't have sentient computers and even daily non-stop flights to L5 orbital stations, but that's only because we, as a people and a group, haven't been given a good compelling reason for doing so. It all comes down to initiative and determination, and if those columnists had either, they wouldn't be in journalism.

You want to travel on a starship? Go back to school and get your engineering degree, and start designing one. You may never live to travel on your very own interstellar vehicle, but your children or your grandchildren may, and they'll be telling tales about their ancestors who took a chance and allowed mankind to visit Alpha Centauri.

You want instantaneous data and matter transmission? Finish that physics degree and find any loopholes in Einstein's General and Special Theories of Relativity. Relativity didn't break Newtonian physics but instead accented it, the same way modern genetics accented Darwin's theories on natural selection. One reader of this column might be the first person to theorize a whole new field of physics that build upon relativity in the same way, or find the one way to slip past the laws of causality and send data or matter into the past or far future. Right now, nobody knows if data can be transmitted into the future more than a femtosecond before it was sent, but the difference between what we know and what we don't know is staggering.

You want to explore strange new worlds? Get an oceanography degree. It was true in the 1950s, and it's still true today: we know more about the surface of Mars than we know about the bottoms of our own oceans, and understanding our own oceans should help us understand how oceans and life in general operate on other worlds. A good percentage of life in the ocean survives not via photosynthesis, but by a combination of chemosynthesis (utilizing chemical compounds for energy; the huge tubeworms of mid-oceanic vents use chemosynthesizing bacteria to convert sulfur compounds into energy) and the constant rain of debris from the surface. Considering that whole ecosystems thrive on the corpses of whales, what could we expect in the oceans of Europa? Could understanding what happened to the seas of Mars and Venus help prevent the same from happening to Earth? If Titan has a sea of liquid methane, as current data suggests, how will a methane ocean differ from one of water, or liquid carbon dioxide, or ammonia? Even with worlds physically identical to Earth, what differing conditions will we see on worlds orbiting gas giants, or those without large moons to generate tides, or those with erratic suns or orbits?

You want colonies on Mars, or geosynchronous orbital platforms, or a fat substitute that doesn't deplete the body's store of Vitamin K, or a space opera movie that doesn't treat its viewers like ten-year-olds? Get cracking yourself, or get together with people who also want these goals, and do something about it. It's really easy to complain about how the world didn't turn out the way we all thought it would twenty-five or fifty or one hundred years ago, and it's really hard to do something to reach or exceed those expectations, but nobody writes history book entries about the people who looked at the world, whined "It's too hard to do anything about it," and went back to watching television. It's up to us to make the future, because if we don't, someone else will make it for us, and I guarantee that if you don't like the present, you're going to loathe the future you're going to get.

—*SciFiNow.com, August 2000*

Postscript: Back at the beginning of the Twenty-First Century, we really had no idea that the decade would be described as a Stanley Kubrick decade. Unfortunately for us all, the decade was equal parts A Clockwork Orange, Full Metal Jacket, *and* Dr. Strangelove.

"On Being Musically Inclined"

This month, a relatively minor concern, but one that's bugged me for years. Why does science fiction, in all of its forms, neglect the arts?

All of this started a few years back while watching an old rerun of *Star Trek: The Next Generation*, when it hit me that Earth's arts in Roddenberry's universe were completely stagnant. Take a good look: occasionally, a few bits of alien music sneak through, mostly when it's essential to the plot, but almost every bit of human music listened to and appreciated by the crew qualified as classical. By "classical," I mean at least two hundred years old at that point: lots of concertos, a bit of blues, and some classical guitar, but all work that made about as much sense in this context as everyone speaking Latin. Where's the new stuff?

Music isn't that much better off in literary science fiction. New music features prominently in John Shirley's novels and short stories (particularly in *City Come a'Walkin'* and *Eclipse*), we have Deadheads in Allen Steele's *Orbital Decay*, and we can't forget the Wrackers in Bradley Denton's *Wrack and Roll*. We have lots of characters in literary SF who say that they're musicians, but we get precious little of it being played, and even less described as being drastically different or derived from existing styles.

Now, if fantasy and horror suffered the same lapses in artistic endeavors, we could assume that music just doesn't translate to written fiction. However, anyone who has so much as read *The Hobbit* knows that fantasy has a long and rich history of incorporating song and poetry into the prose, and although horror has had a tendency to focus on more heavy metal as of late, focusing on the emotional aspects of music isn't necessarily lacking there, either. So why doesn't more science fiction feature music?

For anyone thinking about it, just the history of rock and roll alone presents all sorts of examples of how music could go in the future. From its origin in the blues, which itself wouldn't have existed without spirituals, rock rapidly split, rewove, and cross-pollinated from its own sources and plenty of outside stimulation. The British invasion of the Sixties wouldn't have happened if American rock and roll from the Fifties hadn't made it over the Atlantic, and the increasing engineering of album rock in the Seventies led to both its logical conclusion in disco and its antithesis in punk. These joined together in techno, and received further stimulation in any number of other musical movements of the past and inspirations in the present. Some bands realized that not that much of a difference lies between punk and country, and the mixing of styles continues.

While it's foolish to try to shoehorn popular music into categories the way the music industry does, nobody can point to one particular form of music and say "This is the music of Earth."

And if you think such diverse acts as The Crickets, Tangerine Dream, the Butthole Surfers, and Shonen Knife (to name a bare handful) would be enough to drive alien xenologists insane, just consider the wealth of new inspirations if Earth was just part of a federation or an empire. Unless any alien species we contact have no grasp of music, their musical styles are going to influence ours and vice versa, leading to whole new experiences. Even if we really are alone and have no intelligent cohorts anywhere in the universe, each world we colonize is going to develop its own particular attitudes, and the music will reflect this. But we don't see much of this in science fiction.

A lot of this is probably due to the source: a lot of science fiction writers come from hard science backgrounds such as physics or astronomy, and not that many have the understanding of music that translates to the written page. Also, truth be told, coming up with a believable alien musical form is tough: fantasy and horror benefit from being able to borrow from existing human music, but how does a writer describe a pop song for aliens that echolocate? Or creatures that "see" tones and "hear" colors?

Music isn't the only branch of the arts similarly neglected. Games are a good example: many science fiction writers have incorporated various forms of chess into their stories, but where are the variations on backgammon, poker, roulette (Russian and otherwise), Scrabble, Twister, and Clue? One of the few recent novels to experiment with painting techniques is Ernest Hogan's *Cortez on Jupiter*: what new painting media will zero-gee denizens have to invent to keep control of the paint? And then there's sculpting, and dance, and decorative architecture, and animation, and...

As one can see, I could go on for days. I also make this a challenge to the new generation of science fiction writers: not only will serious thought on this subject help stimulate new stories, but any of the ideas generated by the consideration of the arts just may lead to a new real-life style. In a hundred years, when the Mars colonies finally settle to the point where residents can worry about such nonessentials such as art, a brave new musical movement might just take all of mankind by surprise, only with the founder saying "Well, I got the idea off an old science fiction story published in 2001..."

—SciFiNow.com, September 2000

"You Don't Know Scary"

Well, October is upon us, and alongside all of the "Halloween: Remember The Reason For The Season And Keep It Holy" bumper stickers are the usual film critics' lists of what constitutes proper Halloween video-watching. Alongside the Hitchcock and John Carpenter stalwarts, it's the usual list every year, usually compiled by people who dismiss horror films as being beneath them. Even with the ones who know and love horror films, the chosen movies are more comforting than terrifying. After spending a day fighting the traffic and crowds at the local shopping mall, most of us watch *Dawn of the Dead* and *Mad Max* to relax. Even considering that Halloween is for me what New Year's Eve is to Keith Richards (i.e., strictly for amateurs), it's hard to see anyone getting into the proper spirit: way too many vampire wannabes imitating Tom Cruise in *Interview With The Vampire* and nowhere near enough copying Bill Paxton in *Near Dark*.

To make things worse, most "horror" films and TV shows don't even come close to the nightmares in the "Comedy" section of the local video store. (Let's put it this way: somebody actually paid money for *It's Pat: The Movie*.) Those who doubt the alien conspiracies in *The X-Files* and *First Wave* should just wonder exactly how Norm MacDonald manages to keep getting film and television gigs if he and Pauly Shore weren't the vanguard for the joint kzinti/Dalek war fleet currently heading toward Earth at just under light speed. Dark Lovecraftian forces aren't threatening the precious bodily fluids of Earth's denizens? How else do we explain *The New Movie Show With Chris Gore* stealing time away from perfectly good reruns of *Married...With Children* on FX?

With this in mind, we still have enough mindnumbing horrors in our genre to give everyone a good taste. They aren't being pitched as such, but they should be. Forget *The Blair Witch Project*: just try reading this list out loud without the hair on your back standing on end. Reading this in the dark around a campfire is almost as frightening as waking up strapped into a chair *Clockwork Orange*-style and forced to watch *Inspector Gadget* on a tape loop. (See? I knew I could get you to scream already.)

- Is Paul Verhoeven actively campaigning to become "The Ed Wood of the New Century," or did he start solely to keep Joel Schumacher away from the title?

- History will probably refer to the Clinton Administration as the first *Star Trek* Administration, with a paunchy, womanizing captain and an emotionless alien first officer looking at the future through the lens of the Sixties. (Of course, to offend everyone else, George W. Bush looks as if the only thing he really wants to do is watch MTV videos with his best friend Beavis.)

- Simply make a comparison between the nominees for "Best" in the Saturn Awards and the "Worst" nominations in comparable categories in the Golden Raspberry Awards this year and note the overlap. (The fact that the eighth-rate *Mallrats* ripoff *Free Enterprise* managed to beat *The Iron Giant* for the "Best Home Video Release" Saturn isn't a horror: that's a crime.)

- Based on current rates of presentation, the one millionth showing of the Roland Emmerich-directed *Godzilla* will run on Showtime in May 2004.

- Thanks to the overload of *Episode One* action figures clogging up toy store aisles, enterprising hobbyists with Exacto knives and filler putty can now start their own sets of *Trainspotting, Pulp Fiction, Velvet Goldmine*, and *The Professional* action figures.

- Thanks to the legacy of *Aliens* and *Spawn* toys, *Meet The Feebles* lunchboxes are the wave of the future.

- Anyone notice the disturbing similarities between the animated James in *James and the Giant Peach* and the animated Johnny Rotten in *The Great Rock 'n' Roll Swindle*?

- Ten words: *Star Wars, Episode Two: The Return of Jar Jar Binks*.

- Somebody still thinks that *Superman Reborn* is a great idea, and that making it (in the words of producer Jon Peters) "just like *The Matrix*" is even better.

- If *Battlefield Earth* was allegedly propaganda for the Church of Scientology, why weren't *Orgazmo* or *Dogma* considered propaganda for the Mormon or Catholic faiths? (Not that I have anything against any of these religions; I just figure that we should be consistent.)

- If the song "Blame Canada" from the *South Park* movie could get an Oscar nomination, how many Oscar voters pushed for the other obvious choice from the film: the Terrance and Phillip song with the title that can't be published in a family magazine?

- Lastly, the "Rant" column has been running for three years now, and nobody's tried to put a cap in me yet. (After this column, that may change…)

–SCI FI, October 2000

Postscript: That last sentence was incredibly prophetic, but whether my firing was due to my comments about the Saturn Awards or those about George W. Bush is still unclear. Either way, seeing as how the magazine, in its form at the time, died four issues later, it wasn't a crushing loss.

"Ageism in Hollywood and Science Fiction" or "Why Johnny Can't Attain Escape Velocity"

Without doubt, the 2001-2002 television and movie season is going to be one of the most interesting in years, and not because of the shows and films being offered. The contracts for members of both the Screen Actor's Guild and the Writer's Guild of America come up for arbitration next year, and everyone in Hollywood who isn't a member of either union is in an utter panic over the possibility of both unions going on strike. After all, the 1980 SAG strike crippled the fall 1980 television season, and the film and television industries have only now recuperated from the 1988 writer's strike. Most entertainment news sources mention the number of studios stockpiling scripts and speeding projects through development in the hopes of buffering the worst of the strikes, should they happen, and studio execs are moving much more quickly than usual to complete deals, mostly so they don't get caught without product to release by the end of 2001. If the SAG strike over advertising issues is any indication, both unions have a long and justifiable list of grievances against management in both television and film, and unless management starts negotiating now, each respective strike may last for months.

(On a personal note, one point of the Writer's Guild arbitration has my unalloyed adoration, and that's the banning of vanity credits on motion pictures. This is an understandably sore spot with most writers, especially when they write a screenplay and effectively see the director take credit for everything. Writers take enough grief with every goofball in a studio who makes a minor suggestion wanting a "Written By" byline on the poster or in the opening credits, but anything that ends the ridiculousness of seeing "A Film By Steven Spielberg" or "*John Carpenter's Trip To Disneyland*" when said director never would have come up with the concept in a billion years is all right by me.)

Well, this is part of the impending situation facing fans of a multitude of television shows, but not all. Mixed in with all of the other entertainment news coming from the Reuters News Service on October 24 was a very intriguing gem of an article. According to the report, twenty-eight television writers over the age of 40 filed a class-action lawsuit on October 23 against the major television networks, most of the big movie studios, and talent agencies such as the William Morris Agency, Creative Artists Agency, and International Creative Management. The suit alleged that these groups intentionally engage in age discrimination when making hiring decisions. The Writers Guild of America magazine *Written By* regularly runs articles about the problems facing middle-aged writers in Hollywood, but this was the first time anyone had pressed for a lawsuit of this scope. Not only did the suit allege violations of the federal Age Discrimination in Employment Act, the Labor Management Relations Act, and the California Fair Employment and Housing Act, but it seeks damages and injunctive relief.

The individual comments that accompanied the lawsuit, combined with a decade of tales of ageism in Hollywood, are pretty damning. Besides a comment made by the late Brandon Tartikoff, former head of NBC, who said that he'd never hire any writer over the age of 30, the push toward young and hot goes beyond the pretty creatures infesting the cast rolls on the WB. Astute readers may remember the minor stink made two years ago about a writer hired for *Dawson's Creek*, where both the WB and the production crew made much of the fact that she was only 18 and therefore much more likely to understand issues of the young than some old fuddy-duddy thirtysomething. Well, surprise: she turned out to be 30 herself, and had lied about her age knowing that she wouldn't have stood a chance at getting any assignments on the show any other way. Although her scripts were held as being exceptionally good (of course, the definition of "good" on *Dawson's Creek* is a matter of opinion), she was fired once her real age became an issue, and the fact that the crew was looking only for pro writers under the age of 22 went quiet once again.

As can be expected, the idea that older writers have nothing to say is a crock, and it can be examined by comparing writing to other activities. Obviously, most sports are for the young. When Muhammad Ali went against Leon Spinks in 1977 to regain the world heavyweight boxing title, everyone figured that Ali was way too old at 33. Between 35 and 40, most football players (both American football and real football) are looking at retiring and letting new players take over. In artistic endeavors, rock music is generally considered to be a sport for the young. Let's be honest: The Who singing "Talkin' About My Generation" was rather strange when all of the members were in their late thirties, and Mick Jagger pretending to be an everlasting 25 when he's pushing sixty is just plain wrong. But what's old for a rapper or a baseball player is still adolescence for a writer: Harlan Ellison is currently 66, and compared to most of his contemporaries in the genre, he's still considered the angry young whippersnapper.

Now why this should matter to fans of most science fiction television and film came up with the premiere of *Gene Roddenberry's Andromeda* in the States a couple of weeks ago. Oh, plenty of other examples are available, but this one is particularly poignant.

Science fiction writing is particularly dependent upon the mellowing aspects of experience. Science fiction isn't just a form of literature: good SF requires both a grasp of character and motivation AND a good understanding of "What If...?" to work. Good SF also requires that the writer know enough to build a convincing world or situation, as well as knowing what has been done before. While it's possible to find a true 20-year-old literary prodigy, the odds are pretty poor, and one or two prodigies simply cannot produce the volume of genre work demanded in Hollywood or in overseas film and television productions. Ergo, the slack would have to be filled by writers who think they know how to write science fiction, fantasy, and horror, and if they all have to be under the age of 30, that means a whole crop who have done little but watch television.

Now, one could make snide comments about the growth industry of Gene Roddenberry projects based on fragments from his files, or that Mr. Roddenberry is seemingly as prolific as V.C. Andrews and L. Ron Hubbard were after their departure from this mortal coil. The obvious snickerings about the show could come from the abysmal acting and the pathetic makeup effects. The most pertinent complaints about the show, though, come from what falls in the writer's purview: the characters are all so two-dimensional that they'd disappear if they turned their profiles toward the camera, and the dialogue would have been embarrassing had it appeared in an episode of *Battlestar Galactica*. The main thrust of the storyline, such as it is, gives the impression that everyone involved fervently hopes that nobody remembers Terry Nation's *Blake's Seven* from 25 years ago.

Excusing the fact that the problem with *Gene Roddenberry's Andromeda* is itself, the whole show just reeks of young and/or inexperienced writers trying to create a science fiction show, and basing it on examples they'd seen on television. Nearly every TV show created since *Star Wars* has the usual impossible audible explosions and visible lasers in space, so we get lots of those. *Babylon 5* had lots of CGI work to keep the costs down, and so we get CGI poisoning in damn near every scene, particularly involving the title ship, the *Andromeda Ascendant*. *Star Trek: Voyager* had great success with using Jeri Ryan's Seven of Nine to lead male fans around by their libidos, so we get a holographic representation of the *Andromeda*'s AI that shows more skin than a pictorial in *Maxim*. When the first episode after the pilot is pretty much a third-rate ripoff of the second half of *Mad Max Beyond Thunderdome*, with a gaggle of kids keeping the faith that their savior would arrive and save them from life aboard a forgotten space station, you know we've boldly gone where *everyone* has gone before.

Now, *Andromeda* could have been prevented, or at least fixed, with a judicious use of writers who know something about science fiction. Since it's a Canadian production, the crew could hire Robert J. Sawyer to act as a script consultant or "conceptual consultant," or it could bring in any number of willing writers from the States or Australia. Of course, most of these writers are older than thirty, so they obviously don't know anything about reaching the youth audiences so desperately sought by advertisers. And besides, science fiction fans will watch anything, no matter how insulting, right? All we need to do is spend fifty times as much money on FX work than on a legible or coherent script, and the hypnotized fannish masses will just stare and whisper "Cool..."

Based on the age rule, most of your favorite SF writers would be ineligible to write for Hollywood. Look at fantasy: if not for previous successes, Ray Bradbury and Michael Moorcock would be considered too old for the job. In horror, almost anyone writing horror today with any level of exactitude fails to survive that arbitrary "don't hire anyone over thirty" rule. Even existing screenplay scribes, such as J. Michael Straczynski and Rockne S. O'Bannon, don't qualify, their successes with *Babylon 5* and *Farscape* be damned. The best writers from the original *Star Trek*, such as Dorothy Fontana and David Gerrold, weren't in their late teens when the show premiered. The same situation with your favorite comic writers: the last time I checked, almost every successful comic writer around, from Chris Claremont to Warren Ellis, passed the great three-decade divide some time ago.

Now, Your Humble Columnist has been kvetching for years about the fact that Hollywood is overrun with MBAs that make deals based not on what they read in college (as if a business major could be literate in the first place) but on what television shows they watched as kids, which explains why somebody thought that movie adaptations of *The Brady Bunch* and *McHale's Navy* were good ideas. Honest: we're seeing films like *Inspector Gadget* because some exec used to watch that show when s/he was in high school, and that was only five years ago. These decisions aren't any dumber than those made by execs thirty years their senior, and considering the youth-obsessed culture in Hollywood, we'll probably be seeing pre-teen producers by the end of the decade. But to get decent material, one needs to get decent writers, and for anything other than quick-and-smartass sitcoms (which help keep much of the journalism departments of Columbia, Harvard, and Yale off welfare), this means writers who actually know something about something besides being young and hip in the big city. If these same producers want science fiction shows that just might last more than one season, this means hiring writers that just might be middle-aged or older, or else we'll be up to our eyeballs in *Cleopatra 2525* and *Gene Roddenberry's Andromeda*.

In conclusion, I for one hope that this ageism class-action lawsuit goes through, if only to teach producers and studio heads that "over 25" doesn't mean "washed-up" when talking about writers, or actors, or anyone else. Besides, they might want to take this into account when the current crop of hot young writers see that little red gem in their palms start flashing, and all of the talent scouts in the world aren't able to find high schoolers able to rewrite scripts for *Lexx* and still get to bed by nine.

—*SciFiNow.com, November 2000*

"A Final Thought On The Twentieth Century"

Well, in another month, it's here. 2001. Those readers old enough to remember the hype over 1984 rolling around now have to deal with it over again, in between "Thus Spake Zarathustra" blasting over every sound speaker on the planet. If you thought hearing Prince's "1999" every five minutes was annoying, wait until you see crowds of Microsoft employees at the local cinema, bawling their eyes out when HAL 9000 hums out the last bars of "Daisy." (Secretly, I understand: I still bawl my eyes out at the end of *Alien*, when the only interesting or developed character in the whole film besides the cat gets blown out the airlock.)

If science fiction was supposed to be prophetic, we've dodged a lot of bullets in the past decade. New York wasn't turned into a maximum-security prison in 1994, Khan Noonien Singh didn't abandon his empire in 1996, SkyNet didn't take out most of humanity in 1997, and we go into 2001 being reasonably sure that we won't lose our luggage on Pan Am flights to the moon. (If we do, you just know the luggage will get rerouted to New Jersey.) 2001 won't be the future we expected even ten years ago, but it's our future all the same.

Even so, it's hard not to get disappointed over the possibilities we were promised years before, when manned Mars bases in 1980 and artificial intelligences by 1995 seemed perfectly reasonable. We have a global communications network and handheld computers, and our biggest worry comes from all of the radio transmissions we're beaming toward space. (Let's face it: the moment aliens start picking up Edie Brickell and Pauly Shore transmissions, boy, are they gonna be mad.) But that's not the same thing.

Since every decade should end with a good encompassing New Year's Resolution for the next, and since the Gregorian calendar is giving us so many good excuses for a party this year, it's time for one that will literally change the world. This year, instead of resolving to lose some weight or not to fall for the latest *Star Wars: Episode Two* rumor, resolve to help make the world more like the world promised by the best science fiction. The possibilities are rampant, but try these for a start.

Give the gift of science fiction. The best way to deflect criticism of science fiction fans is to convert the other side, so make a point of playing missionary for the genre. Find a particular novel or author that strikes your fancy and make a point of introducing it to friends. If co-workers make noises about attending a convention but don't know what to do, treat them to a three-day pass and a guided tour. The idea is to show that SF and fantasy fans aren't insular misanthropes, and it'll also bring in lots of new blood to the genre.

Don't forget the kids. Contrary to the prattlings of *Fortune* staffers, most high schoolers and preteens don't have any money, and buying a magazine subscription is secondary to having money for movies or video games. With this in mind, make a point of giving magazine subscriptions to children, nephews and nieces, siblings, and neighbor kids. (The subscriptions don't necessarily have to be to this magazine, but they certainly wouldn't hurt.) While you're at it, donate magazine subscriptions, magazine archives, and lots of novels to local school and public libraries: their budgets are already hurting, and every donation guarantees a new crop of readers. Giving an idea of where science fiction came from instills the urge to push it as far as it will go.

Read six impossible things before breakfast. Make a point of reading or viewing something new and different on a regular basis, and encourage your friends to do the same. Read everything ever written by Robert Heinlein? Pick up some Paul Di Filippo or Richard Kadrey for a drastically distinct perspective. Live for *Star Trek*? Turn on *Farscape* or rent *The Prisoner*. Already familiar with SF? Try some fantasy or horror, or switch over to related nonfiction. You can't expect others to change their perspectives if you aren't willing to change yours.

Don't gently dream of the future; make it happen. The future belongs to those willing to expend the time and energy to make it so, and sitting back and wishing for a better world doesn't do anything but contribute to butt bloat. Lead by example: if you aren't willing to put down cash for lunar exploration or nanotech research, how can you expect anyone else to follow? If you don't have money, lead with energy, or teach those who have both.

Again, this is a start, but it's also something that should make 2002 a lot more interesting. Go have fun this New Year's Eve: I'll be the guy waving the bowel disruptor he got for Christmas.

—SCI FI, December 2000

Postscript: This is the original and intended version of the last column I did for SCI FI; *for unguessable reasons, the published version was chopped all to hell, probably to make room for what qualified as one of the ugliest illustrations ever published in a science fiction magazine. Either way, here's the complete version. It's no big deal about the leavetaking, really: it's always best to know when to leave the party before you're unwelcome, and it was a good three-year run. Selah.*

"Eyes Shut, Ears Closed, and Mouth Wide Open: A Variant Perspective on the Decline of Genre Magazine Circulation"

Well, the *Locus* "2000: A Year In Review" issue came out recently, and those either unable or unwilling to look at the breakdowns for science fiction magazines were spared the ongoing horror. Even discounting the terminations of *Science Fiction Age* and *Marion Zimmer Bradley's Fantasy Magazine*, the future don't look too keen for most of the survivors. *Asimov's* is down, *Analog* is down, *The Magazine of Fantasy & Science Fiction* and *Realms of Fantasy* are down...all of the long-running magazines have seen a steady decline from 1990 on, but 2000 was a real bonecruncher for everyone.

The ongoing commentary from people in the field is that outside sources are at fault for the decrease in newsstand sales and subscription renewals. The comics business says the same thing: kids aren't reading SF magazines or comics because of the Internet or television or video games or Elvis sightings. The decline isn't the fault of business practices in either industry, or by changes in society and the available readership. Everything bad is coming from the outside, and the partisans who keep buying genre magazines and keeping the faith keep getting older and older with no replacements in sight.

When talking about the "death of a thousand cuts" facing SF magazines, these paper cuts are a factor, but the unkindest cuts come from ourselves. We could talk about the most obvious factor in the decline of literary SF magazines, and that's the distinct possibility that the magazines and the fiction published therein simply don't have any relevance to anyone other than the geeks who masturbate over CompUSA flyers. We could talk about magazine formats that made perfect sense in 1956 but that are ludicrous in a day when Borders and Barnes & Noble nearly monopolize the US bookbuying landscape. We could talk about an industry attitude that encourages everyone to flood the slush piles at any magazine worth mentioning with all sorts of stories, but can't be bothered to encourage anyone to subscribe or even to pick up a copy before sending off manuscripts. We could mention that the literary side of the genre has done bugger-all to counter the flood of crappy SF films and television with alternatives, or in trying to interest young readers in short fiction. Instead, we're going to talk about promotion and retention.

Back in 1956, keeping the Big Three SF magazines (and yes, I know that

Asimov's has only been around since 1979) in digest format made sense because lots of magazines were available in digest form at the time. Back in 1956, promoting genre magazines almost solely at conventions and through direct mailings made sense, because SF fans were few and scattered, and the few genre-related diversions such as films or television shows weren't anywhere near as good as SF novels and short stories. Back in 1956, SF fans could be depended upon to come close to one demographic, and magazines didn't have to worry as much about retaining subscribers because the alternatives were so poor. Guess what? It ain't 1956 any more, and methods that worked back when new encyclopedias read "one day, man will go to the moon" aren't going to work in a media environment that encourages Attention Deficit Disorder.

To illustrate the situation, I received a mailing from *Asimov's* the other day, one of three apparently due to the company handling the direct mailing getting the mailing lists from the three genre magazines to which I still subscribe. The advertising probably worked on someone so addicted to SF that s/he is saving up to get an ear bobbing in order to pass for Vulcan or elf, but I was just struck by how worthless it was for attracting new readers. Below is the copy on half of the response card: the other half was intended to go in the mail with one of those big "Yes! I want to try a free issue, with the option of buying a subscription if I like this copy" checkboxes with the checkmark already inside and no option for saying "No, I'm happy with my subscription to *Star Wars Insider*." The original copy is in quotes, with commentary in parentheses.

"When you accept your FREE ISSUE of *Asimov's Science Fiction*, be sure that you are ready for some truly gripping, spellbinding storytelling." (And are you prepared for the slight but plausible possibility that you may not get any? I mean, remember when the *New Yorker* was promising all sorts of interesting articles in the wake of Tina Brown taking over as editor, and all we got were puff pieces about Tina's friends and lickspittles?)

"Each issue of *Asimov's Science Fiction* features novellas and short stories from the leading science fiction and fantasy writers. (Mind telling those who don't already subscribe who these people are? And why "the leading," instead of just "leading"?) Plus, you'll enjoy candid, no-holds-barred book reviews and guest editorials, as well as a handy monthly science fiction convention calendar." (Oh boy, just what the people whose whole picture of conventions came from seeing *Galaxy Quest* want: a convention calendar! Do we get an official Klingon uniform if we subscribe for two years?)

"Year after year, the stories published in *Asimov's Science Fiction* dominate the *Locus* Recommended Reading List and carry off the lion's share of the annual

Nebula and Hugo Awards." (This is great for the people who already know or care about the Hugos or Nebulas, but it isn't any help for those people wanting to take a quick splash into science fiction. Besides, years of watching the Academy Awards should prove to everyone that something that clears lots of awards isn't necessarily any good.)

"Don't you owe it to yourself to at least take a FREE look at *Asimov's Science Fiction?*" (Beg pardon? The magazine owes readers a good value for their entertainment dollar, and the readers owe nothing besides the subscription fee if they decide to try it for a year. Telling potential subscribers that they owe it to themselves to try a magazine implies "We're so arrogant about our magazine that anyone who doesn't subscribe is obviously mentally defective," and it'd damn well better deliver on that promise. Or, to put it another way, don't you owe it to yourself to take a bath, lose 100 pounds, and try to find a compatible sexual partner instead?)

Mean? Yep, but with damn good reason. The only other publication with that level of arrogance in its subscription materials is the *Wall Street Journal*, and they can get away with it. The only other publication that can get away with being that vague in listing its contents is *Maxim*, and that's because nobody buys *Maxim* for any other reason than for the barely clad bimbos on every cover.

The point here is that *Asimov's* is not an essential ingredient to life on this planet. The truth is that *no* magazine is essential. The trick is to convince readers that a magazine is essential, if only because they'll miss out on some damn good reading. The goal is to create advertising for a magazine so compelling that junkies are willing to pawn their crack pipes to buy a two-year subscription, and to make sure that the magazine follows through on the promise of that advertising.

This requires subtlety, cunning, and initiative. This requires skipping the conventions, because the people who can afford to spend a weekend at a science fiction convention are already True Believers, and just try getting conventioneers these days to peel their claws away from their cash for anything other than that life-sized Boba Fett figure from The Sharper Image. This also requires focusing advertising money away from the usual targets and going for new audiences. Televangelists realized this years ago, when a growing number of Bible-thumping faith healers with bad toupees realized that milking each others' mailing lists netted a limited number of little old ladies willing to send "seed money" to every grinning dingbat in a polyester suit who came calling. Instead, they went for new crowds and new techniques, and it worked: corner anybody on the street and ask them to name at least one televangelist and at least one science fiction writer.

The direct mailing system currently used by magazines makes plenty of sense, seeing as how direct mail is still much more efficient than any other advertising medium, but genre magazines keep missing the target. Instead of going after people who already subscribe to one or another SF magazine, they should be going after magazine readers who may be sympathetic to SF (subscribers to *Wired*, *Popular Science*, and *MacAddict*, for instance), and experiment with web-based subscription methods. We already know that SF readers tend to be well-educated and relatively well-off (to the point where one wonders if Web surfers are predisposed to SF or SF fans are predisposed to being on the Web), so making a push for "Subscribe on our Web site and get a free T-shirt!" might be plausible and profitable. Most of all, it's a matter of being ready for dabblers and random browsers of SF magazines who came across a copy in a bus station or in a doctor's waiting room, who aren't ready to commit to a full subscription but who wouldn't be averse to checking out the latest issue online while on a lunch break.

The other side to the acquisition of new readers is retaining existing ones, and efforts all throughout the magazine industry are abysmal. Everyone talks about how hard retention is, but very few seem to go to any effort to ascertain why those new subscribers let their subs lapse, and we're missing out on very important data on the slide in SF magazine circulation by ignoring reader perceptions.

Here's an example. About two years ago, I subscribed to a genre literary analysis magazine of some repute because I figured that now was the time to quit buying individual issues and try it for a year. Toward the end of the subscription, I received the usual request to renew, and I passed on it: the magazine had about one really great article a year, and most of the rest of the articles were dry, humorless pieces with all of the flavor of refried cardboard. I didn't hate the magazine: I just didn't like it enough to plunk down another $20 for another year. Over the next four months, I received four more notices from the editor reminding me that my subscription was about to lapse. Not once did one of these notices come with a query asking "Was it something we published?," no questionnaire on what spice was necessary to turn that refried cardboard into pheasant under glass. This wasn't a big magazine that could afford to pass up on asking: the publication was and is small enough that every sub cancellation should be a cause for concern. *Entertainment Weekly* can afford the attrition of new subscribers who tire of the incessant *Star Wars*, *Star Trek*, *X-Files*, and *Friends* articles every bloody issue, but *Entertainment Weekly* also gets subscriber numbers every week for which most genre editors would sell their souls to Elvis or run a Paul Riddell article to get, and most genre magazines aren't getting subsidies from AOL Time Warner to keep publishing.

(As a sideline, let's forget once and for all the conceit that "Letters to the

Editor" give an editor or publisher a good idea of where to go with a magazine. The people who write letters to magazines do so because something moved them to do so, or they're hoping for the ego boost of seeing their name in print in the "Letters" section. Most readers aren't going to bother writing to complain if a magazine doesn't meet their expectations: they'll simply let their subscriptions lapse or quit picking up copies on the stands, and editorial policy will continue to be dictated by the blowhards with a machete to sharpen or the sycophants who figure that lots of gushy letters will give them an easy in when they start submitting stories. The idea here is that we need information from the folks actually *buying* individual copies and subscriptions, not the readers already mentally spending the $1 million advance they expect from their first short story sale.)

Since I already savaged the subscription flyer, let's take on the renewal notice. Almost every renewal notice, from big or small magazines, starts with the guilt trip of "If you don't subscribe now, you'll be missing out on great new stories from..." Well, suppose that the authors supplying those "great new stories" are the reason why the subscriber let the magazine lapse? This is like promising "If you don't come to dinner now, you'll miss out on this great cowpie milkshake we have for dessert," and then wondering why the only person coming to dinner is Aunt Phil with the coprophilia fixation. Or the reason could be that the reader loves the short stories but can't stand one of the columnists, or that the editorials rode that one last nerve. For all we know, everything was great except for the godawful covers every issue, or that subscribers receive their copies a full month after the issue appears on magazine racks in the local bookstore. The typical renewal notice takes none of this into account, and while the implied guilt trip may work with some subscribers, it's enough to convince others never to renew. Sending multiple renewal notices just cements the decision.

Here's an alternative to the standard renewal notice harangue that should save a fair amount of postage and a lot of potential good will. Instead of the usual three to ten subsequent reminders to renew a subscription once it's in danger of lapsing, just send one. In that renewal notice, instead of just the ecstatic "Yes!Yes!Yes! I'd pawn my crack pipe to purchase another year of *Zizzle-Swump!*," include a "No, I think I'll pass this time" checkbox. Better yet, include three options. The first is "I'm still thinking about it, so could you give me a little while?," for those who may be able to renew in a month or so but need some time to consider the financial situation. The second is "I think I'll pass for a while": all of these responses go back into the mailing list in a year, after which they may be amenable to starting up again. The third is "I'd sooner eat broken glass than see another issue again," and make a point of removing the names and addresses of these former subscribers from the mailing lists. They aren't going to resubscribe now and they're probably never going to resubscribe again, and any further queries are likely to make them glue the Business Reply Mail envelope to the side of a cinder block and drop that in the mailbox. (For those little magazines that can't afford Business Reply Mail envelopes, don't rest easy. Another query to re-up is just as likely to get that same cinder block with a one-cent stamp on the side and a terse note from the Post Office requesting the difference in postage.)

Now here's the innovative aspect of the "No, I'll slide" checkboxes. On the back of the renewal notice, include a space for those subscribers to explain why they're declining to buy another year. The answers will likely be surprising, and definitely valuable. Without this feedback, editors may not know that readers are tired of stories with the same theme appearing in issue after issue, or that another magazine offers stories they prefer, or that they don't have time to read any more. These subscribers may be offended by a particular columnist, or dislike the editor's constant tirades, or just simply grew out of the genre. Either way, every magazine doing this has real, hard data to back up why their readers are leaving, and without blaming the Internet, video games, or *Farscape* reruns. Smart editors and publishers will pay attention to this information, because the writers have nothing to gain by making their comments and therefore offer more reliable advice. Most importantly, asking for feedback from former subscribers makes them more likely to renew in the future, after they see that someone actually implemented corrections to their complaints.

All of these issues are going to require a lot of work from large and small magazines, but this beats the only other option, and that option is the gradual extinction of every genre magazine with a circulation over 200. Instead of pretending that it's still 1956 outside and that the last thirty years in publishing were just a nasty dream, it's time to take the initiative and fight for audiences with the same intensity as other publications. Either that, or let the existing readers die of old age, close up shop, and go home.

—*Science Fiction Chronicle, June 2001*

Postscript: While this essay received a bit of response from people involved in magazine sales, particularly the head magazine buyer for Tower Records, it didn't get a response in the slightest from the producers of those magazines. And why should they bother? They're too busy going to conventions and expecting fans to try to touch the hems of their robes. It's no big deal: even Entertainment Weekly *is on its way out as I write this, and nothing of value was lost.*

"A Bestiary of Fanboys" or "Arguments for Genocide: Six Reasons to Preserve the Second Amendment"

I generally work in the science fiction field, writing essays and articles on the state of the genre, and quite a few people ask me why the whole supergenre of science fiction, fantasy, and horror sucks farts from dead cats. It's not for lack of interested writers: were the universe to have a modicum of justice, such talents as Misha Nogha, Ernest Hogan, and Don Webb would be outselling Stephen King, while David Drake, Larry Niven, and Piers Anthony busied themselves by building shelters underneath highway overpasses with abandoned cardboard boxes. We can kick magazine editors in the balls (in many cases, all one of them) until our legs drop off for cowardice and flat-out contempt for the genre, but we still find a goodly number who care about what they print – David Truesdale of *Tangent* and Chris DeVito of the late, lamented *Fuck Science Fiction* being sterling examples. We can go after publishers, distributors, and the editors of trade magazines with plans to turn them into Viking Maypoles until the end of time, but removing them from the equation doesn't cure the problem. They wouldn't be in business if someone wasn't buying their shit.

So here comes the question: why is the genre at such an all-time high for producing boredom? Why is it so fucked up right now? Could it be...the fans?

Actually, "fan" isn't the right word for the twerps who make *Star Wars* novels bestsellers: "fanboy" is. Fans are the people who enjoy a particular subject but don't let it rule their lives: fanboys are the people who ruin things with their fanatical overkill. (Interestingly, they always think William Shatner's "Get A Life" speech was directed toward someone else.) For instance, a comics fan might get off on old issues of *Justice League* (preferably from the funny days circa the turn of the decade), but only a fanboy would take the time to make an authentic Green Lantern uniform and wear it to work. Fifteen years ago, I might have done the same thing; however, fifteen years ago, I was a runny-nosed high school sophomore.

We've all seen fanboys in our travels: you can't walk into a comics shop without running into the fuckers. Yeah, the toad in the corner with six weeks of food stains down the front of his official *Next Generation* uniform (the outfit with the thick stripe of human grease running under his armpits and over his hip joints) and the complexion best simulated by sticking No. 2 pencils into facial pores and breaking off the points is a fanboy: if you couldn't see that he had no life outside of science fiction, you'd be able to smell it, because he thinks that water and napalm have the same effect on the human body. He's either 50 to 400 pounds overweight and wheezing like a beached pilot whale, or he weighs in at 23 pounds, has no chin, a neck that looks as if it were broken and reset at a 45-degree angle, and a face that resembles Viking orbiter photos ("My God, that's either the Tharsis Plateau or he's suffering from leprosy!"). The females of the species are even worse: only in fandom can one encounter a woman who can corn-row her moustache.

One might assume that all social menaces who just don't get the hint that activities besides buggering sheep and biting the heads off chickens exist are fanboys: nobody could argue that Joe Coleman and G.G. Allin are fanboys. The fanboy typically possesses a fanaticism comparable to the most rabid Southern Baptist: Nyarlathotep help the poor bastard who chooses to point out logic holes in *Deep Space Nine* with a fanboy. Combined with their already truncated social skills, this fanaticism makes them deadly in certain situations, and anyone bored to tears with a fervent discussion of the Romulan cloaking device can attest. They also have a tendency toward violence: merely express the opinion that the world probably won't see another *Star Wars* film in our lifetimes, and you'll get a squeal of "Nyuh-UH!" (sounding exactly the same as that produced by a four-year-old told on Christmas Eve that Santa quit, the reindeer were all chopped up into Alpo, and we're all getting coal to eat for dinner), followed by a punch to the mouth. Thankfully, most fanboys are in terrible physical shape: just as in George Romero zombie films, they're only dangerous in large numbers.

Now, if only one breed existed, modern developments in genetic engineering would remove the threat with a minimum of muss, fuss, and bother. (Figuring that they won't breed is counterproductive: although fanboys wouldn't know what sex was, they reproduce by budding, like sponges. Two fanboys can produce thousands in a lifetime, thus explaining why Steven Spielberg hasn't had to pick up any minutiae such as talent.) At the very least, a judicious application of nerve agents at a WorldCon would cut the breeding population down to manageable levels (to quote Raoul Duke, "CS gas slaps at the problem; nerve gas solves it."); otherwise, the fanboy threatens to become a health hazard comparable to the cane toad in Australia or the fire ant in Texas.

Unfortunately for us, I managed to identify six distinct species of fanboy, with some overlap in habits, attitude, and effective countermeasures. In order of population, these are:

The Trekkie. The most common form, these are the ones the TV camera crews home in on whenever doing one of their "look at the freaks" reports on science fiction conventions for the evening news. The most common form of Trekkie lives for *Star Trek*, of course, but they also live for *Star Wars*, *Space: 1999*, *Battlestar Galactica*, *V*, and *Doctor Who*, among many others. For the most part, if it ain't a TV show, movie, or comic book, they've never heard of it. As a general rule, the more insulting the TV show or movie is to their intelligences, the more they love it: they loathe *Babylon 5* and *Brazil* because both have a plot to get in the way of the special effects, but they lose bowel control over *Space: Above and Beyond* and *Independence Day*.

For the most part, Trekkies are relatively harmless: they're clicking their heels together, wishing reeeeeeeealy hard, and hoping to wake up as senior officers aboard a starship. Never mind that the ones who passed the physical to Starfleet Academy wouldn't pass the psych tests; they're all gently dreaming of the future and their place in it. Were Hitler to rise from the grave and take over the North American continent, the Trekkies would be perfectly happy so long as the new regime instituted regular showings of *Robotech* and *seaQuest*.

How to Annoy A Trekkie: Recreate the stoning sequence from *Monty Python's Life of Brian*, only replace the word "Jehovah" with the phrase "*Star Trek* is only a TV show!"

The Metalhead. Out of the six major species of fanboy, the Metalhead has the most opportunity for accomplishment. I add them because of their influence on the horror field: if not for the thousands of angst-ridden Pantera fans out there, Clive Barker and Dean Koontz would still be working their day jobs, Anne Rice's fans would consist solely of frustrated female English majors who read all of Sylvia Plath's work back in grade school, Brian Lumley would return to writing crappy Lovecraft pastiches, and Poppy Z. Brite's only opportunity for an interview would come by stripping in front of Howard Stern.

On the bright side, Metalheads have the best sense of humor out of all fanboys, even if that humor is exceedingly twisted. Metalheads also bother to get driver's licenses and real jobs, and they have the best chance of getting laid at a private party. (They also have the best chance of getting crabs and other venereal wildlife, but them's the breaks.) The bad side is that the combine a nearly complete lack of imagination (which usually manifests itself in parlor tricks involving kittens and Sterno) with a xenophobia that rivals that of a Klan Grand Dragon. Most of them don't realize the irony of *Beavis and Butt-Head*, and the ones that do don't care, because they're trying to figure out ways to make a living by making incoherent comments about MTV videos. Even more so than Trekkies, Metalheads are easily identifiable in crowds: just watch for the long uncombed hair; the tattoos and T-shirts with an emphasis on eagles, swords, demons, and Harley-Davidson logos; and the uncontrollable drooling over the unrated version of *Hellraiser III*. Quite a few Metalheads take on theatrical makeup as a potential career; for those without musical aptitude, the only other option for steady employment is working in an auto parts store.

How to Annoy a Metalhead: Point out that Clive Barker came out of the closet, and imply that Ronnie James Dio is next.

The True Believer. If the Metalhead has a sense of humor about his/her interests, then the True Believer is the obverse: the TB spends his/her life believing that UFO aliens killed Kennedy and kidnapped Elvis, and the government has proof in classified files. Or the TB might claim that the world's scientific community is committed to the complete and utter coverup of any information that might confirm the theories of Velikovsky, von Daaniken, or Richard Hoagland (the twit who claims that the famed "Mars face" is an alien artifact). True Believers really get torqued out of shape if anyone suggests that UFOs have mundane explanations, and they really lose it if they hear the phrase "Oswald acted alone." Many TBs believe in the oxymoronic "scientific creationism," and will explain in depth how Paluxy River trackways show that man coexisted with dinosaurs in Cretaceous Texas.

The worst problem with the little hummers lies in their similarities to Trekkies: I once nearly gnawed off an arm trying to escape one hybrid who planned to reveal to me how Gene Roddenberry designed the Starship *Enterprise* after viewing top-secret documents pertaining to Germany's experiments in building flying saucers. The underlying question that should be thrown at these booger-eating morons is this: How the hell do they get their information? Contrary to the impression given by *The X-Files*, most government organizations employ extensive psychological testing to screen out loonies like these, and no secret agent worth his James Bond decoder ring would entrust his career to some dingleberry who plans to expose the whole conspiracy in a letter to *Starlog*. If any group listed herein needed a good lobotomy with a Roto-Rooter, the True Believers would qualify above and beyond the call of duty.

How to Annoy a True Believer: Note that Whitley Streiber still hasn't caught on that "Klaatu barada nikto" really means "Squeal like a pig, boy! SQUEEE!." Thereafter, refer to Streiber's book *Communion* as "Deliverance: The Next Generation."

The Avant-Poseur: So far, the assembled gaggles of fanboys deserve to be clubbed like a baby seal, but none deserves it so much as the Avant-Poseur, because this phenotype thinks that it's the hope of the future. The Avant-Poseur is best caricatured in the character of Rick in the British comedy series *The Young Ones*: the pseudo-anarchist and would-be revolutionary poet whom, upon finding that he can't write his lawyer because he's an anarchist, screams "Then I'll write the lead singer of Echo and the Bunnymen. 'Dear...Mr. ...Echo...'" Avant-Poseurs are the reason why cyberpunk has none of the pith and moment it had before it became a cover story for *Time*: the bastards turned cyberpunk into a fashion statement.

Like Metalheads, Avant-Poseurs are fashion casualties, with wardrobes inspired by reading too many issues of Neil Gaiman's *Sandman* comic. They prattle on and on about alternative film, but they've never seen anything but David Lynch's last three films, and they actually sat through every episode of *Twin Peaks* and Oliver Stone's *Hairy Palms*. (Everything else they know about alt film they picked up from reading *Film Threat*, but only the post-1991 issues, after editor Chris Gore decided that people read the magazine for his commentary alone.) They also made Greil Marcus and Douglas Coupland celebrities by believing every last bit of tripe in *Lipstick Traces* and *Generation X*. Although most are in their early twenties, they claim with a straight face that they saw the Sex Pistols at the Longhorn Ballroom in Dallas in 1978 (to quote Barry Kooda, whose band the Nervebreakers opened for the Pistols, "Their babysitters took them"). In the same way, they glibber and meep about William Gibson, but have any of them read any of his books?

Underground filmmaker Edgar Harris summed it up best when he said "You've got to be fucking kidding." Avant-Poseurs are the sort who honestly believe that Duran Duran, Pearl Jam, Stone Temple Fuckups, and Porno for Pyros are "the cutting edge of rock," just because *Spin* and *Mondo 2000* say so. Need we say more?

How to Annoy An Avant-Poseur: Giggle at how nothing's going to make them real vampires, no matter how badly they may want to be. Alternate this with yelling "Vivian! You utter bastard!" in a British accent.

The Technoweenie: Some may say that this is a subspecies of the Avant-Poseur, but I disagree: the Avant-Poseur tries to exude the impression of knowing what the future holds in store based on the current hot cyberpunk writer, while the Technoweenie tries to make these surmisals into reality. We're talking about the gits who cream their pants while reading *Wired*; the ones who experiment with virtual sex and chop their dicks off by using an upright vacuum cleaner for the necessary stimulation. They managed to get a different picture of the future: they're the ones who long to interface with exotic computer systems and leave the meat behind because they couldn't get laid in Tijuana with $100 bills in their jockstraps without the help of virtual reality. For most Technoweenies, Bruce

Sterling and Bill Gates are separate incarnations of God: one made a literary career by writing about new developments among the socially retarded, and the other became an bullying geek who makes millions across the globe want to put out lit cigars in his eyes. Both were necessary for the Great Computer Parasite Dream, and the Technoweenies know it.

Technoweenies are the most likely of all six types to get a well-paying job, but that's because most people would prefer not to copulate with a Unix box for sixteen hours a day. Most of them are the modern-day equivalent of a court wizard: pompous tricksters whose twin fears are that either the King will discover their utter incompetence, or that another, more competent wizard will put them out of a job. The surge of the Internet allowed far too many of them to get salaries way out of proportion to their knowledge or social skills, seeing as how far too many of them failed to complete college careers because the university Board of Directors refused to acknowledge mastery of FORTRAN or COBOL as the "foreign language" requirement. Ever wonder why 99 percent of the World Wide Web is utter crap? Look at the frustrated wannabe *Analog* writers pumping out Web content and find enlightenment.

Now, if the Technoweenies actually produced anything, we might forgive them and remove them from this *Scala Naturae*; unfortunately, they have about the same chance of success in doing something with their lives as any other breed of fanboy. One in 500,000 might create something that makes life more interesting or more tolerable, but the remaining 499,999 waste their time masturbating about smart drugs and the number of Web sites dedicated to Terri Hatcher. Fuck them: onward.

How to Annoy A Technoweenie: Loudly and proudly declare that you'd take a hot Clorox enema before you'd buy Windows 95. If said Technoweenie makes noises about writing a computer book, ask him about the impending publicity tour ("So what do you plan to do with all of the groupies?").

The Gamer: The Gamer is the bottom-feeder of the fanboy food chain: they usually get the hint of what's going on in the upper biomes when it's shit out as a role-filling game. I'm not talking about the casual RPG player –a lot of casual gamers treat gaming as just another goddamn hobby. The Gamer (with a capital "G") is the twit who has no life outside gaming: given a choice between climbing a local hill for real and climbing Olympus Mons in a game, he'll (invariably, Gamers are male) take the game every time. Achievement in reality requires risk, and it's much easier to stand back, roll dice, and play the skin flute than actually take a chance on failure or rejection.

Gamers even take crap from other fanboys. I was once a guest at a science fiction convention where the hotel presented an Easter petting zoo, complete with lambs, goats, and chickens. Seeing it, a friend commented "Oh, *look!* They brought farm animals for the gamers!" This is closer to reality than many jests: most women at such conventions would rather pass out drunk in the middle of a Hell's Angels rally than fall asleep in the middle of a gaming tourney. At least children born of an Angels' union should have useable skills, while a Gamer child deserves nothing more than a quick backhand with a machete before cremation.

How to Annoy A Gamer: Ask if "Dungeons and Dragons" promotes gross obesity instead of suicide or Satanism.

Now I know I'm going to get lots of death threats from this essay, but this ties into the mention of the Second Amendment of the title. To quote one of my favorite movies, "You don't have enough ammunition, Captain, to shoot them all in the head. The time to have done that would have been at the beginning. But we let them overrun us. They have overrun us, you know; we're in the minority now. Something like 400,000 to one by my calculations." Or to borrow from Chris DeVito, "The objective is to slaughter as many of them as you can before they get you."

—Proud Flesh, October 1994

Postscript: The original version of this essay appeared in the first and only issue of Proud Flesh, *but it was extensively revised in 1996 for publication in yet another stillborn magazine. These days, the specific terms for the worst sort of science fiction fan have been compressed into the universal description "Cat Piss Man," which is a term that most non-SF people get right off the bat.*

"The Final Word About Deadlines"

"It ain't none of your business/where I'm goin',
It ain't none of your business/who I'm seein'"
—Missing Persons

To start off, Harlan Ellison is a friend of mine. Lots of people are friends of mine, including a lot of folks who don't deserve the shame and disgrace of being associated with me, but Unca Harlan is one of those people who make me proud to say "Look! He had the opportunity to plant a rock hammer in my skull, and he chose not to!" Lord knows, he deserves the opportunity. It's bad enough that I've been playing Steve Irwin to his Frank Buck (or Robert Bakker to his Edward Cope, or Guy Gardner to his Alan Scott: choose your own comparison) for my entire adult life, but when some snotnosed twerp comes along and manages to top his story on how he was fired from Disney for suggesting an animated Disney porno film, well... (Let's just say that I have an FBI record for allegedly selling government secrets to the Daleks, okay?)

Well, because of the fact that Mr. Ellison hasn't scooped me out and used me as a portable barbecue smoker, I get lots of people who seem to think that I am my brother's keeper. (I have two biological brothers, and I'm not their keeper, either.) Besides the usual "What does Harlan think of..." and "Do you think Harlan would..." questions and the variations of "Could you get Harlan to..." that assume that we're Siamese twins joined at the brain, and the ubiquitous "Could you give me Harlan's E-mail address?" (often uttered right after the man says that he doesn't have one and doesn't want one), I always get one smartarse. This is the equivalent of the intern who just discovered that catatonics tend to remain in one position and thereby positions every catatonic in a psych ward so they flip the bird at passersby. It always starts with a smarmy, whiny "So...you gonna ask when Harlan's going to get *The Last Dangerous Visions* out?"

Ah yes, true wit in action. That's right up there with the scintillant geniuses whose idea of charm is to pronounce my last name "Riddle." (For those who may actually give a damn, it's pronounced "Rih-DELL," and the last time it was spelled without a double "D" or "L," my ancestors were passing out shirts that read "My family went to Agincourt, and all I got was smallpox.") They don't really want an answer: they just want to get a rise out of someone. It's not like the guy's going to buy a copy if it comes out tomorrow.

Ergo, here is my standard answer: it's none of my business as to when *The Last*

Dangerous Visions comes out, or *Blood's A Rover*, or the next issue of *Harlan Ellison's Dream Corridor*. This is the same way it's none of my business as to when Steve Bissette gets out a new issue of *Tyrant*. It's none of my business as to when George Romero plans to film *Twilight of the Dead*, or Terry Gilliam starts work on *The Defective Detective*, or Stanley Kubrick on *AI*. (Yes, I know Kubrick's dead: it's just the thought of Steven Spielberg replacing Kubrick as director brings on the same mental image as letting Jeffrey Dahmer take over cooking duties for Emeril Lagasse.) And unless you have some serious financial interest in the final product, it's none of your business, either.

Usually, when I drop that ketamine-laced bonbon in someone's lap, I get the immediate whine of "Well, I've been waiting..." There's the problem. Not any concern over whether the creator is suffering from personal problems, or that undefeatable mishaps are keeping a project from completion. All the whiner is complaining about is that product isn't dropped in his or her little flippers fast enough. And if it isn't in their paws now now NOW, then they're flapping their lips or pounding the keyboard on Usenet about how their lives are ruined because they didn't get their fix right then.

(The more extreme examples are the characters whose little voices tell them that they've been chosen to fulfill the sacred quest of bringing those responsible for the delays to justice. To use Harlan's example, they're the ones who appoint themselves representatives of the authors whose stories were accepted for publication in *Last Dangerous Visions*, with whether the authors or their estates requested this being moot, and that they'll force everyone involved to drop their claims on those stories. These are usually the same characters whose little voices tell them to play copyright cop at conventions with any dealer selling bootleg anime tapes, and who know their holy quest supercedes chats with the police and restraining orders. To use a Chris Rock quote and re-reference it to Joan of Arc, "I'm not saying they should have killed her, but I understand.")

What's really annoying comes with knowing all too well what happens when a delayed project finally comes out: the same people who whimpered and threatened beforehand, usually swearing upon God and Elvis that they'd be the first in line to buy the first copy on the stands, look at the final product and let loose a mealymouthed "Oh, I thought it was going to be different" and dump it right there without buying it. These are usually the same exact people who demand free samples of comics because they swear that they're going to review or otherwise utilize that sample, and then throw it away once they get it. (Just a tiny note: this is the reason why most bookstores and comic shops that take special orders expect those customers to pay in advance.) No matter what the outcome, they aren't going to be happy, and once one project they've clamored for is completed, they'll find something else to complain about.

The quite simple fact of the matter is that creators owe nothing to the consumers of entertainment other than a decent value for their money, and creators don't owe jack shit to those who didn't pay for it. If Kevin Smith idly mentions that he'd like to write *Green Arrow* one of these days, DC Comics is not obligated to fulfill the longings of the crazed fanboys who want to see a Smith-penned *Green Arrow*. Alternately, if DC and Kevin Smith sign a contract so that he can write *Green Arrow*, and the project gets canned before it starts, Smith and DC don't owe fans that miniseries, no matter how it was hyped before things fell through. Even if DC and Smith sign a contract, and Smith takes the advance money and parties in Perth for six months without writing a script, the only people really out of anything are the folks who make up the comics company. They don't have a product they can sell to make back that advance, and that's all. The fanboys awaiting the new *Green Arrow* may be upset, but the project has all of the effect upon the universe as if nobody had ever agreed to anything. Life goes on.

Now, on the other hand, those with a serious financial stake in an upcoming project have a reason to be upset over delays, but they don't need help in expressing their ire. Comic shop owners deserve to get pissed if they pay for a gigantic graphic novel set in advance and it doesn't show up for six months, but the last thing they need to get the point across is a swarm of little nitpickers whose idea of gentle persuasion consists of E-mailed messages along the lines of "you dumb shits wheres my collection you suck and yr mothers gay." If a creator's late with a new comic, the publisher has ways of reminding the creator of contractual obligations, ranging from querying phone calls to various interesting combinations of household alternating current and jumper cables attached to the nipples. They don't need, and they didn't ask for, fans to call up and bug said creator as well.

Finally, someone needs to express to fans the concept of stalled or failed projects. Every writer and every artist worthy of the title has a whole file cabinet full of concepts that they started but never got around to finishing. The publisher could have gone out of business, a lengthy convalescence from Dutch Elm Blight could have interfered, or they simply decided to file that individual project and work on it when the spirit moved them. It's guaranteed, though, that if said writer or artist makes even the slightest mention of any of these projects in public, fans will hound them for years. Just ask Steve Bissette one of these days about the number of fans nagging him for the abortive adaptations of *Night of the Living Dead* or Clive Barker's *Rawhead Rex* that fell through years ago.

Here's the summation. I know it's hard to understand this, being from a world where Mommy and Daddy made sure that your every idle request was fulfilled in seconds and still continue to wipe your soiled bottom even though you just turned 45, but pretend, just for a moment, that every comics project that comes along may never see daylight. You can joke about seriously delayed projects, the way wags made fun of Windows 95 and *Star Wars: Episode One* before they finally hit their respective venues, but also consider that you wouldn't be anticipating these projects if you'd never heard of them. Ergo, they are not *your* responsibility. Don't sulk and pout because you aren't going to get them when you expect them. And for those who feel that they have nothing better to do but get on Usenet newsgroups and bitch about the situation, all I can do is quote one of the great philosophers of the Twentieth Century and yell "Aaaaaaaaaah, SHADDAP!"

—Savant, November 9, 2000

Science

I very seriously suspect that my original attraction to science fiction was due to my long-running love affair with science. This was before I discovered that pure science has better stories, better characterization, and many fewer deus ex machinas *than skiffy. These days, who has time for fiction when nonfiction is so much more fun?*

"The Apple of Eden As More Than A Metaphor: An Overview of the Problems with Introducing Plants and Animals To Alien Worlds"

Throughout most of the history of science fiction, the concept of human colonization of alien worlds has been simplistic at best. Either the world in question just happens to be perfectly suited for human occupation without biohazard suits or breathing apparatus, or it's a rugged world that just needs a few crops and farm animals to support a lively population of pioneers. Looking at the reality of the probable incompatibility of any alien ecosystem to our own, an engineering solution presents itself: instead of taming the wilderness, why not develop self-contained ecosystems and live therein? After all, the wilderness will still be outside tomorrow, while needs for food, water, and shelter are a bit more immediate. A combination of the two suggests the terraforming of a world might make sense: a planet may be uninhabitable today, but by engineering conditions preferential to Earthly life, it might be made into a new Earth with the right application of agriculture and applied science.

The first concern with such terraforming, interestingly enough, lies with ethics: if a world has life, even in microbial form, what right do humans have to wipe it out or replace it with terrestrial forms? More importantly, would native life pose a direct hazard or hardship to terrestrial forms? Alien bacteria or algae don't have to be deadly to make a colonization effort an ordeal: alien and terrestrial biochemistry may be completely incompatible, which may prevent infection but won't do anything about allergies to alien pathogens. The "lost" H. Beam Piper story "When In the Course" mentioned the artificial habitats on the planet Yggdrasil, where the only source of food for humans came from hydroponics and carniculture vats. A bacterium regularly infected the growth media on both; the bacteria died on contact, but it left the food tasting absolutely foul. This scenario is inherently more plausible than any story of alien life hunting or eating humans.

In any possible interstellar colonization effort, the colonization of worlds where life already exists will probably be banned for any number of ethical reasons, as well as for financial reasons. A much more attractive target would be a world with a reasonably thick atmosphere and plenty of water, but without any indigenous life. A world that resembled the Earth of 4 billion years ago might be ideal: large, open bodies of water, a methane-nitrogen atmosphere, and (if the colonists were lucky) an oversized moon perfect for catching a good portion of the asteroids and comets still floating around a given planetary system. Even if such worlds are rare, worlds similar to Mars might make good colonization material, and Mars itself may make a good experimental lab to understand exactly what would be necessary to make a marginal planet attractive to Earth life.

For the sake of this argument, let's say that Mars is completely sterile: it has no life today, and it never had so much as a microbe during its history. (Based on recent understanding of Martian geology and climatology, this is fairly unlikely. However, the evidence presented so far for Martian life is minimal, as with the famed Martian meteorite "fossils," or flat-out ridiculous, as in the Cydonia "face.") If one wanted to go through the tremendous engineering efforts to liberate enough volatiles from Martian bedrock and the polar caps to restore a thick atmosphere and liquid water on its surface, it might be possible to see oceans and lakes in the southern hemisphere within a century. The problem then facing any colonists is the introduction of life to what is, after all, a sterile biosphere, and what organisms should be introduced, as well as in what order. The engineering of a future Mars colony is relatively easy compared to the biology of a self-sustaining colony.

Let's assume that someone collects or donates the money necessary to build a permanent base on the Tharsis Plateau of Mars, and the base's main intent is to make the planet habitable within a thousand years, where unsuited humans could walk free on the surface without any special equipment. This has been tackled before in science fiction, with Kim Stanley Robinson's *Mars* trilogy as the most recent and most detailed example. However, we're going to concentrate solely on the biological aspects of the terraforming of Mars, not with lifeforms genetically engineered to survive under Mars' current conditions, but with the introduction of organisms as conditions become more Earthlike.

The bioengineering of Mars has a precedent in human history with the dual colonizations of New Zealand. New Zealand was first described to Westerners by Dutch traders in the 1600s, but it was first discovered by humans approximately 600 years before, when Polynesian explorers landed somewhere on the country's North Island. Before that, New Zealand was the most isolated chunk of continental crust on Earth: it separated from the ancient continent of Gondwana about 85 million years ago, taking with it a representative biota that it shared with South America, Australia, Africa, India, Madagascar, and Antarctica.

New Zealand's geology and biological history is still being studied (most of its original terrestrial fossil deposits eroded away when the islands started sinking about 40 million years ago, and were further worn during the last Ice Age, which covered all of South Island and most of North Island), but it became unique for one major aspect. Mammals were and are common on Australia (mostly marsupials, but early placental mammals arrived during the Cretaceous, only to be forced out by unknown causes), but New Zealand had no terrestrial mammals besides two species of bats at the time of its discovery. So far, no mammal fossils have been discovered (however, dinosaurs were unknown from New Zealand until 1979, and some six different dinosaurs are known today, so early mammals may be discovered yet), and the only other mammals in the vicinity were fur seals and whales. In their place, birds filled every available ecological niche.

The natural history of New Zealand is a fascinating subject in its own right, but the main consideration in this essay is that the flora spent some 65 million years adapting to the depredations of birds instead of mammals. This meant that when the ancestors of the Maori, the indigenous people of New Zealand, first arrived, they found a land with an incredible number of food sources...for anything with a gizzard. Polynesian explorers traditionally brought stores of plants and animals on their expeditions, as most islands were notoriously poor larders for humans, but the cooler weather of New Zealand and other, unknown, factors stunted or killed off most of the new crops. Of the 36 known species of plants generally brought by Polynesians, only seven survived to the present day, and of the animal imports, only two. The introduction of the dog and the *kiore* (the Polynesian edible rat) may have hastened the extinction of many species of native animal and plant, but their effect was minor compared to the cornucopia brought to the islands by European colonists after Captain James Cook first circumnavigated the islands in 1769.

Cook himself left quite a few plants and animals during his second voyage to New Zealand in 1773, including the goose and the goat, and subsequent French expeditions introduced the pig (which was probably brought as well by the Polynesians, but didn't survive its initial introduction). Cook also introduced the potato: although the *kumara*, or sweet potato, was a staple of the Maori diet, the white potato was much easier to grow and store in the local climate, and rapidly became a favored food. (The same thing happened when the Rev. Samuel Marsden introduced the peach: missionaries were responsible for many of the fruit and vegetable importations during the early days of colonization). For a time, New Zealand became a haunt for whalers, who introduced tobacco and dock (since the seeds are nearly identical, unscrupulous traders offered dock seeds as tobacco, leading to the weed's spread across the islands), as well as Norway rats and mice. As a proviso for transportation to New Zealand, most colonists were expected to bring seeds, tubers, and bulbs for their personal gardens, and many also required that each colonist grow hedges around houses. The transport media for the bulbs and tubers, usually soil or peat moss, crawled with small animals and fungi, and all were dumped to the side when the colonists planted their gardens.

The real efforts, though, came with the formation of the Acclimatisation Societies. The first and most influential of these, the Canterbury Acclimatisation Society, was formed in 1864 with the intent of introducing and acclimatizing plants and animals from around the world. In retrospect, the Societies went about their business in a haphazard and even chaotic way, but in a day when the ecology of England, much less New Zealand, was poorly understood, the Societies performed a vital service to the survival and success of New Zealand. The Canterbury Society itself became famous for introducing such diverse animals as trout, red deer, pheasants, and bumblebees, and the Hawkes Bay Acclimatisation Society became involved with the importation of birds, seeds, and vine cuttings. Until after World War I, the Acclimatisation Societies were responsible for the introduction of a simply incredible number of new plants and animals to New Zealand, as well as the review and consideration of even more. The New Zealand government authorized the efforts of the Societies, and even in some cases donated land for animal and plant husbandry.

By the mid-Twentieth Century, though, naturalists began to notice the extent of the damage to New Zealand's original ecosystem. Foreign transplants replaced huge stretches of native bush, with logging and farming being the main causes of native decline, and many native animals and plants became extinct on the mainland. The tuatara (the two known species are the only living representatives of the Sphenodontia, an ancient reptile group that once ranged worldwide but died out elsewhere for unknown reasons) is now found only on several offshore islands due to predations by rats and feral cats, and the weta (a large relative of the grasshopper and New Zealand's largest insect) was similarly threatened by mice that competed for its ecological niche. With the failure of some acclimatization attempts, and the problems caused by others, many groups worked just as hard to keep non-native species out as they did previously to bring them in.

Our hypothetical Martian colony set up on a sterile world, but each introduction of a new animal or plant during the terraforming process would act in a similar way. In many ways, the introduction and reintroduction of terrestrial life to Mars would set off a series of mass extinctions, only occurring every few years instead of every few million years. The addition of blue-green algae to any beginning Martian seas and lakes would hasten the extinction of anaerobic bacteria introduced to help break down rock into component compounds, and the algae would in turn be threatened by the introduction of more developed plants for both the oceans and land. Plants and animals chosen for their hardiness during the early days of Mars' terraforming may be replaced by others as the planet becomes more Earthlike, but many might also usurp the introduced species and retain their grip on their particular biomes. Furthermore, some new introductions may not react to the Martian environment in the way intended by human engineers or ecologists, requiring efforts to control or remove them.

Even though any terraforming effort will be unique, based on local conditions such as gravity, atmosphere, and local resources, a few lessons may be gleaned by studying the biological history of the European colonization of New Zealand. While these are generalities, they should be considered by anyone contemplating the development of any terrestrial ecosystem on any planet other than Earth.

The easiest introductions will be animals and plants already adapted to life with humans. No matter where humans go, they bring life with them. Rats, mice, cockroaches, mosquitoes, pigeons, cats...all of these are great opportunists, and rapidly reproduce despite all efforts to keep them under control. Rats and roaches adapt well to any human environment, and short of leaving spaceship cargo bays open to deep vacuum, they *will* get into ships, outposts, and any other area where two or more humans congregate. Others simply take advantage of environments created by man: pigeons became cosmopolitan with the advent of cities, where buildings simulated their natural cliff environments, while mosquitoes utilized flowerpots and open water containers as breeding media, thus spreading themselves and their young anywhere with access to stagnant fresh water. Still others, such as the Mediterranean gecko, may be very static as adults, but lay their eggs on any suitable surface: many geckos use artificial light to hunt insects, and they attach their eggs to suitable areas on trucks, boats, and anything else they can find, with the hatchlings often emerging hundreds or thousands of miles away from their original laying site.

Based on history, the most likely animal intruder on a new Mars colony would be the roach and the gecko: considering that both can survive longer without food than any mammal, and both can survive levels of hard radiation that would kill a rat or mouse, both would take advantage of climate controlled areas and breed prolifically long before Mars had a breathable atmosphere. Taking advantage of water sources from condensation (inevitable no matter how efficient the air processing equipment), both could thrive alongside humans, and if current efforts to eliminate roaches were any indication, would be impossible to eliminate. As most pet shop owners would explain, efforts to use geckos to control roaches would be inadequate: the geckos may hunt and eat roaches, but the populations would stabilize after a few years, with an unabated plague of roaches and an equally annoying horde of geckos chasing them.

Although blue-green algae technically qualify as bacteria and not plants, unwanted flora and fungi are another concern. Without a thorough sterilization, rest assured that any human colony would deal with growths of algae, mold, fungus, and moss in the most inopportune places, as their spores are exceedingly resistant to radiation, desiccation, and the other hazards of space travel. Many of these may make ready food sources for escaped animals, such as the aforementioned roaches, acting as a substitute larder when human food was unavailable. After a time, these would become oases for larger intruders, such as rats and mice, and become self-sustaining so long as heat and water held out. They might also become problems for the human colonists: maintenance crews in skyscrapers on Earth have similar concerns with outbreaks, so Martian maintenance crews very likely will deal with any number of wildlife-induced breakdowns, as well as allergies set off by fungus and mold spores in the ventilation ducts.

An interesting sidenote to the problems with contemporary animals is the Maori nickname for European: *Pakeha*. Originally applied to the introduced flea, the name means "little stranger," and the flea became an unwelcome visitor to Maori villages. Making a connection between the fleas and the colonists who spread them, the Maori transferred the nickname to the carrier, where it remains to this day. Considering the resilience of the common cat flea, and the flea larva's ability to eat nearly anything organic, the flea will be another "little stranger" aboard any Martian colony in short order, especially if the colonists bring small mammals such as cats and dogs.

The introduction of foreign plants and animals to any colony, either self-enclosed or otherwise, is inevitable. Short of cloning humans from frozen ova, any colony from Earth is going to bring unwanted or unnoticed intruders. Considering the jungle of flora in the human gastrointestinal tract, the herds of dust mites on bare skin, and the plethora of bacteria and metazoans that call the human body home, the only way to prevent any possible problems is to sterilize each and every human that leaves Earth, and the treatments necessary might be fatal. The problems increase with the introduction of any animals or plants to the local ecosystem: again, short of cloning, no animal or plant can be guaranteed to be free of any commuter brought from home, and any items used by the colonists would need to be made from local materials.

Many introduced species may become essential exports. While New Zealand boasts many unique organisms, its economy is inextricably tied to exotics. The California pine grows much larger in New Zealand than in the United States, thus making lumber an essential cash crop. Likewise, the famed Kiwi fruit is actually a

Chinese gooseberry: a combination of savvy marketing and perfect growing conditions have made this berry synonymous with New Zealand. Due to the relatively mild weather, dairy farms are exceedingly popular, as cattle are able to feed on fresh grass year-round instead of hay, and sheep and the resultant wool and mutton were some of the first exports from the islands in the Nineteenth Century. New Zealand streams contain brown trout, an American import, which draw sports fishers from around the world for their size and tenacity. Even pests such as rabbits became exports, with the New Zealand Giant becoming a popular breed for pets.

Martian agriculture might use examples from New Zealand's history, especially during its early days, for ways to promote and develop new goods for Earth markets. Just as New Zealand dairy farmers understandably brag about the high quality of milk and butter due to clement weather and rich grasslands, Martian poultry ranchers might brag about chickens grown in low-gravity conditions being more tender or larger than those raised on Earth. Some others might prove popular solely due to attentive farmers or ranchers: the Granny Smith apple is now grown elsewhere, but the first orchards grew in New Zealand. Since New Zealand beehives have never been exposed to diseases and parasites such as European foul brood or the bee mite, its beekeepers promote the fact that their hives are generally chemical-free, and Martian exports could follow a similar attitude.

Want a great way to introduce unwanted organisms? Try homesickness. While many introductions to New Zealand were deliberate attempts for agricultural purposes, quite a few came from individuals who missed the sights of home. Most of the available land is covered with introduced plants from the British Isles, and the skies are as infested with sparrows and starlings as those of America, thanks to well-meaning bird lovers who wanted familiar birds in their yards. During the days of the Acclimatisation Societies, these were encouraged: today, the threat of introduced diseases means that the Ministry of Agriculture and Forestry spends a considerable amount of time and effort to inform the general public of the dangers of any new introduction. A single rose, a handful of seeds, or a lone apple may not appear threatening to most, but in a country where most of its wealth is tied to agriculture, the possibility of diseases or insects being brought in without controls, as well as the deliberate planting of flora that could compete with native plants or threaten cash crops, keeps the Ministry very busy.

Considering the versatility and tenacity of Earth life, any imports to Mars, of any kind, desperately need extensive inspection before release. After all, if a wheat rust wipes out half of the food supply during the early days of our hypothetical colony, the colonists won't have the option of going home and trying again later. Other nonfood items will have to be checked as well, since molds and bacteria produce spores that could survive in dormancy for years until exposed to the proper conditions, and insects and other animals are notorious for hiding in spaces in almost anything manmade. A famed New Zealand case involves a boring beetle that managed to get to the islands in a shipment of cricket bats: had an inspector not noticed the wood dust at the bottom of the bag from the beetle's burrowing, the damage caused by its escape to the lumber industry could have been incalculable. Now consider that any item shipped to Mars could contain a similar menace to the welfare of the colony, and we no longer need to talk about adequate quarantine procedures being essential.

Even with laws against the importation of potentially hazardous life, one constant of human nature will always dog any inspector, and that's the philosophy of "Well, just one won't hurt." NZ inspectors regularly slap customs violators with fines for trying to smuggle in fruit or vegetables, but just as many assume that they'll be all right. New Zealand is snake-free, a major selling point to tourists afraid of snakes, but the Ministry inspectors still find individuals who try to import snakes and other reptiles as pets. Even NZ zoos have to be exceedingly careful with animal imports: as illustrated by a recent incident where a box turtle that arrived in an airport due to a shipping error. Although zoos volunteered to adopt the turtle, the Ministry ultimately had to ship it elsewhere: turtles are known carriers of salmonella, even if they show no symptoms of the disease, and the last thing anyone wanted was a new strain of salmonella on the islands. Martian inspectors will probably have to deal with any number of terrestrial souvenirs, samples, and pets being brought by visitors or new colonists, and each of these could threaten the success of the colony.

Some of the biggest pests may come from previously unconsidered sources. Since Mars has a barely noticeable magnetic field compared to Earth, and has no ozone layer, a lot of high-energy particles and waves hit the surface with no loss of power. Even with a lively magnetic field, its current atmosphere can't keep ultraviolet light from slamming everything on the surface, threatening most animals and plants with tissue cancers in very short order. The obvious solution is to introduce plants originally from mountainous areas (being higher in the atmosphere means more exposure to UV, and most mountain plants have safeguards to protect their DNA from UV damage) and nocturnal animals, at least until an ozone layer starts building in the upper atmosphere.

One of the few lowland plants that adapts well to high levels of UV light is *Cannabis sativa*, better known as marijuana. In fact, the active ingredient in marijuana, THC, is produced as a direct response to higher levels of UVA light, so its introduction could offer interesting side-effects on Martian society. Marijuana might become as much of a cash crop on Mars as on Earth: growing in marginal soil, it would make a good erosion preventative and ready source of fiber for clothes and other textiles, and the seeds used to produce animal feed and vegetable oil. Grown in rich soil, it might make a desirable import to countries on Earth where its purchase and possession is legal, and the sales potential of "Space Pot" might make it a luxury item that brings hard currency to the Martian colony.

The introduction of marijuana could happen either by deliberate cultivation or by smuggling: one individual trying to start his/her own little pot patch may find that it grows wild with little or no encouragement. "Wild" is the word to watch for. With its current tolerance of UV, combined with the Martian gravity, marijuana could go berserk for a generation or more, growing into impenetrable forests across the Martian surface. As far as the production of free oxygen is concerned, this would be a godsend for the colonists (the first known tree, *Archaeopteris*, did the same thing for Earth about 400 million years ago, when vast stands helped increase the oxygen level of the atmosphere and incidentally probably encouraged the development of land animals), but the plants' effect upon human activities might be drastically different.

A similar situation became apparent on New Zealand in the 1800s, when Scottish colonists began farms and villages on South Island. They planted oats, the traditional Scottish cereal crop, and introduced heather, the seeds of which were an unavoidable contaminant of the sown oats. Heather rapidly grew all over South Island, reaching previously unknown sizes and becoming a menace to horse and train travel in many areas due to the absolutely impenetrable stands in which it grew. Heather eventually died back and became manageable, but not before some disgruntled colonists suggested that the heather invasion was a deliberate attempt by the Scots to cover New Zealand with the Scottish national flower. Similar incidents occurred with watercress and willows, as introduced stands rapidly went wild and choked waterways before declining in numbers and density.

Many of the most pernicious pests in New Zealand's ecosystem today were introduced in a comparable manner, and similar threats face any future extraterrestrial colony. Spores and eggs trapped in clothing, worms brought in potting soil, seeds in the guts of animals that are later expelled: all of these are new arrivals whose appearance may aggravate current problems or start new ones. Anyone who uses uncomposted cow or horse manure on a garden, and then deals with the new crop of weeds sprouting from seeds swallowed by the animals producing said manure, can attest to this.

Biological controls for one pest may aggravate problems later on. The history of biological controls for accidental imports to other countries is well-mined with predators that ignored their intended prey. The introduction of the mongoose to the West Indies and the cane toad to Queensland are telling: the cane toad was introduced to Australia from its native Caribbean islands in an effort to control the grey cane beetle attacking sugar cane fields in the earlier portion of the century. Although the toad readily ate beetles in the lab, their life cycles prevented them from meeting in the wild, and the cane toad's catholic diet (literally eating any animal it could jam into its mouth) and prolific breeding habits made it a menace across northern Australia. The cane toad is also very toxic, and any native predator that tried to eat or even taste a cane toad usually never survived the experience

One of New Zealand's biological controls is responsible for the impending extinction of the flightless *kakapo*, the world's largest parrot. The "owl-parrot" thrived in New Zealand until shortly after the introduction of the rabbit. Rabbits and foxes were imported to offer colonists the opportunity to try the sports of the British gentry back home, as were deer and elk, and rabbits came very close to becoming as much of a pest in New Zealand as in Australia. (Foxes themselves preferred hunting native birds to hunting rabbits, so the foxes rapidly became unwanted arrivals as well.) In an attempt to use biological controls on the rabbit populations, the stoat was introduced to New Zealand, where it ignored the rabbits and hunted the *kakapo*. Since the *kakapo* lives in burrows, the stoat was able to crawl down those burrows and kill the otherwise defenseless birds, and the *kakapo* now lives only on predator-free islands. Today, about fifty of these birds survive, and considering its slow reproductive rate, the *kakapo* will probably be extinct by 2020.

A simple consideration generally forgotten when considering biological controls is that predators of any type will attack and eat the easiest food source around. Stoats, foxes, and rabbits are well adapted to each others' habits, with the rabbits offering a challenge in the hunt. Given a choice, the stoats and foxes generally went after New Zealand flightless birds, supremely unadapted for dealing with hunting mammals, instead of expending the effort to chase after quick and alert rabbits. Martian colonists would not only have to deal with predators and herbivores preferring an unintended food source, but with those animals that preferred human handouts over having to forage on their own.

New colonies could act as "DNA banks" for other worlds. One of the strangest tales of introduced exotics comes from the parma wallaby, introduced to Kawau Island during the days of the Acclimatisation Societies. This species became extinct in Australia in the early portion of the Twentieth Century, and was assumed to be lost forever, until the discovery of this "lost colony." This was especially good news to the residents, as the wallabies had become pests, and they were just as glad to give away as many of the wallabies as they could as Australians were to take them.

For all of the reasonable concerns about importing intrusive or potentially dangerous organisms, one aspect of a biodiverse colonization project in favor of introducing as many animals and plants possible lies in protection against extinction. For instance, say that a virus wipes out every horse on Earth. Any horses kept on Mars would be unexposed to the virus, and they become breeding stock to revive Earth's horse population (after the appropriate inoculations, of course). This is an extreme example (as the first European colonists to New Zealand discovered, horses are very hard to transport across very long distances, and many equestrians spent an obscene amount of money to bring them to the islands), but it also applies to small plants and animals under similar situations. It's not impossible to consider a period a thousand years in the future, after humanity travels to and establishes colonies around any number of stars, where the locals keep exotics long extinct on the mother world.

Finally, some organisms, no matter how well-treated, may not survive anywhere outside of captivity. The history of New Zealand is rife with examples of successes in biological introduction, both deliberate and accidental, but some of the most intriguing stories deal with the failures of organisms to take root, as it were, in the islands. One of the best examples is the guinea pig. Over the past century, several attempts were made to introduce the guinea pig to New Zealand: one botanist wanted to introduce wild violets, and thought that guinea pigs would crop back the vegetation that intruded upon them, so he raised dozens of them and let them run free in his garden. In this case, and in several others, the wild guinea pig colonies gradually faded for unknown reasons, and the guinea pig lives today on the islands solely as a pet and experimental animal. A similar fate awaited its South American contemporary the llama: although the llama seemed to be a perfect fit for the grassy, mountainous steppes of South Island, it either couldn't compete with previously established elk and goats or lost out for other reasons, but it never established itself. The llama thrives on farms, though, where it does very well as a pet and pack animal.

Any effort to import organisms to Mars will face much worse: since Mars has little to no magnetic field, animals such as pigeons that use Earth's field to navigate may find themselves hopelessly lost, and rapidly disappear. Many probably won't adapt well to the lower gravity, and still others need the right combination of sunlight, water quality and soil conditions impossible to reproduce on Mars. Trout and salmon adapted to New Zealand conditions rather well, but all efforts to grow lobsters for the seafood trade were a dismal failure. The reverse may be true for Mars.

Inevitably, any successes in the introduction of terrestrial life to Mars or any other planet are directly dependent upon the efforts of the individuals importing them. The same is true of any efforts to control or exterminate unwanted life. Any attempt to colonize a new world will be a unique experience, but history shows that many of the problems facing such a project have been dealt with before.

–Most of the research for this article came from a variety of sources, but the most helpful in understanding the biological impact of the European colonization of New Zealand was Exotic Intruders: The Introduction of Plants and Animals Into New Zealand by Joan Druett (Heinemann, 1983). The Web also contains considerable resources for understanding current efforts to keep New Zealand pest-free: most of these are located at the New Zealand Ministry of Agriculture and Forestry at http://www.maf.govt.nz, and specific considerations for border inspections and quarantines may be found at http://www.maf.govt.nz/MAFnet/issues/pest/border.html.

—Event Horizon, December 1999

Postscript: After the magazine OMNI collapsed for the final time, fiction editor Ellen Datlow started her own online magazine, Event Horizon, and this essay was one of the last pieces to appear in Event Horizon before the publication went on "indefinite hiatus" at the end of 1999. Considering that Datlow's work was one of the reasons why I started reading OMNI back in 1980, I was honored and flattered that she asked me to do so, and if she ever gets involved with a new magazine, I'd honestly have to consider returning to writing just to write for her.

Oh, and the first Aotearoan mammal fossils showed up a few years back. The real mystery is why they never got established, in the same way that placental mammals once lived in Australia but were stomped by the marsupials.

"Back Lots of the Lost: The Implausibility of the Clichéd 'Lost World'"

Since the Victorian period, shortly after the discovery and scientific description of the first recognized examples of the class Dinosauria, individuals have speculated on the possibilities of areas where dinosaurs and other prehistoric creatures may still exist. Back before aerial surveys and satellite photographs, the idea of lost continents brimming with tyrannosaurs and pterosaurs fevered the imaginations of fiction writers and readers. After serious exploration efforts turned up no signs of previously unknown saurians, speculation turned toward parallel evolution of dinosaurs on alien worlds, or in isolated patches of jungle unknown to humans. The "lost world" cliché soon became almost universal, demanding a Frank Frazetta canvas: mention "lost world" to nearly anyone and ask for the first images that pop up, and invariably the first response concerns cavemen (and rather shapely cavewomen) watching as a *Tyrannosaurus* and *Triceratops* duke it out in a landscape shadowed by giant volcanoes and fern trees.

The perception is popular, and certain lost worlds exist today. However, the prediluvian world of the Galapagos rift vents, with animals and bacteria probably related to the first organisms that left the confines of the vents and struck out for the wide, cold ocean just don't have the same appeal. If we don't get dinosaurs, then at least we need prehistoric mammals (usually saber-toothed cats and mammoths, although titanotheres and creodonts have their possibilities), or maybe some of the reptiles that predated the dinosaurs. They're not as impressive as *T. rex*, but being chased by a *Lycaenops* or a *Dimetrodon* still offers adventure and suspense. For those seeking the less familiar, the creatures of the mid-Devonian are passable, between giant four-meter-long sea scorpions and early amphibians on land and gigantic predatory fish like *Dunklosteus* in the oceans, and then there's always the singular (if diminutive) animals of the early Cambrian as preserved in the Burgess Shale.

The fascination with the concept of areas where animals extinct elsewhere survive and thrive began in the 1700s, when theologians and naturalists started discovering fossils of animals otherwise unknown. Thomas Jefferson, best known for his political contributions to the early United States, was an avid scientist at a time when the word didn't exist: as well as making contributions to statecraft and technology, he spent considerable time on the study of wildlife in America. At a salt lick near his Monticello estate in Virginia, Jefferson discovered the bones of mastodons (distant relatives of the modern elephant), and the bones and claws of a completely unknown animal in a nearby cave, which he assumed belonged to a giant lion. Although the great French naturalist George Cuvier argued at that time that many animals known from fossil records were in fact extinct, Jefferson rejected the idea of extinction, and favored the idea that the beasts has simply retreated to areas inaccessible to man. When sending Lewis and Clark on their expedition to explore the Louisiana Purchase, Jefferson included directions to document all plants, animals, and minerals of note, and instructed them to keep an eye open for mastodons and his giant lions. (The bones of his "lion" in fact belonged to a giant extinct ground sloth from the Pleistocene; the beast is known today as *Megalonyx jeffersoni*.)

The concept of dinosaurs surviving to the present day started shortly after their formal description, as people worldwide latched onto the popular descriptions of fossil beasts collected in England and the United States. Sir Arthur Conan Doyle's book *The Lost World* is most famous for jump-starting the popular idea of prehistoric oases, but it wasn't the first: among others, an obscure short story called "The Monster of Lake La Metrie" developed around the idea of a surviving plesiosaur in a lake in the American West. Jules Verne experimented with lost worlds in *Journey to the Center of the Earth*, and Edgar Rice Burroughs took the concept of lost worlds further with his books *The Land That Time Forgot*, *The People That Time Forgot*, and *At The Earth's Core*. To the former two books, Burroughs added the then-popular idea of ontogeny recapitulating phylogeny, where all evolution was a steady climb to the perfection of modern man. In books, movies, and film, the idea of vast swamps and valleys where an enterprising explorer could still come across dinosaurs and other prehistoric reptiles became somewhat of a cliché over the years, but an immensely popular cliché.

Well, the possibilities are fascinating, but the realities are a completely different matter. As man keeps exploring the planet, the likelihood of finding prehistoric beasts on land becomes less and less likely, but the existence of a lost world isn't impossible. Improbable, yes, and definitely implausible.

For the purposes of this discussion, we're considering only dinosaurs, as considering the logistics of any number of other prehistoric animals would make this essay overly complex. More importantly, we're going to talk about dinosaurs surviving to the present day in previously uncharted areas of Earth. This means dinosaurs that grew in isolation in their original habitat, which was isolated from the outside world due to natural forces. Robert Sawyer's *Quintaglio* series of novels contains a world where dinosaurs never became extinct, and in fact developed intelligence. However, their presence involves the *deus ex machina* of an alien intelligence transporting them to that world: while lost worlds of this sort are possible, as are prehistoric ecosystems created via DNA manipulation as presented in the book and film *Jurassic Park*, they lie beyond the scope of this essay.

The first assumption that must be made is that any dinosaurs survived the great K-T extinction of 65 million years ago. (The "K-T" stands for "Cretaceous-Tertiary" after the geologic periods separated by the event; the "K" is used to distinguish this period from the Cambrian Period of 600 million years ago, which itself ended with a massive extinction incident.) While circumstantial evidence argues that some individuals may have survived for a time past the main extinction date, no incontrovertible dinosaur fossils of any type have been found after that date. If any dinosaurs survived, they apparently weren't able to sustain a sufficient gene pool necessary to repopulate, thus leaving the planet free for mammals to take over.

Now, some survivors might elude extinction and survive in pockets where conditions never changed. Most known survivors are plants, though. The stinking cedar of the Appalachians survives in isolated areas, having previously covered good portions of the eastern United States during the Pleistocene, and the town of Aquarena Springs, Texas is world-famous for preserving the flora of the surrounding area circa the last ice age, before most of Texas dried out about 10,000 years ago. The most famous botanical survivor is the ginkgo: almost all ginkgos were gone by the K-T extinction except a small population in China, and Chinese monks cultivated the tree for centuries before introducing it to the West. Today, the ginkgo does very well in cool, wet environments such as the Pacific Northwest of North America, thus demonstrating that most extinctions are not a sign of evolutionary failure but a sign of swiftly changing conditions.

In discussions of cryptozoology, the study of animals previously unknown to science, much is made of the modern coelacanth, *Latimeria chalumnae*. All other known coelacanths died out at the same time as the dinosaurs, but *Latimeria* lives today off the Comoro Islands and off Indonesia in the Indian Ocean. (The second population of coelacanths was only discovered at the end of 1997; both groups rarely have contact with man.) Since its rediscovery, *Latimeria* is often used as an argument for the continued existence of dinosaurs or other prehistoric creatures. *Latimeria* is a trap, though: while all shallow-water coelacanths died during the K-T extinction, almost all marine fossil deposits on land were formed in relatively shallow water, and *Latimeria* and its predecessors left no traces of themselves in those sediments. Bones and other remains of *Latimeria*'s ancestors are probably readily available to any paleontologist able to excavate the ocean bed, but not many bones may be available. Due to the mechanics of plate tectonics, where seafloor is subducted under continental plates and new seafloor formed as the continents moved about, the oldest areas of modern seafloor are approximately 150 million years old, with many areas being considerably younger, and *Latimeria* isn't all that common in the first place due to its rather exacting habitat requirements, so the odds of finding deep-sea coelacanth bones are exceedingly remote.

Another consideration presented by the coelacanth lies with the ocean itself. Water covers seventy percent of Earth's surface, and its average depth offers more hiding spaces for unknown species than a comparable area of land. Since all known dinosaurs were terrestrial (and all known Mesozoic sea reptiles were residents of relatively shallow oceans), all hunts for them have to be undertaken on the surface. This limits searches to the continents and islands, and only areas that existed 65 million years ago or more.

That timeline removes the possibility of many survivors, as many of the best (or the most sterotypical) habitats amenable to dinosaurs haven't been around that long. Dr. Louis Jacobs, author of *The Search for the African Dinosaurs* (1993), points out that most of the jungles in Africa are far too young to have been homes to dinosaurs, and the idea of "darkest" Africa being a throwback to the Mesozoic is a myth. If dinosaurs live in the Congo today, they had to have migrated there from somewhere else, and again, no definitive dinosaur bones or other remains have been discovered past the K-T boundary. (The same argument may be used against the existence of prehistoric creatures in Loch Ness or Lake Champlain: considering that both lakes were covered by glaciers during the last Ice Age, and that glaciers were in fact responsible for helping to carve out the distinctive shape of both bodies of water, any large animal living in either location today would have had to have entered from elsewhere within the last 10,000 years.)

That's another consideration rarely contemplated by fiction writers: what sort of dinosaurs would have survived? Almost all known dinosaurs were lowland dwellers, as the conditions were more conducive to the preservation of their remains. Dinosaurs almost definitely frequented every available ecological niche open to them, but erosion destroyed the haunts of highland dinosaurs long ago, along with their remains. The actual location of a "lost world" would have directly affected what dinosaurs managed to survive in them: the cliché of *Tyrannosaurus* and *Triceratops* in such a lost valley would work only if that valley were in Montana or North Dakota. Valleys in, say, Australia or Antarctica would have drastically different fauna and flora. For the most part, the best candidates would be the descendants of dinosaurs from the Triassic and Jurassic periods of the Mesozoic Era, when the continents were still joined and a dinosaur could theoretically walk from Antarctica to Greenland without once touching salt water. This means no horned dinosaurs outside of North America and Asia, and the same for tyrannosaurs and dromaeosaurs: an explorer in South America could tangle with an allosaur or a titanosaur, but not with a *Deinonychus* or a hadrosaur.

Another factor in the development of a lost world lies with its size. The larger an animal, the larger the range required for it to get enough to eat. Giant brontosaurs survived quite nicely in a habitat of floodplains, where they had plenty of room to travel without depleting their food supply, but living in a valley or on a plateau would have affected them in two ways. A suitable herd of brontosaurs would probably strip clean any area smaller than the state of Massachusetts, thus starving to death, and a smaller number of brontosaurs probably wouldn't offer a large enough gene pool to ensure longterm survival.

(An interesting corollary involves the argument whether dinosaurs produced their own internal body heat or depended upon the sun for warmth. As fond as we all are of the concept of active, warm-blooded dinosaurs, the odds of finding a decent population of dinosaurs increases if they were all cold-blooded like modern reptiles. Warm-bloods simply need too much food in order to keep a consistent body temperature: not only does a Nile crocodile or Komodo dragon the size of a small bear need about one-tenth of the food necessary to keep the bear alive, but the crocodile and dragon have more available energy for producing eggs and young because they don't need to maintain a mammalian metabolic furnace. In limited areas, those who can get by with smaller amounts of food generally live long enough to pass their genes on to future generations, thus helping to favor cold-bloods. This phenomenon occurs in the Komodo Islands: the islands are bare enough of prey animals that a coldblooded predator like the Komodo dragon can get enough to eat while preserving a viable gene pool. Any mammalian predator of that size or larger would either eat all available prey, thus starving, or suffer from the effects of inbreeding and die out.)

An alternative comes from fossil remains. The wooly mammoth was assumed to have become extinct approximately 10,000 years ago, but a small herd survived on Howell Island off Alaska until apparently about 4,000 years ago. These mammoths were a fraction of the size of mainland mammoths, and they survived because they no longer needed quite so much food to support a decent herd. A similar situation was discovered by the flamboyant paleontologist Baron Nopsca on his estate in Transylvania: he uncovered bones of dinosaurs that lived on an island themselves, and were correspondingly smaller than similar species found elsewhere. Islands and other areas isolated from the general world tend to see a change in size of their inhabitants: large animals generally shrink to deal with diminishing resources, and previously diminutive species enlarge to fill new ecological niches. Our lost world may have miniature brontosaurs and gigantic flightless birds, both competing for domination.

Again returning to the clichéd lost valley, we have the assumption that any animals and plants remaining within haven't changed in 65 million years ago. While some individual genus of animal and plant may survive relatively unchanged, this is due to the fact that its environment is also unchanged, and that rarely happens. The volcanoes mentioned in the beginning of this essay have a tendency to dump ash and lava, not to mention poisonous gases, all over the surrounding landscape, and that obviously would stress any population of dinosaurs to the point of extinction.

For an example, New Zealand would seem to be the perfect lost world at first. It separated from Gondwana (the prehistoric supercontinent that once contained the masses of South America, Africa, Australia, Antarctica, India, and Madagascar as well) about 85 to 90 million years ago, and it took a comparable amount of Gonwana's life with it. Some of this survives today: the native podocarp trees became extinct elsewhere around the end of the Cretaceous, as did the relatives of the tuatara, the sole surviving member of the reptilian Class Sphenodontia. (Today, the tuatara consists of two species indistinguishable without DNA analysis, but before their relatives died out for unknown reasons, these reptiles once filled many of the niches held today by lizards.) The extant kiwi and the extinct moa are members of the ratite family, an ancient Gondwana bird group that also includes the African ostrich, the Australian emu, and the South American rhea, and the ancestors of the kiwi and moa probably stowed aboard New Zealand as it separated. New Zealand separated before the development of snakes, so the only snakes anywhere near the islands are sea snakes, and until the arrival of Polynesian explorers about one thousand years ago, the only native land mammals were bats.

By all rights, New Zealand should have had dinosaurs on it at least until the arrival of humans. The terrestrial fossil history of New Zealand is still sketchy, but at least six different species of dinosaur are known from fragmentary remains, including a large sauropod, a predator probably identical to *Allosaurus*, a much smaller predator, an ankylosaur, and at least one herbivorous ornithopod related to the English *Hypsilophodon*. This population is comparable to the dinosaurs of Australia, and further research may turn up other groups endemic to Gondwana. One thing is clear, though: barring the effects of a global catastrophe that killed off dinosaurs and other large, specialized animals, New Zealand's dinosaur population should not have been affected by the factors offered by some palaeontologists to explain the K-T extinction, such as disease and lowered temperature. New Zealand is now the most isolated chunk of continental crust on Earth, and it definitely had enough area to support a lively assemblage of dinosaurs up to the present day.

Well, that would be true...if New Zealand hadn't changed at all in the last 85 million years. The reality is that the islands suffered severe erosion after their separation from Gondwana, and until about 40 million years ago, they had weathered into little more than barrier islands. At that time, the oceanic crustal plate bearing New Zealand connected with another plate, and when New Zealand's mass impacted this plate, it started a round of volcanic activity that continues today. Australia is very geologically stable today, but New Zealand is a roiling mass of active volcanoes, geysers, and hot springs, and the resultant activity raised the islands up to their current positions.

If any dinosaurs had managed to survive the erosion of their original habitat and the stresses of the volcanic reconfiguration of the islands, the last Ice Age would have finished them off. Due to its antipodean location and the prominent mountains on South Island, New Zealand became just as glacier-encapsulated as North America or Europe in the Pleistocene, only the life of New Zealand had nowhere else to go. By most estimates, all of South Island and almost all of North Island were covered by glaciers before the end of the last glacial period, and the current biosphere of the islands descended from the survivors at the northern tip of North Island.

In a way, dinosaurs survived in New Zealand: their descendants, the birds, colonized the islands and filled many of the niches abandoned by their ancestors. The moas, second only to the Madagascar elephant bird in size, took over the large herbivore niche left by the brontosaurs, and predatory eagles twice the size of the golden eagle took the top predator niche filled by lions or jaguars elsewhere. All throughout the islands, birds (along with the tuatara, geckos and skinks, and a relative of the grasshopper called a *weta*) took advantage of the lack of mammalian competition, with many species going flightless. A fraction if this survived the colonization by the ancestors of the Maori, and even more of the biota became extinct due to European colonization in the Eighteenth and Nineteenth Centuries, but many endemic New Zealand birds survive, and some even thrive. However, non-flying dinosaurs definitely didn't make it.

Even if the environment didn't change, the animals and plants inside have no reason to follow along. The basis behind Stephen Jay Gould's and Niles Eldridge's theory of "punctuated equilibrium" is that new species develop when small groups are isolated from the bulk of a population. With a smaller gene pool, mutations or changes in behavior accumulate, and this group gradually develops into a new species, being unable or unwilling to mate with members of its ancestor species in the wild. Paleontologist John Horner argues that punctuated equilibrium helps explain the explosion of new species of dinosaur in North America during the Cretaceous: as the Rocky Mountains started to form, the buckling and warping of the Earth's surface formed any number of valleys and plateaus, isolating groups and accelerating evolutionary trends. Considering the size of any "lost world," basic dinosaur body plans might remain unchanged (among predatory dinosaurs, for instance, the body plan remained essentially static for 130 million years), but the species themselves would rapidly specialize and evolve. The ancestors of the giant panda are a perfect example of this: as its structure shows, the panda developed from carnivorous ancestors, but its isolation in China ultimately allowed enough modifications to appear for it to survive on bamboo. (Interestingly, the same thing happened in the mountains of New Guinea, only the bamboo-eater was a descendant of marsupial herbivores distantly related to the wombat called diprotodonts.) Greg Bear's sequel to Doyle's *The Lost World*, *Dinosaur Summer*, touches upon this: with the dinosaurs in his lost world, the main predators were descendants of allosaurian predators, but they were becoming wiped out by a new predator evolved from birdlike dinosaurs called avimimids. While some species in a lost world might appear the same over the intervening centuries, others would probably evolve in ways scarcely imaginable.

Something else to consider with a lost world ecosystem concerns the introduction of new species. No matter how isolated from the rest of the planet one may be, a lost world will always be affected by the changes on the outside. Windborne seeds and spores, not to mention flying animals, will always get in, and many might find the conditions quite amenable.

Many lost world stories involve a nice cross-section of dinosaur evolution from the beginning of the Triassic to the end of the Cretaceous, with no explanation as to why, for instance, tyrannosaurs and stegosaurs would be contemporaries, much less contemporaries with saber-tooth cats and humans. (Probably the worst example of this is Harry Harrison's *West of Eden* trilogy, which not only mixed-and-matched species and genera from all across the Mesozoic, but left them in stasis for 65 million years afterward. Somehow, though, humans, mammoths, and saber-tooths were able to develop in North America after mammals larger than mice had become extinct elsewhere.) To come across this sort of strange mix, which resembles a collection of prepackaged toy dinosaurs than a viable ecosystem, one has to assume that the lost world isn't quite as isolated as was believed. If it were, the introduction of new species, no matter how seemingly innocuous, could have devastating ramifications.

The threat against a lost world might be as massive as mammalian predators, or it may be as meek as grass. Grasses didn't evolve until after the K-T extinction, and the main forms of ground cover throughout most of the Mesozoic were mosses. Even by the end of the Cretaceous, the most common form of ground cover in North America consisted of bushes closely related to the raspberry. The evolution of grass directly affected the development of many groups of mammals, including horses and humans, but no dinosaur had seen a blade of grass, and none had the adaptations necessary to deal with eating it.

Let's say that our lost world was a cross-section of life in the Cretaceous before it became isolated from the rest of the planet: the plants are mainly flowering plants like today's cottonwoods, dogwoods, and raspberries, with relics similar to the ginkgo or New Zealand's kauri pine throughout the mix. A high-flying bird accidentally drops a grass seed stuck to a leg feather into the lost valley, and that seed germinates. Within a very short time, the valley is covered with grass in every available area, choking out the native mosses and bushes and taking nutrients from other plants. If the plants affected are food plants for the herbivorous dinosaurs, the dinosaurs starve unless they independently developed adaptations that allow them to eat grass. For this argument, let's say that the lost world has hadrosaurs (better known as duckbilled dinosaurs), which are able to adapt to eating grass, which is notoriously nutrient-poor and very tough. Every other herbivorous dinosaur starves to death, leaving nothing but hadrosaurs in our little world. The hadrosaurs begin to radiate out and fill all of the old niches, until the next catastrophe occurs.

If grass can cause these problems, imagine what could happen to a lost world if aggressive predators or omnivores showed up. Until about three million years ago, South America was an island continent, and its fauna was drastically different than that today. At the time, the herbivores were all placental mammals, but the predators were marsupials called borhyaenids that roughly resembled the Tasmanian devil (epitomized by their most famous member, the "marsupial sabertooth" *Thylacosmilus*) and gigantic flightless birds called phoruschids. When what is now Panama connected North and South America, a progression of North American animals migrated into South America and wreaked untold havoc. Some South American animals reciprocated: the ground sloths, the armadillos (including the giant herbivorous glyptodonts, heavily armored armadillos the size of a Volkswagen Bug), the Virginia opossum (North America's only living marsupial) and porcupines, but not much else. Within a million years, the borhyaenids were extinct, the indigenous herbivores wiped out, the phoruschids reduced to one species that migrated to North America, and all of their niches replaced with naturalized immigrants from North America. Jaguars, ocelots, peccaries, and camels did very well in South America, and left no descendants of their competition.

Under normal circumstances, dinosaurs might have been able to hold their own against mammals in close quarters. Based on studies of nesting sites and population densities, dinosaurs kept dominion over Earth for so long not because of their size, but because of their fecundity. An elephant requires nearly two years of gestation to produce one baby, while an elephant-sized dinosaur could have laid up to 100 eggs a year in those two years. Saltwater and Nile crocodiles demonstrate this as well. Slow-breeding dinosaur species, though, would have been doomed: if (and there's absolutely no basis for this summation, so take this as a hypothesis) sauropods produced one nest of eggs every two to four years, that nest contained ten eggs on average, and the mortality rate of baby sauropods rated around 70 percent (pretty light, compared to crocodile and alligator mortality), losing an additional two babies per nest per year would wipe out the species. Even if they squeaked by, a good catastrophe such as a volcanic eruption or disease could drop the population down to a level where it could never recover.

Now it's possible to get an ecosystem full of mammals, reptiles, and birds that became extinct elsewhere: Australia managed to pull that off for millions of years. Australia even managed to get new invaders that adapted to the conditions and sent life on new directions: both monitor lizards and rodents reached Australia approximately 20 million years ago, and monitors are now the main terrestrial predators on the continent after snakes. The effects of humans on an ecosystem, though, still aren't fully understood, but the aftermath is well documented.

Now it must be said that early man did not set out on a pogrom to destroy animal and plant species, but man's population growth and use of tools meant disaster for numerous Ice Age species. Many species, such as mammoths, North American horses, and North American camels were already highly stressed by the sudden end of the last glacial period (some estimates suggest that the glacial caps may have melted in as little as twenty to fifty years), and human hunting may have accelerated their decline. In many other cases, though, human hunting and habitat destruction led to the annihilation of much of the megafauna of the planet in as little as 1000 years. Merely by hunting more than could be replaced by normal reproduction, man probably eradicated the mastodons, mammoths, ground sloths, horses, and camels of North America. (Today's North American horses were introduced by Spanish explorers during the Sixteenth Century, and their wild descendants recolonized the old habitats quite nicely.) In Europe and

Asia, the same happened with the mammoths, the wooly rhinoceros, the English hippopotamus, and the cave bear. In Australia, the arrival of man coincided with the disappearance of many of its indigenous species: the diprotodonts, the short-faced kangaroo, the monitor *Megalania* (imagine a Komodo dragon the size of a grizzly bear), the "marsupial lion" *Thylacoleo*, and a host of others. By inadvertent overhunting, man also doomed the big predators: a population crash among the mammoths probably led to the starvation of the saber-toothed cats in North America, and the same thing probably happened to *Megalania* and *Thylacoleo* after the diprotodonts died.

The final proof of the effect of man upon large fauna happened when man first discovered New Zealand. As said before, all of the large animals on the islands were birds: by the time the islands were first discovered by Dutch explorers in the 1640s, the moas were probably all gone, as were the giant eagles that fed upon them. The eagles were a special case: since they normally hunted birds that stood between one and four meters tall, they probably looked at the ancestral Maori as nothing more than funny-shaped moas, and their extinction was probably a matter of justifiable self-defense. Either way, though, the only moas on the islands by the time Captain James Cook circumnavigated the islands in 1769 were probably fossils. One moa skeleton is highly controversial because it seems to show evidence of having been butchered with metal knives, thus suggesting that it died after Europeans started trading steel knives and axes with the Maori, and a few residents still claim to see live moas from time to time, but no incontrovertible evidence exists to show that the moa lived to see the European colonization of New Zealand.

In a dinosaur-filled lost world invaded by humans, one of two things would happen. The first possibility is that the humans would be eaten by the current residents. (Interestingly, while science fiction is full of stories of tyrannosaurs and other large predators chasing, attacking, and eating humans, seemingly nobody considered the threat of smaller predators such as the dromaeosaurs until David Drake's novella "Time Safari" and Harry Adam Knight's novel *Carnosaur*. To humans moving into a lost valley, though, the smaller predators would have been much more dangerous than the big predators: consider the likelihood of being attacked by a wolf or wolf pack in Nineteenth Century North America compared to encountering a grizzly.) However, the use of tools and fire could compensate for a lack of natural armament, and if this happened, the humans would rapidly take over.

The first real damage would hit the big predators. Humans naturally look at any animal big enough to eat a full-grown man both as a threat and as a competitor, so picture hunting parties that went out of their way to kill juvenile carnosaurs before they became a threat, or raid nesting sites to destroy eggs before they hatched. Even the full-grown predators would be susceptible to traps or poison, and as they became rare, some enterprising St. George wannabe would always try to head out to collect a trophy of the biggest predator around. At the same time, as the human population increased, the sources of easy meat from herbivorous dinosaurs would disappear, and all of the large dinosaurs would be gone in as little as 100 years in a smallish lost valley. As they declined, the smaller dinosaurs would become targets, and as they disappeared, the remaining human population would either start domesticating them or face starvation. By the time any explorer from outside found that valley, the resident dinosaur population would consist of bones and artifacts, and zoologists would regret not getting there sooner.

Sadly, in a day of global positioning satellites and spy planes, the likelihood of a large population of previously unknown animals surviving anywhere is increasingly remote. A few survivors, comparable to the last few members of the Java rhinoceros recently discovered in Vietnam or the coelacanths of Indonesia, may pop up, but if dinosaurs still lived anywhere on the planet, we'd have heard about it by now. Even so, the stories of Edward Challenger still stir those who dream of a lost world somewhere in the wilds of South America, Africa, or Antarctica. The problem is that any dinosaurs in one would probably end up like the dinosaurs in Greg Bear's *Dinosaur Summer*, where the world went crazy for dinosaurs and then soon became bored with them as zoos and circuses became full of temperamental, potentially dangerous beasts. Besides, isn't the real thrill in the imagining?

—*Revolution SF, February 2002*

Postscript: This essay was an orphan from Event Horizon, *having been finished shortly before its hiatus. Two years later, it saw print in* Revolution SF, *and it became one of my last published articles before I quit writing.*

"Applied Genesis, Volume 1: The Problems With Cloning Dinosaurs And Other Animals Of The Distant Past"

In the past few years, SF stories about the advantages and disadvantages of genetic engineering have proliferated almost as well as conjectures about real applications of genetic science. At the same time writers consider the possibilities of manipulating DNA to create new life forms, legal battles go on about the same thing: do companies have the right to patent life forms? Do they have the right to release altered life forms, whether they be animal, vegetable, or protist, into Earth's ecosystems without studying the effects? And do individuals have the right to alter life forms in the first place?

The legal and ethical ramifications have produced some interesting quandaries. One group added pig genes to strawberries to improve their transportability: does this addition break Muslim and Jewish dietary practices forbidding the eating of pork? And what other problems might surface in the pursuit of "improved" life forms?

In SF, at least, the most popular possibility with this new technology lies in the ability to re-create extinct life forms through rebuilt DNA. This isn't a new idea, but it really reached the public through the publication of Michael Crichton's book *Jurassic Park* in 1990. Suddenly, editors want stories looking at the possibilities and writers are submitting them, mostly because the other two ways of meeting dinosaurs (time travel and the exploration of "lost worlds") are so unlikely. Through the magic of DNA manipulation, readers of these stories might actually meet real dinosaurs in their lifetimes.

But how easy is this? Most writers merely mention extracting fossil DNA and using it to clone extinct beasties, a process comparable to getting a ton of steel, a tank of gasoline, and four tires and blithely building a car. In actuality, cloning a dinosaur would be comparable to cloning a cow from a packet of lime Jell-O: it's possible, but will the cow actually work like a real one? This is the question this essay hopes to answer.

An Extremely Short Primer on Genetics

To understand the problems with cloning a dinosaur, one needs to have a little understanding of genetics and cellular structures. Those having taken a college biology course can leave the room and take a break: I won't be long.

The underlying base to terrestrial biology is deoxyribonucleic acid, or DNA.

DNA has a singular ability to reproduce itself from compounds found in its vicinity, although it needs several unique enzymes to catalyze these reactions, and it dictates the workings of the cell it occupies. Viruses are nothing more than DNA in a protein sheath: viruses penetrate the wall of a cell and inject their DNA, making the invaded cell do nothing but replicate more viruses, and the new viruses escape when nutrients run out and the cell has nothing left.

(Backtracking slightly, maybe I should explain the workings of a cell. For the purposes of this essay, we will ignore many of the specialized structures in the cell, and focus on those directly influenced by DNA replication. Each cell is an independent entity of sorts, each containing a nucleus, which contains its basic DNA; protoplasm, which supports the nucleus; and a cell wall, which allows nutrients and water to enter while trying to keep harmful substances, waste products, and attacking viruses and other predators out. Two major forms of cell exist: the prokaryotic cell, which is used by bacteria, and the eukaryotic cell, which is used by all known multicellular life, including us. The eukaryotic cell allows an advanced form of sexual reproduction, in which two cells combine half of a DNA strand, producing an offspring which contains the traits of both parents.

(Eukaryotic cells contain one more vital element: the mitochondrion, which converts nutrients into usable energy for the cell. Standing theory holds that the mitochondria once were free-ranging cells, but they combined with eukaryotic cells in an act of symbiosis: mitochondria have their own DNA, reproduce in the same way as a normal cell, and are maternally inherited. Remember this: it will be important later in the essay.)

Because of the way DNA replicates itself, it has a tendency to goof up every once in a while and change itself slightly; radiation helps this process (one of the reasons pregnant women are encouraged to stay away from X-ray sources), but what really causes variations is recombination events, when the DNA molecule changes itself, which are frequent and sometimes quite lengthy. The change is called a mutation, and it's both bad and good. Few mutations are favorable (most cause the death of the mutant in a very short time, and others, such as albinism, are slightly slower-acting death sentences), but the variety of terrestrial life would be impossible without them. Sex plays a major role in mutations, if all life reproduced parthogenically (that is, without a sexual partner), then mutations would pop up, but much more slowly, and they would need a considerable amount of time before the mutants became a major element of the local population. With sexual reproduction, if one or both parents have the potential for a particular mutation, then the child has a much higher chance of manifesting it, and it may carry the trait for this mutation and pass it on for generations before it actually manifests itself. Many forms of cancer are similar phenomena: for reasons not well understood, the DNA goes haywire, with genes called oncogenes causing nearby cells to become infected with the changed DNA, ultimately leading to death of the cell or organism.

Now, a typical DNA molecule is very long (a typical DNA molecule varies with the organism, with the human length being about four feet), and each of the "rungs" on the helix structure (composed of the amino acids adenine, thymine, cytosine, and guanine, but you should have known that already) corresponds to an area which produces a particular protein. Each of these units is called a gene, and the DNA itself is organized into structures known as chromosomes. Each gene dictates a certain trait, such as blonde hair or flippers, and in a particular species, these genes may be found in certain chromosomes. The whole packet of genes is known as a genome, and the genome is quite literally the building plan for an organism.

Still with me? Good. Now, the further up the evolutionary ladder, tree, or bush (depending on what analogy meets your favor) one goes, the more genes an organism has. Or so it works in theory. Humans have 48 chromosomes, while red foxes have 34. If members of two species with the same number of chromosomes mate, the offspring is called a hybrid, which may or may not have the ability to bear offspring of its own. Mules are the offspring of horses and asses, for example, and mules are completely sterile. The mating of species without the same number of chromosomes produces nothing, as the DNA doesn't match evenly, the reason we don't see human-cow and human-sheep hybrids in hellholes like Tupelo, Mississippi and Lewisville, Texas.

Now what makes the chromosomes interesting is that the further up the evolutionary tree, the more genes that exist to suppress traits that ancestors needed. For instance, these suppressor genes occasionally disappear in the replication process at conception, which allows us three-toed horses. The South American hoatzin is a normal-seeming bird as an adult, but its hatchlings possess three-clawed fingers which allow them to climb trees to escape predators, a legacy of their dinosaurian ancestry. These suppressor genes sometimes fail for humans as well, causing such traits as fur, short tails, or gill slits to manifest themselves. Most of the DNA in any strand is used for cell replication; very little variation exists between, say, humans and Komodo dragons, but the variation that exists allows the differences.

Okay, this is the extremely simplified version of cellular function, and anyone interested further should check out any textbook on molecular biology. Now we get to the meat of this article.

Because DNA is such a complex molecule, one can't just bump a few amino acids together and create a life form; they need some order, or they don't work. To determine the order in which the genes go, molecular geneticists use a process known as sequencing, in which (in its most popular form) DNA strands are separated by alkaline denaturization, primers (either random or specially constructed) are annealed to those strands, and an enzyme then replicates the DNA using a radiolabeled amino acid. Then a gel bed to contain this is made and an autoradiograph is done, at which point the actual sequence of the bases (the adenine, thymine, cytosine, and guanine again) is readable in X-ray film. Again, this is an incredibly simplified version; the process is much more complicated and horrendously expensive.

Now, for the sake of argument, let's say we want to re-create an extinct animal. Let's select a wooly mammoth: it's big, impressive, and readily accessible. Frozen chunks of mammoth are found to this day in Siberia, where the permafrost preserves the flesh in good (in some cases, technically edible) condition. Furthermore, due to palaeontological research, we know what it ate, how it acted, and its relationship to modern elephants. If we wanted, we could even let the resultant mammoths loose in Alaska and Canada to wander with the musk-oxen.

This almost happened: back in the 1970s, Russian biologists planned to take a complete cell nucleus from a frozen baby mammoth named Dima and inject it into the egg cell of an Indian elephant. The injected cell would then be implanted in a female elephant and the resultant baby mammoth brought to term. Unfortunately, Dima's cells were too badly damaged by ice crystals to find an intact nucleus, and the researchers dropped their plans. The basic process, when done correctly, is called cloning, and it's much simpler to talk about than to implement. Some organisms do it naturally (every time you take an aloe or jade plant leaf and repot it, you're cloning the original plant), but cloning of mammals didn't happen until recently, and nobody has tried to clone birds or reptiles so far.

Okay, so we can't find a complete nucleus, but we do have tons and tons of mammoth flesh, skin, hair, and bones. This is where the sequencing comes in. After extracting the necessary DNA, it's sequenced and charted, and the resultant mapping allows us to know what mammoth DNA, genes, and chromosomes look like. We can then compare those genes to those in a living elephant (Indian elephants are the closest living relatives to the wooly mammoth) and decide where the differences lie. Then, with the appropriate equipment (and still again, I'm simplifying this horribly to keep from making a book of this essay), we rebuild the mammoth DNA and inject it into the host ovum.

Sounds simple? Wrong. Unlike creating computer programs (which is essentially what a DNA molecule does: it acts as the program for a construction sequence), it's very hard to tell what may go wrong when bioengineering organisms. A series of genes may be incorrectly placed or accidentally deleted due to a lack of evidence (and the sequencing is not 100 percent accurate either, which is the reason more and more courtrooms disallow their use in identifying murder and rape suspects) and the poor geneticists end up with a creature that incidentally resembles a mammoth. Therefore, one series of sequencing isn't enough, so let's run through the task twice more in order to make sure we did everything right.

Now we get to real problems. By way of example, the human genome is so complex that it cannot be handled by human operators: computers are absolutely necessary, both for the replication and the translation of DNA. This is why the much-vaunted Human Genome Project is taking so long: even with Cray supercomputers, the researchers expect to finish sometime within the next five to fifteen years, and this is with a creature that has more than five billion living examples scurrying across the face of the planet. Anyone trying extinct animals had better have a lot of idle time to waste on such a project.

Let's assume that the next 20 years bring unprecedented advances in the ability to manipulate DNA. It's now 2014, and we want to build a dinosaur.

Firstly, we'd better work on living animals for a good while, and then on extinct animals that left lots of traces, because we're going to need all the practice we can get. We'll start out with reptiles and birds, and then work our way up to replicating passenger pigeons, great auks, and Steller's sea cows. They didn't die off too long ago, so their DNA is still pretty much intact in feathers, hides, and bones. Let's bring back the mammoths, and the long-horned bison, and the giant ground sloths for good measure: in one way, the last Ice Age was very good for us, leaving us all of these freebies in frozen and dried flesh and skin. And then let's prepare to be extremely disappointed.

We now have two major problems to face before we go on. Some molecular biologists theorize that fossil DNA might be found that dates back to the development of multicellular life, some 600 million years ago, but this is like physicists theorizing possible ways to surpass the speed of light. It may be possible, but it's awfully unlikely. As of this writing, the oldest extracted DNA comes from a bee and a termite, both trapped in amber (fossilized tree sap), and from magnolia leaves from a singular fossil bed in Idaho (the leaves fell into an extremely stagnant pond and soon became covered in mud; when split, the rock reveals leaves that still remain green, even though they rapidly oxidize when exposed to air), all dating to about 30 million years ago. To get dinosaur DNA, we'd have to extract it from fossils some three to seven times older, depending upon the dinosaur. If we wanted *Tyrannosaurus*, we'd need the technology to extract DNA from 65-million-year-old bones, but if we wanted a *big* dinosaur, we'd have to go back about 150 million years. That's a long way from 30 million: the great apes split off from the monkeys about then, and our closest known relative was a little fellow called *Proconsul*.

Since we're throwing around assumptions, let's assume we want a *Seismosaurus*, one of the biggest of the sauropods (long-necked dinosaurs, also known as brontosaurs) and definitely the largest known animal on the planet, with an estimated length of 150 feet. Furthermore, let's assume we found a whole burial ground of the damn things, so we don't have to destroy the only known skeleton to get our DNA. Now what do we do?

Well, first, we start grinding up bones, and flushing out the proteins we need. Proteins are not DNA: DNA is the template for the construction of proteins by the cell, but we can sequence them using a process called reverse sequencing. It gives us only an approximation of the DNA sequence, due to the redundancy of the genetic code, but it's a start, and it'll come in extremely handy when we go to synthesizing our DNA strands. If we actually find some DNA in those bones, so much the better, but we're still going to need lots and lots of bone and lots of time to flush the proteins and DNA out of them, so while we have a team of Bachelor's degrees looking for fragments and logging them into our computer, let's look for other sources of DNA.

If we're looking for complete bodies, say frozen in ice, we're shit out of luck. The oldest ice fields on the planet date back a full 400,000 years, and the seismosaurs throve in a period when ice *might* have formed at the poles in winter. The temperature on Earth averaged 26° F warmer than today, and Antarctica didn't exist where it currently is, so cold ocean currents couldn't swirl around a trapped southern continent and bring down the temperature of the whole planet. Mummification won't work either, because a creature that big would become allosaur food long before its body had a chance to dry out that completely. Also, the few known "dinosaur mummies" don't have a scrap of real skin on them. The skin was replaced, bit by bit, with dissolved minerals, and it's now about as organic as a block of granite. But we can check anyway, if you insist.

We do have two other options. Much has been made about amber, that fossilized tree sap I mentioned earlier. Pine trees date back to the seismosaurs' heyday, and in fact were likely food sources for them and other sauropods. When injured, pine trees leak lots of sap, which occasionally traps small animals, such as insects, spiders, and even small lizards and frogs, and the sap tends to outlast the tree. In the Baltic Peninsula, amber mining is a major industry, and a piece containing animals can command interesting prices. Michael Crichton made quite a deal about hunting down amber with biting insects in it and extracting DNA from the remains of their meals, which may have been dinosaur blood, but not only is it not certain that the victim of such flies was a dinosaur, but it's not likely that we're going to find amber from the period and place we need. The best-known dinosaurs are from North America, including *Seismosaurus*; Baltic amber would contain insects that fed on Baltic dinosaurs, and unless *Seismosaurus* also ranged through Russia, we're in tough shape. We're going to need amber from North America, from about the right area and the right time, and a whole lot of luck in finding a biting animal entrapped therein. The trapped animals are rare enough, and we'd better have lots of money to buy pieces from collectors if we find ones to our liking. And if they contain fossil blood from early mammals or crocodiles, well, them's the breaks, ain't they?

(I might also add that Crichton's idea about using amber isn't new, although quite a few book reviewers, myself included, thought it was. A tip of the hat to Gregory Benford, who pointed this out.)

Since we're making so many assumptions about our seismosaur that we could rebuild Windsor Castle were they bricks, let's assume we luck out and get a big relative of the horsefly that bored through seismosaur hide, took a big drink of seismosaur blood, and then landed on a glob of pine sap while cleaning itself and was covered with richly flowing sap. Let's assume that the hardening sap didn't crack and allow any oxygen in, and let's assume that the amber containing this big fly got into our sweaty little hands at the same time we were grinding up those bones. Better yet, assume we found some seismosaur coproliths (coproliths are fossilized feces, and seismosaur coproliths would give whole new meaning to the expression "What a load of shit") and were able to extract some usable DNA from them. (This is extremely unlikely but possible, were a few cells from the lining of the intestine to survive the bacteria of the gut. Colonic bleeding, say from hemorrhoids or colonic cancer, might help the odds a bit, but it's still unlikely.) We carefully drill a hole through the amber to our fly, poke around in his tummy with a needle, break off what we assume was his last meal (in 150 million years, while his outside looks okay, the inside is all dried up and crumbly), and sequence the blood. If what we get is seismosaur blood, we add the sequencing information to the other pieces of seismosaur genome we've been able to construct from the coproliths and the bones, and build the DNA to our specs.

Now we come to one last hurdle, one I've saved for last to illustrate one of the biggest problems with sequencing fossil DNA. I already pointed out the problems with sequencing, and I mentioned the problems with DNA that was battered, split by heat and weather, and otherwise in little fragments. What I left out is that, for unknown reasons, nuclear DNA doesn't preserve very well. The DNA from those insects and magnolia leaves was mitochondiral DNA, which is quite different. If we didn't know any better, we'd sequence and build our DNA, and become the proud parents of a spanking new seismosaur mitochondrion. We're going to need that mitochondrion later (and that's another point Crichton and associates forgot; you can't run a eukaryotic cell without one), but we can't clone a dinosaur from it.

All is not lost, though. As I mentioned earlier, mitochondria are really houseguests in the eukaryotic cell, but they mutate, too. It's possible to compare the mitochondrial DNA of two species and determine if they are related based on the similarities in the mitochondria. With our seismosaur, mitochondrial studies would settle once and for all the arguments as to whether birds are dinosaur descendants, and even allow us to ascertain where the seismosaurs belonged in classification systems such as cladistics. Were we to sequence enough dinosaurs, we could discover quite a bit more about relationships, and this might be reason enough to do it in the first place.

Actually, it's already been done, but with humans. *Science* (September 1992) published a report about a team that developed a way to help identify skeletal human remains using traces of mitochondrial DNA in tooth canals and bones, thus helping to identify accident and murder victims if dental records didn't match and no other forms of identification existed. Also, mitochondrial studies allowed one anthropological team to discover "Eve," the early human from which all living humans descended. The jury is still out on both of these developments, but the possibilities are fascinating.

The New Zoo Revue

Now that we've made enough assumption bricks to make a six-lane freeway to Alpha Centauri, let's assume further that we succeeded in getting nuclear DNA, assembling two full strands and placing it in reptilian or avian host ova, and bringing the young zygote to full term, whereupon it hatches and peeks out into a world 150 million years older than the one its kind lived in. Hurry up: I want to get to the Andromeda Galaxy by lunch time.

Firstly, we're going to have to learn how to make an amniotic egg in the lab. Seismosaurs were probably egg layers, although noted palaeontological gadfly Robert T. Bakker surmises that sauropods gave live birth (in reptiles, the eggs are retained in the body without benefit of the mother offering nourishment to the embryo; this is called being ovoviviparous. Rattlesnakes and garter snakes are ovoviviparous, as opposed to the oviparous box turtle and the viviparous woodchuck. Seismosaurs may have been ovoviviparous, but without good fossils, it's hard to be certain), so we have to build an egg to meet the standards of a growing seismosaur embryo. We'll have to learn the constitution of seismosaur yolk, the main food source for our growing boy, as well as to build a functioning allantois, the waste removal structure in the egg. We'll have to use real eggshell as opposed to Crichton's plastic ones, as the embryo will depend upon the calcium in the shell to grow strong teeth and bones, and we'll have to be extremely careful about eggshell thickness. Too thin, and the egg breaks under its own weight; too thick, and the hatchling can't break the shell at birth. We'll have it easier after we have some practice, but it's still a tough proposition. Replicating egg layers is much harder than replicating creatures that bear live young.

We're going to have problems, just because of what it is. Seismosaurs were little more than feeding machines. Whether one accepts the theories supporting endothermy or exothermy in dinosaurs, our charge is going to eat at an outrageous rate. We're slightly better off if seismosaurs hatched from a football-sized egg and were cold-blooded; Bakker surmises that all sauropods were warm-blooded and gave live birth. This gives us a spectrum between a baby the size of a cat and able to convert as much as 25 percent of its feed to body weight (about the average for iguanas, a good model for coldblooded herbivores) to a 100-pound baby able to convert maybe 2 to 3 percent of its forage to body weight (using an elephant for a model this time). One way or another, we're going to need lots of food for Junior. If he's cold-blooded and kept warm, he'll grow at about the same rate as a warmblood allowed to control his own temperature, which means he's going to double his weight anywhere from every three days to every month. We won't know until we observe him: I once had a savannah monitor that grew from five inches to three feet in a year, merely by keeping him warm and stuffing lots of high-protein food down his gullet, and if Junior keeps up that kind of growth, we'll be busy feeding him. If he grows at avian levels of growth, we'll probably collapse from having to move truckloads of forage day in and day out.

Another problem lies with the forage. All of the plants living today have one defense or another to keep them from being munched down to the soil line, and a lot of them depend upon subtle poisons that herbivores cannot digest. Millions of years of evolution offered herbivores better enzymes and better processing techniques to take out those poisons, but occasionally the genes don't manifest themselves, which is why George Bush doesn't like broccoli: he can't digest it, and his body signals that it can't as a yucky taste. Our seismosaur probably won't be able to eat any flowering plant, as they didn't exist when his kind last roamed, and it's pretty unlikely he'd be able to handle contemporary redwoods and jack pines, either. Either we get him used to eating kibble, and lots of it, or he'll starve. While we're at it, let's make certain we immunize him from nearly everything: we've had 150 million years of bacterial, fungal, and viral evolution, too, and we'd have blown billions of dollars on a dinosaur that dies from athlete's foot.

We've been worrying about Junior's physical state; now we'll have to worry about his mental state. Palaeontological evidence shows that most dinosaurs were hopelessly social, and all of the big brontosaurs apparently formed herds with the babies in the center to protect them from the depredations of *Allosaurus*, *Ceratosaurus*, and *Epanterias*, three extremely nasty and extremely big predators wandering the same floodplains *Seismosaurus* favored. As we know from human and animal research, babies from social species deprived of contact with members of their species develop in weird ways. Wrens raised by humans don't sing like their parents: they sing a garbled version, proving that while instinct gives the basic template for bird songs, the nuance is learned. Gorillas and pandas raised in captivity alone have no grasp as how to care for their young, and humans raised without contact at an early age become stone sociopaths, found in either jail or multimedia science fiction conventions. We'd better hire some animal behaviorists, and quickly, just in case we don't recognize dangerous tendencies in time. And while we're at it, let's breed some playmates for Junior, so he won't be completely alone. His new friends might not be experienced, either, but they're a lot closer to his worldview than those funny dun-colored two-legs who pick and prod at him.

As this demonstration shows, surmisals such as Crichton's *Jurassic Park* and Gregory Benford's "Shakers of the Earth" fall through very quickly, because who in their Technicolor mind is going to finance this? It's not just the idea of blowing $10 billion on the replication and the raising, but on the idea that this money will never be earned back. No zoo or preservation park could ever get that kind of money from tourism; Disneyworld doesn't make that kind of money, and it has films, television programs, and lots of rides to fall back on. Having dinosaurs in the here-and-now might be nice, but we either start charging about a hundred grand a head for every person who comes through the door or we close up shop.

With this in mind, why should we clone dinosaurs? Scientific curiosity is a good one, but scientific curiosity won't pay the bills. Our space program depends upon government assistance for everything, and its scientific payback is immense: only a fool would assert that the Apollo, Viking, and Voyager missions didn't kindle some of humanity's adventuring spirit and curiosity, and I for one heartily look forward to the Galileo probe sending back data. However, I doubt any government, no matter how rich, is going to throw away the billions necessary to stock a wildlife preserve with saurians without getting some payback. Even the

Superconducting Supercollider, theoretically one of the best tools for understanding subatomic physics available (damn pity it's named after Ronald Reagan, a move comparable to starting the Madalyn Murray O'Hair Institute for Biblical Studies), offered lots of free pork to Texans living around its construction site. The folks in Waxahatchie and Avalon don't give a damn about science; all they want is government money, and a dinosaur preserve won't offer that same money.

So let's consider other reasons. Since I now want a freeway to the next pulsar, let's say that McDonald's wants to explore the possibility of putting dinosaur meat in its burgers. McDonald's might be able to finance this little venture, if it liquidated most of its holdings, so we go to work planning to turn Junior into Seismosaur McNuggets. After all, if dinosaur meat is similar to bird flesh, it'll be a lot healthier than beef or pork, right?

Maybe, but it won't be more efficient. Carnivorism has a hefty price when we're talking dinosaur. To simplify things immeasurably, a bundle of wheat needs ten weeks of sun to reach maturity. It then gets eaten, along with other bundles of wheat, but a herbivore with one metabolism or another. As I pointed out earlier, an iguana is able to convert about 25 percent of its food into body weight due to its being cold-blooded. It isn't wasting precious calories trying to keep warm, so as long as it stays warm, it's happy. A steer not only has an extremely inefficient digestive system, but it's warmblooded, so only 2 to 5 percent of its feed becomes USDA prime sirloin. A steer and a steer-sized iguana may reach slaughter weight at the same time, but the iguana needs only one-tenth of the food to do so. This is about the only reason why human vegetarianism is a good idea, aside from trying to keep from accumulating toxins through the food chain: cattle eat too much for what they produce, and most other mammalian food sources aren't much better, aside from the Irish, if Jonathan Swift is to be trusted.

Either way, we're in trouble with Junior. If he's cold-blooded, he's still going to eat a good three tons of forage every day at full body weight, and he might eat as much as 12 tons a day if he's an endotherm. Let's say it takes three years for Junior to reach sexual maturity (cattle take two); that works out to a staggering 13,110 tons of Purina Seismosaur Chow that goes into Junior's gullet before McDonald's slams a bullet into his brain and tries to bleed him. For a mere 100 tons of undressed meat (figure anywhere from 50 to 60 tons dressed: Junior's bones and viscera are going to be heavy), we've just cost McDonald's a hell of a lot of money. And for them to realize a profit sometime within the next billion years, we'd need to give McDonald's a whole herd of seismosaurs.

Of course, we could mess with smaller dinosaurs, but we'd still have the same problems with replicating and raising them, and we'd have the same grief with financing. Anyone wanting dinosaurs would have to be both philanthropic and obscenely rich, and even with the advances to be found in 2014, the payback would be utterly impractical for any corporation or government agency to handle. We're right back where we started.

Not exactly. We may not be able to replicate dinosaurs in actuality, but the knowledge we gain by building the DNA would be invaluable. Let's look at it this way.

For starters, I mentioned the value of using sequencing to ascertain relationships between dinosaurs and contemporary animals. Not only could we answer the questions about dinosaur-bird relationships, but we could determine approximately how long ago birds split from the dinosaurian stock, and what relationships dinosaurs had with their only living archosaurian relatives, the crocodilians. Crocodiles are almost-dinosaurs: they have a semierect stance, they possess a four-chambered heart, and they show maternal care for their young. By comparing DNA strands between crocodilians and dinosaurs, we might be able to ascertain when the two groups diverged a bit more soundly than by using just fossil evidence, and if dinosaurs were warm-blooded, when they became so. One way or another, intact dinosaur DNA would solve many questions.

Okay, so this is all fine and good, but it isn't going to give us real dinosaurs to display in zoos and wildlife parks, and all of the previous complaints about the problems with replication aren't going to change the minds of those who want living dinosaurs. Forget the problems with disease, feeding, or the (very slight) chance that some might escape. (Not that we have such a worry about the big ones, anyway: ol' *T. Rex* may have been the biggest predator known, but a couple of LAW rockets would turn its thoracic cavity into about two tons of hamburger and tripe, mixed with bone splinters and explosive residue. Yummy.) We still need to see if we can bring them back alive.

Well, we can, and without the necessity of terraforming a whole planet just to make optimum living conditions for our charges, which is what we'd have to do to do this right. All it takes is a bit more computer power than what we'd have to use to replicate them in the flesh.

A lot has been written about the wonders of virtual reality lately, almost as much as on the replication of extinct beasts, and the supporters fall into two distinct camps. The first crew, the *Mondo 2000* bunch, are all gung ho about hooking themselves up and living out their fantasies in cyberspace, while the second crew, the *bOING bOING* gaggle, support a bit more moderation. Virtual reality to them is fine and good for teaching and training, as well as experimentation with consciousness expansion without chemical side effects, but they note that it's all too easy to crawl into one's belly button and forget the real world outside. This latter attitude is what we need for our dinosaurs.

With enough computational power, we could do everything we planned to do with replicated dinosaurs and then some. With the appropriate amount of work on living genomes, it should be easy to extrapolate how a dinosaur genome would act in vitro, and then extrapolate the appearance of the grown dinosaur. We already assume we have the DNA; now we see how it works, and without the horrendous cost.

With virtual reality booth/hoods/cyberjacks, the ante gets a bit bigger. A hookup into cyberspace would present "real" dinosaurs without the attendant cost that all zoos face. They don't eat, they don't try to kill the nice man who cleans their cages, they don't escape, and they don't die for exotic reasons. We can experiment with models of their assumed environment (did *Brachiosaurus* lie submerged in swamps, or did it tromp around floodplains as a true land-dweller?), see how various groups would react, and even test our theories of how they might survive in today's world. Back in the early Seventies, children's books assumed that a good-sized Kodiak bear could take on and kill a *Tyrannosaurus*; now we can test this without murdering two otherwise innocent animals.

One of my personal favorite tests would be learning possible evolutionary trends in the dinosaurs' future, had they survived the end of the Mesozoic Era. Dougal Dixon did a terrible book exploring some of the possibilities, but we'd have the power to try other permutations of the DNA. This would be a dream for chaos theorists: imagine taking a typical ecosystem and giving it a heavy dose of hyperevolution, and examining the resultant plants and animals of 30 million years later without leaving the chair. By adding what we know of changing weather patterns and continental drift, we could see if the tyrannosaurs could have survived until the present day, or what animals took their place if they didn't. This system could even simulate one of the biggest pipe dreams of the SF community: whether one branch of the predatory dinosaurs known as troodontids had the capability of developing intelligence as we know it. Canadian palaeontologist Dale Russell surmised that one such dinosaur might have evolved into a tool-user (the resultant pictures of Russell's "dinosauroid" made a big impression, especially on tabloid writers); now we can see if his theories were correct.

Of course, we don't have the capabilities to do this right now, as computer technology is about comparable to genetic technology, but twenty years of computer R&D should give us systems surpassing our expectations, and our grandchildren might have the opportunity to see real dinosaurs, even if they live in cyberspace. Where they belong.

Addendum

Quite a bit has happened since this article was originally written in early 1993, the most important being a team of molecular biologists collecting DNA from a weevil entrapped in 145-million-year-old amber. Much was made of this by the popular media, especially Universal Pictures, which used the development to hype up the release of the film version of *Jurassic Park*. Interestingly, although the team released its paper to *Nature* nearly a year before, it didn't see publication until the day before the film's release, for unknown reasons. Equally interestingly, all of the popular articles failed to point out that only one gene was extracted from that weevil, making it extremely unlikely that we're going to see prehistoric weevils (or prehistoric anything) any time soon.

In fact, *Scientific American*'s November 1993 issue wan a very interesting article entitled "Ancient DNA" by Svante Paabo, which acts as a very good layman's guide to how DNA extraction and identification works. One of the facts brought up (and regrettably omitted from this article) was the reason fossil DNA breaks up so readily: a process called autolysis causes enzymes to digest dying tissue. This process requires water, so DNA is available only from tissues that dehydrated beforehand (hair, epidermal skin, feathers, and nonbony armor plate), and even then the preservation isn't perfect. Even recently dead DNA decomposes into fragments of only 100 to 200 base pairs (those collections of thymine, adenine, cytosine, and guanine again), while fresh tissues yield fragments of more than 10,000 base pairs. The analogy of cloning a dinosaur as reading a book with missing pages and words is untrue: a closer analogy is trying to piece together a herd of cattle from a truckload of hamburger.

Dr. Paabo finishes his paper with this comment: "The resurrection of lost species will remain beyond our power. The furthest step toward 'reanimation' that one can imagine would be the isolation of a single ancient gene. Such a gene, introduced into existing species, might create animals that mimic an aspect of an extinct species. In this way, one could test the function of an ancient gene. Yet such experiments do not in any sense preserve or re-create lost species or ecosystems. Extinction is and always will be forever." So much for Steven Spielberg's whining of "This isn't science fiction; this is science eventuality."

—*Fuck Science Fiction, April 1994*

Postscript: *Well, a few developments have changed portions of this assessment, but the main thesis remains valid: we aren't going to see cloned dinosaurs in this lifetime or any other. While several teams of geneticists claim to have isolated dinosaurian proteins, that's still a long way from a complete genome. However, I'd like to go back and revise this article one of these days, if only because of so many new revisions that need to be made. As of late 1993, when this was first revised, this was pretty accurate; amazing* *how dated science articles get in a few years, isn't it?*

A few other points of interest: part of the thesis of extracting fossil dinosaur DNA from amber-encrusted insects goes to hell when one considers how little Mesozoic amber exists. The two main amber-producing regions, the Baltic Sea area and the Dominican Republic, both produce amber that's about 30 million years too young. While Mexico recently started exporting amber that's the right age, very few of the insects in it are the biting insects sought. However, one might be able to replicate extinct plants from these herbivores.

And for the record, this essay was written for Science Fiction Eye *as a response to the godawful Gregory Benford short story "Shakers of the Earth"; after Steve Brown sat on it for nearly a year, I sent it in to Chris DeVito at* Fuck Science Fiction. *Interestingly, nearly two years after this essay first appeared in* Fuck SF, *Michael Crichton added the problems with socialization to his sequel to* Jurassic Park, The Lost World. *Funny; the dinosaurs in the original didn't seem to have any problems with socializing then...*

"Anarchy and Palaeontology: Two Great Things That Go Great Together"

A notice to the youth of today: if you really want to aggravate your parents, don't pierce body parts or perform new atrocities with your hair. Merely tell them you want to become a palaeontologist when you grow up. If they don't have immediate heart attacks, they'll disown you. It worked for me.

America's anti-intellectual stance has finally paid off: we now have a new generation who consider science to be a worthy interest just because everyone else shuns it. The local coffeehouse has just about as many Stephen Hawking proponents as fans of the Dead Kennedys, and chaos theory is a new growth industry among gonzo graphics artists and T-shirt illustrators. However, the true sign of being outré is having an interest in and knowledge of palaeontology, thanks to the parents, teachers, and employers who dumped on it for years. No longer marred by the traditional view of it being a nerd science, palaeo students are just as likely to wear Butthole Surfers shirts and motorcycle leathers as polyester short-sleeves and nylon windbreakers.

The best example of this is dinosaurology: while the young hellraiser of the 1970s was content with tattoos of Harley Davidson logos and ribald slogans, the anarchist of today is more likely to have a *Tyrannosaurus* on his/her chest. An artist acquaintance of mine had the incredible luck to discover one of the youngest ichthyosaur fossils known in a stream bed near Dallas; he celebrated by having an ichthyosaur tattoo drawn on his arm. Similarly, dinosaur designs in jewelry, skateboard art, and posters, while not overrunning the traditional rock 'n' roll versions, are welcomed as a sign that the individual wearing or displaying them is not a business major from Southern Methodist University.

The explanation for this shift among the avant garde? Well, the well-documented proficiency of dinosaurs and other ancient life among the young has some bearing, as most of these characters brag about never having left childhood (this author counts himself among them), but more may figure into it. For most of our lives, we hear the same refrain from our parents: "We don't care what you do with your life; just don't pick something that shames us, makes you bail us out of jail every other week, or leaves you unable to make a healthy living. And we'll hold you to it."

Well, to the child who wishes to spite said parents, an interest in palaeo offers infinite possibilities. While the careers of lawyer and crack dealer hold similar loathing among parents, they also offer the opportunity to amass considerable money. The only difference between a starving palaeo student and a starving art student is a much less pretentious attitude and a knowledge of Latin, and film studies are no fun unless the professor gives an overview of Ray Harryhausen. Finally, getting the much-purloined degree not only offers the new graduate an opportunity to experience severe suffering and starvation for his/her discipline, but it offers that last touch of shame: not only do they have to admit their child's chosen profession, but they have to endure the constant questions of "Palaeo-whatzit?"

Even for those who never came close to getting that degree, an interest in palaeo makes the individual stand out. Anyone between the ages of 13 and 25 can list the most popular new bands in Europe or the coolest new skateboard shop, but how many can stop a science class with a discussion of the Burgess Shale? The Burgess oddballs are perfect for the young anarchist: they're ugly yet fascinating, with just the right sense of exotica to blow the minds of interested friends. Small wonder the illustrations in Stephen Jay Gould's *Wonderful Life* see so much use in garage band promo flyers.

And the role models! Robert Bakker alone offers an infinitude of fashion comments to the brave and angry: he proves that someone in his forties can wear long hair and not get fired for it. Even the nerdiest palaeontologist gets the respect due his/her field: these are people who stuck to their interests and never let anyone change their minds, and even the angriest punk respects that. And it should be noted that looks are secondary to writing ability, as one is likely to see copies of *Wonderful Life* and *The Dinosaur Heresies* alongside *Fear and Loathing In Las Vegas* and *The Anarchist Cookbook* in a typical thrasher library.

For this reason, we should not shun or deride the alien in our midst, but in fact embrace him. The fellow with the blue Mohawk and bicycle chain-embroidered leather jacket may be singing "Anarchy in the U.K.," but he's probably contemplating the causes of the great K-T extinction or the diversification of Permian amphibians.

—*Fuck Science Fiction, April 1994*

"A Study of Theropod Dinosaur Psychology and Social Habits Using Unorthodox Sources"

Although the study of dinosaurian palaeontology has advanced exponentially since the early 1960s, thanks to groundbreaking by such notables as Robert T. Bakker, John Horner, David Weishampel, John Ostrom, and others, one facet of Mesozoic remains a mystery: sociology and behaviour. While we have some clues thanks to recent discoveries, such as Dr. Horner's famed hadrosaur nesting sites in Montana, we know far more about archosaurian physiology than archosaurian psychology, mostly because habits and social behaviour don't fossilise. The best we have to work with are scattered hints from the fosssil record, as well as informed speculation based on the habits of birds and crocodilians, which is akin to studying the capabilities of the space shuttle by comparing it to DC-10s and Model T Fords. Palaeontologists desperately need new sources of information in order to obtain a well rounded view of the Mesozoic fauna.

Thankfully, thanks to a new technique developed by Dr. Edgar Z. Harris, doctor of journalism at the University of Texas at Flower Mound, palaeontologists now have a means of studying dinosaurian psychology without long hours in the field or the lab. Dr. Harris originally developed the technique to study the behaviour and motivations of extraterrestrials: by watching videotapes of popular films, he was able to chart some seven basic mental traits among ETs. For instance, after watching *Communion*, *Invaders* and *Fire In the Sky*, he ascertained that the famed alien phrase "Klaatu barada nikto" translated to "Squeal like a pig, boy!," while study of *Alien*, *Invaders From Mars* (both versions), and *Attack of the Saucer Men* indeed proves that ETs are here to eat us, enslave us, and steal our wimmenfolk.

After months of correspondence, we finally set up our basic protocol, and performed a smash-and-grab raid on the local Blockbuster Video branch while obtaining other necessary supplies. (One note: the initial stages of research precludes the use of alcohol and narcotics, as some of our videotapes, when combined with a case of Dr. Pepper, picante sauce, and chocolate-covered peanuts, caused hallucinations after a mere twelve hours of viewing. Jolt cola and Doritos cause tremors, and Pepsi and Hostess cupcakes induces parthogenic birth.) After setting up, we sat back with notebooks and took copious notes with the help of handheld recorders.

Since our data show an extreme bias toward theropod dinosaurs, we decided to focus on this branch, as almost nothing is known about the habits of carnivorous dinosaurs from the fossil record. Even with this taken into account, our research held an extreme bias toward North American theropods, such as *Tyrannosaurus*, *Allosaurus*, and *Ceratosaurus*, but with scattered examples of the smaller coelurosaurs, such as *Velociraptor*. No examples of African, Australian, or South American theropods were found, and the only example of Asian theropods came from one species, *Godzilla latex* from Japan. The latter, however, comprised a statistically significant portion of our data, suggesting that this species is extremely prolific.

The first observation we made was that the work of Bakker et al concerning endothermy in dinosaurs was correct: nearly every theropod species we observed literally raced about, ready to attack anything in sight. The Japanese specimens were an exception, but they also reached phenomenal size due to the ingestion of radioactive isotopes, thus explaining the paucity of these elements in modern Japan. This ability to convert hard radiation to energy and size was shared by other members of its biome, such as the pterosaur *Rodan plasticine* and the previously unknown arthropod *Mothra fiberglass*. (We found another case of potential exothermy with a new species, *Barney imbecilis nonsapiens*, which we discovered while channel-surfing past our local PBS affiliate. It apparently attacked by inducing terminal diabetes and narcolepsy on its prey and then feeding at its leisure. *Barney* was apparently extremely successful at this, as it no longer possesses the sharp teeth of its fellow carnosaurs.)

During our study, we noted innumerable examples of theropod territorial and hunting behaviour, with some interesting variations. Enemies and prey included the expected ornithischians such as *Triceratops*, *Styracosaurus*, and *Stegosaurus*, but also included a previously unknown species of giant ape, Asian elephants, and even Cro-Magnon men. The Japanese data show that we know considerably less about this biome than previously thought: the authors recommend that reputable institutions immediately instigate expeditions to recover the remains of the three-headed space aliens, giant spiders and praying mantises, and humanoid robots we observed. The costs of these digs might be mitigated by cloning them from fossil DNA and placing them in an amusement park in downtown Tokyo, the apparent native habitat of these species.

We also observed nesting behaviour among theropods, with both altricial and precocial young. According to *Jurassic Park*, the dromaeosaur *Velociraptor* was extremely precocial, being able to leave the nest moments after birth in preparation to chow down on unprepared human tourists. Our one known Japanese carnosaur, however, was extremely altricial, needing nearly constant care from its parent in order to protect it from local predators. It also lacked an adult version of the radioactive breath weapon possessed by the species, being able to blow "smoke rings" unless subjected to extreme pain, such as a tromped tail. We hoped for more information on the last, but the videos needed to return by midnight, and Dr. Harris and I had to work the next morning, so this fascinating research must wait for another paper.

We made one last observation before returning them, though, which threatens the entire dinosaurian palaeontological community. In our witnessed encounters of dinosaurs and humans, we noted that while theropods are attracted to persons with blonde hair (Fay Wray in *King Kong*, James Franciscus in *Valley of Gwangi*, and Laura Dern in *Jurassic Park* are three examples), they actually find it easier to catch and eat brunettes, while ignoring redheads. Since most of the most active dinosaurologists are brunettes (such as Drs. Bakker, Horner, and Weishampel), we suggest all parties in university-sponsored dinosaur hunts carry red wigs in order to escape detection. (We desperately need data on baldness and dinosaur attraction: please send all possible sources directly to UTFM. We promise to credit all research conducted by others.)

CONCLUSION

While not all-inclusive, we find that the use of videotapes to study theropod psychology and sociology offers great rewards without the tiring and tedious field and lab work. Besides the ease, we find considerably more data than other sources provide, and the technique offers ways to relieve work-related stress as well (in the tradition of midnight showings of *The Rocky Horror Picture Show* and *Dawn of the Dead*, we found *Jurassic Park* to be improved immeasurably by adding Dennis Hopper's dialogue from *Blue Velvet* in place of the tyrannosaur's roars). We await further discoveries using Dr. Harris' technique, and hope that it helps advance the study of palaeontology.

−The Annals of Improbable Research, Spring 1994

Postscript: This paper was originally written for the Journal of Irreproducible Results, *one of the most prestigious scientific journals around. However, due to the original staff leaving to strike out on their own, it appeared in the new journal, the* Annals of Improbable Research. *Either way, the final paper was, as is usual with scientific journals, butchered beyond all recognition: this is its first appearance in its original form.*

On Mass Media

My writing career, such as it was, started with coverage of mass media, and many of the most notable articles came from commentary about movies, television, comics, and magazines. In fact, my obsession with mass media for a good portion of my career allowed me to cross from science fiction magazines to more mainstream publications, because who else was going to shove that much garbage into their heads?

"The Wrath of Cat Piss Man"

It's a distasteful subject, not fit for family reading, but it's time. It's time to relate the origins of everyone's least favorite comic shop fixture, Cat Piss Man.

Back about three-quarters of a decade ago, I was a regular at a local comic shop in Dallas, and was yakking with the staff about the new issue of *Fuck Science Fiction* (yes, that was a real magazine, and I bawled like a baby went it went under) when I met my first Cat Piss Man. Every comic shop in every city has at least one, all seemingly grown off this one like cuttings off jade plants. About six foot four he was, weighing in at least 200 kilos if an ounce, and the perfect cliché of the comics aficionado. The lank, greasy hair that wasn't long enough to tie back but also wasn't so short that it took care of itself without combing. The heavily abused "Marvel" T-shirt, with holes that suggested that cotton polyblend was the only fiber he got in his diet, since most of the rest was covered in a thick layer of Cheetos crumbs. Facial pores that suggested that gnomes sneaked into his bedroom in his parents' house and broke off the tips of No. 2 pencils in them. Beady little eyes behind Buddy Holly birth control glasses. If one's dental apparatus was a city, his mouth obviously took a direct hit with an H-bomb, and the mixture of nose hairs and crusted boogers protruding an inch past his nostrils and down his moustache guaranteed that he breathed through his mouth, producing a charitable impersonation of "The Creature From the Black Latrine." The last of the Olmec had taken to living in cliff dwellings in the shelter between his double chin and his gut, reasonably assured that nothing would disturb their mushroom and cave cricket farms.

However, Cat Piss Man's name was pure olfactory onomatopoeia. The first time I encountered him, he was walking up to the store door when one of the staff said "Oh God, it's Cat Piss Man." I was about ready to ask why he said that when Cat Piss Man stepped inside. Now, Texas heat has a tendency to make everyone exposed to it somewhat less than fresh, but this was the end of December, and his odor literally brought tears to my eyes. This wasn't a minor case of body odor: he literally smelled like a mile-wide overloaded litter box, left out in the Australian outback to cook in the sun, with enough power to kill a silk ficus. This stench wasn't just an affront to God, Satan, and Elvis: this was positively Lovecraftian in scope. I suddenly attained insane insights into the magazine distribution business, and I think a lack of available oxygen had something to do with it. Other customers would simply run the moment they saw him waddling toward the door, and he could clear the entire shop within seconds if the store's air conditioner wasn't on at full blast.

If this wasn't nauseating enough, his behavior was even more horrifying. Since this store didn't carry "adult" comics, he didn't disappear into the back area to wank off (to steal from the *Republicans Attack!* trading card set from Kitchen Sink, I doubt if he nor anyone else had seen his genitalia since 1984), so he felt compelled to follow people around. Someone would be reading the back copy on an issue of *The Comics Journal* when he'd come trucking over, not saying anything, and just kinda stare. Every time the customer would move away because Cat Piss Man was melting their Mylar baggies, he'd just follow along, not saying a word, and reposition himself like a corpulent vulture over a dying prospector. And Arioch help us all if the customer was female: Cat Piss Man would sidle over closer, trying to stun her with his natural perfume, and apparently he once tried to feel up one woman who wasn't able to get away fast enough.

The last time I ever saw Cat Piss Man, he was at a science fiction convention in Austin, Texas a few years back, hogging space in front of a dealer's table, doing the same thing. This time, he was dressed semi-formal, in a homemade *Star Trek: The Next Generation* uniform with a thick layer of human grease clogging the uniform's fabric in a band starting at his armpits and ending at the tops of his hips. He apparently couldn't afford or find a prop communicator pin, so he had one appliqued with Elmer's Glue-All and glitter, and the grease was making the symbol peel free. For some reason, this made his assaults even more terrifying.

Oh, and did I mention that this guy almost never bought anything during his regular visits? Or if he did, he nitpicked everything in an effort to scam as much free stuff as possible?

Okay, so you think it's cruel to make fun of the socially challenged. We've all been there at one point or another in our lives (I can't read one of Evan Dorkin's *Eltingville* strips without getting flashbacks to 1985, and when I remember how much I used to be like Bill from the Eltingville Club, I want to borrow a time machine just so I can kick my former self's ass into the next time zone), but this is different. This isn't making fun of someone different from us. This is explaining why so many people stay away from comic shops.

Let's put it another way. If Cat Piss Man were to act like this on the street toward random passerby, he'd probably get arrested or at least given a stern warning by a local cop. If Cat Piss Man were to do this at a restaurant, he'd be thrown out for bothering the customers. If Cat Piss Man were to do this at a nightclub, about eight big burly guys would take him out back and beat the shit out of him. If Cat Piss Man were even to smell like this in the Army, he'd get a good scrubdown with lye soap and wire brushes. (I had Cat Piss Man's brother in my Basic Training platoon in the Army, and we finally had to give him a blanket party a la Private Pyle in *Full Metal Jacket* to convince him that bathing and changing clothes were good things, because every other method simply didn't work.) In a comic shop, though, this isn't only tolerated, but its example just acts as encouragement for others. Every time I mention Cat Piss Man to a comic shop owner, no matter where in the country the comic shop is located, s/he laughs and says "Oh yeah: he's in here all of the time." It's not the same guy (sometimes Cat Piss Man is skinny, and sometimes he actually combs his hair), but this new Cat Piss Man is a glob off the original.

I'm willing to concede that Cat Piss Man buys something every once in a while, and that we can't afford to alienate customers in this depressed market. However, even if his Mommy's allowance gave him the opportunity to buy $200 or more in comics and other goodies a week, Cat Piss Man drives off easily twice that many paying customers, who would come back to a comic shop again and again if they weren't subjected to nasal rape every time they walked inside. This also holds true for the "Tragic: This Gathering" players shrieking at the tops of their lungs in the back (that is, except in the comic shops where the owners realized that they lost less money in sales to card game players by closing the gaming areas than they lost from items that "liberated" themselves when the gamers left for the day), or the guy who pesters customers into buying loose action figures out front because the store owner didn't want a box of dog-chewed *Spawn* figures. And let's not forget the fanatics who threaten violence upon anyone who dares scoff at the idea of an *Action Girl/Witchblade* crossover event. Comic store owners just don't seem to realize the lesson that the shantytowns out in front of movie theaters for *Star Wars: Episode One* taught movie theater managers: the last thing most patrons wanted was to be harangued by some dork in a Jedi costume who had been living in it for the last four months, and the fear of even getting close to the *Episode One* line meant that customers didn't come to see other films, either.

And for those store owners and patrons who don't think that Cat Piss Man and his brothers are a problem, look at it this way. Imagine going into a pet shop in a world where every pet shop had a big, smelly incontinent St. Bernard in the back. The dog doesn't belong to the store: it's just some stray that comes in every day, eats straight out of the bulk dog food bins, drools all over the copies of *Reptiles Monthly* and *Tropical Fish Hobbyist* up front, rapes the hamsters and dry-humps the legs of every customer that comes in, and doesn't contribute a thing to the operation of the store. If anything, it gets in the way of normal operation, and pet supply proprietors find that their business is directly affected by customer perceptions of the ordeal of trying to get around the St. Bernard shit piled around the front entrance. This world doesn't exist, although I've seen some pet shops that have come close. One of two things happen to pet shops like this: they go out of business, or the owner does an *Old Yeller* to the mangy beast and burns its carcass in a big bonfire out front.

The latter is what comic shop owners and managers need to do to their resident Cat Piss Man: throw the bums out. Don't joke about the stench or put on gas masks while Cat Piss Man is in the store, because he's spent years ignoring the comments of every other human about his appearance. Simply say "I'm afraid I'm going to have to ask you to leave until you take a bath and leave the customers alone," and back it up. In the best scenario, he realizes that cleaning himself from time to time is at least as important as wearing pants, and comes back after realizing that his body isn't made from pure sodium and that soap and water don't necessarily burst into flame on contact. Otherwise, he'll throw a temper tantrum and stomp off to another comic shop; the other comic shop gets his pittance, and his old shop gets a whole passel of customers who apologize "I would have come in sooner, but that guy in here was melting the windows..." Either way, the problem is solved, and his old shop may even get a whole new contingent of customers who say "I used to go to that shop across town, but this guy who smells like he sleeps in a cat box came in and took over."

I'm not advocating setting up a dress code for comic shops, although I have to say that a dress code for comic shop managers and customers might not be a bad idea. (C'mon, guys: you don't need suits from Barneys, but have you ever wondered what people think when they see you behind the counter in sandals, ratty jeans, and a *Lady Death* T-shirt?) What I am advocating is considering the benefits of getting the shop Cat Piss Man to bathe or getting him to leave. And since none of the other customers are going to say anything, he's there until the store staff gets rid of him, and he'll cost you. Oh boy howdy, he'll cost you.

–*Savant, August 31, 2000*

Postscript: Since publication of this essay, the term "Cat Piss Man" moved beyond the comics industry as an automatic description of the worst sort of science fiction or gaming fan. I suspect that this is because even people outside of the genre have an immediate understanding of the term: I have to explain the concept behind "fanboy," but "Cat Piss Man" is something that anyone can grasp. It's even inspired two card games so far, and the Cartoon Network animated series can't be too far away.

"Shopping Through The Movies"

Since this last year was as crippled as it was as far as filmgoing is concerned, the ongoing talk in Hollywood follows what films, if any, will make the short list for the Oscars. We had a lot of films released this year, but not all that many are worthy of Oscar inclusion, and some critics talk about how they can't come up with a Top Ten list for the end of the season. Everyone pretty much agrees that this wasn't a good year for filmgoers: even the films that made back their costs didn't pull in the orbital revenues that everyone saw last year.

One can chalk this up to any number of factors: moviegoers being burned out on spectacle films, a receding stock market, not enough methamphetamine or too much saltpeter in the water supply, or other concerns that will only be identified by epidemiologists trying to understand the correlation between David Spade cameos and an increase in irritable bowel syndrome. This doesn't stop pundits from seeking out surefire ways to spot impending dud films and trying to warn others of the dangers. Some methods do indeed work (any time more than two writers get credit in a movie poster, especially when at least one is also the executive producer, is guaranteed), but we need methods that the average person, cut off from copies of *Variety* and *The Hollywood Reporter*, can use at will.

Several years back, Roger Ebert noted one system that worked surprising well, to a point: he noted that the big hits of a given summer always marketed their tie-in promotions with McDonald's, while the major disappointments sign on with Burger King. This seems to work most often than not, such as in 1993 when McDonald's snagged *Jurassic Park* and Burger King relegated itself to *The Last Action Hero*, but it's not a foolproof test. For instance, when animated films are concerned, the reverse is true (look at the success Burger King had with *The Lion King* in 1994 versus McDonald's with *Tarzan* or *Dinosaur* in 1999 and 2000), but with all of the others, it's a crapshoot. Although the American *Godzilla* was a flop, Taco Bell made quite a bit of money from selling Godzilla cup holders, but the company lost a large fortune with tie-ins with the seemingly sure-thing *Star Wars: Episode One* a year later.

Even with the flaws in the system, Ebert unwittingly came across a way to spot the big successes and failures of a movie season. Considering that the big films are intentionally constructed to appeal to as large a crowd as possible (thus explaining why we didn't see *Mallrats* coffee mugs and *Run, Lola, Run!* Happy Meals), we have to look at the one common factor to almost all of the American moviegoing public: the grocery store. Ten minutes in a grocery store, poking about, will tell more about an impending release than millions of words in trade magazines and hundreds of hours of analysis in entertainment news shows.

To wit, here's a handy guide to spotting the probable stinkers coming to your Multiplex in this or any given moviegoing season. Remember that this is not in any way all-inclusive: just because the film is bad doesn't mean that it won't be successful, and a good film sneaks through regardless of the amount of merchandising. (After all, just because Wendy's carried *Armageddon* tie-ins didn't guarantee that the film would flop.) However, the more samples available for inspection, the more likely a final analysis is possible. Just go from aisle to aisle in the local supermarket, and tally up the number of points as examples present themselves, either by choosing a film and looking for these items, or by counting everything in sight and sorting it by film. Ready? Start with:

Every five tie-in products promoting the film: 5 points (in addition to other specialty points)

Every month in advance of a release date that action figures or other toys are on the shelves: 5 points per month

Promotional tie-ins that feature only a body part of the title character (the Grinch's hand or Godzilla's feet): 5 points

Every cardboard standup in the front doorway: 10 points

Every tie-in product where the film's URL on the packaging is more prominent than the product's URL: 10 points

Big tubs or dispensers of tie-in candy or other snacks: 5 points per tub or dispenser

Every surprising or unconventional tie-in (the Grinch on posters for US postage stamps, for instance): 5 points

Every promotional tie-in on products unapproved for consumption by humans (cat litter, light bulbs, motor oil, tampons): 5 points

Every fast food toy offered in a promo tie-in: 5 points each

Fast food promotion through McDonald's: minus 10 points

Fast food promotion through Taco Bell/KFC/Pizza Hut: minus 5 points

Fast food promotion through Burger King (excepting animated films): plus 5 points

Fast food promotion through Wendy's: plus 10 points

"Free trading card in this box!": 5 points

"Mail-in Toy Rebate!": 10 points

Any sugared cereal with the official mascot replaced with a movie character: 5 points

Front cover of Entertainment Weekly: 5 points for every cover after the first

Front cover of TV Guide: 5 points per variant cover

Front cover mention on any unexpected magazine (Maxim, Scientific American,

Martha Stewart Living, Tropical Fish Hobbyist): 5 points per incident

Special Starlog Press "Official Photozine" in main magazine rack: 20 points

Special Starlog Press "Official Photozine" in checkout line magazine rack: 50 points

Every announcement on the store Muzak system, announcing "From the new hit movie...": 10 points

Have fun at the supermarket? Now it's time to count the points from all of the examples seen while wandering the aisles. Here's a handy guide:

Less than 20 points: Either it's not a family movie, or someone at the studio publicity department was sleeping on the job.

Up to 30 points: Probably not a sure thing, but someone's at least making an effort.

Up to 40 points: Pretty reasonable these days; could go either way.

Up to 50 points: Someone at the studio knows something that we don't, and they're hoping to snag at least a little money to offset the film costs so they won't lose their jobs.

Up to 60 points: Uh oh.

Up to 70 points: Why didn't they make tie-in urinal cakes while they were at it?

Up to 80 points: I think they made the urinal cakes, too.

Up to 90 points: Someone would have licensed a tie-in brand of crack cocaine if they thought it would bring in a buck.

More than 90 points: "Run! Run! Run for your lives!"

See? It's informative, entertaining, and infuriating. At least, it's infuriating to the store assistant manager who can't understand why anyone would be laughing at the market potential of Pink Flamingos 30th anniversary Pooper-Scoopers. For the rest of us, though, the only thing funnier is seeing the metric tons of Episode One Fruit-By-The-Foot being given away with every purchase. And who says that capitalism doesn't work?

—SciFiNow, December 2000

"Phoning It In"

In the esteemed pages of *Savant*, we all talk about ways to improve sales of comics, and talk about ways to make stores more customer-friendly. In all of this, though, one of the most obvious solutions to the problem almost literally smacked me in the mouth a couple of weeks ago, and odds are that most comic shop owners and patrons never even consider it.

It started out simply enough: a week ago last Tuesday, I was suddenly smitten by the idea of going out to the comic shop and blowing a hundred dollars or so on my favorite biodegradable addiction. (I'd just received a series of paychecks from writing assignments, and since the bills were all paid up, I figured that I could afford to splurge and do my best to keep Slave Labor Graphics solvent.) Of course, this is about 7:45 Central Daylight time, so the question was "Is the comic shop still open, or is Tuesday one of the days they close at 7?" To find out, I did what most people would do: I reached for the Yellow Pages and went in search for a phone number.

It's been several years since I went looking through a Yellow Pages guide to look for a comic shop, and what the Dallas directory had listed shocked the hell out of me. This was the 2000 edition, and yet it still listed shops that I knew had shut down years before. (The Comic Zone in Lewisville, for instance, was not only the place that introduced me to comics other than DC and Marvel, but also one of the only venues for books to be found outside of the local grocery store within a twenty-mile radius. Considering the money I plunked into that place during and after high school, I was honestly shocked when I moved back to Texas in 1997 and found it dead for a year.) I went looking for my shop, with no success: lots of other shops I knew were dead or had moved in the last five years, a big listing for a fairly decent shop down the road, and a big ad for a chain store run by one of the biggest assholes in the comic business. (You'd probably recognize the name if you're a regular reader of *The Comic Buyer's Guide*; the owner is one of those people so worried about "protecting the little children" that he refused to carry *Strangers In Paradise* for six months because it wasn't meant for kids, and only started carrying Vertigo titles when customers went elsewhere for their *Preacher* fix. Even so, his stores have a ratings system that prevents anyone under the age of 13 from buying standard superhero comics, and the good stuff is rated "I-18," meaning that nobody under the age of 18 is allowed to look at the covers. I know that the Southern Baptist influence in Dallas has made the local culture positively poisonous, but still...) Now I was starting to get worried: why wasn't my store listed?

You may notice, in this point in the narrative, that I haven't named My Store. This is deliberate. While My Store isn't perfect, all of the staff members are good friends, and they do their damnedest to watch out for their customers as best as they can. Therefore, they don't need to be embarrassed. I did enough of that when I mentioned that I was going to use them as an example.

Anyway, while scratching my head in puzzlement, I suddenly remembered that I had a postcard the owner had printed up a couple of years before, complete with the store's phone number. Better yet, I knew where it was, so I ran to my office, grabbed it, and ran back to the phone. Punched in the number. Let it ring...and ring...and ring...obviously, nobody there. Presumably, the shop closed at seven. But I got no answering machine telling me "Thank you for calling My Store, located at Somesuch and Thereabout, open seven days a week...," and no way of knowing that I had the right party in the first place. For all I knew, I had dialed the cell phone of some drunken BMW brat currently driving up Central Expressway, and my call had distracted him from his discussion of "101 Drinks That Go Well With Rohypnol" with one of his frat brothers from SMU that he'd spun out on the highway and started an 83-car pileup that would make the national news. I was raised Catholic, so guilt and paranoia run my life.

Well, they don't run my life that much, so I figured "Okay, I guess they're closed," and went back to knocking squirrels out of the trees in my back yard with a Super Soaker. (I have to, you see: they travel in hordes, capturing humans, paralyzing them and implanting eggs, with the squirrel pups chewing their way out of the humans' chest cavities...oh, forget it.) Two days later, when I knew the store would be open until nine, I asked about the lack of an answering machine: the response was "We used to have one, and then when the last manager left, he took his phone and answering machine with him..."

Now, for those who could get through my turgid and indulgent prose, we see three major obstacles to a comic shop trying to get new customers. The guys running My Store promptly fixed the situation when they realized how much potential business they were losing: no excuses, no whining, no rationalization. A lot of shop owners will whine and rationalize, and that's why they'll either collect as little business as is possible, or they'll just go under.

Obviously, my little quest went on much further than it would have if conducted by a casual browser. Let's take a look at the three major roadblocks, shall we?

Firstly, I took the time to check the Yellow Pages. For all of the shops that make a big deal about setting up a Web presence, an ungodly number of them forget that while Web access is still a luxury for many, most people in America have access to a phone. It may be at work, and it may be a pay phone around the corner, but they have some sort of access to a phone that allows local calls. (Compare this to the still relatively tiny number of occupations that allow employees to Websurf, either on company time or otherwise.) Even with unlimited Web access, most people are going to use the Web to discover the address for a comic shop in the opposite hemisphere but use the Yellow Pages for a comic shop that may be just around the corner. This is why paying for a Yellow Pages ad, and keeping it current, is absolutely vital.

By neglecting the old dead-tree phone book, comic store owners and operators are neglecting a huge potential audience. Most kids who might have an interest in comics but no easy access to a store will peruse the phone book, if only to argue with their parents that "it's just on the way to soccer practice." Former readers who might want to get back into the hobby will poke through the Yellow Pages and decide to visit a shop based on a particular listing. Most importantly of all, those moving into a community will probably search out a comic shop through the phone book in the same way they'd search out an attorney, a dentist, or a mechanic.

Because of this, keeping up a current phone number in the phone book is vital. Most Yellow Pages will continue to run basic listings for any number of venues long after they've gone out of business (five years ago, my personal phone number belonged to a methadone clinic, and although I've contacted damn near every venue passing out that number and informed them of the clinic's shuffling off that mortal coil, I still get at least one phone call a month from someone who found the number in the GTE Yellow Pages and needs to get into a substance abuse program), and the phone company usually won't correct the old phone number if the area code or the whole number changes. If a retailer used to run three shops in a town, and two of them go out of business, I guarantee that not only will the other numbers remain in the phone book until Elvis rises again, but that customers will try to call the numbers of the other two stores and give up before finding the one store that's still open.

Secondly, I went searching for another source for a phone number. If potential customers don't know about a store, they naturally won't go searching other venues to glean the number for a place they don't know exists. If they do know about a store, they aren't going to hop in a car and gleefully go driving in the middle of the night if they can call to find hours of operation. If the phone works but they get no message, they're likely to blow off heading out for a while...maybe forever.

Now, having all of the pertinent information about a comic shop (address, Web site, E-mail, phone number, and hours) on a flyer or postcard is great, but this presupposes that the person receiving it didn't just ball it up and throw it away, or give it to a friend, or leave it in the car or on the bus. It presupposes that this flyer or card is in an accessible location, and that the person receiving it remembers where it is at all times. In other words, while they're great to attract new customers, they should not be depended upon as the one source of information. Just go out and buy a damn Yellow pages ad, you cheap bastard.

Thirdly, I went to the store to ask why it didn't have an answering machine. My comic shop is about fifteen miles away from home: not a tremendous distance for Dallas, but not one I'd want to cruise in summer without a car. However, I knew the store existed and that it had certain hours: even if a new customer had an address, this person might be averse to driving, walking, or bicycling all that way only to discover that the store was closed. If the store was closed, then the odds that this person is going to come back just dropped by at least fifty percent.

Even more importantly, let's consider the new or casual comics buyer who's looking for one thing in particular. Given a choice between driving to every comic shop in town to look for a particular item and calling up every shop in town, the phone is going to be a saner choice. If one store doesn't have a phone, or at least a message stating its hours, that buyer is going to go down the list until s/he finds someone who bothers to pick up the phone. This is good for the phone-bearer, but bad for all of the other stores that could have made a sale. Or series of sales.

As an alternative to nail the point home, let's just say that the person doing the calling isn't the actual customer. In this example, we have a parent trying to hunt down a particular comic for his or her kid, and this person is usually going on what the kid may have mentioned in casual conversation a week before. Or the kid is a Pokemon junkie, and Mom is trying to feed the kid's addiction. Not all parents are this way, but most of us at least know parents who will expend the absolute minimum amount of effort on any interest their children have of which they personally disapprove. Mom will make the call, and if nobody answers, tell the kid "Sorry, but nobody was there" in the hopes that the kid will give it up. Now, if the store was closed but the answering machine had the store hours on its message, said parent is much more likely to make a second call, if only because the kid is likely to call to check up, or even drive out the next day and peruse the store. And if this shop followed the patented *Savant* guides to making a store newbie-friendly, Mom may run across something that catches her interest, and the store has two new customers instead of one. Hell, she might grab Dad and the other kids and make a family outing of it: it's impossible to tell.

Even in the most extreme cases, that answering machine will generate business. Let's say that Mom is calling up, asking about Pokemon cards, and has no intention of buying a single thing other than those all-important trading cards. She may not, but her kid will remember the store, and come back when s/he has the first opportunity. Even if the kid never comes back after burning out on Pikachu, s/he may tell friends, or Mom just might if asked by someone searching for a comic shop for their kids.

This is why a phone with an answering machine is an essential purchase in a comics market as depressed as this one. Considering the amount of money the average shop spends on overhead, the $50 spent to buy a decent answering machine (or to get CallNotes if the local phone company offers the service) should pay for itself in a month just in the number of new customers willing to take a chance after listening to a friendly and professional message. Even better, adventurous shop owners can decide to let the machine take messages as well: imagine the surprise when a newbie calls up at around midnight, says "Well, I'm looking for a copy of the new *Barry Ween* collection, if you have it..." and gets a call in the morning of "Yes, we do, and we have all of the back issues of the second series as well..."

Trust me on this one. Any retailers wanting to keep their stores alive need a phone and answering machine. More importantly, they need to know how to use them. Even more so than a cash register, a phone is probably the most important sales tool they'll ever get. Phone. Answering machine. Current Yellow Pages listing. Do it. Now.

—*Savant, August 10, 2000*

"Bungles In Advertising"

We all have those questions that beggar rational answers or analysis. We wonder why Americans were willing to settle for Spock and McCoy or Beavis and Butt-Head as the only choices in the Presidential election (which still hasn't been decided as I write this, but Spock is tied with Butt-Head at the moment), or how Norm MacDonald and Pauly Shore manage to keep from being put up against a wall and shot by real comedians. We wonder why *Star Trek: Voyager* managed to last as long as it did, even though it regularly cops Nielsen ratings that would kill any other UPN show in a week. We wonder why "classic rock" radio stations gleefully play Bon Jovi but not the Ramones, or how extraterrestrial intelligences are supposed to consider us worthy of being anything other than a meat animal after we've been blasting soap operas and Edie Brickell across half the galaxy. (Just think: the folks on Alpha Centauri are just now catching "The Macarena" in our radio transmissions, and they're even more pissed than they were when the only thing they could pick up was The Bangles' "Manic Monday.") Most of all, we keep wondering "Why don't comics advertise?"

A couple of weeks ago, writer Chuck Dixon asked that question at his Web site, and he has a really valid point. For all of the noises in the comics industry about how comics readers are giving up on comics in favor of movies, TV, and cyberporn, nobody even considers plunking down a few bucks and advertising comics. Hell, even basic promotion seems out of the question.

Here's an example for consideration, and proof that I'm willing to maul the hand that pays for my comics habit. (I've become convinced that I was a Gila monster in a previous life.) I currently work for *SCI FI*, the house magazine for the SCI FI Channel, writing the "Rant" column inside. Every two months, when a new issue comes out, I go through both it and the competition and compare content. Not just the articles: I go through the letters to the editor, the graphics used, and particularly the ads. If you thought the gimps who send in letter bombs if any writer dares admit that *Gene Roddenberry's Andromeda* is anything less than the pinnacle of achievement in science fiction television are scary, you haven't seen anything until you see the advertising.

For instance, ads from book publishers are few and far between, except when you have somebody like Del Rey pitching some rot like *The Art of Star Wars: Episode One* or ads for the latest L. Ron Hubbard reprint from Bridge. You might see a few dotcom ads for genre-related sites, usually for sites that require every visitor to have a T3 line and a 1-gig processor to see the home page, much less go anywhere. Lots and lots of video game ads, whose misogyny is only exceeded by the psychic laughter of the ad company who put it together as they spend the gigantic check they received on booze and hookers. (I remember seeing one about a year ago that intimated that the only thing better than whacking off in a restroom stall was doing so with a game controller in the other hand; the last I checked, this company was no longer in business.) Lots of ads for prop companies, such as the guy who sells "unauthorized" light sabers for all of the wannabe Jedi out there. A few ads for pay-per-view genre movies and DVDs, as if anyone is dumb enough to pay real money to see the R-rated cut of *Supernova*. A few ads for "Russian Ladies Seek Marriage" and the like, but precious little for print media. Absolutely nothing for comics, except from companies willing to help collectors find back issues.

The really funny part is that all of the comics companies pass up great opportunities to hype up their comics with a minimum of effort. Last summer, for instance, damn near every magazine from *SCI FI* to *Maxim* ran cover stories on the *X-Men* movie, and you'd think that Marvel would have jumped all over that business like Scott Weiland on a kilo of heroin. Instead, aside from some silliness in *TV Guide*, nuthin'. No ads for the main comic, no ads for "*Ultimate X-Men*: Coming Soon," no ads for action figures or graphic novels, no calls to check out the official Marvel Comics Web site. For all intents and purposes, the movie was released in a vacuum, and anyone not already familiar with the comics industry would have been hard pressed to know that *X-Men* was based on a comic in the first place.

Now, this happens on a regular basis, where the promotion of a comic-related project such as this falls right into the heart of the True Believers anyway. Not that anything could have saved the *Tank Girl* movie from fuelling the careers of a million smarmy film critics anyway, but aside from a few mentions in the press material going out to journalists about the film (which nobody reads anyway), the only mentions that the film was based on a comic came through comic shops. The same thing with *Judge Dredd* or *Barb Wire* or *The Mask*, to pick three examples: all the general public knew was that they were based on comic books, with all of the "I'm too cool for this" snickering that this entailed, and anyone who might want to know more had no idea where to look for more info. Yeah, Dark Horse collected the early *The Mask* stories in a graphic novel, but readers were only going to come across these if they poked through the "Sci-Fi" section of their bookstore, and not because they were informed that it was available.

Right now, take a look at the sources for advertising comics. Chuck Dixon noted that while DC sees nothing wrong with licensing its characters for all sorts of generic bullshit that tells the general public nothing about the characters or their situations (my personal favorite was the Kraft Macaroni and Cheese packs that incorporated *Justice League* character icons but made no mention that they were actually based on a comic or anything), the company can't be bothered to advertise its main business: it sells comics. If DC (or Marvel, or Dark Horse, or Image or Top Cow or any other company you can name) advertises its comics, that advertising is already going to the people who buy comics. These are ads in *Previews* or *Wizard* or those little floppy handouts that are supposed to be slipped in each comic shop customer's bags but end up piled somewhere. (I literally tripped over a pile of flyers for Vertigo's *The Girl Who Would Be Death* miniseries the other day, two years after that series came and went, that were slowly being compressed into diamond by the pile of other material stacked atop them.) Either that, or they're ads in the company's own comics: I'm starting to suspect that most of the company crossover "events" are nothing but an excuse to get advertising in a competitor's title, or is there actually another excuse for the *Aliens/Predator/Witchblade/Darkness* crossover?

The preceding goes doubly true for the idea that promoting comics at conventions is good enough. Bollocks on that: giving out comics at a convention doesn't help sell them. All it does is draw a crowd of cheap greedy bastards who will either throw them away once they realize they don't have an interest, or who plan to fence them at the local comic shop right after the convention. All of those booths and banners and half-nude models in San Diego won't bring new readers into the comics community: anyone willing to pay for plane fare, hotel space, and a three-day pass is already pretty damn likely to be a frequent denizen of a comic shop anyway. We need new blood.

Advertising in different sources falls under what I like to call "the iMac effect," which states that many people don't know what they want until they see it. Three years ago, if anyone were to ask a fledgling computer user what s/he wanted from a computer, probably one in 20,000 would say "a five-minute plug-and-play system in cool colors," but a lot of folks who saw the iMac suddenly knew that this was The One Computer for them. Likewise, merely pitching the old "Visit your local comic shop" does nothing without any idea of what to expect: even if the potential customer finds a great comic shop within an easy commute, and the local Cat Piss Man is either at home or driven off with flamethrowers, s/he's going to step inside and be completely lost. The average person isn't going to know the difference between *Strangers In Paradise* and *Danger Girl*, and probably won't find out, because that poor person is going to shoot out of the store rather than ask questions and run the risk of asking a stupid question.

Now, I'm not advocating that every little company with a single title needs to go out and buy an ad in the Super Bowl, but if the National Association of Newspapers can sponsor LL Cool J telling TV watchers to "read a newspaper to your kids every day," why can't every company that buys space in *Previews* collectively plunk down some cash to convince general folk via a TV or magazine ad campaign that walking into a comic shop won't make you go blind and grow hair on your palms? Or is it easier to bitch about how the audience for comics is dying than to take any pro-active effort?

—*Savant, November 16, 2000*

"Culling The Card Geeks"

Well, the Christmas buying season is upon all good comic shops right about now, and comic shop retailers have enough crap on their plates right now. The toy industry is imploding, meaning that no one toy in the store window is enough to bring in customers, and Pokemon is finally revealing itself as a slightly longer-lived version of Pogs, so two previously dependable sources of alternate income will probably bring in considerably less money in 2000 than in 1999. (Last year, I was able to get the neighbor kids to rake up leaves through half of the area just by paying them in Pokemon cards: this year, they're asking me if I know anyone who wants to buy their collections.) Even if this Christmas season is, hope of hopes, the best the comics business has ever seen, the impending collapse of Marvel Entertainment Group should encourage everyone to save their holiday profits in anticipation of a very long, dark recession in the field. Right now, the comics industry is in the same limbo currently holding the movie and music industries: nothing's a particularly breakthrough hit right now, and everyone's waiting for an impending swell to show up so they can make plans to swim toward or away from it.

Because of these factors, good comic shops need every bit of help they can get. We customers can help, but one major suggestion on how to increase profitability is one that needs to be undertaken by retailers themselves. Trust me on this: get rid of the card geeks this season.

Now, I'm not talking about Pokemon players: most Pokemon collectors come in with their parents and walk right out as soon as they get their next fix. At least they pay money for their addictions. I'm talking about the "Tragic: This Gathering" nits, as well as the Kallikaks wanting to get together gaming groups for everything from GURPS to "The RPG That Ate Kankakee." Kick 'em out for the season: if you're smart, you'll keep them out for the rest of the year, too.

By way of analogy, my best friend and I used to go to an Irish bar here in Dallas every Wednesday, partly to catch up on current events and partly to catch a bit of music. This club used to host Celtic musicians every Wednesday, and it was a nice way to take a break from writing and relax. That is, before it was discovered by the local Renaissance Festival flakes, who promptly moved in, medieval garb in Texas summer and all. Within about three months, this huge club was packed solid with what the manager called "Scarborough Fairies" every Wednesday, which would have been fine if any of them had actually purchased so much as a beer. Instead, if they weren't cackling about costume making or the latest Society for Creative Anachronism scandal loudly enough to drown out the music, they were either ordering plenty of food and beverage and then skipping on the bill, or one would order a single glass of water and share it with eighteen others and then bitch if s/he was charged for it. After three months of this, the bar's owner had no choice but to shut down the music nights: not only were paying customers not able to get a seat among the little *Dungeons & Dragons* cliques on Wednesday night, but the pittance the bar made from the few who squared away their bar tabs was less than the cost of cleaning up the horrendous messes left when the Scarborough Fairies finally went home at closing time. (He quietly started them up again a few months later, only to put them on a staggered schedule to keep the RenFest dweebs from collecting critical mass again.) Best of all, it made everyone at the bar incredibly biased against anyone remotely connected with that pack of losers, which is why I still apologize for my associations and why I still tip heavily whenever I visit.

(Based on previous experience, making these comments guarantees that some flat-footed fantasy fanatic is going to write up, sniffing "Well, I'm going to do everything I can to make sure you can't join the SCA, and we'll keep you away from the Renaissance Festivals, too." Oh, please, Brer Fox, don't throw me in that briar patch.)

In the scale of general fandom, gamers are the bottom-dwellers thanks to the pedantic and obsessive nature of the more vocal members of the population. (I used to play *Call of Cthulhu* back during my sordid youth, and I saw far too many gaming groups splinter and die because of one rule-waving geek or another who got his way by dint of overpowering volume and/or breath, and these are always the ones who proclaim themselves to be the spokespeople for the business.) Gamers are even beaten upon by other fans: back in 1991, I was at a spring comics convention held at a hotel with a big petting zoo in the lobby for the Easter holiday, and a friend looked at this and sighed "Oh, look: they brought farm animals for the gamers." A good percentage of gamers are rational, decent folk, but they're usually crowded out by the wankers and pocket psychotics who make one look back fondly on the local Cat Piss Man.

Because of the good people in the gaming industry, a surprising number of comic shops start up little gaming spaces so that gamers may collect and have a friendly territory for their chosen hobby. Because of the pocket psychotics, many of those comic shops close down the spaces in short order. The ones that don't either have nothing but good people using the spaces, or simply don't care about the impression the pocket psychotics give passersby about the store's clientele.

The first reason to consider pitching the gaming table is for immediate financial gain. Besides the obvious aspect of how the space dedicated to a gaming table could be used for displaying merchandise, just compare the amount of money the gamers bring in versus the amount they take away. Even without considering the costs of shoplifting, and I once demonstrated to a friend who owned a shop exactly how easy it was to sneak out a couple of hundred dollars' worth of merchandise out under the nose of his partner, look at the cost of cleaning and maintaining that area every night and then check to see if sales of cards and games justifies the expenditure. Even if they don't steal merchandise outright, look at the gamers who figure that books and comics on the shelves are community property while they're in the store, and ask "Do I make more from selling Magic cards than I lose from copies of *Cry for Dawn* with the pages all glued together?"

(Just before I left Oregon in 1997, I had the opportunity to talk to a comic store owner who was shutting down his store about the gamers, seeing as how one had just stormed out in a hissy fit. Said gamer had been nagging the owner about opening up a gaming space, and the owner pointed out that the money he made from the gamers taking up that table for twelve hours was considerably less than the cost of the electricity necessary to heat and light it, and he couldn't afford the extra staff necessary to keep order. To this, the gamer volunteered to take care of everything, and did the owner have an extra set of keys so the gamer could open the store at 7 in the morning so he and his friends could get an early start on the gaming day...?)

Next we have the wear and tear on the staff. Comic shops already attract one of the most strange and wonderful casts of characters this side of an episode of *Farscape*, and the store staff has enough to deal with without having to break up fights and put out fires started by gamers in the back. A couple of weeks ago, I was at My Comic Shop in a pretty impressive line snaking from the cash register toward the front door, when this peanut-headed gamer comes waddling from the back and gets the attention of the poor guy manning the till.

"You see that guy who just left?" the chickenhead asked, assuming that poor Bill memorized the entries and exits of every customer in the store. "He threatened me."

Bill was desperately trying to ring up another customer, but he broke free long enough to ask, "What did he say?"

Peanuthead smirked. "He threatened me. I want you to kick him out of the store."

Bill pardoned himself, saying "I'll take care of it in a minute," and Peanuthead started whining about how he wanted it taken care of now now NOW, and finally settled for waddling back and continuing his interrupted game. Nobody had any idea of what the threat was, or if it existed in any form other than the little voices echoing through Peanuthead's skull, but Bill gave the impression that this was a regular game that he was tired of playing.

This was just one incident, and dealt with easily that time, but does any comic shop have the necessary time and energy to deal with this level of bullshit once a week, much less on a daily basis? More importantly, what if Peanuthead had become violent, or decided to set the back room afire because he didn't get satisfaction? Is he really that good a customer that the store can justify tolerating his tantrums?

And then we have the public relations issue. Just close your eyes and pretend that you're a normal interested bystander to the comics scene, and you're walking into a comic shop for the first time. Just as you wouldn't want to visit a bookstore if a local radio station was hosting a "Battle of the Bands" competition on the next aisle, could you concentrate on seeing what comics had to offer if a gaggle of crazed gamers were shrieking and arguing and laughing in the corner? More importantly, if you saw them for the first time, or had to deal with them as they tried to start a conversation at nothing less than 250 decibels, would you necessarily want to remain? Okay, so store owners may not be bothered by the gamers in back, running around in their "authentic" Klingon uniforms until the store closes, but don't let them disrupt the store's operations and then complain about how "normal" folks won't go into the store. People are funny that way.

With all of these factors in mind, make an informed decision, and Do What Thou Wilt. Just remember, though: crack dealers generally don't allow their customers to crash over at their houses and indulge their various nasty habits, and why should those selling games do the same thing? Likewise, Target and Wal-Mart sell Pokemon cards, and they don't offer gaming space for customers, so why should a comic shop? The smart money says to shut down the gaming section and tell the denizens "GO HOME." Everyone will be happier that way.

—*Savant, November 30, 2000*

Postscript: Oh, yeah, I got more than a few death threats from this one. How dare I advocate shutting down a vital sacrament of the Church of Saint Spock the Pointyeared?

"Two Minutes To Midnight, The Marvel Way"

Something about former champions in a field being beaten like redheaded stepchildren brings out a particularly nasty streak in all of us. Back three years ago, the little *King of the Hill* snipe "Dallas is crawlin' with crackheads and debutantes, and half of 'em play for the Cowboys" was nearly blasphemous: these days, it's creepily prophetic. Show me one person who figures we should be nice to Leona Helmsley or Donald Trump, and I shouldn't even have to mention musical examples like Vanilla Ice or the Bangles. (Yeah, they're jokes *now*, but *somebody* bought their albums.) And man alive, the people planning to beat on the carcass of Marvel Entertainment Group are starting to get ugly.

The current discussion, among the feces-flinging bands of apes known as Usenet and the convention circuit, is on the impending death of Marvel Comics. Oh, they deserve it, the chimps scream, and I'm going to have a party when they go under. Some people even talk about a "Marvel Death Watch," in which they await the collapse of the company as if the comics industry was a variation on the French Revolution. (We could have used a revolution four years ago: the thought of Ron Perelman being dragged up the guillotine steps like Louis XVI is a particularly comforting one.) These aren't people who work for the company, own stock in the company, or even read any of the company's comics: these are folks who are convinced that Marvel is The Great Satan, and that we'll all be better off once its monolith has been blown clear off the planet, never to darken our horizon again.

Okay, even considering that a world without Marvel just means that *Comics Journal* publisher Gary Groth will have to find another straw horse to beat (from what I understand, a couple manning the lighthouse on Stewart Island south of New Zealand are the only people on the planet that Groth hasn't insulted yet, either in print or in person), wishing for the collapse of Marvel is Wrong, and not for the reasons you may think. Yes, it's been a horribly mismanaged company. Yes, it puts out crap. Yes, it helped flood comic shops with lots and lots of poorly-thought-through product intended solely for twelve-year-olds and those with the maturity of twelve-year-olds. The problem is that the people who made the mess are never going to clean it up, and they're never going to be held accountable for their actions. The folks who will pay are the ones whose only mistake was working for the perps who left the mess.

By way of corollary, look at all of the hype about the collapse of the dotcom industry. Damn near every paper and every news Web site is practically crowing about the demise of goofball dotcom companies such as Pets.Com. On one point, they should be crowing that bad businesses are going under, but it forgets one particular point. The people responsible for the goofball ideas, and the ones who collected the money while it was still coming in, aren't going to be held accountable for their excesses. The people who pay are the rank-and-file, who may have busted their asses for months or years on promises of riches in the future only to get a layoff notice. Meanwhile, the ringleaders skip merrily on to their next big scam, usually getting a job at another company within days or even hours, while everyone under them sits in the unemployment line.

Here's another example. Three months ago, Dallas' last independent weekly newspaper was bought out and shut down by New Times Inc., which regularly buys up weeklies all over the US and either guts them of anything that makes them unique or interesting, or shuts them down so they won't compete with their own papers. This paper wasn't the greatest, and in fact had been laboring under a revolving door of editors and a publisher who thought that the perfect slogan for it was "The Paper For People Who Don't Read." (Considering that the publisher was reaching for an audience of frat boys from Southern Methodist University, business majors, and any mouth-breathing inbreed who wanted nothing more than bimbos on the front cover and drinking tips inside, the slogan should have read "The Paper For People Who *Can't* Read," but why get nasty?) In its six years of publication, this paper had managed to burn through damn near every freelance writer or artist in the Dallas area, and was subsisting on a diet of interns who frantically hoped that they would become full-time staffers if and when the publisher let the paper be successful. The publisher and his investors, who made one idiotic business decision after another, weren't punished for their stupidity: they walked with $2 million from the buyout. The people who were punished were the few full-timers, who were given a month's separation pay in one of the worst job markets for journalists in history. New Times made a big deal about promising to hire staffers for its papers, but New Times made that same promise in 1991 when the *Dallas Times Herald* went under, and they didn't keep that promise, either.

That's why a Marvel Death Watch is Wrong. The people who led Marvel Entertainment Group into the toy business, who pushed for Marvel to go public with its stock, who came up with silly-ass ideas like the Marvel Superheroes fast-food chain, who bought up SkyBox just as the trading card and Pog business was declining, who pushed for the idiot distribution deal that crippled the entire direct market, who let movie licenses go for pennies on the dollar...are never going to pay. Even if Marvel were to go completely bankrupt tomorrow, with creditors barging into the building, shoving artists away from drawing tables and kicking secretaries into the street, you can be reasonably sure that the board of directors won't be resorting to eating dog food by the weekend. Unless every one of them blew every last penny they made on black tar heroin and $10k-a-night hookers, you can be reasonably sure they won't be broke for a while. If Marvel goes under, the people who are going to be hurt are the writers, artists, support staff, custodial crew, and general support who were working for peanuts. Most people in the comics business work in it because they love the medium, not because they expected to get rich on it, so rest assured that they won't be sleeping on a mattress full of $100 bills when Marvel locks the doors for the last time.

(Last summer, *The New York Times Magazine* ran an article written by Herb Trimpe on how he had reinvented himself as an art teacher in the wake of the Marvel shakedown. Even for those who weren't particularly impressed with his work, his article should be taken as a very serious warning to those in the comics business who don't have anything to fall back on. His editor wouldn't admit for months that Herb was on the way out, along with Arioch-knows-how-many other artists and writers, and he took the initiative to find something else before he found fifteen former Marvel artists all fighting for the same job. I'm seeing the same thing in the tech industry, which is why I'm going back to school to get my veterinary medicine degree this fall.)

This isn't intended to be an apologia for the company, nor is it an entreaty for everyone to buy lots of Marvel comics to keep the company afloat. Marvel's management brought all of this horror upon itself, but Ron Perelman and Carl Icahn managed to weasel their way into cushy deals, so they aren't going to starve for their arrogance. The people who are going to be hit are the folks lower down the food chain: if the artists and writers are out of work, then that cuts into the revenues of distributors, news vendors, store owners, and everyone else who depends upon Marvel for at least a portion of their paychecks every month. These people hitting the job market are going to make things that much tougher for those wanting to get into the business, as well as for those already in the comics business. And considering that Marvel Comics are generally the gateway brand for new generations of comics buyers, the company's demise could keep us in turmoil for decades.

Besides, you really want to stick one to Marvel? Buy up Marvel stock, each and every one of you, and vote out the slimesuckers and dogfelchers who put the company into this situation at the next stockholder's meeting. The stock's really cheap right now, for obvious reasons, and I don't see why we can't start our own Alice's Restaurant Massacree Movement and buy up at least a significant portion of the stock floating around right now. If the inmates run the asylum, we might get the chance to make the changes that everyone wants to do, and we'll be responsible if the plan fails. But hey: that's why Charlie Chaplin and Mary Pickford started United Artists.

—*Savant, December 14, 2000*

Postscript: Marvel bailed itself out in subsequent years, mostly due to income from a succession of movie adaptations such as Spider-Man *and* Iron Man. *Increasingly, though, the comics are secondary to the movie projects. And so it goes.*

"Does Artist's Alley Turn Into Easy Street or Suicide Slum?"

Back at the end of November, I was invited to be a guest at a major multimedia science fiction convention. Never mind which one: the convention staff did its best, and I have no intention of slandering its efforts by naming it. All that matters is that, for the first time in over eleven years of being a guest at these things, I was given a table in the dealer's room in order to sell my dubious wares. It was at this locale that I learned that one of the most oft-repeated bits of folk wisdom about promoting oneself in the comics business was a blatant lie.

For those who have never been to a science fiction convention, a comics convention, or one of those collector fairs that somehow reads "Country Mayfair" on the marquee in front of the hotel, most people attend conventions for one of two things. Either they arrive to be able to meet the varying guests (usually one to ten stars for an extant or defunct science fiction or fantasy TV series and a whole crew of second-rans, usually hailing from literary or comics backgrounds), or they come to clean out the dealer's room. At most of these, the dealer's room is the largest room rented for the event, and it's usually packed solid with any amount of amazing crap from all corners of the genre. At many of them, the dealer's room is the only reason to attend, and the organizers arrange to have guest signings and minor events in the main room so that people will come to get their picture taken with their favorite *Star Trek* star and leave with a critically depleted MasterCard and a forklift full of toys and collectibles. At shows dominated by comics dealers and comics writers/artists/publishers, a certain amount of space is left in back, generally entitled "Artists' Alley," for creators to show off their work and maybe, just maybe, sell some of that work.

The basic idea behind Artist Alley is that this is a way for comics creators and publishers to meet up with existing fans and make new ones, and it works in a strange petting-zoo sort of way. The creators (almost always artists, but the occasional writer appears in the mix) are stationary except when called to do their dancing bear impersonations at panels or other sanctioned events, or when calls of nature or nicotine addiction force them to leave for a time. Through all of this, a never-ending wall of vaguely bored people walk by, and after three days of this, I understood why the cattle and chickens at the State Fair of Texas had that touch of bloodlust in their eyes.

As a PR exercise, Artist Alley is a joke. Even considering the number of people who want to see their favorite artist in the flesh, the emphasis is on seeing. Every creator attending a convention hopes to have hordes of adoring fans rampaging through the dealer's room in a mad panic to be the first to say hello, but that almost never happens. If it does, those rampagers are usually hauling handcart after handcart of stuff to be autographed, and they tend to get rather persnickety when they're told that the object of their affections literally doesn't have all day to autograph two metric tons of comics. (My most vivid autographing story happened at the summer 1993 Dallas Fantasy Fair, with Clive Barker as the guest of honor. Among the usual hordes of *Hellraiser* fans was one guy who came up to Barker during an autographing session, handed Barker a fresh scalpel, took off his shirt, and turned around, tapping his back and saying "Sign this." Naturally, when Barker declined, the guy threw a hissy fit, thus helping to explain why Barker doesn't do autographing sessions of this type any more.) For everyone else, while they may want to see the human face behind their comics, courtesy or even shyness keeps them from coming up and introducing themselves: after all, what else are they going to say besides "Hey, I really love your stuff..."?

Oh, and then we have The Thing That Wouldn't Shut Up (he described with self-loathing, having channeled for this parasite quite often in the past). We're talking about the guy (sometimes the Thing is female, lest ye think I'm being sexist) who assumes that because the creator touched him in some way in the past, that said creator is his friend. Because far too many of us were raised to be polite in conversations, we'll see a creator in Artist Alley talking with someone else and wander on, feeling confident that the creator doesn't want to be disturbed by a random fan while having a conversation of import. Usually, though, what happened is that the Thing crawled up, wanting to blather about everything and nothing, and the creator is stuck not wanting to be rude but also wishing that s/he could crawl on buttocks away from this purgatory. The Thing won't take a hint to go away and bother himself for a while, and it's bad enough when a guest at a convention is stalked by a fan who wants some attention while the guest is perusing items in the dealer's room, trying to talk to someone else, trying to track down someone else, trying to get something to eat, or trying to use the toilet in peace. When The Thing That Wouldn't Shut Up is on the prowl, a comics guest behind a table in Artist Alley has a lot in common with a wooly rhinoceros trapped in a tar pit.

As if The Thing isn't enough of a menace, then we have the ongoing horrors of being Second Fiddle. This usually happens when a new or moderately successful comics creator ends up with a table in Artist Alley next to one of the convention headliners: picture, say, Jim Mahfood getting a table next to Rob Liefeld. Within minutes, a line of supplicants spreads throughout the alley, usually blocking off access to any other guest with a moving wall of humanity. Some creators may feel "Oh, good: I have a captive audience," but that doesn't happen, either, as those mendicants are there only for the healing touch of the creator at the other end of the line, and most of those waiting couldn't care less about anyone else at the convention. In the meantime, because of the wave of Liefeld zombies, anyone wanting to talk to Mahfood, or anyone else on the other side of the Great Wall of Fandom, in many cases literally cannot get through without whining of "No cutting" or physical violence.

In my case, I wasn't bothered by the lines, seeing as how I was literally giving stuff away. (I was out with lots of work on my own projects, including big fat stacks of *Savant* and other magazines I had written for in previous years, as well as flyers for friends' projects and even some candy as an extra incentive.) I had big signs up saying "Free...To A Good Home," and I actively encouraged people to help themselves. That was when I learned the one overriding law of conventions: *Everyone Wants Everything For Free Except When It Is Free, In Which Case They Don't Want It Any More.* By way of example, I was sharing a table with Mark Murphy, creator of the exemplary *House of Java*, and he was trying to sell graphic novels and individual issues. Without fail, if anyone came by to poke through my freebies, they'd start pawing through Mark's comics, whining "Is this free, too?"

"Nope, sorry," I'd respond cheerily, "you have to pay for that. I'll tell you what, though: if you want a copy, I'll buy it for you." (Mark had put up with my antediluvian honk for two days, so I figured that getting another reader hooked on *House of Java* was the least I could do to make reparations.)

The attendee would then look at the comic, sniff "Oh," in that nasal way that anyone who attends conventions knows so well but can't explain without sounding it out, and left without getting anything. (And before anyone notes that maybe I wasn't offering anything of interest, I tried an experiment where I left out samples of the same stuff I had on my table on the "Freebie Table" out in front of the dealer's room. Everything invariably disappeared within fifteen minutes to an hour.) After one of these incidents, I suddenly understood and felt for the people manning the booths at tech conventions, where the attendees grabbed for every gewgaw they could, but only if they didn't have to make eye contact with the people offering the gewgaws.

For the first time as well, I understood the motivation behind having "booth bunnies" at a comics table, even if I still don't agree with their use. With all of the intervening distractions in a typical dealer's room, even the most patient of us ends up suffering from an otherwise debilitating case of Attention Deficit Disorder, making it impossible to conduct coherent conversations, much less stay on focus. About the only thing that draws the attention of a typical convention attendee is a pair of barely covered mammaries, and considering that attendees won't stop to look at good artwork, the only way a lot of marginal work stands a chance is by hiring a few girls from the local Hooter's to show off their talents (as Joe Bob Briggs would have put it) to slow down the lemming rush for a few moments. Yes, it's sexist, and yes it's degrading to both women and the comics industry, but the booth bunnies fill the same niche that Jeri Ryan's addition to *Star Trek: Voyager* did: they use the rampant and unused libidos of the audience to keep them from fluttering to the next attraction. Those comics creators who didn't have characters that could benefit from being modeled by denizens from the local strip club...well, they're fucked.

The worst part of this sojourn through the Alley was that most of my fellow sides of meat were resigned to using the Alley as their sole form of promotion. Never mind that artists and writers should be among the crowds, pressing flesh and making friends, or that if artists feel the need for a table showing off their work, then that work should be on display in the Art Show along with business cards and other contact information. Never mind that a lot of creators wasted half of their available time trying to drive off The Thing That Wouldn't Shut Up so that someone else could get a chance to say hello. Never mind that the same people who didn't think anything of going to the Sharper Image and blowing $10,000 on a life-sized Boba Fett model suddenly became misers over the thought of paying for a $2 comic that they thought they should get for free. Never mind that most of the audience that the comics industry is desperately trying to reach either can't afford or can't justify blowing $15 for a one-day pass or $35 for a three-day pass to go rooting around the basement of a hotel in search of the one comic that might make them regular readers. Never mind that the people who do show up are already faithful martyrs to the cause, so long as the cause is advocating lots of physiologically impossible superheroines. Oh, and never mind that when we're talking about people who see nothing wrong with sleeping 30 to a single hotel room, we're talking about people who are so incredibly cheap that they try to use both sides of the toilet paper, and usually won't buy comics at a convention unless they know that said comic will be worth Harry Knowles' weight in platinum once it's signed. In the meantime, the smaller publishers are screwed: even those who can afford to give out free copies of the latest issue of their latest title don't necessarily get a return for their promotional efforts, and since most creators are dead-poor and buy copies for promotion at the detriment of their grocery funds, only a very lucky few make enough at a convention to cover lunch in the convention hotel, much less enough to pay for their time and energy. It's been like this from the beginning, and so it shall be until the end of time: if you want to promote your comic, or at least get a few more fans, you have to do your time in Artist Alley.

Well, bollocks to this. What should replace the standard comics convention as a gathering place for creators and a showcase for publishers is a very good question, but the convention as it stands ill-serves the comics community. Conventions are great for fans to get together, exchange gossip, and pretend that the outside world doesn't exist for a weekend or so, but when creators and publishers depend upon the big San Diego show or innumerable little conventions as one of their only venues for reaching the general public, then it's time to come up with an alternative. Otherwise, the industry remains at the mercy of the twerps who have nothing better to do on a Thanksgiving or Labor Day weekend than drool over booth bunnies and argue over Silver Age versus Golden Age minutiae while fighting over the latest *Spawn* action figures.

—Savant, December 21, 2000

"Rapid-Fire Magazines"

With the ongoing and thoroughly depressing collapse of the comic direct market, quite a few voices have started questioning the need for the standard 20-page comic format. The graphic novel is definitely coming in on its own, and online comics have their own particular joys and horrors, but a few souls are starting to ask about using the standard print magazine format again. It's not as if the format is new (after all, *Heavy Metal* has been using that format for nearly thirty years, with its predecessor *Metal Hurlant* going back even further, and older readers may remember the uneven but sometimes brilliant *Epic* from Marvel in the late Seventies and early Eighties), but just because the format had limited appeal before doesn't mean that it couldn't work now.

That said, though, some of the suggestions being made about successful comic magazines are...well, naïve. That is, they're good suggestions, but they come from people who have no idea of the pit of horrors that is the magazine publishing industry in this foul Year of Our Lord 2001. They're suggestions that don't take into account the incredible amount of money and manpower necessary to get any magazine going, and they're suggestions that not once ask about ongoing profitability. These factors don't make the suggestions any less valid: instead of deriding them out of hand, this essay intends to help answer these concerns in the hopes that someone will find work-arounds to the standard responses.

Right at the moment, the magazine industry in the United States is in about as bad a shape as the comics industry, only the people in the magazine business don't air the dirty laundry quite so much. The distribution system is a mess still mired in procedures and policies instigated back just after World War II, the number of venues that sell and distribute magazines are steadily decreasing, and most Americans can't be bothered to read magazines at all. That is, while industry trades ranging from *The Industry Standard* to *Variety* to *Nature* still command a reasonable readership, the number of people reading magazines purely for pleasure are declining. The only exceptions are mainstream sex magazines, with *Cosmopolitan*, *Maxim*, and their clones marking the only noticeable increases in magazine sales and circulation in the business. Everyone else is right out of luck.

Part of the situation with magazine sales is due to a changing demographic. With the Web and television offering more alternatives for a cheaper price, not to mention a population for whom reading has long been considered a chore, the successful magazines are the ones with as few words as possible that get in the way of the pictures. Even for those who have the inclination to utilize basic literacy in a contemporary setting, the problem is finding time to read. In this category, the best sellers are those magazines that offer content that can be read on the bus, in a doctor's waiting room, or in the john. (This is what I call the Crap Rule: most magazine articles should be just long enough that the reader can finish it while taking a potty break, without that break going on for so long that the reader gets in trouble for excessive reading at work.) This is one of the reasons why self-help and news magazines have expanded in the last twenty years, while fiction magazines are relegated to a tiny portion of the general literary landscape.

The other part of the situation comes from the assimilation and deconstruction of the magazine market by superpublishers. AOL Time Warner and Conde Nast are two perfect examples of large publishers that rule the magazine industry like tyrannosaurs, and their predations directly affect everyone else. The first influence comes when they observe a newcomer that puts out an interesting and successful magazine and immediately flood the market with competition. Even in the best of times, magazine racks have a limited amount of space available, and the Big Guys have plenty of influence in getting booksellers or magazine distributors to carry ALL of their products. Ergo, if Conde Nast decides to put out five new ripoffs of *Stuff* (and just out of curiosity, when are we going to see a men's magazine with the honest titles of "Dry Hump" or "Masturbating Like Caged Apes"?), five spaces for five different magazines are going to disappear.

(This, incidentally, is the reason I laugh at apologists for the science fiction industry about the relevance of SF magazines. If genre magazines were anything but tax writeoffs or attempts to keep anyone else from trying to horn in on a few spare shekels, don't you think that Time Warner would have put out at least one literary science fiction magazine by now? Hell, they don't even bother trying to compete with TV and film SF magazines like *Cinescape* and *Starlog*, which should tell you something about these magazines' audience recognition or profitability.)

And before I forget, we need to take a look at those magazine sellers themselves. As anyone with even the slightest interest in books already knows, Borders and Barnes & Noble have already altered the bookbuying landscape beyond all recognition, which helps explain why *Publisher's Weekly* regularly features articles on the latest lawsuit concerning both chains' predatory buying practices. (Both have been charged with working out deep discount deals with big publishers, receiving a higher discount for books than what is being offered to independently owned bookstores, and thereby explaining how both chains can afford their discounts on bestselling books. We don't have time to go into that now.) Because these guys order more magazines than most, their buying practices are going to affect what a distributor wants to offer: if Barnes & Noble doesn't want to order a particular magazine, the odds that a distributor is going to keep pushing for it are pretty slim.

(Here's a corollary for the situation, this time using the school textbook market as an example. Texas at the moment is one of the biggest purchasers of elementary and high school textbooks in the United States, and for years it was held hostage by Mel and Norma Gabler, a duo of self-appointed book censors down in Longview who regularly critiqued textbooks up for consideration in Texas schools. By the Eighties, the Gablers had become a national joke, and not just because of their ongoing efforts to remove evolutionary theory from science books and sex education from every possible niche: in one of their most famous incidents, they rejected a dictionary because it defined "bed" as "a place where one or more people sleep." Even with this idiocy, book publishers such as Houghton Mifflin knew that they had to deal with the Gablers, and so books that were suitable for sale in Texas were the de facto standard for the rest of the country. And you thought that a comics market dominated by superhero fanatics was bad.)

Backtracking to comic sales and making comic magazines, the biggest consideration for anyone contemplating starting one is that the comics business isn't the magazine business, and it never will be. Let me explain.

Even though it's ill-serving today, the concept behind the comics direct-sales market was a clichéd but accurate stroke of genius. Before the direct market allowed comic shop buyers to order comics directly from the publisher (or, as in the current system, from a series of distributors), comics were treated just like any other magazine. These days, comics are a nonreturnable commodity: once a store ordered its comics, those comics were and are nonreturnable, and it's up to the store to move them. If they sell poorly, well, the publisher and distributor take no direct responsibility. (Actually, they do, but only when the comic shops of the world realize that they're stuck with thousands of copies of *Silicone Implant Girl* #1 and decide to cut back on their next order. However, in most circumstances, the store owner isn't allowed to ship back all of those unsold copies and demand a refund or credit.) This tends to work because of the perceived collectability of new and old comics, but magazines don't have that level of collectability unless they feature nude photos of celebrities taken when they were unknowns.

(In a recent interview in the magazine *Nova Express*, no relation to the paper in *Watchmen*, Neil Gaiman related that the main reason why most comics publishers don't bother advertising new comics is because they're already sold under the current system. The comic shops have already paid for those comics, so the only interest Marvel or DC have in advertising new or ongoing titles is to get new or increased orders in the future. In their perception, they'll only lose money by advertising the first issue of *Silicone Implant Girl*, but they'll run ads in their own comics in order to stoke enough interest so that the shops will order the second and third issues. After the third, generally people will keep getting it out of habit.)

In a typical newsstand situation, though, magazines are usually returnable. Take a look at a typical magazine stand and look at the publication date right below the magazine title: ever notice how the date on top is always anywhere from two weeks to three months in the future? Well, that's because the date is not for the potential purchaser. That's to help the guy (or gal) who stocks the racks: that date is to denote when that issue is to be pulled and replaced with the new one. (Comics generally still work on that system, and this also ties into that color-coded bar on the top of most older comics. It's all designed to keep old product from hogging space that could be used by titles that will sell.) That person then counts all of the copies left, compares them to the number sold, and sends out two reports. The first one goes to whomever is responsible for paying for the magazines sold in the store, and that person usually cuts a check that goes back to the distributor which ultimately gets to the publisher. The second report is to the person or people who make new orders for magazines, and they use that report to decide how many copies of a particular magazine they should get next time. These latter folks are usually pretty unforgiving: if they order ten copies of a new magazine for a store and it sells only three, they'll usually cut back the order to three and might consider raising the order to four a year or so down the road. In the meantime, the magazine might become famous or otherwise in-demand between issues two or three, which means tough luck for the new readers trying to find a copy and tough luck for a publisher who has to wait until the buyers decide to take a chance again.

Anyway. Back to "returnable." After those reports go out, the magazines themselves are supposedly returned to the distributor handling them. Some places still cut off most of the front cover and send that back to the distributor as proof that the copy didn't sell and receive credit on their next order (paperback books get their covers ripped off in the same way; many of these still end up in garage sales and flea markets, as do the mutilated magazines). Others ship back the whole lot to the distributor, who is then responsible for tallying sales versus returns and sending the publisher a check minus returned copies and the costs of shipping. Those returned copies generally disappear (more often than not, they're sold in bulk to recyclers who grind them into paper towels and toilet paper, right alongside poorly-selling paperback novels and prayer requests to televangelists), and the whole system holds together because the publishers trust the distributors in their bookkeeping.

Now, other factors figure into the profitability of a magazine, starting with the point of sale. Until relatively recently, newsstands and magazine sellers were held responsible for any copies that were damaged or stolen, which is part of the reason for the clichéd "This ain't a liberry" newsstand hawker attitude. About two years ago, though, Barnes & Noble started keeping exact tabs on what magazines and newspapers came in and which ones were rung up on their cash registers. (This is why Barnes & Noble won't touch magazine without one of those little funny UPC codes on the cover, and why all comics sold in comic shops have that "DIRECT SALES" notice on the top of the UPC. The first is to keep exact track of what magazines came in and left the store, and the second is so that some comics geek doesn't pick up comics from his/her store and try to exchange them for cash or credit at the local B&N.) That part wasn't so bad, but then B&N decided that the chain was no longer responsible for magazines that were stolen or damaged while in the store. This meant that the cost of magazines that were rendered unsaleable because some dolt poured coffee inside it while reading it in the store Starbucks, magazines gummed by a customer's toddler, magazines with pages ripped out by some fanboy who couldn't live without that pinup of Jeri Ryan in the latest *Femme Fatales*, and/or magazines that walked out the door in the backpacks of employees (and the last is rumored to be the number one factor for missing magazines at any Borders or Barnes & Noble) were to be eaten by the publisher. Imagine the shriek from Toyota if car dealers were to tell the company that the costs of idiot Lexus test-drivers wrapping a 2001 SUV around a telephone pole were to be assumed by the manufacturer, and then consider that Lexus has a much better profit margin than most publishers. With that, the lack of noise from publishers is deafening.

This said, the return on selling magazines is pretty poor. Even under the best of arrangements, only about half of the cover price goes back to the publisher. Most bookstores pay about or less than 50 percent of the cover price every time a copy of a magazine sells, and that's if the store can return unsold copies to the distributor. If the magazine is nonreturnable, the stores generally pay 40 percent, and let's not forget that the distributor gets a percentage on the copies that do sell. And that's if the store decides to pay its bills in the first place: Barnes & Noble in particular is notorious for paying its bills if and when the company feels like it, so the money from a sold-out first issue may finally arrive as much as three years after the magazines arrived. (And unlike small stores that bail on their bills, the big stores have lots of lawyers that keep people from dragging the CEO into court over $200 in magazines that were never paid for. The small stores aren't perfect, either: I'm still owed money from Powell's City of Books in Portland, Oregon for copies of a magazine named *Tangent* that I sold to them on consignment back in 1997, and I have yet to receive a check or even a letter explaining why they never paid.)

Because of the low return on magazines, the big magazines take advantage of advertising to offset the dips in the revenue stream. The money that AOL Time Warner receives from a copy of *Time* sold on the newsstand is gravy: that issue was already in the black when it went to the printer thanks to the full-page color glossy ads that infest it. *Time* can justify the ad rates it charges because of its planetwide circulation, and very few niche magazines make more than operating expenses from selling advertising. Running advertising requires its own little empire of ad reps to get it, though, and many potential advertisers will probably look down on a comic magazine as being beneath them.

This essay has already gone way over length as is just for a preamble, so come back next week for the second installment, complete with an explanation why the Ultimate Marvel magazine line is an excellent idea that came along at the worst possible time.

—*Savant, March 8, 2001*

Postscript: We were a very naïve people back in 2001. Here in 2009, the magazine market is collapsing, in all categories, and Time Warner (which ditched the "AOL" some time back) is still trying to sell most of its house magazines, such as Field & Stream *and* Popular Science. *They haven't been successful so far, but they won't shut them down, either.*

"'Keeping the Columnist's Ego On A Short Leash' and Other Surefire Ways To Keep A Comics Magazine Afloat"

Last installment, we started to discuss how certain members of the comics community, looking for alternatives to the standard 20-page comic sold through direct-sales outlets, are talking about moving to a standard magazine format and a standard magazine distribution system for new sequential art. This is a noble and laudable goal, and that last installment was intended to encourage the idea while warning of the real concerns that anyone switching from comic to magazine format should consider before jumping in. Those who didn't read it last week should go back and read it: I'll wait.

Back so soon? Nice to know people who read faster than I do.

The idea of doing comics in magazine form isn't new and never has been. The most obvious example is *Heavy Metal* and its French Siamese twin *Metal Hurlant*, but we can point to Marvel's *Epic*, the UK's *Warrior* and even (if you want to stretch the definition of "magazine") *2000 AD*. The last was closer to a standard tabloid paper, but it's still an alternative to the standard comic in size, distribution and content. Most of these combined standard articles and interviews with the comics, thus producing a magazine with much more general appeal than a magazine that simply reprinted comic stories. Size wasn't necessarily important: the Seattle-based *Glyph* (which reintroduced all of David Lee Ingersoll's characters from the sadly defunct comic *Misspent Youths*, along with a whole crate of new characters) and the Austin-based *Chaos* (edited by Deanne DeWitt and Deborah de Frietas, the real brains behind the now-defunct Adhesive Comics) were closer to traditional zines in size and circulation, but this didn't affect the product inside. We can also mention the Warren Press magazines from the Sixties and Seventies, and even a few Marvel products such as *Savage Sword of Conan*.

All of these had a few commonalities. Most worked as anthologies for a varying number of stories per issue, some serialized and some not, and they mixed a variety of creators and a variety of forms in a way that the good ones had at least one feature for everyone picking up an issue. Most of these were going for more adult audiences (or, in the case of *Heavy Metal*, sixteen-year-olds who couldn't get the key to their fathers' collections of *Hustler*), and most made a pretense of trying something different. Even the magazine-sized comics such as *Savage Sword* took advantage of the magazine's larger size and better paper to run longer storylines than what were available in a standard comic format.

With this as a start, not much is necessary to make your own sequential art magazine. Just get artwork and copy together, reproduce it onto 11x17 paper at the local Kinko's, fold it in half, put a cover on it, and you have a magazine. Pure Scott McCloud territory. The problem is that we're looking at trying to produce a magazine that might actually sell when put on a newstand shelf, and nothing screams "UNPROFESSIONAL!!!" more than a cover made of construction paper. A real sequential art magazine requires a staff that knows what it's doing, and a revenue source behind it that won't dry up in a week, and a reasonable understanding of what audience it can strive for and what audience it can expect. Lots of magazines die because someone in that chain didn't understand the audience, and we're trying to avoid death for as long as we can.

Since this is the sort of essay that it is, it wouldn't be complete without a list of points That Must Be Obeyed Or Else Failure And Damnation Will Envelop You All. Actually, that's not fair: these are intended to scare away the poseurs. Anyone serious about trying to get a professional comic magazine going will already understand these: these are intended for the wankers who figure that they can get fame and fortune with a minimum of effort, money, and consideration of the realities of publishing.

Numero Uno: Magazines are disposable. The only reason why comics have a shelf life is because of their perceived collectability, and this is part of the crutch of direct sales. Order too many copies of *Silicone Implant Girl*, the logic goes, and you just keep them around the store until they sell. This works great for comics, or at least the market for back issues is such that it seems to work great, but magazines have a limited shelf life no matter the content. Unless it's chock full of porn, very few people are as interested in buying a magazine collection as they are in buying a comics collection.

Here's a direct example. My Comic Shop orders quite a few magazines from Diamond Distribution, and they're put in the "New Arrivals" section right alongside the new comics. These include new issues of *SCI FI*, *Wizard*, *Cinescape*, and *SFX*, along with more specialized magazines like *Cinefex*, *Locus*, and *G-Fan* (and if you don't recognize these names, don't feel bad). Since Diamond sells its magazines and figurines and toys on the same non-returnable basis as its comics, those magazines sit until they sell, which may be years. Maybe some will leave over the decades as serious collectors find the one issue they needed for a college thesis, or someone finds a copy of a magazine that was legendary to them in their youth, but they're otherwise hogging up space that could be used for other product.

Comic shops can still profit on the occasional magazine sale, but any bookstore or magazine stand that operated like this would be buried, literally, in tons of unsold periodicals. Just consider the number of daily papers that sit unsold in a typical magazine stand, and then combine all of the weeklies, monthlies, quarterlies and semiannuals and consider the number of unsold copies of *Maxim* with the pages all glued together in themselves. Standard magazine outlets have no interest in acting as collectors: even if the magazine's publisher goes out of business, sooner or later someone manning the racks will note "Hey, this has been sitting on the shelf for the last two years" and throw it out.

The reason why is that magazines are intended to be ephemeral entertainment. Someone with thirty years of comics in a collection is given marginally more respect than someone with boxes and boxes of old magazines: the latter is usually discovered a decade after s/he died in a pile of those old magazines and newspapers, rats having gnawed most of the flesh off those bones and the bones of the 37 cats kept in the house. Everybody weeps over a family member throwing out a comic collection: only obsessives weep over a twenty-year collection of *Cosmopolitan* going to the dump. Most magazines get cut up for art projects, read to death, used for kindling, or bundled with the rest of the recyclables, which is why magazine collectible value has some real connection to demand instead of the crazed speculation in the comics industry. (Hey, just look at the number of weirdzos who want that one copy of *Life* with Lee Harvey Oswald on the cover.)

Because of this and the general situation with profitability, a sequential art magazine cannot treat itself as a comic, because relatively few people are going to collect it. In fact, the opposite effect is necessary. The idea here is to make sure that one magazine gets passed through as many hands as possible. Not only does it make the advertisers happy (after all, if eight people read an ad, then that ad makes more of an impression than it would in a comic where the purchaser immediately seals it in Lucite after paying for it), but it improves the odds that these people will want their very own copy of the next issue.

Numero Two-O: When you edit a magazine, you're in it for the long haul. Contrary to popular impression, nobody makes money by publishing a magazine right away. Most magazines don't start to make a profit for about two years: they may be making money before they see print, but that money has to go into payroll, insurance, and debt reduction. (I've worked for several magazines with a rich benefactor who decided three months in that he wasn't making millions of dollars right away the way he figured, and he pulled his backing right about the time the magazine was starting to become profitable. I'm certain that he'll be sunk up to his nose in boiling hyena vomit in the deepest pits of Hell, standing on the shoulders of the editors and publishers who can't be bothered to inform their staffers and freelancers that the publication is going under until they've strapped on their golden parachutes and left for a new job.) Even if the magazine is a blowout hit right away, getting new advertisers and new subscribers is going to take a while: far too many people and businesses have been burned by buying subscriptions or advertising packages for magazines and papers that shut down right after the first issue.

What this means is that a good, serious sequential art magazine is going to need a regular source of income for at least a year, instead of assuming that everyone can pay for the next issue with the income from the previous issue. (Remember what I said about Borders and Barnes & Noble paying their bills when they feel like it? Well, you can call and write and E-mail until your eyes bleed, and they still won't expedite their money, no matter how badly you need it.) This means making sure that writers and artists get paid right away, instead of that nebulous "when we start making money" crapola. This means having enough cash to pay the printshop first and paying for the editor's fancy office second. Hell, this means getting a real editor, instead of some prima donna whom gets pissy because nobody recognizes his name or that of the magazine. This means doing something that seems to be in very short supply in the comics field: planning for the future.

Numero Three-O: Subscriptions and decent customer service shall be the whole of the law. Right now, most comics publishers ignore or downplay subscriptions. Back about 25 years ago, subscriptions were often the only way to guarantee that readers could get every issue of *Howard the Duck*, and even then the service wasn't all that great. (Hunt down any Marvel comic published in 1976 and turn to the "Subscriptions" form. Notice that they make a big deal about how "Now all issues mailed flat!" because they used to just roll them up in a tube and mail them that way.) These days, though, with the joys of pull boxes, subscriptions aren't the huge moneymakers they used to be, and subscriptions don't make any sense at all with the plethora of miniseries put out by damn near everyone.

Well, bunkie, when switching to magazine format, subscribers are your lifeblood. These are the folks willing to trust you with $25 or more of their cash in exchange for some good or at least interesting reading material. Considering that newsstand sales bring on a pittance, and since a comic magazine is going to be too much of a niche market to draw the likes of Lexus or Crown Royal, that's seed money for the future. And there's no better way to have to eat that seed corn than to screw over subscribers.

As an example, I try to make a point of buying subscriptions to the magazines for whom I write, because I figure that every writer or beginning writer who pays for his/her magazines helps guarantee that the magazine will still be around for the next submission. Anyway, I had a column in one magazine that had and has a horrible track record for getting subscriber copies out into the mail: right now, the current issue has been on the stands for a month, and I still haven't received my subscriber copy. The assistant publisher and I discussed this many times when I was working for him, and his general attitude was "oh, well."

This sort of attitude was reprehensible even when times are good, but magazines are never necessities. Now that everyone is spooked about the near future and the state of the world economy, they're starting to look long and hard at their expenditures, and nothing (and I do mean nothing) gets cut out of the budget faster than resubscribing to magazines with consistently shitty service. (I did this with *Entertainment Weekly* about two years back: I could almost tolerate the "all-*Star Wars*, all the time" coverage, but when my wife would go a month without an issue arriving and the idiot customer service rep for Time Warner kept claiming that those last five issues had been mailed off, renewing the subscription wasn't worth the cost of calling every month because we received one issue out of every four.) Remember: a sequential art magazine is a niche luxury, and the real money is made on subscription renewals, so this requires a whole new level of customer service. The most beautiful artwork in the world is never going to make up for a snotty attitude toward potential purchasers.

Numero Four-O: The only thing keeping you alive is advertising. Remember what I said before about how little money a magazine makes from newsstand sales? Subscriptions will help the bite a bit, but the overriding concern of one and all is to get enough advertising, or enough sponsorship, to ride any slow selling issues. This means getting people who know a little something about ad layout, and most importantly people who know something about selling advertising. A few potential advertisers will contact you, but any rational magazine staff will work in the opposite direction.

And as an amendment to this, try for a bit more upscale clientele than what you think you can get. DC in particular has been getting a higher grade of advertiser for the Vertigo line than what anyone conceived a decade ago. (Go back to your comic collection, pull out any comic published in 1991, and compare the ads to any comparable comic published today. Okay, so Pennzoil and hair gel aren't as fancy as we'd like, but don't they beat the hell out of candy, "Odd-Balls," and Saturday morning cartoon lineups?) This is even more vital for any magazine gunning for adults and other non-traditional readers. By getting advertisers with a bit of class, people thumbing through a copy at the local Borders won't be quite so embarrassed to be caught with it, and that's halfway to a sale.

The other thing to consider is that by making a good impression as a magazine with a future, advertisers might buy a whole ad campaign instead of individual spaces, and that's just as important as subscriber money. As soon as one potential advertiser hears that his/her competitor just bought a year's worth of advertising, they'll call up and ask about jumping in on what appears to be a good thing.

(And for those purists who don't believe in advertising, I have a way out. Make your magazine so incredibly good that junkies in Seattle will pawn their crack pipes to buy a subscription. In fact, follow the tradition started by some of the better public television stations in the US: simply threaten that you'll start running advertising if the subscriber base drops below a certain level, and watch the scramble. Hey, it beats all hell out of waiting for some incredibly rich but fannish dotcom billionaire to subsidize the whole thing, and you'll feel better about it in the morning.)

Numero Five-O: The real sign of success is when you can pick up your magazine at O'Hare Airport, not when you win the Harvey Award. Winning niche awards is all fine and good, even if they don't really mean a damn thing in sales or circulation, but the main goal here is to expand comics' readership. That's why the real underlying goal is to work toward getting that new sequential art magazine in the newsstands at airports.

Airport newsstands are easily the toughest market to crack for a new magazine. They're generally dominated by big publishers and big distributors, and the stands' management is completely unforgiving of poorly selling magazines, or to anything sufficiently controversial that they have to deal with irate travelers threatening boycotts over "inappropriate material." These are frequented not by diehards who will go to any distance to buy your magazine, but by people looking for a diversion from a boring flight or looking for an hour to kill while the previous passengers disembark. All of the magazines therein are intended to be disposable, with Arioch-knows how many copies being left in restrooms, on gate seats, and left on the planes themselves, and most serious travelers only bring home the magazines that they want to share with others. They'd be willing to read comics if they didn't fear the disapproving glances from fellow passengers, or if they didn't find themselves buried under years of continuity or lousy, breast-infected artwork. Most importantly, if their first experience aboard the Southwest 6:45 to Phoenix was good enough, they just might take a chance and head out to the local newsstand and keep buying.

This, kids, is our intended market, strange as it seems. Getting existing comics fans is all fine and good, but anyone who can produce a magazine that can survive the depredations of the airport zine rack and make a profit will be a Force To Be Reckoned With. Get that kind of success, and everything else is gravy.

Next week: The realities of the magazine industry today, and why *Ultimate Marvel* is the right idea at absolutely the worst possible time.

—*Savant, March 15, 2001*

"The Ultimate Insult to *Ultimate Marvel*"

Update for the Unwary: Three weeks ago, this essay started discussing the merits of comic magazines. The idea was that standard-sized magazines that just happen to contain sequential art already have a longrunning tradition in both the US and the rest of the world (although more stunted in the US, thereby proving that the rest of the planet is more civilized), and the only thing keeping comics magazines from being a success lay with the subpar distribution system inherent in the magazine industry. We start the last part of the trilogy, already in progress.

Back in November, Marvel Enterprises (comprised of the wreckage that was the Ron Perelman kamikaze vehicle Marvel Entertainment Group) announced something different. Marvel had prior experience with standard format sequential art magazines: admittedly, its last, *Epic*, died in 1985, but this wasn't *terra incognita*. *Ultimate Marvel*, though, was *different*: in an effort to get more exposure for the new Ultimate Marvel line of comics, the *Ultimate Marvel* magazine was to contain segments of the comics, complete with explanations of what had happened in the previous issue. Instead of focusing on one comic, say *Ultimate X-Men*, the *Ultimate Marvel* magazine contained serials from several of them, all in one package. Best of all, *Ultimate Marvel* was intended to be sold through standard newsstand distribution systems, so potential customers didn't have to find a comic shop to read the new lineup.

This was intriguing, and not because I'm a huge fan of superhero comics. With the ongoing debate as to whether the current direct market for comic distribution is a dead end for the medium, anything that either tried a whole new direction or recycled a neglected concept was welcome news. The magazine format could have saved ensemble comics such as Dark Horse's incredible *Instant Piano* from 1995: comic shop denizens didn't like it because it didn't have superheroes (the first issue featured the first US appearance of Evan Dorkin's Eltingville Club, so that may have been an issue as well), and humor fans and others who would have appreciated the material weren't about to brave the local comic shop even if they had known about it, so it was dead coming and going. The magazine format also was something rarely used in the US, so the novelty value alone made it worth seeking out. Either way, it was a brave move from a company not generally known for initiative, so I spent weeks trying to find a copy.

That search took a little longer than I expected, seeing as how the first issue wasn't released until January. Even so, nobody seemed to have copies except for my local comic shop, and the crew at the shop sheepishly admitted that they only ordered copies for the people who specifically requested it. That made good business sense to the store, seeing as how the magazine was full of reprints of comics that its customers probably already had, but it didn't help my quest. I finally contacted Bender Helper Impact, the publicity company handling press relations on *Ultimate Marvel*, and asked about its availability, and they were kind enough to forward a press release and a copy of the third issue.

About the magazine. It's a beautiful piece of work. It combines good printing and good layout (which are not always found in the same comic), and it's a good hefty size, just perfect for a road trip or airplane flight. For those who appreciate or have any interest in Marvel superheroes, it's worth the money. Had this come out in 1993, it probably would remain one of the bestselling magazines of its type around, and it probably would have inspired efforts from DC, Dark Horse, and just about every other comic publisher wanting to get away from the comic shop ghetto. Unfortunately, since it premiered at the end of 2000, it's doomed.

Part of that logic lies with the distributor handling *Ultimate Marvel*. As mentioned in previous installments, most of the magazine business in the US is handled by Ingram Periodicals, and the little guys rarely get a chance to show their stuff these days. (This is part of the reason why nobody sees too many zines in the local Borders any more: Fine Print Distribution, the largest zine distributor in the early Nineties, went bankrupt in 1997, and competitors such as Desert Moon are finding that Borders and Barnes & Noble just quit ordering zines when Fine Print died, rather than finding a new distributor.) This makes things really interesting for magazine buyers at times: when living in Oregon, I found myself frequenting a newsstand that did ninety percent of its business from hardcore porn (and I mean HARDCORE: stuff whose covers peeled the enamel off my teeth just by walking by) because it was the only place in town that carried *Reptiles Monthly*. *Ultimate Marvel* is distributed by Curtis Circulation Company, a company that I'd never heard of, but this shouldn't be held against them. Even so, if most of the stores I was frequenting were purely Ingram venues, then it helped explain why finding the magazine was such a pain.

(Dallas is already well-known for similar blacklists. Back in 1987, when Jolt Cola first came out, it was an incredibly popular soda that suddenly and without warning disappeared from store shelves all over the city. According to several sources, Jolt disappeared because Coca-Cola and PepsiCo had special deals with most of the soda distributors in town: "carry Jolt, and we'll make sure that you pay more for Coke Classic and Mountain Dew than your competitors" and the like. Buying Jolt in a typical convenience store in Dallas is impossible, but the shutout started up a very enthusiastic and profitable operation from teenagers and twentysomethings who drive up to Kansas City, load up on as many cases of Jolt in as many flavors as possible, and then drive back to Dallas and sell it at raves, parties, and science fiction conventions at a fair profit. I just love to see enterprising kids making money by smuggling stuff that's legal.)

Anyway, calling up Bender Helper Impact was very informative, and not just because BHI isn't stingy with its information. (Trust me on this: just try to pry information out of a movie publicity company unless that information is for an obvious bomb like *Joe Dirt.*) *Ultimate Marvel* has a current print run of 60,000, which isn't half-bad, and the rep I talked to said that it was out and freely available. I saw no reason to disbelieve him: he was going on sales reports that showed that it was selling well throughout the US, particularly in the Southeast. This makes sense: when selling to teens, you have to remember "bang for the buck," and when a whole huge magazine like this costs about as much as two standard issues, they're getting lots of bang. This made me redouble my efforts, and I started searching through newsstands and bookstores in the hopes that somebody had seen a recent copy. No dice.

The reason that *Ultimate Marvel* is doomed isn't just because the US magazine market has changed since 1992, when Borders and Barnes & Noble took over. It's that even when the ordering is taken care of by the home office, the responsibility of actually setting out magazines usually falls on some 22-year-old pothead or Trekkie who, more often than not, will lie out his/her ass rather than take the time to see if a magazine is in. Just try this sometime: walk into one of these great emporia of literature and ask the person in charge of the magazines about a magazine that's either dead or nearly impossible to find in the States (my three big tests are *Granta*, *Eidolon*, and *Mondo 2000*), and only rarely will you get someone who (a) cares to know anything about the magazines being carried or (b) will expend any other effort than to say "It isn't in right now; it'll be in next week."

That "It'll be in next week," particularly with one magazine stand at the local Tower Records, was the mantra. (To give an idea of the sales skills of the people being hired by Tower, ostensibly the zinester's best friend in the States, I also asked the magazine guy if they had the newest copy of *A Reader's Guide to the Underground Press*, formerly *Zine World*. He mumbled the request to his boss, who told me "I'm sorry, but we don't carry *Reader's Digest*," and then gave me the phone number of "our magazine buyer" when I corrected him on the magazine's name and told me to talk to her after the weekend. Naturally, this person had quit some six months before. Double the amount of paraquat being sprayed on Maui's marijuana crop, and Tower might actually be a tolerable store again in six months once natural selection took effect.) If they even knew they were carrying *Ultimate Marvel*, they weren't telling, and even the magazine stores that carried Marvel and DC comics didn't have any idea of what I was talking about.

This situation can be fixed, but this'll cost money, and that's something Marvel can't afford to hemorrhage away right now. Getting top placement for a new title in a comic shop is pretty easy: most comic shop owners are routinely entertained by cardboard standups and posters, and handing out a few tschochkes will keep many owners giggling for weeks. (One shop I know in the Dallas area makes most of its money off freebies like this: why hang them up where they could get damaged when you can take those freebies and sell them at insane prices to some Cat Piss Man who just can't live without a *Shi* life-sized cutout?) The big bookstores and magazine stands, however, usually demand some kind of compensation for good placement, the same way supermarkets charge manufacturers for the eye-level spots in the Frozen Foods or Pasta aisle. Ever notice how most magazine and book chain stores have that big stack of *Maxim* or *Rolling Stone* right at the cash register? This isn't largesse from the store: either these are already big sellers that sell even better as impulse purchases (and impulse buys are critical for some magazines: care to name any other reason why anyone would pick up *TV Guide* or *Entertainment Weekly* if not held at gunpoint?), or, more frequently as of late, the publishers paid a pretty hefty chunk of chump change to get their magazines stacked by the register.

The other problem ties right back into that old bugaboo of comics: promotion. Outside of the comics community, nobody knows or cares that *Ultimate Marvel* exists, and the only promotion for the title has been internal. Even then, Marvel's been slacking: take a look at the official Marvel Web site and try, the way I did, to find any information on *Ultimate Marvel* the magazine. The site has a big banner ad at the top screaming "HEY KIDS! Watch *X-Men: Evolution*," but the WB already does more promotion for that cartoon than Marvel could conceive of doing, and that space could be used to promote the magazine and the locales from where it could be purchased. And yes, Marvel's publicity team has done quite well in pitching new information to people in the comics community, and they should be commended for this. However, promoting *Ultimate Marvel* to the comics community kindasorta ignores that the purpose of the magazine was to introduce Marvel comic characters and situations to people outside of the comics community. The level of promotion for *Ultimate Marvel* blows the bejeezus out of promotion for most standard titles, but *Ultimate Marvel* is supposed to be trying to steal reader attention away from *Talk* and *Newsweek* (or at least *MacAddict* and *Cinescape*), not *Powers* or *Green Lantern*. We're talking about ads in *Time* or the occasional billboard: television advertising is way too much to hope for, but a couple of well-placed ads on the SCI FI Channel during *Farscape* or on ABC during *The Drew Carey Show* would do more in a minute than twenty years of product placements.

Now, if some farsighted person at Marvel back in 1991 had seen the possibilities of a standard magazine format and pushed it instead of action figures and Pogs and fast food restaurants, *Ultimate Marvel* would have been well-established by the time the comics speculation market fall down and go "Boom." Since it isn't dependent upon comic shops for its distribution, its sales may have dropped when the dolts who polybag Taco Bell *Episode One* wrappers stopped buying ten copies for their collections, but probably not much. A lot of the discussion on changing the form of the standard comic going on today never would happened, because participants in this debate could argue the success or failure of *Ultimate Marvel* on real data, not speculation. In the spirit of building dream castles and measuring for drapes, magazines like *Ultimate Marvel* might have helped buffer some of the real shocks of the speculation bust by giving a venue for new writers and artists who were just a little too unknown to be trusted with their own titles, as well as offer a comics venue for kids and adults who had no access to traditional comics shops. Shoulda, woulda, coulda.

The reality right now is that *Ultimate Marvel* is making all of the right moves, but will probably be held as a failure. This is a shame, and has nothing to do with the magazine's viability: it has to do with uncontrollable forces in the outside world that may kill it before it finds an audience. A lot of magazines right now are dying or limping along, and unless the powers at Marvel Enterprises can think of a good way to get magazines into the hands of potential customers and bypass the potheads and burnouts manning the magazine racks, *Ultimate Marvel* is going to be just another name on the casualty list. And that hurts the comics community at large as much as it hurts Marvel in particular.

—*Savant, March 29, 2001*

Postscript: If the first time you heard of Ultimate Marvel was from this trilogy of essays, then you see how well Marvel decided to promote the magazine. Contrary to original promises of how this was going to be a mainstream newsstand magazine, it reverted to a direct market-only magazine with its fourth issue, and it promptly disappeared shortly afterwards. Goddamn, there are times where I hate being right.

"Taste-Testing Dog Crap"

It's one of the most commented-upon maxims of the comics industry: we don't remember our past. Of course, this is usually in reference to the long-forgotten classics of the field. It's a valid concern: a lot of good titles and stories lay moldering in long boxes and in "3 for a Buck" bins, unrecognized while the latest one-hit wonders get the accolades. In this case, the comics industry is just like the music industry (has anyone who actually listened to rock music in the Eighties wanted to scream at the "Sounds of the Eighties" format making its way across the radio dial, where the B-52s apparently existed solely to produce "Love Shack"?). However, we're just as guilty of ignoring the worst of the field, and in this case, we keep repeating the past because we forgot it.

When talking about bad comics, it's easy to succumb to a snotty little list such as the bad music lists every music critic around puts together once a year, beating on little acts that can't afford to buy advertising in that particular publication and therefore make themselves easy targets. It's also easy to use the discussion of bad comics as a great chance to grind a few axes: the real reason why William Castle takes so much shit in Michael Medved's *Golden Turkey Awards* books lies more with Castle having produced *Rosemary's Baby*, which offended Medved's fanatical Catholic sensibilities, not because *The Tingler* and *13 Ghosts* were as bad as Medved likes to convince us. These attitudes must be eschewed: we need to look at the bad stuff, the really bad stuff, because of what it can teach us.

The Web site *Web Pages That Suck* exists not simply to laugh at lousy Web pages, but, as its slogan attests, by "Teaching Good Web Design By Showing Bad Web Design." The *Gone and Forgotten* site (http://ape-law.com/GAF/) works the same way: it's not just enough to tell creators "Don't make sucky comics." The site shows examples of horrible comics, as well as explanations of WHY *Bee-Man* or *Secret Wars II* are not the comics you want dropped into a time capsule so the sentient species that replaces humanity in 100 million years will understand why we obsessed so much over sequential art. *Gone and Forgotten* doesn't just show bad covers with a note of "You may laugh now": the site includes commentary to explain to those new to the field (or to those too young to remember some of the real offenders, such as Atlas Comics, created by Stan Lee's brother Larry Lieber in 1975) the whys and wherefores of how these titles came to be. And by doing so, they protect future generations.

The comic industry isn't only bad at preserving good material for future generations: trying to find copies of the more important seminal works in the business is hard enough, but a lot of material continues to remain in slowly crumbling pamphlet form because while it was good work at the time, and probably would hold up well in the future, it's not seen as being profitable enough to republish in graphic novel format. We're also really bad at preserving the crap: we don't really want to preserve the crap, but we need to remember where we came from so we don't make the same stupid moves every ten years or so. For instance, having CD-ROM archives of every DC comic published in the Nineties would not only dissuade future editors from going crazy with tie-in stories, but show that just because Marvel managed to scam thousands of comics buyers into the non-event that was *The Marvel Mutant Massacre* in 1986 didn't mean that DC had to do the same thing with *Zero Hour*, *Bloodlines*, *Underworld Unleashed*, and *The Way of the Warrior*. As disgusting as publishing a CD-ROM collection of every title released by Malibu or Image (pre-1997, that is) may be, we need to remember, and keep remembering, that just because an artist is good at work-for-hire claptrap for Marvel doesn't mean that s/he should listen to the Cat Piss Men at conventions whispering "You're a genius; you're too good for these guys; you should branch off on your own..."

Because of our unwillingness to remember our mistakes, we forget the whys and wherefores of the new material. This may only appeal to the obsessives who make comics reading so unenjoyable, but for all of the noise about the animated *Batman Beyond* series, nobody seems to remember the first time we had a futuristic Batman running around Gotham City. Of course, that's because this previous Future Batman was a supporting player in the otherwise justifiably forgotten series *Hex*, a *Crisis on Infinite Earths* spin-off which featured Jonah Hex thrown into a post-apocalyptic world full of mutants, robots, and aliens. (This previous Batman had come across the remains of stately Wayne Manor after the bombs had fallen, and decided to become the Law in Gotham when the Law had disappeared everywhere else.) The current *Batman Beyond* series is a great improvement upon the 1985 version, but it begs the question: was *Batman Beyond* inspired by someone coming across an old issue of *Hex* and saying "Hey, this is a great idea, only we have to get rid of the *Road Warrior* mindset...," or was this a matter of convergent evolution by someone who honestly never heard of the previous *Batman: The Next Generation*?

The main purpose of this exercise is to point out that these comics didn't spring from vacuum. Somebody, somewhere down the line, took the editorial or financial responsibility to put these turkeys out on the stands. Someone gave the okay to *Lady Rawhide*. Someone took time from huffing E-Z-Off to green-light Rob Liefeld's *Captain America*. Someone was at the switch when the train wreck that was *Dazzler: The Movie* came whooshing around the bend. A person or persons unknown had the opportunity to prevent *Guy Gardner: Warrior*, but didn't hit the "Abort" button fast enough. And someone, somewhere, still thinks of *US 1* as being good enough to put on a resume. Don't even get me going about the media tie-ins: picking on all of those bathetic Marvel movie adaptations of *Krull* and *Dune* are too easy, but even discounting Marvel trying to bottle lightning after the surprise success of the *Star Wars* franchise, The House of Ideas still pumped out a lot of series based on movies that never should have left the editor's office? It's not just the fact that the Doug Moench/Herb Trimpe *Godzilla* lasted for nearly four years (even after Godzilla took on the Fantastic Four and Devil Dinosaur), but that DC succumbed to the urge and put out *V*, which had the distinction of running for two years and thereby survived the crappy skiffy TV series upon which it was based by a factor of four.

Now let's not forget the other guilty party in this comedy. That's right: we're all responsible. We may not be responsible for the vanity press crapola pumped out by geeks who figure that their clones of Marvel characters will make them fortunes, but we're responsible for everything else. We may laugh at some of the idiotic comics that have appeared in our industry, but we laughed at Vanilla Ice's musical career, forgetting that somebody made "Ice, Ice Baby" a platinum album. We laugh at *Youngblood now*, but is this because we were laughing at it way back when, or because we're hoping that nobody goes poking through our collections and finds that we have a complete set? How many of us helped keep bad series going beyond their intended lifespans because it was easier to keep buying a title in hopes that it'd get better one of these days instead of cutting it free? Most importantly, how many of us kept buying bad series because we honestly didn't know any better and honestly thought Chris Claremont is a master writer?

This is a factor we'd sooner ignore. A lot of the "classic" work in this business is just as bad as the vast majority of the latest titles that hit the "New Comics" section yesterday, only the work in 1959 really was better than the work from 1939 in most cases. That's the clincher, though: we keep going back to the "classics" because of our memories of how it was better back when we were ten years old, without recognizing that our tastes should have improved since we were ten. Arguing that *Ghost Rider* is better than *Omega Men* is still taste-testing dog crap: both of them were and still are godawful, and the only people who ignore that both titles are garbage are those who have come to enjoy the flavor.

With that in mind, head on over to *Gone and Forgotten* and peruse the chronicles of Bad Art. It's not enough to know where you're going by studying where you've been. It's just as important to know where you've been so you know why your boots are covered in cowflop, and to help you decide whether you want to wash off your boots or keep going because the smell makes you nostalgic.

—Savant, August 16, 2001

"The Big Move"

It's always said that wisdom comes in strange forms, and never where you expect it. H.P. Lovecraft always suggested that insanity, suitably applied, broke down the barriers between our perception of the universe and the reality. With one friendly bit of volunteer action, I realized that both are true.

A few months ago, the owners of my favored comic shop discovered that the stripmall in which the store was located was to be demolished at the end of the summer. This spot had been home to comic shops for nearly a decade and a half: it was originally a branch of the Clint's Comics empire from the late Eighties, and when Clint's abandoned Texas, the new owner bought out the inventory and the location and set up shop there. It was high time for a move anyway: the sewer line underneath the strip mall was going the way of all PVC pipe, causing visits from Mr. Hanky the Christmas Poo at the worst possible times. The owners found a new locale right down the street, in a new strip mall loaded with the best video store in Dallas, a really good deli, and a Burger King and a Taco Bell within walking distance. The new location was perfect: now all that remained was to move everything out of the old space.

Now, My Comic Shop (original location) was a rabbit warren, but most of that wasn't the fault of the owners. Besides the ongoing boom in comics-related collectibles shoved in everyone's faces by Diamond Distribution, this store still contained some inventory from the Clint's Era, as well as from the first manager, who never saw an action figure he didn't like. Several other comic shops and memorabilia stores went out of business or otherwise shut down in the last couple of years, and two of the owners' own stores shut down due to the ongoing compression of the comics industry, so all of that inventory had to go *somewhere*. The owners also weren't averse to grabbing really good deals as they became available, so they snagged particularly good collections at particularly good prices. This meant, when the move started, that we had a simply incredible amount of merchandise, display space, and support material that had to be loaded up and relocated. Just the action figures alone filled up a space roughly 20 feet on a side and four feet high, and I don't want to get into the stuff in the "Adult" section: the owners decided to give Garth Ennis, Warren Ellis, Alan Moore, and Neil Gaiman their own sections in the new store just to keep the area under control.

Most retailers should recognize now that any significant move should be done by professionals. It may cost real money, but moving a store across town should not be done by willing volunteers schlepping store inventory in the backs of their

Gremlins. In this case, though, since the new store was literally down the street, this was a reasonable and sane measure: using volunteers to lug the fixtures into pickup trucks was a lot cheaper than professional labor. And that's what we did: the owner put out an open call for volunteers, and we collected one hot Sunday afternoon and worked until dark. We moved only about half of the contents of the old store, but the important and/or valuable stuff (particularly the fixtures) went first, and it was out of the way before the little stuff came though.

While boxing, sorting, stuffing, and pulling out from underneath counters, I came to realize some serious lessons about comic store retail. A lot of these lessons came from strange sources: the store had a simply incredible number of T-shirts, for instance, and every time we figured that we'd snagged the last shirt, another would emerge from a new hiding place. Some were common sense; others would never occur to anyone not moving a store to a new site. Either way, here comes possible wisdom, to be used as anyone sees fit.

Numero Uno: If an item is so old that carbon-14 dating no longer works and you have to switch to strontium-rubidium dating to find out how long it's been in the store, it's probably not going to sell in the future without a drastic price cut. The ongoing mantra of comic shop owners and customers is "We can't get rid of this: it's valuable!" Well, everything's valuable, if you look at the intristic value of noting that the constituent atoms were produced in the death throes of a supernova. The question is if an item has a value other than its basic composition: look at the number of televangelist victims willing to pay ridiculous prices for dirt just because it allegedly came from the Holy Land. Comics and paraphernalia won't help you get into Heaven (or Valhalla or Elysium or Mictlan), though, so if it's been sitting around for months or years, consider why it's been sitting around. Is it because nobody really wants it, or is it because the price is just high enough to keep away most of the clientele?

To look at this another way, some items are only sufficiently dusted by getting them out of the store, preferably in the hands of a customer. My store also had a collection of consignment toys and tschochkes, mostly left over from the previous manager of the location. (Sadly, he bought into every last speculation craze, including buying up lots and lots of *Star Wars* figures at horribly inflated prices, and one of those 12-inch Boba Fett figures remained suspended over the counter for months because he believed the figure owner's boasts that it'd sell for $250, no problem.) The centerpiece was one of the old Mattel Godzilla figures from the *Shogun Warriors* line from the late Seventies, marked $350-As Is." Well, it had sat "As Is" for the previous five years, and it was moving to the new store to sit "As Is" because precious few customers were willing to plunk down that $350. Godzilla got regular dustings (or at least the box did), but nobody ever gave it more than a cursory glance. The obvious solution would be to drop the price or work out some kind of payment program to get the bloody thing out of the way, but Godzilla hung on because of a perceived value that no customer was ever going to match.

One of the worst offenders in this category is the horde of cold-cast porcelain figures and collector's sets making the rounds. DC Direct in particular has been flogging comic shops with model Green Lanterns (with "working" ring), lighted chunks of kryptonite, and bottled Cities of Kandor, all slowly disintegrating in the fluorescent lights of comic shops all over the country. The heart is in the right place, but the price ain't: that aforementioned Green Lantern gets pulled out and inspected on a weekly basis by interested purchasers at my shop, but they always balk at the $250 price tag. It'll probably still be on that shelf in another decade, right alongside the cold-cast Dawn and Lady Death stroke statuettes and other ephemera that someone will maintain is still worth the suggested retail price. Get rid of this: yes, the store may lose money, but the space will be left open for merchandise that will sell.

Numero Two-o: Some items are so badly depreciated that it's cheaper to throw them out than to pay for the storage. The most worthless thing in the universe is a three-year collection of back issues of *Wizard*, and the collectible cards from the late Nineties are pretty goddamn close. Anyone considering a move to a new location should go through everything well beforehand and jettison all of the stuff that will never sell, no matter how deeply discounted. This includes *Youngblood* trading cards. This includes any calendar from a year starting with "19": my cleaning discovered at least seven pristine calendars buried in the back of the magazine rack that had fallen and couldn't get up again. This includes any science fiction movie magazine more than six months old: with the exception of the one copy in the collectible magazine box, any copy of *Cinescape* or *Starburst* that didn't sell when *X-Men* premiered isn't going to sell now. This includes any issues of *Locus, Science Fiction Chronicle, Toy Collector, Comic Buyer's Guide,* or *Amazing Heroes* lying around. Fiction magazines, back issues of *The Comics Journal*, or anything containing interviews or article by or about notable personalities in the comics field are a judgment call: that back issue of *The Comics Journal* with the Evan Dorkin interview is probably going to sell sooner or later, but any magazine with a photocopied cover or with the tagline "New Fiction by Hugo Gernsback!" probably isn't going to go anywhere. Donate all of this to local children's charities, give it to regular customers who express an interest, or set it on fire: just don't let it grow roots in the new store.

(And a personal pet peeve: any action figure based on a comic you've never heard of probably belongs in the Rejects bin. Comic shops aren't the only places with this problem: most of the Kay-Bee Toy Outlets throughout the US are overloaded with action figures supposedly based on "The #1 Comic!," and one gets the suspicion that someone was so worried about the action figures that they kindasorta forgot to do the comic. Besides, if you want to run a toy store that dabbles in comics, don't call it a comic shop.)

Numero Three-o: Regular sales to clear out excess inventory are a Good Thing. In the twelve or thirteen years that My Comic Shop had been in that location, the place had accumulated a lot of merchandise that must have seemed like a good idea at the time. Literally thousands of dollars in action figures, many squirreled away by potential customers who never came by to pick up their nutsacks. Posters. Cardboard stand-ups. Minicomics. All of the aforementioned crap that had been picked up for a song. All of this had already been paid for, and it's capital that's tied up until the item sells. Not only do regular sidewalk sales, customer parties, and sales via eBay help keep the aisles clear, but it helps clear out stuff left over from fads that went nowhere, before it becomes worthless. Trust me: nobody's going to get nostalgic for Pogs, so mark 'em down 50 percent and let them go to a good home.

Numero Four-o: Despite your best efforts, inventory will breed like roaches. This may seem to be a corollary to the previous lesson, but it's not. I'm always amazed at the comic shops that have all of the latest information as to what value a back comic should be, but don't have even basic accounting software to track inventory. Shoplifting tracking is one reason to have this, but another is to keep an eye on what already came into the store so it doesn't get ordered again and again. The idea here is to keep surplus inventory from replicating, so you don't keep ordering those Bat-Mite plush dolls when a full box of them is under the counter where an employee stashed them.

During the move, the amount of duplicate items (and not just comics) that kept coming up was mind-numbing after a while. A lot of these came from the aforementioned purchases of other stores' inventory, but it's still disturbing to open up new boxes to see what was inside, and seeing copies of other items that had just been reboxed and packed into the back of a truck. Keeping tight controls on what gets purchased and when will prevent scenes like these, where pristine boxes, packing tape still affixed, open to display items ordered months and years before, only to be reordered because everyone assumed that they never arrived.

Numero Five-o: It's now time for new promotion. Time for a digression into the world of apiculture. Beekeepers have particular tastes in the bees they cultivate, and each of the various strains running worldwide have their advantages. The two most common are the German and Italian strains, and beekeepers will get into literal fistfights about the merits and disadvantages of each variety. German bees (and I speak from experience, having kept bees for years) tend to be more than a bit crabby, with a tendency to fall on the ground when brushed off comb only to crawl up your pant leg and sting the hell out of your ankles, but German bees always scope out the neighborhood before going on foraging runs, so moving their hives a short distance has little effect on their finding their way home. Italian bees, on the other hand, are much better honey producers, are much less likely to swarm without warning, and are incredibly gentle compared to German bees, but they blithely fly out of their hives when foraging without locking into their brains where home is. Move an Italian hive ten feet away during the day, and all of the gatherers will cluster where the hive used to be for the next few days, until they starve to death. Without assistance, Italian bees will rarely find their hive after a small move, and boy do those gatherers get pissed when anyone or anything gets close to the old hive location.

End of the digression. Comic shop patrons are like Italian bees: no matter how many times you tell your clientele about an impending move, you'll always have at least one or two stragglers who will come to the old shop location, peek inside, see nothing but random bits of garbage and the *Battlefield Earth* poster that nobody was willing to carry to the trash, and assume that the shop went out of business. They won't see the notices on the door or window reading "We've Moved!," and they'll automatically assume the worst. Some people just can't be helped, but try to minimize this by letting the clientele know about any impending move as far in advance as possible. Make up flyers to include with every purchase, complete with the new address, maps, and any new phone numbers. Contact the local Yellow Pages and change your ad if you have one: make sure that new and old customers are going to the new location instead of the old one when they see that ad. Spread the word, through any other media venue you can think of. Believe it or not, Usenet can be your friend. If your town has a weekly newspaper read by more than five people, buy an ad and invite a reporter to come out and write about the move. It certainly can't hurt.

Oh, and while we're at it, a move might be a good time to reconsider your storefront appearance, too. Most comic shops in my area are located in strip malls, and I'm always amazed that they don't advertise in the big billboard in front (the one that always lists the local Radio Shack and KFC). Get rid of the generic sign that reads "COMICS": that only works on the comics junkies that need their fix. Plunk down some extra money for a good sign over the front door that not only tells people what you sell, but encourages them to come closer. Remember that your store is competing with every other store in a strip mall or along a major drag, and that yellowing and peeling "COMICS" sign is going to get drowned out by everything else. (And on another pet peeve, I realize that comics yellow badly in the sun, but have you considered putting UV-resistant window tinting on the storefront instead of painting goofy superheroes or plastering posters across the windows? Quit thinking as if your shop was a porno parlor, and that the only people who want to come inside are the raincoat brigade. If general customers can see inside, they're more likely to come in and buy something, especially if they have no fear that they'll be grabbed and drained of blood the moment they cross the threshold.)

Numero Six-o: Kipple is your Enemy. For those who never read Philip K. Dick's novel *Do Androids Dream of Electric Sheep*, "kipple" is the term used to describe all of the little bits of crap and detritus that starts spontaneously sprouting any place where humans gather. We're talking about dustbunnies, bottle caps, condom wrappers, small unidentifiable scraps of paper, and other stuff that accumulates. And it'll accumulate and breed, and it'll force you out before you know it.

Kipple in comic shops is pretty much tolerable: it's those bits of paper, lost blow-in subscription cards that fell out of long-dead magazines, flyers for miniseries that came and went ages ago, coupons for local conventions, unidentifiable parts to action figures and toys, and a lot of pieces of plastic and pulp. It beats the hell out of the kipple found in hair salons, fast food restaurants, pet shops, and porno parlors, let me tell you. It's the accumulation that's intolerable: kipple breeds best in between counters, in back rooms, and underneath display counters, and it'll form drifts, slides, and avalanches without regular extermination. In a comic shop, one of its best habitats is in those big slotted display racks (called a "waterfall" in the trade - thanks to Aaron Davis for this piece of information), where kipple herds in the slots. Cleaning out the comics and graphic novels in each of these isn't enough: a good kipple control program includes pulling out any assorted items that may have fallen in the slots and giving each slot a good dusting. I did this with a couple of racks, and the resultant dust and crap was thick enough for planting potatoes.

(As an aside, cleaning out the kipple BEFORE moving items is a very good idea. We'd like to think that leaving a display rack in the back of a moving pickup truck is a great way to blow out all of the dust and schmutz, but that kipple has been breeding in those racks for a long time, and it flies free when exposed to sunlight and air. The last thing you need is a littering ticket because the local Officer Friendly saw you pull out of the old store parking lot and leave a cloud of ancient Cartoon Network minicomics that blotted out the sun for an hour.)

Numero Seven-o: A move is a great time to reconsider your current product arrangement. When many comic shops move locations, they tend to put up the merchandise in a pattern roughly similar to where it was at the old locale. New comics go here, the longboxes go there, the talking Jar-Jar up front. Besides the obvious but distasteful consideration of an arrangement that discourages shoplifting, might it be time to rearrange the comics racks to allow random passersby to view all the way to the back of the store? Do you want to put the best-selling material up front where it'll be spotted by window shoppers, or do you want to put it in back with a big sign to encourage customers to pass through the rest of the store and possibly find something on their way? What about revamping the adult section, no pun intended? Does a strange layout of wall, phone jacks, or electrical plugs hinder some layouts but encourage something else that wasn't possible in the old locale? The new store is now plastic, so don't feel that you're limited to what has been done before.

Numero Eight-o: Learn to cut your losses with customers. This doesn't just mean cutting your losses with the customers so dense that they don't notice the signs on the window and door saying "We've MOVED!!!" and get on their favorite comics forum to bitch about how their shop upped stumps in the middle of the night. This means considering the cost of maintaining a particular line, category, or service compared to the income made by it. The move is a life-altering event: just as you don't necessarily want your psycho ex to get your new phone number when you move to a new apartment or house, you don't necessarily want to encourage the Law of Diminishing Returns.

For instance, I've gone on already about keeping the gaming geek groups out of the local comic store, because just in presence and volume alone, they don't buy enough "Tragic: This Gathering" cards to compensate for the amount of business lost when they scare off new visitors to the shop. Exactly how much they cost my store didn't become apparent until we started cleaning up the former gaming area. The owners already had an idea of how much inventory disappeared in five-finger discounts back in the gaming area, not to mention the amount of merchandise that was used as common property and then flung to the side, but we found all sorts of evil back in that corner. Discarded food wrappers shoved in all available areas: just try to sell that stack of long boxes when some geek has shoved Milky Way wrappers chocolate-side-out between each layer. Even with a garbage can within immediate reach, one space under a display rack was stuffed literally full of "Magic" card wrappers, where their buyer felt that he was too good to get his overly padded arse out of the chair and put them into the trash. A simply amazing amount of gaming books, action figures, T-shirts (clean and used for handkerchiefs and spunk rags), and unidentifiable crap came out of that corner, and the cleaning costs alone would have eclipsed the amount of money that gaming area brought to the store in a year. (To belabor the point, the store had a very noticeable sign on the restroom reading "EMPLOYEES ONLY," mostly because of the sewer line problems, and a clogged toilet was no source of humor. This didn't stop the gamers from going in, stealing the toilet paper to take home, wiping their butts with newspaper or whatever else happened to be available, and leaving the restroom almost literally covered in shit. That behavior alone was the reason why the owners shut down the gaming section, and you should have heard the shrieking and moaning coming from some of the worst offenders about the unfairness of it all.)

This is why a thorough evaluation of everything in a new comic shop is a dirty but essential chore. The move even gives a good reason to get rid of it: "Sorry, but we just don't have room for a gaming section over here. Have you considered going home and playing there?"

Numero Nine-o: A move can be a wonderful thing. My best friend is fond of pointing out that the two times that anyone finds out who their real friends are is when they move and when they're in the hospital. (One could argue that a funeral is a third, but you're usually not in any condition to thank everyone for showing up.) The owners of my comic shop heard lots of people, myself included, saying "Oh, I'll be out there: definitely," but they also knew that people in comic shops say lots, but have no intention of following through if a rerun of *Gene Roddenberry's Andromeda* gets in the way. Imagine their surprise and glee to discover that the vast majority of volunteers showed up, and that the ones who couldn't make it called beforehand to pass on word. In fact, even more people showed than expected, meaning that a lot more was cleaned up and moved than they had planned. In return, the owners fed and watered everyone very well (the spectre of people eating double-cheese and pepperoni pizza before handling comics might bring shrieks of terror to most owners, but we were all very careful to wash our hands afterwards), and we finished that night knowing that while we hadn't finished the job, we had made a really impressive dent. We felt like the guys building the pyramids when we were finished, and walking into the new store will always make us think "Hey, I was the guy who lugged that display counter into the store, and the first person to leave fingerprints on it is a dead man." We're always talking about building communities in the comics field, and what better bond is there than that between people who saved each other from kipple avalanches?

—Savant, August 15, 2001

"Jamie Rich and Other Editorial Lessons You Don't Read About In *Writer's Digest*"

Okay, so you just got back from the San Diego ComicCon or Dragon*Con or whatever venue you planned to use to pitch your latest comic endeavor. You followed all of the advice given by established professionals in the industry. You bathed, used deodorant, and cut your hair. You wore something besides your favorite "I (heart) the Unabomber" T-shirt, and you put on the slacks without the holes that let your nutsack dangle in the breeze. You took diction classes so editors knew what you were saying without having to translate from Chipmunk, you spent months training yourself to emit a coherent sentence that doesn't contain the word "fuck" somewhere within, and you took that special tranquilizer to keep the random profanity and squeaking noises to a minimum. You've learned not to start conversations with "Hey, yuh wanna see my infected anal gland?," and you understand that humans don't *have* anal glands. If you're an incipient writer, you brought samples and lots of business cards; if you're an artist, you brought portfolios, samples, and lots of business cards. You looked at this as being as important as a job interview, not an opportunity to freak out Aunt Phil so badly that your parents never take you on family outings again. You're ready to set the comics world on fire, and you pitched yourself to every editor willing to listen to your spiel. After shaking hands and dropping proposals or sketches in their hands, you're blasted into their brains, and you've make such an impression that they can't help but remember you years or decades afterwards.

Don't you believe it.

Trust me. Even if you set yourself on fire and went running up and down the aisles of the dealer's room screaming "I'M JOHNNY STORM! GIVE ME YOUR ATTENTION OR I'LL FART ON YOU!," this is no guarantee that a comics editor will remember you past that initial encounter. Comic and science fiction conventions induce Attention Deficit Disorder in the best of us, and while you may remember yakking for hours with the editor of the hour at DC Vertigo before selling him the charms of your barely pubescent sister (and get her back, at the end of the convention, covered in old axle grease and porcupine quills and several appliances of unknown composition and function sticking out of her nostrils), the editor may have no further recollection of you an hour later, much less a year later. Even if you were the only one to offer your sister in exchange for fifteen minutes of conversation, rest assured that this was only because everyone else was offering their brothers. Editors just have to deal with way too many people at conventions, seminars, and general get-togethers, so unless your physical deformities are so overwhelming that you eclipse even the foulest attendees (which gets us into the realm of extra heads, bat wings, and the surprise appearance of "Melvert the Happy Buttplug"), they probably won't connect a face to the name.

Now, I'm cursed with a packrat memory. I say "cursed" because while I can remember line and verse on conversations held with others a quarter-century ago, I also assume that everyone else has the same level of recall. I'm the guy who gets called up to make introductions at class reunions, who has to remind two people that they were high school sweethearts and in fact had been married for four years before that distasteful incident with the cheerleader and the thoroughbred. This gets in the way of being a writer: sure, I remember that conversation, but the editor has no recollection, even when prompted with videotape. And then there's the Jamie Rich story.

To begin, I moved to Portland, Oregon in the summer of 1996 to work for a Web design dotcom on the southwest side of the city. Seeing as how Portland seemed to have plenty of literary opportunities, I plied my wares as previously published freelance writer to all of the venues up and extant at the time. I finally managed to get the attention of the publisher of a monthly arts and entertainment magazine that had just started up, and my packet of samples led to a submission request, and the completed submission led to my being invited to the next editorial meeting. That meeting fell the day I was laid off from that dotcom, but that is a different tale for another time.

I'm not going to go into detail about the situation with the magazine, mostly because it's been dead and gone for years (not to mention most of my comments about the parentage and social skills of many of the staff could be used as material in a possible libel suit, especially amongst those members without a sense of humor and/or skills that would allow them to get off welfare) , but I learned a lot for the short time I was there. Firstly, I learned the lesson of the Psychic Editor: the dolt who regularly demands new content and then rejects it, saying "I don't know what I want, but this isn't it." I learned about what locals call "The Portland Coma," where nobody can be bothered to get off their asses to start any creative endeavour but everyone jackslaps each other to take credit once someone decides to get going. I learned that some editors don't seem to understand that writing for a nonpaying venue is a secondary consideration when unemployed, and that I wasn't going to drop four job interviews a day to slap together something that was going to be replaced at the last second by the editor's ignorant babblings. On the better side, I met Tiffany Brown, the hottie in the Mohawk on the front cover of the otherwise execrable *The Cyberpunk Fakebook* by R.U. Sirius and St. Jude, who was one of the few editors there who actually did anything besides expect the freelancers to bask in the glow of their genius. And most importantly, I met Jamie S. Rich, the resident film critic.

Regular readers of *Savant* already know Jamie Rich: he and James Lucas Jones are the two ringleaders of Oni Press who appear in the public eye. Yes, that Oni Press: the guys who helped introduce the comics world to Judd Winick and Jim Mahfood, among many others. Back in the latter days of 1996, though, Jamie was still an editor at Dark Horse, back when Dark Horse published something besides *Star Wars*, *Aliens*, *Terminator*, and other movie tie-ins. Because of those "others," I was practically giggling: wowsers, talking to an editor for a local comics publisher, and one that didn't put out shit!

Anyway, after the editorial meeting, the weather was getting nasty. Portland weather from Halloween to about Easter is best described as "suicide-inducing," but this rain wasn't the usual drizzle that seeps down the back of your coat and down your neck. This was about as close to a honest-to-Elvis thunderstorm as Portland gets, and I knew that Jamie had to walk across town to get home, so I offered him a ride. Basic human courtesy, and besides, he was quite fun to talk to, so we got in my wife's car and headed out toward the far west side of town.

The discussion on the way out to the outskirts of West Portland was entertaining. I was doing my best not to get all slobbery fanboyish on him ("Gee, Mr. Rich, I'd do anything, and I mean ANYTHING, to get published!"), and he was trying his best to be courteous and not stab me in the neck with a bowling ball for insisting on talking shop. We were right in the middle of a conversation on how Dark Horse management was at that time willing to look at new creations by new writers and artists only after they'd written or drawn a few *Aliens* stories when we came very close to dying.

To explain, Portland is mostly a pedestrian town. That is, pedestrians always have the right of way within the city, and most people rest assured of getting across the street without some mad yuppie in a horribly overpriced SUV popping them like a catsup packet. It even goes in the opposite direction: pedestrians regularly jaywalk or trot across intersections regardless of what the "WALK/DON'T WALK" pictograms say, and they stare at drivers who suddenly blew out their brakes trying to stop like they're the Little Prince and the driver is pushing a manure cart. In a city like Dallas, where the car is the top predator of the local ecosystem, natural selection would remove that attitude within days, but it was practically encouraged in Portland.

That attitude also extends to bicyclists. I used run in bicycle races on a regular basis back in my sordid youth, and I learned everything I know about bike safety from the streets of Dallas, where riding a bike is even more of a crime than walking. This meant watching lights and signs, paying attention to that alter kokker in the turn lane who suddenly decides to slam into reverse, and listening for the slow rustle of the tailgating SUV driver who considers bicyclists to be a threat to his manhood, such as it is. (As it stands, I'm one of the only people on the planet to ride a bicycle down Central Expressway, once listed second only to the Autobahn as the world's most dangerous freeway, but that was due to an honest mistake, and I'll never do it again.) These attitudes were completely alien in Portland, where bicyclists sashayed back and forth between sidewalk and street, ignored stoplights, and flipped off anyone who complained. When I moved to Portland, I loved the idea of a bicycle-friendly town, but after six months of near-misses and verbal abuse from innumerable Eddie Vedder wannabes, I was starting to shop for caltrops and naginatas.

In this situation, Jamie and I were heading down a one-way street to his apartment. In the middle of the night. In pouring rain. The weather was so foul that we kept expecting to see Barry Bostwick and Susan Sarandon on the sidewalk, trying to find someone with a phone. Thanks to all of the illegal parkers on either side of the street, we're down to one lane, offering barely enough room for a Saturn, and I kept wondering how the hell people got Ford Explorers up that street. Suddenly, at the end of the effective reach of the headlights, I see a bicyclist coming right toward us. Going in the wrong direction, with no lights nor reflectors, and wearing nothing but black: the only reason I saw him was because of the chrome on his handlebars. He was also right in the middle of the road and accelerating: he apparently thought we were going to stop for him.

Well, Bill Cosby is right: first you say it, and then you do it. I screamed. Jamie screamed. I hit the brakes, feeling the tires hydroplane underneath us. The car started to fishtail, and I still can't believe I managed to keep control of the car and keep us from slamming into the cars around us. I finally managed to get us to a complete stop, and the cyclist squeezed between us and the parked cars on the driver's side, giving us the finger as he did so. I tried to open the car door and bodycheck him into his next incarnation, or at least into a body cast, but he was already well out of range.

After this lovely experience, I managed to get Jamie home without incident. He was still twitching, but I wasn't sure if this was because of the cyclist or my general conversational skills. After shaking hands one last time, we parted ways, and I never saw him again.

Two years later, I was back in Texas, and I was working for a small media science fiction magazine with a fairly decent readership. At about that time, my local comic shop started shoving lots of material by Oni Press under my nose, particularly the first *Clerks* comic by Mahfood and Smith, and I saw Jamie Rich's name on the masthead. "Goody!" I thought, and sent him a packet with copies of the magazine and a little note. I figured that he'd contact the comics reviewer or otherwise send a note back reminiscing about our near-death experience, because who forgets something like that? Several such mailings, as new issues became available, and still nothing: I figured that maybe he was busy, or that he didn't want to talk to me, or he thought my column in back was a load of horseshit. (Well, it was, but that's not the point.) I finally started joking about that when I started talking about how few comics companies take advantage of potential publicity: Jamie was justified in ignoring anything that came from me, because after all I had tried to kill him that dark December night.

You can imagine my surprise when I discovered that Jamie didn't remember me, and only recollected the incident when reminded. He'd received my packages, but kept asking himself "Who the hell keeps sending me these magazines, and why?" I just chalked it up to poor communication on my part and reminded myself that not everyone has the sort of packrat memory that I do. For God's sake, my family tries to forget that they have any connection to me, so I can understand Jamie Rich getting a perfectly reasonable case of amnesia brought on by a fear of bicyclists.

The lesson? No matter the stunt, no matter the incident, don't assume that any comics editor is going to remember you after a convention. The work will speak for itself: odds are, after a few incipient car crashes, that editor is going to pull that business card out of his/her satchel and go "And who the hell is this?" Even if they don't, they'll probably ask "Was this the first guy who tried to kill me by running into that deer, or the fourth?" Don't worry so much about the schmoozing and concentrate on making your final submissions as good as possible, and you'll be much less disappointed.

—*Savant, November 1, 2001*

Postscript: About a year after this piece came out, Jamie Rich left Oni. He's publishing his own work these days, and I ran into him at a shindig about three years ago. Sadly, as fond as I am of him, I still have enough of an aversion to comics themselves that I haven't read any of his work.

"Ziggy Jordan and the Spiders From HEAT"

Way back in 1994, the forces that be at DC Comics did a very bad thing, according to many readers. That was the year after DC killed off Superman and then brought him back: lots of people bought the *Death of Superman* comic, but those who knew how the comics industry worked knew that Supes would be back, if only because nobody was going to kill off DC's most famous cash cow. The beginning of 1994, though, featured a major change in the DC Universe that involved the Green Lantern Corps.

For those who stuck with Marvel titles at the time, the Green Lanterns were one of the big icons in DC's stable. Since 1959, when editor Julie Schwartz first pushed for revamps of classic Golden Age DC superheroes, the exploits of Hal Jordan, Green Lantern of galactic Sector 2814, were featured all over its titles. If Hal wasn't in *Justice League of America*, he was in his own title or somewhere else, continually wrangling with a power ring that could do anything except affect the color yellow. If he wasn't, then another Green Lantern would take his place. No big deal, though: at one point, the GLs had 3600 members all roaming the universe, ready to fight evil in all of its forms.

In 1994, that changed. That was the year that editor Kevin Dooley and writer Ron Marz presented, with DC's blessing, the *Emerald Twilight* storyline. In this arc, Hal snapped after his home town was destroyed (if you weren't already keeping up with the whole *Death of Superman* story, don't worry: it's too long to get into) and wanted to use his ring to "make things right" again. His masters, the Guardians of the Universe, told him that he was abusing his power, so he made haste to Oa, the home of the Guardians, and managed to kill off his GL comrades and drain off the power of the Central Battery, the source of power for his ring. Hal went on to further interference, ultimately dying and coming back as the newest incarnation of the Spectre (as I said, if you weren't into it, you won't understand), but one Guardian lived, took the crushed remains of Hal's old ring, and gave a newly reconstructed ring to a ne'er-do-well artist on Earth by the name of Kyle Rayner.

The situation behind the scenes at DC doesn't matter in this retelling. Neither does any commentary on the story itself, as contrived as it was. What matters is that the fan base reading *Green Lantern* went bugfuck. Patty Jeres, head publicist at DC, related the death threats that came through for Marz and Dooley, as if they had killed off a real human being instead of a fictional construct composed of ink lines and pages of dialogue. To this day, comics readers who couldn't tell you who was the President of the US will gleefully give their interpretations of why Hal Jordan was a better GL than Kyle Rayner, and vice versa. Until DC stopped accepting unsolicited story ideas, any intern working there would relate how most of the DC slush pile consisted of scripts and proposals for "Elseworlds" stories that somehow reversed the Marz storyline and brought Hal back.

One group of fans decided to go further, forming the group "Hal's Emerald Advancement Team" (HEAT for short, with their headquarters at http://glheat.cjb.net/) with the intent of convincing the Powers That Be At DC to dump Kyle Rayner and return Hal and the rest of the GL Corps to its former glory. The site has a petition and instructions on how Happy Hal fans can write DC and express their displeasure at the current state of affairs, as well as links to other sites that support their efforts.

To many, especially to those who look at comics as being reading material and not the basis for a life or lack thereof, the efforts of HEAT come off as pathetic or obsessive or ridiculous. However, are they wrong? Why should they be? They're simply playing by the rules, and nobody bothered to tell them that the rules changed.

A lot of effort and energy has already been expended on the subject of letter columns in comics. Several years back, DC publisher Jeanette Kahn cut the letters columns from the Vertigo line to make room for more advertising, and many argued persuasively that this was A Good Thing, and not just for the additional ad revenue. A lot of readers complained about the lettercol removal, but for others it meant that one more distraction was removed. For instance, by removing the letters column from each issue of *Preacher*, new and existing readers could get past the ego trips of young psychotics who assumed that profanity was a substitute for eloquence and *concentrate on the story*. In the days of yore, when letters columns were the only way that comics fans could make contact, they'd go on for two to four pages of incredibly tiny type. These days, though, when any idiot can start up a fan site on GeoCities and many do, most of these sections have been cut back to one page, and they keep running because the fans feel more comfortable knowing that they have some way of expressing their opinions and proof that someone cares enough about those opinions to set them to type and print them.

To some observers, graphic novels are just a different vehicle for comics. You don't hear about letters columns in graphic novels, do you? That's because we need to focus on a graphic novel being a novel. This means that the story has a beginning, a middle, and an end. You may need multiple graphic novels to tell a long story, but the idea is that each is supposed to be self-encapsulated and ready for general consumption. Since the author already knew how the story was going to end before the book saw print, nobody writes to the author and suggests "You know, this character would be best off doing this…" Well, some may make suggestions for future books, and a few braindrains may suggest rewriting the existing volume to protect their fragile sensibilities, but the only time anyone takes these braindrains seriously is when the book in question is a Texas high school biology textbook with a chapter on Darwinian evolution. The only time a publisher takes suggestions from readers seriously are for publicity stunts, such as that Baen Books contest nearly a decade ago that asked fans whether or not Robert Heinlein's original ending or the ending-as-published was the best for *Podykane of Mars*. Otherwise, they get roundfiled.

(Back about a decade ago, Byron Preiss Visual Media published a series of books intended as sequels to Ray Bradbury's short story "A Sound of Thunder," and each book came with a little notice in the back asking readers "Like what you just read? Let us know what you think!" Considering that books generally aren't supposed to be written by committee, the basic idea of soliciting letters was ludicrous, but that's why Byron Preiss continues to muck about with interactive media in forms that really don't need interactivity.)

With typical pamphlet comics, though, we're looking at several different standards. Firstly, as Scott McCloud likes to point out, comics are bastard magazines: they were originally handled through standard magazine distribution outlets, and they are most assuredly periodical publications. Secondly, even in the days where most comics had a self-contained story in each issue, readers were encouraged to write in to express their enjoyment of what they were reading. Go pick up one of those *Green Lantern* hardcover editions DC put out and read the end of each story, making sure to note the number of times that little panel "If you want more *Green Lantern* stories, be sure to write care of DC Comics" appears. The easiest way to ascertain whether or not the writers and artists were doing their jobs was by going through letters to the editor and counting the number of people who liked Hal Jordan futzing about on Earth versus the number of readers who preferred him bouncing around the galaxy. Well, sales figures were the real factor, but reader responses gave good warning as to whether or not a new story twist might alienate more readers than it would retain.

Unfortunately, the letters column was and is a trap. All publications that depend upon letters work on a fundamental fallacy: they assume that this is an accurate gauge of the publication's readership. Actually, the letters are only representative of the number of readers sufficiently stimulated to offer a response. Many readers are perfectly happy to read a magazine, laugh at the sections where they're supposed to laugh, scrunch their brow at the sections where they're supposed to think, and go on to the next stimulus in their universe, and most will never ever take the time to write a letter to the magazine's editor. The usual occasion that produces a letter is either something appears that almost demands a "Well done!" response, or something that causes enough outrage that the reader wants to engage in the civilized human equivalent of flinging feces.

The problem? The problem is that editors assume that a lack of response means a lack of readership. This is one of the main reasons why magazine and newspaper editors tend to hang onto annoying or obnoxious columnists and guest writers. Yes, the responses range from vitriolic to libelous, but at least they prove that someone is reading. Of course, after a while, the publication gets an equilibrium of sorts, where response dies down because the readers either agree with the writer or because the writer is being ignored, so the editor pushes for more edginess and obnoxiousness. Some writers can manage this: if they can, the escalation continues until the number of readers canceling their subscriptions in outrage outnumbers the number getting subscriptions, in which case the writer is told to tone things down or gets fired. With free publications such as weekly newspapers, the odds of the firing happening are drastically decreased, because those letters are proof to advertisers that the weekly is being used for its stated purpose instead of being used as bulk insulation or birdcage liner. (I used to work for a weekly newspaper whose editorial staff manufactured most of the letters printed in the Letters Page for its first year, partly because nobody was writing in, and partly because the paper's star columnist would pout if he didn't see letters every week telling him what a genius he was. In a way, seeing letters in the Letters Page encouraged more letters, even if the originals were all fakes, because the average reader didn't know they were fakes.)

On a slight tangent, this is why so many radio station morning shows are full of rancid trolls blathering potty-talk instead of music, and any attempt at a "More Music In The Morning!" format rapidly slides back into yammering again. Listeners who hear music all morning are less likely to call in to agree or complain, and if they don't like what they hear, they'll simply change the station. In the cases of successful trolls such as Howard Stern, the audience stays put, even if they can't stand the message or the messenger, just to hang on for what he's going to say next. In the case of Stern wannabes, the death threats are used as corroboration of positive ratings numbers, which means that the station can justify charging advertisers more because it assumes that listeners are staying tuned during commercial breaks instead of switching to another station. It's only in cases of extreme embarrassment that threaten the advertisers' comfort, such as with the two former Dallas deejays who started the rumor last year that Britney Spears had died in a car crash, that they'll actually get cut from the payroll. Everyone in radio assumes that nobody is listening at 3 ayem and that the people who are listening don't matter, which is why most radio stations play a better selection or at least more music than during drive time.

In a way, letters columns in publications are a proven sales technique. Let's say that you make a comment about an article in the latest issue of *Scientific American*. You send a letter to the editor, and you keep checking back through subsequent issues to see if your letter was printed. If you aren't a subscriber, then you'll definitely buy a copy if your letter appears, and even if it doesn't right away, you may come across something else in the magazine that catches your interest, so you buy it anyway. (If you have a subscription, the magazine already has your money, but you'll probably tell all of your friends that your letter appeared in the current issue, so they'll all rush out and take a peek, with the same chance that they'll buy a copy themselves.) Those letters columns are great ego boosts for those who have the time to write and kvetch about just about anything: an ungodly number of comics magazines (the *Comic Buyer's Guide*, *Comics Journal*, and the late *Amazing Heroes* in particular) are little more than letters columns with a few features intended to generate more letters. In these extreme cases, these aren't magazines: they're Usenet newsgroups and Delphi forums in search of a computer. Most of the letters in the *CBG* aren't about material that appeared in previous issues: they're letters bitching and moaning about how Superman's costume changed or Buddy Bradley isn't as much of a slob as he used to be, all written by fans who hope that someone at *CBG* cares enough to let them share their worries with the rest of the readership. One good nasty letter produces letters in response for the next year, long after the comic that started the debate was canceled and dumped into the "3 for a buck" bin at the local comic shop.

These factors explain why HEAT was inevitable. Comics publishers encouraged letters columns. It was a great ego boost for the writers and artists, as well as for the editors, even if the letters were all nasty, because of Oscar Wilde's comment that the only thing worse than being talked about was not being talked about. In return, the creators were more likely to consider fannish commentary if it meant more letters. Just killed off a character? Wait to see what the next month's letters are like. If the response is positive, Silicone Implant Girl stays dead. If the fans go ballistic, you can bring her back, no matter how artificial or silly the situation. As the old saying goes, this is comic books: we can do anything. Because fans learned that they can get their way by writing and calling and sending strippergrams, they'll continue to do so, secure in the knowledge that if the Hulk was blown to individual atoms with a thermonuclear suppository, someone will rationalize a way to bring him back if enough angry missives clog the Marvel

Comics mailroom. If that someone wants to keep the Hulk dead, well, we'll just turn up the volume a bit, won't we?

What everyone forgets in this little game of nuclear escalation is that this sort of creation process prevents any kind of real storytelling. It's the same as with soap operas or *Star Trek* franchises: if the decisions are being dictated by letters from crazed fans, then what are the odds that the story will ever end? What chance is there that a writer will kill off a popular character permanently when a write-in campaign will bring him/her/it right back? In situations such as these, the only time anyone takes a chance at telling a STORY, instead of running stunts intended to keep readers or viewers, is when everyone involved figures that they have nothing to lose by taking that chance. If this means that characters never age, never die, and never advance, so be it, because a certain percentage of the fans of just about any entertainment venue would be perfectly happy if everything remained the same for ever and ever, and they're the ones who write early and often if their favorite obsession dares change.

Unfortunately, the format of standard comics keeps encouraging this dichotomy. Just think of the number of comics, everything from *Elfquest* to *Fortune & Glory*, where the creators knew exactly where the story was going. The only things that were going to change were particulars, because the main story was nailed down long before the first page was laid out. If that's the case, why did these and other comics series bother with letters columns? Was it because the creators were so stricken by their own egos that they had to share comments from their fans and detractors with the world? Or was it, and I emphasize this, because comics always had letters pages, and nobody bothered to ask why they were necessary when letter-writing campaigns weren't going to change a damn thing?

Many of the arguments in favor of original graphic novels instead of standard comics have merit. Accessibility in standard bookstores instead of limited distribution in comic shops, more value for the entertainment dollar, improved quality of paper and printing, better likelihood of being read by someone other than traditional "comics fans": all of these have merit, and their proponents are right in arguing for the change. However, OGNs have one additional advantage, and that's immunity from the assumption by readers that they get some sort of say in how the story turns out. Nobody assumes that fans get any say in how standard novels and art collections turn out, so why should sequential art be any different?

—*Savant, February 28, 2002*

Postscript: Because there's a buck to be made, someone at DC decided to reverse the 1994 events, and the Green Lantern Corps exists again. Back then, it would have mattered to me. Now? I have other things to do.

"The Art of Journalism As War" or "Why So Many Dipshits Make Mainstream Media Unreadable"

Let's look at a hypothetical situation that isn't so hypothetical for a lot of the editors whose literary children are held up for review in *Factsheet Five*. Let's pretend that you're the editor/publisher of *Zizzle-swump*, an eclectic zine full of poetry, pithy commentary, and other joys, and you're doing a good enough job at it that you're starting to get noticed in the zine community. Maybe your commentary is sufficiently vicious enough that it singes off the eyebrows of anyone reading it, or your cover illustrator is an unsung genius, or you managed to score a coup and get an interview with an old friend who suddenly hits the big time in whatever endeavor he/she engages, or you get an interview with a famous sod who dies two days after you send the proofs of the article off to the printer. Whatever the reason, you're suddenly a name in the small press, and your local daily or weekly newspaper wants to interview you for a story. You send off samples of everything you've ever done to the reporter writing the interview, and the two of you set up a time for lunch and a few questions.

After what you assumed was a successful interview, maybe with a photo session at the end, the cheery reporter who just took down your life story buzzes off to make the deadline for the Wednesday edition, swearing that "If I have any more questions, I'll call you." In many cases, you'll call the reporter, asking "Hey, when's that interview going to run?," and you'll get a response along the lines of "Oh, we had it scheduled for Wednesday, but the editor has a frat brother who just started up a Web design company, so that story appeared instead." A lot of times, you won't get a response at all: believe it or not, you've lucked out.

The reason you've lucked out, of course, is if you see the final interview, it's usually a mangled piece of trash that mocks your work, makes you out to be a heroin-peddling pederast, misspells your name or the name of your zine, or all of the preceding. At your day job, if you aren't fired because the boss doesn't want anyone literate on the staff (in most grunt jobs, chronic drunkenness is all right, but not creativity or intelligence), you'll have to deal with co-workers who laugh and ask "What's the matter: can't you spell your own name?"

It happens more often than most readers know, and zine editors aren't the only ones who suffer from crappy reportage. To understand why anyone involved with zines keeps getting lousy coverage in mainstream media, you have to understand some basics about journalism today.

The bare beginnings are the basics of any first-year high school reporting student. Stories in the typical daily paper fall under two categories: news and features, with sports reportage bridging the two and adding a few unique features. News stories consist of the usual "who, what, where" facts, while features are a little more freeform. An interview with Jim Goad of *Answer Me!* over the recent Washington censorship trial is a news story; an interview with the editors of *Carpe Noctem* over why they started a goth magazine is generally a feature.

Now that I've simultaneously bored to death and insulted every journalism major reading this, one has to remember that features are considered "easy work." Getting an exclusive with the President of the United States is a major deal; getting an exclusive with the president of the Dallas Orchid Society is something that can wait a day or two before it sees print. Not to say that every news story is highly researched (look at all of the stories that try to link high school shootings with Marilyn Manson), but features are generally able to slide with the facts a bit.

(As an aside before I go any further, most of the examples I'm going to bring up to illustrate my points come from Dallas journalism. Having lived in this city for most of my life, these are the examples with which I'm the most familiar, but most of these tales could apply to any daily or weekly paper, or local magazine, in the country.)

And now we get to another major factor in American journalism today, which is why so many of us are writing and printing zines instead of working for newspapers. The days where daily papers were the sole source of news ended fifty years ago with the beginnings of the television industry, and now a sizable portion of the American public doesn't read a daily paper at all, as they get their news from television and the Internet. The demographic of newspaper readers keeps getting older: a longrunning joke has it that the main readership of the *Dallas Morning News* consists of alter kokkers who sent their grandchildren off to fight Sherman and Grant. It's a slight exaggeration, but it explains why daily newspapers are becoming more reactionary: these little old ladies have all the time in the world to write nasty letters to the editor about how the editors need to keep liberal filth such as *Mallard Fillmore* off the comics pages.

(Just the other day, I saw an ad sponsored by the Newspaper Association of America titled "Read A Paper To Your Child Every Day" which made me laugh for a solid hour. This ad was akin to those telco or electric company ads that try to make you feel all cuddly about your local monopoly: rather than spend the advertising money on improving the product, the NAA would rather guilt-trip viewers into reading papers to their kids, regardless of how bad the local paper might be. After all, the phone company, electric company, cable company or newspaper has no intention of improving their services without an act of Congress or God, but they want you to feel that they care, just so you won't decide to do anything crazy like try to live without them.)

Another point to consider is that increasingly fewer cities have two daily papers any more, and the ones that died were generally the more liberal in tone. When the *Dallas Morning News* won its war against the *Dallas Times Herald* in 1991, the *News* had support from every right-wing plutocrat in the state, but not as much respect as an actual newspaper. While the *Herald* was a long way away from its peak when it died, it was still the paper that brought us Jim Lehrer, Molly Ivins, and Joe Bob Briggs; the only famous writer the *News* ever produced was Elizabeth Wurtzel, the author of *Prozac Nation*, and she got her ass fired for plagiarism while she was there.

Because of inadequate coverage from dailies, the weekly paper stepped in: for a while during the early Eighties, seemingly every town with a population above 25,000 had its own weekly newspaper. However, thanks to the increasing cost of newsprint, weeklies are becoming just as much a monopoly business as the dailies; one can complain about the miserable music and arts coverage in the typical weekly, but the staff knows perfectly well that nobody else is going to step in and compete with them with anything less than $100,000 in capital behind them, and the upstarts that try usually don't last more than one issue before folding.

Because of these factors, reporters are learning one thing about weeklies and dailies both: the job market isn't safe. When yuppie-magnet magazines such as POV list the newspaper journalist as one of the worst jobs to have as far as pay, advancement opportunities, and resistance to layoffs are concerned, it's pretty goddamned bad. Because of the costs of running a newspaper, those papers that survive nowadays are usually pretty conservative, if not flat-out reactionary: they aren't going to run anything that'll scare either the little old ladies still reading papers, or the business execs buying advertising in them. More papers are being bought by big media conglomerates, which either have a right-wing agenda or just want a hefty profit on their investment (this includes weeklies, as demonstrated by the New Times Corporation in Phoenix buying out weekly after weekly across the US), or their current management figures that it's time to sell out and collect some cash before the market falls out. Whatever the factors, reporters know that crossing the bosses means a really rough time trying to find comparable work somewhere else.

And now one last factor. Reporters are like high school teachers: the ones who have talent could make much more money doing something else with a lot less stress, so the ones that remain in newspapers are either young and naive, true believers in the powers of journalism, or lazy hacks who have no other job skills besides running the counter at McDonald's. This is especially true at weekly papers; it's generally pretty safe to say that anyone working for a weekly for more than three years (especially as a music critic or "humor columnist") is unfit for gainful work anywhere else.

Oh, and lest I forget, the reporter isn't the only person responsible for a godawful article about zines or anything else. We've neglected to mention the editor, who usually rewrites articles to fit his or her ideological bent, with no concern as to accuracy or responsibility. In my years in journalism, I've met maybe three editors, either chief editors or department editors, who were anything but cowardly little martinets who wanted to make the world suffer for not acknowledging their genius. These characters love taking credit for their "contributions" to stories, but blame the writer when they screw up.

(An example: about four years ago, I was asked by one such editor to write a piece on a local comic convention, and I wrote a little missive on how Clive Barker was one of the guests. When the story finally saw print, I think I recognized individual words I had written, with the editor-added comment "Clive Barker, director of *The Texas Chainsaw Massacre*" in it. Now, I knew that Tobe Hooper directed *Chainsaw* and Barker directed *Hellraiser* and *Nightbreed*, but since the article had my byline on it, I spent the entire weekend fielding phone calls from smartasses asking me "Gee, Riddell, Clive Barker didn't direct *Chainsaw*," to which I responded "I know that, but the capon who edited me didn't." Naturally, due to the nasty letters the paper received, the next issue ran a correction that absolved the editor of any such blame. Take my word for it: any correction a paper runs with one of those "[The paper] regrets the error" comments usually means an editor screwed it up and refuses to take the blame.)

So where does this lead us, the valiant zine writer, editor, or reader? Well, it leads the more prudent of us not to trust any mainstream journalist, but we need reasons why we shouldn't trust anyone asking for an interview. With that in mind, let me give you my three catchall rules about journalists: these points don't cover all of them, but it covers enough to make the real offenders squeal.

Number One: Journalists Is Lazy. The only thing that runs a paper, weekly or daily, is the all-important deadline, which dictates that a certain number of column inches will be filled; with what, nobody really cares. All that matters to most journalists is that this space gets filled with something bearing their byline, which means grabbing at whatever idea happens to pop up at a brainstorming session. If the editor asks for a zine article, this usually means "I want an article on zines, and I want it Thursday." So, rather than taking the time to research a credible article, the reporter grabs a few zines off a shelf somewhere, no matter how out of date, and writes something.

(Another example: about seven years ago, I watched the music editor for one Dallas weekly walk into a local record shop and grab a handful of ostensibly local zines, and produce an article about Dallas zines three days later. Never mind that two of the zines she mentioned had gone under about a year before; they were on the shelf, so they were still viable for a story.)

Another illustration comes from what I call the "Look At The Freaks" story, which comprises far too many features on zines, piercings, or anything else not considered mainstream. (I came to zines through science fiction, so I saw entirely too many "Look At The Freaks" stories through coverage of SF writers, magazines, or conventions.) These stories all go the same way: Reporter goes to an event and interviews the goofiest dingleberry in the area, promises to do an honest interview, and ends up comparing the rest of the field to that lone goofball. This may be an article on a new arts community, where the reporter interviews a few trust fund babies who wish they would be accepted by everyone else, or it may be a story on a science fiction convention, where the reporter goes after the Trekkie who got his ears bobbed so he could pass for Vulcan or elf. Either way, the stories have the same effect: the little old ladies at home read about those ridiculous nutcases who edit zines or pierce their privates, and get a good laugh at those psychos who don't live according to mainstream American values.

(The "LATF" effect is doubled when the reporter obviously has a loathing for the subject in question. Right after the release of his book *The Redneck Manifesto*, the *Oregonian* up on Portland ran an interview with *Answer Me!* editor Jim Goad about his book and life in Portland in general. Instead of getting a reporter who either knew or cared about Goad, the twit who wrote the interview made Goad out to be a sociopath, and the editors refused to run any "Letters to the Editor" except those that ragged on Goad over the last issue of *Answer Me!* being allegedly offensive to women. Damned twice, was Goad.)

Number Two: Journalists Is Arrogant. One of the basic rules all writers must learn sooner or later is that Nobody Reads Your Work. This isn't necessarily true, but if more writers worked toward improving their writing, rather than expecting fame, riches, and groupies, literature and journalism would be much better. I knew one editor who used to introduce himself to freelance writers with the line "You, of course, know who I am, don't you?," and then would badmouth these freelancers in print if they said the understandable "No, and should I?"

Journalists live under the spectre of producing disposable reading material: not only does nobody read it, but the few who may see it later forget the subject and never care in the slightest about the author. (I learned this two years ago, when I wrote a cover story for one weekly and made the mistake of showing it during a job interview. The darling who was interviewing me not only had never heard of the publication, although it was given away free all over Dallas, but looked at me and said "Well, maybe I don't know what you mean by 'cover story', but this looks like a graphic to me," referring to the actual cover illustration.) Because of this immediate obsolescence, many don't take well to the thought of some damn zine editor or writer getting more fame than they get, especially when they work for a major daily or weekly and the zine is read by a few hundred very impressed individuals.

Insecurity and arrogance make a pretty lethal combination, especially when the person inflicted with them has some power to go with them. A few years back, I was working as a Web designer for a Dallas weekly, and I made a big mistake: when a review appeared in *Factsheet Five* for a science fiction magazine called *Tangent*, I made a copy of the review and I gave it to the editor. The reason I gave it to the editor was because the review read, in part, "Any zine with a Paul Riddell article in it is worth reading, and this one has two!," and my mistake was in assuming that this quote would make a nice blurb for advertising the paper as well, as in "Hey, *Factsheet Five* likes Riddell, and he works for us!" Nothing of the sort ever happened, but that isn't the story.

About fifteen minutes after I gave the review to my editor and I went back to work, the "humor" columnist came stomping in and demanded of me, "Where did this come from?" He looked furious.

"*Factsheet Five*," I said, not understanding why he was angry.

"*Factsheet Five*? I've never *heard* of it!" This wasn't an "I've never heard of it; tell me more" yell; this was a "How dare you!" yell.

Naive fool that I was, I continued on: "Yeah, *Factsheet Five* covers all sorts of small press magazines. This was a review for a magazine I work for, called *Tangent*."

The columnist finally stomped off, and I understood a basic problem with journalists: nobody dares upstage them. After all, I hadn't gone to his college (nor much of college at all, truth be told), and I didn't hang around with the right people, so how dare I get better reviews than he did? Ergo, any zine editor is automatically at a disadvantage, especially if that journalist has power of any sort, especially a film or music critic. (We've all known critics who essentially refuse to write good reviews unless they're paid off with freebies, but I met one critic who refused to give a good review to one film solely because she showed up fifteen minutes late to the preview and the projectionist wouldn't rewind the film for her to see the beginning.) If you aren't willing to kiss reporter ass and let them know they're special, you're in trouble.

Number Three: Journalists Is Scared Shitless by Zines, The Internet, and Anything Else That Might Force Them To Get Real Jobs. We've all seen the constant articles about how cyberporn will rot children's minds, and we've probably seen the articles connecting little high school underground newspapers to rape, arson, or Satanism. Part of this bias is due to laziness (after all, a nice sensationalistic tirade about the Internet is easier to write than a well-researched article about its potential benefits, and it draws in more readers), but it's also due to fear. Editors demand more articles about the evil of other news media because it's the only option they have to try to get readers to take newspapers seriously again.

With this in mind, zines are easy to shoot up. Television is pretty much a standard medium, and the only people who still complain about TV are the gits who argue that letting children watch Mr. Hanky The Christmas Poo on *South Park* will rot our collective psyche. Enough people get on the Internet daily to realize that porn is generally available only to the televangelists and newspaper editors who go searching for it in mass quantities. Rock music has been around long enough that nobody seriously worries about whether Bob Dylan's lyrics are mumbled profanities or just mumbles (although papers can get a little free mileage from displaying Marilyn Manson or Pump 'N' Ethyl to an audience that still considers Buddy Holly to be too risque for television), and *Dungeons & Dragons* has been dead long enough that nobody cares whether it promotes anything but gross obesity, much less Satanism or suicide.

Zines, though, are a great target. They're generally blue-collar publications, meaning that the staff was hired based on merit rather than having been part of a journalism class at Southern Methodist University or USC; the publications themselves tend to be a hell of a lot more liberal or at least anarchistic than the paper covering them; and the successful ones tend to be successful without a major ad campaign or a distribution plan. Not too many people can tell the difference between any number of local daily papers, but you can always tell the difference between zines. Because of this, they must be stopped: if a zine can offer better coverage of a subject than a mainstream paper or magazine, then that takes money, even a few dollars, away from the mass-produced product, and we can't have that, now can we?

This isn't to say that all zine coverage is going to be rotten, but the odds are against it. Journalism in America and elsewhere rewards the generalist who can make deadlines, rather than the talent who knows something about a particular subject: if a feature can't be written from thirty minutes' worth of interview, then the subject can't be too interesting. The big positions at a daily, such as political commentary, fall to specialists, but who cares if the resident film critic can't tell the difference between Tim Burton and Tim Allen but feels up to writing about them anyway? Hunter Thompson was right: journalism is neither a profession or a trade, but a catch-all for fuckoffs and misfits, and it'll remain this way so long as quick and smartass will always get preference over methodical and respectful.

Now, after this tirade, any "real" journalists who take offense to this will probably start shrieking and raging about how this was an inaccurate and biased assessment of their life's work. Well, now you know how *we* feel.

—*Angry Thoreauan, June 1999*

Postscript: This essay was originally commissioned for the zine review magazine Factsheet Five, *and was all ready to go...until publisher Seth Friedman decided that his magazine was worth $70,000 and put it up for sale. Let us never mind that he still hasn't received $70k for a magazine he received from founder Mike Gunderloy for free: he put out one last issue without telling any of his advertisers or subscribers, and awaited the bidding war. Since he, of course, had to give his unique history of* Factsheet Five, *this essay was cut to make room for an extra page of masturbation. I'd be tempted to hunt him down and beat the kill fee he promised out of his hide, but his death in utter poverty and obscurity is much more satisfying. (Me, bitter? Naah.)*

As for the situation with most of the newspapers mentioned or alluded to? These days, newspapers are becoming about as topical as disco, midnight movies, and milkmen. The only thing more likely to disappear before 2020 than the standard daily newspaper is the standard weekly newspaper, and good riddance to bad rubbish.

"At The Late-Night Double Feature Picture Show"

One of the most entertaining generation gaps around comes with science fiction and horror movie buffs of a certain age, centering right about 30 right now. Those older than 30 remember the days of all-night late-night movie marathons on television, catching all sorts of strange and terrible films from all over the world, and have the common connection of remembering when CBS delayed its "CBS Late Night Movie" presentation of *Dracula Has Risen From The Grave* to broadcast Nixon's resignation. Those younger than that, particularly the film buffs in their early twenties and even their teens, not only don't get nostalgic for late-night movies, but can't remember a time when they couldn't fall back on video and cable. I can't help but feel pity for them, because they missed out on the best venue for great and great atrocious moviewatching ever created.

The Late Show was an obvious concession to the realities of early television broadcasting. TV and big radio transmitters are sufficiently expensive that most stations leave them on 24-7, running a test pattern all night rather than taking a chance on the transmitter tubes blowing every time someone turns it on. Some stations decided to run movies into the wee hours rather than the test pattern (even late-night movies draw a bit of advertising money), and science fiction and horror films were cheap and easy to get. Best of all, those late night "Creature Features" usually drew enough viewers, either insomniacs or those deliberately staying up to catch *The Green Slime*, to justify both higher ad rates and hiring a host to introduce each film. If not for late-night movie hosts such as "Chilly Billy" Cardille in Pittsburgh or the pseudonymous "Ned the Dead" up in Wisconsin (to name just two of dozens), a lot of current movie buffs never would have gone on to learn more about their favorite films.

The infomercial put paid to the late night movie, when the FCC in 1989 allowed the current glut of real estate and "Sounds of the Eighties" presentations to run on both cable and regular television. We can't blame the broadcasters: they aren't idiots for foregoing having to hunt for advertisers to fill the commercial breaks in *This Island Earth* when advertisers were willing to buy whole chunks of broadcast time. Also, remember that the idea of 24-hour broadcasting is still relatively new: even pay channels such as Home Box Office didn't run all night until the beginning of 1982. In the process, though, the old SF and horror films got crunched: even with the advent of digital cable, obviating the need for traditional transmissions, most late-night programming consists of infomercials. (Time zone differences make this intolerable for those living west of the Mississippi, at least in the States: for the longest time, viewers of the Sci-Fi Channel in Hawaii would come home from work, turn on the channel...and get hours of infomercials after normal broadcasting hours in New York ended. Multiple feeds for larger channels, such as TNT and USA, is improving this somewhat, but individual feeds for each time zone worldwide is still a long way off.)

Oh, they aren't dead yet: American Movie Classics still runs old (and relatively new) horror films every Friday night, and everyone starts running the old Hammer Dracula films right around Halloween, but the days of staying up late every Friday night to watch old and old bad films into the wee hours have been gone for a decade. In the process, we're getting a new generation of film buffs that never saw great old films without enough commercial appeal to justify a video release within the last ten years (anyone remember *The Asphyx* or *The Monolith Monsters*?), or really good bad films such as *Equinox* or *Children Shouldn't Play With Dead Things*. Even if the films exist, most video stores pass in order to carry thirty copies of the latest Tom Cruise monstrosity, so potential fans come across them after a determined search, rather than stumbling across them while channel surfing. Even the existing horror film shows run on cable, automatically leaving out the starving college student or anyone living too far away to get a cable hookup or unable to afford a satellite dish.

And why should this matter? Look at the number of noted directors who grew up on a diet of late night movies, both the good ones and the irredeemably bad, and wanted to improve upon that level. Because many of the older genre films had no budget to speak of, they help demonstrate the power of subtlety and suggestion in an age where nobody thinks anything of making a $200 million remake of *The Haunting*. (I heartily recommend a viewing of the original *The Outer Limits* or the entire Jon Pertwee period of *Doctor Who* for anyone considering a career in genre television: sure, the special effects were cheesy even then, but these show what a dedicated crew can do with a tiny budget but unlimited imagination.) The bad ones teach what not to do, including building spacecraft models with rockets that spew obvious smoke. Most of all, all of these uncover an age in filmmaking when people made films partly for profit and partly for fun: when a typical summer movie release today can draw in $30 million in its first weekend and still be considered a failure, it's nice to look back at the reign of American International, when a movie could make a profit of $500,000 and everyone involved was ecstatic.

With this in mind, I call for public support of the return of the late night movie. Where else will we get our fill of Godzilla and Gamera (not to mention Yongary, Gorgo, and Gwangi), Lovecraft and Poe adaptations, and all of the other mutants that made staying up until 5 ayem on Saturday morning so much fun? In an age when Norm MacDonald can get his own sitcom, why can't we get a few horrors we can stand?

—SciFiNow.com, July 2000

"Kvetching About Comics And Comics Adaptations"

The cover of *Wizard* in the supermarket said it all: "How Batman Beyond and Six Other Comics Adaptations Are Going To Rock Hollywood," or some similar trifle. Every year, we get the same piffle on how a hot new movie or TV adaptation of someone's favorite comic is going to gain the industry the respect it feels it deserves, usually written by closet comics obsessives at the local weekly newspaper who want to come into work wearing a *Lady Death* T-shirt but still be considered cool by their co-staffers. In 1990, it was *Captain America*. In 1995, it was *Tank Girl* and *Judge Dredd*. The names *Watchmen* and *Elfquest* have come up every year since 1742. This year, it's *X-Men*, *Spider-Man*, and *The Fantastic Four*.

Trust me on this one, folks. The universe does not need a big-budget adaptation of *X-Men*. What the universe and the comics industry need are adaptations of Alex Robinson's *Box Office Poison* and David Lee Ingersoll's *Misspent Youths*. Forget *Spider-Man*: we need Terry Moore's *Strangers In Paradise* and Jhonen Vasquez' *Squee*. And bollocks on *Superman Reborn*: we desperately need Warren Ellis' *Transmetropolitan*, Alan Moore's *The League of Extraordinary Gentlemen*, and Kyle Baker's *Why I Hate Saturn* to hit movie screens before it's too late. (We really need an adaptation of Brian Michael Bendis' exemplary *Fortune and Glory: A True Hollywood Comic Book Story*, but that's asking too much, isn't it?)

Part of the reason why the big adaptations of superhero comics aren't going to make that much of a difference lies with the audience. Even with the big popular superhero comics, the general readerships are insignificant compared to the moviegoing public. Sure, we can make lots of noise about making adaptations "for the fans," but "the fans" aren't going to goose Nielsen ratings or box office receipts as much as a good story with a common appeal. After all, if Todd McFarlane's incessant hype about *Spawn* being "America's #1 Comic!" was true, don't you think the film adaptation would have done better? That is, if it hadn't been directed and written solely for the twerps who collect the action figures?

Let's put it another way. Only a tiny proportion of the people who went to see *High Fidelity* or *Trainspotting* ever bothered to read the novels beforehand, and most of 'em never bothered to read them afterwards, either. A new superhero film isn't magically going to fill comic stores with recent viewers who want the comics; they might buy the soundtrack or the toys, but they honestly don't really care about the source material. If the source is full of characters and situations that appeal to the general moviegoing audience, they'll go, but if it doesn't appeal, all the fanboy shrieking about the importance of Kyle Rayner versus Hal Jordan in an adaptation of *Green Lantern* isn't going to make a damned bit of difference to the rest of the world.

The really funny situation is that some of the best comics adaptations in the last ten years were ones where the general public didn't know that the source material came from a comic or graphic novel. Hands up: how many general moviegoers read Dark Horse's *The Mask* or Jim O'Barr's *The Crow* before the movie came out? How many even knew that *Men In Black* started out as a comic in the first place? (Of course, nobody knew *Barb Wire* was based on a comic, so maybe I should stop while I'm ahead.) Out of all the people who gleefully watch reruns of *The Tick* on Comedy Central, how many have dared enter a comic shop to pick up the original material? Better yet, for the five people who actually read *Mystery Men*, how many actually preferred the movie? The fans of these either didn't care about their origins or would have run away screaming if they realized that they were about ready to spend money on a movie about a funny-book, but went because the characters and/or situations appealed to them. One of the reasons so few people read comics in America today is because of the perception that all comics fans are maladjusted middle-age dorks (whether or not it's true doesn't matter), and the comics adaptations that survive that tarring are the ones that sneak past the audience's expectations.

Comics-based films, like science fiction and fantasy films in general, could be so much better than they are, but so long as the bellyaching of obsessives keeps influencing what gets made, the adaptations will be just as bad as the comics that spawned them, no pun intended. In the meantime, I advocate keeping the bellyaching to a minimum by starting every big comic adaptation with a live-action short of Evan Dorkin's *The Eltingville Comic Book, Science Fiction, Fantasy, Horror, and Role-Playing Club*: if that doesn't shut up the fanatics, they'll go nuts trying to figure out why the rest of the audience is laughing so hard.

—*SCI FI, October 2000*

Postscript: Some of the adaptations I mentioned that we needed actually saw screens, and some, particularly the film that received the name The League of Extraordinary Gentlemen, *cemented the basic thesis of this essay. Shortly after it saw print, I realized that comics fans will watch anything that's connected to their pet obsession, so I gave up: they're the ones paying money for* Catwoman *or* The Punisher, *not I.*

"Horrible Horror and the Delusions of Crowds"

Back in 1985, horror author Joe Lansdale wrote an essay for the sadly defunct *Twilight Zone* magazine about the return of the drive-in theater. Years later, he noted that what seemed to be the resurgence of drive-ins (as others did about midnight movies) was actually a death rattle that offered the illusion of vitality: by 1990, the drive-in and the midnight show were pretty much murdered by suburban sprawl, video stores, and multimegaplexes. Eight years after that, *USA Today* announced the return of horror films from the dead; I fear that this alleged revival is another death twitch.

Part of the decline of the horror film has to do with changing social mores and situations. Here in my beloved Texas, the locals laugh at giant bug movies because of the native cockroaches and praying mantises: a good friend commented that *Starship Troopers* could have been shot for a pittance in Houston. In Dallas, *Dawn of the Dead* is quaint, considering that the zombies outnumbered humanity in our shopping malls decades ago. (Sometimes the obverse is true: any former resident of the town of Lewisville can be brought to screaming hysteria just by mentioning the film *Deliverance*, but that's mostly because "Dueling Banjos" is the fight song of the Fighting Farmers, the local high school football team.) When Senator Kay Bailey Hutchison returns home, smiles for the TV cameras meeting her at the airport, and elicits the universal response among her audience (including her staff) of "Where the hell are Sigourney Weaver and a forklift when you need 'em?," it's kinda hard to be scared of a goddamn movie.

Another crippling blow is due to the disdain for horror in Hollywood, both among filmmakers and critics. Horror is considered too lowbrow, unless it's loaded with big-name actors, and even then, studio publicity departments start describing an upcoming film as "It's not a horror movie; it's a (fill in the blank)." Okay, so *Silence of the Lambs* is suspense using this logic, but *Friday the 13th: Jason Takes Manhattan* is "action-adventure-suspense"? It was a horror film, folks, and so was *Near Dark*, *Event Horizon*, *Bram Stoker's Dracula*, and any number of other films that shied away from the big "H" word. Even *Showgirls* qualifies as horror: one of my biggest fears is that Elizabeth Berkley and Jerry Seinfeld will marry and produce children that could gnaw through a mature redwood.

The main reason why the horror film is dying, though, lies with simple economics. Almost all of the best horror films of the last century were made on the cheap: when the budget is $1.49, the filmmakers have to use their imaginations, and shoveling cash at a project doesn't compensate for a lack of ideas. Unlike SF films, horror films require mood and concept more than anything else: by tapping into the little pit of terror in everybody, a good horror film can hotwire the suspension of disbelief and make the viewer consider, just for a moment, that the events on screen could happen. Just try to argue the logic of *Alien* or *Night of the Living Dead*: they make no real sense, but they scare us anyway.

The problem with the current crop of "horror" films, such as *Scream*, *Halloween H2O*, *I Know What You Did Last Summer*, and *Disturbing Behavior*, is that they aren't really horror films. Sure, they offer cheap scares, but they're designed for the teenage audience, and that audience wants a carnival haunted house ride where everything is all right at the end, but with just enough spookiness so that the guys just might get lucky with their dates later. *Hellraiser* and *Phantasm* and *Day of the Dead* aren't make-out films, and any films made today that try not to be are forced to become so by the studios distributing them. The original *Return of the Living Dead* became a comedy only in post-production, when Orion Pictures realized that, thanks to the incompetence of director-writer Dan O'Bannon, audiences were laughing at the scenes that O'Bannon intended to be terrifying. Unfortunately, far too many filmmakers nowadays assume that horror and humor are synonymous: Peter Jackson can pull off that fusion (as evidenced in *Dead Alive*), but not too many others.

Due to the lack of sympathetic distributors, the increasing costs of feature films, the increasing cowardice of the studios that make them, and an audience that screams to Donald Wildmon about any film spookier than *Toy Story*, the horror film as we used to know it is pretty much dead. Of course, so long as characters like Jackson, David Cronenberg, and Sam Raimi are still alive, it'll keep trying to claw out of that grave, hungry for the flesh of the horror aficionado.

—Sci-Fi Universe, December 1998

"Making Margaritas With the *Titanic*: An Overview of the Implosion of Comics Distribution"

At the beginning of 1994, the American comics industry was in one of its biggest booms since the 1950s. By most estimates, the comics industry, comprised of icons Marvel and DC and an ever-expanding supporting cast, managed to do $840 million in business in 1993. Marvel Entertainment Group was literally at the top of the heap, pulling in money not only on sales of comics but on related toys, action figures, collectible figurines, trading cards, cartoon series, and the promise of feature films. Three years later, the comics business was rapidly imploding, with titles and whole companies declaring bankruptcy, being assimilated by other companies, and simply disappearing. Marvel was at the top of this heap, too, having declared Chapter 11 bankruptcy in December 1996. As of 2000, many in the field are making bets as to how long Marvel will survive before being bought out by a competitor, broken down for parts and sold to any number of prospective buyers, or simply fading from the scene. Former CEO Ron Perelman, who orchestrated first Marvel's buyout and then its sea-change from a publisher to a manufacturer of toys and collectibles that incidentally publishes comics, now admits that his involvement was a mistake, but he still left Marvel a rich man.

The particulars of the collapse of Marvel have been covered in detail elsewhere, but two factors are worth repeating. Most of the blame for the immolation of the comics industry lies with the obsession with speculation in "hot" titles, but much also lies with failing to understand the vagaries of their distribution. Many in the industry assumed that the Nineties Boom was going to run forever, and when speculators realized that their mint copies of *Silicone Implant Girl* were never going to sell for what market guides said it would, they left comics entirely, taking their money elsewhere and leaving publishers and retailers with millions of dollars' worth of unsellable product.

Comics fill a strange twilight zone in publications, in that they really don't qualify as magazines nor newspapers, and so generally fall between the cracks in general publication distribution. Most of the current comics situation started with the "direct market" movement in the late Seventies. Previously, when sold on newsstands, comics were returnable, with either the comic or just its cover being returned to the distributor if it didn't sell. Direct market retailers, almost always comic shops, receive a slightly better percentage of the retail price of a comic in exchange for forgoing returns. Since all inventory that didn't sell had to be stored or otherwise disposed of, direct market retailers made a point of ordering only the number of copies they could reasonably sell. Naturally, this meant that if a title suddenly became popular, the demand for available copies went up, and comic shops rapidly moved into comic collecting and preservation supplies. The stores also inadvertently accelerated a speculation boom that presumed the value of certain "hot" comics would always increase.

The Nineties boom wasn't the first in the comics industry: back in the mid-Eighties, retailers were buried by the "black-and-white boom," instigated by the surprise success of Eastman and Laird's *Teenage Mutant Ninja Turtles*. Printing comics in black-and-white instead of four-color had long been an economic way to make comics considered too esoteric for the big comics companies, but the growth of the direct sales market meant that many of them were available outside of head shops. The steady increase in popularity of black-and-whites such as *Cerebus* and *Elfquest*, as well as decreasing costs in printing and production, and an increased demand for creators to keep the rights to their creations, made independent publication much more popular, but the surprise success of *TMNT* and the first issue's subsequent jump in value produced an overflowing toilet of black-and-white parodies of *TMNT*, Frank Miller's *The Dark Knight Returns*, *X-Men*, and damn near anything else wannabe comics moguls could produce. Some of these parodies, such as the unreadable *Adolescent Radioactive Black-Belt Hamsters*, became valuable in their own right as speculators hoped to make a quick dollar by buying up the first issue of every new b&w that came out. Some others, such as the critically acclaimed *TrollLords*, took advantage of the crazed market to get their messages out, but even the more successful titles faltered and died as the boom did. By 1988, many comics shops refused to carry any b&w titles, and others had such a backlog of titles ordered based on customer expectations that never materialized that they were *very* selective of what they ordered. Dark Horse Comics managed to break the stigma of b&w comics thanks to its licensed *Aliens* series, but the medium remains a relatively minor portion of general comics sales.

The current boom was not solely Marvel's fault, but Marvel's activities were the catalyst in the exothermic reaction that followed. Thanks to Marvel's insistence on retaining the rights to all characters and situations in the comics it published, many creators bailed out, either to work for DC's Vertigo line or to form their own companies. The most famed of the new companies was Image, founded by a collective of former Marvel creators who claimed that their comics were composed of characters and situations that they thought were too good to waste on Marvel. While the final products frequently gave lie to this claim, Image titles rapidly became subject to the same levels of speculation as Marvel product, and many of the new companies initiated or perfected a fair number of the gimmicks that fueled the speculation boom, such as variant and foil or hologram covers, guaranteeing that collectors would pick up multiple copies of the same comic solely for the differing cover art.

In 1993, the war escalated when Marvel Entertainment Group announced that it was buying, and would distribute Marvel comics solely through, Heroes World Distribution. The basic logic behind the buyout was incredibly simple, and might have worked if the comics industry wasn't already facing a slowdown. Before the Heroes World buyout, comics retailers had a choice between twelve different distributors, and many put in orders of varying quantities with different distributors in order to get what they perceived to be a proper mix of comics and related merchandise, including magazines, toys, collectible figures, and any variety of other items. Since anywhere between forty and eighty percent of a typical comic shop's business was in Marvel titles, this meant that retailers who were happy with their current distributors found that they either dealt with Heroes World or stopped carrying Marvel, and not carrying Marvel usually meant bankruptcy.

In the short term, Heroes World's business spiked, as retailers had no choice but to work with the company to take care of their customers. However, Heroes World was simply unprepared for the work necessary to fill these orders, and it rapidly crashed under the number of unfilled orders. As a counterstroke, Diamond Distribution signed similar exclusive agreements with DC, Dark Horse, and a plethora of others, leaving the rest with nothing to sell. Before the Marvel/Heroes World alliance, comics retailers had twelve distributors from which to choose: two years after, only Diamond remained, and it promptly cut costs by phasing out more and more of its non-comics inventory. (Diamond also publishes a regular catalog, *Previews*, which is the de facto guide for upcoming comics and related products. Since Diamond is the only game in town, tales of new comics being neglected or ignored in the catalog because the publisher refused to pay for additional advertising in *Previews* keep growing.)

What nobody considered in all of this was that the comics market was finite, and most of the sales were based on already existing readers or those looking to make money from speculation; the comics industry, much like the science fiction magazine community, is notoriously poor in promoting itself outside of its immediate sphere. The market also depended upon what comics professionals derided as "Marvel zombies," usually preteens who recently discovered comics collecting and were encouraged for a short time by their parents, but who generally left after reaching puberty. By 1994, fewer comics collectors were coming into the hobby than were leaving, and many of the speculators, realizing that their collections were worth a lot less than what they paid, and sold them off at fire sale prices. This paralleled the collapse of the trading card market at about the same time, as too many companies pumped out marginal material with the assumption that the market would continue to expand with the influx of product. This couldn't have been worse timing for Marvel, as the company had just purchased trading card manufacturers Fleer for $250 million and SkyBox for $150 million, and SkyBox's attempt to enter the Pog market fizzled as a multitude of companies flooded a market that simply did not exist. Marvel subsequently sold Fleer/SkyBox for $26 million in 1999.

Right now the comics market is a zombie, with many openly wondering if it will still exist in its current form in another five years. Of the approximately 4500 comic shops in the United States in 1994, approximately half of these remained in 2000, with the survivors generally limiting their collectible card inventory to Pokemon. Many in the industry, such as *Transmetropolitan* creator Warren Ellis, are pushing for a move away from the standard 22-page format to full-sized graphic novels in order to move into existing bookstores. Considering the radical slash-and-burn of the bookselling industry over the last ten years, another subject entirely, moving comics into chain stores may complicate the current situation.

Marvel itself took the hardest strike from the collapse of the latest speculation market, mostly because Marvel Entertainment Group was a publicly held company. The company squandered millions on trading cards, toy lines, and even development of a Marvel Superheroes fast-food restaurant chain (the last thankfully never made it to market), and as of this writing is creeping along under a debt of approximately $250 million. Since the company declared bankruptcy in 1996, its stock price has declined from $24 to $2.50 a share, it fired dozens of writers and artists, initiated incredibly unpopular cost-savings measures, such as forcing employees to leave at 5:00 PM (in order to save on the costs of heating and lighting the offices) and charging previous creators for long-forgotten expenses, and pushed even harder for movie adaptations of its comics in the hope of delaying a complete shutdown. In order to sweeten Hollywood interest in adaptations of its other comics, the company let the rights to X-Men go for a nominal price, and Marvel made no real money from the recent X-Men movie. Seeing as how the anticipated surge in sales of the comic thanks to audience curiosity never materialized, all Marvel's hopes lie with the success of Sam Raimi's adaptation of *Spider-Man* due out in the summer of 2002. Marvel reported a fiscal 1999 loss of $32.3 million, and in October announced that its results for 2000 would be even worse. According to its August 15 SEC filing for the period ending

June 30, Marvel had $46.2 million in cash as of June 30. With a burn rate of more than $10 million per quarter (according to that same filing, but some reports hold this burn rate at as much as $10 million a month), Marvel may declare bankruptcy before the middle of 2001 if it is unable to find further funding.

Right now, the future of the comics industry is impossible to predict. While some publishers, such as Slave Labor Graphics, are looking at alternate distribution venues (Slave Labor is currently pushing its goth titles such as Jhonen Vasquez' *Johnny the Homicidal Maniac* and Roman Dirge's *Lenore* through the Hot Topic mall chain), most are waiting for the fallout from any decision Marvel may make. However, the basic conditions that caused the collapse of comics distribution in the US still exist, with trade magazines such as *Wizard* still extolling the alleged payout of comics speculation. Whether the comics business will ever reattain the sales levels of the mid-Nineties or though, is anyone's guess, and whether the current depression is of benefit to the industry remains a subject of vitriolic debate in the comics community. While comics will continue to be published, the attempt to move beyond their current marginal niche in popular culture will depend upon finding a way to get comics to readers outside current buyers, and so long as publishers are tolerant of the current situation, this is exceedingly unlikely.

—Nova Express, Winter 2000

"Fandom Sound and Fury"

Well, the new *Star Trek* franchise *Enterprise* has been out for a week, and damn near everyone who feels fit to comment upon it has commented. Bitching about too much near-nudity or too little, bitching about continuity holes, bitching about the continuing shoddy makeup designs from Michael Westmore, bitching about that sappy opening theme song...hey, let me tell you about sappy opening songs. A few outside of the UK may remember a BBC series called *Starcops* that saw syndication through PBS in 1990: now *that* had a sappy opening song. Compared to the "shiny happy people" opener for *Starcops*, the *Enterprise* theme could have been penned by the Butthole Surfers or GWAR.

More important and more pertinent was all of the before-the-fact kvetching about how Paramount and producer Rick Berman had better not screw it up. One of the more obvious examples was Mark Altman's recent "Mark My Words" column in the newly resurrected *Cinescape*, where he gave his edicts on where *Enterprise* should go. (Mr. Altman has a problem with assuming that because he once edited a long-dead SF magazine and wrote or co-wrote any number of unauthorized *Star Trek* guides, he gets some leverage with the crew at Paramount on how any *Star Trek* franchise turns out. I write a lot about Texas culture, but Governor Rick Perry doesn't come to me to ask my opinion on tourism ventures.) Outside of the humor inherent in Altman's impersonation of Josh Levy from Evan Dorkin's fandom spoof *The Eltingville Comic Book, Science Fiction, Fantasy, Horror, and Role-Playing Club* strips, this column had one valuable shining truth: the success of *Star Trek* lies behind the people.

It hurts to admit that he has a point. One of the reasons why *Star Trek* survived in reruns as long as it did, and why it still continues to enjoy as much popular success as it does, is because of the characters and situations. *Star Trek* and M*A*S*H* were two television shows that survived as long as they did because of the interaction between interesting and unique characters, which is especially rare in science fiction productions. Don't believe me? Just point to any one episode of *The Invaders* or *Time Tunnel* (or *Battlestar Galactica*, *War of the Worlds*, *Lexx*, or *Gene Roddenberry's Andromeda*) where the character development was enough to get anyone not already obsessed with science fiction to sit down and watch. That's the clincher here: the real money doesn't come from fans. It comes from everyone else, and that's why nobody at Paramount gives a fart in a high wind what the fans think.

See, if anyone at Paramount thought that fan commentary was valid, they'd have asked for it. This isn't a slam on the value, real or imagined, of that commentary: it's just a statement. If Berman and associates wanted outside influence, they'd be hiring established science fiction writers to produce scripts, the way Gene Roddenberry encouraged Theodore Sturgeon, Harlan Ellison, Norman Spinrad, and Robert Bloch to write some of the most memorable episodes of the original series. Instead, the sole opportunity for genre writers is in cobbling together *Star Trek* novels, where all of the characters and situations are still under the control of Paramount's legal department, and those writers are used solely to attract readers familiar with their other work. (Just as how John Waters chuckles about the fans of *Crybaby* picking up *Pink Flamingos* for the first time, I chuckle over the *Star Trek* fans who read a K.W. Jeter-penned *Star Trek* novel and then reach for a copy of *Dr. Adder* or *Death Arms*. You can smell the subject matter burning the flesh off their faces from here.) If Berman and associates wanted new blood in the scripting department from young and eager *Star Trek* enthusiasts, they would have opened the doors to those enthusiasts. Instead, they took advantage of that enthusiasm with the notorious "scriptwriter's workshops" at science fiction conventions back in the late Eighties and early Nineties, where Paramount paid pittances for contributions, high-graded all of the best ideas ("high-grading" is a term used in paleontological circles for fossil hunters who take the best or rarest fossils and leave the degraded site behind), and left the "winning" writers with little but the satisfaction of saying "That was my idea" when the episode featuring that high-graded idea finally aired. The only time the producers listened to fan commentary was in getting rid of Wesley Crusher from *Next Generation*, and that was only because Roddenberry was dead and therefore in no condition to do anything about it.

The thing to remember here is that *Star Trek* is a cash cow for Paramount, both in ratings and in licensing. If it weren't, then *Voyager* would have been cancelled alongside all of UPN's other offerings during that first season in 1995. Because of this, everyone there knows that fan complaints mean little, because you're going to watch anyway. We all act like the Comic Shop Guy in *The Simpsons*, watching every episode solely to get online to the nearest chat board or Usenet newsgroup to tell everyone "Worst. Episode. Ever." Even those fans who say "Oh, I never watch (fill in the blank)" are liars, because they're sneaking peeks when they figure nobody else is watching them (C'mon: be honest. If you really were skipping out on bad skiffy TV, we wouldn't be facing new seasons of *The Lost World* or *Andromeda*.)

And this is why Berman and crew don't care about what we have to say about *Enterprise*, because after we've finished venting spleen, we'll be right back in front of the idiot box for the next episode. The repeat kvetchers, alongside the hopelessly deluded who figure "Okay, it's bad now, but it'll get better some day," are the people who will carry the series through the ratings. We're the core audience, and we won't leave, so every new viewer who comes on board while channel-surfing is gravy. The only way they'll pay attention to us is if ratings drop all the way across the board, and considering the syndication deals already worked out, the ratings will have to drop into negative numbers before Paramount execs start calling for focus groups to "reimage" *Enterprise*. If the last couple of seasons of *Voyager* were any indication, the scripts and acting will have to become really insulting before the suits descend to asking fans what they want. More likely, the UPN affiliates will resort to chopping out random seconds here and there to make way for more advertising space rather than admit that the current *Star Trek* team needs a forced retirement: fans bitched for years about John Nathan-Turner's disastrous run as producer for *Doctor Who*, too, and the BBC let the show slide into cancellation rather than fire his worthless carcass and bring on people who knew what they were doing.

That said, though, don't let me or anyone else stop your viewing. Considering how *Deep Space Nine* kept following three steps behind *Babylon 5* (remember how suddenly *Deep Space Nine* had a linear storyline about halfway through its run, and how Berman claimed that Paramount had planned at the beginning to shut down the show after seven seasons?), it'll be interesting to see what parts of *Farscape* get grafted onto *Enterprise* in the following months. Just don't think that any complaints, appearing in print or online, are going to make the slightest bit of difference. If they did, then we would have seen cameos of Lieutenants Arex and M'Ress from the animated series sometime in the last fourteen years, or even a lone Andorian or Gorn. And those are just *my* yodels: imagine what would happen if they came from someone with writing ability.

—*Revolution SF, October 2001*

Postscript: The only thing funnier than reminiscing that anybody thought that Enterprise *was worth fussing over was viewing the characters who thought it was worth saving when it was cancelled in 2005. One of the best examples was one Cat Piss Man who decided to start a whole "Save* Enterprise*" campaign, soliciting funds from fellow fans to "convince" Paramount to bring it back. Apparently, he refused to accept that Paramount specifically asked him not to solicit funds. He actually made news in 2008 for announcing a media convention in Dallas, buying up radio ad time to promote it, and then coming up with all sorts of excuses as to why attending guests weren't paid for their time. This was the convention that was shut down at noon on Saturday because the hotel still hadn't been paid for the convention space, and where dealers, guests, and attendees were told that they had a half-hour to clear out.*

"The Sargasso of January"

The ads start roughly before Christmas, and don't let up until mid-February. The ads promise the moon and stars, and they tempt. Oh boy, they tempt. They convince otherwise rational people to partake of their forbidden pleasures, and they keep promising until they've snared enough suckers, after which they disappear. No, we're not talking about the latest wave of dotcoms trying to snag some business before the board of directors scoot to Rio and leave the bills for the creditors; we're talking about the January movie dumping season.

Back in the old days, before 1984, the movie industry had two traditional dumping seasons, where studios would do their best to pawn off their marginal titles. We're talking about the films that cost a little too much to be consigned to a shelf somewhere, but bad enough that pushing for a full release during summer or Christmas was suicide. Back then, we had two dumping seasons: mid-October, when the big summer films finally start disappearing due to lack of interest, and January, when cabin fever after Christmas convinces millions that anything is better than staying home and watching reruns of *Frasier*. 1984 helped destroy the idea of the October dumping season when *The Terminator* came out of nowhere and convinced studio execs that a decent film could make a killing in the fall. Anybody who thought *The Terminator* was a fluke was converted when *Crocodile Dundee* came along two years later and took the fall moviegoing season away from the art films. Ever since 1986, fall is considered the third big season: considering the number of college and high school students looking for an escape from class after the beginning of the school year, spring break is now relegated to dumping otherwise unreleasable animated films on parents desperate to get their screaming children out of the house for at least an hour or so.

These days, the really bad films go directly to video or DVD in the hopes of scamming a few bucks from Blockbuster Video customers who don't know any better, so the films being dumped aren't the really awful atrocities along the line of *The Demonoid*. These usually star big-name actors such as Denzel Washington or Gary Sinese, and these folks aren't cheap, so throwing a finished film starring Famke Jannsen onto the storage room shelf will put the production company behind just a bit. However, someone's focus group testing showed that the fifteen twits willing to volunteer for audience surveys at the local shopping mall didn't like the subject matter, or the movie cost so damn much for so little that the studio developing it figures that spending serious money to promote it is a waste. Advertising during Christmas is serious money, so buying up a saturation ad campaign in January is cheap, seeing as how innumerable broadcast and cable channels are almost literally giving the time away.

And thus comes the reference to the January Sargasso. For those without an oceanography background, the Sargasso Sea is a large stretch in the middle of the Atlantic Ocean formed by the circulation of the Gulf Stream up the coast of North America and down the coast of Europe. The Sargasso Sea is full of sargassum weed, a floating seaweed, drawn there by prevailing currents along with other oceanic detritus. Derelict but still seaworthy ships would be drawn there from time to time, and sailors' legends held that ships that traveled into the Sargasso would find themselves trapped in the weed, unable to leave, ultimately leading to the crew dying of starvation or insanity. Considering the films generally released during January, many of the people involved can appreciate the metaphor.

Now that we've established that January is a no-man's-land for films, and considering that the vast majority of those lousy films are going to be science fiction, fantasy, and horror films, what to do? The typical skiffy dweeb (what is referred to in the comics industry as "Cat Piss Man," because these characters tend to smell like they sleep in a litter box) won't care, because even a godawful genre film is still a genre film. It is hoped, however, that Cat Piss Man isn't the sole representative taxon in the fannish ecosystem, and not all of us like to live off the waste products and other effluvia of the movie industry. Because of this, following are some of the surefire ways to spot the occasional pearls in the sea of sewage. The idea isn't so much that we're looking for treasure: most of the denizens of the January Sargasso aren't great films by any stretch of the imagination, but they generally beat the rest of the pack by an appreciable margin.

Numero Uno: if the release coincides with a cover story in a genre movie magazine, it's a dump. As a general rule, studio publicists only contact the editors and writers of *Starlog, SCI FI,* and *Cinescape* when they've been rebuffed by every other news venue on the planet. Likewise, considering that the fanboys at *Entertainment Weekly* usually get first dibs on interviews with the cast and crew of the big productions, the genre magazines don't have the influence they used to have. Of course, that isn't saying much, but these days the genre magazines get a bit less respect than *The National Enquirer* and a bit more than *The Watchtower* when it comes to publicity consideration.

This said, the January Sargasso is catnip to the crews at these three magazines, because publicists who previously wouldn't bother to return phone calls are suddenly kicking the doors down in the hopes of selling their latest stinker. The star reporter at *SCI FI* told that there's no press accreditation for *Star Wars: Episode*

One? No problem, because the same flunky keeping the reporter away from George Lucas at all costs is more that willing to arrange a full on-set interview with the cast and crew of *Supernova!* Even nasty reportage won't affect the bright and cheery smiles of these publicists, because if the film is that bad, even bad publicity might draw in a few more paying customers before this carcass is cut loose and steered toward HBO. In return, the magazine staffs are so glad that someone is recognizing them for their genius that the final article will probably end up on the front cover, alongside seven or eight pages of gushing commentary that never once mentions that the movie went through eight directors and forty screenwriters before the producer's son finished it so he could get his Director's Guild card.

(As a corollary, want a good gauge of what the worst films due out are going to be, no matter what the time of year? Look to *SCI FI*. If *Starlog* and *Fangoria* cover anything, rest assured that the movies are going straight to video, if they ever get released at all; *Fangoria* in particular is notorious for publishing ecstatic write-ups on films you'll never see because they're some college student's Super-8 project. Until recently, most of the smaller films covered by *Cinefantastique* were the same way, especially since the editor/publisher saw nothing wrong with letting directors or producers write up their own takes on the production. *Cinescape* at least has enough LA connections that it can snag a bit of real news from time to time, even if its staff is far too obsessed with the *Austin Powers* series, anything also being covered by *Ain't-It-Cool News*, and the alleged genius of Mark Altman for safety. *SCI FI*, though, has an incredible propensity for missing the surprise hits of a given year because it was too busy covering the absolute tripe. No coverage of *The Blair Witch Project* but plenty of coverage of *Blair Witch 2*, and way too many trees killed for coverage of *Battlefield Earth*, *Titan A.E.*, *Dungeons & Dragons*, and *End of Days*, among many others. If "exclusive" coverage of a film appears in both *SCI FI* and *Cinescape*, run for the hills.)

Numero Two-O: Look at the ads. I mean it: look at the ads. Count the number of ads that run for a particular film in the space of an hour of television. Listen to the radio ads. Check out the ads in the newspaper. If the newspaper ads appear more than a week before the film's release, it's a dump. If the radio ads tell you absolutely nothing about the film, but run lots of clips of the actors' voices, it's a dump. If the TV ads run more than once every fifteen minutes on American television, if the ad's editing is so flashy that it brings on headaches, if fifteen different ads still focus on the same special effect, and if the ads relate absolutely nothing about the storyline but focus on the really great CGI effects, it's a dump. If the ads keep emphasizing the appearance of the latest hot actor or actress (who probably finished work on this aberration a year or more before starting on the film that gained that fame), it's a dump. Sometimes a fairly decent film can slip through, such as *Deep Rising*, but don't bank on it.

Numero Three-O: Look for the action figures. Considering that Hasbro, which usually handled the licensed tie-ins to most big films, has cut back on the number of licensing deals in the light of its losses from *Godzilla*, *Star Wars: Episode One*, *Small Soldiers*, and *The Lost World* action figures, the number of action figures out on the shelves at the local Toys 'R' Us are starting to drop. Well, the Hasbro-manufactured ones: this won't stop the little companies from trying to buy into what seem to be sure things. Well, there's the rub: they'll keep their side of the bargain, and then suddenly the studio will move the release date back four or five months. This means that enterprising toy collectors will come across figures from films they've never heard of as much as six months in advance, with no clue as to when the film is scheduled for release. *Stargate* was such a dump that actually turned out well: the action figure lines were in the stores in the middle of summer, but it finally saw release in October 1994. One that turned out poorly was 1998's *Virus*, where Resaurus was stuck with a confirmed shipping date on its figures before Christmas when the film came (and went) later. What's really entertaining is the action figure line that comes out without a movie behind it at all: these are usually pulled and hidden away.

Numero Four-O: Look to the critics. Yes, most film critics these days are psychotic scum who aren't fit to steal oxygen away from bacteria, but you can learn a lot by studying their habits. Before the Web helped spread word of the practice, a surefire way to spot a dud was that the studio wouldn't hold a critics' screening beforehand: dumps such as *Cool World* this way got at least three days of good box office before word of mouth killed them. Since far too many critics are so cheap that they use both sides of the toilet paper, only the most dedicated would actually pay out-of-pocket to see a film on which they were slighted, and even then, coverage in a daily paper wouldn't appear until at best Saturday or more likely the subsequent Monday.

Again, things have changed. The latest stunt to minimize the damage from lousy reviews is to hold the preview screening the night before the actual release date. This way, most daily and all weekly newspaper critics miss their deadlines for the next issue, and the general assessment from most editors is "Oh, who cares about a review: it's only a crappy sci-fi film anyway." The upcoming Gary Sinese film *Impostor* was recently scheduled for a Christmas Day release before being bumped to January 4. Before the change, would you believe that the publicity company actually scheduled a Christmas Eve evening screening for critics?

(By the way, you can ALWAYS, without fail, spot a crappy film if critics report that they were required to sign a disclaimer stating that any negative reviews cannot appear, in any form, before the opening date. This usually only happens with big releases, not during January dumps, but consider this an Easter egg. Since the number of critics for online publications keeps increasing, the people who invested money in unreleaseables such as *Tomb Raider* are just trying to protect their money.)

Numero Five-O: Look to the calendar. For those obsessives who follow a film's scheduled release date all over the place, the last and still best way of spotting a January dump is looking at the number of times it bounces in and out of a January release. *Alien 3* was a classic January dump back in 1992, and was only moved to a May release for various reasons depending upon to whom at 20th Century Fox one talked. Again to beat on *Impostor*, you have a film scheduled for a Christmas release that is suddenly, within days, moved to a January release date. This is a classic sign that the studio was so lacking in confidence in the film's success that someone figured that it couldn't hack it against *Harry Potter* or *Fellowship of the Ring*. This could be typical studio cowardice, but maybe not.

No matter what the signs, this January's Sargasso is going to be like many others: lots of films trapped in bad press and worse publicity, hoping for a break. A disturbing number of them are going to be science fiction, fantasy, and horror films, because SF films get dumped if they aren't "just like *Star Wars*," fantasy films get dumped because some idiot exec doesn't understand them, and horror films get dumped the moment the latest spam-in-a-cabin *Scream* ripoff flops. At this point, discerning moviegoers should be able to spot the trapped vehicles that only need a push to get on their way again, and the waterlogged hulks that should be sunk at the first opportunity.

—*Revolution SF, January 2002*

"The Great *Episode One* Closeout Sale"

Pity poor Tricon. Pity poor Toys 'R' Us. Pity poor, poor FAO Schwartz and HarperCollins UK. A year after they got burned by George Lucas, they're realizing that the scab's gone infected. Most of all, pity the poor toy speculator, because we'll be hearing him whine the loudest and most frequently.

In the year since *Star Wars: Episode One* polluted the shores of every country on the planet, the folks who bought into the merchandising deals not only woke up with a hangover but with an empty wallet and a good case of the crabs. Tricon, the restaurant spinoff of PepsiCo that includes Taco Bell, Pizza Hut, and KFC, reported a loss last year, partly due to a gigantic tie-in contest with *Episode One* that flopped faster than Burger King's tie-ins with *Wild Wild West*. The upscale toy retailer FAO Schwartz, already stuck with huge orders of merchandising from *Godzilla* and *Small Soldiers* that it couldn't give away with free beer, is now flooded with Obi-Wan Kenobi banks, Darth Maul calendars, and Jar Jar Binks glow-in-the-dark condoms that may finally sell out about the time our sun expands into a red giant. HarperCollins UK recently reported that it made estimates of sales on the movie novelization upwards of $14 million...only to sell approximately $4 million, even with the four different covers issued to convince the faithful to buy more than one. (Naturally, the response had nothing to do with author Terry Brooks, whose book *Sword of Shannara* is generally considered as derivative of the works of Tolkien as Lucas' is of the works of Frank Herbert and H. Beam Piper. As the saying goes, imitation is the sincerest form of plagiarism.) And we don't even want to pick on Toys 'R' Us too badly: after announcing extended hours when *Episode One* merchandise first saw release, the store ordered millions of dollars of goods tied to the film, only to see demand for Pokemon goodies stomp *Episode One* kipple like a redheaded stepchild. Even typical grocery stores bought into the scam, only to be stuck with caseloads of action figures and Pez dispensers that still rot on shelves after being marked down to "90% Off Listed Price!!!"

The situation with toy collectors is obvious to anyone who attends science fiction conventions, toy shows, or any other get-together where dealers of rare and not-so-rare toys gather to display their wares. The view from all of these is the same: kilometer upon kilometer of *Episode One* figures, their packaging fading and peeling under the harsh fluorescent lights, while the sole dealer with *Fear and Loathing In Las Vegas* figures or *Meet the Feebles* action playsets sells his/her entire stock in minutes. All of these dealers went berserk and bought up everything they could, and Lucasfilm and Hasbro accommodated by supplying action figures and alarm clocks and enema bags of each and every minor and peripheral character in the film. (In this context, *Episode One* was inevitable, as Hasbro had made figures of every character, no matter how miniscule, in all three previous films, and the company had resorted to making figures based on characters from the various tie-in novels to keep the swindle going as long as it did.) One could comment that the characters were created with their marketability first in mind and their viability second, but how could we say this about the man who conceived the Ewoks?

What's really terrifying about the whole scenario is that the same folks who ruined the comics industry by speculating on dubious superhero crap just moved over to toys. The same geeks who saw nothing wrong with buying twelve copies of the same comic because it had six different covers one week (two copies each, natch, so as to sock one away for future trade) and helped the collapse of the comics industry when they realized that those boxes stacked up in temperature-controlled rooms were worth all of their weight in used toilet paper, are now moving in on the toy trade. In anticipation of their business, alongside the assumed presence of the typical toy purchaser, all of the folks bitten by Lucasfilm figured that they could unload tons of *Episode One* crap on the world, starting with the crazed speculators. Well, the speculators bought it at first...and then cut out when they realized that nobody else was interested.

The really sad and ironic part about the *Episode One* toy fiasco was that it started with a rise in sales of the old, circa 1978, figures from the first film. The secret to toys, comics, or any other collectible becoming valuable is that they have to be rare, and considering how rough kids are with toys and comics, the only examples of the early stuff are the ones saved by accident or design. If everyone saved their childhood toys in hermetically sealed canisters made of UV-blocking glass, full of argon, helium, or some other noble gas, then nobody would regret the loss of their childhood and try to buy it back. Back in '78, *Star Wars* figures were simply toys instead of valued heirlooms, and many a "Luke Skywalker as X-Wing Pilot" met its early demise in a battle with a firecracker or the family dog, not to mention the number buried in school playgrounds, dropped out the back window of the family station wagon, or sunk in ponds as they piloted paper boats encountering high seas. Only a few lunatics cared to save their figures "still in the box," which is why the 12" Boba Fett is in such demand today.

With this in mind, I call for the collectors of America to become kids again. Judicious application of gasoline, gas-powered hedge trimmers, BB guns, and sparklers should remove a lot of the *Episode One* backlog, and nothing brings a tear to the eye of the fanatic collector than someone playing with a "collectible." Myself, I just spent $40 on the remainder bin at Toys 'R' Us and a similar amount on Estes model rocket engines: anyone want to see Jar Jar Binks in low Earth orbit?

—*Previously unpublished*

Postscript: *This essay was supposed to see print in a long-forgotten Canadian publication and it never saw print for reasons that never made their way to the writer. The former editor for said publication contacted me a while back, wondering if I was willing to come back to writing for an online venue "that might pay for articles one of these days, once we're established," and it shouldn't be surprised that I dropped the ever-useful Proverbs 26:11 on him. (In other news, this was originally written when I was working as a technical writer for one of the big companies buying licensing for Episode One, and that company lost just short of a billion dollars just on its lonesome. Considering that this company was just one branch of a multinational consumer goods corporation, this should help explain why nobody was bashing the doors down to buy licensing for Episodes Two and Three.)*

On Writing

In retrospect, giving the time of day to beginning writers on the subject of writing is akin to asking Jeffrey Dahmer to manage a vegetarian restaurant. However, I honestly thought that I could pass on a few suggestions to beginners on what to avoid without getting into the paranoiac theories: I'm a firm believer in what's now called Riddell's Theorem, which states "Any sufficiently developed incompetence is indistinguishable from conspiracy." You don't need conspiracies to explain how most magazines operate and why they publish the writers they do: far too many of them published my glibberings, right?

"This Is What You Want, This Is What You Get"

About a month ago, I managed to stumble across the Web site for *Crank!*, one of the better SF magazines on the market. Its editor, Bryan Cholfin, is best known for publishing some of the more...ah, esoteric fiction in science fiction today: we're not talking as deliberately overstimulating as Chris DeVito's *Proud Flesh*, but it's definitely designed to make the average reader of *Analog* choke on his or her Batman Spaghettios.

Anyway, as I went tromping through the site, I naturally gravitated toward the "Guidelines" section, which listed what Bryan did and did not want from possible contributors. (Hey, it's only natural.) At the bottom of the page was this letter, in response to a rejection letter. It read:

"This is nothing but a scam to sell your rag! Your form letter is offensive, elitist, and insufferably snobbish. Forget about killing the TV, try trashing your form letter. And don't try to force people into buying your rag, it won't work."

Naturally, this was anonymous, but considering how many submissions any magazine receives nowadays, it probably fit the attitudes of any number of wannabes that dream of getting paid for their words. (The poor dear was probably complaining about getting rejected over some Asimov pastiche or something similar: I've seen the type all too often.)

Not only did this response illustrate how thin-skinned some wannabe writers can be, but it also demonstrates an all-too-common attitude among writers, both wannabe and established. How *dare* an editor ask potential contributors to buy a copy of a particular magazine, much less a subscription? Never mind that the magazine might be on its last legs and might depend upon revenues from samples to pay printing bills: editors are supposed to send writers checks, not the other way around, dammit!

Aside from quoting the Golden Rule, the best response to this anonymous writer is to ask him/her who told the world that writing is a big get-rich-quick scheme. Talking to beginning writers, you'd think that it was: all one has to do is put lots of words onto paper and send it in to an editor, and money comes back in the return mail. These darlings would never pass up the opportunity to go through market listings in *Writer's Digest* or *Science Fiction Chronicle*, but they balk at buying or at least reading a copy of the magazine to which they plan to submit, and then wonder why they get rejected.

Illustration the Second: I write a regular column for *Tangent*, a magazine that does nothing but review short science fiction, fantasy and horror. The magazine does not and never has published fiction, and makes that point abundantly clear in its submissions guidelines. However, when the last issue was reviewed in *Factsheet Five*, editor Dave Truesdale found himself receiving fiction submissions sent blind by potential writers who either didn't take the time to understand their market or thought that he'd break his guidelines just for them as soon as he saw their brilliant musings. I don't know if Dave sent back a subscription flyer with their manuscripts, but when Chris Lacher of the late *New Blood* did so, he received a shitstorm of nasty letters from those rejected.

Why am I going on for so long about this? Well, besides the fact that our illustrious editor has a death wish, it's to give a few tips to new writers. One of the first tips that I can give, and one that keeps getting ignored, is to Know Your Market.

To look at it with better glasses, consider that you, as a new writer, expect to get paid for your submissions. How, in any conscience, can you expect an editor to take the time to read your story, publish it, and send you a check when you obviously haven't bothered to know what s/he publishes? And how are you supposed to discover what the editor wants without reading an issue of the magazine? And considering the pathetic magazine budgets at most libraries, how else are you supposed to read an issue without buying one?

Here's a parallel comment. You're expecting an editor to send you a check for your story. Contrary to popular opinion, most editors aren't independently wealthy: most of them are publishing out of love or spite, and thereby have to choose between publishing a new issue or buying food. In order to get the money to pay for and publish new stories, they have to sell individual copies and subscriptions. If they can't sell enough copies and subscriptions, the magazine goes under. These are simple economics.

This is an aspect of the perception of writing that absolutely floors me, mostly because I fell for it myself: the same folks who spend thousands of dollars on new computers to save their work, who blow hundreds to hang out at conventions and writer's workshops to schmooze with editors and publishers, and who regularly spend the equivalent of Australia's defense budget on certified mail for their manuscripts can't be bothered to plunk down $20 for a year's subscription to a magazine. I realize that one could end up spending thousands on subscriptions, but shouldn't that be considered part of the annual budget for research?

Okay, so a full subscription isn't feasible or sane: we all know the number of magazines that either go under after the first issue or buy the farm sometime within the first year, and SF magazines are notorious for going as much as five or six years between issues. In that case, send away for a sample issue: this way, you have an idea of the magazine's focus and bent, the current contributors have a new reader, and the editor/publisher has a few extra bucks to help stave off starvation.

With a little modification, this may also be used for anthologies and online magazines. Although very few online SF magazines charge for subscriptions (the ones that did usually flopped within a year), take the time to read the stories therein. Don't just bounce to the "Submissions" section and fire away your latest opus: pore through the whole site and thereby get an idea of what the editor wants and doesn't want from experience. Besides, even if you're just doing research, your visits to the site count toward the hit counts, which means that the sites that charge for advertising can use your visits to justify their ad rates. Even though you aren't directly sending cash to the editor for a copy, you're helping to keep the magazine solvent. (And while we're at it, visit the sites that don't charge for advertising. An ungodly number of magazines, print and online, depend upon reader feedback, so a new genre-related site is much more likely to remain up and available if more than six readers show up every month.)

The same deal holds for anthologies: before sending off your latest short story, take the time to research the editor. Even if s/he has no published fiction available, previously printed anthologies, essays, and even letters to the editor to magazines and Web sites can help understand the editor's mindset. Use the big search engines: HotBot and AltaVista come in very handy in this regard, but don't neglect the print magazines.

This may come off as a reiteration of "Can't we all just get along?," but supporting magazines to which one contributes isn't just an option: it's an absolute perogative if this genre is going to survive. Or, to put it another way, publications are like shareware: if ten percent of the people hitting an editor with slush-pile submissions actually paid for a copy first, the resultant revenues would allow the editor to buy more stories. More stories mean more chances for new authors to be discovered, which means more possibilities for future sales. Even if you can't afford to buy a whole subscription, take the time to send a couple of bucks the way of a harried and overworked editor or publisher: the morale boost alone should keep your name in his or her memory for a long time.

—*Write Market, December 1998*

Postscript: As with so many other publications mentioned in this chrestomathy, Crank! shut down shortly after I wrote this, and I lost touch with Bryan Cholfin shortly thereafter. The really sad part was that he'd been hired as an editor at St. Martin's Press based on his experience with editing Crank!, and when St. Martins started a round of layoffs in 2000, he was one of the many casualties.

"Visiting Dilbert Territory"

Here's a question that I'll bet money you'll never see in the latest issue of *Writer's Digest*: what does an up-and-coming writer do about a real job?

Yes, I know, I know: we're all supposed to be horrendously rich from the million-dollar advances we receive from our short story sales. That's the public perception, anyway: a few SF writers are lucky enough to make a full-time living solely from writing science fiction, fantasy, or horror. The rest of us have to work for someone else to pay for necessities. A few might collect enough cash to pay the bills: the rest of us, if we get paid at all, make enough to afford a few luxuries, but not enough to yell "Shove it!" at the boss.

The problem with this is that while we all know the realities of trying to balance that need to write with the need for food and shelter, the popular perception among nonwriters is that writing is a get-rich-quick scheme. To these people, writing is something you do if you have enough time, that allows one to exchange paper full of typing for big checks, and that offers the secret to living a life of blissful leisure away from the horrors of the factory or office. This is bad enough when murmurs of that perception come from family members or friends; it's potentially disastrous when it comes from a current or potential boss.

By way of example, I worked as a temp six years ago for a big computer retailer. You've definitely heard the name. On my first day, I was assigned to the mail room, where I spent the next four months sorting invoices for the branch stores. That first day, I made the mistake of revealing that I had a book coming out: never mind that it was through a tiny press, and that I never really received any money from it.

"Oh, that means you'll be leaving us soon," one of my co-workers said.

"Uh...beg pardon?"

"Yeah; you have a book coming out, so you won't have to work any more."

Although I explained to him (and my supervisor) that most books pay a relative pittance for the amount of work expended, I found myself unemployed the very day the book came out. Although my supervisor was happy with my work, the order came down from her boss that I was not to stay on board because they didn't want to risk having someone who could strike it rich and leave at a moment's notice.

Because of dealing with ten years of eating shit from making the mistake of mentioning my allegiance to the written word in public, I have one firm piece of advice: engage in a don't ask/don't tell policy. Whether at an interview or in a position, the best policy is not to mention that you're a writer: don't put it on your resume unless it's vital to the position (don't mention it if you're trying to snag a job at a gas station, for instance), don't bring it up during lunch breaks, and don't come up to the boss and show off your new published story. That's the best way to guarantee a minimum of vocational stress.

Okay, you say, I want to tell somebody about my writing. Fine: go ahead, but tread carefully. One boss who loves what you're doing might be replaced by an absolute monster with a serious ego problem, and you'll spend the rest of your career wrangling with someone who will do his or her best to destroy what self-esteem you have.

See, the corporate environment already encourages tattling, backstabbing, butt-kissing, and anything up to and including murder in order to get ahead, but writing (or music, or art) suggests that the participant is playing outside of the lines. Considering the fact that far too many supervisors and managers are now MBAs with few skills other than drunken carousing and spreading venereal diseases, you won't just be an annoyance. You'll be a potential threat.

This situation is aggravated or relieved depending upon the job arena. Each career will offer different situations, but take a few generalities with your coffee.

Manufacturing: Walk softly here. Not only can the writer find himself/herself working alongside people who haven't read or even seen a book since high school, but the potential for grief from supervisors about writing can get to be intolerable. The first half of the workforce usually won't be too much of a problem except among the aggressively illiterate members of the population, and the most common danger is being blindsided by someone who just happens to have a great idea for a book, and is willing to split the money halfway if you'll write it. The supervisors, though, will usually cull anyone who stands above the Morlocks, giving the excuse of "Oh, well, at least he has something to fall back on."

Medical, legal: Not too bad, actually, if one considers the precedents of Michael Crichton and John Grisham. Just never let on that anything that happens on the job could be material for a story or a novel: this can open up legal concerns as well as just employment concerns.

General office: Good God, never. Even considering the horrors of anyone wanting to work in the inspiration for the movie *Brazil*, office politics are usually so thoroughly evil that the only writer who could survive in such a milieu would also have to be the CEO. Most general office positions are so directly controlled by Riddell's Law ("Nobody ever hires an employee smarter or more talented than they are except when absolutely necessary") that the ground-floor peons shouldn't be able to walk upright; any writer starting in a beginning-level job will probably be there in another five years, with management hoping that s/he will quit and thereby removing a source of managerial insecurity.

On the other hand, I heartily recommend office jobs for beginning and established writers: the work is suitably mindless, usually allowing plenty of time to work out new story ideas, and if Scott Adams can stay off welfare by relating tales of corporate ineptitude, why can't you? Even the worst office position has one merit: any writer trapped in it will work twice as hard to get out of it.

Academic: Being a writer on the side is a great career choice for an academic, so long as the subject isn't science fiction. Some colleges have a relatively enlightened view of SF, and have no problems with professors or teaching assistants who write the stuff, but not all. Anyone taking this tour of duty should invest in a very good pseudonym: not only will you face the potential wrath of the administration, but your students may become familiar with your work, and you'll have to deal with them for an entire semester or more.

Journalistic: A career in journalism might appear to be the choice for an SF writer, but one has to remember that journalists are some of the most insecure, neurotic, and potentially sociopathic people this side of an MBA. Working for a newspaper or magazine where the publisher tolerates or even encourages freelance work is a dream, but a lot of papers and magazines discourage their reporters and staffers from garnering any real fame. I once worked as a freelancer for a weekly paper where the Star Columnist threw tantrums whenever anybody else received more fan mail than he did, and he went berserk when I received more critical reviews than he did. (Admittedly, the reviews were from *Factsheet Five*, but they were two more reviews than he had or has received, and I was just a flunky.) Another thing to remember is that while fiction writing pays little or nothing, journalism pays even less. The only people who remain with a newspaper today are either incredibly dedicated or completely unemployable.

One might also be excused in thinking that writing for a magazine might offer employment opportunities in the future. This may happen from time to time, but the days where a writer could walk into the front office at *Rolling Stone* and get a staff position disappeared about the time Nixon was deposed. In SF, most of the magazines are running hand-to-mouth, and they can barely afford to keep their own immediate staff afloat, much less take on anyone else. I ran into this back in 1991, when I was laid off from one position and then kindasorta received an offer to work for a movie magazine in Los Angeles. When I asked point blank "Are you offering me a job?," the editor responded "No, but we can let you stay with one of us for a couple of weeks while you find a real job." In the middle of Hollywood, in the middle of the 1990-1994 recession.

Technical: This seems to be the choice among writers; technical writers in particular have no choice but to improve their skills by any means necessary. Not only does a stint as a tech writer pay much more than a comparable journalistic or secretarial career, but tech writers usually gain some aptitude that helps with story research. Think about it: getting paid to research stories: where do you sign up?

Well, there's an obverse, and that lies with your fellow employees. While many techies are the salt of the earth, quite a few are paranoiac to an obscene degree, and many are very familiar with science fiction. The fact that they haven't been able to sell their fantasy tetratology or their pitch for a *Star Trek/Quantum Leap* tie-in novel might affect your life to an adverse degree, and your suggestions might make things worse. I once worked for a programmer who co-wrote a book on the Perl programming language, and who blew a gasket when he realized that he wasn't going to get publicity junkets and groupies from that book. I was only getting articles published at the time, but I was still getting published when he wasn't, and getting fan mail to boot, so I found myself out of a job about two weeks after his book bombed.

Anyway, as I was saying, the choice of mentioning your choice of alternate profession is up to you. If you find a boss who enjoys your work or even (gasp) encourages it is someone who deserves loyalty, because he's rarer than swan teeth. However, be warned: the business world is ugly and nasty, and not all of us are able to find those perfect positions. Gives whole new meaning to the phrase "Don't quit your day job," eh?

—*Write Market, March 1999*

"Dead Stories (And Other Things About Which You Won't Read In *Writer's Digest*)"

Any number of guides on how to be a writer contain information on markets. They contain information on getting a good contract, and on how to deduct expenses for tax purposes. However, almost none will contain advice on one of the biggest aggravations to beginning and established writers: stories and articles canceled or rejected at the last minute.

In all genres of literature and journalism, but particularly in science fiction, the spectre of getting stories rejected by editors is expected. Far too many people compete for too few markets for a writer, newbie or veteran, not to get at least one rejection notice in his or her lifetime. That's usually par for the course: the really aggravating rejection, though, comes when the story or article receives the okay all the way down the line, and then never sees publication for one reason or another.

Most of the time, the reason for the rejection is beyond anyone's control. An editor who accepted a story might be replaced by another who detested it, or a publisher scales back on the amount of fiction or nonfiction being published, or the magazine goes under. Sooner or later, especially in a genre as small as science fiction, everyone will end up in this situation. The best thing to do is keep plugging along. In some cases, the author will receive payment for the article (or a percentage, known as a "kill fee") and the rights to the story will revert back to the author, but most of the time, a writer will be lucky to receive notice that it won't be printed in the next issue, if ever.

This isn't to say that editors and publishers are always blameless: some editors (especially for more mainstream magazines, and I refuse to name names) are notorious for calling for articles from freelancers, rewriting them beyond recognition, and then skipping out on printing them after multiple rewrites. Some publishers have a tendency to micromanage the publications under their control, and an article that went past editor after editor may suddenly die because the publisher didn't like one element or another about it. Publications may go under due to plain old bad luck or diminishing sales, but others die because of incompetent management, and the promise of payment or publication from any of these characters is worth its weight in used toilet paper. To be sure, they'll use any letters or entreaties from starving writers as toilet paper, and without the slightest sense of remorse or apology.

Writers have always been compared to prostitutes; the only difference is that we may get paid after we're screwed, and we're rarely, if ever, paid beforehand unless we're famous. It's a rotten deal, especially for beginners, but it's nearly unavoidable. The upside is that, in some cases, a dumped article can sometimes be salvaged; hell, in some cases, it can receive more recognition if it gets neglected than if it saw print the first time.

Because your dear old Uncle Zonker has been shafted by any number of editors and publishers over the years, here's a not quite complete strategy for minimizing the damage when an article or story doesn't get published. It can't be inclusive (as the joke goes, it can't be idiot-proof because publishers are so goddamn ingenious), but it should act as a fairly decent warning.

Firstly, remain calm. If you haven't heard anything from a particular editor, a gentle phone call asking about the situation does a lot more good than assuming the worst and blowing up in the editor's face. Especially in the science fiction business, printing deadlines find themselves pushed back, and a magazine scheduled for publication in October may see print the next May. A delay of up to a year between submission and publication isn't unheard of, and a good editor will let his/her writers know that the next issue may be a little late. However, since any magazine that takes more than a year to put out an issue isn't really a magazine, you're within your rights to scream and yowl if you've waited two years and the editor still puts off the question of a new issue.

(Example: In September 1998, I submitted an article to a magazine on the request of the editor. Because her budget was shot by a push for distribution in Barnes & Noble, she didn't have any cash, so I told her that I'd be glad to do this first article for free, as I'd always enjoyed the publication. Anyway, the article was scheduled for publication in October, and I waited to see my contributor's copy in my mailbox. Finally, in March 1999, I finally decided that it was high time to contact the editor and publisher and ask kindly if anything was holding up the new issue. By making this decision, this meant that the new issue appeared that day in my box, with the article completely unchanged. If I had been a jackass and called up to rant and scream back in October, I probably would have buggered any chances of getting published at a later date, as well as of getting that original article printed. Good editors put up with a lot of crap, but they don't tolerate too much abuse.)

Secondly, put your faith in Allah, but tie up your camel. Since the SF business is so small, most publishers of genre magazines are on cutrate budgets, and they can't afford to put out full contracts and upfront payments for submissions. (A lot of them can't pay at all; this is why so many people write SF because they must, and not because they plan to make any money from it.) Most agreements for publication are gentlemen's agreements (although I must say that most female editors have a better understanding of this than most males), and some editors and publishers aren't gentlemen. Because of this, although most editors don't want to see a manuscript submitted to multiple markets, keep a backup lying around if the editor chickens out or the magazine goes under without notice.

(Example: back in 1992, I wrote a series of articles for a magazine for which I was already a columnist, with the editor's alleged blessings. After waiting nearly two years to see them in print, in which time the editor refused to make a definitive answer as to whether or not he would print them, I finally gave up and gave them to another magazine, which published two of them in its second (and sadly last) issue. Although the magazine's circulation itself was pretty small, enough copies went out to people in the science fiction business that these articles led to my current reputation in the business, such as it is. As for the original magazine, it's published a whole two issues in the subsequent five years, so I probably made the right decision.)

By the way, here's where writing fiction and nonfiction go completely different ways. The advantage to fiction is that, barring developments that make the story obsolete, it could be sold at any time. Nonfiction is much worse: interviews and essays tend to get very dated, and nothing is more worthless than an old review. If an editor requests a 1500-word essay on the latest summer movie and s/he wimps out in November, you're pretty much forced to eat the essay. Larger and/or more reputable magazines offer "kill fees" (in the event of an article being killed at any time, the kill fee pays a percentage of what the article would have offered; it's less than full pay and publication, but it's better than a kick in the butt), but many don't, and usually the only reward you'll receive in this case is a good dose of bitterness over seeing yet another article go unseen.

Thirdly, if you decide to take back a story and try it somewhere else, and the editor gives you a routine of "Well, you know, you probably won't get it published anywhere else/you're burning a bridge/I'll do everything I can to make sure you never get published again,," ignore the twit. If the story or article is any good, it'll find a discerning editor; any editor who makes that sort of claim is usually a martinet full of delusions of his/her importance in the cosmos, and therefore safe to ignore. The only time you shouldn't ignore them is when they make crank calls for daring to usurp their authority; in that case, tape the phone calls and print out the E-mail, and slap a harassment lawsuit on the bastards.

Fourthly, as tempting as it may sound, don't mention lawyers or legal action unless the editor sits on the article and refuses to return the rights to you upon request. Threatening to sue an editor is like trying to screw fog: they're generally broke (otherwise, they wouldn't be editing SF magazines), so a monetary settlement is usually impossible, and any revenue gained by suing an editor who didn't publish your story will be absorbed by legal costs. Just send the editor a letter stating that you wish to publish your story elsewhere, and do just that: if s/he wants it, then it'll either get published or you'll receive notice that the rights have been returned to you. If the editor publishes that story or article without your permission, and you didn't sign a contract stating that the editor had that option...well, that's when you call a lawyer, because that's a point of protecting a writer's rights and interests.

Finally, it's always something. Make a point of never throwing away articles, stories, and essays if they don't get printed the first time, because you'd be amazed at future uses. In this business, the best revenge for dealing with an incompetent or malevolent editor is to garner success somewhere else, so keep on plugging.

—*Write Market, April 1999*

"It Ain't Valuable If They Ain't Buying"

Over the last decade, I've been asked by quite a number of beginning writers about what the editors of genre magazines want in the way of stories and nonfiction. Even though I'm the last person in the world whose advice they should trust, I keep getting the question "Well, I have a story; do you think (fill in the blank) would buy it?"

Firstly, remember this basic point: don't write a story unless you want to do so. Although a lot of writers, newbies and established ones, labor under the delusion that they have to write solely what editors already want to publish. The real trick is to offer a story that an editor didn't know s/he wanted, but that s/he, in retrospect, wanted to see in the slush pile. Writing with that goal in mind is actually a safer prospect than poring over market reports on what an editor will buy now: 1500 people may read that an editor is buying Brand X stories and flood the magazine's mailbox with crap, but you, and only you, may come up with that one story that changes everything.

Even so, beginning writers in this business have a tendency to offer stories that they assume are innovative and new, but have been done to death for the last fifty years. The only fault lies with not understanding the market: only the naive and deluded figure that anyone can make a living from writing stories for SF magazines any more, so only those who look at writing as a get-rich-quick scheme send in one of the Grand Clichés (the Adam and Eve story, the dinosaur hunt story, the shock ending story, among others) and expect it to sell.

Even though editors are open to innovative stories, one has to remember that they generally have no interest in material unrelated to the magazine's purview. In other words, know your market: if the story doesn't have a hard scientific base, don't bother sending it to *Analog*, because it'll come back about as quickly as a hardcore porn story from *The Magazine of Fantasy and Science Fiction*. When you receive submission guidelines from a magazine, read them: if an editor says "No horror" or "No fantasy," this usually means that, no matter how groundbreaking your story may be, it'll come back on the mail truck with a big fat pink rejection notice on top. More importantly, if said story is a cliché as well as something outside their purview, you'll get it back even faster.

Now, the last time I dared to make an assumption about genre editors, I never heard the end of it from the Science Fiction Writers of America. That won't stop me from giving a reasonable list of what the vast majority of editors really don't want to see in their mailboxes each morning. We'll always find exceptions, but I'm offering generalities.

Numero Uno: *If it's based on something you saw on a TV show or in a movie, don't bother.* Most newbie writers are told to write what they know, which explains why everyone tries their hand at fan fiction. Editors usually see nothing wrong with fan fiction; they just don't want to see it in their mailboxes. Unless the editor specifically asks for a particular story from you, don't send him/her your 300-page *Star Trek, Star Wars,* or *Babylon 5* novel. Don't send crossover fiction; nobody really wants to see your *Star Trek/The Young Ones* crossover spoof, and just because Patrick Stewart would like to see a crossover between *Star Trek* and *Beavis and Butt-Head* doesn't mean that the rest of the world wants it from *you.* Unless specifically requested, don't send your Ph.D thesis on the parallels between *Star Wars* and *Less Than Zero* and expect to get anything but a rejection notice. Most of all, nobody wants your *Star Trek: The Next Generation* porn stories, even if they involve Wesley and Worf. *Especially* if they involve Wesley and Worf.

This point also applies to attempting to one-up the storyline of an established movie or TV show. Just because *Jurassic Park* was popular does NOT mean that an editor is interested in tales concerning cloning dinosaurs, titanotheres, trilobites, Neanderthals, space aliens, or TV news anchorpeople from fossil DNA. We also don't want to see stories on how the *Titanic* was sunk by a chronal vortex, a time-travel plot, or a Godzilla attack. Trust me: it's been done.

Numero Two-o: *Leave your poetry at home.* This is nothing personal, but the reason why so many editors put "No poetry" on submission guidelines is because they'd be buried in lousy genre-related poetry. I'm not saying that your poetry is bad; I'm just saying that very few editors are willing to pay for it. If you feel that you must write poetry because your soul demands an outlet, that's okay; practice your craft to the point where you receive offers to become Poet Laureate before submitting it to a genre magazine.

Numero Three-o: *When a submission guideline says "No horror," it's for a reason.* Don't get me wrong: I like horror. Scratch that: I like *good* horror, and so do quite a few editors. Unfortunately, most non-horror magazines have to reject horror just because their readers don't want to see it (if you remember how badly readers of *Science Fiction Age* bitched about the occasional fantasy submission before Sovereign Media started *Realms of Fantasy,* consider how many would shit blood over a good old-fashioned horror tale appearing in *SF Age*), no matter how great the story may be. And that's assuming that your story is great: most horror stories received by an editor are flat-out godawful, and that's just an accurate assessment of Sturgeon's Law. Just pay attention to those submission guidelines, and you'll save a lot of return postage.

Numero Four-O: *Skip the* Twilight Zone *endings.* Rod Serling (and the cadre of screenwriters who worked for him) managed to get quite a bit of mileage from surprise endings; of course, he and his writers were geniuses. A well-written surprise ending is a welcome joy to an editor: however, if that surprise ending is "And they called themselves Adam and Eve," that story probably won't see print, no matter how good it was. Or, to put it another way, the ending to the original *Planet of the Apes* movie was impressive and startling for about fifteen seconds. Of course, that was over thirty years ago.

Numero Five-O: *If you feel compelled to submit Ferdinand Feghoot tales, don't be surprised when they get kicked back.* For those not old enough to remember, in the days before Shawna McCarthy became editor, the pages of *Asimov's* used to be full of Ferdinand Feghoot stories. FF tales were attempted humor stories whose punchline involved a really dumb pun, and the entire story was nothing but preamble to that pun. If you want to write humor, write something with some pith to it, and skip the dumb puns. (Yes, I know that SF fandom is inordinately fascinated with puns, but not every reader is a literary coprophagist.) Try wit: it's the sniper rifle of humor, and it leaves longer-lasting marks on its targets.

Numero Six-O: *No wish fulfillment fantasies.* Every editor has to deal with a certain number of these: they're fairly obvious to spot. The most common are the so-called "Lieutenant Mary Sue" *Star Trek* short stories, where the new member of the *Enterprise* crew (amazingly named after the author of the story) not only falls in love with the crew member of his/her choice, but manages to save the day while the rest of the crew sits around with its collective thumb up its collective butt. Everyone puts a part of himself/herself into a story, but that doesn't mean that we want to read about how you want to get even with the jocks and cheerleaders you knew in high school, how you wish that you could get a perfect job instead of the minimum-wage nightmare you found yourself in, or how you'd love to bang that member of your chosen sexual persuasion until his/her eyes bled. Or, if you do, we want it in an intriguing or at least entertaining way: we all have our demons, and unless yours are a hell of a lot more interesting, we don't want yours moving in for the weekend.

Numero Seven-O: *Just because you know all the in-jokes doesn't mean that everyone else does.* The main limitation to a good in-joke is that it'll only make sense to a limited percentage of your readership. A well-constructed inside joke is one that will convulse someone familiar with the subject, but won't disrupt those innocent of that knowledge. A story that depends upon a particular in-joke that applies to, say, spot welders or entomologists is going to fall dead if your potential editor is ignorant of those professions. If you can't help but use them, use them as a garnish, not as dessert.

Actually, here's a good guide to the addition of jokes to any story: should you find yourself being asked to add a glossary to your tale in order to make it accessible to readers, it probably won't work. Some stories work very well with a glossary for non-English words and phrases (Harlan Ellison's "Looking for Kadak" comes immediately to mind), but they're generally written by people who know how to use a glossary to its best advantage. A good writer generally uses glossaries as a minor reference, but any story that needs a glossary to explain a punchline is going to be exceedingly weak.

Number Eight-o: *Don't try to usurp the staffers.* This is a notice for those preferring to write nonfiction. If a magazine is interested in nonfiction submissions, and you have the idea for an essay or article that hasn't been covered before, send in a query: the worst thing that could happen is that one editor may say "no." However, if you're trying to write something under the jurisdiction of a staffer, you're usually wasting your time.

In the food web of journalism, film and music critics are generally and rightly considered to be the bottom-feeders of the business. Since every idiot considers himself/herself an authority on pop entertainment, editors get lots and lots of offers for movie and music reviews. A writer with a unique interpretation of a particular film or book (for instance, as Ernest Hogan did several years ago, noting the parallels between Cervantes' *Man of La Mancha* and Thompson's *Fear and Loathing In Las Vegas*) may get invited to submit a guest review, but sending your unsolicited review of *Star Wars: Episode One* to *Analog* could generally be considered to be a waste of time. Columnists are generally chosen for their ability to enhance the experience of reading a magazine: damn near everybody wants to write a regular column for a magazine or newspaper, so generally those spots go to those with the talent or the connections. Nothing personal, you understand: it's just that most columnists are pretty goddamn insecure as it is, and a good editor won't replace their articles with those from a complete unknown.

With this in mind, try to concentrate on more functional works than something already covered by an existing columnist. Likewise, if an editor says that s/he isn't interested in film, music, book, or magazine reviews, respect that decision.

This should be a mantra: these comments naturally don't cover all situations, but they should be used as basic guidelines. Ignore them at your peril, or the peril of your postage budget.

—Write Market, May 1999

Postscript: I don't know if it was because Shawna McCarthy really liked the general subject, or the fact that she personally banned Ferdinand Feghoot stories when she took over as editor of Asimov's *many moons ago, but she actually bought and reprinted this column for* Realms of Fantasy *in September 1999. Nobody was quite so surprised to see my byline in* Realms *as I was.*

"Advice for Writers: The True Story"

The onus of being a (reasonably) famous writer lies with helping those more unfortunate types get up to my alleged pinnacle of success. Never mind that I managed to get to this summit by breaking every rule I found in *Writer's Digest* (although you have to admit that gaining a reputation by kicking one's potential employers in the figurative nuts has its advantages; I rarely have a problem with collecting payment checks after the incident with *Cinefantastique*); everyone assumes that I have advice to give. Well, not everyone: just those poor sods intent upon literary suicide.

This came up when I received a letter from Paula Fleming, who herself tired of holding the hands of newbies as they plied their careers. She comments that she's up to her eyeballs with queries from well-meaning folk who try to read some meaning into rejection notices. I understand, having tired of explaining that just because a notice reading "SEND ME ANOTHER STORY AND I'LL CUT YOUR GODDAMN HEART OUT" appears on pink paper doesn't mean that the editor sending it will take the story if the lead character changes the color of his hair. However, nobody ever collects these questions and gives them the answers they deserve. Once again, it's up to me.

"I'm worried about someone stealing my ideas. Should I make copies of my stories and mail them to myself?"

Of course not: look at the number of successful writers who also work at the post office. Just as with the postal worker in Tulsa who stole innumerable envelopes full of "seed offerings" intended for Oral Roberts for years before getting caught, plenty of postmen take time from reloading their Heckler & Koch PK5s to sneak a few submission envelopes from the *Asimov's* mailbox. Microsoft is doing the same thing with E-mail: any electronic submission sent via Windows 95 is guaranteed not only never to reach its destination, but to appear in the new anthology *If I Wasn't A Billionaire, I Couldn't Get Laid In Tijuana* by Bill Gates, due out this December from Baen.

Remember that the best way to keep a secret is to make sure that nobody gets hold of it. Always print out your stories on sheets of the purest osmium, burn the computer or typewriter used and scatter the ashes, and bury the manuscripts in hermetically sealed containers well away from any fault zone. (Repel psychic plagiarism by putting a two-inch layer of Crisco on your hair, covered with at least five layers of aluminum foil; for some reason, dog feces smeared around the edges of the foil keep out even CIA mindprobe beams.) With luck, these stories may be discovered by palaeontologists some 65 million years in the future; they sure as hell won't be stolen by some editor.

"I received a letter from Gordon Van Gelder that included the word `alas'. Is this good?"

My dear, you have to remember that Mr. Van Gelder, the editor of *The Magazine of Fantasy & Science Fiction*, is a dreadful tease. Of course this is good; this is his way of saying "Come and get it like a big funky sex machine." All editors use code phrases to transmit their true feelings: the following comments demonstrate the power of the codeword.

"Regretfully": "I'm taking this over to *Playboy* so you can snag some real money, not the pittance I pay."

"Unfortunately": "You just want me to talk dirty to you, don't you?"

"No fucking way": "Will you take $20 bills, or just gold bars?"

"We are currently overstocked in new fiction": "I have tickets to the new Iggy Pop show and you don't, so nyah nyah nyah!"

"Tighten it up a bit": "Your mother and I are getting a divorce, and we're both declining custody of the kids, so you'll have to move out next week."

"It's a bit too derivative of another author's work": "That goddamn Riddell sent you, didn't he?"

"How do I get published?"

All right, you've figured it out: the science fiction industry is purely based on connections, and the only way you'll ever get published is if you either join the Science Fiction Writers of America (SFWA) or stand on a corner in Times Square in a horse suit and sing all of "Paradise By the Dashboard Light." The real trick is keeping the job.

Y'see, since publishers can afford to print only so many novels, articles, and short stories a year, we members of the SF/fantasy/horror community have to keep out everybody else, or else we all go back to selling storm windows door to door. To determine who gets to stay, everyone has to be able to impersonate at least one cartoon character, and each writer gets only one impersonation; hence, because Harlan Ellison does an incredible Mickey Mouse impersonation, nobody else may do Mickey until he dies. Sometimes it gets tough: a few people remember the war between Brian Aldiss and Michael Moorcock over which writer did the best Olive Oyl impression. (Moorcock lost, but managed to get into the SF community due to his stunning take on Underdog.) Myself, I took advantage of a clause that allows nonfiction writers to reserve three impersonations, and I had a lock on Beavis, Barney Gumbel, and Eric Cartman before anyone knew what happened.

Because of this, the best advice I can give to new writers is that they spend as much time as possible watching Saturday morning television. I understand Space Ghost and Buzz Lightyear are now open.

"I started work on a story, and somebody else beat me to the idea. Did they steal my idea?"

Yep: you didn't put on enough Crisco and dog crap. Next question.

"If I sell a short story, should I quit my job and write full-time?"

Of course you should: doesn't *Writer's Digest* say as much in every issue? Just make sure you invest that money in a profitable and conservative venture, just in case the writing doesn't pan out and you run out of ideas. For instance, I'd be glad to sell you three-acre lots of my exclusive oceanside property in Oklahoma, for a really reasonable price. I also have deeds on the Statue of Liberty, the Astrodome, and Seattle's Space Needle, just in case you want something more collectible.

"You have so many ideas. Where do you get them?"

Upon hearing this question, many writers claim that they order story ideas from a firm in either Schenectady, New York or Arkham, Massachusetts that delivers the ideas in handy six-packs. They then decant the ideas and plug them into the typewriter (the carriage return doles out small doses like an insulin pump). I've never had to go to such extremes: I just search out young beginning writers at conventions and writing workshops, take them back to my hotel room for a few drinks, and play Viking piñata with a baseball bat until they tell me everything. Then, after sacrificing the broken bodies to my lord Nyarlathotep, the completed manuscripts ooze under the editor's door and congeal into readable form. At least, that's what Scott Edelman at *SF Age* tells me, and he's never lied to me before.

"In what form should I submit my manuscripts?"

Well, this depends upon whether you plan to keep the stories for your own personal edification and entertainment, or if you have delusions of getting them published. In my experience, good stout typing paper with double-spaced text in an easy-to-read font is great for home, especially if the dog gets bored one afternoon and wants something to kill the time before *Daria* comes on. However, for publication, one should always carve stories onto authentic Olmec basalt heads and leave them on the editor's front doorstep. It works for editors, and it works for filing my income taxes.

Now, if the editor is willing, a writer may send electronic manuscripts via E-mail, disk, or jumper cables to the nipples. Always ask the editor if sending short stories in this fashion is all right, generally before demanding a $1 million advance and after asking about the publicity junket itinerary and whether that includes

Australia.

"Should I mention to an editor that another writer recommended me?"

Sure, if you want to catch half of the shitrain coming down on the other writer. My sister Erin made that mistake: she almost had a four-book deal through TSR, and then she mentioned "You know, my brother is..." After that, she couldn't get her phone number printed on restroom walls. To her regret, her married name won't protect her, and she's now such a pariah in Wisconsin fandom circles that even the gamers refuse to talk to her. Learn from her example, and shut your piehole.

"What do you do to get inspired, and will it work for me?"

That was my dilemma as a beginning writer, so I decided to copy the techniques of one of my favorite writers. I discovered that while I had some interesting experiences doing this, rounding up a red Cadillac convertible, a 300-pound Samoan attorney, and a pint of raw ether is rather difficult on what I make as a writer. (It could be worse: I could have borrowed another author's relaxation techniques, but I rapidly discovered that shooting up heroin in Tangiers with naked teenage boys after shooting my wife in the head during "our William Tell routine" just wasn't for me.)

The simple fact is that other writers' techniques probably won't work for you: different body chemistry or something. Besides, considering that most SF writers are perverts, you could get twenty-to-life for doing things like that with a lobster.

"Do I stand a better chance of getting published if I go to an SF convention and talk to an editor about my story?"

This works from time to time, but you're better off just going directly to the bribes. $100 bills in packets of 50 are best. If that doesn't work, tell the editor that you'll do anything to get published, close your eyes, and think of England. If they demand that you squeal, go along with it. You could be on your way to a Hugo.

The trick to dealing with editors at conventions is that they're people, too, with dreams, hopes, and delusions just like yours. This means never sticking your hands in the cage, never making sudden moves in their vicinity, and never letting them smell your fear. (Of course, they got that way by dealing with wannabe writers like you all day, but that's not your fault. Yet.) They won't understand what you're saying, but they can follow the tones of your voice like a dog, so speak smoothly and gently, and you could get a couple of contracts for *Star Trek* novels like the best of `em. Just remember that editors generally don't bite. They may not be housebroken, but they don't bite.

"This advice is all bullshit, isn't it?"

Hey, I said that I'd give free advice. I didn't say it was any good.

—*Write Market, June 1999*

"Taking Oneself Seriously And Selling Oneself Dear"

Ever feel like the little guys in Dr. Seuss' *Horton Hears A Who* when trying to expand your writing career? This hits almost everybody, and not just beginners: established authors deal with this all the time. Not everyone has the clichéd meteoric career from writing fanzine stories to the top of the *New York Times* Bestseller List: in fact, that's pretty much a myth in the first place. Yeah, you know you're good, and your current editors think you're good, but how do you let the rest of the world in on your work?

Well, promoting yourself is a start.

I know, I know, you don't know how to do this. You're too busy writing stories and articles and novels to take the time to promote your work. If you had the money, you'd hire a publicist, who would do almost nothing but put your name in front of the world. Unfortunately, almost nobody in the science fiction business has that kind of money, so it falls upon each and every one of you to do this.

What to do? Well, not everyone has a degree in advertising, but any reasonably creative individual can do what s/he can to improve visibility in today's crowded publishing scene. It all depends upon how much energy one wants to expend. Quite a few venues are open just because nobody knows that they exist.

Firstly, as a note of caution, don't bother with trying to snag radio, newspaper, or television interviews unless you feel really confident. While these are what everyone thinks of when the word "promotion" is mentioned, trying to get a television interview on *Good Morning America* or some other such rot is almost impossible without some sort of hook. Generally, when a writer gets invited to appear on television, it's part of a national publicity campaign to promote a new book, and usually that book has to have some sort of interest for the viewing audience (which, in the case of morning news programs, the most common interview format, consists of retirees, housewives and househusbands, and the unemployed). As a general rule, science fiction is going to run second to diet books, kiss-and-tell biographies, pseudoscience potboilers (any variation on the *South Park* episode "Cartman Gets An Anal Probe" is good for an interview), and repressed-memory incest memoirs. Even if you're lucky enough to get an interview, don't expect the interviewer to have read your book in advance, so be prepared to perform like a dancing bear instead of answering serious questions about your work.

(Another reason why relatively few writers appear on the radio or television is due to media limitations. Almost nobody wants to hear an author reading his or her work: what audiences seem to want is something more akin to a standup comedy routine. If you're reasonably witty and quick when being interviewed by a radio DJ suffering from a horrendous hangover, then go for that interview; if you stutter and fumble when being asked questions while a microphone gets shoved down your gullet, ask for more controlled conditions or forego the entire interview. The last thing anyone wants is a writer who becomes so flustered by a microphone or TV camera that s/he can't remember to tell the audience where to purchase copies of the pertinent book/magazine/chapbook.)

Newspapers are another sore point: nowadays, most papers go for the same demographics as morning news programs. If any reporter bothers to ask for an interview, it's usually involved with some big news story ("Did Sci-Fi Contribute To the Littleton Massacree?"), or with a look-at-the-freaks report on a local SF convention. Sending promo material is usually a folly for anyone short of a bestselling author: trust me when I say that most arts and entertainment editors are inundated with press kits, review copies, and other crap, so you need to have a really good angle to get past the noise on a reporter's desk. Also, considering the fact that far too many reporters are closet fans (they want to admit that they watch *Star Trek: Voyager* every Wednesday, but they're afraid that they'll lose their coolness if anyone finds out), this sort of publicity can backfire if the reporter wants to use you as an object of ridicule.

(Another corollary: don't even bother trying to contact a radio or TV station or a newspaper without a few books under your belt or without a significant body of periodical work. Trust me: nobody at your local newspaper is going to give a damn about your impending publication in a magazine, unless it has that "hook" mentioned previously.)

Nope, the best way to promote oneself is to start small. Ernest Hogan (author of *High Aztech*) makes a point of drawing flyers promoting his upcoming stories in magazines such as *Science Fiction Age* and sending them out to friends and relatives. While not every writer has Ernest's art ability, this is a very good start: make up a flyer with the story or article title, your name, the name of the magazine, and information on where to get a copy. This works very well for garnering interest at SF conventions: the difference between you and every wannabe who wants to snag a guest badge is that you've already been published, and the convention committee can confirm it. (With books, contact the publisher and ask about any promotional material: if the publisher already made up flyers or press kits, offer to send them off yourself. If the publisher didn't, offer to make them, and then spend a little cash at the local Office Depot or Kinko's and make the best flyer or package you can afford. Yes, it may cost a bit, but this may be the difference between a wildly popular book and one that barely sells its initial print run.)

Promoting books is a bit rougher, but an industrious writer can improve the odds on its receiving a good response. The problem with sending books for review is that by the time a book review appears, the book may be long out of print, as months or even years may elapse between the writing of a review and its publication. John Stith and Robert Sawyer both mentioned years back that the best way they discovered to beat this time lag was to print up proofs of their books and send them off as soon as possible to every likely venue willing to review them: this way, the reviews appeared at the same time as the books on bookstore shelves, and a reader could go straight from the review in, say, *Analog* to the bookstore and snag a copy. Modern technology might help keep the cost down by using such applications as Adobe Acrobat to make files that could be E-mailed to reviewers, but try to stick with dead-tree proofs as much as possible. Critics are vain creatures, and they tend to appreciate hardcopy books for review.

The same trick may be used for magazine stories and articles, especially if the editor/publisher doesn't have the time to submit copies for review. Consider buying a few copies (either from the publisher or from the newsstand), putting them in an envelope with a bit of bio information and a contact address and phone number, and send them to the SF news magazines. ALWAYS send material to *Locus*, *SF Chronicle*, and *Tangent*, but consider sending copies to any other genre magazine that strikes your fancy. At the very least, someone might take down the name and address and contact you later. They might not, but hey, the point is that you made the effort.

If the magazine is out of print, the particular issue that published your story is sold out, or the article therein becomes a point of contention (for instance, someone quotes it out of context), be prepared to spend some time at the copy shop. A standard practice among music acts is to include photocopies of previous reviews and interviews with press kits: sending a copy of a previous article might convince an editor that you happen to be the one person with the expertise to write a similar piece in the near future. This doesn't always work (once again, editors have enough to read as it is), but the idea is to get your work read by as many people as possible, and if the magazine that originally published it went under or saw very limited distribution, well...

Web sites are another possible way to promote previous and upcoming work, and will be the subject of next month's article. In the meantime, remember these basic rules about promotion.

Remember to whom you sent material, and when. Keep a notebook or database of contact addresses and phone numbers: this not only prevents redundancy in mailing materials, but it gives a good idea of who received what and how long ago. This way, if your address changes, you'll know exactly who knows, and who doesn't know.

Your editor may not be your friend, but s/he should be a partner. Back in the early Seventies, when Harlan Ellison was writing stories like "Croatoan" for *The Magazine of Fantasy & Science Fiction,* he noted the number of people who cancelled their subscriptions solely because of his stories and asked editor Ed Ferman why he kept publishing Ellison's work if it kept bringing this response. Ferman replied that for every subscriber who cancelled, he received at least three subscriptions because of Ellison's work appearing in the magazine.

This is an important consideration that far too many writers (and editors) forget: the best situation between a writer and editor is that of partnership. The editor takes a chance on your story being interesting enough that readers either buy a copy on the newsstands or renew their subscriptions, and s/he certainly won't pass up any (legal) opportunities to increase sales. If your story draws enough popular response, either in sales or reviews, this is an incentive for the editor to buy your next story, or to keep you in mind for special projects.

This is why it never hurts to let others know about good experiences with editors, and not just the teeth-clenching nightmares. If an editor takes the time to get a really good cover illustration for your story, let your friends and colleagues know (this'll also help out the artist; artists need love and money as well). If an editor makes suggestions that improve a story, be willing to give the editor credit; s/he'll remember this. Best of all, do your best to convince friends and colleagues to buy a magazine or a subscription. As I've mentioned elsewhere, the best way to get published again is to help keep solvent the magazines that published you the first time around.

This isn't to say that editors and publishers do nothing to promote your work: they just don't have the time to emphasize your work to the exception of every other contributor. If a particular magazine doesn't have a section mentioning upcoming stories and articles appearing in the next issue, make a subtle plea for one. Many magazines can't justify giving up the advertising space, and many editors won't make decisions about content until long after the previous issue has gone to the printer, but a plea can't hurt.

Another possibility is to buy copies of magazines from the publisher. Many editors and publishers have no qualms with selling copies of their magazines at cost, so call or write and ask about the cost of 100 copies, or whatever you can afford. Some larger magazines may give you copies on the explicit condition that they are to be given away instead of sold, but most will ask for some kind of payment. This works out well for you (you've just managed to get 100 copies of your article without ransacking the local bookstores) and for them (these are guaranteed sales, and considering how most SF magazines make back their cost and little else in newsstand distribution, payment at cost is more certain than the eventuality of receiving payment from a bookstore chain when Accounts Payable feels like honoring the bill). In most cases, even if the magazine goes under, those copies are yours to do with as you will.

(Another sidepoint: quite a few SF magazines, if they do promotion of their own, dump copies of an older issue on the "Freebie Table" at a convention and hope for the best. Whenever possible, try to drop copies in the hands of potential readers, as magazines or books left on the Freebie Table usually get snapped up but almost never read. Make a point of giving magazines or books to individuals who plan to read them, instead of people who just want to snag *gratis* goodies.)

The best things in life aren't always free, but they can seem that way. Most people are suckers for free stuff. Trying to convince people on the street to go out and buy a magazine with your story in it is usually a waste of time and energy, but give ` em a free copy and point out your article, and several things happen. Firstly, they have a face to connect with the name, as in "Hey, this crazy person gave me a free copy of his/her magazine, and the story in it was really good!" This may lead to nothing, but it sometimes causes readers to keep an eye open for your name on a magazine cover. Secondly, they haven't had to take a chance with $5 (or whatever the magazine costs) to see whether they might like it: they have a free copy, so they'll know. Thirdly, even if they have no interest in the magazine, they probably have a friend or relative who does, and that person will remember your kindness and generosity.

The same thing can be said about writing articles or stories on a pro bono basis. Far be it for me to advocate writing solely for pleasure instead of compensation, but sometimes holding out for cash when starting a career is a mistake. If an editor offers payment for an article, TAKE IT (don't hesitate, don't backpedal: just take the goddamn money and be appreciative), but if the editor doesn't have a real budget but happens to be working on a project that may offer rewards in the future, work out something so everyone goes away happy. The smartest decision I ever made was contributing a series of articles to Chris DeVito's *Fuck Science Fiction* back in 1993: he didn't pay a dime, but I liked his magazine, and I have to admit that the obnoxious punk in me enjoyed the idea of appearing in a magazine titled *Fuck Science Fiction*. Those articles (and one for the fiction-only *Proud Flesh*) did more for my career, such as it is, than anything else. I attribute a lot of work in the subsequent years as being due solely to my articles in *Fuck Science Fiction*: it may not have been approved for families and the easily disturbed, but that magazine was read by a lot of folks in the business, and it did get my name in front of quite a few people who became friends or colleagues later.

Never, ever, EVER forget the reason for the publicity. Yes, it's very easy to get hooked on promotion: first it's sending copies of articles, and then a bounce to radio interviews, and then it's temper tantrums if you don't get top billing on *Politically Incorrect*. Just remember that, unlike far too many celebrities, writers actually have to produce something to justify this attention. Nothing looks more foolish than a wannabe writer who demands a complimentary guest badge at a local SF convention because s/he is currently working on his/her first short story and thereby qualifies as a pro. Likewise, established authors who flood every media venue with press releases and cute photos may find themselves blacklisted and slapped with a popular backlash faster than they can say "Kristine Kathryn Rusch."

The writer's best promotional tool is the actual written work. If your work holds up, then word of mouth will do more than anything to improve your career. If it doesn't, then all the hype in the world isn't going to sustain a career. As Pasteur noted, "Chance favors the prepared mind," so a good promoter knows when to back off and let an audience digest the press releases and banner flyers. Besides, that gives more time to write, and that's the reason why you're doing this, right?

—*Write Market, August 1999*

Postscript: I back everything I wrote here with the exception of the suggestion about buying copies. I wrote this before writing rather large checks for bulk orders of magazines where the publishers decided to have a party with the windfall before disappearing forever. At the time, I was angry, but now I just relax and remember Proverbs 26:11. I'm going to have to get that carved on my tombstone one of these days.

"Yes, The Internet Can Be Your Friend: A Serious Internet Strategy for Writers"

Seeing as how most writers are vain yet insecure creatures, the urge for an author to set up a personal Web page is almost irresistible. For a few dollars a month in Web access and the use of a decent Web editor, nearly anyone can set up an information-rich, aesthetically pleasing site, full of information about the writer (including addresses and other contact information for editors and/or groupies) and his or her works.

Mind you, this works in theory. In reality, well...

A well-constructed author Web site, constructed and operated by the author or a knowledgeable employee or fan, allows fans and interested bystanders to read previous and new works, query about buying copies of new or older books, get fellow fans in contact with each other, and gather feedback on novels, stories, and articles. The focus here is on "well-constructed." As with too many sites on the Web, many author sites, both author-run and fan-run, are confusing warrens of broken links, bad graphics, and poor design elements, with new material appearing every few years or so.

Web design is still so new that many so-called experts argue endlessly about what qualifies as good design. Moveable type has had centuries to perfect the look of the printed page, and most of the concepts behind that layout go back even further. Since Web construction techniques are so new, it's easy to abuse them. The big question anyone should be asking when starting up a Web site is "Why?" Why set up a site? Why add these elements? Why focus on sales? Why focus on content? Why are we expecting this new site to make a difference? Why should Web surfers visit this site, as opposed to the millions of other sites available?

Well, you didn't ask for answers, but you're getting them anyway. While not intended to be all-inclusive, let these points act as a guide for further "Why? Questions.

If you're just starting out as a writer, then you probably don't need a Web site. Setting up personal pages are all fine and good, and we're all proud of your "Hi, my name is Skippy and here's my cat Skippy" site. However, the idea here is that we're trying to promote previously published material on the Web. This means the material is paramount, and if you don't have any material, you're wasting your time. Oh, and don't bother with those "Under construction" banners for new material, either: wait until you have at least twenty stories, articles, or reviews to present, or at least one book, before even considering a Web site to promote your work.

With that done, consider what you plan to do with your site. Are you trying to promote a new book, or just send readers to Amazon.com to buy a copy? Or did you have enough leftover reference material that you want to offer an additional experience to those who already bought a copy? Are you reprinting stories to build up a fan base, or are you reprinting them because the original publishing magazine had a total print run of twenty? Are you publishing previously unpublished material because your files are full of material from stillborn magazines, or because you're so full of energy that you can't resist throwing out free stuff to incoming visitors? Take these into account, and plan accordingly. Try to consider what you plan to do with your site in one year, two years, or even five years: if spending at least a few hours every month to update and upgrade a site seems like too much time, save yourself and your visitors grief and bail out now, or get someone else to do all of the design tasks for you.

Learn something about Web design before starting. Far too many Web sites of any kind subscribe to the "Chimps With Shotguns" school of Web design: giving a Web editor such as Adobe PageMill or Microsoft FrontPage to someone unfamiliar with even the basics of effective Web design is like giving shotguns to chimpanzees. It guarantees a mess, and someone may get hurt. Many Web sites may have a message, but it's buried under bleeding-edge technology that doesn't work half of the time, or irritating animations, or banner ads for any number of ridiculous get-rich-quick schemes and affiliate site programs. Even if it's relatively free of these menaces, more work went into text in funny colors or poorly scanned photographs than to basics such as navigation or even content presentation.

Plenty of free Web design guides exist to help the Web-ignorant help themselves. Both *Webmonkey* (http://www.webmonkey.com) and *Web Pages That Suck* (http://www.webpagesthatsuck.com) are stuffed with guides for the beginner and the advanced Web designer. *Web Pages That Suck* is in many ways the better guide: as it teaches "Learn good Web design by looking at bad Web design," a few of its examples of what NOT to do should cure any new Web author of the usual clichés, such as black backgrounds, funny-colored text, and home pages that run on forever. Also, both sites offer plenty of links to other guides to design and technology, so that anyone feeling compelled to try something really exotic, such as dynamic HTML or dynamic content generation, can decide if this is a good idea for a particular site.

For those unfamiliar with even the basics of Web design, contemplate this scenario. A Web site and a magazine are roughly similar, if magazines needed special readers to access them. Picture a magazine that is printed in color, which does absolutely no good for anyone with a black-and-white reader, and has a built-in strip that plays music...which does no good for someone with a reader that either plays in mono or with a volume knob turned off. With this magazine, large articles require the reader to wait until s/he can turn the page, and big ads slow reading beyond all endurance. A real-time magazine like this wouldn't last more than a few seconds, but this same lack of consideration is standard for many Web sites.

Consider the bells and whistles, but don't go crazy. Considering the focus of the site is essential, because it allows you to decide what needs to be done next. Here's where things get interesting.

First and foremost, consider the advantages and disadvantages of getting your own domain name. Four years ago, when the Web was young, domain names made sense for those with free server space at their employer or for those with plenty of money to burn, but now the price has dropped to where one can buy a truly obscene amount of storage space for as little as $25 a month. Reserving a domain name itself is pretty easy, with sites such as Register.com (http://www.register.com) offering free application; all a new designer has to do is pay the $70 registration fee (which is good for two years) and then reserve space on a server to store the site.

Getting a domain name has its advantages. Many Internet service providers offer free Web site space on their servers in exchange for membership, and many colleges give out free E-mail and Web services to students, but consider the problems with relaying a URL as long as your arm to someone over the phone. One misspelling and the person at the other end gets either the wrong page, or a "Page Not Found" notice, and gives up. (Fess up: how many readers have had to explain what a "tilde" was over the phone, hm?) Also, most ISP server space is limited to 5 megabytes of data: this is great for "This Is My Cat" sites, but a serious site full of content (both graphic and text) will eat through that pretty quickly.

Another reason to reserve a domain name lies with the state of business on the Web: I went through four ISPs in a year, when I moved from Oregon to Texas (one), set up shop with a new ISP that promptly declared bankruptcy and shut down (two), switched to another that was bought out by a competitor (three), and finally settled on the current location (four). That's four different URLs in the same period: with a reserved domain name, I could switch ISPs thirty times, and traffic would still get to the proper location. I have no idea how many readers I lost with each of these moves, so learn from my mistake.

Now that the need for domain names has been established, what domain name should be reserved? Welp, that's up to you. I'd recommend reserving two domain names: your name (in my case, "www.paultriddell.com") and the name of your site ("www.hpoo.com"). This way, it keeps domain name speculators from trying to scam your name if you become famous or at least rich, and it allows more than one entryway to a site. (After all, readers might not remember some obscure in-joke of a URL, but they can be expected to know how to spell your name, so get your ISP to redirect traffic from your name URL to the one you plan to use.) Something descriptive works well: Robert Sawyer saw some of the possibilities when he reserved http://www.sfwriter.com. One way or another, it's better than wasting time on a URL like http://www.cheapasspages.com/users/web/homepages/writers/~sucker/index.html, isn't it?

With the domain name situation resolved, it's time to concentrate on what's actually going to go into the site. Lots of folks make noises about how E-commerce is where the money is, and it may be, but what do you plan to sell? If you plan to use your site to sell copies of your new book, you're going to have to prepare to set up a secure server system to protect credit card numbers, as well as have a way to process those credit card numbers when you get them. If only three people buy a copy of your book from you, you'd probably be better off joining an affiliate program with Amazon.com or your favorite bookseller and have them take care of the details of sales tax, shipping and handling, and returns. However, if you have a body of work comparable to that of Isaac Asimov or Harlan Ellison, and your house is creaking with cases of out-of-print books that fans desperately crave, then setting up a secure purchase system makes sense. (At that point, having someone else set it up makes even more sense, but that's another acid flashback.)

As an aside, consider the problems with the Internet being an international medium. An American ordering books from Australia, or vice versa, has to deal not only with shipping costs, but customs regulations, currency exchanges, and a lot of other aggravations, and rest assured that you'll get at least one order coming from at least 1000 klicks outside your mother country. Once again, better to let someone else handle the transactions, unless you enjoy cashing checks from all over the world.

Let's make an assumption of a middle ground here. Let's say that you're a moderately famous writer: one or two books under your belt, a good smattering of short stories sold over the last fifteen to twenty years, and plenty of nonfiction essays and articles. At least one of the books is out of print, but the other is readily available at most book superstores. Of the magazines that published your short stories and articles, half are currently dead, but all reverted rights back to you after publication. How does this affect the design of your Web site?

Vincent Flanders, the co-author of *Web Pages That Suck*, makes a very obvious mantra for anyone going this route. He argues that the one question that should be asked whenever anything gets added to a Web site is "Will this addition ultimately cause someone to write me big checks with lots of zeros to the left of the decimal point?" This means setting up an outline of both books, complete with ordering information and a scan of the cover, is essential: visitors may like the outlines, but they won't buy copies if the purchase information consists of "Available at smaller bookstores everywhere." (For the out-of-print book, set up a link with a used bookstore with a good collection of material and will notify a buyer when a copy of a desired book comes in. The best example that comes to mind is Powell's City of Books in Portland, Oregon: book collectors worldwide make trips to Portland solely to buy and sell at Powell's, and if they can't get a book, it's usually completely unavailable.) Make things easy for visitors, and they'll reward you.

The short stories and articles are a bit problematic, considering the market for single-author anthologies and collections is close to dead right now. Publishing the entirety of stories and articles from long-dead magazines is prudent, but never publish material from magazines currently out on the stands. A good rule to use is "Wait 60 days or until the appearance of a new issue, whichever comes first." If the magazine has a Web site, make a point of offering a link to that site instead: giving a visitor the opportunity to buy a copy of the magazine not only helps keep a particular market solvent, but impresses upon the editor that you have a base of readers who can and will buy magazines based on your work appearing therein.

Other additions are dependent upon personal taste, but should be used sparingly. Authors should always include one photo to a site (after all, you never know if a fan will recognize you by sight and buy you dinner), but keep them to an absolute minimum unless you're a fashion model or carny freak on the side. Don't worry about video or audio files unless they're recordings of radio or TV interviews, and always make sure that visitors know the exact size of each file. (Remember that most visitors are still puttering around the Web with 14.4 or 28.8 modems, so nothing drives them crazier than getting locked into a download for an hour for something indulgent or silly or pointless.) Keep graphics to a manageable size, and stay away from cheap clip art: yes, a pro artist is expensive, but you get what you pay for. Most of all, always, always, ALWAYS include at least one way for a visitor to contact you. The resultant cascade of E-mail may be mostly crank mail, but what if an editor comes a'callin'?

Skip the hit counter. Just leave it off: until word of mouth gets out about the great content on your site, it'll just depress you. Concentrate on offering material that gets people to come back, not on how many people visit once and then leave.

Update, update, update. Most Web magazines like to refer to "Web years": the idea is that time on the Web goes by seven times as fast as "normal," so sites age in dog years. It's not too inexact an analogy: print magazine subscribers will wait up to a year before giving up on a new issue, but forget to update your site for a month and watch the hit counter. After three months, unless you cut up an editor with a hacksaw and made the CBS Evening News, the number of daily visitors should be a tenth of what they were after first announcing the site. After six months, the only people visiting are those forlornly seeking new content, and they'll just peek in, look at the "Last updated" date, and skulk off. After a year, the only visitors will be the people connecting via links from other sites, and the only site connecting after that will be "Ghost Sites" at Disobey.com.

It's not absolutely necessary to offer new, compelling content every day or even every week, but it should be updated at least as often as the seasons roll around. The more new content that appears on a regular basis, the more likely visitors will return, if only to see what's new.

After the site is done, the real work starts. Many companies and individuals assume that once a new Web site goes online, everyone can relax. Anything but. Besides the obvious effort to garner listings in the big search engines, the first and foremost responsibility of the new Web parent is to let the rest of the world know that the site is alive and running.

Five years ago, the Web was so new that any company or individual that went online was a news story (hey, that's how I ended up on the front of the business section of the Dallas Morning News back at the beginning of 1995), but now the surprise comes from the companies and individuals who aren't online. Even so, take the time to contact friends, neighbors, and organizations and let them know. Belong to SFWA? Send a message to the SFWA Bulletin and let the staff know, and they might list the URL. Spend a little bit of time to print up a decent announcement sheet and include it in standard mailings. Let your editors and publishers know, and they might pass on the word. Whatever happens, though, don't sit on your hands and wait for visitors to come to you. This is as foolish as quitting your day job the moment you sell your first short story.

Take constructive criticism as it was intended, and not as an insult. A while back, "Web Pages That Suck" gave its Daily Sucker award to the home page of an author who shall remain nameless. The Daily Sucker normally goes to corporate Web sites that displayed consistently bad design and not to personal sites, but seeing as how this author regularly wrote tech articles and columns, the idea was that he should be at least a little knowledgeable about design for the Internet. (The author deserved the criticism, as the site was horrid: a godawful olive green background, with a tacky "E-Mail Me" button, a graphic of the author that was entirely too big, and other faux pas.) Instead of taking a hint and improving the navigation and appearance of the site so that it was more useful to visitors, said author put a snotty "This is not a course on web design" notice on the front and continued on. (To be fair, the site improved mightily since then, and it's no longer physically painful to view. However, it still has that notice, as if to say "I'm a big writer, and I don't give a damn what anyone else thinks about my design.")

Opening up a site naturally opens a writer up to criticism, but this is the wrong take. Slap down the rude gits who giggle "Dontcha know bout desin?" with "Yes; don't you know about spelling?," but pay attention to constructive comments about the layout and presentation of material. If visitors kvetch about an overabundance of animated graphics or misspellings or dead links, listen to them, thank them profusely, and *do something about those problems*. Even considering the ease of Internet communications, consider that every complaint means an average of twenty to thirty people who noticed the same problem but didn't bother to say anything. Better still, those twenty to thirty people may have done something: they may have left your site and gone somewhere else. In extreme cases, such as the use of Java applets, strange Javascripts, or other components that crash browsers, they'll go somewhere else, never come back, and tell all of their friends to stay away as well. So much for getting new visitors. Pay attention to user complaints, because they usually won't repeat them.

Don't let Web site maintenance get in the way of writing.. The urge to redecorate or rearrange can become irresistible, and many find themselves trying out new technologies because it looks cool on the page. Resist this temptation: if you have time to write or upgrade, but not both, concentrate on writing. Don't become trapped inside a beautiful Web site refurbished with brand new cascading style sheets and a full search engine if no new content has been added since 1997. Trust me: visitors would rather have a stale interface containing scintillant stories than the opposite. Besides, what's the point of setting up a writer's Web site if nobody is doing any writing?

—Write Market, September 1999

Postscript: Nearly a decade later, you could take just about everything written here about personal Web sites and apply it to blogs. All this new technology, and it gets used for oversized photos, videos of authors' cats, and absolutely idiotic meme polls.

"Writer's Indigestion On The Web"

Without realizing it, I managed to come across one of the best comedy magazines on the stands today, and it wasn't in the section one might be expect. For only $US4.99, you too can pick up one of the funniest reads put between glossy covers in years. It's not *The Onion*, it's not *Harper's*, and it's not an issue of *Wired* with one of those sillyass prediction interviews with Faith Popcorn or Douglas Coupland. It's not even an issue of *Cinescape* trying to convince the world that a big-screen *Battlestar Galactica* film is in the planet's best interests. The magazine is the *Writer's Digest Special Edition: Writing For the Web*, and it's a hoot. I picked up a copy about two weeks ago at a local Barnes & Noble, and I started laughing so hard that the tears started running down my legs (or maybe I pissed myself with laughter; I'm not sure), and I was asked to buy the magazine and leave the store, in that order. I've read some ridiculous guides intended for beginning writers before, but this is one I had to buy, solely to read sections out loud to friends. Folks, this is one of the best prank guides this side of those *Dirty Tricks* collections, especially since anyone taking the advice in here to heart won't realize they've been scammed.

Okay, enough with the laughter. Whenever I'm asked for advice by beginning writers on how to go about the craft of writing, the first comment I make (aside from the obligatory "Make sure you're writing because you can't conceive of doing anything else, not because you figure that writing is an alternative to a real job") is "Ignore anything you may have read in *Writer's Digest.*" Most magazines that dwell on writing are by nature evil: if they don't start the urban legends of writing being one great grand get-rich-quick scheme, they certainly perpetuate it. Although allegedly intended for writers of any level of expertise, most of the advice is pitched toward those who plan to start writing one of these days, even though most of said advice really only works for those who've already been published. All of its articles are happytalk: no articles on how to contact a lawyer about nonpayment by editors, or what to do when an editor screws up copy and refuses to take the blame for any misrepresentation therein, or even a listing of the more notorious scams inflicted upon beginning writers. Coming from *Writer's Digest* and its staff, writing is a lucrative, honorable business where anyone can step up to the plate and present a bestselling novel. Better yet, judging by the number of articles aimed at writers of SF/fantasy/horror, this fantasy world is one where anyone can make a great income by writing science fiction short stories.

My all-time favorite *Writer's Digest* story, from several years back, was the famous "How To Increase Your Writing Income By 60 Percent!" cover story, which definitely caught the attention of droves of beginning writers working for comp copies or maybe one to two cents a word. The actual advice was a lot more prosaic: when an editor calls an author and asks for a magazine article, the author should wait until the editor mentions money, because we all know that authors undersell the value of their work. Considering the real world, where magazine editors rarely have more than a pittance to offer for articles and most beginning authors expect Stephen King-sized advances on 500-word stories, worrying about authors underselling themselves is a minor concern. An honest article should have suggested that the author keep his/her mouth shut until the editor mentions a paycheck because authors have a tendency to overinflate the value of their work, but that wouldn't jibe with the shiny happy people world as presented in *Writer's Digest*. The magazine generally sells only to beginning writers, because established writers know better, and the only established writers who take *Writer's Digest* seriously are the ones trying to sell articles for the next issue.

Which leads us back to the new "Writing for the Web" special edition, and all of the horrors facing the poor fools who take its advice. Well, that's not fair: some of the advice is reasonable, but it's also common sense that any beginner could get for free from any number of sources, instead of paying $5 to get it here.

As is its wont, this special edition starts out with a self-congratulatory riff on the future of writing, gasping and sighing over the future of writing as an electronic activity that incidentally the other articles in the magazine cover in detail. It would have been a great article...in *Wired* circa 1992. The overwhelming impression is that all writers should get rid of their Olympia manual typewriters and jump onto the electronic bandwagon now, because the digiterati are going to ride up their asses! Never mind that many writing markets still require hardcopy manuscript submissions: if it's high-tech, it's obviously better.

Mind you, I'm not arguing from a Luddite angle: I was arguing the merits of online publication for authors back when most newspaper publishers were still arguing that the Internet was just a fad that would fade by the end of 1996. I for one would love to see more online magazines, and more opportunities for beginning writers. However, there's a big difference between some of the rampant speculation that infects the *Special Edition* and the reality of the publishing industry. Considering the ease and advantages of E-mail over Snail Mail, a good computer is nearly essential to writers with tech-literate editors. Assuming that buying a computer will open up any number of online markets is as much folly as assuming that buying a television will turn the buyer into a successful teleplay writer. (Of course, when you look at the number of twits who assume that their memorization of errata in *Entertainment Weekly* and *Ain't It Cool News* makes them players in Hollywood, and the equal number of twits who assume that setting up a Web site will cause them to produce material someone might actually want to read, the delusions are all over.)

The first intimation of trouble lies with the explosive ejaculation of S. Joan Popek's article on E-books. Since Ms. Popek's credentials include being a publisher of E-books, her impartiality on the subject is a little suspect, but it's no worse than the amount of rot written elsewhere by individuals with a vested interest in the product they're pitching. (After all, do you honestly think that any of Microsoft's technology guides are going to admit that products by Sun or Adobe might be better tech solutions?) While the idea behind E-books is intriguing, especially with the potential of storing dozens of novels in a single reader and cross-referencing them, the reality is that E-readers aren't going to crowd out standard paper books any time soon. Considering that books and magazines are still cost-effective to publish, only the obsessively technophilic are going to spend $500 on a reader and then pay another $5 to $50 per book downloaded onto the E-reader. Music offered online makes more of a connection to the average person, and the new MP3 players are now dropping below $100. Joe Average can justify plunking down $50 for a new, improved MP3 player in a year or so and being able to plug it into a car stereo for tunes all the way to the beach. Reading is a much more participatory activity than listening to music, and it usually requires some free time (increasingly rare today). Also, while music fans are willing to pay exorbitant prices for improved delivery and improved sound, reading doesn't require high-tech solutions: funny marks on paper have been a standard requirement for centuries, and considering the number of people who print out Web pages to read later, standard printing is going to remain the core of publishing for years after that. After all, a standard paperback doesn't need batteries, it can be dropped from a great height without significant damage, and it's technically disposable or recyclable. Once E-books reach that level of ease, they might take off, but right now they're nothing but playthings for rich geeks with terminal cases of gadget penis envy.

The same level of technophilic credulity suffuses Keir Groff's article on software for writers. I'm not talking about the justifiable software for screenplay writing that helps keep a screenplay in standard format: I'm talking about variations on the notorious "story wheels" that every wannabe writer drags out in lieu of a real inspiration. Okay, for those who obsess over details with their characters, having software that catalogues particular traits and motivations might make some sense, but this software is a little more subject to crashes and power outages than a handful of 4x6 cards, and a lot more expensive. Besides, story wheels are for suckers: anyone needing a crutch like this in order to write needs to reconsider his or her motivations for writing in the first place.

On the basic common sense level, we have Michael Ray Taylor's "How to Be a Web Writer," which promises us the secrets to the sorts of material that online editors crave. The secret? Editors want material that's quick, short, and smartass. Hell, anyone reading Suck.com on a regular basis could tell you that. And, of course, we get no mention of what happens to writers who may want to be steady, lengthy, and serious: presumably, they're taken behind the CGI bins and shot.

The most aggravating and infuriating material comes with two articles that end up diverting beginning writers' resources away from writing. The first, Mitchell Bard's "Building Your Web Site," is a waste. As I've said before, beginning writers have no business putting together a Web site to show off their work: if you have enough material to justify a site with more than five or six pages, then a Web site makes sense, but a beginner with no published writing credits is expending time and effort on Web design that should be used for writing. Pagan Kennedy's accompanying article about the merits of Web publicity suffers from the same syndrome: she can justify setting up a Web site to promote her newest book because she has six books and a lot of other material to choose from. A beginner who sets up a Web site with a bio photo, a mention on how s/he wants to become a writer, and nothing else isn't going to get editors flooding the E-mail box with requests to contribute to a new magazine or anthology.

Or, to be a bit more mean, we can look at it this way. I've been running my site since April of 1997, and I've received a few requests to contribute to various venues because of it, including *Write Market*. Of course, almost all of those offers came within the last year, after the site had some 125 articles on it. Most of them don't pay a dime, which is fine with me because I'm more interested in writing than with making money from writing, but I've been paid a few times for original articles and reprints. The material stands on its own: editors can peruse it on their own and decide if they want to talk to me about new articles, or tell me to go to hell when I submit proposals. If I just set up a basic site with my name, E-mail address, and a notice reading "I am a writer! Please love me!," I'd be laughed off the Web. You may be a very serious beginner, and may have some excellent stories in you, but look at the number of people who also claim to be writers (and whom you know perfectly well will never get anything published or even written in their lives, as they get off on bragging about being writers) and see why content is more important than anything.

Also, on a psychological level, as related in Pagan Kennedy's article, a Web site is a great way to stay in touch with one's readership, but that implies that there's a readership out there. Beginning writers should never set up a Web site and expect thousands of visitors in its first week of operation: the first head count of actual visitors will just depress them.

Paul Singer's article "How To Succeed In E-Business" is another bit of inspired lunacy, and the first article that made me laugh so much when I first picked up the magazine. The thesis is that any writer can step up and write advertising copy for business Web sites, as well as build the sites themselves, and I know that this is an utter crock. Besides the obvious point that experienced Web designers are having trouble with getting work because of the business majors who assume that they can get a copy of Microsoft FrontPage and build a site themselves, it assumes that a writer can get a job as a copywriter without prior experience. Getting work in Web copy writing (generally called "content development," as "writing" is apparently a dirty word in the New Media Economy) or tech writing is possible for a beginner, but most employers are going to want experience and/or a comparable degree. It's theoretically possible to break into content development or tech writing without any comparable experience, but it's also theoretically possible that Elvis Presley is alive and rooming with Jim Morrison, Stevie Ray Vaughan, and Sid Vicious.

Finally, we get to the money shot on the front cover: "Plus: More Than 40 Sites That Will Buy Your Writing." Yeah, that's true, depending upon the definition of "buy." The problem with content sites, particularly ones that publish fiction, is that they generally don't pay, or if they do, they pay a pittance. This is not to disparage the content of *Dark Matter* or *The Orphic Chronicle*, but anyone who plans to get rich from writing for the Web is (in the words of Bugs Bunny) going to get a biiiiig surpriiiize.

As with the rest of this Special Edition, the real revelations are not what gets listed, but what gets neglected. For instance, although quite a few SF magazines now have their own Web sites and include Web publication in contracts to writers, the only Web markets mentioned for SF and related literature are small venues such as Gothic.Net (which I fully expect to be inundated with lousy vampire fiction after this mention), and not a peep about *Event Horizon*. The definition of "paying market" gets stretched to the limit: the listing for *The Oyster Boy Review*, a literary magazine from San Francisco, mentions that payment is in "2 copies," and doesn't mention whether that's in the print or online version. We have lots of venues for specific material, but I don't see too much of a market for standard fiction in *MacAddict* or *Top Recruits Online*. Even more importantly, it contains almost no information on foreign markets, and a typical market listing in *Science Fiction Chronicle* or *Write Market* has more real info on paying magazines and sites. For all of the promise of the Web, this listing is not only incredibly poorly researched, but most of the markets listed are looking for established writers, not newbies.

The preceding wasn't written to discourage any beginning writer from writing for the Web: considering current magazine distribution concerns, publishing on the Web makes more sense than ever. However, until the Web starts attracting more of a readership, and particularly until the Web attracts enough of a readership willing to pay for content (or at least pay attention to advertising), it won't be a preferable venue over print. Since any idiot can claim to be published via the Web, even if it's a personal GeoCities site, getting published on dead tree pulp is always going to look better on a resume. Even with the more reputable content sites, such as *Salon* or *Feed*, since anyone can submit an article or (try to) submit fiction via E-mail, editors have to look even harder for good material among the dross in the slush pile. It's just as possible to make a career from writing for online publications as it is for print publications, but making a living from it is pretty damn unlikely for now. And with garbage like this Special Edition, *Writer's Digest* isn't making things any easier for anyone.

—Write Market, November 1999

Postscript: Writing as the US economy goes into its worst downturn since the 1930s, I can always count on a few absolutes when the layoffs start. At the top of the list is that Writer's Digest *will always clean up on selling subscriptions and individual copies to all of the goofballs who figure "Now that I'm unemployed, I now have time to start my freelance writing career!" Amazingly, when the Unemployment checks run out six months later and the goofballs still haven't sold a single article or story, they rationalize how much they learned from their two-year subscription.*

"Smack My Columnist Up"

In the magazine business, everyone wants a column. The sign of premier status in most mainstream magazines is to have a page dedicated to a particular writer's ponderings, usually with the author's name in big type and a flattering photo right alongside. It's no different in the science fiction industry, only seeing as how most magazines are small-press operations without the money accorded to, say, *Mirabelle*, the column is usually its own reward. While many columns go to respected members of the science fiction community, others go to complete unknowns, and some go to those completely unsuited for the job. Just look at the wanker who writes the "Rant" column for *Write Market*.

Now, everyone wants a column because of the impression that it's a position of authority. Film critics want a column because their impressions on the state of science fiction film are presumably more important than those of some schlub who just walked in, and having a column allegedly confirms this. The same is true of book criticism, or market issues, or damn near any subject that may apply to the lives of readers of a particular magazine. Because of this, columns are usually some of the most abused sections of a magazine: the success or failure of a column is considered to be an indictment of an author's ability. And most of this abuse is due to the impression of what a column is supposed to do.

In traditional journalism, columns are generally offered in two situations. Music and film columns (as well as those for architecture, gardening, real estate, and stock market tips) are generally given to those with special knowledge or expertise. It's not always true (look at the number of music columns at daily newspapers given not to knowledgeable music buffs but to anyone under the age of 30 willing to put up with the abuse at a daily paper), but that's the idea. The other situation is the general op-ed column, usually given to an older reporter who stuck out the incessant turnover at a paper and deserves a reward in his dotage. Because of the vagaries of standard journalism, these give the impression that most columnists are bitter cranks determined to get even with the rest of the universe for real and perceived injustices against the authors. The impression is usually right, but this gives other columnists the erroneous idea that all columns need to be vicious or vindictive.

With a standard newspaper, all of that bitterness serves one function: to sell newspapers. Actually, it's not so much to sell newspapers, but to generate discussion about the paper, which is why columnists for freebie weekly newspapers are generally some of the most obnoxious people using the English language this side of shock jock DJs. The purpose is identical: by letting these twerps froth and kvetch and whine, the idea is to offend as many people as possible, thereby causing a big stink in the local community. Readers may complain all they want, but they'll keep coming back to the column to see if the complaints did any good, and they'll also complain to their friends and acquaintances, which means they pick up the paper to see what the fuss is about. One columnist with verbal diarrhea can keep a paper going for weeks, and such intangibles as talent or a point are usually missed in the glee of both sides trying to kill the other.

Now, with a daily or weekly paper, this works because even a piss-poor weekly can be assured of a premeasured circulation and reader base, and since a newspaper or print magazine can't measure the pages read versus pages not read (one of the reasons why editors love Web sites is that readership can be measured through hit counts), they depend upon reader response. Even if all of the letters to the editor received are negative, it still means that someone read the paper, not to mention the subject of reader wrath. Sadly for papers, even in the days of E-mail, very few readers every bother to take the time to respond to anything, so editors keep pushing for more controversial material on the assumption that they can gauge the number of readers by the number of calls for the columnist's head.

The astute reader may recognize that this assumption is gibberish, but that explains why so few individuals under the age of 50 bother to read newspapers any more. This also explains why so many magazine columnists go berserk in print: all they're doing is imitating what they've read elsewhere, and most of what they've read elsewhere was inspired by newspapers and their attitudes.

In the case of science fiction magazines, the idea of the balls-to-the-wall, I'll-say-anything columnist sounds like a good idea, but consider the medium. Since a reader buys a newpaper for local and national news, very few readers will decide to stop reading the paper entirely because of a columnist. (Many papers respond, though, to reader responses, so even if the fifteen dittoheads who threaten to cancel their subscriptions because a paper runs a column critical of creationism never follow through, the editorial department assumes that they will, and usually pulls the columnist before s/he can cause more damage.) With a magazine, though, the reader pays a significantly higher amount and buys it for entertainment and more thoughtful news coverage, so columnists are significantly more prominent. With a science fiction magazine, since (with the exception of *Locus* and *Science Fiction Chronicle*) it's being read solely for entertainment and edification, one columnist who comes off as an arrogant nit can cut into a significant proportion of the readership. I have friends who refuse to buy one magazine solely because of its columnist. (And it's not any magazine I write for, so stop your snickering.)

The thing for any science fiction columnist to remember is that the available readership is ridiculously small, and nobody especially gives a damn about the columnist unless the writer established his/her credentials somewhere else. This means that nobody gives a damn that you think that every genre television show sucks farts from dead cats, or that you feel that you should be the producer of the *Star Trek* franchises, or that you thought that *Star Wars: Episode One* got a bad deal, just because you're a columnist. Nobody's going to jump through hoops to grant you interviews just because you're the columnist for some xeroxed fanzine with a total circulation of 250, and nobody's going to give you a press junket to Antarctica just because you're columnist for a Webzine that purports to have 300 visitors per annum. Considering the news and entertainment options available to readers today, both in print and in electronic format, nobody's going to waste too much time with a narcissistic brat who does nothing but throw tantrums because the universe won't acknowledge his/her greatness.

The alternative? For those who either have a column somewhere or want to have one, always assume that nobody reads your column nor cares to do so, and then intend to wow them. Write with honest intent, make valid points, and always intend to make at least one person who may stumble across your work whistle in appreciation. Instead of hammering the same five points over and over again, take different perspectives. And for Arioch's sake, at least try to be entertaining. If you're planning to make readers angry, try to get them to laugh at the same time, if only so they'll remember the point of the column. Better yet, they'll read the column all the way through: usually, when faced with a humorless tirade, readers just dump the damn thing.

The important thing to remember about columns is that they're like any other piece of writing, and that they're never disposable. I realize that deadlines keep a writer from making an absolute masterpiece, but anyone who starts treating regular columns as a chore instead of a calling really shouldn't have started in the first place. Always, always, ALWAYS write a column as if you're dying fifteen minutes after it's finished, and that it'll get quoted in your obituary. Trust me: the readership will notice, and sufficiently passionate writing will find an audience after a while. Now if more columnists would heed this advice...oh, that's right, I forgot. Nobody's reading this either, right?

—*Write Market, February 2000*

"Quit Conning Around And Get Back To Work!"

With the passing of Spring Break in the Northern Hemisphere comes the traditional spike in the number of science fiction conventions the world over. From now until the start of the next school year, the entire planet will be overloaded with conventions of any variety and form. Not that they stop after September, but the vast bulk follow holidays, vacations, and other free times for students and wage slaves.

For those not interested in writing, particularly those who attend conventions to buy toys, to flip through new or used novels, or to see old friends in garish or surreal garb, never mind all of this. The folks who have the most fun at cons are usually the ones with no delusions of doing anything approaching gainful work, unless that work consists of polishing off a triple platter of buffalo wings at the bar down the street. Going to conventions is intended to be entertainment, so the only people who have the right to consider it a chore are the poor schmucks lassoed by Paramount to star in the *Star Trek* franchises and appear at forty of these things a year. For everyone else, if attending them is a chore, it's time to find another line of work.

That said, however, the subject at hand is looking at how a beginning or established writer can use a convention to improve one's writing. The established writers tend to use conventions either for networking or for saying hello to old friends; beginners and intermediates need to make those contacts and friends, and this is about the best way to get noticed.

The biggest problem with conventions, at least for a beginning writer, lies with expectations. Trust me on this: no matter who you are, you're a worm. A dolt. A nobody. Your work is crap, and nobody would waste their time to read it. This may not be true (and I'm hoping that anyone reading this doesn't take my commentary on this seriously), but you have to look at your work this way, and then work on ways to prove that assessment wrong. Don't just march in, sneer "Well, I'm a W*R*I*T*E*R*!!!" and expect everyone to genuflect in your radiance, because the odds are pretty damn good that nobody's heard of you and nobody particularly cares who you are.

Now, if you come in with a big armful of flyers and a bigger smile on your face, and introduce yourself along the lines of "Hi! I'm Joe Writer, and I'm here to learn more about the business and the people who are in it," then both conventioneers and staff are much more likely to listen to what you have to say.

Or read what you have to write, which is a hell of a lot more important.

The other thing to remember is not all cons are the same. The advice to follow usually fits all conventions, but we have to remember the categories. Ignore these at your most desperate peril.

Literary conventions are generally just that: they're dedicated to the literary aspects of science fiction. This means lots of panels on the history and future direction of science fiction, a dealer's room full of books and not much else, and lots of authors with guest badges. Readercon in Boston is one of the more famous examples of a literary convention: they've built up a reputation for being professional enough that they have standing orders to escort anyone in costume to the door and tell them to come back when they're properly attired for the con. (After 11 cons, someone finally broke that code last year and showed up in costume, and I heartily recommend that the bastard who did so be bright to swift and terrible justice. Just ask the Readercon staff about this dingbat: he's a blight upon conventions the world over.)

Media conventions usually cover the non-literary aspects of the genre, but generally cross over into other categories, such as comics and gaming. The most pure of these are the big *Star Trek* shindigs that travel from town to town over the space of a year, but most of these are dedicated to genre television or film, with guests coming from the ranks of TV show casts. They may have room for literary fans, but these are generally cons for fun for serious literary types. Project A-Kon in Dallas, with its emphasis on all aspects of anime and animation, is a good example of a media con.

College conventions are a progressively rarer animal these days than they used to be: time was when many large colleges ran conventions for both fans and interested bystanders who wanted to see *2001* or *Star Trek* bloopers and couldn't get them anywhere else. In the aftermath of the video revolution, lots of college conventions died off due to lack of interest, but a few still run and draw in respectable audiences. AggieCon, hosted by the Cepheid Variable group at Texas A&M University, is one of the longest-running cons of its sort in the United States, and manages to incorporate all of the aspects of the other con somatypes and a few aspects all its own. This means lots of eager and interested college students who may not know the history of the genre but are willing to learn, along with a lot of casual visitors who heard about the convention from friends and acquaintances from A&M.

Gaming conventions almost solely for strategy or role-playing gaming: even the biggest of these, such as GenCon, are reserved for gaming and thereby offer little for those wanting to sell stories or books. However, for those who want to write

Dragonlance novels, they have possibilities.

Finally, anti-cons are a unique animal for those tired of the usual fannish bulldada at other conventions. ExotiCon in New Orleans is one of the best examples of an anti-convention: don't expect to do much writing, pitching, or much of anything else besides recreating whole chapters from *Fear and Loathing In Las Vegas*. Anti-cons are actually quite good for making contacts, but those without type-A personalities should generally stay away if they don't like to jump into the middle of a slamdance session to say hello to a fellow writer.

Have the distinctions between conventions firmly in your head? Good, because now it's time to keep a few tips in your head about what to do at a convention. These all come from long, painfully earned experience, not must from me, but from a lot of other writers who learned the unique value of conventions. Have fun.

Don't waste your time with inappropriate cons. This means "Do your goddamn research," just as you're supposed to do with markets and submissions requirements. If you honestly enjoy gaming, then by all means go to a gaming convention for the fun of it, but don't go to one expecting to talk to fellow literary SF writers. Now, if you want to write novels for Wizards of the Coast or Chaosium, that's a horse of a different color, but you're still pretty likely to be talking to editors of the games, not editors for the literary division.

An easy way to do your research is to look at the guests invited to a particular con. If they're all literary types, and the convention advertises itself as a literary convention, then by all means put together your portfolio and reserve a hotel room. If your specialty is writing about SF film and television, that literary convention may not be as comfortable a fit, but this depends upon whether or not you have other projects to work on.

Don't start shoving manuscripts under editors' noses. Lots of editors of genre magazines show up to conventions, but this doesn't mean that they have nothing better things to do than personally accept submissions for the slush pile, nor are they there to tell you if your story is worth printing. They're certainly not there to cut you a check for your story, no matter how brilliant, and they absolutely don't have the time to read your 2000-page novel. You want editors to remember you, true, and they'll certainly remember you for attacking them in the restroom with your scintillant novella while they were trying to use the urinal. Whether those memories will help your career is a matter of contention.

Should you feel the need to schmooze with an editor, take it easy. Introduce yourself after a panel or at the local watering hole, and nicely talk to him/her. Don't criticize or insult the editor's choices of articles and stories unless specifically asked, and remember that the editor has other places to be and other people to see. Always have a business card on hand, and give it out in lieu of a manuscript. Send the manuscript later, with a cover letter stating "We talked at WhozitCon last week, and you said that you wanted to take a look at this story..." This still won't guarantee a sale, but it *will* jog the editor's memory.

Don't throw fits over getting a guest badge. Even if you're already well-established in the writing business, and you have a good dozen novels out on the shelves at that moment, buy a damn badge unless someone offers you one. The same deal with panels and lectures: don't push the issue. If someone wanted you to appear on the program guide, they'd have asked. (This being said, your job, if you really crave to appear at a convention as a guest, is to give the convention staff a reason to make you a guest. Do this by sending copies of your previously published work to the con staff, not by yelling "Do you know who I am?" at the registration table. I've seen this happen: nobody was impressed then, and they won't be impressed now.)

The logical thing to do is just the opposite: offer to pay your own way. Convention staffs are usually up to their eyeballs with twerps trying to cadge free admission, so running into someone professional enough to pay for a badge without being asked usually impresses the hell out of them. You may not get a guest badge then, but they'll usually be impressed enough to give you one at the next year's convention.

Don't dominate panels unless you really have something to say. Yes, we all know you have all sorts of entertaining anecdotes and parables about any damn thing in sight, but unless you're a wit on a par with Groucho Marx, all it'll do is turn everyone off. This means laying off the heckling unless the person being heckled really deserves it, shouting over everyone else, or otherwise acting like a member of the Washington press corps. Convention attendees tend to have long memories, so you might run into an editor years later who remembers "This guy hogged that panel for hours, and never said a damn thing, and he kept talking over me..."

Give the benefit of the doubt, but always verify. Most of the people at a convention are going to be (generally) well-adjusted folks out for a good time. Some will be there to do serious, legitimate business, and may be interested in publishing your book or short story, or otherwise have dealings with you. Others, though, are hopeless flakes who make grand promises but never come through, and some are even deliberate, malignant crooks and thugs who will lie up a storm to get something from you and then rip you off. The real trick in this business is to tell the difference between the legitimate businesspeople and the trolls.

Remember to remain on your best behavior if you want to impress someone important. Okay, so that editor you want to meet is known for ribald jokes and a touch of acid wit. It still isn't good form to insult him, spit in his face, pee in his coffee, and still expect to sell a novella to him afterwards. That sort of behavior, even when it's used against the people who deserve it, generally reflects badly on you later.

Oh, and there's a little thing about the dress code. Besides the usual admonitions about bathing, using toothpaste and dental floss, brushing your hair, and popping plenty of Gas-X before talking to an editor or publisher, pretend to be getting ready for a job interview. Technically, that's what you're doing: you're trying to convince an editor or publisher that you're sane and dependable enough to be trusted with deadlines, and you're hoping to turn the end products at those deadlines into potential paychecks, so dressing for success is very important. Don't go out to a convention in a business suit, but at least consider something that says "Serious Writer" instead of "Crazed Fanboy." This means leaving the *Star Trek* uniform at home and bringing stuff that looks best on a hanger. Dressing "business casual" signals that you're professional enough to take the time to make a decent presentation and that you have enough respect for the editor/publisher to try to make a good impression. Take my word for it: no editor is going to be impressed with anyone sporting a Klingon headdress, a full suit of chain mail, or artificial fangs so long that they permanently pierce the wearer's lower lip. Well, they may be impressed, but not in your potential writing ability.

(The dress code is really important to those who for unguessable reasons still expect to get groupies at conventions. Go for professional but interesting, and so long as your personality isn't so foul that it scares off syphilitic warthogs, you stand just as much a chance as anyone else with getting groupies. The personality is 90 percent of the battle, but why not improve the odds, eh?)

Learn to listen. The best way to get information about markets, editors, and possible trends is to go in costume...as Silent Bob from the movie *Clerks*. This means shut up and listen to what everyone else has to say. If you have questions, ask them, but don't go spouting off about how editors don't want your magnum opus unless you're sure that everyone else wants to hear about it. Just listen and learn, and act on the little pearls of wisdom down there among the pig crap.

Free stuff is a good thing. Have a Web site full of your material? Don't go around yelling the URL and expect everyone to write down a URL as long as your arm. Instead, hand out flyers with the URL and all of the other pertinent information on your career. It won't necessarily lead to a 12-book deal right off the bat, but the idea is that people will remember your name and associate it with getting interesting material.

Continuing with the analogy, try any number of other freebies. Have a new article in a magazine? Buy copies from the publisher and give them out to interested bystanders. Want people to read your new short story? Make up a flyer with a short excerpt and pass it around, complete with full ordering information for the magazine if it isn't easily available. What about a new book? Make up a flyer or pamphlet, include an excerpt and quickie synopsis, and spread the wealth. Even if nobody who receives it orders a copy directly from the publisher, they'll try to keep an eye open at the local bookstore, or even nag the local store to order a copy. This also includes the carryover effect: the person who received the flyer might not do anything with it, but they may pass it on to someone who not only orders the book/magazine/whatever, but tells all of his/her friends about it as well.

That's the biggest thing to remember about conventions: connections go both ways. The people you talk to at a convention may just be fans today, but they may become influential later, and no better word of mouth exists than a popular writer or editor saying "Oh, and I was really inspired by Joe Writer's work when I was a fan, and he was nice enough when I was just a fan that it encouraged me to start writing..."

As with all of the other advice from this column, this doesn't even begin to cover all of the particulars of con-going, but for those with an extroverted personality and just a slight touch of ego, cons can be an effective way of improving business. Just remember to keep con-going under control: the main point of being a writer is to write, and you need to take time from your busy con schedule to write, right?

—*Write Market, April 2000*

Postscript: When I wrote this, I was spending more on attending various conventions than I was making from writing in a given year. At the end of 2000, I decided to take a hiatus from conventions for a year, and still had the ditz running one big convention writing me to ask "I know you said you aren't going to any conventions for a year, but are you still going to [her convention]?" I now advocate that all beginning writers go to as many conventions as possible. The ones that wise up and realize that they get a better return by staying home and writing are the ones who might make it as writers.

"Etiquette Around Authors"

(Note - This essay originally started out as a posting on UseNet that Mary Anne Mohanraj saved for edification of writers, fans, and interested bystanders. She was considerate enough to save that original dump in the aether and post it on her site, and in return, I recommend that everyone reading this hunt down some of her fiction. She writes mostly erotica, but trust me on this: it's good erotica.)

Normally, this space is dedicated to advice for authors, both beginning and established. This installment is going to be different: this is advice that writers should copy and mail off to everyone else.

The actual physical and mental effort of writing is already known to all of you: the carpal tunnel syndrome and bad backs, the constant migraines and cataracts, the ink poisoning and psychotic binges on goat blood. The problem is that most non-writers don't understand that this is work: to the outsider, writing is easy. Without other information, they buy into the bullshit that writers make $37.50 an hour; that we have nothing better to do than ghostwrite their story ideas; that we can drop everything to yak with them on the phone because they're contemplating getting into the writing business themselves. It's not that co-workers and friends and spouses know any better: they just need someone to explain that most of us are trying to carve what we laughingly call our callings from the time that they use for watching television, drinking beer, and improving family ties. And since I respect and love the whole bloody lot of you (even *you*, with your thumb jammed up your nose to the fourth digit), I volunteer to take the heat.

Now, in the interests of having it apply to those who write science fiction, fantasy, and horror, this is written for fans of those genres. I joke about the pathetic twits who think that they're going to get publicity junkets and groupies from their new book on programming in Perl, but I don't know of any technical writers who get fan mail and groupies in real life. (Well, Vincent Flanders and Michael Willis of *Web Pages That Suck* may, but they deserve the groupies.) However, I actually get a few phone calls in the middle of the night from fans, and I know that better writers than me (and that comprises most of the population) get a lot more. This is intended to make their lives a little easier.

"What Every Fan Should Know"
by Paul T. Riddell

You! Yes, you with the worn and well-used paperback under your arm. You want to meet your favorite author? Of course you do, but are you ready to?

Honest to Arioch, this isn't a dig. I understand the situation. You want to meet an author whose work has influenced you or moved you in some way. You may want to converse with an author on a subject of mutual interest, or ask about an upcoming work, or simply introduce yourself and go to your grave happy. In the interests of making both fan and author happy, here's a few tips about dealing with pro writers, most learned from years of long experience.

Firstly, remember that the writers you admire are normal folks, too. After you see them at a convention, they'll go home and most likely (save the ones lucky enough to make a living off writing) return to their day jobs. I know you admire them, but don't go all worshippy when you meet them. Most of us have serious self-confidence issues, and we can't tell if you're serious or if you're mocking us.

Secondly, remember that they have real lives. Just because you get Joe Haldeman's phone number or Piers Anthony's fax number from a friend doesn't mean you have to use it (however, if someone happens to have H. Beam Piper's or Fritz Leiber's phone number, please call me. Collect). If you call while they're busy on, say, a new novel, you'll almost certainly interrupt them while they're on a roll. They could be doing other things, like washing dishes, playing with the kids, making love, taking a shower, or dissecting the Jehovah's Witness who won't leave them alone, and they'll feel lots less antic and friendly if you call just because you have their number and want to chew the fat. You may think that you know them, but they don't know you, and they may have more important things to consider than keeping a fan happy.

The best way to tell a writer's intentions is if you yourself gets that phone number dropped into your misshapen paw, and that still doesn't give permission to pass it on or abuse it. Let's put it this way: I've had Harlan Ellison's phone number for ten years, and I've used it three times, after he's called me first. I'd never consider calling just to shoot the breeze, mostly because I hate being interrupted while working, and I'd sooner jam stingray spines through my urethra than interrupt him.

This point goes double for E-mail. Those of us with E-mail addresses usually don't mind getting letters from fans (some of us, present company included, positively dote on them), but that doesn't mean that we can respond to everything we get. Write all you want, but consider that messages get lost or caught in filtering software, and some of us may be too busy to check our mail every fifteen minutes, so don't get upset when we haven't read your latest letter. Maybe we have, and just haven't been able to peel away from writing that new novel to write back.

Oh, and here's a tiny bit of advice to folks who think that a quick "let's do lunch" at a con or at a local reading is an invite to move in: go out and rent

Martin Scorcese's film *The King of Comedy*. If you find yourself imitating Rupert
Pupkin in any way, you've usually overstepped your welcome as far as most pros
are concerned. There's a fine line between adoration and stalking, and what may
seem to be perfectly reasonable behavior to you may be considered a crime in
many locales. Even if you have a home address, don't show up at a writer's house
without a prior invitation, no matter how badly you want to say "Hi, I was in the
neighborhood." This is nothing against you, but the propensity for people to do
this, as well as some of the...how shall I put this...unsavory elements of the fan
community, are two reasons why so many of us get PO boxes and mail drops.

Thirdly, if you want to make friends with a pro writer, don't drink all of his
booze at a party, try to get the name of his agent, swipe his books and steal his
girlfriend, get up in his face and say "Your last book/story/review was a lump of
wombat dung," hit him in the face with a cup of warm vomit, or any of the other
lovely things fans have come up with over the years to express their feelings toward
their favorite writers. If the pro is female, don't make a pass at her; she's most
likely not interested, and she'll probably take you out. If she's married, her
husband will probably finish the job, and you'll remember that moment well while
in traction. This goes double for male writers: Hell hath no fury like the wife of an
author who sees her hubby being mauled (against his will or otherwise) by a well-
meaning but amorous fan. I speak of this from experience. Any of these offenses
are good arguments for a good whomping with baseball bats, but the more
civilized of us will just make sure never to grace your life with our presences again.

Fourthly, NEVER send stories or story ideas to a writer, no matter how well-
intentioned the act may be. Most fans forget that ideas are a dime a dozen; the
difference between an idea and a finished book is about six months to five years
of hard work. Most fans forget that, and so they tend to get antsy about a book
appearing by an author they were chummy with that contains an idea they
thought was theirs. 99 percent of the time, it's coincidence, but don't throw out
the plot to your 15-book magnum opus to your favorite pro unless you really want
him or her to hear about it. Most of the time, they really don't anyway, but they'll
be polite.

Fifthly, NEVER EVER take advantage of a pro's politeness. When a pro
stands back and lets a fan go into a 40-minute rendition of the biology of
Andorians or something like that, they're probably just being nice and don't want
to hurt the fan's feelings, but they're probably thinking "I wish lightning would
strike me dead." If a pro breaks off and says "Sorry, but I have a panel, I have kids
on the stove, and I need to take my Thorazine," don't follow them down the hall
rattling away. Take a hint and let them have some time to themselves. Most of all,

don't follow anyone into the restroom, unless you want to get peed on. (I know some of you little perverts actually enjoy this, but just don't go there.)

Sixthly, don't ask, nag, or kvetch about freebies. A few of us have enough spare cash on us to hand out copies of magazines or books to fans who ask nice and don't beg, but most of us are lucky to get a couple of copies of our new book, and we don't have the money to get any more. Even if you've known an author since the two of you had adjoining stalls in the maternity ward, don't come up and start nagging about "Where's my free copy?" Go out and buy one of your own, you cheap bastard.

Lastly, remember this: if you really want to make a pro happy, buy his/her work. Nice postcards and letters are fine, but they'll appreciate you a lot more if you buy 500 copies of their latest books and give them out to friends and relatives, or convince a publisher to reprint a forgotten classic. We need to eat, too, and we can't survive just on the love of our fans. With that in mind, the next time you see your favorite writer, ask him/her politely if you can buy them dinner. If s/he's at a convention, that's usually to the detriment of writing, and since most writers aren't writing for anything but a love for the genre, the recipient will remember. You probably won't get a book dedicated to you for it, but you never can tell.

–*Write Market*, May 2000

"They Hate You! They Really Hate You!"

As has been noted in this space, *Writer's Digest* is notorious for telling beginning writers about all the wonderful and fascinating things about being a writer. The World of the Writer, according to *WD*, is a fascinating place where editors call writers and request articles and stories for much more money than they'll ever make working the front line at McDonald's. This is a world where magazines and weekly newspapers are just falling all over themselves to publish the first essay of a newbie writer, and where the only real concern the writer has is in plotting the best tax writeoffs for his/her writing income in a fiscal year. It's a really nice place, and one day I'd like to get a ticket there, when I've finished my obligatory pilgrimages to Oz, Melnibone, and R'lyeh.

Yes, it's flippant, but *Writer's Digest* feeds on telling wannabe writers what they want to hear. No established writer pays any attention to *WD* after they've become familiar with the reality of being a writer, unless they figure they can make some extra spending money by cobbling together some "How To Write Science Fiction" guide or similar rot. The reason real writers don't pay any attention to the multitude of books and pamphlets *WD* puts out is because the advice is either common sense (Don't Set Your Price, Because The Editor May Offer More"), or it's completely bogus ("You, Too, Can Make Money By Selling Science Fiction"). *WD* doesn't handle the real concerns of writers, such as what legal venues a writer should consider when screwed by an editor or publisher, what to do about idiot copy editors who feel compelled to rewrite an author and then blame the writer when the editor gets the facts wrong, or how to turn that payment check into a year's supply of ramen noodles. So far as I know, *WD* has never dealt with that most important of concerns: what to do about hate mail.

Yes, hate mail is a major concern, and one that every writer should be warned about before s/he starts writing, because everyone gets some of it sooner or later. Even those who try to cultivate it, such as myself, often can't deal with it when it comes in. It impacts with the force of a kidney punch from a wrecking ball, and it can cripple or even kill the careers of those unprepared to deal with it. No matter how often one gets it, it still hurts, and that's the point of it.

As a slight digression, I might also add that this advice also applies to reviews of a writer's work. In the perfect world of *WD*, any negative reviews are ones intended to show a writer the error of his/her ways and gently steer the author back to the right and true path. No mention is made of negative reviews made for political or purely vindictive reasons, and negative reviews as a rule are generally ignored. They shouldn't be, but I'm getting ahead of myself.

The two reasons a writer writes, to strip the urge down to purely selfish reasons, are to get paid or to get recognition. We all hope and pray that our short story or article made a difference, and that someone takes the time to write and tell us this. We don't necessarily want the letters of "I really like your work; could you lend me $20?," but the simple, honest letters telling us that we're writing what someone wanted or needed to read often make up for a lack of pay or other remuneration. Let's face it: most people writing science fiction aren't going to get groupies, so we take what we can.

Because of this hope for recognition, it's only inevitable that a writer will sooner or later receive some hate or crank mail. Quite often, it's nearly illiterate ("Yur story suks and yer gay"), but most of it is along the line of "You're not as funny/literate/accomplished as you think you are, so why don't you do us all a favor and drop dead?" This is to be distinguished from criticism, constructive or otherwise, of the work: most of the little bastards who send hate mail are too cowardly to include return addresses or even real names, so they're sending it out of a primate attempt to get a rise out of the target. Almost always, they succeed.

Because of my attitude and subject matter, I get quite a few of these missives every month, and I've found one way to deal with them. That method doesn't include hunting down the author and beating the shit out of him/her, or writing back to try to inflict as much damage as the letter-writer intended to inflict on you, or using the critic's name for a future story where his/her namesake comes to a nasty end. The best advice I can give is to ignore it and move on, because the best revenge against the assassins is to keep on writing and getting published.

That said, I have to make a few caveats, because some of us have a problem with the difference between constructive criticism and assault. More often than not, that nasty letter wasn't intended to be as nasty as it may have read, and paying attention to the letter writer may be necessary. Several months ago, I received a bit of mail from someone reading a column of mine that was a little more strident in its criticism than I would have liked. However, I gave the author the benefit of the doubt and used that basic bit of wisdom imparted by H. Beam Piper: "If you disagree with someone, don't say he's crazy. Ask him what he means." I did that with the author, and Aaron is now one of those people whose opinion I implicitly trust. He wasn't trying to be nasty when he criticized my attitude: he pointed out that I don't necessarily have to use the howitzers on every problem, and I like to think that my writing has improved as a result.

Therefore, hate mail can be fun, if using the right attitude. Just follow these simple tips, and run with them.

Numero Uno: If the author is illiterate or worse, don't even bother. Most hate mail falls in the category of the twerp who can barely spell, and paying attention to their brayings is like listening to a blind person for fashion advice. The same goes for the obviously humorless: if you wrote a satire and some jerk writes in to complain about scientific inaccuracies or the usual "What's the point of your story?," just let it slide. Don't even bother to write back: all that does is encourage the little dears, and your mailbox will be full of similar bat frothings. Either file these under "Hate Mail," or make copies and pass them around, but don't waste your time in trying to get a rational discussion out of one of these types, because you never will.

Numero Two-O: Distinguish between constructive criticism and nastiness. People have a tendency to write off nasty notes now and think later, especially when E-mail is concerned. If the person writing that nasty letter has legitimate, honest complaints about your work, pay attention, because this person may have a point that you ignore at your risk. If the writer sent a note solely to get you angry, though, just let it slide.

Numero Three-O: If you feel you must write back, keep it short, sweet, and concise. Some of us can't leave an insult without an appropriate response, and some of us just can't stand to go without the last word, but most nasty letters just beg for a response of one sort or another. If life just isn't worth living without giving the jerk a piece of your mind, keep it to about two sentences. If the letter came by mail, send back via postcard, and file or throw away any letters that come back. You'd be amazed at the twerps who are so thrilled that an "enemy" wrote back that they'll keep the abuse coming for months or even years, but an appropriate putdown is usually enough to shut them up for good.

Numero Four-O: Keep copies of the hate mail if appropriate, because it'll come in handy later. Several years ago, David Lynch ran an ad campaign for his film *The Lost Highway* that ran nothing but negative reviews (of which there were many), and an enterprising writer could use that to good effect. At the very least, the poor ones are always good for a laugh, especially if it criticizes a story or article that goes on to win awards.

Numero Five-O: Don't mess around with threats. Fun's fun, but always treat any serious threat of bodily injury or death seriously. I used to laugh at death threats after my first book came out, until I found someone had driven by my apartment one night and popped off three .25 rounds into the wall. I still have two of the three slugs.

Dealing with these is quite easy, in several ways. If the threat was sent through standard mail, take a look at the postmark (most of these characters aren't smart enough to mail threats from a different area) and contact the police in the town or city where the ZIP code originated. At the same time, make a formal report to your police of the threat, if only so that the police have ample warning if it happens again or if you go to the grocery store and never come back. If receiving threats by phone, try to tape them, or use Caller ID if available in your area. Dingbats who use the phone for threats usually screw up sooner or later, so they're relatively easy to catch.

E-mail's even easier. If the crank letter came from a free E-mail service, such as Yahoo or Hotmail, go to the main site and look for an "Abuse" address. Most of these are set up to deal with spam, but forwarding a death threat is usually enough to get a free account shut down, and most of these free services report letters like these to the police as well. If the letter came from a standard ISP or company server, contacting the admin will usually get some sort of results, unless the admin was the person sending off the threat. In that case, a quick phone call to someone else at the ISP or company will get results.

A little warning about this is that some characters love nothing more than to make threats while using someone else's E-mail address or home address. Just report everything to the police, and don't play superhero by yourself. You'll feel awfully stupid if you beat the crap out of someone whose identity was borrowed by a crank and you get arrested for assault yourself.

Numero Six-O: Always, ALWAYS go with your gut. The big thing to remember is that hate mail is intended to tear you down, and make you question your abilities. If you know instinctively that the crank is full of crap, run with that conviction.

By way of personal example, this didn't qualify as hate mail per se, but it definitely qualified as abuse. I used to be an acquaintance of someone still operating in this business whose advice I used to take about writing. Without fail, she would bitch and scream about articles I wrote, to the point where I took a diatribe about an article as an endorsement. Without fail, the articles or columns she kvetched about turned out to be my most popular, and if I'd listened to her, I would have thrown out quite a few articles that made an impression on others.

With that in mind, don't dread the inevitable piece of hate mail. Embrace it and make it your own. You may not have earned it, but it's still yours.

—Write Market, June 2000

"If We Didn't Kill and Eat Editors, Wouldn't They Breed Out Of Control?"

In Hollywood, the eternal mantra coming from busboys, telephone repairmen, and anyone with any delusion of getting into the movie industry is "Ultimately, I'd like to direct." In the science fiction business, the mantra is "Ultimately, I want to be able to make a living by writing science fiction." Even among the obvious laughter and rolled eyes, one sees the occasional ratfaced mutant in the shadows that doesn't follow that philosophy. In Los Angeles, their cry is "To hell with directing: I want to be a producer." In science fiction, it's "I'm going to be an editor."

Now, people become editors of science fiction magazines for various reasons. The first and most honest stereotype is the person who can't find a magazine with the sort of fiction and nonfiction that s/he wants to read, and starts a magazine to collect all of this. We have the people who discover the joys of desktop publishing or Web design and figure that it's high time to start a new publication. We have the people who quit or are fired from an established publication, and figure that they can hoof it on their own. And, of course, we have the thankfully rare twerps who think that they'll get fame, riches, and groupies by editing a science fiction magazine with a circulation of about 50.

(At about this point, I need to interject that I'm using "editor" and "publisher" interchangeably at this point, mostly because these positions are held by the same person at most science fiction magazines. The editor is usually in charge of the day-to-day operations at a magazine, including assigning stories, proofreading, and getting everything ready to go to the printer or Webmaster. The publisher takes care of the business side of the magazine: writing checks, paying bills, writing checks, coordinating with distributors, writing checks... In any case, since so few magazines have enough of a budget to require two people to do these jobs, the editor is also the publisher. However, publishing is the focus of an upcoming essay, so I won't deal with it here.)

If the Web has done any one thing right, it's minimizing the people who shouldn't be editing or publishing a magazine in the first place. Back ten or twenty years ago, you'd see a lot of characters who kept piling up rejection slips from the larger magazines and not realize that they were getting rejection slips for a reason. Instead, they'd start into some paranoid fantasy about how the world wasn't ready for their genius, and start a magazine full of their stories to show the universe that Everett C. Marm was a force to be reckoned with. Back then, they'd probably go on for a couple of years, leaving a swath of burned writers and artists who dared get more fan mail than the editor, until the magazine was a running joke or until The Law of Diminishing Returns forced them to stop publishing. Nowadays, these same people will just set up a Web site, fill it full of their diseased stories, and leave the rest of us alone.

Even with this natural elimination from the editorial pool, editors everywhere aren't exactly the most popular critters on God's green Earth. In a recent story in *Salon*, Sean Elder noted that nobody in New York can find an editor who can actually edit any more: most "editors" seemed to be perfectly happy doing nothing more than attending parties and chasing interns. Lest anyone laugh at that impression, just remember that most editors, for any sort of publication, not only have to fight that impression but also make sure that they never suffer from that level of poisonous hubris.

The first thing every wannabe editor should ask is "Why? Why do I want to be an editor? Why do I want to edit a magazine? Why do I want to sink myself up to my armpits in slush pile manuscripts, field any number of phone calls from leeches and hangers-on who want a free writing coach, and surround myself with fellow wannabes who take a professional rejection as a personal insult?" Be honest with the questioning: make certain that you really want to become an editor before making that jump.

The second question for every beginning writer is "Will I have the time to do this right?" Again, working on the stereotype of the magazine editor (a carefully contrived cliché that has about as much to do with the realities of publishing as the movie *Independence Day* has to do with the SETI movement), editing is just as easy as writing (and I'm assuming that the audience of this essay knows the fallacy of "writing is easy; anyone can do it"), and that a few minutes a day can go into actual editing. Don't you believe it.

For most SF magazines, the editor is Stable-Shoveler Extraordinaire. The editor is the person who has to go to the mailbox in search of submissions and queries; who sends off press releases to *Locus* and *Science Fiction Chronicle* about new contributors or changed situations; who contacts people about late stories or missing artwork; who ultimately has to sift through piles and piles of manuscripts looking for the few that will comprise the next issue's content. If the magazine is a paying venue (and a lot of SF magazines don't pay a dime), the editor is in charge of sending contracts to contributors and mailing off sample copies to other venues. In short, even for a minor Webzine, editing is nearly a full-time job.

Even after asking this, an unnatural number of people figure that they can be editors: judging by some of the baboons who edit weekly newspapers, all that's required for the position in some cases is the capability to fling feces at will. However, there's a huge difference between being an editor and being a good editor, and here are the obligatory tips to making sure that a reign as a Good Editor is long and healthy, because the only cheer made to a bad editor is something between "Ding dong, the witch is dead!" and "Let's frag the lieutenant!"

Guess what? Nobody cares. When talking about science fiction magazines, the only people who give a damn about the editor are all the freelancers looking for a submission address in the latest *Scavenger's Newsletter*. The world is not going to jump back in awe if you stand up and declare (in tones reserved for the Second Coming of Elvis) "As you know, I'm the editor of *Zizzle-Swump!*" Trust me on this: the sun will not set in the east just because you started a new SF zine. It may if you and the magazine are really, really good, but not until about the third or fourth issue.

(As a sidebar, if you become the ex-editor of a magazine, the world cares even less. Publishing is like Hollywood in that you're only as good as your last project, and anyone still crowing about being the editor of a magazine that died three or five or twenty years ago isn't worth listening to if they haven't done a thing since the magazine went under. When *OMNI* died, Ellen Datlow didn't go to conventions, begging for drinks while bellowing in her best Al Bundy tones "As you know, I used to edit *OMNI!*" Instead, she immediately jumped up and went to other projects and kept looking beyond *OMNI*. Ellen Datlow is a great example of a Good Editor to emulate anyway, but pay particular attention to this attitude.)

This is even more important to Webzines, partly because Web-based magazines are considered less professional (after all, anyone with a decent grasp of Web design can produce what appears to be a long-established site), and partly because of the incredible variety of options on the Web. Six years ago, announcing the formation of a Web-based magazine was a big deal: a lot of those early Webzines have gone under since then, and a lot of others are in perpetual limbo (what longtime Webheads call "Ghost Sites") when the editor ran out of interest, ran out of money, or gave up because the multitudes weren't so busy typing in the URL that it slowed Web access across two continents.

The solution? The same one I give standard writers and columnists both. Always assume that nobody cares, and give them a reason to care. The magazine may never take off, and it may die after about two or three issues, but at least someone tried hard enough that it was remembered after it went under.

Put up or shut up. I've spent years of my career dealing with wannabe editors, who plan to put together a magazine that'll blow the world's condoms off once someone gives them enough money. Most pro writers know better than to deal with walking dingleberries like this, because the money will never come through (or if it does, enough only for one issue) and the writer (or artist) has to wrangle for months to get work back from an editor who can't be bothered to return phone calls or E-mail. Don't go around bragging about how great your magazine will be one of these days, all the while expecting perks because "I'm the editor." The only thing you're going to get is a series of small claims court suits from people who bought subscriptions but never received a single issue.

Don't bogart the stage. While a "From the Editor" featurette is perfectly acceptable or even understandable, anything running longer than about 800 words says two things: the editor is too cheap to pay for writers and depends upon his or her own material, or the editor is an egomaniac. Or both. Readers don't need to read about how the editor blew every penny from his/her paycheck to pay for the printing on the current issue, they don't need to read about how the editor hasn't been laid in four years, and they don't need to read constant tirades about how anyone even mildly critical of the content is The Enemy.

The editor is there to make the writers look good; the writers are not there to make the editor look good. Several years ago, *The New Yorker* started yet another subscription drive with a bulk mailing of little subscription cards full of reasons why someone in Kokomo or Tigard or Cross Plains should bother to subscribe to a N'Yawk publication. One of the biggest, in large white type on a dark brown background was "Now Edited by Tina Brown!" If the name "Tina Brown" makes no impression upon your psyche, then join the club: this made as much an impression upon everyone else reading that card, and Ms. Brown fell upward from *The New Yorker* under dubious circumstances to helm the new magazine *Talk*.

The only reason why anyone should care about an editor is because of the editor's reputation. Contrary to the egos of any number of editors, nobody reads a magazine (or a paper, or a Web site) for the editor. They read a magazine for the writers and their contributions, and the only way the editor gets any credit is for having the sense to buy a particular story or article that brings praise upon the magazine. A Good Editor is the sort who subsumes his/her ego in order to let the writers shine: an editor who hogs the spotlight not only finds a lack of writers willing to put up with that abuse, but also finds that the readers go elsewhere for those writers. Good Editors are generally never seen and never heard, but their influence is everywhere within the publication: Bad Editors are the ones who cut other writers' work so their or their spouse's work gets the front cover.

Now, a Good Editor wouldn't have put that bit of hubris on the *New Yorker*: instead, s/he would have exalted the names of the great writers and artists working for the magazine, and let the praise trickle down. They'll get the recognition, and also a lot of respect from writers who are frankly sick to death of grandstanding editors throwing tantrums because they aren't the sole reason why people read the magazine.

Rewrite at your peril. Considering that most editors start out as writers, it's amazing to see the number who would shriek and moan over the slightest rewrite of their darling prose but see nothing wrong with butchering someone else's. These are also the characters who blow gaskets if someone else rewrote them and screwed up facts or dialogue, but see nothing wrong with rewriting another writer, dropping serious flaws in the revised material, and then foist all the blame back on the writer. These are people who deserve to have their editing pencils removed, along with most of the attached arm. But that's just me.

The thing for genre editors to remember is that writers will put up with one form of abuse, but not too many. Many writers will grumble about being rewritten if they're getting paid for their troubles, but they'll tolerate it; rewrite someone who contributes out of a love of the genre and then let him or her take the blame for the rewrite, and you've just made an enemy. This also applies to micromanaging writers, calling them up to harangue them, adding all sorts of "Editor's Notes" and rebuttals when disagreeing with the writer's points, and threatening them if they want to write for another magazine. Many writers are willing to put up with a lot of garbage just to have a dependable venue for their work, but abuse their trust and suffer.

And another point: when accepting an article or story and then realizing that the magazine doesn't have room, contact the writer right then and there and explain the situation. Nothing makes writers bolt for the door faster than being told that a new story will be in the next issue, and having them discover that it was put off indefinitely when they get the new issue and wonder where their contributions went. And if that article was replaced with something else, pray that the replacement doesn't have the editor's byline on it: under the best of circumstances, the writer won't bother to contribute ever again, but many writers are known to mail dead gophers to the editor via fourth class mail for that stunt.

Get it out the door on time. The final plea for beginning editors is to set up a deadline system and stick with it. Don't hold off on a print date for two weeks to get in a review of the latest *Star Trek* film, don't tell contributors that the current issue is on a truck going from Wisconsin to North Carolina (by way of California) and the truck broke down unless it really happened, and don't leave the writers having to explain to friends and family that they have no idea when the new issue is due out. If the magazine is supposed to be a quarterly, get it out on a quarterly basis; whatever happens, don't let two years slip between issues.

Besides making advertisers very happy, this has the effect of making writers very happy, because they know when they're expected to get in their submissions. For instance, nothing is more worthless than year-old film reviews, so when calling upon the magazine film critic to hand in a column, do so a week before going to press. Don't sit on timely articles for months or years on the vague hope of printing again someday: in many cases, those writers could sell their stories and articles to other magazines and then offer new material if they knew in advance that the issue is going to be drastically late. Besides, promising a regular schedule and then delivering magazines whenever everyone feels like it is not only horribly unprofessional, it's a guaranteed way to keep that magazine from being carried in most bookstores.

And that's the final comment: **keep the lines of communication open.** No matter how bad things may get, don't screen phone calls and ignore E-mail if writers are trying to make contact. Don't make up fibs to conceal the real situation, and don't play anyone for a sucker. The science fiction community is sufficiently small, and the Web sufficiently fast, that word about incompetent or malicious editors gets around in hours instead of months, and you really don't want that nightmare on your back. Just apply the Golden Rule (and not the version that states "He who has the gold makes the rules"), and editing should be a relative joy. It may pay nothing, and make all the hair on everyone within a twenty-mile radius fall out, but it beats getting dead gophers in the mail.

—Write Market, August 2000

Postscript: No, I didn't write this based on experience, nor have I ever run into that same attitude the few times I've had a relapse and returned to writing. Why would you ever ask such a horrible thing?

"Delaying the Revolution (Or At Least the Execution)"

Last installment, we discussed the situation of writers wanting to become editors. This time around, we discuss writers and editors wanting to become publishers. The jobs aren't necessarily the same.

To compress everything down to its most simplistic form, an editor is the person who handles the content going into a magazine. That is, the editor solicits submissions, proofreads the submissions received, cleans and generally edits them (after all, they don't call the editor "the proofreader," do they?), and otherwise prepares them for publication. The editor is also generally responsible for layout, graphics and ad placement, and all of the work on the actual magazine. The publisher, on the other hand, is the business person in charge of the publication. Again, in its simplest form, the publisher is ultimately responsible for getting the money together to print the next issue, paying staff (writers, editors, and anyone else involved with publication), and making sure that the publication sees print after the editor is finished.

The problem with publishers, more often than not, lies with the money. I've either seen or worked for any number of publications where the publisher suddenly decided "My money is better used elsewhere," and the whole publication went kaput, usually at the brink of profitability. Since the publisher controls the money, the temptation to tinker with the product to "improve" the investment is almost irresistible. In either case, writers and editors stand back in horror as the publisher decides to invoke the Golden Rule: "He who has the gold makes the rules."

Not that we have this much of a problem in science fiction publishing: it's not like anyone has any money. However, a publisher who tends to flip-flop on a magazine usually produces one thing: a dead magazine. If the publisher was particularly good at messing around in areas best left to editors and writers, s/he gets something else: a reputation as someone whose troops' battle cry is "Hey, let's frag the lieutenant!"

Again, since most science fiction magazines are small enough that the editor, publisher, layout editor, publicist, and janitor are the same person, the separation between editor and publisher is rather indistinct, and those seeking both jobs at once really need to have a distinct grasp of each position. A great editor can also be a thoroughly terrible publisher, and a great publisher may not have the instincts necessary to make a half-assed editor, but someone who goes slapping through both usually ends up becoming a horror for staffers and freelancers. The rules don't change between print and the Web, so pay attention, because what comes next is important.

It's the business, stupid. For all the protestations to the contrary, publishing a magazine is a business, or at least it should be. That means that the publisher is ultimately responsible for filling subscriptions, getting advertising or other revenue, running ads in other publications or on the Web, and otherwise making sure that the editor and writers don't have to wrangle with the day-to-day operation of the magazine. This also means having a basic business sense.

Most science fiction magazines have a business plan: it's just seemingly cobbled together from too many viewings of *The Producers*. Printing costs money, so budget it to make sure that the money is available when the issue is ready to run. Printers need to fill a particular schedule, so make sure to meet that schedule. If someone calls offering to pay for advertising, don't turn them away with some pansyass babbling about "keeping the art pure" by rejecting advertising if that advertising gives enough money to publish a new issue. Most distributors and booksellers are run by pathological liars who have no intention of paying for magazines if they can possibly help it, so keep records of what went to whom and be prepared to use legal force to get Barnes & Noble to pay their bills. Paying writers for articles and stories ultimately flags the IRS or Inland Revenue to somebody who might not be paying their fair share of taxes, so keep those records in neat and clean form, and not in a pile under the bed.

Along those lines, a lot of publishers tend to have...ah, shall we say, an *intriguing* idea of what qualifies as prompt payment. Many writers (or at least the good ones) are willing to forego pay if they're allowed editorial freedom, or the opportunity to write for a venue they've admired for a time, but this should be spelled out. Don't promise a paycheck to a writer and then mumble, six months down the road, "Oh, gee, we blew all of the money on a table at WorldCon." If finances are a problem, lay down the situation to everyone all at once, and NEVER let the writers discover the money woes only after they've threatened legal proceedings. By that time, it's way too late.

First, do no harm. In the same way editors have a tendency to rewrite articles without concern for the author's feelings, publishers have a tendency to assume that they can tinker with a final magazine however they see fit. Sure, it's your money on the line, but remember that nobody really reads a magazine because of the publisher. This means keep your nasty picture out of the magazine (if you want to see your picture in a magazine, do an interview for another one, preferably in a different genre), don't push the editor into accepting articles or stories written by your girl/boyfriend or mom or roommate from college, and no cutesy editorials telling us all about your personal life. Readers honestly don't care if the publisher blew his last $50 on getting the magazine out or that he hasn't been laid in fourteen years: all that matters is that they exchanged money for product, and publisher vanity is a great way to guarantee that this exchange won't happen in the future. If you don't like that, and you want accolades for your work, become a rock star, because publishing is a thankless business where neither you nor anyone else doing it should expect anything at all. Certainly not groupies or money falling from the sky.

(Several years back, I worked for a trust-fund brat who decided that he needed to become a publisher because being a trust fund baby isn't quite so cool when you're pushing 35, and is usually kinda creepy. He financed several magazines, and grabbed all of his blocks and went home six months later because the world wasn't beating down his door for being a publisher. In the process, he crippled one magazine and killed two others, and most of his staff had to take him to court to get back pay, seeing as how he felt he wasn't responsible because he hadn't made the millions of dollars he expected. Copping a bad attitude like that was bad enough for him, mostly because everyone in the general community then realized what a flake he was. Pulling that sort of attitude in the science fiction community is a good way to get your knees broken, your wife rustled and your cattle raped, and your car turned into a four-wheel paperweight from all of the Minute Rice in the radiator and gas tank. Writers and editors will put up with a lot of crap, but flat-out abuse triggers a swift and terrible vengeance.)

Keep the money under control. Every publisher I've ever known has reason to celebrate the birth of a new magazine or Web site. This doesn't mean burning through six months' operating expenses for the party. It also doesn't mean spending thousands of dollars on new equipment and office furniture (or even an office) when contributors aren't making a dime. Unless you're running *Zizzle-Swump* on the money you made from Microsoft stock options, and you have literally millions of dollars to throw away, always finance developments as if they guarantee that everyone will be living off Ramen noodles, dead cockroaches, and hope for the next six months if those developments don't work.

Better yet, keep your promises. Anyone becoming a publisher should look at your word being your bond, and consider that breaking that word could very easily lead to people walking in to your bedroom in the middle of the night with horse heads under their arms. If you promise to put $10,000 of your own money into a magazine, don't wheedle and hem and rationalize: do it. If you promise to bring people onto the payroll once conditions are right, don't back out or welsh on the promise: do it. If you promise to get an issue out by such-and-such a date, don't prepare excuses that blame the editor or distributor or the guy who ships the magazines from the printer: drop everything to get it done. If you promise to give the editor a new computer or give whoever's doing your promotion a big order of postcards with the magazine name and info or even pay the freelancers on time, don't finagle. Just keep your promises, and watch your employees (and let's face it: they're employees) jump through hoops to keep theirs.

Even more so, keep your schedule. This is the most critical point that most science fiction magazine publishers forget: keeping a regular schedule is the best way to ensure that everyone takes the publisher and the magazine seriously. Tattoo it on the inside of your skull: "If I say that the magazine is quarterly, it's quarterly, goddamn it!"

Most science fiction magazines started as zines, and zines have always been a hobby. If the editor and publisher are the same person as the sole contributor, and the magazine is given out free with no internal advertising, nobody's going to give a damn if the new issue is a few weeks late. However, when you have bookstores that already ordered hundreds of copies and have to deal with the constant customer nagging for new product, and subscribers who are quite understandably pissed because they already put money down up front for the next issue, and writers who handed in articles ahead of deadline so as not to jam up the works at their end, none of them are going to be really thrilled when the magazine comes out two years late.

Again, money problems always happen, but be honest with everyone involved. Don't sing-and-dance about the next issue coming out any day now when work and family issues keep it from coming out for months. If subscribers ask about a delay, answer truthfully, and give them the opportunity to get a refund on their subscriptions if they so choose. (That offer alone will give enough subscribers enough faith to give everyone another chance; stalling or lying about it just guarantees that they'll start pulling in lawyers to get that refund.) Send letters to all of the subscribers, explaining the situation. Most importantly of all, don't screw over the writers on this: at least give them a proof of the upcoming article, so they see something has been done. I once quit one once-prominent SF magazine because the editor/publisher's whole attitude about terminal tardiness was "Oh well."

Finally, if you aren't going to make it a long-term commitment, don't even bother. Writers have any number of idle little things that bug the shit out of us, and one of the worst comes from working for a magazine where the publisher started with the best of intentions, and then got bored and decided to shut down everything four issues later. More often than not, it ties right back to money: either the money being spent wasn't coming back into the publisher's pocket fast enough or the publisher wasn't getting attention commensurate to the financial support. Either way, it leaves writers, printers, editors, and damn near everyone else in the lurch because the publisher couldn't commit.

Publishers refer to their magazines as children with good reason, and just as we all know that one person who had a kid for the absolute worst reasons ("I want a tax writeoff," "I want something that will love me unconditionally"), writers all know one person who decides to become a publisher for the absolute worst reasons ("I want a tax writeoff," "I want respect," "I want something that will outlive me"). Writers produce enough of our own troubles all by ourselves, but we've nearly all been burned by writing for a startup publication that died out, leaving their stories and articles homeless, solely because the publisher found a better tax shelter or a new TV show to watch. It's not just print, either: Web or CD-ROM publication requires just as much effort as print, and the Web is festooned with dead zines that seemed like a good idea, but died out when the publisher decided that it was too much effort.

That said, please don't let this discourage anyone honestly and truly interested in becoming a publisher from doing so. The idea is to weed out the poseurs and wannabes, not the determined ones. Considering how the science fiction industry is becoming increasingly dependent upon small magazines as an outlet for beginning writers, we need new, able publishers now more than at any other time in the genre's history. Just don't be a jerk about it, or we'll hunt you down.

—*Write Market, September 2000*

"Time, Precious Time"

Dedicated to Alex Jay Berman

Time is the most valuable asset to a writer. All of the talent and all of the motivation in the universe won't compensate for the inability to put down on paper or phosphor dot a concept or conversation. Since most writers, especially science fiction writers, are working day jobs to feed our irrational obsessions with writing, what time we have is more important than it is to most. The normal reality, that of coming home from work, bitching about co-workers, eating dinner, and falling asleep in front of the television, is denied us. Our evenings, mornings, and weekends are shot, because we have to keep feeding our compulsions.

Admittedly, when most of us talk about not having enough time to write, this is a matter of time management. Saying "I'm going to write all weekend" and then settling in for a six-hour *South Park* marathon on Comedy Central before finally getting in front of the keyboard at a little before midnight won't get any sympathy from me, mostly because I'm all too likely to do this myself. In this case, don't go whining about how you figure that you'd do great work if you didn't have to deal with the time wasted on a job: most likely, that additional eight hours a day would go into a slow search of everything available on television, long walks for "inspiration," and damn near every other possible excuse to keep from working. That's what writing is, folks: it's *work*. You may enjoy it, and you may love it, but anyone considering doing it for a living should always look at writing as a job. This means setting aside particular times and sticking to a general schedule.

When people ask me how I start writing, I usually relate Joe Lansdale's advice: (1) Put chair in front of typewriter, (2) put ass in chair, and (3) repeat as necessary. That's actually not quite true: I start out by getting my choice of stimulants (Diet Pepsi in a BIG glass), get comfortable (T-shirt and shorts), keep a Super Soaker in a holster on the back of my typing chair for the cats and the wife, crank up the stereo, and start tearing into the newest deadline. Otherwise, I have enough gibberish going on that I have to watch the time, and I still find myself at four ayem, with the possibility for maybe an hour's sleep before having to get up and go to work again, still going strong. As with the clichéd writerly use of exotic pharmaceuticals, tankards of alcohol, or tender young buttocks to put out cigarettes on, this is just my take on ritual, and should not be copied by anyone else, because it probably won't work for anyone else.

Even with Lansdale's advice running through our skulls, we all still hear the excuses. Sometimes, it passes through our lips. Let's go through the excuses, shall we?

"I don't have the time."

Here's where some decent time management pays out obscene dividends. Lots of people talk about how they don't have the time to write, but they never bother to look at how much time they waste on other things. Yeah, I'm talking to you: if there's nothing on television, shut it down and get to work instead of flipping around to find something to watch. If that time gets burned up with three-hour phone calls from friends, disconnect the phone or explain to them that you have to work: set up a five-minute egg timer by the phone to convince the clueless that it's time to hang up. Get a timer for yourself, so those fifteen-minute potty and lunch breaks don't drag on any longer than they're supposed to. (Business majors can justify four-hour lunch breaks, but business majors are soulless scum who will be crushed like grapes when Jim Henson rises from the grave to reclaim His kingdom.) Schedule all of your errands and other events for one day out of the week, so at least a couple of hours a day are dedicated to writing. One way or another, time should be managed like money, and I always laugh at the twits who micromanage every tax expense on their in-home offices but never get around to writing anything.

"I have so many things I have to do."

No sympathy from me, bub. As members of a technological society, we all have our societal and social obligations, but the question is once again "Do you want to be a writer, or do you want to be something else?" Now, some activities are more important than writing: attending your child's college graduation, for instance, is just a little bit more important than working on a new short story. However, a surfeit of important activities should give the impression that a serious decision is in order. If attending art openings or drowning kittens is taking up too much time, and it's at least as important to you as writing, it might be time to drop writing for a while.

"I'm too tired after I get home from work."

Aw, poor baby. Not that I can't empathize: my regular commute only needs a few Australian motorcycle punks in bondage pants to make the image complete, and something in Dallas air sets off random bouts of Tourette's Syndrome, because my throat is raw from screaming at idiot drivers. (You know the sort: the ones who go plugging along in the fast lane of the highway, babbling into their cell phones while running well below the speed limit.) If writing is important to you, find a way to recharge. I'd never advocate the use of crystal meth, but if it's necessary, snort up a kilo or two: me, I settle for quick naps right after I get home and I start writing well after sunset, when it's cooler and quieter.

An alternative that those who work with PCs should consider is bypassing the trip home and writing at work. A lot of employers don't mind their workers using computers and internet connections on their own time, and some don't mind use during working hours during slowdowns and other non-peak periods such as lunch breaks. Always ask about this: some bosses may have problems with a two-meg file containing your next novel being bounced back and forth across the E-mail server, and others may have real problems with that ZIP disk that contains your trilogy being perceived as company property. Otherwise, work can be an excellent environment for creativity: you usually have no choice but to plant your butt in a chair for eight hours anyway, and using that downtime for writing is a lot better than using it for surfing HotSluts.com.

The problem here is that fatigue is usually an excuse to keep from writing. Real physical and mental exhaustion is an understandable reason to skip out on writing for a while, especially when the hallucinations start to kick in from a few weeks of sleep deprivation. Procrastinating because you'd rather lie back on the couch and watch television does not qualify.

"People interrupt me while I'm trying to write."

Now, this is a perfectly understandable situation, and it's easily cured. Get a cattle prod and an AC adapter, and keep it next to your seat. Nothing says "I need time to write" quite like the smell of seared human fat. Some people actually like this sensation, though, so keep a can of pepper gas handy as well for these perverts. I have one of those big cans for riot control that's the size of a fire extinguisher. I could soak down a herd of grizzlies with this puppy. Unwanted phone calls are best dealt with through the use of air horns, and I just bought a special virus for ICQ abusers that replaces all existing files in a computer with audio and video clips from Pauly Shore movies.

Seriously, this is perfectly understandable. The only option is to remove these interruptions from your work schedule. Obviously, not all of us can afford a secretary to sift through our phone calls and keep unwanted visitors away, so it's time to be creative. This means big signs on the front door reading "WRITING IN PROGRESS: INTERLOPERS WILL BE EATEN" and messages on the phone answering machine to the same effect. Better yet, should you have access to voice mail, direct all phone calls to voice mail and disconnect the phone entirely. If that's not possible, shut off the ringer. The same goes for cell phones and pagers. If you have a separate office or room that allows you to shut out the rest of the living area from roommates or family members, close and lock the door. If you have problems with animals (dogs, cats, rabbits, savannah monitors, etcetera) crawling into your lap, kick them out of the room, let them outside, or otherwise get them out of your sphere of influence. The same goes for kids, spouses, or any other loved ones that may require a good soaking with pepper gas if they get in the way.

For those who keep their Web connections going while they're writing, remember one thing: ICQ Messenger is A Force of Evil. After you've exorcised all of the other interruptions and annoyances, the last thing you need is a string of petty "Hihowaya" notes from folks who may care about you but also want to drain off what little attention span you still have. Personally, I bundle ICQ with cell phones as having crawled out of Satan's backside (I'm constantly telling people that I'm against cell phones on religious grounds, because I believe the morons who use cell phones while driving should be burned at the stake) and therefore never use it, but it's easy to have this happen with E-mail, too. For those with E-mail applications that beep the user whenever a new message arrives, shut it down. You'll have plenty of time to answer your E-mail after you get your work done.

Finally, we have to talk about family members and spouses. Anyone marrying a writer should understand that they're getting involved with an addict. For writers, make sure that the other person understands that you may have to choose between them and your writing career, and be prepared to make a hard choice if it comes to a "it or me" showdown. In extreme cases, when the love of your life decides to demonstrate his/her best Peg Bundy impersonation and scream and cry about how writing gets in the way, the option is for the other person to find an activity to occupy them or to start flashing the business card of a good divorce lawyer. Be merciless: it's not like you're out drinking and whoring around.

"I can't concentrate."

An answer to this always depends upon the individual, because each writer's nerves are different. Some can't work in anything but absolute silence, others in any area with any visual distractions, and others could write in a battlefield, propped up against an anti-aircraft gun. (Myself, I've been known to write in packed nightclubs to quite good effect, so long as nobody tried to start a conversation. At the same time, having a television running in the other room drives me nuts.) The idea is to find that perfect balance and stick with it.

"Once I get situated, I can't come up with any ideas."

Sorry: can't help you there. I'm just here to help with organization: when it comes to ideas, you're on your own.

—*Write Market*, October 2000

"The Hair of the Dog That Tripped You"

Most beginning science fiction writers are looking for that angle that will allow them to beat the odds and get their work published when all of their counterparts are wallpapering their bathrooms with rejection notices. A lot of them assume that going to conventions and buying drinks for editors is enough: they get a reputation with the editor, all right, but not necessarily one that's complimentary to them as a writer. Others assume that they need the blessing of an established writer, or a subscription to the right writer's market magazine, or the right Web site showing off their work. All of these have merit from time to time, but here's a surefire way not only to impress the hell out of editors but to beat out most of the beginner competition.

Learn to spell.

This isn't all, but it's a start. Take the time to learn the differences between and the uses for "there," "their," and "they're." Learn never to start a paragraph with "there," unless it's for specific effect. Discover the basics of constructing a paragraph. Understand the different characters used for punctuation, and when they should and should not be used. Make a point of learning how the parts of the language fit together, and then worry about using them to tell the story you want to tell.

Considering how being a writer requires at least a tenuous grasp of understanding of English (or Portuguese or Farsi or the writer's language of choice), I'm always amazed at the lack of concern shown by beginning and wannabe writers toward learning the parts of speech. I'm not one of those obsessives who diagrams sentences until they scream: at times, I take great glee in carving my initials on Strunk & White's tombstone. The difference, though, is in knowing the rules and deliberately flouting them, or in producing clunky material without knowing any better.

Now, some famous writers were notoriously poor spellers: Alfred Bester, for instance, was well-known for his atrocious spelling. He was able to transcend this both with the power of his ideas and with sympathetic editors correcting his manuscripts. A newbie writer might be able to transcend a lack of spelling ability in the same way, but in a writing market as competitive as this one, most editors reading through a slush pile will simply reject any manuscript they come across without immaculate spelling, punctuation, and sentence structure. Considering that the editors for the larger SF magazines receive literally thousands of unsolicited manuscripts every month, editors cannot afford to do anything else, and a talent without spelling skills is going to get stomped by a mediocre writer who understands the old "I before E except after C" rule.

The number of beginning writers who are poor spellers is paradoxical but understandable, considering how most schools teach writing. From grade school through college, writing is a chore, a drudgery, and a punishment. C'mon: how many teachers punish students by forcing them to determine the square root of 2014 or finding the capital of the Solomon Islands? The same teachers who decry corporal punishment and the resulting psychic trauma discipline students by making them write "I will not [throw spitwads, defecate in the urinal, charge the assistant principal with sexual harassment]" 500 times, and then wonder why those students loathe composition later in life. It's only when money is involved that everyone perks up about spending hours in front of the typewriter or computer, and as with any other item or procedure seen as an easy way to wealth, a good number of the participants jump in without any concern for the amount of time and effort that needs to go into it to get a payoff.

Many confuse typing ability with writing ability, and so a lot of programmers and general office laborers start playing around with word processing software and "story generators" the way they play around with making graphics with Photoshop or Macromedia Flash. Sorry to be so cynical, but I have yet to run into a computer programmer who could write or spell for shit. (I'm willing to give a lot of slack to those for whom English is their second language, but not when their first language is C++ or Perl.) Programming is a valuable skill which should be encouraged, but programming and writing are skills about as similar as cutting horse training and iguana ranching. Knowledge of one does not automatically grant proficiency of the other. Even so, the same programmers I meet who sneer at managers who think that programming in machine code is easy see no problem themselves with pumping out story after story, and then scream about evil cabals in the magazine industry when they get rejection letters.

(As a digression, ever notice how beginning writers are certain that some conspiracy exists solely to keep them out of the field, and established writers are certain that some conspiracy exists solely to keep mediocre writers in?)

Now, most writer's guides don't teach this. Most guides on how to write science fiction start with cultivating that great concept and turning it into a story. Well, that great concept is worth all of its weight in used toilet paper if the verbiage is impossible to tolerate. Look at a well-constructed story as a gem-encrusted tiara, with the concepts as individual diamonds. Without taking the time to design and complete the underlying structure, all you have is a handful of rocks, which may be pretty but are harder to sell on their own. And when the undercarriage is composed of aluminum foil and dental floss, well...

The first and most important consideration toward doing this is to learn how to spell. Learn: don't depend upon spell checkers. Most spell checkers are limited in scope, and they'll only catch obvious misspellings. They won't catch homophones, such as the "there/their/they're" triplets mentioned earlier. Unless they're exposed to a correct example, they won't catch an obvious error as anything more than an unfamiliar word, and most are notorious for ignoring words missing letters, so "One" is just as acceptable as "none."

The spelling and syntax are even more important in cover letters and E-mailed queries to editors. Sending a letter to the boss written all in lowercase to save time may be all right in the corporate environment, but always look at a query letter as a job interview, and make sure that it's the best. Is all of the copy spelled correctly? Does it make sense? (You'd be amazed at the number of query letters and cover letters that make almost no sense whatsoever.) Does it come off as abrasive, arrogant, whiny, demanding, or otherwise annoying? Most importantly, does it make the reader want to give the story any consideration, or does it make the reader return the manuscript unread?

After working on spelling, work on the other aspects of the use of English. Know your punctuation marks and when to use them. Know the correct times to use a colon and when to use a semicolon. Remember that quotation marks are your friends when used in accordance to manufacturer's guidelines. Always remember that exclamation points outside of quotation marks should be used as sparingly as plastic explosives in dentistry. Unless recreating the recreating style of a crank or crackpot, never use more than one exclamation point or question mark per sentence, and know that shoveling them on doesn't make the sentence more intense. Gene Roddenberry liked to boldly split infinitives, but this shouldn't be held as an endorsement of the practice.

And for Arioch's sake, please note that one does not pluralize a subject with an apostrophe-S. If I see that one more time, especially in advertising copy, I'm going to have to kill someone.

—*Write Market, November 2000*

"A Handy Metaphor For The Life Of The Freelancer"

Back in my pre-high school days, I worked as a lawnmower. The summer and fall of 1979, I was in Chicago, racing through the neighborhood with the family lawn mower, charging $3 per mowing. Simple service: no trimming, no edging, no bagging of spare cuttings, and no lip. I came in blasting, tearing through grass, weeds, and small trees, and left with a basic chop-and-run. I was running the Supercuts of lawn care maintenance, and I made just enough per lawn, after covering lawn mower maintenance and fresh gasoline, to cover the basic requirements for a thirteen-year-old. Namely, comics, the occasional paperback book, and money for family members' birthday presents.

In the spring of 1980, after moving to Dallas, the situation repeated itself, only the lawns were much larger, and the challenges greater. The subdivision in which I lived was brand new, which meant that most yards consisted of a touch of grass atop the native Texas clay, and any topsoil that existed above that red gunk had been scalped by the grading bulldozers that flattened out any irregularities in the local geology for miles around. Texas clay is a notoriously poor growth medium for anything but flowerpot manufacturers, and the grass had to compete with huge clusters of sandburrs. Sandburrs were weeds that produced cockleburrs from Acheron: while most burrs simply caught in clothing and animal fur like the scratchy part of Velcro, sandburrs had points on them sharp and strong enough to puncture bicycle tires, and they grew in amber waves all the way to the horizon. Mowing sandburrs simply spread burrs throughout the yard, and being pelted with them was much like being stoned to death with prairie dog-scaled throwing stars. The trick was to keep the lawn well-mowed at least every three days, as green sandburrs were minced quite nicely by a well-maintained mower, and the weeds needed at least a week for the sandburrs to mature to their potentially lethal condition.

1980 was also the year that the fire ant came into its own in Texas. The Argentinean fire ant first became an exotic intruder in 1956, but the huge boom in construction thanks to the oil boom in the late Seventies was a godsend for the vermin. Bulldozers scraping the landscape removed any competition, and since fire ants were already adapted to flooded winters and blazing summers, the Trinity River floodplain was a perfect habitat. Fire ants construct softball-sized mounds of extremely fine and fluffy soil, and the slightest touch on a mound extruded thousands of furious warriors, each capable of stinging multiple times. Mowing over a fire ant mound also simply spread the monsters all over creation, so the trick was to minimize the damage and blow the debris over the areas that had already been mowed. Any other tactic simply allowed the fire ants time to crawl up pants legs and into socks, and one fire ant bite felt like someone stubbing out a soldering iron on bare flesh and left a nasty pimple-sized welt that usually became infected. Dozens of stings generally meant that the victim didn't go out in public until the sores healed, and that could take weeks.

In both Dallas and Chicago, most lawns were quick and easy, and the customers understood what they were getting, and I generally understood what I was getting into. They didn't expect a Better Homes & Gardens front yard, and I didn't expect a freshly-squeezed glass of lemonade at the end of the job. They didn't have to supply their own lawn mowers, and I didn't clean up dog crap and random toys except those toys that directly threatened the mower. I charged $3 (or $10 in Dallas), and they didn't have to deal with wheedling and negotiation. Some customers, though, always tried to get something more after the fact, and that's when we had problems.

Two jobs in particular come to mind. In Chicago, I was used to thick and rich yards, especially those belonging to people with large dogs, and finding spare Great Dane landmines in ankle-high grass was one of the hazards of the business. Just mow through it and keep going, and if the customer complains about the smell, point out that s/he should get that pony housebroken. One woman in the neighborhood, though, called up to get her lawn mowed late one September afternoon, and she had let the back yard slide for most of the summer. The grass came nearly to my knees, and it choked the mower three times before the job was done. At that point, darkness was falling fast, and I was heading home when she called me back. "Aren't you going to rake up the cuttings?"

Mind you, the back yard at that point was nothing but cuttings: if I were charging what pro landscaping outfits charged, I'd have felt guilty about leaving mounds of green hay all over the place, but I reminded her that the $3 was for just the mowing, ma'am. She threw a ruckus, and I figured "What the hell: she's old and alone, and I'll do this as a favor." I raked that yard under the back porch light until well after my curfew time, and got a good chewing out when I got home for missing out on dinner. I didn't collect my money due to the time, but eight big black plastic garbage bags sat out at the curb, proof that I hadn't been idle.

The next day, I went to collect my fee, and the woman looked at the bags and the back yard, sniffed, and said "You didn't edge it. I'm not paying you until you edge it." At this point, argument was impossible, and I simply stomped off, looking at all of this as a learning experience. She kept calling my house for three weeks, trying to get me to come back and mow again, telling my mother that "he did such a good job, and I want to get him to mow every week." I never got my fee, and I was always afraid that I'd get drafted into installing a sprinkler system for free if I went back to collect.

The other incident came in Dallas, with a neighbor down the street. Since he was out of town most of the time, running a profitable business in cable descramblers and satellite dishes, his yard took on most of the characteristics of a Schezwan bamboo forest *sans* pandas, and he called to see if I was interested in making an easy $10. I took him up on it, mowing a half-acre lawn in the beginning of the worst heat wave in North Texas history. The crippling heat wasn't so bad: the problem lay with sandburr colonies the size of a picnic table, fire ant mounds the size of a basketball, and cotton rats the size of small dogs. The rats apparently nested in a woodpile at the end of the property but roamed free throughout the yard, and since I started at the outer edge and spiraled my way toward the center, the center of the yard was quickly surrounded with a no-mans-land of freshly cut grass that terrified the rats in the center. For some reason, they would only break and run for safety as I was passing by, and although the mower made an incredible racket, they apparently assumed that safety lay underneath, and they dove for the perceived security of the spinning blades. Or maybe they despaired of being picked off by hawks and committed suicide: both way, the regular roar of the mower motor was punctuated with the occasional ker-CHUNK, and the stench of rat guts in the afternoon heat was obscene.

Two hours later, I finally finished mowing, and went in to collect my pay, only to find that the neighbor had gone to run an errand. Well, he was gone for two weeks, and by that time, the rat guts spread over the yard had helped fertilize any amount of new alien growth. When he came back, he called me to ask about getting another mowing, swearing that he'd pay me for both jobs when I was done. No surprise: when I finished the second time, he had already taken off again, and so now I'm out $20, no small change for 1980, and no small change for an incipient high school freshman. I had never heard the phrase "Once a philosopher, twice a pervert" at that time, but I now understood its meaning, especially when he called again and wanted a triple or nothing.

Now, I certainly would have been within my rights to do any number of horrible things to that man's lawn, especially since our neighborhood lay along a major flight path leading to DFW International Airport and passengers looking out their windows could see quite a bit of detail in the neighborhood back yards. Instead, I simply let all of the neighborhood kids of legal mowing age know about his little scam, and while I never mowed his yard again, I finally got my $20 when he couldn't find anyone in the county dumb enough to get burned themselves.

And what does this have to do with writing? Read the fine print, and use these examples as an object lesson in how not to let someone take advantage of your work. At the very least, you learned something about fire ants, didn't you?

—*Write Market, December 2000*

"Photo Finish"

Shortly after crawling from the primordial slime and pulling in that first lungful of air, the Beginning Writer wants to do several things because of the popular impression of what a writer does. The successful Beginning Writer starts by writing something sufficiently interesting that someone wants to publish it, and goes from there. The rest, though, worry about the small stuff: obsessing over getting an agent willing to work for ten percent of a nonexistent writing revenue, or getting tax writeoffs on home office space and new computers that will be used more for prowling Web chat rooms at three ayem than in advancing the state of Earth's literature. One of the top pseudopriorities comes with the bio photo, intended to be plastered across the back of that first novel or throughout the "Contributors" section of any magazine in which they appear. These range from little Instamatic snaps that leave everyone with the eyes of a demon-possessed jaguar, all the way to staged spectaculars that would have embarrassed Cecil B. DeMille or maybe even James Cameron (although the latter is pretty damned unlikely). Then, with a little bit of Photoshop work to conceal the liver spots and the gill slits, they're ready to draw an unsuspecting crowd of frantic fans, editors, and publishing deals.

To one extent or another, everyone in publishing has made this assumption at one point or another. We're all guilty of this: writers, editors, artists, the custodial help, and everyone else involved with a magazine. (Editors in particular seem to be obsessed with getting their pictures in their own magazines, especially in the science fiction industry. About the only editor I know who isn't compelled to plaster his 8x10 glossy at the top of every "From the Editor" column around is Scott Edelman, formerly of *Science Fiction Age* and currently of *Science Fiction Weekly*. With a few, I'm amazed that they have time left to edit their magazines, what with all of the photo shoots they do and all.) Some of us get sucked in because our editors want photos to show off their staff of new and regular scribes: a notorious one of me was taken on Dallas' Grassy Knoll five years ago because an editor wanted a still, and never mind that my smile makes everyone around regret ever leaving Ripley and Parker behind to look for the ship's cat. (I had another that started as a fun shot I sent an editor purely for grins and giggles: I had no idea that he was going to use it as the opener to a triad of essays in the next issue, and if I had, I wouldn't have been flipping the bird quite so enthusiastically.) Others, though, seem to think the world wants to see our image and fall in love with it, and incidentally get around to reading our prose.

Trust me on this: nobody really wants to know what you look like. Not anyone who matters, anyway. Don't send the bio photo with your submissions, and bury that portrait from Glamour Shots deep in your Web site where nobody will ever find it. If anything, making sure that nobody knows you by face will only increase your allure in the writing community: anyone remember all of the people trying to get one good peek at James Tiptree, Jr.? And that's not even counting the number of people who study your bio photo after reading something of yours that deeply angers and disturbs them, just on the offhand chance that they may run into you in a dark, silent alley one day.

To put this in context, here's a little quote from a childhood role model:

"A group photo of the top ten journalists in America on any given day would be a monument to human ugliness. It is not a trade that attracts a lot of slick people; none of the Calvin Klein crowd or international jet set types. The sun will set in a blazing red sky to the east of Casablanca before a Journalist appears on the cover of *People* magazine."

-Hunter S. Thompson

Introduction, *Generation of Swine*

Coming from a journalism background, I know of what the good Doctor is saying. One of the big perks in the newspaper business is the column in the Op/Ed section with the big photo alongside the byline, and that perk is so entrenched that nobody will even consider the possibility that those photos scare off twice as many readers as attract them. If the columnist doesn't look as if s/he crawls up through sewer lines into houses to bite babies in the night, his/her tighter-than-a-chicken's-asshole mug looks as if s/he sent off the grandkids to help fight the Boer War. (My local paper, the *Dallas Morning News*, regularly runs old, old, OLD photos of its columnists, much to the screaming horror of those watching their new television ads. Their high society columnist, for instance, doesn't even look human: she looks like someone put a condom over the head of Tutankhamen's mummy and added makeup with a paint roller and grout trowel. To steal from Jennifer Saunders, one more facelift and she'll have a beard. Her photo, though, looks as fresh as it did the day it was taken, back when she was sending her boys off to take on those horrible Yankees at Gettysburg.) And if you think that journalists are ugly enough to stop a sundial, just take a look at the photos *Locus* feels compelled to run of each year's Hugo winners. Mind you, these are of the big guns in the genre: the response to these photos is "Man, I always loved [fill in the blank]'s work, but I had no idea that [fill in the blank] could scare a pack of starving dogs off the back of a meat truck," so just think of the potential damage to a tyro's ego were someone to write back "No offense, but based on your photo, do you catch flies with your tongue, or do you snap them out of the air with your teeth?."

By way of example, a couple of weeks ago, I came across an ad in our local weekly newspaper for Earthlink Internet services, and someone got the bright idea of using the *Ain't It Cool News* site to help promote the need for Earthlink services. Unfortunately, instead of running an ad that brought up the supposed merits of *Ain't It Cool News* and how having Web access would allow movie junkies to get the latest gossip about *Star Wars: Episode Two*, it ran a full-page photo of *Ain't It Cool News* head honcho Harry Knowles. For some reason, Mr. Knowles seems compelled to put photos or cartoons of himself all over his site, and this ad was no exception. Not only was the ad a waste of good money as an argument for getting Web access, anyone coming across Knowles' three chins, scraggly beard, and beady eyes would probably succumb to the cliché that Web users are no-life dweebs and decide against ever signing up for Earthlink services. The same could be said of many of the bio photos of writers, artists, and editors in most magazines; the only time Harry Knowles' face should appear in an ad is to sell condoms.

The fact is that readers are interested in writers because of what they write, and that's it. If you want to pose for the camera, become a model. If you feel compelled to yack and sing incessantly, be a musician or a politician. If you feel compelled to let everyone check out your buff bod at every available opportunity, get into the porn industry. If you can do these and write, do these as a sideline, but don't let it interfere with the writing. The world is already full of good models and musicians and porn stars who seem to think that they can write as well, and they do it so poorly that it reflects upon the rest of us.

And let's be honest: most writers started writing as a holy calling, but also as a way of garnering attention from the world. We couldn't compete on looks, so we didn't get into modeling. Our voices bring forth the image of a cat in a cement mixer, which is why we didn't get into radio or the music industry. (If your local favorite radio station has a Web site, and the management is dumb enough to put photos of its deejays on the site, look and learn. These people are being hired for their husky, soothing voices, not for their visual appeal. There's nothing quite like seeing a listener who fell in love with a deejay solely on voice quality alone, who now sits in a corner, weeping and gnashing of teeth rising in the air, after seeing the object of his/her affections in the flesh at a "Bring In The Weekend" party or at a movie preview.) We weren't athletic enough to become an Olympic gymnast or an Airborne Ranger, dexterous enough to choreograph music videos, or arrogant enough to run a business. The only skill worthy of recognition for the most of us, aside from being able to belch the first five lines of "Mary Had A Little Lamb" and fart the last three of "Blitzkrieg Bop," is the ability to link together twenty-six characters (or as many happen to be in your alphabet of choice) into strings of words that make people feel something after they've scanned them. As such, the time expended in getting that photo doesn't even come close in making up for the time wasted on that instead of a new novel or short story.

Even with this warning, some editors and publishers insist on including bio photos in their publications, so here's the best solution possible. Go out and invest in some stock images, either by buying them from an image company such as Eyewire, or just buy a picture frame and pluck out the person on the little printout intended to help sell that godawful frame. Find someone that will fit your general body image, and use that. The stock image route can be a bit expensive at times, but it offers the advantage of having everything in Internet-ready formats; the frame model route is cheap, but it requires a scanner to send an electronic version to editors and/or fans.

A little warning before you start: ALWAYS GET ROYALTY-FREE MATERIAL. Sure, you gals can use a photo of Cindy Crawford and the guys can use Andy Dick, but the owners of those faces tend to get just a little pissy if someone decides to borrow them to go on the back cover of a book without permission. That's why I recommend Eyewire: its images are guaranteed royalty-free, so they can be used for everything short of selling pornography. Best of all, Eyewire sells individual images, so anyone trying to live on a writer's income doesn't have to plunk down $300 or more on a CD archive that never sees any other use. Just download it off the site, trim it to size on any image editing software, and keep it on hand to print out or E-mail to any editor who specifically requests a recent photo for a new book or magazine.

And there you have it. By going this route, everyone is happy. Editors are happy because they have something to run alongside their own photos. Readers are happy because they have a positive image to go with their positive impressions of the author's work. Writers are happy because they're able to concentrate on writing, and because the wannabes are going to be too busy arranging studio shoots to clog up magazine slush piles more than they have already. Best of all, just wait until some reader comes across that picture frame photo and writes back "I didn't know you were a model, too!"

—*Write Market, January 2001*

Postscript: Eyewire died a long while back, and was sold to Fonts.com. Other than that, everything I write is the truth, including what I'm writing now.

"Celebrating the Absolute Worst"

A few weeks ago, the Golden Raspberry Awards Foundation announced the 2001 Golden Raspberry Awards nominations. The Razzies are a long-running tradition in the movie industry: since 1980, the Razzies have celebrated the absolute worst of the movie industry. These were the folks who rained down ridicule and brimstone on such cinematic abortions as *Wild Wild West*, *Showgirls*, and *Rambo* by presenting them the only award that no amount of publicist schmoozing can buy. The Razzies generally don't target the little direct-to-cable belches that deserve pity instead of scorn, such as *Summer of the Monkeys* or *Free Enterprise*: they go right for the biggest films of a given year. In most years, it's no surprise that the films with the most Razzies are also some of the biggest hits, but the Razzies are usually remembered long after the last videotape of *The Lost World: Jurassic Park* is dumped in the "Free To A Good Home" bin at the local Blockbuster Video.

Now, by taking a look at the archives of previous winners and nominees at the official Razzie Web site (http://www.razzies.com), one tends to notice that a disturbing number of past and present nominees are science fiction, fantasy, and horror films. The 2001 awards nominations, for instance, were a landslide for the adaptation of *Battlefield Earth*, just in time for the revised DVD edition. Last year, *Wild Wild West*, *Star Wars: Episode One*, and *The Blair Witch Project* tore through the Razzies like a double-spoonful of Ex-Lax. The reasons for these are probably impossible to understand or even comprehend, but I suspect it's because the producers and directors of genre films have a major blind spot. The cynics who make genre films to cash in on what they perceive is a trend are at least honest about their greed, but to hear George Lucas defending *Episode One* or John Travolta defend *Battlefield Earth* suggests a bout of utter denial in their parts in making two of the worst films, of any sort, in the last decade.

And what does this have to do with the literary aspects of science fiction? That's simple: it's time to apply the healing flame of ridicule and scorn upon the literary side of the genre. It's time to recognize the worst published science fiction in a given year. It's time for the Elwood Awards.

For those too young to remember, Roger Elwood was a rather prolific editor of science fiction anthologies. Not quite as prolific as Martin Greenberg, who bundles anthologies the way Anhauser-Busch bundles 12-packs of Budweiser, but Roger tried for that scale. During the late Sixties and the early Seventies, Roger flooded the industry with any number of anthologies: paraphrasing from Michael

Bishop's *Light Years and Dark*, aside from *Six Science Fiction Plays* (which included the only publication in twenty years of Harlan Ellison's screenplay for his sole *Star Trek* episode), all of Elwood's collections glutted the market with mediocre anthologies full of forgettable stories that poisoned the well for paperback and hardcover anthologies for years. These days, Elwood's contributions to science fiction lay in forgotten tomes in high school libraries, slowly crumbling under the onslaught of silverfish and ultraviolet light. (Since they were cheap, my high school library's SF section was packed full of Elwood-edited collections, so I had firsthand experience with the foul stories therein.)

Considering that the Hugos are named after the acknowledged founder of modern SF, the Elwoods are the best way to commemorate the contributions of one of the most reviled people in the industry, if only to act as a warning to those who follow in his shadow.

Science fiction is a very schizophrenic genre, mostly because of all of the neuroses of the people who write it and edit it and publish it and read it. With very few exceptions, we were the people who hid our copies of *Twilight Zone* and *Locus* behind a spare copy of *Coprophiliacs Monthly* while reading them in school because the teachers wouldn't rag on us quite so badly if we were reading porn. Because of the ridicule and abuse and flat-out hate, we tend to be rather defensive. At best, we give the benefit of the doubt to shoddy stories because "criticism brings down the whole business" or similar twaddle. At worst, we have folks in the genre that don't know bad fiction when they read it, and who will gleefully go for trash. Speaking from experience, pigs prefer good food to slop if they can help it, but humans are the only animals that willingly and repeatedly gobbles down shit even when given better choices. This helps explain *Maxim* magazine, Wendy's hamburgers, and new episodes of *Lexx* on the Skiffy Channel every Monday.

At about the same time as the Golden Raspberry nominations last year, the Saturn Award nominations were announced in Los Angeles. The Saturns are awards for the best science fiction, fantasy, and horror television and film of a given year, and last year's Saturn nominations weren't that much different from the Razzies. George Lucas and *Episode One* received nominations for Best/Worst Picture, Best/Worst Director, Best/Worst Screenplay, and a plethora of others. The Saturn response seemed to be "Oh, we know it's bad, but it's still science fiction," which is the same exact defense used by diehard fans of both literature and film in our esteemed genre. This is why we need the Elwood Awards, if only to remind ourselves that this genre isn't so grandiose that it can't laugh at itself.

And yes, yes: I know all about the Hogus, the alleged anti-Hugos that run at the same time. The Hogus don't count because of a lack of publicity. As it is, the

Hugos really only matter to the people winning them, and it's damn near impossible to get audiences to stick around after the announcement of the "Best Dramatic Presentation" Hugo anyway. If such a thing is even conceivable, the Hogus have even less of an impact upon the science fiction community and popular culture in general than its opposite. The idea here is not to hide crippling shame and abuse under a bushel basket, but to let it light the world.

So here's the assignment. It's time to look at the absolute worst short story, novella, and novel published in 2000. It's time to look for the worst Dramatic Presentation, the worst professional and semi-professional magazine, the worst pro editor, and the worst pro artist. It's time to list the worst nonfiction book of the year. It's time to nominate the one person or group most responsible for keeping science fiction in the dumps. Seeing as how this award is based on pure nausea, malice, and rage, it'll be inherently more honest than the Hugo nominations, because nobody is going to vote in order to suck up to (or suck off) the recipient. It's time to follow in the steps of the Golden Raspberries in demonstrating the advantages of good writing by illuminating examples of bad writing. Most of all, it'll probably demonstrate an old adage about most of the entries and people nominated for and winning Hugos each year: the winner of a particular Hugo and the person involved with the most bloated, unreadable, or otherwise intolerable product could probably be hit with the same bullet.

And to add spice to this award, seeing as how we all love to help rag on a victim, this needs to be a well-publicized event. The Hugos are so poorly promoted that a couple of former *Grit* paperboys on a syphilitic warthog could do a better job of spreading the news, so a few effective yet gonzo PR people could get twice as much attention in the national news solely by letting news venues know about the ceremony. (Contrary to popular impression, the Hugos are not publicized by SFWA flacks psychically beaming the press releases into the aether, but that approach might actually improve the coverage.) This includes ads in all of the trade publications in the genre (all two of 'em), Web coverage, and even videotapes if interest leads to enough money in admissions tickets. We get a has-been genre actor who sings like a cat in a cement mixer (the Saturns already have William Shatner, so I nominate Butch Patrick) to open, and wait to see if any of the nominees are dumb enough to collect their prizes. Even if they aren't, a good time could be had by all.

Now, one may argue that this is a cruel, heartless prank that doesn't do anything to improve the state of science fiction. Anything but, my dear: by illuminating the worst published science fiction in a given year, this will make people hunt it down and read it. The Elwood voting will be based on the number of impersonations of cats coughing up I-beam hairballs that ensue over reading these short stories and novels, followed immediately by the comment "WHO IN THEIR EVERLOVING BLOODY MIND PAID MONEY FOR THIS PIECE OF TRIPE?" With the works that simultaneously win Hugos, the basic question of "Did anyone actually *read* this?" will echo throughout the land. Editors may actually win Hugos based on their editorial ability, and not because they threw the best party at the previous WorldCon. By reading the worst, readers get an appreciation for the best, and will start searching for it. Best of all, it sows dissention, and good serious discussion of the genre and its future is exactly what the genre needs if it's going to survive or even (gasp) grow.

Besides, recognition of bad writing never kept anyone from continuing to write. I'm living proof.

—Spicy Green Iguana, March 2001

"The Secret Word is 'News'"

Well, the end was nigh for a long time, and now it's all coming down hard. Internet-based SF magazines, long held to be the one hope of preserving the science fiction magazine well into the 21st century, are either dropping like dead ticks or barely squeezing through. When times were flush, everyone started moving to the Web in the hopes of finding new audiences for science fiction, and a lot of ill-earned cash went into trying to turn one site or another into The Portal for all things science fiction. Well, that was then, and the sites that aren't dead already will probably go the way of all electrons before too long.

It's not as if Web-based SF magazines had a particularly good chance to begin with. Way from the beginning, editor Algis Budrys moved *Tomorrow SF* to the Web back in 1995, only to fall because nobody was interested in paying subscription fees to read short stories. (Six years later, the news site Salon.com is experimenting with charging a subscription fee in return for access to special subscriber-only material and an absence of banner ads. If *Salon* succeeds, it'll be the first news site besides *The Wall Street Journal* to make a subscription-based model work in real life.) Quality had nothing to do with sites' success for failure: Ellen Datlow's *Event Horizon* published some incredible fiction and nonfiction, but ad sales couldn't justify keeping it going, and it shut down in 1999. Any number of factors were bandied about as to why SF sites couldn't be profitable just yet, but that didn't keep high-financed sites from popping up in 1999 and 2000, as witnessed by the launches of *DistantCorners* and *Galaxy Online*.

Now, the problem with a lot of these sites is that they copied (or continue to copy) one of two formats. Nothing against the sites: print magazines have been following these formats for years. We have either the all-media, all-the-time sites, where almost all of the content is somehow involved with television, movies, and other non-literary media, or we have the all-literary sites that contain nothing but short stories and novellas. Quite a few sites cross these boundaries (the most obvious is *Science Fiction Weekly*, as edited by Scott Edelman), but they're all missing or deficient in one element that could justify repeated returns for new material. That element is news.

Yes, yes, I know all too well that many of these sites carry news, or what they'd like to call news. Unfortunately, most of this news consists of preformatted, predigested "news flashes" about the latest rumors concerning the next *Star Wars* film or cast changes in *Farscape*, usually made available to every possible venue all at once. Very rarely does literary science fiction (or fantasy, or horror) rate a mention, unless an author dies or someone sells the film rights to a classic or popular novel. (Just look at the amount of "news" space dedicated to the possible film adaptation of *The Hitchhiker's Guide to the Galaxy*, and never mind the number of times the book had been optioned since 1980 or how little Douglas Adams has written in the last fifteen years.) A few places cover literary news, but it's either reprints of press releases or news so full of snide commentary that it's practically useless. Anyone willing to start up a real SF news site has a product of immediate interest to readers and writers, and anyone willing to write news of this sort has free run of a category of SF writing that has practically been ignored.

Some sites that provide real SF news exist, but the coverage is a bit...well, lacking. *Spicy Green Iguana*, for instance, contains great thumbnail reports on publishers and magazines, as do competitors such as *Speculations* and *The Gila Queen's Guide To Markets*, but they remain thumbnails. Sure, they keep tabs on dead magazines, but nothing on why they went under. Did a magazine die because the editor/publisher no longer had time to keep up with it? Did it die because of poor distribution? Did it die because the people with the money figured that they'd be better served by spending the cash on cocaine snorted off the butt of a teenage prostitute in Rio? We very rarely get any follow-through on these, partly because all of these sites are horrendously understaffed, and partly because nobody considers asking the right questions.

One of the most lacking items in SF news lies with analysis. Listing synopses of press releases and running small articles are essential, to be sure, but the closest many of these sites come to serious in-depth articles comes from interviews. Those interviews are important as well, but a lot goes on in this business that rarely if ever gets covered, much less dissected to understand future trends. A good example of this is the decline of the publishing midlist. Most of the news about publishers cutting back on buying books from authors whose books sold well but not according to sales estimates has come from understandingly disappointed authors, not from anyone willing to prognosticate the side-effects of this practice and how it impacts other authors, other publishers, and booksellers. A few people do a good job with analysis and public-service articles (A.C. Crispin's articles for SFWA on fraudulent agents would be up for consideration for awards in any other genre, and *Science Fiction Chronicle* regularly runs serious essays by Allen Steele and others), but the examples are so rare that they're really exceptions.

(One could make an argument that book, television, and film reviews qualify as journalism, but not any more than editorials do. The problem here is that good reviews require a basic understanding and knowledge of the subject being reviewed, and reviewing positions are usually snagged by idiots who watched Roger

Ebert on *Sneak Previews* and assumed that reviewing is easy work. Well, yes it is, which is why the Web is full of review sites that tell audiences nothing other than that the author likes the sound of his/her voice, he said with self-loathing. Unfortunately for these characters, good reviews require more than ecstatic plot synopses based on the amount of free swag sent with the item being reviewed, and if they don't get their freebies, they get violent.)

Right now, news about science fiction literature is much like that in the newspaper, if your local newspaper consisted solely of police reports, interviews with noted citizens, and movie and TV reviews and gossip. This is fine for pure entertainment purposes, but more insightful reportage is something that SF's practitioners could use. Here are some perfect examples:

- Right now, everyone in the publishing industry is prattling about E-books, but small press publishers are expanding, and nobody is looking at how small presses may be the only venues publishing older SF novels and those by beginning and midlist authors in another five to ten years.

- Just what, if any, value comes from joining the Science Fiction Writers of America? This isn't intended to rile: for all the noise made about joining or not joining, if anyone has written a serious, nonpartisan evaluation of any advantages to joining SFWA as opposed to remaining out of the organization, it hasn't seen general dissemination. A good article on the positives and negatives of joining SFWA, as well as a breakdown of costs versus benefits and a thumbnail history of SFWA voting, could be of inestimable value to beginning and established writers who now consider joining in the near future.

- Two years ago, the Barnes & Noble superstore chain instigated a policy whereupon magazine publishers are responsible for lost, stolen, or damaged magazines in all B&N stores. Aside from an editorial or two in *Locus*, nobody of any importance in the field has written anything about the effect this policy may have upon small-press magazines and large magazines with tight profit margins.

- SF is becoming more international in scope and circulation, with more magazines and books coming from Canada, Australia, New Zealand, and other countries other than the United States. Both *Locus* and *Science Fiction Chronicle* cover the British book scene, but aside from Jonathan Strahan's coverage in *Locus*, precious little is reaching the rest of the world about the Australian publishing community, with about as much attention paid to Canada. Any of these countries, or any number of others completely ignored in current SF news venues, may become a major nexus for publishing in the next ten years.

- All of the news magazines and sites make much of movie companies buying the film rights to classic novels and new short stories, but nobody reports on the projects that don't go to production. Considering the number of production companies that buy the rights to stories and novels solely to keep competitors from adapting them, a caution to those willing to sign away their rights in perpetuity, only to find that those rights are filed away in some Hollywood storage shed, is in order.

- The comics industry regularly reports on the precarious state of comic shops, especially concerning the number of comic shops that have closed since 1994, and this same sort of analysis is necessary for bookstores specializing in SF. What stores have declined or died due to competition with the superstore chains, which ones have survived or even grown, and what are the successes doing right? With the death of small-press magazine distributor Fine Print, how are bookstores getting genre magazines, or have they cut out magazines altogether? Are buyers continuing to return out of habit, or are stores attracting a new clientele? If they're attracting new readers, are they coming to SF bookstores looking for TV or movie crossover material, were they originally brought in by established SF readers, or are they finding the stores for reasons yet undiscovered?

These are issues rarely if ever covered in established SF journalism. The odds of, say, *Locus* moving into serious investigative journalism are miniscule right now, and there's not that much incentive for anyone to take it on as a paying career. Journalism is already a poorly-paying and disreputable business (as the joke goes, most journalists pray for a sibling to become a crack whore so they have someone to look up to), and since writing SF novels is already a good way to starve to death with the blessings of society, well...anyone wanting to get in on this racket had best do so for love of the genre, not hopes for financial gain. Readers, writers, and editors are all notorious for being thin-skinned (poke at a few of 'em, and they pop like a zit), so writing anything that might be construed as negative usually garners nothing but crank calls and nasty letters, not accolades.

On the other side, beginning writers always ask about what direction they should go when starting out, and SF journalism is a venue with a decided dearth of competition. We all know of at least one author, book, magazine, or event that deserves wider recognition, and many beginning writers might be better suited for journalism than fiction, at least while starting out. Besides, nobody's getting paid to write for most SF magazines and Web sites anyway, so now's the time to start writing in anticipation of the SF market getting better.

Okay, go ahead and laugh. It's a silly idea, comparable to suggesting that the crew at *Entertainment Weekly* actually gets its collective tongue out of George Lucas' ass for at least one issue. But I'll say this: combine enough people with stories to tell with people willing to write about them, and that's enough material for a news site. If enough people think that it's viable, and the site manages to attract enough readers tired of publicity releases masquerading as news, then it just might be able to pay operating costs. Either way, it'll be a change for the writers, and it can only improve the genre.

—Spicy Green Iguana, April 2001

"Ascertaining the Difference Between Horses and Zebras Without Dissection"

Having been a writer for twelve years now, I really feel for doctors and lawyers. Without fail, anyone being introduced at a party or other social occasion as a doctor finds himself/herself surrounded by gits who start up with "Well, doctor, I have this funny pain running from my armpit to my big toe; what do you think it is?" When the doctor explains that it's impossible to make a diagnosis without an examination, and that the doctor covers all of the overhead on offices, equipment and student loans to get that degree in medicine by charging for diagnoses, the git gets indignant. Lawyers get it worse: if they don't offer free legal advice to anyone who asks, they're subjected to eight hours of lawyer jokes. (I really feel for veterinarians: they not only have to offer diagnoses at parties, but diagnoses from second parties: "My Lhasa Schnookums keeps yelping whenever she eats road tar and fishhooks, and I think that maybe she has a vitamin deficiency that makes her stomach tender. What do *you* think it is?") Seeing as how I look at doctors and lawyers as two essential elements in a technological society (yeah, you can laugh at the "tough smart lawyers" at 1-800-GREEDHEAD who advertise on daytime television all you want, but the first time you get hit with a lawsuit, or the first time you find that someone else is making money from your hard work without compensation, you'll be GLAD for a good lawyer), I'm usually the guy at parties who makes the running tackle to save doctors and lawyers from that sort of aggravation, usually by asking the git "Gee, have you gained weight lately?"

And why would I do this? It's because I get the same exact sort of idiot questions the moment I'm introduced as a writer. And so does everyone else in this business.

Now, writers get a lot of questions, and many of them deserve answers, even though we have dreams at night that we've died and gone to Hell, and our eternal punishment is to answer questions from people who weren't listening the first or fifth or 117,298th times. The aggravation comes from those who (to steal from David Gerrold) want a partner for masturbation by asking for confirmation instead of answers. It's not even the "Hey, I have a great idea for a novel: if you write it, I'll split the money with you" saw: It's the "I'm working on a story, and it's about..." They don't want critiques, they don't want acknowledgement, and they don't want dismissal. All they want is the writer clapping hands together and gleefully chirping "I wish I'd come up with that! When it's published, I'll be jealous!" (It's always easy to spot wannabe writers, and people who will be wannabes until they last draw breath, because they'll always get paranoid if they don't get that exact response. Naturally, if they don't get it, it's because that writer is planning to steal his/her idea, damn it!)

In writing science fiction, fantasy, and horror, this declaration is always especially annoying for one reason. Without fail, the mendicant will pop up with a "It's about..." and go on for the next six hours about an idea. In SF, the idea is almost always a technological wonder that would change the world, and that the author has researched for years to check for absolute scientific accuracy. In fantasy, it's a magical or political wonder. In horror, it's always a Menace From Outside that nobody could *ever* copy. Either way, the discussion isn't about the story that wraps around the Idea: it's about the Idea itself.

To save time, here's the thesis for today's column: An idea is not a story. Write this 500 times and keep it in memory. AN IDEA IS NOT A STORY.

The problem here is that science fiction, fantasy, and horror are literatures of ideas. Writers in these genres are expected, nay, demanded to stretch the imaginations of readers and make them consider situations that never would have occurred to them in a billion years. The mundane, the average, the normal are to be eschewed in these stories, to a point. However, unless a writer specializes in nonfiction, those ideas require a framework to support them. (This isn't to excuse nonfiction from this, either. Really good nonfiction borrows liberally from standard storytelling structure to impress the importance of the material upon the reader.) In this model, ideas are much like eggs: they're good for you, and they have quite a bit of value, so long as they get to the recipient in an edible form. Now, you can swallow eggs whole, but they're pretty unappetizing to anything besides a Gila monster, so they need to be transported in one form or another.

Quite a few science fiction writers make the mistake of building a scaffold for ideas, much like an egg crate. One of the best examples of this that comes to mind at the moment is Larry Niven's *Ringworld* series: ostensibly, each book is an ongoing story, but in reality they're collections of Ideas that have a story built around them to keep them from cracking. These sorts of stories are notable for the amount of infodump necessary to make the story, as it is, move forward. When the story stops for more than a paragraph to bring the reader up to speed, usually with one of those lectures "As you know, in the 29th Century, we got rid of/implemented/had sex with...," you're looking at a classic case of infodump. The story doesn't affect the flavor of the ideas, and it's still just as necessary to swallow those ideas, complete with the shell that holds them together and all of the stringy nasty bits, whole.

The alternative method of egg or idea transportation is to incorporate eggs or ideas into a composite so that the essence gets to the recipient, but they are inseparable from the rest of that composite. In cooking, a great way to move eggs is to bake them into a cake: the eggs are still there, only they're impossible to remove from the cake mix, and their inclusion, along with all of the other ingredients, makes the assemblage much more valuable than the separate components. A science fiction story requires Big Grandiose Ideas, but the trick is to mix them with characters, situations, and locales that pass on those great ideas without the reader realizing it. Everyone agrees that the best teachers are those who made learning fun, and the best way to make learning fun is to impress those lessons in the context of other activities, only to have the student realize "Hey, I learned something" after the fact. Good stories should be the same way.

Background is another Big Idea that many writers, tyro and experienced, tend to overload on without realizing it, once again creating Egg Crate Stories. Fantasy stories in particular are vulnerable to this phenomenon: while it may help you, the writer, to visualize a dynasty of warrior kings, complete with names, deeds, and idiosyncrasies, the last thing most readers want to do is to slog through genealogies and histories unless they're absolutely essential to the plot. In this case, if this history was melded, in little bits and pieces, to the story as it was needed, the story would be much more interesting.

(Here's an example that may help illuminate the situation, and help explain why movie adaptations of great stories are not always the best. When Universal Pictures released the extended version of David Lynch's adaptation of *Dune* in 1988, someone at Universal felt compelled to add a foreword to the film, bringing the viewer up to speed on the situation before starting the movie proper. Because of this, the viewer was "treated" to twenty minutes of explanation of the Butlerian Jihad, the development of the Mentats and Bene Gesserit, as well as all of the political machinations that led us to the conflict presented in the film. Compare that to the novel: the movie runs for another fifteen minutes before it reaches the novel's starting point. *Dune* the novel, while not exactly light reading, manages to disseminate a lot of the history of the known universe ruled by Shaddam IV in bits and chunks, partly through character discussions and partly through the characters' thoughts. The book didn't need a huge infodump at the beginning to explain what was going on: while the reader had no idea of the scope of the story at the start, anyone with a remotely decent attention span was able to relate the general social and political situation by the end.)

Melding of ingredients in horror is just as important: in fact, it depends upon story more than either science fiction or fantasy to work. Characterization is exceedingly important: not only does the threat imposed in the story have to be terrifying, but the reader needs characters with an immediate interest in escaping from that threat, and that requires characters with whom the reader can empathize with or at least understand. Setting fire to a gaggle of dolls made from clothespins has nowhere near the emotional impact of setting fire to one's family and neighbors. Timing is also incredibly important in a horror tale: just as a joke is ruined by revealing the punchline too early, a good horror writer will give the reader just enough rope, and only just enough, before springing a good surprise. Just as how a good horror film is one that makes the audience scream instead of oohing "Wow, great special effect," a good horror tale makes the reader forget that s/he is reading in the first place.

All this, though, seems to slip by beginning writers. Yes, we're all inspired by outside events, and many of us can relate how we came up with one great sequence by listening to one perfect piece of music, or seeing one perfect piece of art, or mishearing one perfect conversation. The difference here is that the sequence is not the story, unless that sequence is so self-contained that it would make a good 2000-word short-short story. For anything running over 2000 words, a single idea won't carry the story. As Joe Bob Briggs used to describe any number of particularly bad drive-in films, "Absolutely no plot to get in the way of the story," and this can be paraphrased to read "Absolutely no story to get in the way of the idea." And this simply won't do.

—*Spicy Green Iguana, July 2001*

"Should You Care That It Ain't Christmas?"

And now for a very distasteful idea in writing circles. The horrible reality of having to work for free. To quote Ralph Steadman, teddible, teddible.

You don't have to be a Rhodes Scholar, or even a member of SFWA, to realize that the literary science fiction market is in, well, deep shit. Out of the magazines that survive, most pay what are ridiculous rates anywhere else: argue all you want, but ten cents a word for a story in Asimov's is pathetic when most magazines on the stands pay an average of 60 cents a word. And that's if you can even get into these markets in the first place, because you're up against thousands of other established, beginning, and wannabe writers all fighting for a spot in one of those "prestige" markets. Just do the math: if you figure that each of the Big Three digests have an average of six stories a month, and they come out monthly, that's only 288 spots in the space of a year, and most editors have a pool of stories they've already bought but haven't found the right time to run. This isn't counting the bimonthlies, the quarterlies, the biannuals, and the Magazines That Come Out When The Editor Damn Well Feels Like It.

Of course, Western culture keeps presenting the cliché that writers are perpetrating the best get-rich-quick scheme since the invention of the televangelist. We trade big reams of paper with funny marks on them for big fat checks with lots of zeros to the left of the decimal point, don't we? What everyone conveniently forgets is that to get those checks, a writer has to submit stories to publications that will pay for those reams of paper, and even if they pay, they won't pay the ridiculous rates that passersby assume writers collect. With the magazines that pay, most are looking for only the best and brightest (and far too many, in New York, anyway, for the editors' former classmates from Columbia or the *Harvard Lampoon*), leaving precious little room for beginning writers to learn how to knock off the rough edges. One also has to realize that due to ongoing neglect, genre magazines are the worst sort of niche publishing: each issue of *Reptiles Monthly* pulls in subscriber and general newsstand circulation that most SF editors would kill and eat their grandmothers to get. Because writers are perfectly willing to submit stories to a magazine but balk at actually buying a copy, lots of genre magazines are running on the bare edge of survivability. It's a tough choice: pay writers for their work and come out every few years, or ask them to write out of their compassion for the genre and publish on a quarterly schedule.

Here is the razor's edge. Contrary to what *Writer's Digest* would like us to believe, writing for free is not an inherently evil undertaking. For those writers who are more worried about being a WRITER, and whose day job pays enough that they don't have to depend upon writing revenue to pay the rent, working for free is not inherently wrong, so long as the writer understands the advantages and disadvantages of the situation. Most real writers (that is, the ones who think of getting published as a way to disseminate their ideas and dreams) might consider working for free if they feel that they'll gain something from the transaction, such as working for an editor they admire, seeing a story rejected everywhere else get printed, or moving into another area of writing that they hadn't considered previously. The trick is to decide when the benefits aren't worth the trouble, or when it's time to move on to all-pay, all-the-time.

To start, take a quick peek in the listings here at *SGI*. Quite a few magazines and Webzines listed pay in something besides good will and the eternal appreciation of the editor, and some pay quite well for SF venues. However, beginning writers should also assume that those paying venues are already flooded with pro writers, semipro writers, writer wannabes, and geeks who heard that *Asimov's* is paying top dollar for *Star Trek: Voyager* fan fiction. This time around, look at the other publications listed, and don't immediately let your eyes glaze over when the listing doesn't include a payment of less than 15 cents a word. The beginners aren't going to get that kind of money anyway unless they're channeling for Hemingway or Steinbeck, and even the established folks may have something in them that defies classification in other magazines.

First thing first, though, the most important lesson. Any editor who says "We can't pay right now, but we hope to do so in the future" is lying, even if s/he doesn't realize that s/he's lying. Both the deliberate and accidental liars always use this as an incentive to get work for free, and they should just be honest about it. In both cases, the idea is that they'll start paying once a magazine starts to make a profit, and anyone familiar with magazine publishing knows that most magazines don't make a profit until their second year or their tenth issue, whichever comes second. Either way, since most magazines are lucky to see a second issue, and very few of any type survive to see their tenth issue, most die due to inattention or neglect long before they could ever make a profit.

The deliberate liars are reasonably easy to spot: they're the ones always pleading poverty while collecting subscription and retail revenues and then pumping them into new computers and equipment. When times are good and everyone is flush, the money goes into the newest computers and associated toys, as well as plane fare for conventions for "promotion purposes" (it's amazing how much promotion goes on at conventions with the participants passed out under a barstool and clutching an empty bottle of vodka) and new clothes to make the best impression on convention panels. When times are bad, the money's still coming in, only the deliberate liar gets on the contributors' cases about bringing in new subscribers because he needs to pay for car repairs or a new computer. When times are flat-out rotten, the deliberate liar will shut down the magazine without bothering to tell the writers, and the contributors only find out about the death of the magazine from other sources.

The inadvertent liars are just as bad, but they honestly mean well. Unfortunately, a combination of economic woes, changes in distribution systems, and inexperience with running a business (and magazines should always be treated as a business if the magazine wants to be taken seriously) take out far too many of these venues as well. The danger here isn't from having stories and articles disappear (although this happens with disconcerting regularity for those working in SF), but with the fanaticism usually involved in these labors of love. Sooner or later, most good editors and publishers realize that they have to offer something to their contributors to keep them writing: if money is an issue, then complimentary copies of the magazine, T-shirts, and other goodies may be offered and sometimes accepted. (Lots of writers are willing to forgo cash in exchange for review copies of books, magazines, computer games, toys, and just about anything else you can imagine. A good writer can get more value from these than from a standard paycheck, especially considering the cost of hardcover books these days.) Otherwise, contributors who were initially enthusiastic about contributing find themselves sliding along: if they dealt with editorial interference without pay, they usually quit. It's not a constant, but far too many editors putting out an SF magazine out of their love for the genre tend to get really cranky when their writers say "I'm tired of the rewrites/two years between issues/your standing at the front door at WorldCon in a Sailor Moon outfit singing 'I'm A Little Teapot'" and walk. Too many contributors leave, especially the more popular contributors, and the whole magazine generally goes under.

Advertising is a particularly sore issue when talking about nonpayment. Since most SF magazines don't have much in the way of advertising, most of the ads inside are trades with other magazines to get more exposure (thereby taking space away from paying advertising), or they're from stalwarts who have been running advertising for years and are still charged at the 1952 rate. Most genre magazines don't have the staff or seemingly the inclination to hunt for advertising: one magazine of my acquaintance had advertisers calling up on a daily basis after a write-up in *Wired*, only to be rejected because the editor wanted to keep the magazine "pure." Never mind that he could have used that money to pay his writers or put out the magazine more than once every two years: he had no intention of ever making a profit, but he sure as hell wasn't going to share that with the contributors.

Now, in lieu of financial remuneration, editors have to offer some sort of compensation for their contributors' time and effort. Editorial freedom is always a good one, as quite a few writers are willing to work for free if they can see controversial or noncommercial articles or stories published in their lifetimes. Some are willing to work for free if they can get in a few licks on the established powers, and others are willing if they figure that they can write ten articles a year for free instead of one every two years for a paying market. Some just want to work for a respected or interesting editor, and damn the paychecks. Some will even jump on board because of intriguing subject matter or even a good name: I still rate my experiences with the late great *Fuck Science Fiction* as one of the best writing experiences of my life.

The second lesson is that while working for free may not be wrong, whoring yourself for free is. In the beginning days of the Web, everybody jumped onto the concept that Web-based magazines would transform science fiction, because it was possible to reach a gigantic audience with a relatively tiny expenditure of money. Well, technically, this was true, but reputable editors soon learned that they had to spend just as much on promotion of their sites as they would have spent on paper for a print edition, and writers were a bit leery about contributing to venues that could evaporate in a moment's notice with the unplugging of a server. Working for a defunct magazine or newspaper still left writing samples as proof: as the Web site *The Museum of E-Failure* will point out, when a Webzine dies, everything goes.

Even so, far too many of these beginning sites were like far too many zines: since they couldn't pay for top-line writing talent, they offered newbies the opportunity to "get exposure," as in "We can't afford to pay, but your story will get you lots of exposure." Suuuuuuure it will. If that story appears for free in a magazine with the circulation of, say, an in-flight magazine like *American Way*, it might actually be read by more than three people. If it appears on some GeoCities site with a URL as long as your arm (and that's just to get to the home page, not to your posted story), it's not going to get read by anyone other than your friends and relatives, and that's if they're able to get the right URL the first time around. A corollary to that "you'll get exposure" yarn is that somehow editors of all stripes are going to go sifting through a GeoCities site looking for the one diamond in a sea of pigflop. Sure, that could happen: Ellen Datlow and Gordon Van Gelder may be sufficiently bored enough with the day-to-day operations of their current publishing commitments that they'll want to go plowing through a poorly-designed fan site and come across your story, herald it to the world, and stand at your side when you win a Hugo for it. However, the good money says that you're better off waiting for someone to present you with an operational Green Lantern ring.

As a slight tangent that ties back into everything else, just because you worked for free on one publication doesn't mean that you should work for free on every other. Just as there's nothing wrong with working for free if you feel that you're getting something from one venue, there's nothing wrong with being compensated for your time and effort. With the Web in particular, writing for one Webzine will get letters from editors asking to write for their Webzines, and if they don't pay anything either, don't feel guilty in telling the editors "NO" if you're not up for it. The one true sign of a poor writer is one that only appears in venues that don't pay a dime: even with the gentleman-writers who write for the love of telling a good story, don't you think that they'd be appearing from time to time in paying publications if they were any damn good?

The third lesson is that any editor or publisher who sees a particular magazine as a Holy Calling is bad news. I've put this in other essays over the years, but this is a point worth noting again. Most paying publications don't really notice when a writer quits, save for swearing that the writer will never work there again, but the editors/publishers of nonpaying magazines have a disturbing tendency to make threats when a writer leaves, especially due to editorial interference. These can range anywhere from snivelings of "Well, I'm going to tell everyone I know that you were completely unreasonable about this, and I'll do everything I can to make sure that you can't get published anywhere else" to crank calls and random threats of violence. Report any death threats to the cops immediately, but otherwise blow off the other threats. If these geniuses had any power, they wouldn't be publishing out of their garages, and their whining usually has very little to do with whether or not you'll sell something somewhere else. The editors at The New Yorker generally couldn't give a fart in a high wind if you were blacklisted by some sword-and-sorcery zine with a total readership of 200 back ten years ago, unless the zine editor somehow became editor of The New Yorker.

This leads directly to the fourth lesson: don't be afraid to walk away. If an editor treats you well, and you get recognition for your work from readers, money shouldn't matter all that much (or it may, depending upon whether or not you pay your mortgage in money or in body parts of random victims you poleaxe in the streets, drain of blood, and present to your banker). However, if the editor turns out to be a taskmaster or a petty tyrant, just pick up and leave. If family or work schedules prevent you from putting out as much work as you would like, explain the situation to your editor, and anyone who throws temper tantrums because you can't manage fifteen movie reviews a week is someone you really don't want to work for. If your editor spends more time plotting the violent overthrow of the local government than in getting a new issue out the door, you can be reasonably assured that nobody's going to be reading your work anyway, because nobody can read unpublished material unless it's sold door-to-door. Contrary to the shrieking, leaving a nonpaying publication won't destroy your writing career: in some cases, it can only improve your reputation. Just don't be the prima donna, okay? This genre has enough of them already.

—*Spicy Green Iguana, August 2001*

Postscript: My old friend Joey Shea had the same attitude about doing art for free that I had about writing for free. He finally came to his senses about the same time and quit, after the thirtieth snotty request for free artwork and the thirtieth snotty response to payment of "You have to earn your dues." As Joey noted, "I've been doing this for twenty years. When do I stop paying dues?"

"Conventions and Other Forms of Vocational Suicide"

So you've finally made the big time. You beat the slush pile, and your first short story was published in a magazine that pays real money instead of copies or Burger King coupons. Or your first book came out to rave reviews. Or you've been publishing for a while, and you're itching to meet other writer-persons in neutral ground. Now, you might make your mistake by looking in the back of certain magazines and seeing the listings. You might run across a local one and volunteer to cause trouble. Hell, you might get a letter from someone involved in it, asking you if you're amenable to attending. One way or another, you just got suckered into being a science fiction convention guest.

Even with the worst stereotypes of the denizens and activities of a con (and most of these are true, mostly because nobody cares to do anything to change it), it's not all bad. If you're planning to go to a convention in order to meet old friends and wander around in what is, for all intents and purposes, a flea market that charges $30 for the weekend, help yourself. If you're going to a convention to get drunk and loud and get beaten up by hotel security, *vaya con Dios*. If you're going to a convention because you get a cheaper rate on a hotel room in a city you were planning to visit anyway, and you honestly believe you'll be able to get outside the hotel during the convention, good luck to you. If your literary career is sufficiently advanced, or you have enough of a dancing-bear stage presence that compensates for lack of experience, that you can justify charging speaking fees, have fun so long as the check clears. For those who honestly think that they're going to promote their work at a convention or talk to an editor, don't bother. You'll only get an empty wallet and an urge to shoot at school buses for your trouble.

Think I'm kidding? The days where science fiction conventions were dedicated to literary science fiction are as dead as the days where you could run into indricotheres in your back yard. Go poking through those convention listings in the back of *Locus* or *Asimov's*, and you'll see lots of conventions that call themselves "science fiction conventions," and you'll find that most have a focus on television or movies, or costuming, or polyamory, or anything other than science fiction that utilizes funny marks on paper. The ones that promote literary efforts are usually so poorly promoted that nobody besides the con staff even knows that they're happening, and they only survive because of word of mouth from previous attendees the year before.

Even showing up to talk to fellow authors at a con is a hassle: half of them are frantically scurrying to panels and events, and the other half are sufficiently upset that they aren't being noticed that this is all they talk about. Be honest: you became a writer so you could get a little attention, right? Don't be shy: you wouldn't be wasting effort on writing science fiction if you could get attention from other venues. Well, just consider that you're sharing space with anywhere between ten to 100 people just like you. The only difference between you depends upon whether or not you have a namebadge with some variation of "Guest" on it. If you have it and they don't, you'll spend the weekend with them pumping you for information while wishing you dead at every footfall. If the reverse, you'll spend your time wondering why they won't let you in the club, because you certainly won't be treated like a fellow writer. (This, of course, skips the problem with the pathological liars that infest conventions like belly worms. We're not talking about those with more enthusiasm than execution who just haven't quite sold a story yet: we're talking about the nutcases who either impersonate another author well enough to fool the gullible, or the psychotics who talk a great game until they start ranting about the Zionist/Papist conspiracy that keeps their stories from being accepted. I haven't even gone into the recruiters for the Libertarian Party yet.)

Even with this much warning, there are those who think that going to conventions is a good way to get that all-important name recognition. In some rare cases, this actually happens, but usually only after a writer already has recognition. Let's take a look at the reality for a bit.

The first and foremost thing to remember about science fiction conventions is that there's precious little money to be made off them. If they were lucrative, you'd be seeing much more professional conventions, because it's in the best interest of a profit-seeking organizer to maximize the profit. Most fans are so cheap that they use both sides of the toilet paper, and the reason why such a security presence is necessary at most cons is to keep our slans from stealing everything not Superglued to the rafters and keep hordes of Cat Piss Men from walking in. (This happens anyway: just sit at the registration desk at a big con one of these days and listen to the hourly 500-pound sociopath howl that he DESERVES a free guest badge because he runs a GeoCities *Buffy the Vampire Slayer* fanfiction site.) Fans may have money, but they aren't going to spend a penny of it unless absolutely necessary. Cut into the budget set aside to buy *Star Wars* action figures or Asian porn videos with a sufficiently high admission, and the typical fan won't bother; nobody else is going to be caught dead at the con thanks to the stereotypes, so anyone who claims to be making a living by running conventions usually has a second job or unorthodox sources of income.

This means that you have two things to consider. The first is that since profits are secondary to most convention committees, they aren't going to be run by professionals. (Actually, I lie: they may be run by people who manage professional events such as rock concerts or auto shows, but SF cons are a side business they do for fun, like a software designer who runs fan Web sites for grins and giggles. These people are usually the most honest about the odds that a convention will turn a profit, and they're usually the best to work with because they know the importance of having the trains running on time.) Most conventions are run by amateurs who think that it'd be cool to run a convention, or by those amateurs who figure that they could do a better job than that other pack of amateurs running another convention across town or across the country. Some amateurs take the job seriously, but sadly they're usually outnumbered (by about 400,000 to one) by egomaniacs who get off on telling their fellow fans that they're running a convention. Nobody's getting paid for their efforts, so the con gets varying efforts, which is why most cons these days expect their volunteers to pay for their admission badges beforehand. (Far too often, especially when it comes to members of Con Security, the only time anyone would see some of those volunteers is on Thursday night, when they showed up to pick up their badges, and on Sunday night, when they'd show up for the after-con party.) This means that while the head of Guest Relations may be an absolute angel who manages to smelt uranium with her bare hands and mix up the best Caesar salad you've ever tasted, the person in charge of getting information to the head of Guest Relations could very well be a human-sized slug who can't be bothered to do anything because he's too busy Web-surfing anime porn.

(TRUE STORY THE FIRST: A couple of years ago, I was hoping to attend a big convention out East. If you follow the convention listings, you'd know the name. Anyway, my car decides to blow out the water pump, head gasket, and the head, in that order, along a hot stretch of Texas freeway about a month before the convention, so I get online and try to pass on word to the con staff, via E-mail, that I'm now out $1500 and attending the convention would be impossible. I found out much later, as in about three days befor the con, that attending wouldn't be a problem because the con had a fund set up for the one guest who was too poor to be able to afford to make the trip. Why did I find out so late? Because the person in charge of checking the E-mail account wasn't doing his job and hadn't bothered to pass on any of the mail he received, and the convention chairpeople only found out from a mutual friend that I was too busy nursing a dying Cavalier back to automotive health to do the convention. If he wasn't doing his job, why was he allowed to run that account year after year? Because, as one of the few competents on board put it, "he's been with the con for years, and he complains if anyone tries to take it away from him." Those competent folks have retired to the sidelines, and the remaining staff wonders why the con has such a mediocre reputation these days. In fact, this guy now runs the convention, and lists himself as a guest solely by dint of his Being In Charge.)

The second thing to consider is that these fans aren't going to part with a penny unless they can't avoid it. At the big Comdex computer show in Las Vegas, the joke is that Comdex attendees show up with one $20 bill and one set of clothes, and neither get changed the entire week long. This means that writers are going to get screwed. Figure that you're going to rent a table in the dealers' room to promote your newest novel? Don't bother: all you'll get are people grabbing copies and asking "Is this a free sample?," people trying to sweet-talk you into giving them a free copy, people demanding a free copy "for review purposes," people throwing a tantrum because you can't afford to give them a copy "for review purposes," and people blatantly trying to steal them. If you give them out, rest assured that the same people with their grubby mitts out for those free copies will immediately turn around and trade or sell them to a dealer, and you'll see your autographed copy on a dealer's table other than your own sometime during the con.

And there lies one of the major issues for writers at conventions. Most conventions are nothing more than a dealers' room with attempts to pretend to have activities and lectures on the side. With the exception of the headliner guests, everyone else is filler: if you've just sold your first short story to *Analog*, nobody really cares. This isn't cynicism: this is reality. Even if you've been writing for years, the odds that anyone has read any of your work are passing slim in a genre community where nothing gets promoted and people only read magazines to get contact information for story submission. Attending a big media con, especially one with a major subtext such as a particular TV show but that makes room for authors, is a waste of time. The dream of showing up to be greeted and feted by convention staff and fans gets crushed within minutes of finding yourself in an empty panel room because too many of the attendees suffer from Attention Deficit Disorder to spend any time watching and listening to someone they don't know read from a book or story they haven't read. And these are under the best of circumstances: just wait until straight con staff incompetence sends you to one panel room and the schedule sends your potential fans to another.

(TRUE STORY THE SECOND: Shortly after the first TRUE STORY, I was scheduled to be a guest at a local con run by acquaintances and staffed by a few friends. Being the sort of writer who didn't pass up the opportunity to promote his work, I volunteered to show up and pass out lots of copies of a magazine for which I was writing a column at the time. Months and months before, I'd passed on my biography information and suggestions for programming, and only discovered on the Friday night of the convention that my bio information, as well as that from almost all of the guests, had disappeared from the program guide. Y'see, the person who normally laid out and edited the program guide for this con had other things to do at the time, so the con chairperson went looking for someone else who could lay out the program guide for the proper price: free. She finally found someone willing to lay it out for free, but the job was so incompetently done that the center of the book, the guest biographies, never made it to the printer. Lots and lots of fan art drawn by the con staff made it to the program, but it wasn't like the attendees were paying for that guide solely for that bad fan art.

(This was also the convention where most of the guests weren't listed in the actual programming schedule, and when this was brought up, said guests were told "Oh, don't worry: just look for a panel that you'd like and crash it." Since the local guests got a poverty sob story about why the convention couldn't afford hotel rooms for the guests, those who made the mistake of commuting from home to the con hotel found that the hotel had a tiny fraction of the parking necessary for a hotel that size, and I for one gave up after circling the parking garage for an hour in search of a space. After all of this, the con chair still can't believe that I'd sooner eat broken glass than show up to any of her shindigs any more.)

In any of these cases, the writers are the ones who get it in the butt, over and over again. The writers are the ones who get panels opposite Opening Ceremonies, or opposite the standing-room-only appearance of the big media guest. The writers are the ones whose biographies magically disappear from the program guide, along with the locations of their events and activities. The media guests don't show up until the check clears, and they sure as hell don't have the con staff pull fast ones about paying for the hotel room, so the writer guests are the ones who come down to the hotel front desk when the convention is done and find that the con chairperson said that the writers were covering the costs of their hotel rooms. (Don't laugh: it's happened to me at least once.) The writers are the ones who get invited to conventions that may or may not happen, with lots of whining along the lines of "Oh, we'd love to have you here, but we can't afford to pay your way, but we'll have plenty of things for you to do if you show up...," only to discover that the whole con was just that. Finally, if any writer finally blows up from the poor treatment, the Internet is full of stories about how he or she "doesn't play well with others." Let us never mind that the second-list writers aren't really wanted around, because they get in the way of the conventioneers and con staff being able to schmooze with the guests of honor.

Truth be told, there's one panel at just about every convention around where writers will be welcomed: the obligatory "How To Get Published" panel. The problem is that the attendees don't want to hear the problems and issues with being a professional writer at a time when it's harder to sell books and short stories than ever before. No, all they want are shiny happy people stories about how editors are just waiting to pay six-figure advances for first novels or five-figure sums for short stories through online magazines. They're waiting to find out the magic codephrase that'll allow them to get "in" at *Realms of Fantasy* or discover which editors are willing to exchange a few rounds of "Dick Puppet Theater" for publication of a three-part novella. They don't give a fart in a high wind about the authors behind the table if the subject goes elsewhere, and many will go from petulant to violent if those authors don't feed their delusions of lifetime ease from strife and toil the moment they sell their first story.

Considering all of this, keep in mind the guides above. If having snorting fanboys with poor hygiene and worse haircuts is your idea of a vacation, go to that next convention with all my love. However, if you're expecting to accomplish something other than wander a dealer's room for three days, take the money that you planned to spend on the convention and run it through a tree mulcher. You'll get as much satisfaction and a lot less aggravation.

—*Previously unpublished*

Postscript: For various unguessable reasons, this column never appeared in the venue for which it was intended, and considering how my life was going straight to hell at that point, I didn't push the issue.

"The Truth, The Horrible Truth, About The Lives of Writers"

When established writers are first asked by potential writers about the process of writing, the pros tend to be nice. Daring not to wound the darlings' little sensibilities, they spin tales of what to do with manuscripts and what to do with editors, trying not to discourage the beginners but also trying to warn the beginners about the ordeal of being a writer. The emphasis is on encouragement, though: after all, we don't dare tell a beginner that s/he may not have that strange spark that makes an entertaining writer. It'll hurt the little dear's self-esteem.

Well, bollocks on that.

Here's the simple fact of life: most of the characters who believe that they could become writers should be discouraged. Hell, they should be horsewhipped, but that's another tale. I am, of course, talking about the twits who look at writing as an alternative to working a real job; the dingleberries who pass on those great tales about how writers make that proverbial $37.50 an hour. We're talking about the dolts who spend their time prattling about editors and publishers, but amazingly never get around to writing anything. These are the ones who bellow at the top of their lungs about how everybody has a story in them, but forget that (a) that story might not be worth preserving on paper and (b) the story might be worth something, but its promoter probably won't do it justice.

The myth of the writer, as opposed to the sad, pathetic reality, is one of book tours and TV interviews, of turning a few inspirations into a never-ending well of gold. Never mind that a real writer would never sell that line of crap; that's the impression. The reality is a lot more somber for the wannabes: being a writer usually means putting in a full forty hours a week on a soulkilling job before turning around and putting in another forty hours (or more) on a novel or essay. It means having to kick family and friends out of the house in order to satisfy the muse. It means getting laid off from jobs the moment the boss discovers that you have a master on the side, and that the boss isn't absolutely necessary. It means having to make a circle of friends who understand that you only have so many hours in the week for your one true love, or else having no friends at all. It means being ridiculed by complete strangers, abandoned by lovers and family, and having to wonder if the effort was worth all of the pain.

If I make writing sound more like an addiction to opium rather than a career, that's the intended effect. Writing is an evil, filthy, horrible, insidious habit: if you thought smoking was hard to quit, just try to quit writing if you've been hooked.

Last year, I quit writing and went back in three weeks; I quit drinking twelve years ago and haven't had more than a beer or two since.

Now, I've been writing in something approximating a professional attitude for nearly ten years, and I've learned something about the process. More importantly, I've learned a little about attitudes, and this essay is intended to correct what you, the reader, may believe about the nobility of writing. Read all the way through: we will have a test afterwards.

For the sake of this essay, I'm going to talk about writing science fiction. Part of this is because I'm familiar with writing SF; part of it is because SF is the only genre remaining where one could sell short stories and get them published. (Unless specifically noted, what I have to say also applies to fantasy and horror; unlike, say, mysteries, Westerns, and children's stories, the supergenre of SF/fantasy/horror is the only literary genre where more than one or two magazines still exist.) The upcoming advice still applies elsewhere, but seeing as how the vast majority of beginning writers I see are ones who want to break into science fiction, it's a good start.

By the way, all of this applies to that alleged great break all writers are supposed to get sooner or later in their careers. All of this advice could also apply to musicians and artists, or anyone with a creative bent, but beginning writers are the worst offenders. Uncle Zonker's Three Laws of Writing are simple: *You Ain't Gonna Get Rich*, *You Ain't Gonna Get Famous*, and *You Ain't Gonna Get Laid*.

The first law, You Ain't Gonna Get Rich, is self-explanatory. Wannabe writers assume that writing is a great get-rich-quick scheme; after all, all you have to do is put words to paper and checks come in the mail, right? This is the reason writers find themselves attacked at parties and at work with that old horse chestnut of "I have this great idea: you write it up, and I'll split the money with you." (My usual response is a variation of a comment made by David Gerrold: I usually look the character right in the eye and respond "I have this great cesspool: you turn it into a Jacuzzi by licking it clean, and maybe I'll let you swim in it.")

Well, it's possible to make money using a variation of this plot: it's called ghostwriting, but the ghostwriter or collaborator gets paid up front. (Anyone who waits to get that cut is known as a "goddamn fool" or a "fucking moron" by anyone who knows better.) For everyone else, writing pays nearly nothing.

One of the great lies told by nonwriters about writing is that an average writer makes an average of $37.50 an hour. Compared to making $7 an hour at the average office position, this sounds like great money. Let's dissect it, though. Assuming that a writer could get enough assignments to remain in a forty-hour week, 52 weeks a year, with no time for research or reading or rest, which comes to a grand total of $78,000 a year. This money is possible, if you've been writing for years and you never get any rejections. In reality, though...

Again, let's take a look at science fiction. The average magazines pay from seven to 15 cents a word, with an average short story running about 4500 words in length. *Science Fiction Age*, for instance, pays an average of ten cents a word; that means that an average story offers a full paycheck of $450. Sounds good, right? Well, discounting the fact that you're competing with literally thousands of other beginning writers for space, the fact that the average SF magazine has space for maybe five stories per issue, and the fact that only the most incredible writers stand a chance of getting more than one story a year published in any given magazine, that $450 might be all of the money you pull in over a given year. Writing may pay after a while, but not right away.

Okay, so you assume that you'll skip out on writing short stories: all the money is in writing novels, right? Well, it is if you're already established, and people will crawl through broken glass to buy one of your books. Almost every book publisher that handles science fiction pays a whole $5000 per novel for a first-timer: if everything you write turns to gold and disappears from the shelves, you might be able to make that $37.50 goal...if you write a full novel once every three weeks.

To consider that goal, let's look at it this way. The average novel runs about 350 pages. Someone as prolific as Stephen King still only gets about six pages a day on average: on a good day, I might get nine pages a day, but that's also usually a week's output. (Of course, I usually write nonfiction, which has completely different requirements than fiction.) Let's assume that you're as fast as Stephen King: making that 350-page count would take you just short of 60 days, assuming that what you've put to paper is any good. A more realistic goal is about six months per novel, which, assuming that you're able to sell your novels, means an annual income of $10,000. That's below the poverty level.

The main fallacy of writing as revenue generator is that you'll constantly produce material that will sell, from the moment you start. In his book *Stalking the Wild Asparagus*, Euell Gibbons pointed out that those who wish to collect wild-grown food must go into it with a love for it: those who look at wild gathering solely as a means to save on the grocery bill will end up with a foul-tasting mess that satisfies half of their hunger. Writing (or guitar playing, or blacksmithing, or computer programming) is best done by those who look at it with love, instead of merely a way to collect a paycheck. Trust me: if you don't love writing, it'll show.

To sum up, when people ask me what they should do if they want to become writers, I say "Don't quit your day job." This isn't a smartass quip: I'm deadly serious. Regardless of what *Writer's Digest* may tell you, quitting your job the first time you sell something to write full-time is a guaranteed method of dying of starvation underneath a highway overpass, unless you have a considerable inheritance stashed away somewhere. Forty years ago, it was possible to make a passable living from freelance writing after a year or so; nowadays, unless you have the connections to get past the slush piles, you'll be lucky to make enough to cover a dinner and a movie every month.

All right, so writing doesn't pay. That might be reasonable, but you're writing for the publicity. You want to be invited to speak at college lectures; you want to appear on David Letterman or *Politically Incorrect*; you want to stand on a podium and hear crowds stretching toward the horizon chanting your name. In short, you want the fame normally attributed to rock stars and/or Charles Manson.

Well, good luck. For the most part, if you had the charisma or the self-confidence to gain that kind of adulation, you wouldn't be writing. Unlike music, politics, or business, writing doesn't require contact from the general public. A writer doesn't have to perform on cue for his/her audience, and that's exactly the talent that this sort of fame requires. It's especially important to consider this as a first-time writer: sitting around waiting for Jay Leno's crew to call, just because you sold a short story to some little magazine that pays two cents a word, is going to get lonely after the first year or so, and calling them to ask about a booking will usually get a response of laughter, unless you have some sort of gimmick.

Let's put it another way. A very dear friend of mine is one of my favorite writers, and I have yet to see him put out any work that wasn't his absolute best. The man's a bloody genius, and yet he has one thing that keeps him from taking over the literary community: he has a slight speech impediment. I've watched him do readings at science fiction conventions, and it breaks my heart to watch an audience trickle out because they can't get past his stammer. If not for that attitude from listeners, I'm certain that he'd have to turn away people from admission-only readings nearly anywhere.

Audiences are notoriously fickle beasts, and getting those TV and radio interviews you crave so much require a completely new set of skills than those used by a writer. A typical audience expects a dancing bear routine: lose its attention for one minute, and its members scurry out on little rat feet and disappear into the night. Harlan Ellison gets invited back to *Politically Incorrect* and *The Late Show* because he's a fascinating conversationalist and tireless agent provocateur; Hunter S. Thompson got on *Late Night With Conan O'Brien* in '97 because he wanted to blow up things with his personal arsenal on national TV. None of 'em, nor any writer you could mention, was asked "Read some of your recent work for us, please." Unless you also worked as a public speaker or standup comedian at some time in your life, most radio and TV talk shows don't have much of an incentive to invite you to speak.

Garnering publicity is much like going to a job interview: you have to promote yourself constantly if anyone will remember you, which is something that constantly flusters wannabes who assume that promotion is beneath them. On the other hand, excessive promotion can blow up in your face: the main reason why Kristine Kathryn Rusch receives so much derision in the science fiction industry isn't due to her being a bad writer, but instead mostly because her picture kept appearing over and over in trade magazines such as *Locus*. Had those pictures been connected to legitimate events, it wouldn't have been a problem, but when those photos were showing off her new softball uniform, for instance, it got to be a bit much.

(Of course, I can say all this because I've been lucky enough to do one morning rush-hour radio show interview and one college lecture. Ooh, ain't I hoity-toity.)

Besides, are you sure that you really want people to see or hear you? One of the best advantages to being a writer is that nobody has to see or hear you: the sort of fame you're demanding requires a face and a voice to go along with the printed words. I've seen fans of one particular writer literally scream and run out of the room because their impression of their hero was destroyed by actually laying eyes on him; I have a voice that Fran Drescher finds nasal and annoying, so the folks who come to my readings usually leave when their seeing-eye dogs drag them out.

Which leads us to the tertiary lobe of this essay: the likelihood of getting laid because of your writerly talents. In response, let me drop a few comments from two disparate sources.

Back in 1993, when his book *Virtual Light* came out, a reporter from *USA Today* asked William Gibson if he got any groupies thanks to his books. Gibson said (and I paraphrase, not having the interview directly underneath my nose at the moment) "Oh, yes, can you imagine some blonde in a teddy in the middle of the night, saying to herself 'I'm lonely; why don't I call some middle-aged, married science fiction writer?'" Nine years before, when Dee Snyder's band Twisted Sister was more than a trivia question, a different reporter (we hope) asked Snyder about groupies, and he said "They weren't interested in me before I was famous, so why should I go after them now?"

Trust me (and this isn't bitterness talking), writers don't get crowds of screaming groupies following them everywhere, especially when they're first starting out. You WON'T get a multitude of readers wondering "Gee, I like this person's writing; I wonder what they're like in bed?" after your first short story gets published. I should amend that: you might, but are these the sort of people you want to sleep with in the first place?

Some of the people reading this essay are going to get all huffy and puffy, as I've just destroyed most of your illusions. All I can say is "Good." A few others will decide to give up on writing as a career: if you want fame, riches, and sexual partners of your choice, go start a band and stay the hell out of writing. A few, though, will get angry at my presumption of their motivations, and decide to show me one. These are the hope of literature.

Writing isn't easy, nor is it glamorous: it's almost literally painful. Writing fiction requires the author to pull out big bloody chunks of his/her psyche and shape them into something presentable to the public at large, and that's not a job for the typical computer programmer or waitress who assumes that coming up with an idea is all it takes to become successful. A successful writer is one who can get past the distractions, bypass the self-doubt, and still put ideas, characters, and situations onto paper in a form that might interest others. These are the people whom, when they receive rejections, don't scream about conspiracies to keep their work from publication but ask themselves "What could I do to make this better?," and throw out work when they realize that the characters or motivations have fatal flaws. Considering the ease of telling everyone within the immediate vicinity that "I'm a writer" without ever having to write anything, the real writer is the one who writes first and gets accolades as they're earned.

Now, this essay won't discourage a single wannabe writer: as with music, art, and business, the capacity for self-delusion is infinite. However, for those who really want to become writers, maybe this will piss you off to the point where you try to prove me wrong. That was the point, and I hope I succeeded.

—*Ellison Webderland, October 1998*

Postscript: This was a guest rant on Harlan Ellison's Web site Ellison Webderland, where Webmaster Rick Wyatt invited me to submit a tirade about anything that struck my fancy. As might be told, I was having a really bad month at the time.

"The Psychic Editor And Other Horrors"

Being asked on a regular basis for advice on being a writer is sometimes an exercise in patience. For every person who wants to write because s/he is compelled to do so, I deal with twenty wannabes who don't know what they want to write, have no knowledge of any subject besides advanced alcohol poisoning and masturbation, and spend their time spending the massive royalty checks they assume they'll make once they sell their romance novel, *Star Trek* novel, or computer manual. They're not the ones that worry me, mostly because as soon as they discover that writing is hard work, they usually scurry back to more profitable ventures, such as playing the Lotto. The ones that always worry me are the ones that peer up with dewy innocence and ask "So how do I keep editors from stealing my ideas?"

Dear child, I always say, editors have better things to do than steal your ideas, because more often than not, your ideas aren't worth stealing. That is, the miniscule amount of cash to be made from selling a short story or article isn't worth the legal expense of a charge of plagiarism. That's not to say that it won't happen: certain movie magazines are notorious for listening to freelancers pitch article ideas and then assigning those articles to staffers so as not to have to pay any more than the staffer's salary. Even then, though, this is minor: any writer worth his or her word processor could make ten pitches a day based on vague ideas that come up during breakfast. The real expenditure of energy comes from the actual writing, not the concept generation.

What beginning writers should worry about instead of idea theft is time theft. The real frustration to an established writer doesn't come from his/her ideas misappropriated by others; it comes from busting tail for days on a story or article, only to find it mangled by the rewrites of an idiot editor. Better yet, to work for days to make a particularly tight deadline, only to discover that the story isn't in the new issue and nobody has any idea if and when it'll appear. Still better, to discover that the editor/publisher decided to shut down the publication or move it to another format (print to Web, for instance) with no mention of a new release date. For those of us who work on spec, we're lucky if we get a kill fee: instead, we're stuck with an article or story that can't be sold anywhere else, or that will be painfully obsolete by the time it finds a sympathetic market.

Conventional logic holds that all writers are by necessity prostitutes, but we're the only whores willing to work on IOUs. Because of the logistics of the publishing industry, we have no choice but to trust the editor at the other end of the phone or E-mail connection, and trust that we've received all of the information we needed when starting an article in the first place. Most editors are good people (let me repeat that: Most Editors Are Good People) (Repeat again: MOST EDITORS ARE GOOD PEOPLE), but the dolts and greedheads are the ones that make most writers want to quit the business and make a living by herding cats. Cat-herding is less work and more emotionally satisfying.

(Not that we writers are any better: I know plenty of editors who want to kill writers, with some justification. Nothing quite like having a writer miss a critical deadline because he was too busy taste-testing the strippers at the local Lapdance Emporium, eh?)

Bad editors come in all sorts of breeds, such as The Mole (who pretends to be buddy-buddy with writers, only to take pains to screw them over), The Slug (who makes all decisions with the speed and grace of a curare-addicted sloth), The Mute (who amazingly can never be reached, especially when payment checks are due), King Log (who always blames the writers for his/her mistakes), and The Brat (who threatens to "destroy" a writer's career if the writer doesn't eat the tasty shit sandwich the editor just served up). The worst, the most aggravating, and the most wasteful of the species, though, is the Psychic Editor. Apparently hailing from a planet where everyone is born with innate telepathy, they have serious problems with any writer who can't read their thoughts at any given moment. These characters usually became editors because they went to college and/or slept with the publisher, so the concept of burning hour upon hour on rewrites and revisions is completely alien to them.

The conversation usually goes like this: Writer calls up Editor and pitches story idea. Editor keeps mumbling "Mmmm-hmm" over the phone, and gives the okay to do the story. Writer rushes to the writing implement and manages, against colossal odds, to finish the story before deadline. Writer rushes to the editor with the manuscript, and after Editor reads it, Writer asks "So what do you think?"

Editor: "This isn't what I wanted."

Writer: "I gave you everything you asked for."

Editor: "Yeah, but this isn't what I wanted."

Writer: "So what do you want?"

Editor: "I don't know, but I don't want this."

This happy dance usually continues until Writer gives up in disgust, where Editor usually transforms into The Brat and swears that Writer will never work for another publication again. If Writer concedes to Editor, Editor sends out psychic vibrations warning Writer that "Hey, my girlfriend's article just got precedence, so we're chopping down your article from 3000 words to 250 words. Hope you don't mind." Of course not, so long as Writer gets paid for the 3000 words instead of the 250. In real life, this never happens, and Editor has the nerve to look surprised when Writer goes ballistic.

So my advice to beginning writers? Better to work for free for an editor who respects writers and their work than get paid to work for a budding young sociopath. Also, beware of trying to treat or cure a Psychic Editor: since the best cures involve baseball bats, cigar trimmers, and Claymore mines fitted rectally, be sure to check with local laws before attempting. If you're lucky, the cops will want to help.

—Spark Online, April 2000

General Culture

Because of my masterly grasp of popular media, I was also asked quite often to comment about the rest of popular culture, and I was certainly willing to accommodate those editors and readers, so long as the checks cleared. It's not bad work if you can get it, and so long as you're willing to get out of the house to experience that culture. My ex-wife also did wonders to encourage me to get out of the house and not spend the entire day watching Buffy marathons on television, but that's because I really didn't want to live by her example.

"Generation X: Wankers by the Wayside"

After the death of Kurt Cobain, the mainstream press went into overdrive over the so-called "Generation X": the generation born to the baby boomers; the demographic group now in their early to late twenties; the gaggle of young adults who can't remember a time when *Star Trek* wasn't on a television somewhere and who skipped out of junior high to watch the first few hours of eMpTyV. If *Time* and *Newsweek* are to be trusted, this generation has its own definitive musical style, clothing taste, and sociological outlook. If we trust most magazines, newspapers, and talk show hosts, the only difference between the hippies of the Sixties and the Xers is that the Xers have more cynicism and more computer literacy. The unspoken hope is that the Xers will go where their hippie parents failed and make everything work right after all.

Bullshit. I have only a few regrets about Cobain's death, and that's before he wasted himself, he should have taken out Pearl Jam, Soundgarden, and Stone Temple Fuckups. (I also wish that he'd blown away Courtney Love: I'd much prefer her to be remembered as the Nancy Spungen of grunge than the Yoko Ono.) The final act before giving that blow job to his trusty 12-gauge should have been to exterminate every twentysomething fool who thought that his music would actually accomplish something besides making record company executives rich by exploiting young angst.

As usual, by the time the mainstream press gets to anything, the original drive and moment of any given movement wafts away in the wind, leaving a gaggle of fashion casualties and general poseurs all too willing to tell reporters any sort of bullshit so long as they get listed as some all-knowing expert. *Time* didn't cover the hippie movement until 1967 and the cyberpunk movement until 1992, by which time the real practitioners had moved on to better things, and the only people left were those who wanted to make a buck by trying to convince suburban kids that this was the real happening thing. People like R.U. Sirius have not the slightest fucking idea what's really going on out there in the real world; they make oodles by selling their bullshit through magazines such as *Wired* and *Mondo 2000* to impressionable zombies who think that the only way to be *avant garde* is to wear flannel and surfing jams while trying to hook one's brain to a computer system.

This is the problem: everyone wants to be different without being too different. Boomers like to claim that they were hippies. Most of the time, they were spoiled little rich kids who wore tie-dye because it freaked out their parents, or they were skinny-tie mail clerks who claimed to be pot smokers after it became cool to do so. A good ninety-nine percent of the people who claim to be hippies never were. Since they know nobody will check up on them, they'll hitch a ride on whatever tired nostalgia trip happens to be going through at the moment, especially when time has rendered the movement harmless. If all of these people were hippies back then, or they supported the hippie movement, then why did Nixon become president in 1968 and 1972?

The situation is the same for the punk movement. If I had a nickel for every snot-nosed twerp who claimed to have caught the Sex Pistols when they played the Longhorn Ballroom in 1978, I wouldn't have to work a real job to pay the rent. Never mind that most of these people were either campaigning for Reagan or just starting to feel the twinges of puberty at the time. (Hell, I was twelve when they showed up in Dallas, and I get hit with this pearl of crap by 18-year-olds, to whom I respond "So how did you get in? Your babysitter take you?") Now that *Never Mind the Bollocks* has gone platinum, it's horribly *avant* to brag about how Johnny Rotten spat in their faces. The only way to burst their bubbles is to ask them if they had any witnesses.

Now it's happening with the GenX crowd. Admittedly, the Seattle scene had something about five years ago, but that was before Nirvana signed with a major label. Right now, the city is awash with sleazy agents, all looking for the next big act, and the walking wounded from across the nation, all seeing some reason for their worthless existence. All over the country, wannabes hook into the urge to rebel yet belong by wearing flannel (hopelessly counterproductive in, say, Dallas or Phoenix) and listening to worthless bands whose only digression in style from the Bee Gees or Phil Collins is that they call themselves "alternative."

That's the problem with rebellion nowadays: instead of copying the statements of the leaders of any movement, they copy the fashions. Look at the Nixon Youth, who wore tie-dyes and flared pants; the Reagan Youth, who wore black leather and torn jeans; and then look at the grungers who slap "Dan Quayle in '96" bumper stickers on the bottoms of their skateboards. In their way, they're the safest in any rebellion because they can go both ways: should the rebels win, they can parade around like pouter pigeons and tell everyone within shouting distance that they were in on it from the beginning. If the established forces win, then they just put their pinstripe suits and swastika armbands back on and go back to their jobs as junior business executives.

Real change comes from commitment and courage: no amount of clothing or music videos can change that. Anyone thinking that they can change the world by getting a tribal tattoo, wearing Doc Martens, and getting stoned on bad weed while watching the latest *MTV UnPlugged* special is just blowing clove smoke up their asses. Just put the muzzle of the shotgun in your mouth, and thank you for calling.

—*Chaos, Summer 1994*

Postscript: Nearly fifteen years later, there are few more pathetic things than former grunge babies turned dysfunctional parents and grandparents. Sid Vicious has been dead for 30 years, and Kurt Cobain for half that time, and yet these twits somehow think "the scene" is going to come back to rescue them.

"And Now A Word About Spooky Uncles and Aunts"

One of the basic tenets to "Spooky Parenting 101" is that one can be both a good parent and a free spirit, without compromising either lifestyle or children. However, many readers may find themselves reaching middle age and beyond without having children at all. This should never be considered a slight; if anything, many darklings make much better aunts and uncles instead of parents.

A very lucky few have aunts and uncles who have more in common with them than they do with their parents, especially with parents who happen to be obsessed with success or with anything besides child-rearing. Anyone raised in a similar situation has an obligation to follow their inspiration: most kids have very few role-models outside of sports or television, and connecting with real people leaves them much better suited for civilized life than the kids raised by Monday Night Football and *Animaniacs*. Although the risk of being accused of "corrupting" kids is real, especially when dealing with yuppie siblings who don't want their children to take after their goth uncle or aunt, the thrill of saving a nephew or niece from a life of insurance sales or house-husbanding will triple the first time a relative dedicates a book or song to you for making a difference.

The first secret to being a spooky uncle or aunt is to remember that you never really grew up in the first place. Grown-ups (and by using this word, I mean those who decided to leave dreams and wishes behind to become what everyone wanted them to be, rather than what they wanted to become) usually can't grasp that children grow up sooner or later, and tend to treat their kids as if they're perpetually five years old. Make a point of treating nephews and nieces as contemporaries, and they'll remember the compliment. This also means laying off the tales of what the old days were like unless specifically asked about it: if you're old enough to remember when the Sex Pistols played the Biltmore and lucky enough to have seen them, tell your nephew all about it, but not as part of one of those "When I was your age..." tales. He's probably heard all he wants to hear from his parents, and hearing them from a potentially respectable relative will bore him even faster.

The second secret is to listen and act upon the knowledge gained by doing so. Parents are notorious for neglecting to listen to their children, so remembering that your niece wanted a microscope set for her birthday will make an impression when her parents bought her yet another tea set. My eldest niece is a palaeontology nut like her uncle, so she has the opportunity to show off the best dinosaur models and books to classmates, as opposed to getting underwear and socks.

With that in mind, science is probably the best way to turn the imagination of a youngster, so long as you catch 'em early. Once your nephew has joined the football team or your niece the cheerleading squad, it'll be nearly impossible to make them decent people, so start when they're young. Dinosaurs are a great start: someone who starts with fossil bones at the age of fine won't see anything particularly morbid about bones, human or otherwise, when they're older. Start a kid out with some of those snap-together dinosaur skeleton kits (the ones that come complete inside their own egg), and it just may convince him/her to make Turner Van Blarcum bone sculptures by the time the kid's 18. Giving a nephew or niece a gift certificate to the Edmund Scientific catalogue is a good start: even if the kid never gains an appreciation for your lifestyle, it should keep the poor child away from a life as an MBA.

Science toys work well with younger kids, but it's those lovely teenage years where your siblings' children need some sort of mentor. We all remember those days, where we weren't sure about anything but had to put that clichéd best face forward and pretend we knew what we were doing. Nobody at that age ever listens to their parents (except those already programmed not to think on their own, and the only mercy you can give these is a bullet in the head), but they have no problem listening to a relative. Better yet, they'll listen to any relative who doesn't pinch their cheeks and bore them with stories about the old country.

It's at those teenage years that you'll be able to spot whether your nephew or niece takes after you or his/her parents. Remember that a basic urge of adolescence is to rebel against everything a parent stands for, which explains why so many of my generation became supporters of Newt Gingrich and Phil Gramm. In turn, their scions will rebel the only way they know how: either by becoming deadheads, or by going dark. Really dark.

Any number of activities will permanently destroy their sense of conformity, but all of these require spending time with the nephew or niece of your choice. They generally don't work long-distance: you have no guarantee that the catalog or gift you just sent will get through to them, especially if your sibling is a control freak. Take the kid out for a ride, or invite them to stay with you for spring break, and they'll usually never be the same again.

A good way to start is with movies. Stay the hell away from the usual blockbusters: take 'em out to see something at the local repertory cinema, if one is available in your neighborhood. If not, the video store is always an option: I've found in my experience that anything by Terry Gilliam or Tim Burton (with the exception of *Batman*) is a good start for younger ones, while *Alien*, *The Fly*, and (believe it or not) Kenneth Branagh's *Henry V* have incredible results. The idea here is to teach that just because something is different doesn't automatically mean it's evil: *Henry V* also works on all of the little budding warmongers by demonstrating that (a) foreign films aren't necessarily boring, and (b) contrary to the popular opinion expressed by Renaissance Faires, the Middle Ages were pretty godawful.

Use discretion with movies: the last thing you want is a catatonic nephew on your hands after a viewing of *Fear and Loathing In Las Vegas*. However, if the kid bawls his/her eyes out at the end of *Alien*, when the only interesting character in the film besides the cat gets blown out the airlock, you definitely have an incipient darkling on your hands.

Books and music are another possibility, but make sure you know your nephew/niece first before making a run on the local bookstore. My godfather used to love buying me books on the Dallas Cowboys, never realizing that I loathed football, and you aren't doing your niece any favors by sending her stuff she'll never read and then guilt-trip her because she hasn't cracked the spine yet. Start out easy: if your nephew likes art books, start with an Edward Gorey or Gahan Wilson collection and then work toward H.R. Giger. If your niece enjoys mellow music, start with a bit of Siouxsie and the Banshees and *then* move to the Unit:187. Take your time, and don't push. Better yet, take 'em both out to the local bookstore or record shop and let them make informed decisions. Instead of having their parents underfoot, disapproving of their purchases, they'll have a like-minded aunt or uncle suggesting "Hey, if you like that, you'll love this..." Give them your accumulated wisdom, but don't push it on them.

(By the way, if your nephew/niece is already hooked on commercial stuff, use that to best advantage. It's really not all that hard to wean a regular *Goosebumps* reader into Poe or Lovecraft, and a kid predisposed to Marilyn Manson has the opportunity to appreciate the good stuff in music as well.)

Another thing to remember is that the average teen grows like the proverbial *Cannabis* plant, so clothes runs also help. Trips to Goodwill and rummage sales help convince kids that just because it isn't new doesn't mean it's bad, and one can never start frugal habits too soon. Alternately, letting your young charge choose his/her clothes at your favorite gothic clothes store works wonders, especially when s/he knows that Mom and Dad would never allow those clothes in the house so long as they still draw breath. The same is true for jewelry, makeup, and hair products: if they're going to rebel against the ready-fabricated fashions available at school, at least show them that they can do so with style.

Due to space constraints, this can't be an all-inclusive listing of everything one can do to turn an unassuming nephew or niece into a fellow traveler of dark domains, but it's a bare start. The main point to remember is to listen to your younger relative: when s/he asks "Aunt Whatzit, how did you get your nails so long?," the kid usually isn't being a smartaleck. Give 'em a little encouragement, and you've probably saved another member of your family from a life in the insurance industry or the Air Force.

—*Carpe Noctem, Spring 1999*

Postscript: Out of all of the magazines I've worked for over the years, only a few have provided, with their passing, more regret than Carpe Noctem. *The publishers had no choice but to declare bankruptcy in 2001 due to a screw job from Barnes & Noble, and while I wasn't overly thrilled with some of the publishers' business practices, I still miss seeing the magazine on the shelf.*

"Preparing For the Future And Terrifying The Help"

With the return of cooler temperatures in the Northern Hemisphere, students return to centers of higher learning. Many emulate the monarch butterfly (leave the birthplace, breed, and die), but others stand a chance of accomplishing a bit more. At the same time, any number of publications offer basic guides to student living, in the hopes that some of the little darlings remember that their parents pay for them to do something besides parade around Padre Island or Fort Lauderdale during spring break in a thong. Not only is this easy work for the author, but they're reassuring for parents. None of 'em teach anything the students can use.

Guiding freshmen and sophomores away from stupid or self-destructive mistakes is a cottage industry: sooner or later, someone will write a *College for Dummies* book that includes fifty recipes utilizing ramen noodles and 100 ways to scam free phone calls back home. Invariably, this guide will never include the real concerns about campus living, such as the fact that those sales reps offering "guaranteed" credit card applications Are Not Your Friends. (Your credit history is the closest thing to a "permanent record" you'll ever see: default on a student loan, and you only lose out on your income tax refund check for the next fifteen years. Default on $60,000 of credit card debt, and you've resigned yourself to apartment living for the next decade.) The same thing goes for get-rich-quick schemes: the frat boys down the street may have managed to clear thousands of dollars in fraudulent tax refunds, but they will get caught, especially since they signed their real names and addresses to the tax returns. Most importantly, any "Dummies" guide will never impart the real wisdom of a college career, if only because misery loves company.

This is the lesson all college freshmen need to learn: Business, journalism, and English degrees are not real degrees. Contrary to what high school guidance counselors may say, a diploma for a BA in English guarantees success as a writer in the same way a videotape of *Armageddon* imparts knowledge of astrophysics or engineering. This is not a degree: this is a license to starve to death with the blessings of society. As much as I love my mother tongue, I have to advocate the clichéd Ph.D in basket-weaving before any English degree, if only because a few cattail fronds and some studiousness offers possibilities for enterprising streetcorner vendors. What choice does an unemployed English major have: standing around red-light districts with a sheaf of manuscripts in hand, whispering "Hey, meester: wanna buy a dirty story?"

Likewise, considering the impending heat-death of the newspaper as we know it, a journalism degree is recommended only because of a lack of federal subsidies for those wishing to drink themselves to death. More than any other business remaining today, journalism is dependent upon the Peter Principle: considering the lousy pay, the poor conditions, and the intolerable colleagues, the only people who make a career of journalism are those too incompetent to better the world with a switch to food service, and move up the ranks as their more talented brethren get real jobs or commit suicide. Consider another vocation: journalists generally wish for siblings or spouses who specialize in kindergarten heroin deals or necrophilia so they have someone to look up to. Have pity upon the longtimers as well: the authors of most film, music, and political commentary columns not only whimper bitterly about how nobody born after 1950 reads newspapers any more, but how they didn't get the groupies their exposure promised. (Of the last we should be grateful: due to appearance if not personality, most journalists couldn't get laid in Tijuana with $100 bills stuck in their jockstraps.)

Finally, the Master of Business Administration, a triple oxymoron, has an interesting pedigree. Originally conceived so the scions of rich families could justify sending Junior and Muffy to college and guarantee that they'd come back with something besides a cocaine habit and syphilis, the business degree rapidly became the road to rapid wealth...of the deans of the innumerable business colleges infesting North America. As with journalism and English degrees, having a business degree guarantees no aptitude in the subject of study: most business courses are a basic attempt to impart common sense and basic job skills upon dolts with brains too saturated with Miller Genuine Draft to function in society any other way. In a way, we should be thankful for the business degree, as it keeps a multitude of otherwise unemployable australopithecines doing their best to keep Scott Adams and the makers of Rohypnol financially solvent. Unfortunately, though, they breed like rats, and their children continue the mantra of "I'll make $100,000 right out of college! I don't know how, but Daddy will think of something"

So where should the youth of today look for financial security and job satisfaction? Beats me: if I knew, I wouldn't be working in the telecommunications industry. Remember, the only two places where individuals get paid to masturbate in public are in the literary arena and the sex industry, and you don't have the build for a porn star. In the meantime, tell the children to pick a vocation that takes advantage of their aptitudes and their interests, and hope for the best. Choosing an art degree over a PoliSci degree may not offer more money, but it decreases the chances of being carried off and devoured by invisible demons in the night.

—Spark Online, October 1999

Postscript: Oh, this essay infuriated more than a few English majors, including my ex-wife, and considerably more English professors, but English grads tend to have a serious problem with self-esteem. After all, it's not nice to read something like that at the library when you're on your way back to your cardboard box underneath the highway overpass.

"Killing Millions With A Sharp Twist of the Tongue"

Today, everybody is a rebel. Correction: Everyone wants to be a rebel. Of course, we're talking about socially acceptable rebellion, which of course includes buying the right consumables, wearing the correct rebellious clothes, and spouting the correct rebellious phrases. Rebellion is cool, so long as it doesn't go too far.

Unfortunately, thanks to the omnipresent efforts of the television news, it's hard to find anything that shocks the general public any more. Fifty years ago, joining an obscure religion was enough to get disowned by the family, especially if the religion wasn't involved with Christianity, but the thrill of joining the Church of Satan or the Church of the SubGenius generally fades at about the age of 17. Right now, getting a Mohawk or piercings or a limb lopped off and replaced with prosthetics offers the appeal of playing with the thermostat in your first apartment: It's terribly thrilling to play around with that sort of freedom for the first time, but if the parents can't punish you for messing around any more, what's the point? Ten years ago, coming out of the closet was an incredibly brave and potentially dangerous act; today, to the detriment of those who put their lives on the line, seemingly half of the people I know who claim to be gay are just straights who want the extra attention.

Instead of messing with Mommy and Daddy's heads by starting a heroin habit or marrying a stripper (male or female, take your pick), try a different strategy. Nothing works quite so well to screw with society than to be courteous.

Try this as an example. With the current employment climate, the only people willing to work retail sales positions don't expect courtesy and they generally get none. The next time one of these characters screams "Whaddaya want?" across a store counter, respond in the most considerate tones possible. Use lots of "Pleases" and "Yes, sirs" and "No, ma'ams," and just listen for the gears in their heads stripping out. After years of hearing incessant howls of "Do you know who I am?," a single "Please take your time" throws off their entire routine. They can't help but move a little faster or refrain from spitting in your meal, because they have no excuse. Play it just right, and smoke starts pouring out their ears.

Here's one I learned from living in Portland, Oregon, a town full of some of the rudest and most inconsiderate people on the planet. Make a point of holding the door open for others. This gets a better response than using a flamethrower at a gas station. Grown adults are so used to others slamming doors and shoving their way in that they honestly don't know what to do. I've had people back up through open doors, facing me the whole time, because they were terrified that anyone holding a door for them was obviously going to shoot them in the back if they turned around.

The possibilities are endless with this tactic. Study the works of Oscar Wilde or Dorothy Parker and use wit to take down the rude and offensive. Wit is the true smart gun; only those familiar with its use can use it as a weapon, and most don't even have an adequate defense. Make a point of dressing up in stylish but classy clothes when reporting in to work. In an office where most of the managers show up in ratty Izods and shorts, nothing rattles them so much as showing up in a shirt and tie or a well-tailored dress. I know it's expensive, but it keeps everyone guessing that you're going to job interviews every day, and this can be a camouflage for the day you have that interview during your lunch break. When driving, make a point of letting people into your lane; when walking, stop to let others go by. Leave tips for good service, and always thank everyone, verbally or in letters. Be especially courteous with police. Between the usual abuse and toadying they receive, an eloquent and insightful conversation usually leaves them stunned, thus giving you an advantage when caught doing something inappropriate or illegal.

This is the true spirit of rebellion: Any dolt can be rude and offensive, and upgrading the level of offensiveness just breeds more people who don't understand the power of subtlety or restraint. ("Pull a phone prank on me, will you? Well, I'll crap on your front doorstep!") However, nothing rattles the slow and arrogant than someone who plays by different rules. Best of all, it's not something easily imitated by wannabes who pretend to be cool. Any idiot can dress up in a black leather jacket and motorcycle boots and walk into a four-star restaurant in this attire, but how many then go out of their way to turn a hostile waiter into a friend? Ibsen said it best: "To live is to war with trolls," and isn't it better to take on the little bastards on your own terms, with the one weapon they could never use?

—Spark Online, November 1999

"The Rats Have Left The Titanic"

With the end of October comes a collision with truth for many people. For high school students, this truth is that one can't depend upon being able to get out of school early on Fridays for pep rallies after football season ends. For college students, it's the realization that many of the assignations made during the early days of the semester were ill-advised at best, and that they'll have to continue sleeping with that teaching assistant if they expect to pass the semester. For those in the working world, it's that most magical time of the year, Layoff Season.

Not many can explain why so many large companies decide to cleanse their payrolls of the rank and file so close to the holidays, but the surmisals are legion. The obvious answer is that for most companies, the fiscal year starts on October 1, but the logic behind that date being chosen to start a company's financial calendar is chicken-and-the-egg reasoning. Others point out, with plenty of evidence, that stock prices jump whenever a company lays off thousands of employees, in the same way the value of a book jumps when its author commits suicide. Still others suggest that American business is so constructed that a manager cannot beat his/her children at Christmas and threaten to return their presents, but s/he takes it out on the employees. The last is the most likely: after all, by jettisoning the workers, a typical manager has more Christmas bonus money to blow on hair implants to replace the follicles burned away by bad cocaine in college.

Considering the number of companies that threaten employees with termination merely for discussing raises or benefits, as if it isn't plainly obvious that the only people receiving Christmas bonuses are the pet asskissers, the average toiler has few methods to use to ascertain an impending downsizing. After all, even the graduates of the Beavis and Butt-Head School of Business Management are catching on and closing their doors when discussing financial matters, if only to keep the crew from hearing the staccato chuckles of "Yeah! Yeah! Profits are cool! Employees suck!," to steal from cartoonist Tom Tomorrow. A little bit of studiousness, though, reveals future plans, allowing the opportunity to snag a new job and leave on better terms than what the MBAs intended.

Firstly, an absolute concerning layoffs is the flight of upper management. Some big high-tech companies, such as Texas Instruments, are notorious for promoting as many upper managers as possible to vice-presidential positions just days before a massive layoff. The reason they receive promotions is, of course, because their predecessors bail out and cash in their stock options before the price crashes. Those remaining behind receive ample compensation, though: between a generous golden parachute and job placement assistance, they're doing much better than the grunts down on the ground floor. After all, the new former VPs won't have to worry about from where they're getting the money for Christmas presents. When major members of the management staff, such as the CEO and CFO, decide to leave "to pursue other opportunities," collect all personal effects and get them out of the building before Security or the Feds claim them. This phrase generally translates to "they're getting ten-to-fifty for fraud or embezzlement, and they're going to take the rest of the company with them."

Another sign of a fiscal bloodletting comes from the loss of long-held perks, no matter how minor. Considering the obscene number of freebies given to employees at high-tech firms, their sudden or gradual disappearance should be taken as an immediate warning of evil on the horizon. The moment the on-site gym starts charging for towels or the ice machines disappear, start polishing up the resume, because it'll get plenty of work within the next month.

Contract workers are the lifeblood of most high-tech firms, considering that most will work like dogs for month or even years with the vague promise of becoming full-time employees. Most managers love contractors, seeing as how they're easily bullied and they often have no recourse in instances of sexual harassment or unsafe working conditions, and current US tax laws give more write-offs to those companies that use nothing but contractors than those who hire their own staff. With this in mind, the moment a company starts a wave of contract hiring, run do not walk to the nearest available position with a different company. Most of these contractors are hired to protect the jobs of those employees with more seniority, and many find themselves without any job at all within months of becoming a full-time staffer.

Any time a company finds itself assimilated by another, and the new parent company sends human resources reps to the site to tell all of the employees that "We respect you, and want you to be happy," get out immediately. Companies that assimilate smaller ones do so solely to replace the newcomers with their own people, as soon as the newcomers reveal the last secrets of the operation. With these companies, they love to wait until a week before Christmas before cutting everyone, guaranteeing that none of those laid off can find a job until the beginning of March.

Most importantly, one of the most ominous signs of an incipient layoff comes from the vending machines. Just watch the company stocking the soda and snack machines: if a new vendor comes onto the scene, followed by a drastic increase in the price of Fritos and Diet Coke, start calling up recruiting firms and ask them for any openings. Do this as soon as possible, so as not to compete with the thousands of fellow travelers left stranded in financial Coventry when they suddenly find that their keys no longer work in the company locks.

Even with all of these possible warnings, holiday layoffs are a distinctive possibility, so be prepared for the absolute worst this Christmas season. Save up enough ready cash to cover at least one month's rent, make sure to have plenty of spare copies of a good resume, and get a good map to the boss' house in advance. Beating the shit out of him with a baseball bat may not reverse unemployment, but everyone should have some reason to be festive on Christmas Eve.

—*NetSlaves.com, November 1999*

Postscript: I really, really, really wish that I didn't write this one from experience.

"Going Postal Under the Mistletoe"

Yes, it's the Christmas season. It's the goddamned Christmas season. It's the one time of year where everyone parrots that "Peace on Earth, good will toward men" crap while blasting away with a MAC-10 at the zombies at the shopping mall. Best of all, it's the time where embittered journalists either complain that everyone's forgotten The Reason for the Season (namely, to engage in drunken debauchery in the name of Saturn, Kali, or Quetzacoatl), or kvetch about the pointlessness of the whole holiday. In the former case, the whining is because nobody invited said journalist to the really good parties because s/he wanders around with a mouth tighter than a chicken's rectum; in the latter, it's because said journalist won't get what s/he really wanted, because most people don't think of a case of Scotch and a good buggering as a suitable Christmas present.

It must be said, however, that while the holiday season causes at least twice as many suicides as it prevents (especially upon the discovery of plans to let Aunt Edna, the relative who smells of cheese, stay with you until Groundhog's Day), it is possible to have fun during the Christmas season. All that's required is a modest budget, a bullshit meter with a hair trigger, and a loathing of hypocrisy as wide as a bus.

The first and easiest way to mess with the minds of your fellows is to go straight for the kids. Ever tire of the parents who feel compelled to take their children into toy stores at Christmas, and then tell them "No" over and over again until the kid starts crying? Just follow a few of these parents around, and then purchase a toy that the kid particularly wanted and wait near the exit. As the family starts to pass by, make a point of giving the child that toy and then leaving: this not only drives the parents berserk, because they can't really forbid a gift given with the best of intentions, but it teaches the kid that some strangers can be trusted. Either way, that family will never be the same.

We all have stories of parking lot madness at the mall. Yes, nobody really wants to park waaaaaay out in the boonies and then hike to the mall entrance via ski or dogsled, but the number of twits who feel that they're obligated to wait for someone to vacate a space keeps growing every year. The ones that merely block a whole lane, with the blinker signifying that that space is THEIRS, are bad enough, but the obnoxious yuppies who start honking if the subject of their displeasure should hesitate are a pimple on the arse of humanity. Seeing as how these are the same slobs who cut to the front of lines inside because "I'm in a hurry," a judicious dollop of justice is in order.

The perfect implementation of this stunt requires a parking space as close as possible to a mall entrance, preferably on a Saturday or Sunday afternoon, and a working car. Should you feel the urge to shop at a mall in that terrible period between the fourth Friday of November and December 24, please indulge yourself, or just simply go wandering around. The idea is to come back to the car periodically, to drop off packages or just to stretch your legs, and get inside. In a crowded situation, a long line immediately forms as idiots jockey for that space, so pull out a newspaper or a book and start reading. Every once in a while, look back at the ever-growing crowd and return to the paper. Should any yuppie start honking, imploring you to bestir thy ass so they can divest themselves of their ill-gotten gains, simply get out of the car, lock it up, and go back inside the mall, in full sight of the honker. The general facial expressions range from incredulity to rage (the more high-scale the mall, the greater the rage), but they're all absolutely priceless. Repeat as necessary, or until the frustration of fighting holiday crowds overtakes the satisfaction of teaching yuppies that they can't have everything they want.

If torturing business majors is too easy, a great way to relieve stress and appear on television is to watch for the inevitable news story about some religious group complaining because the local government won't let them set up a nativity scene on public property. Make a point of supporting their position in public...and then demand equal access for non-Christian religions. Generally, even the most fanatical Baptist will start shrieking "separation of church and state" if equal time for religion means having to share space with Wiccans, no matter how valid a case the Wiccans have, and a dedicated prankster could have real fun with supporting the rights of members of the Esoteric Order of Dagon to display their faith on public land. After staring at a 20-foot effigy of Nyarlathotep the Crawling Chaos hanging over the Baby Jesus, most fanatics will go out of their way to keep public areas secular areas.

And then there's the subject of parties. Most Christmas parties are insanely dull affairs, with everyone slumping around, sipping eggnog, and trying to fondle each other's spouses under the mistletoe. Offer an alternative for those deathly sick of Christmas carols and sleigh rides. Stock up on unorthodox chow and invite the neighbors and relatives over for a night of deranged videos. I usually find that serving barbecue and ribs during a screening of *Dawn of the Dead* works wonders for banishing the last of the Christmas spirit. Whatever runs, from *Naked Lunch* to *Meet the Feebles*, the movies and food will have the desired effect of causing people to care for each other because they want to, and not because of familial or religious guilt trips. Besides, it keeps minds off the idea of renting an anti-aircraft gun, putting it in the back yard or on the roof, and waiting for the first glimmer of Rudolph's shiny nose.

Any way you want to look at it, Christmas can be a bear, or it can be a blast. The trick to getting through the season is to keep remembering that Easter is just around the corner, when we all commemorate the day Christ rose from His grave, looked down at His shadow, and realized that He had to wait six more weeks until spring.

—Spark Online, December 1999

"Still Life With Browser"

In the last few months, economists have been going nuts with recent studies that show that the typical American worker, particularly those in the technical and office sectors, keeps getting more and more productive. After years of decline, suddenly the typical office grunt and programmer is reaching levels of efficiency previously only seen in Japanese car manufacturers, and nobody has an explanation for it. Increased layoffs and consolidation of core businesses don't seem to do much good, and the unemployment rate is still obscene for all of the noise made about how employers need fresh bodies, so it's not the fear of finding a new job in the middle of a depression. Everyone keeps pointing to the computer installed on every desk, but without knowing why.

We can thank Microsoft for this: by claiming that its Web browser is an integral part of the Windows operating system, Bill Gates and crew have managed to develop the first new model of morale motivator and efficiency developer since the invention of the cattle prod and the rectal pear. No matter the company, and no matter the environment, everyone who uses a computer made after 1995 generally has a Web browser on the desktop, and this beauty is responsible for the increase of office productivity.

Surely, you say, the boost in productivity is due to all of the great Web-based work solutions making the rounds? Maybe the addition of browser-run databases and corporate intranets has something to do with it? Nope and nope. Contrary to popular image, the typical American worker is a lazy and selfish brute, often too lazy to pull his or her pants down to take a crap, and the Web browser milks efficiency from that.

Considering a typical office environment, maybe only fifteen percent of the workforce actually does anything approximating gainful work in a typical 40-hour week. It takes energy to wake up after a typical previous evening of watching TV and snarfing Doritos, so the first two hours of the day are pretty much shot. After the first break in the morning, the day is dedicated to personal phone calls and hour-long potty breaks until lunch, which always needs time to digest. After a semi-siesta, it's time to do something to perpetuate the illusion of being a contributing member of the workforce, so a little bit of paper-shuffling appears before the afternoon break, and of course it's futile to expect anybody to do anything that close to quitting time. In the old days, these slackers would get bored around 10 ayem, and go out and pester their co-workers; now, they sit in their cubicles and Web surf all day, leaving the actual conduct of business to the two or three persons in every corporation who feel guilty about not putting in a full day for their paychecks. Better yet, the real indolents spend so much time farting around on the Web that they inevitably lose their jobs, so the workaholics chuckle smugly and redouble their efforts. This also helps in the cases of those addicted to porn or gambling, where they're removed from the worker pool long before they taint the company reputation with their dirty little secrets.

An even more important factor in that increase of productivity lies with the disappearance of management. Before Web-enabled offices became the norm, the explosion of MBAs across the country meant that at least one smarmy manager was micromanaging everyone in sight. Without fail, when left to their own forms of entertainment, these geniuses always presented some new form of "improvement process" that came to them while slipping Rohypnol to their dates in college: this "improvement" invariably slowed productivity to a crawl before the employees privately decided to go back to the old methods, letting the manager or department head take credit and bonus for the plan. Were the US business community an army, the troops would simply frag their idiot commanders and go home, but since this behavior is the same everywhere, the troops simply wait for the MBAs to expire from alcohol poisoning. Nowadays, just give a manager golf scores on ESPN, stock reports on E*Trade, and the obvious benefits of HotSluts.Com and Pharmacy.Com (for their Propecia prescriptions), and the little bastards are all in their offices, masturbating like caged apes and leaving everyone else alone for more constructive venues.

Unlimited Web access also improves the lot for the perpetually disgruntled, leaving them free to jobhunt on company time instead of destroying what little morale remains after the boss finishes with "improvements." Until the Web browser came along, the only outlets for the dissatisfied was incessant kvetching and spraying the office with tracers from an M-16, so now that they're quietly trying to escape via Monster.Com, the collateral damage from their leavetaking generally doesn't take out their co-workers. (This attitude also improves the situation with contract workers: give them the opiate of the wage slave when they have nothing to do, and they're much less likely to boobytrap important documents with macro viruses and install Back Orifice on the main company server.) Access even acts as a relief valve for the burned-out: why take a lunch break to go bookhunting, with the attendant dangers to the company of that person leaving and not bothering to come back, when it's just as easy to buy books through Amazon.Com during lunch?

E-mail is not only one of the great inventions of the modern era, but is also one of the major factors in the current productivity boom. Both E-mail and faxes offer equal opportunities to send every friend and relative on the planet every crackheaded "happy thought" and vaguely ribald joke that comes down the Interstate, minus the expense of fax paper, toner, and the separate phone connection. By sending these as E-mail, not only are huge tracts of the Pacific Northwest saved from paper logging, but the practice saves the eyes of those who would otherwise squint and strain at every thirtieth-generation fax, trying to decide if the image therein was of Julia Roberts, the Loch Ness Monster, or both. Best of all, those tired of receiving the same sappy "Friendship Bear" message can both delete the message and set up mail filters to keep the sender from polluting their mailboxes ever again.

With this in mind, newspapers should stop the incessant articles about "the dangers of Internet abuse" and embrace the concept of unlimited, unfiltered Web access for every American employee. Without the Web acting as a giant filter for the incompetent and malingering among us, the United States would have been taken over by Canada long ago, and only a fraction of us know how to speak Canadian.

—*Spark Online, May 2000*

Postscript: Damn, that was prophetic, wasn't it?

"Vocational Darwinism and the Decline of the Technical Recruiter"

A few weeks ago, the *New York Times* featured an article in its Business section on the decline and fall of the technical recruiter. Two years ago, technical recruiters had so many positions to fill that job fairs featured scores or even hundreds of companies within any reasonably-sized metropolis, all looking for the technical talent that client companies craved. These days, as more tech firms lay off staff to boost their stock price, the recruiters are dealing with a drastically decreased demand for tech workers, both permanent and contract, and more are looking for work themselves.

When the Great Magnet finishes pulling the pieces of the technical industry to and fro, and enough time elapses that nostalgia for the dotcom days sets in, many books will be written about the Good Old Days when every job came with promises of an IPO and profitability was secondary to "eyeball stickiness." One of the most entertaining sagas will come from analysis of the desperate shortage of technical workers reported in the papers versus the actual tech workers who sat unemployed during the height of the boom unable to find a position. One day, some enterprising Jane Goodall of the tech set will compare data, and find out exactly how many jobs went unfilled or poorly filled because companies depended upon untrained, incompetent, technically ignorant, overly arrogant, or flat-out stupid technical recruiters for their IT needs. For a time, technical recruiting was a gravy job for a business or marketing major drawn by the promises of making $150 per hour or more in commissions, and this was catnip to dolt yuppies who gained nothing from college besides alcoholism and syphilis.

These days, the newly dot-unemployed aren't getting phone calls unless they have skills still in demand by real companies, but recruiters kept local and long-distance phone companies extremely profitable in the late Nineties. Within hours of posting a resume on Headhunter or Monster (or any other job site), the calls filled answering machines all over the country. The calls would usually start at about 9:00 and go until 11 at night, and nearly all of them started with a Valley Girl whine of "Hi: like, I found your resume on the In-tur-neeeeeet, and I have a really exciting opportunity that I wanted to see if you were interested in. If you could give me a call at...," followed by a phone number and a company name chosen because it sounded sufficiently Internet-friendly.

At this point, life could go one of three ways. Ignoring the messages meant that somebody didn't fill in the correct field in a database, meaning that the maroon would call up again and again every time a possible position came up and s/he ran a search through CareerBuilder for those same skills. Calling the recruiter back and saying "I'm really not interested in the position/the company/living in Houston" got a response of "Well, do you know anyone else who might be interested in this position?" and disappointment shading to rage if the response was anything less than the names and phone numbers of at least five suitable replacements, especially if that response was "Everybody I know got smart and got the hell out of the business." Calling the recruiter back and expressing an interest immediately led to the first level of the Recruiter Inferno.

The descent into the abyss started innocently enough, when the recruiter called up asking for more info "and a resume in Word 97 format." They wanted a resume in Word instead of the resume straight from the job site because that would require effort in reformatting it for the company's database. The format had to be Word, and not WordPerfect, Word for Macintosh, RichText, or plain text, because said recruiter usually wasn't smart enough to figure out how to open a file without dumping it on a desktop and double-clicking on it, and Office 97 is the *de facto* tool for the busy and lazy office professional. Any other format instigated a phone call where the recruiter would sigh exasperatedly and lecture "I tried to open this file on every computer we have, and it wouldn't open, so can you convert it to Word and get it to us?"

After the recruiter received the resume in the accepted Word 97 format, now was time for the breakdown on the position. This was what separated the MBAs from the real recruiters: the real recruiters would relay the position and the skills necessary, and ask questions of the applicant that implied a working knowledge of the skills in question. The MBAs and marketing majors would bluff, dissemble, and lie, whether stating with a straight face "Well, our client is huge in the technical industry, and they say that Java has been around for eight years, so we need someone with at least eight to ten years of Java experience," or giggling "Could you explain that again? I'm not technical." Many of the latter were fond of reading straight from the job ticket, speaking slowly to sound out the big words, and regularly asking "Do you have CORBA or COM object experience, and could you tell me what those are?" or "So what's the difference between programming and technical writing?" They had no idea, but they weren't about ready to admit it.

The marketing types were particularly easy to spot just because of the little phrase "I can't tell you who the client is until you come down to the office. We don't present anyone until we've met them first." To translate, "We don't have a job for you, and if we do, it's with a company where any rational person would shoot themselves in the head rather than fill a cubicle, but I need to make my quota this week." They would then wheedle, beg, threaten, and guilt-trip their victims into scheduling an interview. This interview was always during the middle of the day, even if the victim had a job and explained that sneaking out at 2:00 was impossible. The real recruiters were always willing to accommodate standard work schedules for employees of companies that regularly fired jobhunters; the MBAs insisted "I'm out of here at five, so if you want the job, you'll have to work out something. I have a spot at 8 tomorrow morning." Much like vampires fleeing garlic and holy water, the one phrase guaranteed to keep these parasites away was to respond "If you have a real job, I'll come down, but if I waste half of my day just to find that you're trying to fill a database, I'm going to punch you in the nose." The last thing they wanted was to experience pain or discomfort.

The interview with the MBA-run firm was always memorable. The usual tipoff as to a placement company being a fly-by-night conceived in a haze of lap dancers and bad cocaine was with the furniture: more often than not, while the CEO always insisted on having an office with a view, the furniture was almost always picked up cheap from the local "Used Office Furniture Outlet," without any interest in it matching any other piece. The office may have been impeccable, located in a $75-a-square-foot skyscraper, or it could have been jammed in the back of an industrial park next to a U-Stor-It and a Discount Cigs emporium. The computer equipment was always state-of-the-art, with flatscreen displays all over the office back before they were practical or even affordable. The furniture, though, was always the same: dents, dings, delaminations, and the occasional bit of carved graffiti reading "Property of..." and the name of a local company bankrupt and dead for at least twenty years. Very rarely, the obverse was true: Aeron chairs and topnotch workstations in a company where the recruiter didn't have business cards and settled for writing down contact information on Post-It notes.

The interview itself was just a continuation of the phone call, where the recruiter would ask "And you are...?" and shuffle through mounds of resumes until finding the pertinent one, so bringing a spare copy was essential. After that initial bit of embarrassment, the recruiter would "reveal" the job and the skills required, feeding the victim information so that the recruiter could report back to the client and say with full honesty "S/he has all of the skills you need." Most of the real fly-by-night places demanded a job application before anything else, thus making the applicant more likely to stick around for the debasement after spending a half-hour filling out a skills sheet that was likely to be at the bottom of a landfill in six months. That done, the recruiter would spend another hour picking the applicant's brain for new codewords and catchphrases in order to pretend knowledge of the technical field, and then say "Well, we'll get this resume right off, and I'll call you the moment I hear anything." A few more honest ones would say "I'm afraid that you really don't have the skills the client is looking for, but I'll keep you on file the moment something comes through." It did no good to make followup calls: the applicant had performed his/her function, that of showing up and giving the impression of the recruiter doing gainful work, and any checkbacks led to a panicky "I said that I'd call you if we got anything!" Again, a few would confess that they didn't have any jobs and instead were trying to fill a database of resumes in order to impress possible new clients: even if they still had their jobs after admitting this, they still never called back.

Since recruiters for contract positions were generally paid by the hour by their clients, whether or not they found an appropriate candidate, these recruiters were the most aggressive, belligerent, obnoxious, and dishonest of the breed, not to mention the most illiterate. Resumes posted on job sites that specifically read "NO CONTRACT POSITIONS" still received calls at all hours asking "I know you're looking for a permanent direct-hire position, but would you be or would you know someone who would be interested in a three-week contract in Los Angeles?" These positions were always *sans* benefits, *sans* privileges, and *sans* guarantees of further employment, but the recruiters would alternately wheedle and sneer that the candidate was "passing up something really good" if they weren't willing to quit a permanent or longterm contract position to jump on this "sure thing." E-mail queries were invariably evidence of the recruiter not knowing or caring about the difference between "there/their/they're" or "to/too/two," as well as the correct spelling of the client company's name, and geographical ignorance was evident with the number of queries of whether a daily commute from San Francisco to Los Angeles or from Boston to Albany was "reasonable." Since the client companies usually weren't particularly fussy about the bodies they used to fill their slots, any contract assignment of more than a three-week duration was forwarded to every company within a certain radius, and the recruiters all used the same job sites to hunt victims, leaving answering machines and voice mail flooded with multiple offers for the same exact position.

Whether for a contract or a permanent position, the interview with the client company was just as entertaining, but only in retrospect. With some companies, the whole dog-and-pony show of interviewing recruits was to pretend that the HR department had gone to efforts to find applicants other than the boss' frat brother/child/girlfriend, who would immediately get the job after all of the "unsuitable" recruits were rejected on spurious or even slanderous grounds. Recruiters were notorious for sending out grossly unsuitable candidates for positions, and then bitching them out for not telling them that they didn't have the skills the recruiter said they had, or for scheduling interviews with applicants without bothering to check with the interviewer. Anyone not willing to drop everything and go to an interview in a matter of minutes, or who expressed concern about the corporate climate after the interview, was immediately listed as Damaged Goods and would never be used again. The lucky applicants were those who had to report back to the recruiter by phone after a disastrous job interview; some recruiters felt compelled to tag along for the interview and interject distorted or fabricated material to help the sale. "Worked on a Compaq PC for four years" became "worked for Compaq for four years," and the really good recruiters would chirp and babble this information three and four times during an interview, no matter how many times the applicant would try to correct the error. (In the same way, "I was making $40k plus benefits on my last position, but I'm flexible" somehow became "The candidate refuses to work for anything less than $95k and ten percent of the blue chip stock in the company.") With this sort of help, the miracle wasn't in the number of technical positions that were filled during the dotcom boom, but instead that any were filled at all with these idiots in charge of presenting candidates.

Well, that's all over now. As tech firms either cut back on new hires or started laying off existing workers, the fly-by-night places suddenly found that new business wasn't coming in at all. Before, an incompetent recruiter could pick up and move somewhere else, claiming to be an ace in filling tech positions, multiple times before reality or reputation caught up or until they made enough money to become boss of their own recruiting company. These days, even the good recruiters are facing a lack of employment, meaning that the dolts are moving back into their parents' houses or going back to business school to wait out the recession. Good riddance to them: with a bit of luck, they'll find another get-rich-quick scheme to share with their drinking buddies, and the good recruiters will keep quiet about their rates. In a few years, the relationship between techie and recruiter can be one of trust, rather than one of exchanged profanities, but only if we start an organized program of MBA spaying and neutering so they don't breed.

—NetSlaves.com, April 2001

Postscript: Yes, it's possible now to find someone with ten years of Java programming experience, but the recruiter game always has been to find a brand new college graduate with at least ten years of experience in a software application that's been around for three months. The old MBAs die of cirrhosis or overdoses, and then their kids take the positions, and the cycle continues.

"Springtime For Jeff Bezos and Amazon"

The old saying goes "History always repeats itself: the first time as tragedy and the second as farce." This may be true, but what happens when that saying runs in reverse?

In the ongoing analysis of the dotbomb, one of the real ironies in the discussion comes from the journalists and commentators who are shocked, just *shocked*, at the amount of waste and ego that kept most dotcoms going far longer than they should have. The irony, of course, is that most publishing ventures have been running on dotcom terms for decades, if not centuries. The fact that most newspapers and magazines make a profit at all is amazing in itself, considering the number of boneheaded and onanistic decisions made by members all the way up and down the management tree.

Dead magazines usually went under for the same reasons that dead dotcoms shuffled off the Nasdaq, but nobody writes huge articles on the front of the *New York Times* about the latest magazine to collapse under poor and excessive management. About a year ago, *Salon* ran a small article asking about where all of the editors who knew how to edit had gone in New York, because seemingly every editor in town did little more than go to parties and hit on the interns. Usually, magazines start when someone sufficiently narcissistic decides to become a publisher, and (rarely) fronts his/her own money or (far more often) cons any number of frat brothers and relatives to buy into "this sure thing." (Said publisher usually stays in until the money is gone and the magazine folds, in which case s/he packs up looking for the next "sure thing," or until the magazine starts making a profit but not the billions of dollars s/he expected, and the magazine is promptly sold to someone else who shuts it down for the tax writeoff or immediately drives it into the ground. Magazines are the original "born to flip" venue, and not just on the Web.) S/he then immediately surrounds himself/herself with professional asskissers (here known as "editors") usually at least three levels deep, and if you're lucky, they'll stay in their offices, surf porn sites all day, and leave everyone else alone. The publisher and editors are the only ones who ever make any money from the venture, but they convince the rank and file to keep busting their asses with the promise of a great reward (a permanent position, a raise, a column) that never comes if they have anything to say about it. Most of the general employees are paid as little as humanly possible in exchange for the delusion that they're doing something that they love, and if editors and publisher can get work for free, they'll gleefully jump all over the opportunity for a little extra beer money. Just as in dotcoms, the interns and freelancers are treated as the worst sorts of scum; unlike dotcoms, the hubristic toads who sit in the back and throw temper tantrums because they don't receive all of the attention that they feel they deserve aren't called "programmers." They're called "columnists" and "critics."

In either case, this situation usually keeps going until the publisher gets bored (usually after about four issues) and shuts down everything, leaving a huge mound of bills he refuses to pay and breaking every promise he made to staff about his involvement. The sad part is that like dotcom CEOs, no matter how badly they screwed up the publication and everything for a four-block radius, editors and publishers of murdered magazines are usually allowed to take over other publications, abuse the staff, ruin whatever respect the publication had accumulated, and drive them into the ground. (I knew one editor who did this repeatedly, at every publication he commanded, and only left town because he didn't have any more new magazines or papers to cripple.)

Even with the smallest zines, this egocentric mentality manifests itself, as if the editors and/or publishers (which are usually the same person) go out of their way not to be successful. You see it with the constant pictures of the editor on the front cover or plastered all over the publication, with irregular publication, poor customer service when readers want to buy magazines, an inability to interact with fellow humans long enough to get an advertising deal, and with the publication itself being shut down without contributors or subscribers ever being informed of the demise. If anyone dares come to the editor/publisher and suggest "Hey, I'd be glad to help you get profitable, and I'll only collect a fee after the money comes in," everyone starts shrieking and moaning about "selling out." (The really foul bastards are the characters who announce that they're starting up a magazine, solicit artwork, advertising, and content, and then never bother to get anything to press. In the meantime, contributors and advertisers end up missing out on agreements and deals that could have gone somewhere while they were waiting for these flakes to get around to doing something. About half of the time, they actually make some kind of belated effort to slap something together, usually far too late to make any kind of difference.)

About two years ago, a magazine that used to publish a column of mine finally decided to shut down, two years after its last issue and nearly four years after the issue before that, and it was the last twitch of a magazine that could have beaten *Wired* and *Mondo 2000* like redheaded stepchildren had the editor/publisher been willing to allow it to become a success. The general comment was "This is what happens when you base your business plan on too many viewings of *The Producers*." Far too many magazines followed the lessons in that film, so why wouldn't the dotcoms?

For those not familiar with the movie, *The Producers* is arguably Mel Brooks' best film besides *The Twelve Chairs*, back before Brooks started believing his own hype on his slide through *Young Frankenstein* and *Blazing Saddles* into the miasma of *History of the World, Part 1*, *Spaceballs*, and *Life Stinks*. The film starts with poor Max Bialystock (incomparably played by Zero Mostel), a successful but desperately poor stage producer who spends most of his time seducing little old ladies to get enough money to put together his next play. When nebbish accountant Leo Bloom (Gene Wilder) goes over Bialystock's books, Bloom discovers that successful plays almost never make money, and that Max would actually make money by producing a flat-out bomb. Jumping on that knowledge, Max goes searching for the world's worst play, and discovers it in "Springtime for Hitler," a musical written by a former SS officer (Kenneth Mars). Bialystock and Bloom then go to similarly extreme efforts to hunt down the worst director in New York, and they figure that they hit paydirt when they cast a brain-damaged flower child named LSD (Dick Shawn, in easily one of the funniest parts in the film) as Adolf Shickelgruber.

Since the idea was that "Springtime for Hitler" was intended to fall, and fall hard, Max manages to make the rounds with all of his elderly liaisons, promising them all seventy to ninety percent of the production in exchange for their upfront money. He then takes that money and blows it on limos, a fresh new office, and a Swedish secretary named Inga, whose grasp of the phrase "Go...to...work" consists of stripping down to a bikini and dancing. Leo is understandably panicked about the excess, seeing as how they'll both go to jail if something goes wrong, but Max blows off every concern. "Springtime for Hitler" is a guaranteed flop, and he does everything he can to make sure it fails, even down to offering blatant bribes to theater critics on opening night to give it a good review, knowing that they'll do anything but.

The problem with "Springtime for Hitler," though, is that it doesn't flop. After the opening musical number, one of the most embarrassing and excessive displays this side of *Star Wars: Episode One* (only "Springtime for Hitler" was *intended* to be excessive), the retreating audience suddenly finds that LSD's Hitler is the funniest thing they've ever seen. As Leo and Max are in the bar across the street from the theater, waiting for the seemingly inevitable screams of rage and cackling in anticipation, the crowd enters and says, almost to an individual, "I never thought that I'd laugh so hard at something called 'Springtime for Hitler'!"

Naturally, the thought of jail time and hefty fines scare the hell out of Leo and Max, and they conspire with the playwright (who spent the opening screaming

"Mein Fuehrer did not say 'Baby'!" and snarling at fellow audience members "I am ze writer. You are ze audience. I outrank you!") to blow up the theater, preventing any further shows and protecting their investments. Naturally, they succeed in blowing themselves up along with the theater, and the film ends with all of them in prison, up to the same tricks while producing a musical called "Prisoners of Love."

Hmmm. A half-rate scam artist promises the world and a hefty profit to any number of naïve investors in a vague and nebulous enterprise, and then works his ass off to make sure that it will never, ever make a profit. Does anyone else read this see the letters "A-M-A-Z-O-N" anywhere? Or how about "F-A-N-D-O-M"?

Obviously, *The Producers* has nothing to do with dotcom reality. Seeing as how Max Bilaystock was in his late fifties, he would have been replaced almost immediately by a 23-year-old MBA with capped teeth and a $400 haircut. He and Leo wouldn't have produced a play: they would have produced a whole entertainment site full of projects that were well-hyped but amazingly never saw release. They never would have hired Inga when they could have had their mitts on any number of party girls (or boys) who would have done *anything* to make it in the New Media business. They wouldn't have had to hit up old ladies for the cash: they would have simply announced an IPO and waited for the same dingbats who paid real money for K-Tel and Boo.com stock to throw handfuls of $100 bills at them. Most importantly, they never would have gone to jail for their greed: they would have been allowed to cash in their stocks just before the production went under, keep the money, and receive book and magazine offers on how to be an Internet genius. They wouldn't have made a rap sheet: Leo and Max instead would have spent their days posing for cover spreads in *Fast Company* and *Upside* while talking about their next and more memorable project. And potential investors would throw more money at them, while they blamed the previous suckers for being so greedy and expecting profits instead of wanting to be part of something bigger than themselves.

As of this writing, Mel Brooks just premiered the stage production of *The Producers* on Broadway, with Nathan Lane as Max and Matthew Broderick as Leo, and it couldn't have happened at a better time. Those that forget the past are condemned to repeat it, so keep it in mind the next time some sleazy business brat starts talking about paradigms and "stickiness" at the next New Media job interview. The brat probably won't understand why you're humming "Springtime for Hitler," but you will.

—*NetSlaves, April 2001*

"Mutiny in the Toy Store"

The words "toy store" bring out the worst in most seekers of the surreal. They bring visions of the dweeb we knew in high school who had the complete collection of *Star Wars* action figures, still in their bubble packaging, and wouldn't let anyone touch them without gloves and dust-free cloths. Or they bring visions of the girlfriend who had all of her porcelain dolls from her pre-Lolita days, and how she threw a skillet at you when you accidentally knocked one of them off the mantelpiece as you reached for your Butthole Surfers tapes. One should jettison these visions, because they get in the way of one of the best surreal looks at Americana ever available. Checking out what toy companies think will be the bestselling for the 3-to-15 set at Toys 'R' Us offers a hysterical high comparable to freebasing Preparation H or clubbing Trekkies like baby seals.

They advertise themselves as "The World's Greatest Toy Store," but Toys 'R' Us is much more: it's a battleground for the minds of preadolescents throughout America, and although the Catholic Church's motto is said to be "Give me your children until they are 12, and they are mine forever," the Church ain't got nothin' on Kenner and Mattel. Between Saturday morning cartoons, Christmas, and promos for the latest Spielberg film, the only groups who buy more utter shit via advertising than kids are Rush Limbaugh's dittoheads and Scientologists.

Thanks to the ongoing recession, the days where parents would spend hundreds of dollars on Teddy Ruxpins and Cabbage Patch dolls are over, but you'd never know it by looking in a toy store. One of the big recent promotions was for a monstrosity called Toby Terrier, an animatronic dog who only reacts to a TV playing a specially made video featuring (you guessed it) Toby himself. Although the people at T'R'U wouldn't let me try this out, a helpful plastic-cased Toby -- complete with a button that starts a prerecorded spiel -- filled me in on what he did: not one hell of a lot if you didn't have a VCR. At a suggested retail price of $79.95, I figure the company that manufactures Toby must spend a lot on drug rehab programs, because someone was obviously forgetting to "Just Say No" with Toby.

Of course, the ultimate symbol of American conspicuous consumption is still Barbie, and most stores offer a whole aisle full of her shit. The button reading "I wish I was Barbie: the bitch has everything" really gets meaning when walking down that aisle: Barbie has not only her traditional Jaguar, summer home, and selection of clothing rivaling that of Nancy Reagan, but she also has a selection of alternating high-tech and low-tech gadgets that make me wish I hadn't quit drinking. F'r instance, the Barbie washer and dryer really works–only needing some hyperactive six-year-old to pump a button on the top to agitate and aerate her clothes–but her dog and cat come complete with sound chips: as the packaging notes, pet their backs to get them to bark and purr respectively. Between her camper trailer and Ken's remote controlled Ninja crotch rocket motorcycle, buying one of everything would bankrupt most Third World countries.

The Barbie and Ken dolls offer laughs in themselves: several years ago, complaints about the two being whiter than David Duke's sheets made Mattel offer alternative colors, so now we have B&K in African, Asian, and Hispanic shades. Fat lot of good it does, because the three other pairs apparently live the same lives of reckless abandon as the white ones do: must be a lot of trust funds going to minority kids these days if these six are any indication. Even more disconcerting are the collector Barbies in such professions as policewoman (sans pistol, handcuffs, or baton), cowgirl, and soldier. The last has her in official Desert Storm camo fatigues, but she's apparently a conscientious objector, as she still doesn't pack a weapon. (As some sort of salve to the many women who serve in the military, she carries a first aid kit and sports Red Cross insignia; why couldn't she be a fighter pilot or an ICBM mechanic? Wouldn't we all love to see Barbie with huge pecs and biceps from lugging around an M-60 in the Marines? Or wielding an M-17 protective mask as she lobbed nerve agents into the enemy ranks?)

The spectre of homosexuality in the Barbie ranks came to light a few years ago with the release of the new Ken doll, who sported a pink vest, a gold chain, and an earring. Mattel promptly withdrew the dolls in the midst of guffaws all across the country, but the two still offer themselves as role models to the gay and bi community. One of the new collector lines is the Locket Barbie collection, which offers a child-sized locket with each doll. Locket Barbie comes with a picture of Ken in her locket, and Ken (in a ridiculous sequined cowboy outfit complete with hat) has a locket with Barbie's face plastered therein. Then comes Locket Kayla, billed as "Barbie's Best Friend." Is Ken playing "hide the salami" with her, warranting a Ken locket? Nope: she has a big full-color picture of...Barbie.

Imagine this situation: Ken comes home to the Dream House after a long night at the Village People show down near the Nintendo aisle. Still with G.I. Joe's lipstick on his vest collar, he opens the door to find the place stripped of its petrochemical-derivative furniture. His plastic Visa is run to the limit and discarded, and his Bank of Anywhere, USA checkbook drained through the ATM card lying at his feet. In the center of the living room, still smelling of gasoline and the Clearasil he uses to keep his complexion clear, is a smoking pile of his stuff –

complete down to the metal spokes of his crotch rocket and the fake fur pelt of his golden retriever. Next to the pyre, which spits out sparks that mar his synthetic good looks and threatens to fuse his pantaloons to his backside, he finds a note fastened to the floor with a Ninja axle that reads: "Dear Ken: I'm tired of you, tired of your slipping off to pork Conan the Adventurer, tired of you having no penis, and tired of having to subsidize your overly indulgent lifestyle. I'm leaving with Kayla to get a breast reduction, so don't look for us, you yuppie asshole. Love, Barbie."

Now, if Ken were a real man, he'd join the Marines at this point: in which case, he'd hie his ass over to the action figure aisle and get involved in the new war effort. Yep, the armed forces have changed in the toy store: with the death of communism: they're now geared up to blow up aliens, dinosaurs, and deserters in their own ranks. War never goes out of style: its practitioners merely find new enemies.

The strangest trend in action figures today is the emphasis on making figures based on R-rated movies. Fifteen years ago, parents had coronaries over Kenner's 18-inch *Alien* figure, complete with extending inner jaws and an accurate H.R. Giger physique: now the kids of those parent are buying the whole *Aliens* line for their kids. The troopers are pretty impressive in themselves, as they carry more armament than a National Guard armory and sport a nasty attitude to match, but the aliens don't have nothin' on them. Kenner offers varying forms of aliens, apparently produced by the facehuggers of the films attacking various life forms, so we have gorilla aliens that grab prey and spit acid, scorpion aliens that blow apart under fire (press a button on its back and the scorp alien breaks apart, over and over, just like Iraqi troops), bull and rhino aliens that butt adversaries, and snake aliens whose flexible bodies wrap around prey while their jaws paralyze or kill. The line even comes with comparable Predator figures, from the film of the same name, whose sole purpose is to hunt aliens and Marines.

Let's go back to our earlier scenario: Ken joins the Space Marines, where he gets assigned to a bug-hunting squad. Thanks to substandard equipment, his troop gets taken out by a band of ravenous xenomorphs and he awakens in an epoxy-lined cave, glued to a wall with alien secretions and facing a huge leathery egg. Across the cave, he sees the still-attached corpse of his lover G.I. Joe, a gaping bloody hole in his massive hairless chest, with an opened and empty egg in front of his gaping sightless eyes. Further in the cave are other one-night stands: Luke Skywalker, Commander Riker, and the Mighty Morphin Power Rangers, and he starts to scream as the egg opens and he sees the horror therein waiting to attach itself to his vacantly smiling face...

Probably the best part of any trip to T'R'U, though, is a wander through the remainder aisle. Just like on the Island of Misfit Toys in *Rudolph the Red-Nosed Reindeer*, this lane collects all of the toys that didn't cut the grey poupon: the ones that didn't sell well enough to have their names put on the cardboard sign out front. Barbie and Ken are pretty safe, as are all the other constant sellers like Spirographs and Etch-A-Sketches, but all of the other toys quake in fear at ending up there one of these days.

The list in here on any given day makes you wonder how many toy designers get fired every year, because the shit keeps getting weirder and weirder. Anyone with more than three brain cells would have figured that New Kids on the Block action figures and puzzles would have fizzled the moment their fans reached puberty, but who the hell thought that anyone had nostalgia for those goddamned trolls from the early Seventies? Or that TV shows such as *Voltron* or *James Bond, Jr.* would have had enough staying power for toys based on them to find their places on the shelves? Or that stores are very quietly setting aside space for the *Jurassic Park* and *Flintstones* action figures next to the *Hook* toys: three casualties to Steven Spielberg's lack of directorial or producer talent?

Sometimes the whole problem stems from bad timing. The remainder aisle is loaded with stuffed talking Ren and Stimpy dolls: when Nickelodeon signed the merchandising contracts, the company hadn't fucked with the show to the point where *Beavis and Butt-Head* offered deeper entertainment. The dolls came out with a wave of commercial hype to a gang who was deathy sick and tired of hearing "Happy happy, joy joy" and preferred hearing "Huh huh huh, he said 'tool', huh huh."

All this leads to the sort of toys we'd really like to see in the stores. Enough with the complete line of *Star Trek: The Next Generation* and *Dumb Shit Nine* figures: I dare a company to release a line of *Day of the Dead* figures, including zombies with action figures like exploding heads and removable limbs. Bugger the tendency to make dolls based on flash-in-the-pan musical act (thank Nyarlathotep that nobody has made a line of Stone Temple Pilots dolls; reality could not handle the strain): I double-dare a company to offer a line of Famous Writer dolls, including Scott Fitzgerald, William S. Burroughs, Ernest Hemingway, H.P. Lovecraft, Harlan Ellison, and Hunter S. Thompson as the first in the series. Best of all, I double-dog dare any toy manufacturer to make toys that don't cost a month's salary and yet don't fall apart the day after Christmas. Anyone who pulls off that one deserves a Nobel Peace Prize, no matter what else they do: one home on Christmas Day without a child screaming about how Barbie now looks like Marie Antoinette will make it all worthwhile.

—*Cyber-Psychos AOD*, July 1997

Postscript: Originally written in 1997, this article has one purpose. It demonstrates that the only thing that ages more poorly than an old article on movies or television is an old article on toys. The Toys 'R' Us empire exploded thanks to the Internet generation, and then it cratered when the dotcom bust hit and millions of slackers had to decide between paying rent or buying the latest set of Babylon 5 action figures. I think it was fun while it lasted, but after selling off all of the crap I bought during that time, I'm still wondering if I should have spent the money on something more productive, like a heroin habit.

The Edgar Harris Papers

For various strange reasons, the most successful articles I've ever written have involved Edgar Harris in one way or another, and he'd probably appreciate the sentiment if he actually existed. Edgar first saw birth at the beginning of 1990, shortly after I combined a severe case of flu with a reading of Doonesbury: A Musical Comedy, *and he promptly moved in and spent his days eating all of my Cheerios and taking my Volkswagen on late-night road trips. Back then, he had far too much in common with Hunter S. Thompson's Raoul Duke and Mike Royko's Slats Grabnik, but he found a regular venue in the now-defunct Zealot.com at the end of 2000 as the science fiction community's very own Libby Gellman-Waxner. When Zealot died in the middle of 2001 when its parent company went the way of all dotcoms, the staff started up a new venue,* Revolution Science Fiction, *and Edgar tagged along, now as "the former Sports Editor of* Science Fiction Age." *After all, who else was going to publish his news stories?*

Anyway, this compendium contains several pieces intended for Revolution SF *that never saw publication for various unknown reasons: they're all at the end. Since most of them were written shortly before I quit writing entirely, I didn't fight it all that much. They're included for completeness' sake: if you don't get the jokes, you obviously haven't had too much involvement with the science fiction community, and for that you should be incredibly thankful.*

Oh, and some readers may note similarities between the names of individuals mentioned in these articles and names of individuals who volunteered their names to help add verisimilitude to ongoing hoaxes. Pure coincidence.

"Raze the Green Lantern"

Deep in the Robledo Mountains of New Mexico works a film crew in the last few days of production. Security is ultratight: the movie in question is scheduled to be one of the big releases of the 1996 summer season and nobody dares release any information that could ruin the surprise and wonder (read: the box office potential) before the opening date. A handful of actors and crew remain; the rest have already returned to Los Angeles for the grueling postproduction work, including special effects that promise to rewrite the book on computer generated imaging.

All that manages to leak out are four things. The film is a Dreamworks SKG project, with Steven Spielberg himself as the executive producer. The project itself is the much-awaited *Green Lantern* movie, adapted from the DC comic of the same name. The Robledos are filling in for the planet Oa, on which most of the action will take place. Finally, the director of this $80 million-dollar production is a newcomer to Hollywood, but a legend among fans of underground film. Dallas auteur Edgar Harris has finally hit the big time.

Harris refuses to be interviewed about the film, and all calls to Dreamworks SKG are answered by a secretary who says "I really don't know what you're talking about," but a few sources have pieced together the story behind one of the stranger alliances to come out of the film industry in a long time. Most unbelievable is that Harris, a known iconoclast (some say sociopath), would take an offer to work under Spielberg, a man Harris once accused of "producing more NAMBLA poster children than any human alive."

A friend of Harris', speaking on the condition of anonymity, said he told her the reasoning behind his abrupt about-face: "He said 'They offered me $5 million as a director's fee. I may be crazy, but I'm not stupid.'"

Edgar Zappa Harris was born February 27, 1966 in the town of Flint, Michigan. In his early years, he gave no sign that he planned to follow in the tradition of fellow Michiganite filmmakers Sam Raimi (*The Evil Dead, Darkman*) and Michael Moore (*Roger & Me, Canadian Bacon*). In fact, his interests ranged more toward science than anything else: at the age of nine, he discovered the nearly complete remains of a duckbilled dinosaur called *Aachenosaurus* while camping with his family. This made national news, as this was not only the first dinosaur known from Michigan deposits, but the first reasonably intact skeleton of the beast known. He went on through school with no sign of his future reputation showing until 1982, when his family moved to Carrollton and he found his destiny.

His ex-girlfriend, local poet L.A. Dorman, summed up the turning point. "He wanted to catch a preview of *The Thing* that summer, and he begged his parents for any opportunity to get out for it. He told them 'I'll walk back home, I don't care; all I want to do is see this movie.' Well, they said 'We're going out, but we're not going anywhere near the theater,' and late that evening they returned and said 'You didn't miss anything, because *The Thing* was really bad.'

"He never forgave them for that. That one incident ran his life from then on. He became absolutely obsessed with film, mostly because it drove his folks bugfuck."

After spending the summer mowing lawns and saving the cash, Harris bought a small Super 8 movie camera and started shooting demos of events. He started out simply: by his senior year at Newman Smith High School, he was well-known for his humorous shorts of events in the school, and he toyed with the idea of directing music videos for local bands. His best friend from high school, Tim Waite, remembers when Harris first brushed with the Powers That Be and won.

"It was during our senior year in high school, and he was having real problems with his girlfriend at the time. At the same time, the homecoming queen, Ellen Gudex, got on his nerves. She started calling him 'Eddie," and nobody calls him Eddie. Well, he kept talking about fixing her overbite with a two-by-four and a can of Bondo, but he wasn't about ready to hit a woman for anything. Anyway, his girlfriend left him, and he kinda snapped, so he came up with a way to get even with Ellen."

The revenge came when the school held its annual Senior Revue, a talent show consisting of the graduating class. Harris entered a lighthearted animated short as his presentation, but switched films on opening night. The revised short featured Gudex in compromising positions, and it nearly brought the law down on Harris.

"Oh, it was great," Waite said. "She was always presenting herself as the sweetest and most wholesome girl in the school, but Edgar got footage of her snorting coke at a party, and screwing two teachers and the president of the astronomy club. Her boyfriend went ballistic over it, and so did the principal. The whole thing used the Sex Pistols' 'God Save the Queen' as a soundtrack, so that didn't help. She and her family threatened a lawsuit, but that was about the time she got busted for possession of ten grams of coke, so she got expelled instead.

"The last anyone heard, she was living out in Eugene, Oregon, working as a stripper because she couldn't get anything else with her police record. Edgar still laughs about that."

Harris finally graduated, much to the relief of the Carrollton school district, and promptly went to film school at the University of North Texas. Within three weeks, he was on his way back home, expelled for allegedly assaulting his professor. "His professor was a real hardass; the sort who thinks that *Citizen Kane* is the be-all and end-all of human achievement," Waite said. "Well, when the professor was ranting and raving about how *Bringing Up Baby* was a prime example of humor in film, Edgar stood up and asked 'Well, what about *Dawn of the Dead*'s use of satire to poke fun at consumerist culture?' The prof started choking, and said that 'crap like that was the reason nobody took cinema seriously any more' and 'if you like slasher films, maybe you'd be better off directing porn reels, too.' Well, one thing led to another, the two got into a shouting match, and it all went to hell when they started swinging. The professor started it, but Edgar whomped him about seven or eight times, so they kicked him out."

Undiscouraged, Harris took the money he saved for his film degree and started making movies. By 1986, he had his own 16-millimeter Arriflex camera, and his shorts were played every other Wednesday at the now-defunct Theater Gallery. By 1987, *Film Threat*, at that time a quarterly magazine dedicated to underground cinema, took notice of Harris' films, and he was rapidly compared to underground legends Richard Kern, Nick Zedd, and Joe Christ. At the same time, he met L.A. Dorman at one of his screenings, and they very rapidly became an item in the newborn Deep Ellum scene.

"I miss those days a little bit, because Edgar was always full of energy," Dorman said. "He was working for GTE during the day, and then he'd get the gang together and start filming right after he got off work. Then he and I would go out around midnight and party until daybreak. He'd get about two hours of sleep, and then he'd get up and go back to work. He'd do this for weeks, editing and writing scripts on the weekends, until he'd finally run out of energy in three months and need to take a road trip. At night, it was like being in a live version of *Fear and Loathing In Las Vegas*."

Although the schedule ultimately took its toll, Harris produced some of his best work during that period, producing some 23 shorts between 1987 and 1992. He took advantage of the encroaching yuppie horde in Deep Ellum to film *Jock Feast* (1987), a rather nasty view of the Ellum fraternity and sorority brats as aliens "slumming" on backwater planets like Earth, a concept paralleled in John Carpenter's *They Live*. His first documentary, *In Praise of the Second Amendment* (1987), was a hilarious take on the culture that surrounds gun clubs and shows in Texas, and *Genesis Flakes* (1988) interviewed residents of Glen Rose, Texas, and sought their views on the claims by creationists that human and dinosaur tracks

402 Paul T. Riddell

could be found together in the Paluxy riverbottom.

"We had a blast in Glen Rose," Dorman remembers. "We went out one Saturday and filmed for a while in Dinosaur State Park, and then we went up the road to the Creation Science Museum, which at that time was an old double-wide trailer with these cheesy paintings of dinosaurs and cavemen all over it. Nobody inside would speak to us because we had cameras; they knew that we weren't going to present them in a positive light. Besides, Edgar had this huge black Mohawk, too, so I guess they were afraid we were going to rob them or something."

By 1989, however, Harris was starting to get infuriated with the Dallas movie industry and the city's tendency to idolize out-of-town filmmakers while ignoring its own. In an unpublished 1993 interview, Harris summed up his situation: "Dallas has an incredible amount of talent it won't use, because the Dallas Film Commission and the City Council just wet their pants every time someone comes out from Hollywood. We have geniuses like Ken Harrison (director of *Ninth Life*), Jim Conrad (cameraman at large and director of *Mondo Texas*), and a good hundred others who have the talent and the ability to make films, and the city craps all over them. Then, when some hack like Oliver Stone or Paul Verhoeven or the shitheads who made *Leap of Faith* comes to town, they take advantage of local scenery, treat the locals like peons, and leave a godawful mess, and the city bends over and willingly squeals like a pig when they want all of these concessions they know they'd never get in California.

"It's pretty hard to make movies in Dallas. Pittsburgh was glad to have George Romero and Baltimore was ecstatic to have John Waters, because they were local boys who made good. Here, though, unless you go to Hollywood and come back, nobody cares. It's just like in the music industry: Dallas couldn't care about all of the local musicians in town until they started getting recording contracts, and all we got for our trouble was the Toadies, Edie Brickell, and Lisa Loeb. I'm certain the planet is doomed because of this attitude: in twenty years, radio transmissions from 1988 will be all over the galaxy, and any aliens forced to listen to Edie shriek 'What I Am' 80 times an hour are going to come to Earth and blow the planet up just to keep from hearing it again when Eighties nostalgia kicks in."

Harris kept ragging on the local film industry, but he made his final statement at the 1993 USA Film Festival. Infuriated because he thought no local talent was featured in the Festival that year while the short film collections consisted of NEA grant projects ("You can always spot the NEA films because they make absolutely no sense. The NEA keeps giving funds to twits who want to make a statement, but don't have the slightest idea what the statement *is*"), he performed what everyone thought was impossible and hijacked a projector at the Fest. "It was really funny," he said later, after the police arrested him and charged him with fifteen counts, including assault and use of incendiary devices in a theater. "All I wanted to do was run Alex Winter's short *Entering Texas* because that was the only short of his you'd never see at the USA. Winter was a guest, and they ran some of his shorts, but they wouldn't run *Entering Texas*. It couldn't have anything to do with Gibby Haynes [lead singer for the Butthole Surfers] masturbating into a pan and the mung congealing into the word 'Satan', could it?"

After the court trial, Harris paid his fines and disappeared; the only charge that stuck was vandalism from where Harris spraypainted 'STOP OLIVER STONE BEFORE HE FILMS AGAIN" on one of the screens at the AMC Glen Lakes, where the Festival has been held since 1987. Aside from a few interviews and articles in small-press magazines such as *Film Threat Video Guide*, *Brutarian*, and *Fuck Science Fiction*, he disappeared from the Dallas scene. The announcement in Variety in 1995 that he was hired as director of *Green Lantern: The Movie* was ignored by both the *Dallas Morning News* and the *Fort Worth Star-Telegram*; the *Dallas Observer* killed the story on the bequest of editor Peter Elkind.

L.A. Dorman remembers the reasoning for the last. "It was right before we broke up, and we were at a party at the Blind Lemon. Edgar was talking to a group of people, and this asshole marches right into the middle of the group and started with "You of course know who I am, don't you?" Everyone else said "No," but Edgar said "No, and if you don't get the fuck out of my way, I'm going to shove this beer bottle up your ass and kick you in the butt until broken glass comes out your ears. I'd kick you in the balls, but I know your ex-wife took them both as a divorce settlement." Well, I found out that he'd just insulted the editor of the *Dallas Absurder*, but Edgar knew the whole time. I had no idea that Peter Elkind could be so petty, but then take a look at the whole paper."

Back in the Robledo Mountains, Harris continues working on what he plans will be the best adaptation of a comic book in movie history. According to sources, he plans a production that will make *Independence Day*, the other effects-laden summer release, fade like a morning glory.

The movie is based on the comic from DC, the creators of *Superman* and *Batman*. The comic follows the adventures of the Green Lanterns, a group of superheroes formed by the mysterious Guardians to protect the universe from all evil. Each Green Lantern carries a power ring which allows the wielder to create anything his or her will imagines in green energy; aside from needing a recharge every 24 hours and a vulnerability to the color yellow, a Green Lantern can accomplish almost anything.

According to a very early script written by Oscar-winners Cordwainer Bird and

John Simon Ritchie, the action surrounds the three Green Lanterns of Earth: Hal Jordan (played by Mel Gibson), John Stewart (Michael Dorn, best known as portraying Worf in Star Trek: The Next Generation), and Guy Gardner (comedian Denis Leary). The plot revolves around protecting the Guardians' home world of Oa from an attack by the evil Sinestro (Edward James Olmos), a renegade Green Lantern leading a force of alien mercenaries to destroy his former masters and take their power for himself. In a tribute to his Dallas roots, local actress Brenda Susan Foster appears in her Hollywood debut as Carol Ferris, Jordan's girlfriend (Foster appeared in many of Harris' films, including *Jock Feast*). If the script is any indication, the film will compare in special effects usage to *Terminator 2* or *Jurassic Park*: out of a 115-page script (where each page is roughly comparable to a minute of screen time), some 83 pages feature one major effect or another.

One source, speaking on the condition of anonymity, said "It looks like *Green Lantern* is going to be a blowout for the summer. Edgar put everything he could into this, and he really got a lot of help from the cast and crew. I mean, Denis Leary was born to play Guy Gardner."

Whether this will happen is open to debate: few pundits in the movie industry can help but remember *Alien 3* (directed by David Fincher, who went directly from directing music videos to the third *Alien* franchise only to watch it bomb), or the adaptation of Kurt Vonnegut's book *Slapstick*. Likewise, few are sure that Harris is the man for the job: although the successes of Richard Linklater and Quentin Tarantino have made things easier for gonzo filmmakers to sell their projects, some wonder if hiring Harris was the same mistake as hiring David Lynch for *Dune*. Also, a huge special effects budget is no guarantee of success, as evidenced by the box office failures of *The Abyss*, *Last Action Hero*, and *Judge Dredd*, among many others.

A few wonder about Harris' motivations for working under Dreamworks SKG on a film he would have derided a few years ago as "derivative garbage." On one point, the move could be for Harris to get the respect he thinks he deserves. On another, Harris could be using the clout from a major success to direct the films he wants to make, much as Tim Burton used the leverage from *Batman* to get the green-light for *Edward Scissorhands* and *The Nightmare Before Christmas*. On a third, the whole story could be nothing but an April Fools' hoax by a minor science fiction writer to satirize how Dallas treats its resident artists. Whatever the outcome, people will talk about Edgar Harris for a very long time.

In his last interview before starting work on *Green Lantern*, Harris said "I get all sorts of smartasses who tell me 'You know, you're not as clever as you think you are.' All I say in return is 'Physician, heal thyself.' "

–The Met, April 1996

Postscript: This little article was written for The Met, *a long-dead Dallas weekly newspaper that ran a hoax article such as this every April Fool's Day. Unfortunately, I never calculated the credulousness and sheer humorlessness of comics fans: for years afterward, I'd be accosted by people at science fiction conventions who wanted to tell me all about the new Green Lantern movie. Denis Leary is allegedly sick and tired of being told all about it, too, but that's just karmic balance for stealing Bill Hicks' act.*

"Edmund Scientific Sells Out: A decided lack of Viciousness and Depravity threatens our future as a leader in the sciences"

As with most people, I like receiving mail. I get lots of it, mostly from complete strangers, and I hang onto the really good stuff. Nude photos, recipes for psilocybin pizzas, random CDs...I got a CD yesterday containing Courtney Love's song "Teenage Whore"; I presume she's singing from experience.

However, one of my biggest joys in life as a child was getting the Edmund Scientific catalogue in the old mailbox. Even in my adolescence, I looked forward to each catalogue appearing alongside the latest *Soldier of Fortune* and *Heavy Metal* (in the latter's case, this was before the goddamn movie fucked up everything, and you actually got decent story and art). Few things cheered me as much as the Edmund Scientific catalogue, save for spiking the punch at my high school senior prom with about 200 microdots of Orange Sunshine.

Seeing as how I hadn't seen a copy since I was forced to leave the state of Texas for religious reasons (the same ones Bob Tilton had), I perused this new copy with all of the attention of a dyslexic reading the Windows 95 operator's manual.

Folks, the forces of Satan are upon us, and they've infected the only resource for enterprising miscreants who can't afford their own guns nor the metalshops for making them.

The main Edmund Scientific catalogue, free to anyone who asks for one, contains all sorts of shit for the "scientifically minded" out there, and most of it is the safe stuff you can pick up on any Nature Store in any shopping mall. Crystal-making kits, gyroscopes, plastic dinosaurs, and stuff like that. Fine for everyone who believes in playing it safe, but I grew up with toys guaranteed to put your eye out. I used to make mortars with tennis balls and gasoline, pool aerators out of raw metallic sodium, and solid-fuel rockets with ranges of up to 50 miles. Hell, my brother and I learned how to make black powder by the time we were five. And now anyone like us can't learn these things.

This is a company that used to carry some of the coolest chemistry sets in the world, and now they're down to the Elementary Chemistry Set from the Smithsonian, which advertises itself as "The Safest Chemistry Set Ever Made." ..".each chemical is enclosed in a protected, spillproof bottle and is transferred to a special 'experiment dish' by special droppers. Chemical strengths are a fraction of (a) regular chemistry set, but are strong enough to achieve the correct reactions in experiments."

Well, what the fuck good is a chemistry set that's safe? Remember the good old days, when you could take the potassium ferrocyanide and use it to poison that dog that kept getting into the garbage can? What about the bottles with those damn-near-impossible-to-remove tops, that always ended up spilling crap all over your room when your mother told you not to do experiments when she wasn't there to help you? What about the alcohol lamps that allowed you to bend and stretch glassware, and left you with at least one good second-degree burn from molten glass landing on your leg and burning through your jeans? What about when you discovered that the phenophalien solution was the same as the active ingredient in Feen-A-Mints, and you spiked the lemonade you sold outside and gave the whole neighborhood a case of the shits? Not any more. The Safety Nazis saw to that.

Things looked better in the catalogue when I got to the lasers: they have a lot more of the damn things than they did when I was a kid. And they're smaller and cheaper, which means you grab a handful of "Our Lowest Priced Laser-Pointer-Just $49.95!" and go out to the local yuppie dance club, where you flash those things in their eyes while they're drunk and burn holes in their retinas. Then we have the Fresnel lenses: big sheets of plastic that magnify light to truly evil levels. You see small Fresnels on the back windows of Grannymobiles to allow the driver to see things at the back of the bus, but did you know that the really big ones can be used to "melt asphalt in seconds"?

Damn right. I'm getting one right now, so the next tine that dickweed in my apartment complex parks his pimp-blue Firebird in the fire lane again, I'll burn "FUCKHEAD" right into the hood's paint job. Either that, or I'll grab his poodle and demonstrate the Fresnel's uses as a solar oven by serving dog s'mores to my fellow residents.

I have to admit, they still have lots of neat stuff in the catalogue, like the dry ice maker ($69.95) that allows you to take a CO2 tank and make your own dry ice (time to fill the swimming pool in July, kids), or the polarizing lenses sold at Pink Floyd laser light shows (the ones that turn every point of light into a mass of rainbows: the ones that save a lot of money otherwise utilized for acid when driving down the freeway at 3 a.m.), but the really good stuff is gone. Most of the good dissecting gear is gone, and so is just about anything that can go boom, with the exception of the "Carbide Cannons." This is what childhood is really all about: burning stuff, mutilating animals, and blowing up their carcasses. If you never put grasshoppers into Estes model rockets, removed the parachute, added a plastique warhead, and then examined what was left after it landed and the flames died down, you didn't live.

The one item, though, that really pissed me off in its absence was the authentic plastic pyramid. For years, Edmund Scientific sold these cheap clear plastic pyramids to allow students to study "pyramid power," and I made a good living in high school by buying them from Edmund for $20 and selling them at psychic fairs for $100. The only people more willing to be burned by hucksters than Moronic Convergers are *Star Trek* geeks, and I made money by selling pyramids to them, too.

The rest of the catalogue was the same way: let's not hurt or rip off the customers. Fuck you! Show me a chemist who still has all fingers, and I'll show you a pussy. Science experiments should be dangerous: the dingbats who don't do them right fall prey to natural selection. The more dorks who think it's fun to mix sodium cyanide and hydrochloric acid, the more worms we feed, because dead idiots don't breed. It's the same way with music: the retards who pay to sit right next to the amps at a Rolling Stones or Pearl Jam show deserve deafness and cerebral hemorrhages as punishment for their bad taste. If we ever expect to take back the position of world leader in science back from the Bolivians and Tierra Del Fuegans, we need to start by demonstrating (a) science can be fun, and (b) only business and law majors think they're immune to the laws of physics. And they're WRONG!

Because of this move, I plan to take the money I'm collecting from film-making and use it to finance a competing catalogue: one that sells blasting caps, napalm, and electroshock therapy kits. It's up to us to make America a scientific giant again, and if that means a few more prosthetic limbs get made, then we're doing our jobs.

—*Fat City News, July 1996*

Postscript: Originally written for the long-dead online gonzo magazine Fat City News, *this was the first article ever directly attributed to Edgar Harris besides a few book reviews appearing in* Science Fiction Eye. *Now do you understand why I wanted to get him a job and have him move out?*

"Product of the Week"

In the nearly one and one-half years since the release of *Star Wars: Episode One*, most of the manufacturers of licensed products have suffered with less-than-stellar sales. Many grocery stores are still stuck with Anakin Skywalker Halloween costumes, and retail toy chains Toys 'R' Us and FAO Schwartz are almost literally flooded with action figures, MicroMachines playsets, Lego kits, Pez dispensers, and Soap-on-a-Rope boxes that store managers privately concede couldn't be given away with a free six-pack of Budweiser glued to the side. However, one licensed manufacturer has by far the most innovative product available, and this product literally cannot be produced fast enough to match the demand. The company is Flusho, a Houston-based supplier of sanitary products for custodians and health care workers, and the product is the official "Jar Jar Binks" urinal cake.

Stan Anthe, Flusho's president, explained the serendipity of the situation. "We patented a way to put an image into a urinal cake that ran through its whole length, so it only disappeared when the cake wore out. Anyway, so we figured that a fella at a urinal don't have much else to look at, so why not use 'em as advertising? We had a few dotcoms call us up and commission some special cakes as souvenirs, but then Vern, our sales guy, heard that Lucasfilm was calling for bids on licensed products, and we contacted them about doing up *Episode One* cakes. This is a really competitive market, so I couldn't believe that we were the only company that put in a bid."

Within days of the release of the cakes, Flusho was the darling of the advertising world, as nobody had noticed the completely untapped advertising niche until then. Not only did the cakes perform admirably in their main function, keeping the urinals sanitary and smelling fresh, but testing found that they were the focus of the users' attentions. To take advantage of the hype surrounding *Episode One*, Flusho also performed the unthinkable and paid for a national ad campaign in the big entertainment magazines, previously unheard of in the sanitary product industry. The ad campaign, "Piss on Jar Jar," became an unqualified hit.

Anthe related the surprise he and the rest of the company felt over the sudden success. "Well, advance sales weren't all that good until the ad in *Entertainment Weekly* ran, and then we couldn't keep them in stock. When we started the ad campaign, people would go to public restrooms looking for the Jar Jar cakes, and we found people stealing them just to use them at home. People were drinking eight and nine two-liter bottles of Dr. Pepper a day just so they could use the cakes

410   Paul T. Riddell

at work. And when Lucasfilm announced that Jar Jar was going to be in *Episode Two*, some custodians would have to replace them three and four times a day because they'd get plumb wore out. We'd never seen people in such a dang hurry to use a urinal before."

As can be expected, some unethical companies started manufacturing bootleg urinal cakes, sold under the "Jam Jam" name. A spokesperson from Lucasfilm denounced the bootlegs. "We have on good authority that these 'Jam Jam' urinal cakes are made from metallic sodium, which explodes when it comes in contact with water, and we read a story on Usenet about several people being burned severely on their nether regions by faulty urinal cakes. We also heard a caller on a talk radio program that these bootleg cakes have radio transmitters that cause anyone urinating on them to worship Satan, and a poster on *Ain't It Cool News* says that they cause sterility, which in the case of *Ain't It Cool News* fans is moot. We beseech anyone using a urinal in the next six months to use only official 'Jar Jar Binks' urinal cakes, or suffer the consequences. We're starting a hotline to help find and prosecute the people bypassing paying our outrageous royalty fees by making counterfeit *Star Wars* restroom products."

Even the official urinal cakes aren't without controversy. Although the cakes are marked "Not For Home Use," overzealous fans have been using them at home, where they have a tendency to cause uncontrollable fires in most septic tank systems. To allay concerns, Flusho is working with Ti-D-Bowl to make home Jar Jar toilet cleansers, available in green, blue, and blue-green sometime in February 2001. Again breaking with tradition in the industry, these are intended to be hung on the back of the toilet bowl, and are being promoted as encouraging young children in toilet-training.

Flusho isn't staying mum on its other licensed products, either: it announced last month that it plans to mine the hitherto untapped advertising market in sanitary products with a series of new offerings. The *Battlefield Earth* bedpans, *Free Enterprise: The Series* colostomy tubing, and *Gene Roddenberry's Andromeda* air sickness bags are already doubling the company's orders, but the *Star Trek: Voyager* home enema kits are the real hope of the future. "We've had literally hundreds of requests for the *Voyager* enema kits,' said Anthe, "and who are we to argue with the public?"

—*Zealot.com*, December 2000

"Saturn and Golden Raspberry Awards To Merge"

Los Angeles - Mergers between corporations handling similar lines of business are commonplace, but industry awards usually remain separate entities. This changed today with the announcement of the merger between the Saturn Awards, the annual award from the Academy of Science Fiction, Fantasy, and Horror Films for achievement in genre films and television, and the Golden Raspberry Awards, which celebrate the very worst of Hollywood.

John Simon Ritchie, a spokesman for the ASFFHF, said in a prepared statement "We give up. This is a year where, for the life of us, we can't find a single science fiction, fantasy, or horror film worth seeing at discount matinees, and we can't continue to pretend that *Red Planet*, *Dungeons & Dragons*, *Hollow Man*, and *Lost Souls* are worthy of awards. As it is, we're certain that we're going to spend eternity in a lake of burning Tasmanian devil dung in the deepest pits of Hell for nominating *Empire of the Ants* for a Saturn in 1978 and *Creature* in 1985, and we can't stand the thought of Brian DePalma actually expecting to win a Saturn for *Mission to Mars*."

"It was bad enough last year that you couldn't tell the difference between the Saturn and Golden Raspberry nominees, to the point where we thought we had a mole from the Razzies in the organization. I mean, George Lucas nominated for Best Director and Jake Lloyd for Best New Actor? What the fuck were we thinking? Were we all on crack? And then when someone from *SCI FI* magazine pointed out that we gave the Best Home Video Release to *Free Enterprise* instead of *Trekkies* or *The Iron Giant*...well, it just made more sense to admit that science fiction film sucks these days and pack it in. Either that, or admit that we were willing to endorse anything so long as it had lots of flashy special effects or dopey fannish in-jokes."

Raoul Duke, representative for the Golden Raspberry Awards, concurred. "It's been a great year for us, and our only problem is trying to decide which of this year's genre films is worthy of being considered 'the worst', so we can hand out two awards and run the same film clip and save money. Normally, nobody actually shows up to the Razzies ceremony to pick up their awards, but can you imagine John Travolta showing up to pick up not one but two awards for *Battlefield Earth* in each category?"

Because of the merger, the revamped Golden Raspberry now has enough money to schedule a live telecast to be shown on the SCI FI Channel in March opposite the Academy Awards. In a concession to Saturn history, the emcee is Golden Raspberry winner of "Worst Actor of the Century" William Shatner, who plans to join Priceline.Com associate and eyewear poster child Lisa Loeb in an interpretive dance adaptation of "Pac-Man Fever" to open the show. This is to be followed by a retrospective of previous Shatner musical numbers at previous Saturn ceremonies, including his unique renditions of "Rocket Man," "Blitzkrieg Bop," "Stairway to Heaven, "Cause I'm A Blonde," and the "Love Theme from *Apocalypse Now*."

Duke explained the rationale. "William Shatner pretty much sums up what both the Razzies and the Saturns are all about, and the fact that he works cheap doesn't hurt. We wanted to get Richard Hatch from *Battlestar Galactica* to host next year, but he's still bitching about the guy on *Survivor* taking his name." Plans for hosts in future broadcasts include Jason Carter (*Babylon 5*), Butch Patrick (*The Munsters*), director Joel Schumacher (*Batman & Robin*), "and anyone else who now makes a significant portion of their annual income autographing glossies at science fiction and comics conventions."

Genre film industry press representatives were enthusiastic about the merger. Mark A. Altman, columnist for *Cinescape* magazine, said "As you know, I used to edit *Sci-Fi Universe*, back when it was good, so I think this is a great move for the science fiction industry. By the way, did I mention that the *Los Angeles Times* called me 'the world's leading Trekspert'?" Paul T. Riddell, columnist for the competing *SCI FI*, concurred with "Let me freebase some Preparation H and I'll have a comment for you that I'll think is clever." And Harry Knowles of *Ain't It Cool News* said "I haven't eaten in ten minutes. Could you hand me that tub of Crisco and a spoon?"

The announcement of the Saturn/Golden Raspberry merger set off the awards community and set off a round of awards speculation; the announcement of the merger between the Grammy Awards and the Britney Spears Fan Club is scheduled for next week, and the merger between the Academy Awards and the Darwin Awards is set to be finalized in late 2001.

           —Zealot.com, January 2001

Postscript: The crew involved with the Golden Raspberries thought that this was a perfect little article, and put a link to it from their Web site for a few weeks, but the Saturn people apparently never responded. Well, they may have responded, but whinings of "I don't think that's funny at all" don't count.

"St. Martins Starts 'World's Worst Science Fiction Imprint' With First Hardcover Printing of *Eye of Argon*"

New York -Many publishers try to preserve the best in science fiction literature, either with the best short stories and novellas in a given year or with the best novels of years past. St. Martin's Press, though, is taking the opposite route, at least for one line of books in 2001. To commemorate the start of the new century, St. Martin's officially announced its "World's Worst Science Fiction" line, starting with the long-loathed fan fantasy novel *The Eye of Argon*, never published in hardcover format until now.

"The whole thing started with Gordon Van Gelder," said Kilgore Bird, editor of the WWSF line and new assistant to St. Martin's science fiction editor Bryan Cholfin. "Back when Gordon was editor, he wanted to sell his bosses on the idea of reprints of Ed Wood's old novels back when Tim Burton's movie was due out, and he made his presentation at a St. Martin's dinner in full Ed Wood drag. He had the skirt, high heels and angora sweater, and we were complimenting him on his angora leg-warmers until we realized that he hadn't shaved his legs. Damn, that man must be half-Sasquatch."

The Ed Wood series never materialized, but Bird noted the interest in seeing all of Wood's nearly unreadable novels in hardcover or trade paperback format. "Everyone works toward preserving the best in the genre, but nobody talks about saving the worst. We need to save the absolute worst in science fiction, if only to teach people not to write garbage like this. It's also a good guide for others: I had a friend describe it as a 'Scared Straight' for the *Writer's Digest* crowd."

Even though the last seventy years of science fiction and fantasy have been deluged with lousy novels and stories, Bird still had a hard row to hoe. "We couldn't get the rights to reprint Hubbard's *Battlefield Earth* or the *Mission Earth* books because the Scientologists would have kicked the snot out of us. Humorless bastards: they're almost as bad as the Church of the Subgenius fanatics. We also couldn't get reprint rights to any *Star Trek* or *Star Wars* novels, although I'd sell my left nut to get the reprint rights to the novelization to *Return of the Jedi* or anything by Kristine Kathryn Rusch and Dean Wesley Smith. We also couldn't get any of the tie-ins, so that meant that we couldn't reprint *Mr. Scott's Guide to the Enterprise* or Craig Shaw Gardner's *Batman* novelization. We even thought of trying a few of those godawful 'unauthorized' *Trek* books like *Trek Navigator* or *Great Birds of the Galaxy*, but used bookstores all over the country are still stuck with thousands of remaindered copies of those as it is, so why flood the market even further?"

After much deliberation, the crew at St. Martin's settled on the infamous *The Eye of Argon* as its flagship book. Allegedly written by a sixteen-year-old with a hideously defective thesaurus sometime in the mid-Seventies, *Eye* is a fantasy novel in the Robert E. Howard tradition, if Howard had first translated his work to Sanskrit, then to French, and then back to English. A long-running joke in the SF community for nearly 30 years, *Eye* was perfect for Bird's plans.

"Back in the days when science fiction conventions were for people who read science fiction, *Eye of Argon* readings were the precursor to *The Rocky Horror Picture Show*. You'd get a room full of people late one night with a single copy of the manuscript, and they'd each start reading it. The first person who broke down laughing and dropped the manuscript had to give it to the next person. By the time they'd get halfway through it, it could have gone through a good eighty or ninety people, all of whom soiled themselves from laughter. We just *have* to bring this tradition back to fandom."

Initial response from SF book reviewers to the announcement was seen by St. Martin's as positive. *Science Fiction Chronicle* reviewer Don d'Ammassa said "Muuh! Muuh! Muuuuuh!" shortly before his eyes exploded, and *Locus* reviewer Jonathan Strahan simply settled for stabbing himself repeatedly in the testicles with a rusty hedge clipper. Because of these and other equally eloquent responses, St. Martins plans to put out twenty titles in its WWSF imprint, starting with the Michael Jahn space shuttle opera *Armada* (seen by many to be the inspiration for the 1996 film *Independence Day*, both in characterization and scientific accuracy), and Whitley Strieber's extraterrestrial anal rape fantasy *Communion*, now released under its original working title of *Deliverance: The Next Generation*. The WWSF line will also include nonfiction, including Robert S. Elrick's *A Beginner's Guide To Science Fiction*, generally considered to be one of the worst guides to the genre ever written, and Paul T. Riddell's *Squashed Armadillocon*, directly linked to an epidemic of uncontrollable rectal bleeding among science fiction readers in 1993.

Bird even plans to go one further: as a counterpoint to the annual Hugo Awards, St. Martin's plans to host the Elwood Awards, named after famed anthology editor Roger Elwood. "Elwood flooded the publishing industry with any number of lousy anthologies back in the late Sixties and early Seventies before going back to religious publishing, and you can still find libraries where half of the science fiction section consists of his godawful collections," said Bird. "We have the Hugos commemorating the best of the science fiction literature field every year, such as it is, but it takes work to choose the absolute worst novel, novella, and short story published every year. The Golden Raspberries take on the worst of film, but if we don't preserve the worst of science fiction literature, who will?"

—*Zealot.com, February 2001*

"Tina Brown to Take Over Editorship of *Asimov's*"

New York – When one mentions magazine editors, the name of Tina Brown appears time and time again as one of the most recognizable. After her stints as editor of *Vanity Fair* and *The New Yorker* in the early Nineties, Brown moved to her own publication, *Talk*, and beat all estimates of the magazine's success and lifespan. Widely criticized for her attitude and her extravagant spending habits, Brown still became one of the most popular editors in the last half-century.

For the last few years, though, Brown had expressed the urge to carve new frontiers in publishing. This helped explain the announcement this week that Brown was replacing current editor Gardner Dozois as editor of *Isaac Asimov's Science Fiction Magazine*.

"The catchline we're looking for is 'sexy'," said Anne Uhmelmehe, spokesperson for Dell, the owners of Asimov's and its sister publication Analog. "Gardner Dozois may be a lot of things, but 'sexy' isn't a word you use around him unless you're aroused by yeti. We figure that by getting Tina, we'll get a lot of readers who just love that sultry British accent of hers. Besides, it's not like Gardner's being left in the cold. He'll probably be able to get an editing job at *Mimosa* or *Star Wars Insider* or something."

Dell's immediate plan is to convert *Asimov's* into a twenty-first century magazine, complete with standard magazine format, glossy pages, and advertising by Saks 5th Avenue and Nordstrom's. However, the editor's job is to determine the ongoing course and feel of a magazine, and Tina had very definite plans for this transition.

"First things first, we're going to work on makeovers on our writers," Brown said. "Science fiction writers are usually such oiks, so we're looking for glamorous people in the field. Snappy dressers and the like. We can't do anything about the readers just yet, but they're next.

"The next plan is to bring on guest editors who aren't generally associated with science fiction but like reading it in secret, so we can draw in new readers. Our first guest editor will be Roseanne, and then we're going to bring in Christian Slater and David Arquette. They'll do a little editorial or two about how much they like the job, and then we'll publish the stories received in a given month that they like the most."

Brown also expressed interest in bringing new artists in to paint or draw covers for *Asimov's*. "Charles Addams is a perfect fit for the new *Asimov's*, but someone told me he was dead, so we're looking at a nice cross-section of experimental political cartoonists and expressionist painters. Everyone except that Tom Tomorrow; he's just dreadful."

Another aspect with the change lay with promotion: already, bulk mail subscription cards have the "Edited by Gardner Dozois!" note covered over with a sticker reading "Now Edited by Tina Brown!," but Brown has further plans. As of April, *Asimov's* will become the first science fiction magazine since *OMNI* to run television advertising during prime time, and Brown and Dell will sponsor a premiere party simulcast on the E! and SCI FI cable channels. Brown has already answered critics' concerns about the excessive costs of this promotion by saying "When you're as fabulous as I am, you don't need to worry about profits. That's what I taught them at *Vanity Fair*."

When asked about possible reader backlash, Brown was nonplussed. "When I edited *The New Yorker*, we took all sorts of harassment from those trolls at *Spy* magazine, and I crushed them like bugs. I dare *Locus* or *Science Fiction Chronicle* to say anything about this, because I'll make them disappear. I guarantee it."

News of the editorial transition caused immediate changes at most of the main magazines in the science fiction industry. Gordon Van Gelder, editor of *The Magazine of Fantasy & Science Fiction*, hired famed screenwriter Joe Esterhaz (*Showgirls*, *Perfect*) to replace current film critic Kathy Maio for an undisclosed but rumored seven-figure fee, and *Analog* editor Stanley Schmidt commissioned a new convention report column by Lake Wobegon author Garrison Keillor. Other editors were more proactive: calls to confirm rumors that Scott Edelman, editor of the late *Science Fiction Age* and current editor of *Science Fiction Weekly*, and Ellen Datlow, fiction editor for *OMNI* and current editor of *SCIFIction*, had challenged Brown to a Bowie knife duel in the Avenue of the Americas plaza were not returned at press time.

—*Zealot.com, February 2001*

"BBC and SCI FI Announce *Absolutely Fabulous/Farscape* Crossover"

Crossovers, the ongoing bane of fan-written science fiction, have previously had limited success in televised SF. Few can forget (or forgive) the introduction of WWF wrestlers to the guest star list of *Star Trek: Voyager*, and the ongoing crossovers between The WB's *Buffy the Vampire Slayer* and *Angel* help fuel ratings during sweeps periods. However, absolutely nobody expected the latest joint announcement between the BBC, the premier producer of British television programs, and the SCI FI Channel in the ultimate crossover: a merger of the acclaimed sitcom *Absolutely Fabulous* and the equally acclaimed SF drama *Farscape*.

"I've been horribly fond of *Farscape* from the beginning," said Jennifer Saunders, co-creator, scriptwriter, and star of *Absolutely Fabulous*, "and when I found that the crew of *Farscape* was all big fans of our show, I figured that I could scam my way into getting free plane tickets to Australia for location shooting. Besides, you can't get this strange in the UK without the drug-sniffing dogs catching you, so Australia it was."

The final plotline for the one-shot show, tentatively titled "*FabScape*," was sketchy, but a photo of the production material appeared on the Internet within a few days of the announcement, and the BBC coordinated a last-minute press conference with Saunders, co-star Joanna Lumley, and *Farscape* star Ben Browder last week.

Based on an early script stolen from Saunders' apartment and given to a Zealot correspondent after the perp died from wounds sustained in the subsequent gun battle with police, *Absolutely Fabulous* regulars Edina Monsoon (Saunders), Patsy Stone (Lumley), Edina's daughter Saffron (Julia Sawalha), and Edina's scatterbrained assistant Bubble (Jane Horrocks) awaken "somewhere in the universe" as a side-effect from eating botulism-tainted mushroom souffles. Seeing as how Edie is a fashion-obsessed former hippie, Patsy a hopeless lush and hedonist, Saffron a rational opposite to every one of Edie's dubious personality traits, and Bubble barely qualifying as sentient, the old Hollywood saw "and hijinks ensue" don't begin to describe the situation when they first come in contact with the gang of fugitives and escapees currently inhabiting the organic starship Moya.

Browder describes it thusly: "My character, John Crichton, is at first glad to talk to someone from Earth again, until he realizes that he's better off in his isolation if he has to go back to an Earth full of these sorts of people. The rest of the crew is more than bemused, seeing as how these folks are more dysfunctional than they'll ever be. When the ship is captured by Scorpius, the scientific genius trying to get into my character's head, Patsy finds the one person in the universe just like her and manages to drive him off just by trying to get him to marry her. Saffron discovers that she's more of a Delvian ascetic than Zhaan is, but draws the line at getting pruned and manured in the spring. And for Edie, well, let's just say that D'Argo and Chiana lock her up in a spare storeroom and let her 'find herself', and she spends half of the episode trying to get stoned off old Prowler fuel."

"Oh, and don't forget Bubble," Lumley nudged.

"Oh, yeah. Bubble meets Pilot and they fall in love at first sight. The poor guy just can't conceive of anything in the universe so brain-damaged and helpless, and she turns out to be a sucker for a guy with a steady job."

As usual, press response was enthusiastic. Mark A. Altman, columnist for *Cinescape*, said "As you know, the SCI FI Channel referred to me as the Onan, I mean Narcissus, I mean Socrates of sci-fi, so I know what I'm talking about. Did I mention that *SF Site* called me 'the Al Bundy of fandom'?" Paul T. Riddell, former columnist for the competing *SCI FI* magazine, said "Christ, you just described my marriage. Every time I go somewhere without my wife, she threatens 'Sweetie, if I can't come, I'll adopt a Hynerian baby.'" And Harry Knowles of *Ain't It Cool News* said "Gigi Edgeley is really hot, and I'm certain that she doesn't know anything about that restraining order. Her manager has it in for me."

Since the television industry isn't known for its originality, expect further crossovers of this sort. The most intriguing rumor making the rounds is that Fox is willing to finance a big-budget redux of *The Prisoner* if at least one episode also functions as a reunion show for the cast of *The Brady Bunch*. (As one executive at Fox put it, "Wouldn't it be cool if we found out that Number One was really Jan?") The Canadian Broadcasting Corporation plans to retaliate by incorporating at least one recurring character from *The Red Green Show* into each episode of *Gene Roddenberry's Andromeda* per week, and the less said about the cast of the British series *The Young Ones* reprising their roles as the Away Team in the upcoming secret *Star Trek* franchise, the better. Either way this trend goes, Saunders and associates have changed the face of televised science fiction, and fans will probably never recover.

—*Zealot.com, February 2001*

"Episode Two Production Actually Front for Different Film, Lucasfilm Says"

Melbourne, Australia – Back in 1983, the Arizona desert was the home for the production crew of the allegedly upcoming film *Blue Harvest*. Few outsiders knew at the time that the "Blue Harvest" sets really belonged to the then-anticipated *Return of the Jedi*, and filming completed before anyone besides a hand-picked cadre of reporters knew of the deception. In 2001, the same subterfuge is going on in Australia. However, instead of using another production to conceal location shooting for *Star Wars: Episode Two*, the *Episode Two* production is itself camouflage for *Taking It Easy*, a romantic comedy starring Freddy Prinze, Jr. and Kirsten Dunst.

Thanks to sources that spoke on condition of anonymity, Zealot has learned that the entire *Episode Two* location shoot was nothing but a front for *Taking It Easy*, which marks George Lucas' first directorial credit for an intentional comedy since *American Graffiti*. When asked about the reasons behind it, the source said "Look at all of the free publicity we'll get. Now have a film we can sell to everyone besides the dolts camping out in front of theaters waiting for *Episode Two*, and we'll get them, too. For God's sake, some of them are actually willing to hunt down *Twice upon A Time* and *Howard the Duck* just because George was involved, so they'll watch anything."

The source revealed that filming *Taking It Easy* was relatively easy once the press was redirected. "We have Ewan MacGregor on contract for the next six films, whether we make them or not, so we essentially paid him and *Natalie Portman* to take a vacation in Australia. About once a day, we'd set up some set made out of stuff we had lying around, put a Jar-Jar Binks mask on some extra, and pretend to film something. You'd figure that someone would have caught on that the cameras didn't have any film in them, but they were so busy posting pictures on the Internet that they didn't notice.

"We got the whole idea from John Waters talking about how he scammed the papers in Baltimore into believing that he was shooting a new film called *Dorothy, the Kansas City Pothead* back in the Seventies. He had reporters following his whole crew all over town, and they not once had film in their camera. We're just taking it to a whole new level."

George Lucas himself seemed unperturbed by the revelation. "I've been pushing off crap from my notebooks for years as work that I had conceived before

Star Wars. Willow was something I came up with back in high school, and
Radioland Murders came from when I was shotgunning Budweiser and blackberry
brandy back when I was 11. This time, though, this really is something I really
wanted to do before *Star Wars*, and not because I had to make the mortgage
payment on Skywalker Ranch."

This bait-and-switch strategy isn't limited to Lucas. Sources close to the
production of *Lord of the Rings* confessed that the entire entourage was really
finishing filming on a sequel to director Peter Jackson's *Bad Taste*, substituting
exploding hobbits for exploding sheep. Sam Raimi's Renaissance Pictures is
pretending to film the long-awaited *Spider-Man* while in actuality completing a
biography on noted artist Ralph Steadman. And in a reversal, Woody Allen is
currently putting the final touches on the adaptation of H. Beam Piper's alternate
history adventure novel *Lord Kalvan of Otherwhen* in Manhattan while luring his
fans with the promise of a new comedy featuring "a neurotic sixty-something
comedy writer living in New York who inexplicably attracts beautiful women easily
a third his age."

The news that most of the photos purporting to be from the *Episode Two* set
are fakes have caused many sites running them to pull them from circulation. In
a prepared statement, Harry Knowles of *Ain't It Cool News* said "I stand by all of
the information presented on my site, no matter how inaccurate it may be." Chris
Gore of the rival *Film Threat* site said "We would've been all over it if we didn't
have a subject of more importance. Namely, me." Finally, noted Australian SF film
critic Robin Pen was unavailable for comment, having been admitted to hospital
for a ruptured appendix "caused by excessive and explosive laughter."

Taking It Easy will see general release in the US and foreign markets on May
22, 2002.

—*Zealot.com, February 2001*

"Gary Groth Hospitalized for Hate Mail Addiction"

Seattle - Controversial and combative comic publisher Gary Groth, best known as the editor/publisher of the trade magazine *The Comics Journal*, was hospitalized today after suffering a seizure at the Fantagraphics offices. Doctors said that the seizure was caused by stress connected to a lack of hate mail from comics fans, opponents, and interested bystanders.

"Mr. Groth's condition is a complex one," said Dr. Seymour Evsise, "particularly considering the age of the patient. His seizure was a specialized and very obscure condition neurologists call a 'temper tantrum', which causes uncontrollable stamping of the feet, incoherent screaming, and an inability to exhale until the victim turns blue. In children, it has a simple and effective treatment, but pulling his pants down and swatting his butt with a peach switch isn't always possible in a man pushing sixty."

Fantagraphics editor Kim Thompson described the situation. "Gary had been going for the last three weeks without any negative commentary on the last issue of the *Comics Journal*. Even challenging [Marvel Comics editor-in-chief] Joe Quesada to a chainsaw duel got no response. Well, he decided to get online and take his case to the people, and nothing worked. He ragged on [comic writer and artist] John Byrne, he ragged on [*Incredible Hulk* writer and *Comic Buyer's Guide* columnist] Peter David, and nothing made any difference, so he went after some of his usual targets. He accused Harlan Ellison of converting to Catholicism, he said that [DC Comics publisher] Jeanette Kahn wore women's underwear, and he even made fun of [*Savant* editor and co-founder] Matt Fraction for living in Kansas City. He was right in the middle of a big editorial calling all comics readers who didn't like Fantagraphics titles 'poopy-heads' when he started bleeding from his eyes, and he back-flipped out of his chair and started gnawing on the curtains. I had to call the paramedics to tie him down; I didn't have a choice."

After being taken down with a tranquilizer gun, Groth was rushed via CareFlight helicopter to Seattle General Hospital, where he was treated and held for observation. "We've never seen a case like this," said Dr. Evsise, but we figure that it was bound to happen. People in the comics industry are just too high strung." All access to paper, pencils, Internet connections, and large bullhorns is closely monitored, and his access to incoming communications controlled to prevent a relapse when he discovers that the seizure didn't make the front page of the *Seattle Post-Intelligencer.*

Fantagraphics was one of the premier publishers of alternative comics in the late Eighties and early Nineties, with Groth introducing the world to the art of Peter Bagge, Roberta Gregory, and Rob Liefeld. With the end of the comics speculation boom in the mid-Nineties, Fantagraphics' stock dropped as comic shops in general closed up shop, and it currently ekes out life via the *Comics Journal*, the Eros line of upscale porn comics, and investment in the animated TV series *X-Men: Evolution*.

The only formal comment on the Groth hospitalization came from Matt Fraction of the comics commentary Webzine *Savant*, who said "I'm really not surprised by this: Groth was just an embolism waiting to happen. He's almost as desperate for attention as one of my writers, but that dingbat's from Texas, so it's to be expected." A search through Usenet archives, bulletin board systems, and chat rooms dedicated to comics for commentary about Groth's condition found that nobody was interested and nobody really cared. Rumors of singalongs of 'Ding Dong, The Witch Is Dead" coming from the direction of the *Comic Buyer's Guide* offices could not be confirmed at press time.

—*Revolution SF, July 2001*

"*Rocky Horror* Fan Leaves Theater, Fifteen Years Later"

Dallas – During the late Seventies and early Eighties, the wealthy Dallas suburb of Highland Park was home to the Highland Park Village Theater, which until 1986 had hosted the longest continuous run of *The Rocky Horror Picture Show* in the United States. That was the year that the owners shuttered the theater, where it remained empty until the early Nineties, when the AMC Theaters chain restored and reopened it. What most patrons of the new and improved Village didn't know was that one of the longtime *Rocky Horror* participants had fought a one-man war to return the famed cult film to the screens without once leaving the theater.

Jon Douglas East, 35, surrendered yesterday to police, acknowledging that his subtle campaign of terror to force a return of *Rocky Horror* to the Village was perhaps a bit too subtle. East had remained in the Village since the last midnight showing in 1986, leaving the air ducts and restroom stalls in the theater only to get food and make harassing phone calls to local authorities.

"He was all set up in there," said Highland Park Deputy Jim Highcastle. "East started out with a backpack full of beef jerky, a couple of paperback books, a rock hammer, and a pack of matches, and he built himself a nice little nest in the air ducts. He figured that he'd be protesting for a week or so, and had no idea that the original owners were planning to sell it out. He was just lucky that the Village was declared a landmark, or he would have been blown up with it fifteen years ago."

For the first few years, East had it rough, drinking from leaking fire sprinklers and feeding on rats and the occasional escaped Highland Park poodle ("which in Highland Park is pretty much the same thing," said Highcastle) and sleeping in ventilation ducts to evade the occasional security guard checking on the property. Then in 1991, when the AMC chain bought the theater with intent to restore it, East realized that the show might start again, but only if employees and management of the new theater never saw him.

AMC Village manager David Golgotha was very familiar with East's attempts to resurrect the audience participation crowds of his youth. "We'd come in and find 'BRING BACK ROCKY HORROR' spelled out in rat bones in the lobby, and someone TPed the main screen something fierce back about two years ago, but we didn't know he was living there. We'd find ropes braided out of human hair hanging from the ceiling fans, but we just figured that a patron had dropped them. I mean, this is Highland Park. The place is full of rich perverts."

Aside from sneaking views of films from the ventilation ducts ("*Jurassic Park* was one of the worst pieces of garbage I've ever seen," East said in a prepared statement), East was completely isolated from the rest of the world. His new food supply was candy and popcorn rustled from the storage rooms after management closed for the night, but he had no source of news other than conversations of theatergoers, and had no idea that so much time had elapsed. Finally, after having to listen to the screams from the main theater's showing of Hannibal for "way too long," East surrendered to authorities, who were as shocked by his appearance as he was by seeing the neighborhood by daylight for the first time in nearly two decades.

At one point, East had considered violence to get his message across. "Most people don't know that the flavoring for 'golden flavored popcorn' can be mixed with restroom air freshener to make a very effective substitute for napalm," said Highcastle. "He had a stockpile for years, and we're just glad he didn't see the need to use it."

"I'm sorry that I didn't come out and say hello to anyone for all of this time," East said at a press conference before his arraignment on charges of trespassing and squatting. "After all of this, I'm going to go home, take a shower, and get on with my life. I understand that Rocky Horror is now on cable all of the time, so I'll just go over to the Northwood Hills Four and get involved with the audience participation crowd for *Dawn of the Dead* out there." When informed that the theater had stopped running *Dawn of the Dead* in 1986 before going out of business in 1989, East broke down and wept.

Rocky Horror creator Richard O'Brien, when contacted about the incident, simply sighed and said "Bloody shame, it is. I could have used him to restore my castle out here in England. It's always a shame when people refuse to let loose of the past. He could have just spent his life watching the movie on VH1 like everyone else."

—*Revolution SF, July 2001*

"George Lucas Sues To Have Missile Shield Named After *Star Wars*"

Washington, DC – In a special meeting with the Senate Committee on Space and the Joint Chiefs of Staff, filmmaker George Lucas announced that he would sue the US government until the Pentagon-proposed automated missile defense shield currently being designed was renamed "*Star Wars.*"

"Yes, I know that I threatened to sue if they didn't quit calling the Strategic Defense Initiative the 'Star Wars' program, but I've changed my mind," Lucas said in a prepared statement. The fact is that nobody's buying the rights to *Star Wars: Episode Two* tie-ins, and every time the missile shield gets called 'Star Wars', I get a royalty. Maybe if I get enough, Linda Ronstadt will come back to me."

Under the plan, any unauthorized use of the name "*Star Wars*" when referring to the missile shield would result in jail time of no less than 10 years and fines of no less than $10 million. Authorization rates start at $10 for casual conversation among friends, rising to $500 million plus a 23 percent royalty per use in newspapers with a circulation over 100,000 and television programs with more than a 5.5 Nielsen share. The cost of its mention in classified documents was not disclosed. If the government would not capitulate, Lucas threatened to make another trilogy about young Anakin Skywalker, with Jake Lloyd reprising his role. Unnamed sources expect that the government will agree to his demands within days.

Robert Michner, doctor of Journalism at the University of Texas journalism department, calculated the potential royalty Lucas would receive based on current news coverage of the Pentagon missile shield. "Just with use of the title in *The McLaughlin Report* on PBS, public television would end up owing billions of dollars a year. Only the *New York Times* and the *Washington Post* could afford to make mention of the system, and God help us if Lucas decides to move this plan to entertainment journalism. One issue of *Entertainment Weekly* would bankrupt all of AOL Time Warner, and that's just with mention of how the missile shield will stimulate sales of action figures."

In last-minute negotiations, Lucas' lawyers removed the Pentagon as a defendant in the suit, and *Revolution SF* has discovered that this was contingent upon the Pentagon switching contract suppliers for several of its needs. Secretary of State Colin Powell, speaking at a Joint Chiefs dinner, said "We're very proud to have Houston-based Flusho, manufacturer of Jar-Jar Binks urinal cakes, in our defense contractor family. I'd like to call on us to follow Flusho's slogan and 'Piss on Jar-Jar': all day long, if necessary."

Even though the Department of Defense is temporarily safe, the suit affects all other aspects of the US government, including the General Accounting Office and NASA. Asked for comment about the suit, President George W. Bush said "Uhhhh...this sucks worse than anything has ever sucked before. Huh huh huh huh." Vice-President Dick Cheney followed with "Yeah, big time. Heh heh heh heh," before the two left the press conference for a quick game of frog baseball. Former Vice President Al Gore said "This suit was pre-eminently illogical," and his former running mate Joe Lieberman (D-Connecticut) screamed "Dammit, I'm a senator, not a copyright lawyer!"

In retaliation for continued US construction of the missile shield, the rest of the United Nations announced that it was passing the hat for a rival space-based defense system, with discussion logjammed on the merits of the "*Brazil*" defense system (where nuclear warhead-lobbing nations were buried under millions of tons of useless paperwork), the "*Mad Max*" defense system (where any attacking country found itself overrun with Australian motorcycle punks in bondage pants), or the "*Dawn of the Dead*" defense system (where any attacking country's shopping malls would be filled with flesh-eating zombies). Although contacted to inform them of their potential royalty windfalls, directors Terry Gilliam, George Miller, and George Romero could not be reached for comment.

—*Revolution SF, August 2001*

"Hunter S. Thompson To Write New *Babylon 5* Telemovie"

Los Angeles – The longrunning series *Babylon 5* is already known for its efforts to encourage fan interest in literary science fiction and in traditional literature. During its five-year run, creator J. Michael Straczynski included references to the works of Alfred Bester, H.P. Lovecraft, Michael Moorcock, and Chuck Jones into his scripts. However, with the approval of the SCI FI Channel, which is commissioning a series of *Babylon 5* telemovies over the next five years, Straczynski is handing over parts of his universe to other established authors, starting with a stint by noted ESPN.com sports columnist Hunter S. Thompson.

"We've been doing our best to convince the great body of science fiction fans to expand their horizons, and short of going to their houses, chaining them to stakes in the back yard, and forcing them to deal with clean air and sunshine, this is one of the best ways. I've always been an admirer of Hunter's work in [the late magazine] *Scanlon's*, and this is his last free period before he takes over as editor of *Vanity Fair*. As he puts it himself, we must do this."

Thompson was equally enthusiastic about his stint as guest creator. "I remember watching the first episode featuring the Shadows and screaming 'Holy Jesus! What are these goddamn animals?' After that, I was hooked. The whole cast reminded me of people I knew back in the Sixties. When I found that Joe [Straczynski] was a fan, I figured that this endeavor would be an example of everything right and true in the national character, but only for those with true grit. And we're chock full of that."

The new telemovie, tentatively titled *Fear and Loathing On Babylon 5*, is based on an obscure Thompson novel generally unfamiliar to science fiction fans. Starting with the line "We were somewhere outside of Centauri Prime, on the edge of hyperspace, when the drugs began to take hold," Thompson's script follows the exploits of human journalist Raoul Duke (played by Johnny Depp) and his 300-pound Narn attorney G'Onzo (Academy Award winner Benecio Del Toro) as they travel in a hallucinogen-influenced race to cover the Zocalo motorcycle race along the main spindle of Babylon 5. In the course of events, the two encounter diplomats, traders, smugglers, and wanderers (as well as bodyguards, groupies, LSD-crazed Barbra Streisand fans, and a very harried security and maintenance force) while Duke struggles to uncover the long-lost Great Earth Alliance Dream.

Explained Thompson, a doctor of journalism with nearly fifty years of writing experience behind him, "Dr. Johnson always said 'He who makes a beast of himself gets rid of the pain of being a man,' and these two find that the only way to understand how *Babylon 5* works is by immersing themselves in the lowest portions of the local culture. After the motorcycle race is done, they come back to crash a Ranger conference on dangerous technologies and find that they know more about the reality of the illegal organotech community than the Rangers do. This is, of course, after discovering that the Zocalo is what the whole hep galaxy would be doing every Saturday night had the Dilgar won the war."

Fear and Loathing on Babylon 5 is not the only B5 film to be written by a noted author or essayist. Salon.com advice columnist Garrison Keillor is currently engaged in a spinoff telemovie about the residents of Lake Pak'ma'ra, Rigel 4, where everyone knows and eats each other. Others will be announced as the deals are negotiated, but all of the contacted authors are enthusiastic about their involvement. Molly Ivins, tentatively signed to write a script involving transplanted Texans and other wildlife at the edge of the galaxy, said "I'd been writing about government [pronounce "gummint"] for years, and I realized that I'd been slacking off for years compared to the effort of writing science fiction." Bret Easton Ellis, whose script is unfortunately under intense scrutiny by the SCI FI Standards and Practices Department, said "Here I've been, writing shamelessly gratuitous stories about young professionals doing massive amounts of cocaine, when I could have been working with Joe Straczynski. To hell with urban angst: I wanna kill some Vorlons." Finally, *Rolling Stone* freelancer Joe Esterhaz joined the burgeoning ranks, saying "You know, I've never written a screenplay that doesn't involve explosions, breasts, or exploding breasts, and doesn't have a single hooker getting an icepick in the eye, until now. I love Joe Straczynski."

—*Revolution SF, August 2001*

"*Heavy Metal 2000* Viewership Reaches 2000"

Los Angeles – *Heavy Metal* publisher Kevin Eastman announced today that his company reached a very important goal: the total number of viewers of his film *Heavy Metal 2000* finally reached 2000 last week.

At a press conference, Eastman, visibly holding back tears of joy, said "All of that effort paid off. The ads in *Previews* for the DVD and video, not to mention the porcelain busts and action figures. The free copies given out to every radio station that plays 'Freebird' or 'Stairway to Heaven' more than once a month. The Julie Strain inflatable sex dolls. The blackmail photos to get the Starz movie channel to run it six times a week. Now if we can get all of these dedicated fans to pay $20,000 per screening, the movie might actually make a profit."

A sequel to the 1981 film *Heavy Metal*, *Heavy Metal 2000*, originally titled *Heavy Metal: FAKK 2* for obscure reasons, had more effort to reach this number than its predecessor. The original *Heavy Metal* gained a mainstream release through Columbia and ran for years on the midnight movie circuit, although its audience of humans (defined as any biped without a mullet haircut) never got about 750. Columbia rereleased the original in 1996 in a limited run before its official video premiere, only to find that the film's audience had grown up and wasn't as obsessed with animated softcore porn as it was when its members were all 12 and 13. Columbia executive David Manning said "The drug war was really rough on that release. If you figure the number of people who saw the movie the first time around without chemical embellishment was at about 35, that's a lot of people who suddenly realized that *Heavy Metal* aged about as well as Night Ranger's first album."

In the 19 years between the first and second films, the magazine *Heavy Metal* switched hands repeatedly, finally being bought by Eastman with his percentage of the royalties from his co-creation of the Teenage Mutant Ninja Turtles. Proving that lightning usually never strikes twice in the same spot, *Heavy Metal* magazine, having become the only magazine venue for sequential art after the deaths of *Epic*, *Eerie*, and *The Warren Ellis Children's Adventure Monthly*, promptly dropped out of upscale venues such as Target and K-Mart and promptly settled in comic shops. Undeterred by the magazine's lack of success, Eastman financed the second *Heavy Metal* film, bypassing the usual venues of movie theaters, repertory cinema, drive-ins, and shadow puppet walls to concentrate on Dragon*Con and the San Diego ComiCon.

"See, that was the genius of it," Eastman said. "I learned from the release of the second *Ninja Turtles* movie that letting an audience see your genius was a mistake. I mean, I thought Vanilla Ice singing 'Go, Ninjas, Go' was a brilliant move and told the director this, but all of the ungrateful bastards at the premiere started laughing. And those were my friends: you should have seen the film critics. This way, by releasing the film directly to cable and DVD, we have no chance of any critic coming across it, and since we want only those people specifically looking for animated women with physiologically impossibly large breasts, we don't have to deal with negative word of mouth."

Buoyed by *Heavy Metal 2000* reaching its goal, Eastman announced his plans to produce a *Heavy Metal* trilogy, connected only by the name. "See, getting Billy Idol to contribute a voice for *Heavy Metal 2000* was a start, but just barely a start. I see each film being constructed around new albums by the Scorpions, Journey, and Quiet Riot, and they're all glad for the work. You hear the 'All Eighties, All the Time' radio stations all over the place, and people who bought the soundtrack to the original movie will just pop when they find out that they can get all-new albums that are also soundtracks. But we're going to have to gun for 3000 viewers this time around: at the rate things are going, that's the year the last film will be released."

—*Revolution SF, September 2001*

"SCI FI Channel Changes Slogan to 'Where Bad TV and Movies Go To Die'"

New York - The SCI FI Channel, once one of the jewels next to the crown jewel in the vast USA Networks empire, is in much better straits than before its purchase by USA in 1996. The Channel now appears in 4 percent of US markets, its Web site is updated more than once every three months, the percentage of staffers living with their parents has dropped through the floor, and it offers two whole nights of original programming after nearly a decade of broadcasting. However, the Channel has had its problems. Its house magazine, *SCI FI*, recently ceased publication, The TNN channel now draws off valuable ratings points with its constant repeats of the *Star Trek* movies (and the impending incessant repeats of the three recent *Star Trek* franchises), and the number of reruns of *Crossing Over With John Edward* threatens the current record for the number of hours in a row taken by one program (the current record is 17 days, 7 hours with *Road Rules* on MTV). While the current tech crash has liberated many of its most dedicated viewers for more *Lexx* marathons on Sunday nights, those same viewers no longer have the money to buy action figures and other paraphernalia from the Scifi.com catalog. Most importantly, the Channel has been seeking further direction. Should it continue to cultivate its current crop of viewers, or should it reach out to new patrons otherwise attracted to reruns of *Red Dwarf* on BBC America?

To this end, USA management has spent the last six months planning a new promotion campaign for the Channel, promising to accent the Channel's core strengths. After considerable deliberation, management settled for its current slogan, "Where Bad Television and Movies Go To Die."

"It was truth in advertising," said USA representative Lucas Trask. "The Channel's original slogan, 'Ever Wonder?', was dumped when everyone in the television industry kept joking about 'Ever Wonder why anyone would want to watch *Battlestar Galactica* reruns and *Sci-Fi Vortex*?' Because of this, we haven't had a tagline since then, but we weren't getting the brand recognition we were expecting. Then it was 'The Best of the World of SCI FI', but the FCC considered that fraudulent advertising, so we went with the reality of the situation. I don't like it, either, but they threatened us with the sulfur pits of Hell if we lied, and I'm allergic to smoke."

While the choice bothered many in the USA hierarchy, the FCC decision was appropriate considering the number of original TV series that migrate to the SCI

FI Channel every year from other venues. Besides the obvious number of old television programs from the Seventies and Eighties that run in the "SCI FI Land" morning-to-afternoon timeslot, thus allowing the tens of people who missed the original broadcasts of *Prey*, *Probe*, and *Space: Above and Beyond* an opportunity to catch up, the Channel is notorious for receiving shows originating on other networks just before final termination. "The main reason why the Channel has such a bad rep is that it picks up shows whose ratings have dropped to the point where only diehard science fiction fans would bother to hunt them down," said renowned media critic Alejandro Riera. "*Mystery Science Theater 3000* had lived long past its lifespan by the time SCI FI picked it up, and you have to wonder at how much ketamine they were smoking to want to take on *Good vs. Evil*, *Sliders*, and *The Outer Limits*. The only thing crazier than picking up Showtime's sloppy seconds with *Stargate SG-1* and *The Outer Limits* was paying actual money for the broadcast rights for *Battlefield Earth*, *Wing Commander*, and *Free Enterprise*, but even *Stargate SG-1* is better than some of the direct-to-cable movies they've been running lately."

Another reason why the new slogan was implemented was because of the Channel's continuing focus. "We kept making noises about 'being the best of sci-fi'," said Trask, "but it's not like we particularly give a damn about science fiction literature. Goddamn writers and editors kept asking when we were going to give them decent credit for their contributions, and everyone kept asking when we were going to bring Harlan Ellison back to do his rants for *Sci-Fi Buzz*. Well, we aren't, you understand? *Sci-Fi Buzz* is dead, and we aren't going to do any news shows, because nobody cares, okay? If you don't like watching old TV shows and bad movies, tough ta-ta, understand?"

Although fans may be insulted or angered by the honesty of the Channel's representatives, the announcement was treated well by cable operators. "We weren't interested in carrying SCI FI because even their best shows did worse in the ratings than *That's My Bush!* on Comedy Central, and we lost our shirts on advertising that piece of crap," said Elissa Gontero, general manager of TSOL Cable Systems, the largest cable provider in rural Pennsylvania. "But now that they're letting everyone know that they have no delusions of making any improvements, so we can tie them to TVLand and run with it. You know, "Come for *My Mother the Car*, stay for *Earth 2*. We'll make a fortune. Well, maybe not a fortune, but we'll at least make back the cost of the billboards we put out by Smitty's place on FM 203."

The new slogan will appear first during the beginning of the new season, starting February 30, and will be used on all official letterhead and official correspondence. Representatives of the FoxFamily Channel, which announced its own new slogan of "All Crap, All The Time" on the same day, could not be reached for comment.

—Revolution SF, September 2001

"Steven Spielberg to Direct *A Clockwork Orange* Sequel"

Philadelphia – Oscar-winning director Steven Spielberg took an enormous chance in the summer of 2001 by releasing his version of *AI*, a project left unfinished by equally famous director Stanley Kubrick after his death in 1999. Although critically savaged and popularly snubbed, Spielberg has gone on the record as stating that he felt that he preserved Kubrick's vision, based on conversations they had before Kubrick's demise. To that end, Spielberg announced today that he was writing and directing the official sequel to Kubrick's adaptation of *A Clockwork Orange*.

"I know Stanley isn't here to argue the righteousness of this decision, but I'm reasonably sure that he wouldn't say a word if he was here right now. Even if he was, it's not like I'm thinking of doing a sequel to *2001*. I've got an Oscar: I don't do follow-ups to Peter Hyams movies for anything."

In keeping with his tradition of working with young actors, *Another Clockwork Orange* stars Haley Joel Osment as Skiffy, a troubled youth with a heart of gold who finds the temptation to push society's buttons at every opportunity. "Lighting flaming bags of doggie doo, setting off firecrackers in mailboxes, and mooning the little old ladies across the way," said Spielberg. Sent off to teen boot camp for smashing pumpkins at Halloween, he confronts Alex, the troubled youth from the original film, now twenty years older and working as director of the boot camp. When boot camp doctors want to reprise Alex's controversial and experimental psychiatric treatment after Skiffy starts a fatal food fight, Alex fights to preserve Skiffy's freedom of choice, and ultimately adopts the boy as his own.

"It's actually a quite affirming story," Spielberg said. "In the sequel, we see Alex all grown up and regretful of his wanton ways in his youth, and when he sees the opportunity to mentor and protect a child going in the same direction that he did, he naturally wants to step in. I wanted to get Malcolm McDowell to reprise his role, but he had problems with the group shower scene at the boot camp, so we're in the process of casting an appropriate Alex. I'd like to give it to Michael Jackson: he's baaaad. But I'll take Sting if I have to."

Response from the film community was swift and terrible. Video critic Aaron Davis, long an opponent of Spielberg's serious films (and of his frivolous films, for that matter) excused himself, and then plucked his eyeballs out with two grapefruit spoons. Afterwards, he said "Why? WHY! Why couldn't he have done this to

Barry Lyndon? Nobody remembers the original; why would they care about a sequel?" The response of other individuals and publications was equally corrosive, except for one unnamed group that only went by the initials "NAMBLA." "We like all of Spielberg's movies," a press release from group spokesman "Kinko the Kid-Loving Clown" said, "really really."

In unrelated news, a team of physicists have been dispatched to the site of Kubrick's crematory urn, where strange phenomena were noted the moment Spielberg made his announcement. According to reports, the contents of the urn started revolving at such high speed that the urn levitated and started showing effects of time-space dilation as detailed in Einstein's General Theory of Relativity. Spokespeople had no comment about the phenomena, but one of the physicists was heard to say "Man, he's pissed. We should be thankful he's spinning in an urn instead of a coffin." Reports that similar phenomena were seen at the gravesite of Anthony Burgess, the author of the original novel, could not be confirmed at press time.

—*Revolution SF, December 2001*

"McFarlane Toys Runs Out of Media Properties For Action Figures"

McFarlane Toys, founded by comic artist Todd McFarlane to capitalize on the success of his creator-owned comic *Spawn*, announced yesterday that it was cutting back production of new action figures and action figure lines. Instead of the usual reasons for the slowdown, such as a slowing economy or increased prices for materials, McFarlane Toys had one overriding reason to rein back: the company has run out of media properties to use as inspiration for more figures.

Aprile Pazzo, a spokesperson for McFarlane Toys, said in a prepared announcement, "We've simply run out of TV shows and movies to license for action figures. Between us, Hasbro, and a few others, we've bought the toy rights to every TV show, movie, comic, book, CD-ROM, PowerPoint slideshow, and shadowpuppet theater on the planet, and we've put out figures based on all of them in the last year or so. The only thing we can hope for now is an outpouring of creativity from the rest of the world so we can have new properties to exploit in 2002 and 2003, or else we're doomed."

Pazzo said that the problems started when McFarlane Toys snagged the bid to produce *Little Nicky* figures based upon the Adam Sandler bomb of the same name. "We really didn't want to do these, but we were still smarting from when Hasbro got the bid for *The Waterboy*, and we honestly figured that we had a hit on our hands. At least we let Playmates take the bid for *Blair Witch 2* toys." After someone in management questioned the wisdom of this decision did anyone realize the sordid truth: the only reason McFarlane received an offer to buy the rights to *Little Nicky* was because every other film of the fall 2000 season was already taken.

Other companies had empathy for McFarlane's situation, but little sympathy. Everett Marm, senior designer at competing toy company Playmates, said "I tried to warn them, even down to showing them the warehouses of *Coneheads* figures we still have left over from 1993. And you'd think they'd have learned our mistakes from watching the sales of *Star Trek: The Animated Series* figures, but you couldn't tell them anything. Over here, we're running on dregs, too: we've gone retro with our *The Questor Tapes* and *Quark* lines, but if our new *Married...With Children* line doesn't sell this Christmas, we'll be up to our butts in Al Bundy figures faster than you can say 'I scored four touchdowns in a single game at Polk High.'"

As it stands, toy and action figure sales have dropped precipitously in the last two years, probably tied to rises and drops in the pay scales in the technical industry. A representative from Toys 'R' Us, who wished to remain anonymous, said "Three years ago, you could put out anything on the shelves, and fifteen collector geeks would start punching each other out just to get five of each figure for their collections. That's how we sold all of our *Small Soldiers* figures. These days, though, we just don't get folks walking in with a $2500 paycheck and no rent to pay who want to buy our *Episode One* display cases. All of the stock boys who used to make three times their salaries on holding the rare or 'chase' figures for collectors are actually having to go back to stocking. We could make a wall around every store just from all of the nonreturnable 'Talking Jar-Jar Binks' room alarms we couldn't give away with free beer."

Only one toy manufacturer expressed hope for the future, and that was Hasbro, which holds the rights to the *Star Wars* franchises. However, it's holding out not for *Star Wars: Episode Two* toys, but the tie-in figures designed for the new Kevin Smith film *Clerks 2: Clerking*. A Hasbro press release said "Smith's new film features a whole menagerie of *Star Wars* figures previously unavailable, including the 'Tauntaun Guts-Covered Luke Skywalker' and the 'Bantha-Sore Tusken Raider'. Thanks to thirtysomething nostalgia for anything related to *Star Wars*, we fully expect that the 'Cantina Barmaid Bea Arthur' figure will be one of our best-selling toys in 2001."

Some people in the toy industry suggest that McFarlane's best hope is to diversify outside of action figures and comic and film tie-ins, but doubt that the company can turn itself around in time. Aprile Pazzo was philosophical about it. "I'll be the first to admit that we may have a problem," said Pazzo. "McFarlane Toys makes action figures predominately for computer science shut-ins who have no intention of taking their figures out of the packaging and instead store them in airtight vaults. Because of this, we've been able to cut back on quality control to the point where most of these figures couldn't stand on their own with lengths of rebar jammed up their asses. We really don't know how to make figures that won't melt under the light from an office fluorescent fixture, much less something that someone might actually want to play with. But it may be time to start."

—*Revolution SF, November 2001*

"Whitley Strieber To Receive Special Hugo"

Philadelphia – The World Science Fiction Society announced today that novelist and alleged alien abductee Whitley Strieber was the recipient of a special Hugo Award to be presented at ConJose in San Jose, California in August 2002. The award, referred to as the "Hubbard," is intended to reward outstanding achievement in presenting science fictional concepts as fact to the general public.

Susan Tankersley, spokesperson for the WSFS, explained the situation. "Through such books as *Communion, Transformation, Majestic,* and *The Secret School,* Whitley Strieber has managed to present concepts once unique to science fiction and turn them into cultural icons. Thanks to him, you simply cannot hear the phrase 'alien contact' without thinking the complementary phrase 'rectal probe'. Admittedly, he's also thrown the SETI movement back fifty years in the process, but them's the breaks."

Presenting the Hubbard at ConJose are *South Park* creators Trey Parker and Matt Stone, who had nothing but praise for Strieber's contributions to popular culture. "If not for Whitley's anal fixation, we'd have never been able to come up with that first episode of *South Park,* 'Cartman Gets An Anal Probe', and without that, we'd still be waiting tables in Burbank," said Parker, taking a break from filming of *Orgazmo Goes To Salt Lake City,* the sequel to his 1999 superhero film. "Trey and I feel that we'd never have managed to squeeze that initial $16 million contract for the first two years of *South Park* without that episode, and we wouldn't have thought of it until we borrowed Whitley's comment 'Why does everything around here involve something going into or coming out of my ass?' Now we have a multimillion-dollar entertainment empire, and we owe it all to him. Well, not really: if he tries to get any of this money, we'll have security break his legs, but we want to let him know how much we owe him in general."

Streiber himself was extremely enthusiastic about the new Hugo, and expressed it in a special segment of the Art Bell AM radio program by speaking in tongues for twenty-three minutes. Afterwards, he said "You know, certain snotty critics have said that the only thing my books have taught anyone is that 'Klaatu barada nikto' means 'You shore got a purty mouth'. Well, this isn't true. It really means 'Hello, sailor'."

With the announcement also came the announcement that Strieber had signed a contract to adapt his second Visitor book, *Transformation,* for the screen. Although the 1989 release of *Communion* was a critical and box-office flop everywhere but in the audience participation midnight movie circuit, producer

Michael Nelson had high hopes for this adaptation to turn out better. "We found with *Communion* that nobody really accepted Christopher Walken as playing Whitley, because he's just a bit too creepy for words. We finally went with an actor who was a dead ringer for Whitley; we were originally considering [former televangelist] Jim Bakker, but then we found that Rick Moranis was free. We already have Comedy Central and the SCI FI Channel fighting over the first broadcast rights to *Transformation*, and we expect to make a fortune on the action figures. The 'Alien Probe Strieber' is a hit in testing groups: they all want to know how the toymakers managed to get that expression on the doll's face."

—*Revolution SF, December 2001*

"UK Census Reconsiders Category for Fannish Religions"

London – It started with the Australian and New Zealand Census. Based on an E-mail message claiming that the Census Ministries of both countries would recognize them as members of a legitimate religious faith, dozens of diehard *Star Wars* fanatics listed their religious affiliation as "Jedi Knight." Even though Australia and New Zealand refused to recognize "Jedi" as anything besides "Other," the rumor refused to die, and instead moved to the United Kingdom, where the UK Census Ministry was noting that citizens could list themselves as Jedi Knights, but the tallies would not be catalogued in any category other than "Other." In a last-minute decision, though, the Ministry has decided to create a whole new category for all sorts of religions influenced and inspired by literary, televised, and cinematic science fiction, based mostly on the response from England's extensive fandom community.

"Well, we knew for years that science fiction fandom was a religion, and a particularly nasty one at that," said Martin Meier, spokesman for the Ministry. "All you need to do is go to a CreationCon, crash the masquerade, and recreate the stoning sequence from *Monty Python's Life of Brian* with the word 'Jehovah' replaced with the phrase '*Star Trek* is only a TV show'. We've found it to be a very quick, effective, and painful form of suicide, and we've considered using it as an alternative form of capital punishment. Faced with being stomped to death by hordes of furious fanatics, most child molesters and cannibals would rather have their innards scooped out and replaced with nests of bulldog ants."

The new category unfortunately will not be available for the current census; however, it will be implemented for the next census, scheduled for 2011. Intended to include Jedi, Klingons, Order of G'Quann, Galacticans, Bokononists, Scientologists, and other made-up faiths, much effort went into a proper name. The Ministry finally settled for the blanket term "Dumbass," and swore that fannish worshippers could count themselves among the Dumbasses at the next census. When asked about other terms considered, Meier said "We had plenty of alternatives, but we had our mouths washed out with soap as children for using those words, and our mothers would be justified in doing it again. I mean, some of the most descriptive terms we came up with actually made some of us physically ill. Besides, we figured that if we settled for 'Dumbass', the Americans might be able to report on the decision for the evening news. The Yanks have no sense of humor: we gave Australia the mother-stabbers and father-rapers, and America the Puritans, and Australia obviously got the better part of the deal."

UK fans were more sanguine. "You can all laugh, but I see little difference between Jews and Klingons," said longtime fan Guy Larson of Manchester. "They cut off foreskins, and we add rubber headpieces. The members of the Ministry may laugh, but I think that millions of fans will be proud to list themselves as Dumbasses in 2011. We've been called that for years anyway."

Spokespeople for the United States Census Bureau had no official comment when asked by *Revolution SF* if the Bureau had any intention of extending similar courtesies to American fans. Unofficially, though, one representative asked "You're kidding, right?" before breaking down into uncontrollable laughter.

—*Revolution SF, December 2001*

"Harlan Ellison: The Ultimate Literary Robot Warrior"

Washington, DC - Popular attitudes in the science fiction field hold that if celebrated author Harlan Ellison didn't exist, then it would be necessary to make him. Recently declassified documents held by the State Department since 1940 show that the latter part of that truism is literally true.

"Simply put, Harlan Ellison is the most sophisticated machine of mass destruction on the planet," said State Department advisor Dr. Lise Ward, an authority on technology and technological trends in the wake of World War II. "He was part of a top-secret program by the country of Freedonia to build the ultimate cultural warrior. When people talk about how Ellison can kill at fifty paces with a sharp twist of the tongue, they have no idea of how true this is. They should be thankful they don't know about the particle-beam weapons, rubidium lasers, and other armaments built into his body, because if someone irritates him enough to use them, we're all in trouble."

Freedonia's project was the brainchild of its dictator-for-life, the tyrannical autarch Rufus T. Firefly. In an attempt to rebuild Freedonia's crushed economy, Firefly declared war on its neighboring country Sylvania, but had more on his mind than mere military might. "Sylvania was known for its writers and artists, and Freedonia's most popular recreation at the time was recently imported to the US as the board game Don't Whiz On The Electric Fence," said Dr. Ward. "The idea was that if Freedonia couldn't import artists, then it could make them. World War II set in before any other prototypes could be made, and several Freedonian scientists managed to smuggle Ellison out of Europe and to the US before anyone realized the potential." After the war, Firefly (reportedly in the throes of addiction to prescription stool softeners) forgot all about the Ellison project and concentrated his country's resources on more vulgar and therefore profitable venues, such as animatronic television newscasters. Today, two-thirds of Freedonia's gross national product comes from the construction and maintenance of such television personalities as Sam Donaldson, Diane Sawyer, and Robin Leach.

According to the declassified State Department documents, Ellison is an absolute marvel. "Lots of conspiracy fanatics like to argue that most of our modern technological developments were 'borrowed' from extraterrestrial sources, but in Harlan's case, it's probably true, because we can't find any other explanation for the sophistication," said Dr. Ward. Overlaying a skeleton composed of a titanium alloy that self-heals when exposed to heat are input, output, and defense systems well in advance of anything available elsewhere during the 1930s, and many are well in advance of today's comparable systems. Overseeing everything is a true AI processor capable of astounding leaps of deduction, thus explaining Ellison's ability to create fascinating characters and situations in such high-stress conditions as on radio programs and in bookstore windows. "It's no surprise that Ellison does all of his work with a manual typewriter instead of a computer, because trapping himself by using a computer would be like strapping yourself to a sparrow and expecting to fly to Australia," said Ward. Powering everything is the secret to how Ellison manages his grueling schedule of writing and lecturing: an incredible waste-free nuclear battery that promises to revolutionize industry if it could be copied. "People ask if he ever runs out of power after one of his 8-hour lectures, and the answer is 'No'. Oh, he might, but only if he keeps going for a while. Like 40,000 years without a potty break."

The explanation for Ellison's creation, as well as the defense and offense capability (most of which are still classified by the UN) makes sense in the context of Freedonian history. "Firefly wanted true cultural warriors, who could present a thesis and defend it to the death if necessary," said Ward. "Many of Harlan's weapons were intended for use against enemies of Freedonia: radio commentators, film critics, know-nothing science fiction fans. Apparently a glitch in his cerebral matrix prevents him from accessing his full mission, but he obviously knows some of his reason for being. His fascination with artificial life forms, as evidenced in his *Outer Limits* screenplay *Demon With A Glass Hand*, is part of it, as is his ability to verbally filet any critic of his work who hasn't done his homework. If he does access his core memories, then his powers will be virtually unlimited, and could be set off without warning. The trick, of course, is not to set them off. Treat him with the respect accorded to any replicant with the ability to wipe out all life in our solar system with a random sneeze, and we'll all be fine."

After Firefly's death in 1977 and the subsequent collapse of Freedonia's economy, some of the technology used to create Ellison was smuggled out of Europe by varying governments. "Canada did the most testing of the original Ellison technology," said Dr. Ward, "with generally disappointing results. The government was trying to jump-start its own literary warrior program in the Sixties, and finally gave up when its best efforts flopped. When people refer to Paul T. Riddell as a third-rate Harlan Ellison clone, it's closer to reality than you know." Britain scaled its program back severely and sold most of the tech to private industry, with the greatest success to date being in pop music. Dr. Ward related "That's why the Spice Girls disappeared right after their movie came out. Those girls were quite literally too 'high maintenance'."

The response to the announcement ranged throughout the spectrum. Ellison's wife Susan responded "Suddenly it explains everything, especially why he speaks machine code in his sleep." Longtime friend Neil Gaiman announced "Well, it's about time that someone acknowledged Ellison's abilities. I spent years trying to write as much as Harlan has, and the only way I can keep up that kind of schedule is by putting powered light sockets in various orifices and flailing away until the neighbors complain about the stench of burnt flesh." Finally, director James Cameron, who locked horns with Ellison in 1984 over plagiarism of Ellison's works in *The Terminator*, fled the country and is currently hiding out in an undisclosed location after receiving word of Ellison's advanced weaponry and tactical software. Before leaving, Cameron was heard to say "I could have ripped off Larry Niven or William Gibson, or someone else who couldn't blast me from orbit, but no, I had to be clever..."

—*Revolution SF, January 2002*

"Apple, Microsoft Start Lines of Action Figures"

Cupertino, California – 2001 was an atrocious year for the entire computer industry, with sales of hardware, software, and peripherals slipping and falling throughout the world. In response, two of the most powerful IT companies in the world, Apple Computer of Cupertino and Microsoft of Redmond, Washington, made separate announcements today that they were going to move into a hithero new market: action figures.

"The tie-ins between computers and toys has been going on for years," said Velvet Delorey, vice-president of Research and Development at Apple, "culminating with the recent interactive Barney stuffed toy developed by Microsoft. The Barney figure didn't work, mostly because every child's request for Barney to tell the child a story launched into a diatribe about how 'Microsoft must be allowed to innovate, no matter how many souls are devoured in the process', but they were onto something."

The new Apple action figure, to be announced at the upcoming MacWorld Expo in New York, is part branding exercise, and part attempt to make children appreciate those in the computer industry. "Apple Management has always been fond of science fiction and fantasy TV shows and movies, and [Apple CEO] Steve Jobs is particularly fond of such shows as *Babylon 5*, so we talked to Babylonian Productions about a fusion," said Delorey. The first such offering is the "Steve Kosh" figure: a 12-inch articulated environment suit containing a perfect likeness of Jobs inside. In addition, the environment suit contains a voice chip that contains some 150 of Jobs' favorite sayings, particularly "If you go to Windows XP, you will die." As Jobs himself said, "We here at Apple are already quite familiar with influencing the development of lesser species throughout the galaxy, and all we require of our charges is order and obedience. In a million years, humans will be just like us."

Microsoft, in turn, announced its own line of figures shortly after the Apple announcement. Although actual production is tentatively scheduled for mid-2007, Microsoft reps promised that the new figures would contain features unique in the toy business, as soon as the company could prove that extrusion plastic molding was an intrinsic element of the Windows operating system. All of the line will use the new Windows TP OS, which promises unilateral connectivity between Microsoft toys, and will allow action figure users to connect to the Internet at any opportunity. (Rumors that the figures would also come with special software to allow office managers to spy on IT professionals, particularly programmers, so long as the toys are within 10 feet of a Windows-running computer could not be confirmed by press time.) The first, a likeness of Microsoft CEO Steve Ballmer, comes with a sensor-covered travel chair that can be programmed for specific motions or run via remote control, and it also comes with a series of Ballmer's favorite quotations. Unfortunately, Ballmer's favorite quotation is "LINUX USERS ARE ENEMIES OF MICROSOFT! THEY WILL BE EX-TER-MI-NA-TED!" This was to be followed by releases of the main villains in the series: the Permatemps, the State Governors, and the brilliant but seditious Doctor Linus Torvalds.

When asked about the new action figure lines, representatives of other noted tech companies expressed everything from surprise to rage. Typical was the response from Oracle, whose CEO Larry Ellison had expressed interest in having a special action figure made of his likeness as far back as 1995. "Larry in particular wanted a life-sized action figure in stores by 1996," said a source that requested to remain anonymous, "but we found later that he wanted a figure that was a life-sized copy of his ego. He was really pissed when we told him that there wasn't enough plastic in the universe for that. He's now settling for having his profile carved into the moon. It still won't be big enough, but it's a start."

—*Revolution SF, February 2002*

"Literary SF Publishers Announce 'International Slushpile Bonfire Day'"

New York - One of the most onerous tasks in the magazine and book trade is the sifting of the slush pile. Slush piles, the collection of unsolicited and unagented manuscripts sent to publishers by beginning or would-be authors, are sometimes the source of future literary successes, but more often than not are the source of headaches and indigestion. Many editors privately complain and scream about the uselessness of slush piles, but fearing a backlash from beginning writers who already assume conspiracies keep their work from being printed, very few speak out about the quality and quantity of the material received.

With this in mind, the international literary community announced a special amnesty day for those long-suffering editors forced to sift through manuscripts where everything but the name of the author was misspelled on the title page. April 31, 2002 marks International Slushpile Bonfire Day, where editors and publishers are encouraged to collect all of the unreadable or unusable manuscripts that have built up in their offices, in some cases since 1968, and burn them while drinking wine and singing songs. Since one of the worst offenders is the science fiction/fantasy/horror triumvirate, SF, fantasy, and horror editors are allowed to place the first documents and light the pile when complete.

"We're burning everything," said Pablo Redondo, the organizer of the event and the only editor willing to appear on television. "All of the manuscripts with no merit other than the tag 'Member, SFWA'" on the cover page. The manuscripts where the author didn't bother to read the submission guidelines and dumped off the copy to a magazine that doesn't buy that sort of fiction, or doesn't buy fiction at all. The manuscripts where the author already registered the story for a copyright 'to keep editors from stealing their work'. The Wesley/Worf slash fanfiction sent in 'just in case we had an interest.' The manuscripts sent in on toilet paper or on Hello Kitty note paper, and the manuscripts sent with death threats against any editor who plans to reject it, and the 3000-page 'sequels' to popular books written because the author didn't like how the original ended. We're making a big pile in the middle of Times Square, and every editor with a slush pile is invited to pitch in. Big magazines, small book lines, Webzines, rantzines, and weekly newspapers: every editor in the world is welcome to start the healing here."

In return, the rest of the publishing community will protect the identity of the participants in the bonfire and blame the disappearance of the manuscripts on the

Postal Service. "After all, they were all contaminated with...um...anthrax!" said Redondo. That's right: anthrax and Dutch Elm Blight! Maybe a bit of tobacco mosaic and some cane toad venom, but anthrax was definitely involved somewhere. Of course, considering the number of manuscripts we've received with any number of bodily fluids all over the envelope, nobody will be surprised in the slightest."

If this seems a bit extreme, the words of an editor who wished to remain nameless explained the situation. "We're constantly reading in *Locus* or *Speculations* about the bad editors who take more than a week to accept or reject a story or novel, but these people don't know what it's like. An intern who takes eight weeks to reject a story is most likely needing that eight weeks to recover from jamming a set of ten Lee Press-on Nails out of her eyes. By the time she's able to see again, that same author may have sent another eight to ten stories to the slush pile, and the cycle begins again. Even at our best, we can only afford to publish three short stories and a novella a month, which means we publish a grand total of 36 short stories a year, and we get eight to ten THOUSAND manuscripts a month. This is the only way we can keep up with the overload without going insane and shooting at school buses once we got off work.

"Let's put it another way," the editor continued. "I hear from one writer who suggests that because of the delay in response to his submissions, we call out HASMAT teams to pluck his envelopes out of the incoming mail and decontaminate them before opening them. I can't bring myself to tell him that we can't afford a HASMAT team, and each and every one of his stories makes me scrub my arms with carbolic acid whenever I open it. Each one of his stories literally takes away my will to live, and I shudder every time I see his return address on an envelope. And he's one of hundreds out there, maybe thousands. I have to buy elbow-length rubber gloves on credit just to keep up."

Electronic manuscripts are no exception. "Since the advent of the Web, we've been receiving material from people who apparently learned to type by throwing their cats at the keyboard, and some of it is so horrible that we don't let it dare escape," said Redondo. "Some of it is so foul that we've decided to include hard drives in the bonfire, because any hard drive or mail server that contained that story is obviously too contaminated for future use. The New York Fire Department had problems with this at first due to environmental issues, but when we explained the evil that would be removed from the universe by its extirpation, they understood."

Surprisingly, no news of this action appeared in any of the journals dedicated to collecting existing and new writing markets, such as *Writer's Digest*, *The Writer*,

The Gila Queen's Guide To Markets, and the innumerable Web sites cataloguing every market that pays in money, credit, advertising space, or raw meat still on the bone. Redondo said that this was deliberate. "The only publication that contained details was the American Editor's Association newsletter *Rum, Sodomy, and the Lash*, and anyone who leaked the details to the general public was to be appointed the person in charge of dealing with the repercussions. I myself am going into hiding in New Zealand after this, and I'm not returning to work until after I've had extensive cosmetic surgery."

The response from the beginning writer community was, as expected, swift and terrible. A representative of the Eltingville (New Jersey) Science Fiction Writer's Circle and Costuming Guild released a statement that read, in part, "We decry any efforts to rid the world of our works, and the ESFWC&CG will start up a GeoCities site to hold all of these orphaned stories until the New York Literary Establishment comes to its senses and buys them back for their full value." When the representative was contacted and asked whether starting up a magazine or book line might be of more value than lambasting the existing editors, the response was "Of course not. They're supposed to pay us for our work; we're not supposed to pay to get it published. It's not our fault that everyone submits stories but nobody pays to read the stories submitted, and we'll all go to SFWA to complain if the magazines go under. Now go away: I have a *Buffy/Farscape* crossover novel that I have to get off to St. Martin's this evening."

Although the editors and publishers in other countries were sympathetic to the idea, it is currently unknown whether or not they will participate. At least one Australian editor expressed support for the bonfire, saying "Australia has only six million people, and between the four science fiction magazines in the country, we've received submissions from at least four million. Either we have a lot of razorback hunters and crocodile skinners with plenty of free time in the evening who will suddenly buy subscriptions so they can see their stories in print, or we're going to have a bonfire of our own in our future."

—*Revolution SF, February 2002*

"Canada Makes Formal UN Apology for *Lexx*"

Ottawa – For years, Canada was known as an inexpensive place to make science fiction, fantasy, and horror television series for cable and general syndication. Many of these productions, though, were for series that never would have received development money in the US, and "made in Canada" quickly received the same derision in the entertainment industry as "made in Indonesia" did in the sports shoe industry. This week, Canada's Parliament took matters into its own hands and formally apologized to all members of the planet for the SCI FI Channel series *Lexx*.

In an emotional address to the entire country, Canadian Prime Minister Jean Chrétien formally took responsibility for the terrible SF television coming from his country. "We're sorry for *War of the Worlds*. We're sorry for *Friday the 13th*. We're sorry for *Gene Roddenberry's Andromeda*. We're even sorry for *The Starlost*, even though it would have been great if the production crew had left Harlan Ellison alone. But most of all, we are very, very, VERY sorry for *Lexx*, and we are taking steps to make sure that geek porn like this never happens again."

Executives at Salter Street Films, production company for the series, were last seen being chased down by professional baby harp seal clubbers from Newfoundland, and the few survivors formally recanted their folly. "We got greedy, is all," one Salter Street executive said before being tarred, feathered, and dragged behind a pickup truck. "We had *22 Minutes* and *Made In Canada* going for us, but we thought that we could take the money from the SCI FI Channel and run with it. We were going to make amends, but it's too late now."

Shortly after Chrétien's impassioned apology, he addressed a special United Nations session to open Canadian film vaults and video transfer rooms to UN inspectors. "We know now that if *Lexx* were shown to enemy troops during a wartime situation, it would qualify as a war crime under the Geneva Convention. Our fervent hope is that independent inspectors can prevent horrors like these and *War of the Worlds* from ever darkening the planet."

As could be expected, some Canadians resisted the unilateral surrender. Velvet Delorey, a former systems analyst in Toronto and current leader of the SOYB (standing for "Sod Off, Yeh Bollocks," the Anglo Canadian equivalent of "May the Lord be with you"), a militant group dedicated to jump-starting Canada's native entertainment industry, is getting particularly forceful. "The Americans kept shoving lousy TV shows and movies at us, and we were supposed to just sit back and watch *Independence Day* and *Space Rangers*. Then they buy up lousy

Canadian productions, and then blame us because it stinks up their cable boxes. Well, too bad: David Cronenberg isn't the only decent filmmaker in the country." Spurred by general anti-US sentiment in all of Canada's provinces, Delorey's plan is to make a science fiction TV series so powerful that it clears through the Emmy Awards, particularly the non-technical awards.

However, Canada may find itself in the same situation as New Zealand did in the early Eighties. Inspired by the success of the Australian *Mad Max*, the country poured millions of dollars into its own attempt to corner the post-apocalyptic road film. The release of *Battletruck* (released in the US as *Warlords of the 21st Century* and everywhere else under the original working title, *Mildly Irate Ian*) started a lightning war between the two countries, going nuclear in a matter of days. To this day, vast portions of New Zealand have no human life other than a few sheepherders, and the final days of the war were so terrible that the entire nation suffers from a nearly universal memory block. Indeed, only one out of every million New Zealanders even remembers hearing about the "Mad Max War," much less fighting in it.

In related news, the SCI FI Channel announced that the production studios for *Lexx* were moving to the Studios at Las Colinas outside of Dallas, Texas. When asked, a spokesperson for the Channel said *"Walker, Texas Ranger* and *Barney and Friends* were just cancelled, and those two shows comprise all of Dallas' television work, so they said they were willing to work cheap. And we like cheap."

—*Revolution SF, April 2002*

"College Recruiting for UNIT Competes with FBI and CIA"

Padre Island, Texas - For thousands of high school and college students, the beaches of Padre Island are the obvious locale for spring break. Following the students are hundreds of recruiters for various Fortune 500 corporations seeking the brightest and best for new positions right after graduation. In recent years, US government agencies such as the Federal Bureau of Investigation, the Secret Service, and the Central Intelligence Agency have joined the corporate recruiters in seeking new members interested in a higher calling. This year, though, marks the first time the United Nations Intelligence Taskforce (UNIT), the organization the world contacts to deal with extraterrestrial threats, has sought new members via standard recruiting.

Founded in 1969 through the efforts of Brigadier General Alstair Lethbridge-Stewart (British Army - Ret.), UNIT is a multi-national military force whose mission is to deal with alien or extraordinary Earth-based threats with the potential to endanger the whole planet. Headquartered in Geneva and placed under the sole command of the United Nations, UNIT currently operates with branches in Britain, the United States, Australia, Brazil, and Antarctica. Most famed for its missions against invasions by Yeti, Daleks, and Cybermen in the early Eighties, UNIT has expanded its operations to include other, more subtle menaces to humanity, such as stubbing out self-cloning "boy bands" and protecting third-rate horror writers from repeated extraterrestrial abductions and anal probes.

"We've actually had it easy this year," said Lieutenant Colonel Meredith Patterson, chief recruiting officer for UNIT-North America. "Two years ago, when we started down in Fort Lauderdale, we were competing against every last dotcom seeking technical graduates, and most of them decided that they didn't like the military lifestyle or the thought of wrestling Sontarans for the fate of the universe. These days, though, we have our pick of computer science, engineering, astronomy, and cryptography majors. The only group we're having problems recruiting are paleontologists: we've had a couple of cases involving buried Silurian and Sea Devil colonies off Baja California, and we can't get enough dinosaurologists to deal with that mess."

Lieutenant Colonel Patterson explained the reason for recruiting new college graduates instead of drawing them from the existing branches of the world's armies. "I'll be blunt. We take on plenty of opponents that the standard armed forces can't handle. New UNIT soldiers can be maimed, disintegrated, hypnotized, vaporized, parasitized, driven insane, left paraplegic, and converted into foodstuffs. On the bright side, it beats working retail."

Because of new threats and new technologies, the new UNIT recruit has to have skills above and beyond those generally cultivated in college. "In particular, besides the usual computer and scientific skills and the aptitudes with various forms of exotic weaponry, we're looking for that extra something. Immunity to hypnotic suggestion, telepathic ability, and resistance to Cyber-conversion are very good pluses, and we certainly wouldn't turn down anyone with aptitudes in public relations. In the early years, we were constantly blowing up old gravel pits in Surrey, and there was always someone complaining about the racket and the mess."

Even in these rough times, competition for top candidates can be fierce. Jeff Holmes, a journalism and cryptography major from Flagstaff, Arizona, related how he had multiple offers from various public and private groups with the same agenda. "UNIT is really interested in me, but I got a call from this new group called Planetary, and they're offering twice the pay for the right grades. It's just they've only been around for about four years, so I'm not sure if they have the job security I'm looking for right now. I have to admit, though, their promise of a 401(k) that's completely free of Enron stock is pretty tempting. Miskatonic University's grad school program keeps calling me as well, and I can't knock a grad program that pays real money to go tramping around Antarctica."

Charlie Chu, spokesman for Planetary, denied that any competition existed. "Hey, we'll take help from UNIT. We'll even take help from the Coalition to Reunite Gondwanaland if the threat is big enough. Now if you'll excuse me, I have to get going. This is a strange world, and Planetary is dedicated to keeping it that way." Miskatonic University representatives could not be reached for comment.

—Previously unpublished

"Bruce Sterling Fitted With Self-Promotion Inhibitor"

Austin, Texas – It's about the size of the battery in a digital watch, and it's powered by the user's own nervous system. Fitted to the back of the user's skull, it utilizes a sophisticated algorithm to detect a certain brain pattern, and an equally sophisticated miniature transformer delivers a shock in excess of 220 volts once that pattern is detected. In preparation for further human tests and ultimate Federal Drug Administration approval, a crack team of surgeons recently fitted author Bruce Sterling, long the darling of the cyberpunk and technolibertarian community, with the Promotion Inhibitor, a device that holds forth hope for all science fiction writers addicted to self-promotion.

"He gets two plugs per day," said head surgeon Charles Chu, inventor of the Inhibitor. "In Mr. Sterling's case, this means he can say 'It's on the Viridian List. Have I mentioned the Viridian List?' twice in a 24-hour period, and every subsequent attempt garners him an electric shock. The voltage goes up each time, so we'll either cure him or have barbecue."

Chu described the origin of the Inhibitor thusly. "Yeah, we all laughed in the *South Park* movie when Eric Cartman was fitted with that V-chip that kept him from using dirty words, but nobody considered the real advantages of such a device. The Inhibitor is very much like one of those electric bracelets that zaps a patient who snores too loudly, only its sensors detect the brain patterns that usually precede a long run of self-aggrandizement. Since Bruce is a long-running advocate of the benefits of technology, we clubbed him upside the head and brought him to the lab. He was fighting us at first, but now he's thanking us."

Sterling himself was enthusiastic about the procedure and its longterm effects. "The thought of writing an article or column without excessive namedropping really thrills me. I was really getting tired of being called 'the Barney the Dinosaur of the *Wired* set' behind my back, and the Inhibitor should help me get my life back on track and encourage me to write something besides self-congratulatory piffle."

Chu's Inhibitor is the end-result of years of experimentation, utilizing any number of notable writers and editors in the science fiction field. "Our first real success, with a very early prototype, was with Kristine Kathryn Rusch. She came to us with a horrible photography addiction: she was posing for photos for *Locus* four, maybe five times a day. Back then, *Locus* had to add as much as twenty pages just to keep up with all of the poses. With that first Inhibitor," Chu said, displaying an implant the size of a baseball, "she was able to cut back to one shoot a month, which left her with more time to write. Now she's cranking out at least one *Star Trek* novel a month, and nobody's seen her picture in years. Our success with her was what gave us enough grant money to miniaturize the Inhibitor and develop a new battery, because she was having to lug three car batteries wherever she went."

Chu wanted to emphasize that the Inhibitor isn't intended to turn writers into couch potatoes. "If a writer really accomplishes something of note, like winning a plagiarism suit or killing a grizzly with a Swiss Army knife, then they have every reason to crow about their accomplishments. We talk to a lot of writers in the science fiction field who are so busy writing or doing that they forget to let the world know, or they're so off-put by the others crowding the TV cameras at the latest WorldCon that they simply give up. They're eclipsed by the people whose main claim to fame is having edited or written for some fanzine years before that nobody really read, and they just won't let go: with all of the bragging of "Well, as you know...," going to a Dragon*Con these days is like crashing a casting call for *Married...With Children: The Next Generation*. My hope is that the promotion-addicted will learn to control their urges, allowing the promotion-disabled an opportunity to get in a word edgewise at a convention panel without being interrupted by some megalomaniac boasting 'Well, Harlan said to me...'"

Chu's next project is a transference system that stores promotional impulses from the hype-addicted in order to transfuse them into the hype-impaired. "Imagine two writers, one with serious problems with promoting new material, and another that just won't shut up about it. With the system we're designing, we can leach off a certain amount of energy: not enough to stop the donor from being able to live a full literary life, but enough to where bystanders can tolerate the donor for more than five minutes at a time. I even have a dream of a networked system, where one blatant egomaniac such as Paul T. Riddell can serve the promotional needs of literally dozens of beginning authors at once, all through wireless access. We're going to need a much better delivery system than what we have right now, though: Riddell burned through five Inhibitors without any effect, including one fitted with an AC cord and emergency generator, so we're working on the next generation of ego buffers and stun devices before we can start to worry about wireless self-promotion."

Charles Chu's biggest ambition, though, is developing a heavy-duty ego inhibitor for science fiction magazine editors. "Far too many magazine editors, no matter the subject, seem to think that they're the sole reason anyone reads the magazine, and too many SF magazine editors are in complete denial over how they have their jobs only because no real editor wants it. The denial and the subconscious self-loathing are what lead to so much ill will in this industry, as the editors blame everything but themselves when the magazine starts to go under, and they throw temper tantrums when the writers get more fan mail and groupies than they do. If we can get every science fiction editor who needs an Inhibitor fitted with one, and we get one calendar year without Gardner Dozois yelling 'Respect mah authoritah!' at a convention, I can die a satisfied man."

Chu was unable to comment at the time about Inhibitor use on non-literary science fiction personages, but hinted that it might allow bit players in the *Star Wars* films and *Star Trek* franchises who now make livings by following conventions to live normal lives. Representatives for Lucasfilm and Paramount were unavailable for comment.

—Previously unpublished

"SFWA Changes Entry Criteria for Membership"

Chesterton, Maryland - The Science Fiction Writers of America, the long-running organization for professional science fiction and fantasy writers, announced today that it was making drastic changes to how it accepted new members, not to mention how it kept older members within the fold.

"The basic requirements for SFWA membership previously required that a writer have three short stories or one full-length fiction book or a dramatic script appear through professional paying markets," said Caroline Crawford, SFWA spokeswoman. "However, over the late Eighties and early Nineties, we found the organization flooded with members who received their accreditation through sales to the Writers of the Future or *Pulphouse* magazine, and although they never managed to get published again, they had lifetime membership so long as they paid their membership dues. Since we find ourselves flooded with members who do nothing more than put 'Member, SFWA' on their letterhead and throw tantrums if they don't get guest badges at local conventions, besides voting in SFWA elections against any provisions to remove members unpublished in a decade or more, we had to go to further extremes to enliven the organization and clear out the dead wood." Those "further extremes" consist of talent competitions completely unrelated to writing.

"Simply put," said Ms. Crawford, "any current or incipient member of SFWA must be able to impersonate a cartoon character to the satisfaction of an independently selected jury. No exceptions."

According to the new bylaws of SFWA, each member must be able to impersonate the voice of a particular character in an animated TV show or film, and each character belongs to that author until the author dies or is beaten in impersonation combat. "Effectively, each fiction writer qualifies for one impersonation. Nonfiction writers get two, and any professional editor gets one to add to his or her total,," said Crawford. "This means that James Arce-Stevens gets one character, while Mike Resnick, being a fiction writer and a pro editor, gets two." Initially, the characters selected would be done on a first-come, first-served basis, but two writers selecting the same character may compete in an arena for that impersonation: the winner remains with SFWA, while the loser has to leave the SF genre entirely unless they have an alternative. "Nonfiction writers get two solely because we can use as many as we can get."

Many extant and former SFWA members jumped on the new rules, with varying results. Harlan Ellison, due to his singular origins [see "Harlan Ellison:

The Ultimate Literary Warrior Robot," RevSF January 2001], promptly claimed three characters: The Iron Giant, GIR from the Nickelodeon series *Invader ZIM*, and Bender from *Futurama*. Said Crawford, "Everybody knows that Harlan goes running around his house on Friday nights impersonating GIR anyway, so this wasn't too much of a stretch." Others had more of an effort. "[SFWA President] Norman Spinrad and James P. Hogan had a hard time of it, seeing as how they both do an exemplary Olive Oyl, and we needed judges after about three hours. They just wouldn't break character. Jim finally managed to win, but Mr. Spinrad managed to get back into the game with a Boomhauer impersonation that left us with tears in our eyes. It was just beautiful. It was almost as stunning as Pat Cadigan's Snow White or Emily Devenport's Stimpy."

Some new and established writers, unfortunately, found themselves out of SFWA. Kristine Kathryn Rusch, unaware that silent cartoon characters were ineligible for consideration, was quoted as saying "Wait, wait...okay, I'm Odie on *Garfield*. ...No? Okay, how about Maggie Simpson? Um. How about Claude Cat? Uh, okay, how about Taarna in *Heavy Metal*? No? Oh, poop." Other characters were retired without consideration due to the authors' reputation. "Fritz Leiber used to do an impeccable Fleischer-era Superman, and ever since he died, everyone else left it alone out of respect for him and his work," said Crawford. Other characters were left alone due to the nasty reputation of the author. "Even though he has no interest in joining SFWA, and we wouldn't take him if he asked, Paul T. Riddell is known for his Beavis, Zorak [from *Space Ghost: Coast To Coast*], and Mr. Hanky the Christmas Poo. And they're right up his alley, so he can have them."

Likewise, some non-American members of SFWA are understandably aggrieved that some of their cultural icons may be appropriated by Americans, and others feel that the battle for impersonations should cross international barriers. On the Usenet newsgroup rec.arts.sf.written, one angry commentator wrote "I don't have any problems with Brian Aldiss getting Dangermouse, but why does Robert Sawyer get both Terrance and Phillip? What if I can do a better Phillip?" The particulars on the competition, and whether impersonations worked alone or in conjunction with automatic weapons, was not available at press time.

Whatever happens, most members of SFWA agree that it's high time for the membership rules change. One SFWA member who wished to remain unnamed said "The way things were going, just about anyone who wrote for a *Buffy* fanzine could get in, and some people were talking about a cull. You know, Thunderdome. This is better, though, because everyone knows I do a better Daffy Duck than anyone else alive. And since H.P. Lovecraft isn't here any more to challenge me, that means I'm set."

—Previously unpublished

"Bridge Publications Announces 'Fanfic Writers of the Future' Line"

New York - Sixteen years after starting the famed Writers of the Future competition, Bridge Publications is at a crossroads. Popular with beginning writers, the Writers of the Future books were at best lackluster sellers, and the quality of the collections in later years suggested that a new course was in order. Inspired by the ongoing move in popular science fiction to tie-ins to popular movies and TV shows, Bridge announced today a brand-new series of anthologies, entitled "L. Ron Hubbard Presents Fanfic Writers of the Future."

"There's been a lot of discussion about what qualifies as fanfiction, and we've heard a lot of arguments about it," said Alex Jay Berman, the new editor of the "Fanfic Writers of the Future" line. "Alan Dean Foster and Kevin J. Anderson and Kristine Kathryn Rusch have made a lot of money on fanfic. A.C. Crispin got the nickname 'the Kenny Loggins of science fiction' from her paid fanfic. Steve Perry brags about how he made the *New York Times* Bestseller List with his *Shadows of the Empire* fanfic. Depending upon your perspective, Terry Brooks has either based his entire career on fanfic or made his fortune on one of the most blatant cases of necrophilia upon the corpse of J.R.R. Tolkien ever conceived. We're just trying to encourage a whole new generation that may be writing the *Buffy the Vampire Slayer* and *The Fifth Element* novelizations of tomorrow."

To allay concerns that the new competition was intended to offer more money to the Church of Scientology, of which Hubbard was the charismatic and controversial founder, Berman said "Oh, don't worry about it. We only went with the name because no living writer of any import would put his or her name on it, and calling it 'Fritz Leiber Presents' or 'Marion Zimmer Bradley Presents' was just setting us up for a lawsuit from their respective estates. Besides, Ron's in a crematory urn somewhere, so it's not like he's going to complain."

Entry into the competition requires one previously unpublished piece of fanfic ("unpublished" includes no prior appearance on a GeoCities site or Usenet newsgroup, which excludes many fanfic classics) and an administration fee of $450. When asked about the administration fee, Berman said "This is how we pay our expenses for the prizes to be awarded to the winners, and cover the expenses of the parties we need to throw at cons to promote them. It wasn't a good party unless the hotel room looks as if Hunter S. Thompson camped out there for a month." Said prize is a plaque comprised of real oak solids with the winner's name and story title emblazoned on it, a bust of Hubbard cast in solid chocolate, and five copies of the individual FFWotF volume containing the winning story. "This way, the author can give out copies to Mom, Grandma, the neighbor across the street, and maybe the old high school librarian to prove that they amounted to something," said Berman. Just as with the original Writers of the Future, authors are encouraged to buy copies of their winning anthology from local bookstores; unlike WotF, FFWotF offers plans for winners to buy cases of those volumes for promotional purposes. "After all, when they're guests at the latest WorldCon after their *Farscape* or *Gundam Wing* story sees print, they're going to want copies to sell to their hundreds of adoring fans while they're waiting at the autograph tables. It works the same way beginning bands go to a vanity press, uh, I mean, an independent CD producer and buy copies to take on tour. If they sold band candy or had a book accepted through XLibris, they'll be familiar with the concept. Did I mention that this isn't a vanity press yet? Because it isn't."

In the efforts to promote the competition and subsequent volumes, Berman and his fellow editors plan to start on a whirlwind tour of the English-speaking world. The FFWotF tour is scheduled to start at anime conventions in the US, ultimately moving to Dragon*Con, and all of the tour stops will contain fanfic workshops hosted by FFWotF winners and editors. "Due to the number of fan-fiction writers, the popularity of our fanfic panel each year (overflowing room), and the fact that some of these people would like to break out into the professional world of writing some day (or even hone their fan fiction skills), we offer programming to help them along as part of our 'real world' programming," read the programming page of one popular US convention. Another read "GET PUBLISHED NOW," and a third said "Screw *Writer's Digest!* This is the way to get professional writing credits!" When asked about these advertisements, Berman said "Okay, so we got a little enthusiastic. When you see the fiction we're putting out next year, you'll understand. These writers will be bigger than the guy who did *The Eye of Argon!*"

Another point of concern about the FFWotF was originally involving whether or not this publication makes authors eligible to join the Science Fiction Writers of America. SFWA representative Caroline Crawford responded immediately "Of course it does. We need every sucker we can get, and fanfic people will keep renewing their memberships even though they'll never get published again. Just look at the dingbats who joined SFWA after winning the Writers of the Future and keep fighting any possibility of a grandfather clause that requires regular publication as a condition for membership. We love these people: they'll keep us going forever."

The announcement of the formation of the FFWotF was greeted with joy from established fanfic writers, as well as amateurs and beginners. "It's great for us," said fanfic writer Charles Wynn, "because it's about time we got the respect we deserve. The folks at Bridge Publications have our best interests at heart. They're offering magazines and books on how to write fanfiction, they have FFWotC videotapes of convention events and fundraisers, and they even have FFWotC ties, bandannas, book bags, and decoder rings. Those old fuddy-duddies publishing original fiction had best look out for us, because we're not going to go away. We're even campaigning for a 'Best Fanfic' entry in the Hugo Awards."

The only individuals willing to speak on the record against the FFWotC were a group of book review critics for *Locus, Science Fiction Chronicle, Bookseller's Weekly,* and *The New York Times Book Review.* One committed suicide by falling on his thesaurus, another screamed at the heavens "Father, why have you forsaken us?," and a third simply stated "If these twits expect me to review 'alternate reality' stories where Susan Ivanova and Christopher Pike had three children together, they're crazier than I am. Now, if they slip me a couple of Ben Franklins per review, I might consider it, because I can't afford good single-malt scotch any other way. And I'm going to need a lot of Scotch."

—Previously unpublished

"Hoaxers Hack Hugo Computer, Change Hugo Winners For 17 Years"

Atlanta, Georgia - The science fiction community was rocked today by allegations that the Hugo Awards, recognizing the best of the science fiction field, have been altered for the last fifteen years by well-meaning pranksters.

"We didn't mean to cause any harm," said James Palmer, ringleader of the unnamed hacker cell charged with breaking into Hugo vote tallies and modifying the results. "We started by seeing if anyone would notice that the best candidate had won the Best Novel instead of the candidate who sent the best freebies to *Locus*. After a while, though, it just became too much to resist. We don't regret a thing, because the stink we started was just too much fun."

Held each year at the World Science Fiction Convention, the Hugos attract the best of the world's failed engineers, slumming physicists, and would-be writers in voting for what is supposed to be the best of science fiction literature, including novels, novellas, short stories, various categories of magazines, and professional positions. Even though the Hugos have roughly the same relevance to the literary community as the Saturn Awards have to the cinematic community, dozens of attendees arrive at each WorldCon each year to vote and to discover the secret words necessary to get a career writing science fiction for a living.

Most of the details on how this cell managed to access the computer holding the Hugo tabulations were unavailable, although Palmer said "The VIC-20 wasn't locked up or anything," but the particulars were clear. Starting in 1984, the cell altered ballot tallies for the Best Novel Hugo, awarding it to William Gibson for *Neuromancer*, and then, after finding out how easily they could tip close votes, delved into serious pranksterism.

"Originally, the *Neuromancer* vote was really, really close, and we didn't want Jerry Pournelle to win. Besides, the irony of a book about high-tech hijinks winning the Hugo was just too good. However, we kept popping back in and noticing that some of the most godawful books, magazines, and people kept getting nominated, mostly due to the nominees throwing the best parties at the previous WorldCon, so we started tinkering with the results to see if anyone noticed. You honestly think that an Eric Cartman clone like Gardner Dozois would keep winning the Best Pro Editor Hugo if there wasn't chicanery involved?"

According to Palmer, the only thing that amazed the cell was the lack of commentary from the real Hugo voters. "Considering that the Hugo nominations don't require that voters actually read or see the nominees, and that any idiot willing to pay $130 to attend a WorldCon can put in a vote for that year and a nomination for the next year, you'd be amazed at how few people bothered to vote in more than one or two categories. Of course, this says a lot about the quality of the work being offered in most years, which is why we pulled strings to make *Harry Potter and the Goblet of Fire* the winner for the 2000 Hugos. It was obviously the best book out of the nominees, and the only reason why anyone made a stink about it was because J.K. Rowling didn't pose for a photo shoot in *Locus*."

Because of the vote fraud, many Hugos may have to be returned and awarded to their proper recipients. Palmer declined to state which votes the cell altered and which ones were left intact, but said "Let's put it this way. We took our lives in our hands when Harlan Ellison found out, but the 1985 Best Dramatic Presentation Hugo belonged to *Brazil*, not *Back to the Future*. Ellen Datlow [former fiction editor of *OMNI* and current editor of SciFiction.com] had also won about half of the Best Pro Editor Hugos, and *Speculations* really deserves those Best Semi-Prozine awards." The cell also considered thoroughly ridiculous winners, but abstained for fear of giving the whole game away. "Everyone should be thankful that we didn't give the 1999 Best Dramatic Presentation to *Run, Lola, Run* if *Star Wars: Episode One* had won the popular vote. Hell, we almost gave the Best Novel in 1993 to Paul T. Riddell's *Squashed Armadillocon*, but that's just silly. Not to mention too disgusting even for us. And if we'd really thought about it, we'd have awarded the 1984 Best Novel Hugo to K.W. Jeter's *Dr. Adder* just to watch the heads of all of the little Trekkies in the crowd spontaneously implode."

"I will say this, though," Palmer said before ending the press conference, "have any of you actually seen any of the winners for Best Fanzine in the last ten years? Do you even know that *Ansible*, *Lan's Lantern*, or *Mimosa* weren't made up just to see how many dingbats would vote for them sight unseen?"

The response from members of the SF community ranged the gamut. In response to the press conference, Gardner Dozois said "Don't give me none of that tree-hugging hippie crap! Respeckt mah authoritah!" Rob Shooter, spokesman for the Hugo committee, simply said "Ha. Ha. We don't find this funny at all. Besides, everyone knows that we switched the entire database to a 286 last week, so I'd like to see how they'll be able to get in next year." David Hartwell, editor at Tor and co-editor of *The New York Review of Science Fiction*, said "Great. Controversy. Excitement. Just when the New Wave people finally shut up, someone tries to liven up the genre." David Truesdale, editor of the three-time Best Fanzine nominee *Tangent*, simply shouted "I KNEW IT! I KNEW IT! 'THE HUGO VOTERS KNOW BEST', MY ASS!" Many other representatives of the SF community responded, however, with "Aah, who cares? We all go to Dragon*Con anyway" and "What's a Hugo?"

—Previously unpublished

"Amblin, Spielberg to Release 10th Anniversary Edition of *Hook*"

Los Angeles – In a year where remakes and rereleases of classic films outnumber new releases, the upcoming 20th anniverary edition of *E.T.* raised few eyebrows. However, eyebrows went sky-high when Steven Spielberg and Amblin entertainment announced plans for major theatrical rereleases of his lesser-known works, including *Sugarland Express*, *1941*, and *Always*. The main shockwave came from the announcement that Spielberg is now scheduling a 10th anniversary release of his 1992 bomb *Hook* this Christmas.

"*Hook* obviously failed because it was ahead of its time," said Spielberg, "because it has everything a great movie needs. Big stars, great special effects, an unrelenting ad campaign, and a huge line of tie-in toys. Robin Williams being rubbed down and painted by preteen boys...ooh, it makes my nipples hard just thinking about it." The upcoming DVD will contain some eighteen hours of outtakes and deleted scenes never intended to be seen by the public, including early screen tests of Larry "Bud" Melman as Tinkerbelle, a part ultimately filled by Julia Roberts, and Spielberg's videotaped inspection and approval of the action figure line. Only ten hours of this will be available in the theatrical release.

After *Hook: Ten Years Ago*, Spielberg plans to go back and work on some of his other less-well-received directorial efforts. "We're already doing the mixing on *Always: One More Time*, and there's always *The Lost World: The Remix*. I'm ignoring films like *Schindler's List* and *The Color Purple*, which I did only so I could sucker everyone into giving me the Best Director Oscar I always wanted, and focusing on the films that mean the most to me. This is why you'll be seeing *A.I.* all over again in 2003, just about the time everyone forgets the ending from the first time around."

Not to be left behind, Lucasfilm subsequently announced its own plans for a line of new anniversary movies. "We've managed to release every one of the *Star Wars* films in video, DVD, laserdisc, and shadow-puppet theater at least five times each in the last three years," said George Lucas, "so we don't have too many options right now. However, we're releasing a fifth anniversary edition of the 'Special Editions' of the trilogy, and we're offering extras so everyone will have a reason to buy them. In particular, we're offering blooper reels this time around. Being a cinematic genius, I don't make mistakes, and any mistakes that were made by my minions were promptly burned, so we've used the wonders of digital technology to make bloopers where none had existed before. This time, Greedo gets in a first shot, and blows a big hole through Han Solo. That'll teach Harrison Ford to go public with nasty comments about my scripting skills." Still unconfirmed are reports that Lucasfilm plans to release the "lost" Lucasfilm animated project *Twice Upon A Time*, last seen as late-night filler on premium channel cable. "*Twice Upon A Time*? I've never heard of the film, and one of these days, my winged monkeys will get the last video copied from cable, and that'll be the end of it. Now can't you write something about how pretty my nose is today?"

Other directors are re-examining their earliest works in light of the possibility of offering "remastered" editions for the DVD market. James Cameron is currently working his hardest to finish the expanded edition of *Piranha 2: The Spawning* for a June 31 release, as is John Carpenter with *Dark Star* and William Shatner with *Star Trek V*. Spielberg himself is getting involved with new remastered versions of Stanley Kubrick's classic films *Dr. Strangelove*, *2001*, and *Full Metal Jacket*. "I've been talking to Stanley from beyond the grave for years," said Spielberg, "and I have his full assurance that he wants me to do this. The doctors say that I'm just hearing voices from an obsessive ego that can't handle being told 'no', but who are you going to trust? Stanley Kubrick or a bunch of quack psychiatrists?"

—Previously unpublished

Self-Destruct Button

We're all taught "don't shit where you eat." We're all given object lessons as to what happens to people who decide to aggravate the individuals upon whom they depend. However, seeing as how the following was based directly on personal experience with one of the two big bookstore chains in the United States, I'm not worried all that much. (Not that this exonerates Barnes & Noble from blame: how the hell do both chains manage to find so many people doing their passive-aggressive best to promote illiteracy?) Not that it'll do much: considering that Borders is promptly going out of business as I write this, I expect that the only people disagreeing with the assessment are going to be the innumerable bottom-of-the-class English majors suddenly unemployed when the liquidators show up to sell off the inventory and the furniture.

"Borders Books and Music Online Employment Application"

(Reporter's note: By now, we've all heard about the ongoing battle between Barnes & Noble and Amazon.Com over the future of the online bookselling business. Borders Books and Music, one of the two leading brick-and-mortar superstores in the United States, got a late start in the online venue, but recently started to amp up its efforts to sell books online. It also apparently plans to start accepting applications for its physical stores from its Web site, and an anonymous source sent along this prototype application. Anyone familiar with shopping at Borders should immediately recognize that the superstore chain plans to retain all of the features that make buying a book or magazine at Borders such an experience. Please feel free to pass this on: after all, the store could use all of the help it can get, right?)

Borders Books and Music Online Employment Application

We at Borders look for the brightest and best people to work at our stores: unfortunately, since we aren't willing to pay for the brightest and best, we have to settle for people who show up without excessive prompting and who don't commit felonies on the clock. We expect nothing but unswerving loyalty from our associates, even though we could and would throw your asses to the wolves whenever it suits us. In return for your slavish adoration, we guarantee a semiregular paycheck, benefits that would be insulting to a maximum-security inmate, and the warm feeling that comes from knowing that you have a job so long as we can't find purple-assed baboons that stock bookshelves. Please answer all questions to the best of your ability and with the understanding of what Borders wants: if we wanted honesty, we'd hire George Washington.

Why do you want to work for Borders? (Circle all that apply)

- Borders drove my independent bookstore out of business
- Borders drove my incompetently run independent bookstore out of business, and I'm unfit for gainful employment
- I heard that working in a bookstore means I can sit around and read books and magazines all day
- I'm a failed writer who still has delusions of making a living from writing fiction
- I'm on probation, and I need a job to keep out of jail

- Any other place would expect me to cut my hair and take a bath
- The Greys and/or pixies told me to come here
- I need something to pay the rent until my record or book contract comes through
- My mom said that if I didn't get a job before I turned 50, she'd kick me out of the house, and my birthday is tomorrow
- The only other job for which I'm qualified is as a morning disk jockey or a weekly newspaper music critic, and even I have *some* standards

Your sexual orientation is:
- Gay/lesbian
- Militant gay/lesbian
- Heterosexual
- Militant heterosexual
- Chickens, sheep, and cadavers
- Once I finally find someone desperate enough to have sex with me, I'll let you know
- I want to work in the Science Fiction section. What do you think?
- I'm going to get fucked blind by Borders anyway, so which hole gets used doesn't matter

Your reading speed is:
- 50 words per minute +
- 60 words per minute +
- 80 words per minute +
- Less than 10 words per minute (Immediate qualification for upper management with possession of MBA diploma)

Describe your personality:
- Slovenly
- Arrogant
- Paranoid
- Neurotic
- Sociopathic
- Apathetic

- Kleptomanic
- Misanthropistic
- Misogynistic
- Suicidal
- Alcoholic
- Too lazy to pull my pants down when taking a crap

Which phrase best fits your perception of Borders and its customers?
- "I'm afraid I can't do that, Dave."
- "Game over, man! Game over!"
- "Resistance is futile. You will be assimilated."
- "If you go to Z'Ha'Dum, you will die."
- "Greed, for lack of a better word, is good."
- "Blanks get the job done, too."
- "Saigon. Shit."
- "Don't make me break my foot off in your ass!"
- "When there's no more room in Hell, the dead will walk the Earth."
- "Squeal like a pig, boy! SQUEEE!"

Describe your feelings about random drug tests:
- A horrible invasion of personal privacy, and all the other stuff I hear on MTV
- A horrible invasion of personal privacy that keeps me from enjoying my Skinny Puppy albums that much more
- I've never touched illegal drugs in my life, but I chug five bottles of NyQuil a day
- I freebase Preparation H, so I'm safe
- Does Zoloft count?
- Knowing that management's urine is nearly pure cocaine, I'm not all that worried about getting busted for that joint I had at Burning Man

What do you do in your spare time? (Check all that apply)
- I try to interest publishers in my *Star Trek: The Next Generation* porn novel, featuring the erotic exploits of Wesley and Worf

- I mourn the death of my old bookstore (the one that used to be located next door, before Borders moved in and drove me out of business)
- I await the signs of the impending Revolution
- I await the saucermen to take me back to the home world
- I try to find a job that pays something approximating a living wage
- I wait until my band makes it big, so I can tell the whole world and everyone in it to kiss my ass
- I dust my ceramic penguins
- I try to pick up (Choose one: Boys Girls) at the local Catholic junior high
- I await Death's sultry embrace
- I sit on the roof of tall buildings with a sniper rifle and cackle "Why, it's a school bus!"
- I search for the one 12-inch Boba Fett action figure that will make my collection complete
- I work on my Polish dwarf porn Web site
- I do incredibly exciting and unbearably cool things that neither you nor anyone else can possibly conceive
- I compulsively masturbate in public (Immediate qualification for upper management with possession of MBA diploma)
- I put aluminum foil and Crisco on my head to keep out the CIA mind control beams
- Well, er, um...damn that short-term memory loss! I gotta buy better buds!
- I refuse to testify on the grounds that I may be incriminated

Expected rate of pay:

- $4 per hour
- $4.50 per hour
- $5 per hour
- Minimum wage and as many books as I can squirrel away in my backpack

Transportation to and from work:

- Walk
- Bus
- Bicycle
- Car (parents gave it to me when I got my English degree, and I live in it)
- My mommy drives me

The main focus of Borders is to:

- Refer to books as "units"
- Give free poetry reading time in the coffee shop to the manager's girlfriend/wife/child
- Keep most of the New York Literary Establishment off welfare
- Torch your perception of bookstores as venues of enlightenment
- Keep Amazon.com from taking over the world
- Encourage the spread of illiteracy

A customer wants to special-order a book not immediately in stock. You should:

- Offer to take his/her name and number, and then promptly throw out the sheet of paper the moment the customer isn't looking
- Claim that Borders doesn't do special orders, despite the notice on the "Customer Service" desk that says "We order anything!"
- Call the manager for more advice and disappear into the back storeroom
- Go digging through papers behind the Customer Service desk until the customer gets frustrated and leaves
- Simulate a terminal bout of Tourette's Syndrome

An attractive customer wants to special-order a book not immediately in stock. You:

- Order the book
- Order the book and tell the customer to meet you around back after closing to pick it up for free
- Order the book in exchange for a blow job
- Refer the customer to the competitor down the street, where the prices are better
- Simply stare and shiver at the sight of a sex object you will never

have

A customer asks for a magazine with an unfamiliar title. You should:

- Immediately state "We don't carry it, but the new issue should be in next week," whether or not the store actually does
- Tell the customer "I'll look in the back for it" and hide in the stockroom until s/he leaves
- Wave in the general direction of the magazine area, snort "It's in there somewhere," and go back to watching *Titanic* on the video screens by the front counter
- Lead the way to the magazine rack, give the customer a copy of your xeroxed music review zine, and say "You don't want to read that mass-produced crap; this is better!"
- Sneer "Well, how are you so sure that the new issue is out yet?" and hide in the storeroom if the customer gives a logical answer

A customer asks for help fifteen minutes before your lunch break. You:

- Dump the customer on another associate planning to take lunch in twenty minutes and disappear in the back storeroom
- Ignore the customer and go to lunch in fifteen minutes: if s/he needed help, s/he shouldn't be in a bookstore
- Roundly curse out the customer for fifteen minutes for being such a parasite, and then go to lunch
- Say "Excuse me for a second" and take off to lunch early

A local author comes in with his/her new book and wants to sell it on consignment. You should:

- Take every copy s/he has, sell them at the used bookstore down the street, and claim ignorance when s/he asks about their whereabouts three weeks later
- Relay management's policy: "If it ain't by Tom Clancy or John Grisham, we ain't interested"
- Put the books in a wholly inappropriate section (a science fiction novel in the "Local History" section, for instance) and then decline to allow the author to bring in new copies because "They didn't sell that well the first time"
- Scuff them up, rip off the covers, pour coffee inside of each copy, and leave them in the back storeroom, then return them to the author as being unsaleable

This same author wants to sell a magazine containing his articles on consignment. You:

- Tell him that all magazine consignments are handled by the magazine rep, and give the name of someone who quit six months ago
- Tell him that all magazines have to be approved by the home office, even if the home office told him to come to you. Lather, rinse, repeat.
- Request a copy "for review" and dump it in the employee break area
- Put a copy on the desk of the magazine rep and pretend to look surprised when it's stolen before the rep can take a look at it
- Without reading it, scoff and tell the author "Oh, we tried to sell this back in 1994, and we didn't sell a single copy." If the author points out that the store first opened in 1996, excuse yourself and hide in the back storeroom
- Claim that the store already carries it and that new copies will be in next week

Which are appropriate subjects for book signings?

- A. TV stars with a kiss-and-tell book pitched by Rosie O'Donnell
- B. Authors of sappy self-help books that don't work half as well as a two-by-four to the cranium
- C. Cookbook authors who promise free food for the staff after the signing
- D. The author of any book with a non-return policy and about 100,000 copies pre-ordered by the main office in Ann Arbor
- E. Local authors, poets, and artists
- F. A, B, C, and D

A customer calls about a book reading by Samuel Clements later in the week. You:

- Tell the customer that the reading is still scheduled, and that all copies of the author's books must be accompanied by a receipt
- Tell the customer that he's going to record a live spoken-word album with William S. Burroughs, Percy Shelley, and Charlotte Bronte, and that seats are available starting at $50

- Tell the customer that all of his books are out of stock, but should be in next week
- Ask the customer if this conversation is going to be on the new Jerky Boys album
- Tell the dolt from *Fringeware Review* to get a life

A customer is seeking a book in the Computer Section on Internet protocols. You:

- Drag him/her into the back and show off your Polish dwarf porn site on the store's T1 connection
- Engage him/her in a pissing contest over knowledge of TCP/IP
- Launch into a 45-minute tirade on how CompuServe and America Online don't offer customer support for users of the VIC-20 any more
- Brag about all the groupies and publicity junkets you'll get when your book on programming in Perl 5.0 finally comes out
- Simply stare at the customer, respond "This isn't my department; let me find someone," and hide in the back storeroom

Shoplifting is:

- A terrible act that takes money from upper management stock dividends
- Absolutely unacceptable unless committed by a fellow employee
- Absolutely unacceptable unless condoned by management as a way to cover employee theft
- The only way we'd ever move books by Monica Lewinsky, Newt Gingrich, Jay Leno, or Piers Anthony

A new book by Michael Crichton hits the bestseller's lists at #1 during its first week. How long should you wait before taking the hundreds of unsold copies and setting them out on the remainder tables out in front of the store?

- One month
- One week
- Three days
- As soon as you hear that Steven Spielberg is directing or producing the movie adaptation

The store receives a book by an author who claims to have received repeated anal probes from extraterrestrials, and that this is an attempt at spiritual contact from the "Visitors." The reviews are overwhelmingly negative, and the American Family Association stages protests to keep the book out of stores in your area. Under which section do you put this book?

- Fiction
- Humor
- Children's Literature
- Sexuality
- Manager's Pick of the Week

Where do you want to be in ten years?

- Manager
- Dead
- Emperor of the Known Universe
- Anywhere but here
- Working for Barnes & Noble

MANAGEMENT QUIZ
Describe your management style:

- Benign neglect (King Log)
- Cold and cruel (King Stork)
- Too stupid to live (King Dork)
- Too stoned to care (King Toke)
- Good cop/bad cop
- Bad cop/bad cop
- The Scourge of God
- Waiting for the inevitable and unrelenting muttering of "Let's frag the lieutenant"
- "Shut up, Beavis. Don't make me kick your ass. Huh huh huh huh."

–The Hells Half-Acre Herald, October 22, 1999

Postscript: When this first came out in print form, it bounced all over the place, and I received two responses from Borders employees. The first, invariably from the people who volunteered to run the Sci Fi/Fantasy sections, was "I didn't think this was funny at all." The second, from the vast majority remaining, was "And how long did you work for Borders?" I never did, and this piece pretty much guarantees that I never will, but 80 percent of this was based on verbatim interactions with Borders staff and managers, so I fully expect that this book will get hidden in the Local History section at Borders if it gets carried at all. No big deal: I just hope, for any Borders bookbuyers reading this, that the Wesley/Worf slashfic gig is working out.

Bibliography (of sorts)

Since many of the publications that contained these articles and essays are now long-dead, the following is a thumbnail guide to each venue, including distribution and general lifespan. Any snide comments are the author's.

Angry Thoreauan (1999-?): A regular commentary and rant magazine published by "The Reverend Tin-Ear."

The Annals of Improbable Research (1994-present): Formed when the staff of the *Journal of Impossible Results* started their own magazine, the AIR publishes scientific articles of research that cannot and must not be replicated. Best known for its IgNobel Awards, given to the most dubious scientific endeavors of a given year.

Carpe Noctem (?-2000): Latin for "Seize the night," *Carpe Noctem* was a magazine dedicated to the goth movement. Today, it's best known as the first venue to publish Jhonen Vasquez's comic *Johnny the Homicidal Maniac* on a regular basis. Due to money issues stemming from the dotcom crunch and a Barnes & Noble "Magazine of the Month" promotion, *Carpe Noctem* declared bankruptcy in 2001.

Chaos (1993-1994): A Texas-based comics and commentary magazine published and edited by Deanne DeWitt and Deborah de Frietas.

Cyber-Psychos AOD (1993-1997): A Denver-based horror and gonzo entertainment magazine published and edited by Jasmine Sailing.

Ellison Webderland (1995-present): The official Web site for Harlan Ellison, this site also invited certain people to contribute guest rants for publication from time to time.

Event Horizon (1997-1999): Online science fiction magazine published and edited by former OMNI fiction editor Ellen Datlow.

Fat City News (1996): An online magazine dedicated to gonzo journalism, published by David Sparks.

Fuck Science Fiction (1993-1994): Science fiction commentary magazine edited and published by Chris DeVito. Gone but not forgotten.

The Hell's Half-Acre Herald (1998-2002): In one form, the *Herald* was a regular E-mail column intended as a house organ for the now-dead Web site *The Healing Power of Obnoxiousness*. In another, it was a print publication (three issues published between 1999 and 2000) in standard zine format. Both are compiled in the collection *The Savage Pen of Onan: The "Best" of the Hell's Half-Acre Herald.*

The Met (1994-2000): A Dallas-based weekly newspaper dedicated to local arts and entertainment coverage. Before being bought by the Phoenix New Times paper chain and shut down in 2000, *The Met's* obsession with subjects only of interest to its Southern Methodist University-trained staff garnered it the nickname "The Paper By SMU Brats For SMU Brats."

MetOnline (1995-1996): Web site for The Met, including some original content as well as reprints of articles in the print edition.

NetSlaves (1998-2002): An online venue dedicated to protecting New Media employees from abuse and exploitation by their managers. Sadly, it didn't work.

Nova Express (1988-2002): An irregular science fiction commentary and review magazine edited and published by Lawrence Person.

Proud Flesh (1994): The fiction-only offshoot of *Fuck Science Fiction.*

Realms of Fantasy (1994-2009): A bimonthly magazine publishing heroic fantasy, edited by Shawna McCarthy.

Revolution Science Fiction (2001-present): An online magazine formed by the survivors of Zealot.com to cover the same subjects as its predecessor.

Savant (2000-2002): A weekly online essay magazine dedicated to comics activism.

Science Fiction Chronicle (?-2004): A science fiction news and entertainment magazine originally published by Andrew Porter, but later published by DNA Publications in 2001 and renamed *Chronicle.*

Science Fiction Eye (1986-1999?): A "quarterly" publication covering nonfiction subjects related to science fiction and its publication. Due to its irregular publishing schedule in the last six years of publication, it finally shut down in 1999, but its last three issues only appeared in 1994, 1996, and 1997.

SCI FI (original version 2000-2001): The house magazine for the SCI FI Channel. Due to licensing issues, *SCI FI* ceased publication in 2001, but was resurrected by the Channel in 2002.

SciFiNow (2000-2001): Web site created by *SCI FI* and *Realms of Fantasy* publisher Sovereign Media to promote its magazines.

Sci-Fi Universe (Sovereign Media edition 1997-1999): Foundering media science fiction magazine purchased from Larry Flynt Publications in 1997 and published by Sovereign Media. Ceased publication in 1999 due to boom in other media-related magazines: as the joke went, it didn't die, but left early to avoid the rush.

Spark Online (1999-?): A Canada-based online arts and entertainment monthly publication.

Spicy Green Iguana (1998 to 2004): An online science fiction writer's resource, including magazine news, listings of dead and comatose markets, and occasional